Nostratic: Examining a Linguistic Macrofamily

edited by
Colin Renfrew & Daniel Nettle

THE McDONALD INSTITUTE FOR ARCHAEOLOGICAL RESEARCH

Papers in the Prehistory of Languages

Publication of this volume is supported by a grant from the **Alfred P. Sloan Foundation,** New York.

Published by:
The McDonald Institute for Archaeological Research
University of Cambridge
Downing Street
Cambridge
CB2 3ER
(0)(1223) 339336

ISBN: 1-902937-00-7
ISSN: 1461-331x

Printed and bound by BluePrint Cambridge, Severn Place, East Road, Cambridge, England, CB1 1HY.
Tel.: (0)1223 314315; Fax: (0)1223 351944

Table of Contents

Nostratic Symposium, July 1998

Speakers

DAVID APPLEYARD
Chair, Department of the Languages and Cultures of Africa, SOAS, Thornhaugh Street, Russell Square, London, WC1H 0XG, UK.

ALLAN R. BOMHARD
151 Wentworth Street, #3B, Charleston, SC 29401-1743, USA.

LYLE CAMPBELL
Department of Linguistics, University of Canterbury, Private Bag 4800, Christchurch, New Zealand.

ROBERT COLEMAN
Faculty of Classics/Emmanuel College, University of Cambridge, Cambridge, CB2 3AP, UK.

BERNARD COMRIE
Max Planck Institute for Evolutionary Anthropology, Inselstrasse 22–26, D-04103 Leipzig, Germany.

GYULA DÉCSY
Department of Central Eurasian Studies, Goodbody Hall 157, Bloomington, IN 47405-2401, USA.

AHARON DOLGOPOLSKY
Hebrew Language Department, Mount Carmel, Haifa 31905, Israel.

CHRISTOPHER EHRET
Department of History, UCLA, Los Angeles, CA 90095, USA.

IRÉN HEGEDŰS
Janus Pannonius University, Faculty of Humanities, Department of English, Pecs Ifjusag u. 6., H-7624, Hungary.

ALAN S. KAYE
Department of English, Comparative Literature and Linguistics, California State University, P.O. Box 6848, Fullerton, CA 92834-6848, USA.

APRIL MCMAHON
Department of Linguistics/Selwyn College, University of Cambridge, Cambridge, CB3 9DA, UK.

ALEXIS MANASTER RAMER (*in absentia*)
4225 Walden Drive, Ann Arbor, MI 48105, USA.

PETER A. MICHALOVE
307 S McKinley, Champagne, IL 61821-3247, USA.

DANIEL NETTLE
Merton College, Oxford, OX1 4JD, UK.

COLIN RENFREW
The McDonald Institute for Archaeological Research, Downing Street, Cambridge, CB2 3ER, UK.

VITALY SHEVOROSHKIN
Department of Slavic Language and Literature, University of Michigan, Ann Arbor, MI 48109, USA.

DENIS SINOR
Indiana University, Goodbody Hall, Bloomington, IN 47405, USA.

S.A. STAROSTIN
Leninski Prosp. 1091, apt 64, Moscow 117421, Russia.

R.L. TRASK
School of Cognitive and Computing Sciences, University of Sussex, Falmer, Brighton, BN1 9QH, UK.

RAINER VOIGT
Freie Universitat Berlin, Seminar für Semitistik und Arabistik, Altensteinstrasse 34, 14195, Berlin, Germany.

ALEXANDER VOVIN (*in absentia*)
Department of East Asian Languages and Literatures, Moore Hall 382, 1890 East–West Road, Honolulu, HI 96822, USA.

KAMIL V. ZVELEBIL (*in absentia*)
F 11160 Cabrespine, Rue moulin à huile 84, France.

vi

Foreword

Colin Renfrew & Daniel Nettle

The 'Symposium on the Nostratic Macrofamily' was held on 17th and 18th July 1998 at the McDonald Institute. Participants had been provided in advance with Aharon Dolgopolsky's *The Nostratic Macrofamily and Linguistic Palaeontology* (Cambridge, McDonald Institute, 1998) and were invited to comment both upon this work and more generally upon the Nostratic hypothesis. The papers which they produced were pre-circulated prior to the meetings and, following revision, have formed the basis for the present volume. Others who attended the Symposium and chaired sessions were Professor Greville Corbett, Dr John Hines, Professor Philip Jaggar and Dr Marianne Mithun. Unfortunately Dr Alexis Manaster Ramer, Dr Alexander Vovin, Dr V. Ivanov and Professor Kamil Zvelebil were prevented from attending the Symposium, but the papers by Manaster Ramer, Vovin and Zvelebil were indeed discussed and are included here.

The Symposium was generously funded by the Alfred P. Sloan Foundation within the framework of the 'Prehistory of Languages' project which it is supporting at the McDonald Institute. Their policy is to encourage projects working at or near the limits of knowability, and indeed to explore the distinctions between what is simply unknown and what is ultimately unknowable. Some may well feel that the 'Prehistory of Languages' project fits such a bill all too closely. We are optimistic, however, that there is much yet to be learnt in the area of overlap between historical linguistics, molecular genetics and prehistoric archaeology, all of which impinge upon the history of populations. Other enterprises within the framework of the project will explore both molecular genetic and archaeological aspects, and it is hoped in addition to examine further linguistic topics. Some future activities may well have an explicitly interdisciplinary nature, but for reasons given in the first paper of this volume it seemed appropriate that the approaches in the present Symposium devoted to the Nostratic hypothesis should be primarily linguistic ones.

We are grateful to April McMahon and Chris Scarre for their advice, to Patricia Salazar for much practical help, to Katie Boyle for considerable input into the editorial process and to Dora Kemp for her much valued work as Production Editor.

Part I
Introduction to Nostratic

Introduction

Nostratic as a linguistic macrofamily

Colin Renfrew

The hypothesis that many of the principal language families of Eurasia and North Africa might be related, themselves forming part of a larger overarching family or macrofamily designated 'Nostratic', is one of the most interesting and challenging in the field of modern historical linguistics. In that field it raises wider issues concerning the whole concept of notional macrofamilies, and the methodological problems associated with their evaluation.

The question has, moreover, a strong resonance beyond the field of linguistics itself. For if the hypothesis were accepted there would certainly be implications for the history and the prehistory of the regions concerned. The acceptance of the notion of an early Proto-Nostratic language, ancestral to Proto-Indo-European, Proto-Uralic, Proto-Kartvelian etc., would raise consequent problems about the subsequent dispersal of that proto-language into the vast geographical territories involved. To the extent that these dispersals involved the dispersal of a Proto-Nostratic-speaking population there would be demographic implications which in their turn one might expect to see reflected in the patterns of variation of DNA markers which advances in molecular genetics are beginning to reveal.

In this introductory paper I shall hope to touch on these problems without, however, in any way implying that the Nostratic hypothesis has yet been established or that the ensuing implications should yet be accepted. As I shall stress below I am not myself a linguist, and the editors of this volume are in agreement that the Nostratic question is in the first instance a linguistic one to be evaluated by competent linguists before it is applied by archaeologists or molecular geneticists to their own data.

The Nostratic macrofamily is among the best known, and certainly among the most coherently argued, of the various linguistic macrofamilies for which claims have been made in recent years, such as 'Dene-Caucasian' or 'Amerind' or indeed Greenberg's concept of 'Eurasiatic', which is further discussed below. Since the early systematic work of Illič-Svityč and Dolgopolsky in the 1960s it has been approached using the traditional 'comparative method' of historical linguistics, first worked out in the context of Indo-European studies (Brugmann 1897–1916). Whether or not the application of that method has been an entirely successful one is a matter which various authors in this volume set out to examine. But the initiative of setting out to meet these accepted criteria does place the Nostratic hypothesis on a different level methodologically from proposals for various other macrofamilies which have been put forward. They have been proposed mainly on the basis of lexical comparisons (e.g. Greenberg 1987) and often without the same systematic attempt to reconstruct the proto-languages of the constituent language families and to establish the phonological regularities by which their vocabularies might be derived from that of the ancestral macrofamilial proto-language. This is a task which the Nostratic school has accepted as a valid objective and has begun to undertake.

For this reason many of those scholars who are interested in the whole issue of the possible existence of linguistic macrofamilies, and in the evaluation of claims to recognize or define them, see the Nostratic controversy as one of considerable fascination. That fascination underlay the discussions which led to the present volume. They will, I think, be of interest to a wide range of scholars intrigued by the macrofamily question, even if the hypothetical Nostratic macrofamily is not their own prime interest. At the same time, however, it is the Nostratic macrofamily which is here the object of discussion. It does not follow, were the Nostratic hypothesis to be accepted, that other claims for macrofamilial relations, like that for 'Dene-Caucasian' or 'Amerind' would be validated or strengthened, any more than a convincing demonstration of a clear genetic relationship between the Sino-Tibetan and North Caucasian language families would directly impinge upon the Nostratic hypothesis. These are matters to be independently evaluated by the relevant specialists. At the same time, however, there are methodological questions, yet to be clarified, which a number of papers here address, which must be common to the status of macrofamilies in general, including Nostratic. The papers here embark upon that task.

Nostratic

The term 'Nostratic' was introduced by the Danish linguist Holger Pedersen (1931), and was used (in the form 'Nostratian') in his discussion of 1924, in which he argues for the existence of underlying similarities between a number of language families of Eurasia. It has since been given much clearer definition by the work of the Russian linguists, in particular Vladislav Illič-Svityč and Aharon Dolgopolsky. Illič-Svityč wrote his fundamental treatment in the 1960s (Bulatova 1989) and was sadly killed in a street accident in August 1966. Aharon Dolgopolsky wrote a number of fundamental papers in the 1960s (Dolgopolsky 1973) and subsequently emigrated to Israel, where he continues to work. Their work has been made known in the west in a number of studies encouraged by Vitaly Shevoroshkin (1989; 1990; Kaiser & Shevoroshkin 1988). The 'Moscow School' continues its work in Russia in the field of long-range language relationships, where the studies of Sergei Starostin on the North Caucasian languages and on the hypothetical Dene-Caucasian macrofamily are of note. In the west Allan Bomhard (1984) has been one of the most assiduous workers in this field, and his recent monograph (Bomhard 1996) must rank as the most comprehensive treatment currently available other than in Russian.

The term 'Nostratic' was coined by Pedersen from the Latin adjective *nostras* (genitive *nostratis*), meaning *of our country, native*. From the standpoint of most Europeans (unless they be Basque speakers or from North Caucasian lands) that might well seem appropriate. But scholars have pointed out that it is nonetheless an ethnocentric designation, implicitly favouring 'us' against 'them' and thereby excluding linguists, for instance the Chinese, whose native tongue does not fall within the Nostratic realm. But while this is no doubt to be deprecated — and Dolgopolsky did at an earlier stage suggest the term 'Boreic' (i.e. 'northern') to avoid the difficulty — the terminology is by now well-established.

As defined by Illič-Svityč and by Dolgopolsky (1998) the Nostratic macrofamily includes the following language families:

Indo-European
Hamito-Semitic (Afroasiatic)
Kartvelian
Uralic (Uralic-Yukaghir)
Altaic
Dravidian

It should be noted that, while the other families in this list command widespread support among linguists as validly defined language families, the Altaic family is itself controversial (Miller 1991). Dolgopolsky would today include Korean and Japanese within the wider Altaic family. Eskimo-Aleut is another family which some Nostratic specialists would regard as close to the Nostratic macrofamily. The present-day distribution of the speakers of the Nostratic languages as so defined is seen in Figure 1. (Territories which were occupied by Indo-European speakers in the colonial movements of the past six centuries are not taken into account.)

There are members of the Moscow School, notably Starostin, who would draw the boundaries of the Nostratic macrofamily rather differently. In particular, while acknowledging the close relationship of the Afroasiatic family to the others within the macrofamily, they would set it adjacent to rather than within

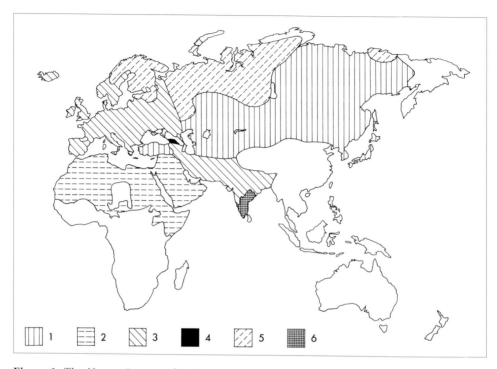

Figure 1. *The Nostratic macrofamily. The present-day distribution of the language groups within the Nostratic macrofamily. The constituent language families are: (1) Altaic; (2) Afroasiatic; (3) Indo-European; (4) South Caucasian (Kartvelian); (5) Uralic; (6) Dravidian.*

the Nostratic macrofamily. The position of Dravidian is also considered by some to be rather marginal. Dolgopolsky himself, while continuing to include these within the Nostratic grouping has at times regarded their status as somewhat peripheral.

At this point it is pertinent to note that the distinguished American linguist Joseph Greenberg has independently sought to define a macrofamily, termed by him 'Eurasiatic', which overlaps significantly with Nostratic. It will be recalled that Greenberg's classification of the languages of Africa (Greenberg 1963) has been very widely accepted, while his comparable initiative for the languages of the Americas (Greenberg 1987) has proved more controversial and can by no means be regarded as generally accepted. He too has developed a coherent methodology, which he terms the method of 'multilateral comparison', based upon the simultaneous examination of the vocabularies of a large number of languages. He has been criticized, however, for not undertaking what many regard as the indispensable preliminary step of reconstructing the proto-languages for the language families in question and for failing to establish the sound rules for the phonological changes involved. As noted above these are widely regarded as forming part of the standard comparative or Brugmannian method of historical linguistics. On the other hand the supporters of Greenberg, notably Merritt Ruhlen (1992; 1994) argue that the underlying historical and in that sense, genetic relationships between languages are sufficiently evident following Greenberg's method of multilateral comparison, and that the comparative method, while valid and desirable, is difficult to apply to language families whose languages have not yet been exhaustively studied and which do not, in many cases, have a legacy of written literature on any scale.

The families which Greenberg would include within his Eurasian macrofamily (Ruhlen 1992) are as follows:

Indo-Hittite (i.e. Indo-European)
Uralic-Yukaghir
Altaic
Japanese
Korean
Ainu
Gilyak
Chukchi-Kamchatkan
Eskimo-Aleut

It will be noted therefore that Greenberg's classification differs from that of Illič-Svityč and Dolgopolsky by excluding Afroasiatic, Kartvelian and Dravidian, and by including Eskimo-Aleut, Chukchi-Kamchatkan, Japanese and Korean (along with Ainu and Gilyak). Japanese and Korean are now included by Dolgopolsky within the Altaic family and hence within the Nostratic macrofamily.

The differences between the positions of the Nostratic scholars and Greenberg on the membership of their Nostratic and Eurasiatic macrofamilies respectively should probably not be exaggerated, since all would see broad underlying relationships, and also significant differences from unrelated (or at this level unrelated) language families such as North Caucasian. This is illustrated by the comments of Bomhard (1996, 4) whose opinion is 'close to that of Greenberg':

> As I see the situation, Nostratic includes Afroasiatic, Kartvelian and Elamo-Dravidian as well as Eurasiatic, in other words I view Nostratic as a higher-level taxonomic entity. Afroasiatic stands apart as an extremely ancient, independent branch — it was the first branch of Nostratic to separate from the rest of the Nostratic speech community. Younger are Kartvelian and Elamo-Dravidian. It is clear from an analysis of their vocabulary, pronominal

> stems and morphological systems that Indo-European, Uralic-Yukaghir, Altaic, Gilyak, Chukchi-Kamchatkan and Eskimo-Aleut are more closely related as a group than any one of them is to Afroasiatic, Kartvelian, and Elamo-Dravidian, and this is the reason that I follow Greenberg in setting up a distinct Eurasiatic group within Nostratic.

In this volume, however, the term 'Nostratic' will in general be interpreted in the sense used by the original exponents of the Nostratic hypothesis, Illič-Svityč and Dolgopolsky. The distribution of the speakers of languages classed by them as within the macrofamily is seen in Figure 1.

What if . . .

Although it may well be premature to regard the Nostratic hypothesis as accepted, it certainly seems appropriate to consider the potential implications were it to achieve such status. Already a number of scholars have sought to do so, and prominent among them is Aharon Dolgopolsky, whose *The Nostratic Macrofamily and Linguistic Palaeontology* (Dolgopolsky 1998) served as the starting point and catalyst for the conference of which this volume is the product. The present introductory paper draws upon my Introduction to that study (Renfrew 1998).

The establishment of a genetic relationship (from the linguistic standpoint) between the constituent language families of the Nostratic language family would normally be taken to imply the earlier existence of an ancestral proto-language, Proto-Nostratic, spoken somewhere within the territories in question. Dolgopolsky would suggest a date of around 15,000 BP for the *floruit* of this proto-language, and in his recent monograph (Dolgopolsky 1998) sets out to show how the linguistic palaeontology of the reconstructed vocabulary is indeed appropriate to the Upper Palaeolithic and Mesolithic worlds of the hunter-gatherer somewhere in Western Asia.

While noting that Dixon (1997, 37–40) firmly rejects the Nostratic hypothesis, we may nonetheless, provisionally suspending disbelief in that respect, apply to the dispersal of Nostratic or Proto-Nostratic his punctuated equilibrium model. If Nostratic were regarded as a true, genetically related macrofamily, its dispersal would, from the perspective which he adopts, be regarded as the result of an episode of punctuation:

> The punctuation may be due to natural causes such as drought or flooding; or to the invention of a new tool or weapon; or to the development of agriculture; or of boats, with movement into new territories; or to the development of secular or religious imperialism. These punctuations to the state of equilibrium are likely to trigger dramatic changes within languages

and between languages. They give rise to expansion and split of peoples and languages. It is during a period of punctuation — which will be brief in comparison with the eras of equilibrium that precede and follow — that the family tree model applies. (Dixon 1997, 3–4)

It is appropriate in this context to note how coherently those observations could bear on the Nostratic case were they applied to it (which Dixon himself would clearly not do). Boats are not particularly relevant here, and 'secular or religious imperialism' are hardly appropriate to the egalitarian societies of the later Palaeolithic and Neolithic periods, but natural causes and innovation, including the development of agriculture, are clearly possibilities.

Already 25 years ago, in discussing the origins and spread of the Indo-European language family (Renfrew 1973) I suggested that so radical a linguistic change should have significant archaeological correlates, and that the most significant episode in European prehistory was the spread of farming. On that basis the Proto-Indo-European homeland would be located in central Anatolia, around 7000 BC. The case was subsequently argued in greater detail (Renfrew 1987), and perhaps finds some purely linguistic support from the recent reiteration of the Indo-Hittite hypothesis of Sturtevant (1962) which emerges from the work of Warnow and Ringe (Warnow 1997). The case has been argued on purely linguistic grounds by Dolgopolsky (1987; 1993).

The language-farming hypothesis, that farming dispersals consequent upon the development of agriculture in various parts of the Old World were responsible for the punctuation underlying the distribution of many of the world's language families, has now been argued in general terms, notably by Bellwood (1996) and by others (e.g. Renfrew 1992; 1996). That it should apparently prove less informative in the case of the Americas may be due to biogeographical factors, as cogently argued by Jared Diamond (1997, 354–9). It was the Nostratic hypothesis itself which first suggested to me that it could be applied not only to Proto-Indo-European, but also to Proto-Afroasiatic, Proto-Elamo-Dravidian and possibly Proto-Altaic (Renfrew 1991; 1998). For it is now well established by standard archaeological means that the crucial area for the origins of farming in Europe and Western Asia was the region originally described by Robert J. Braidwood as 'the hilly flanks of the Fertile Crescent'. This involves the southern Levant (with Jericho as a key site for early farming), the western flanks of the Zagros mountains including southwestern Iran (Elam) where the Early Neolithic is documented, for instance at Ali Kosh, south-central Anatolia (including the Konya plain, where Çatalhöyük is located) and perhaps parts of Turkmenia (with the early farming site of Jeitun). The notion of a 'Great Exodus' around 7000 BC, based upon the dispersal of farming, finds support in the work

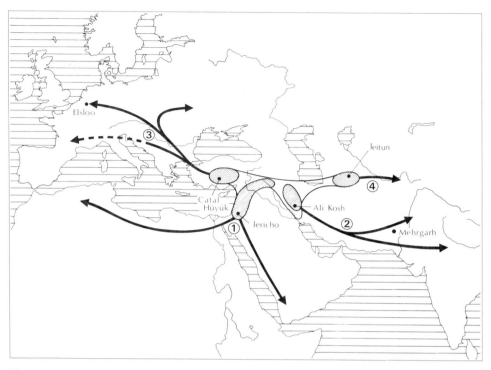

Figure 2. *Hypothetical application of the language/farming-dispersal hypothesis to account for the subsequent distribution of four language families: (1) Afroasiatic; (2) Elamo-Dravidian; (3) Indo-European; (4) Altaic. The shaded areas indicate the suggested homelands for the four respective proto-languages c. 10,000 BC whose dispersals accompanied the subsequent spread of farming along the approximate trajectories indicated.*

If the Nostratic hypothesis were accepted the homeland of Proto-Nostratic, ancestral to the four proto-languages (and to Proto-Kartvelian and Proto-Uralic, not indicated), would lie within the dotted and shaded area c. 15,000 BC. (The dispersal of Proto-Uralic was based on the northward hunter-gatherer colonization of land through climate sensitive adjustments after 8000 BC.)

of Cauvin (1994), although he would give Figure 2 a rather different configuration (Cauvin, pers. comm.)

The pattern has been well established by palaeobotanists and palaeozoologists that the basic farming package of wheat and barley and other domesticated plants accompanied by domesticated sheep and goat (and later cattle) did indeed disperse radially outwards from the nuclear area.

It could be hypothesized, therefore, on the basis of these rather well-established farming dispersals and within the framework of the language/farming hypothesis, that the homeland for Proto-Afroasiatic would be in the Levant, as Militiarev & Shnirelman (1988) have argued, the source area for Proto-Elamo-Dravidian would be in Elam, and, as indicated earlier, the homeland for Proto-Indo-European should lie in south-central Anatolia. The case for Proto-Altaic is much less clear, but Turkmenia could be proposed as the initial locus for the hypothetical dispersal (although farming began there rather later than in the other areas). Comparable arguments could be made for Kartvelian, although biogeographical factors there (i.e. the Caucasus Mountains) would prevent or limit a dispersal. Only Uralic falls outside this picture, and here a later punctuation episode must be proposed. It would be one related to the repopulation of the northern part of the Eurasian steppes following climatic amelioration during the Holocene, and unlike the other episodes would not initially be associated with the dispersal of farming. It falls within the category of 'Northern, climate-sensitive adjustments after 10,000 BP' (Renfrew 1996, 76). These suggestions are shown in schematic form in Figure 2. Some of them have been proposed also by Cavalli-Sforza & Cavalli-Sforza (1995, 160).

The language/farming dispersal hypothesis does not necessarily imply that the spread of farming was brought about by a large number of people, through some process of demic diffusion, although that has certainly been argued. Smaller numbers of migrant farmers might, through their prestige and that of their new economy, have been responsible for processes of contact-induced language change (Zvelebil 1995). Certainly recent molecular genetic evidence for Europe does show indications of human dispersals accompanying the Neolithic, but on a relatively small scale (Richards *et al.* 1998). There is some support within a larger geographical perspective from the molecular genetic evidence (Barbujani & Pilastro 1993; Barbujani *et al.* 1994), but sampling over much of the relevant area has so far been inadequate.

It should be noted that, as formulated here, there is nothing in the language/farming hypothesis as applied to the individual language families which depends upon the Nostratic hypothesis. Nor would the above proposal be invalidated if the Nostratic hypothesis were disregarded.

It is at once obvious, however, that such a view would in fact harmonize very well with the Nostratic hypothesis. For the farming dispersal theory, applied to the four language families in question, requires that, around 7000 BC, the relevant proto-languages (i.e. Indo-European, Afroasiatic, Elamo-Dravidian and Altaic) were all spoken within restricted areas in western Asia which are in effect adjacent to each other, disregarding the intervening Syrian Desert. To the north, in the Caucasus, Proto-North Caucasian would have been spoken (ancestral to the North Caucasian languages as well as to Hattic, Hurrian and Urartian), and very possibly, in the marshes at the mouth of the Tigris and Euphrates, Proto-Sumerian with no known relatives (unless possibly North Caucasian or, following Bomhard (1996, 4), Nostratic itself). The Nostratic hypothesis would therefore hold that during the period between 15,000 BP (if that be the date assigned to Proto-Nostratic) and 10,000 BP there would be gradually increasing linguistic divergence between these different regions, following either some (Nostratic) unity of speech over all this area, or some early dispersal episode from a more restricted Proto-Nostratic homeland situated within the area.

It is tempting to suggest that this very early expansion of the Proto-Nostratic language might be associated with demographic processes following the Late Glacial Maximum of *c.* 18,000 BP (see Otte 1990). Certainly there is evidence from the study of human mitochondrial DNA that there was a significant expansion of population from southwestern to northeastern Europe around that time (Torroni *et al.* 1998). Although the ecological changes may have been less extreme in western Asia than in northern Europe, some climatic factor could have underlain the distribution of Proto-Nostratic. In due course molecular DNA studies in western Asia may help to clarify such demographic questions. Of course the farming dispersal which underlay the subsequent distributions of the constituent language families of Nostratic took place very much later, around 10,000 BP.

Cauvin (pers comm.; see Cauvin 1994; also Cauvin *et al.* 1997) takes the view that the Natufian culture of the Levant is the best candidate for the Proto-Nostratic homeland, prior to the differentiation of the languages in the four lobes of Figure 2. This would set the time range between 12,000 and 9000 BC, some considerable time after the Late Glacial Maximum.

Acceptance of the Nostratic hypothesis would probably entail the acceptance of some such scenario. As we have seen, this would be archaeologically quite plausible. At the same time it would cast the prehistory and indeed the linguistic prehistory of the area in an entirely new light.

Examining Nostratic

The task of evaluating the Nostratic hypothesis is clearly a matter for competent historical linguists. The organizers of the Symposium from which the present work derives consequently made the deliberate decision not to involve archaeologists or molecular geneticists at this stage of the ongoing debate. The papers which follow initiate, in their different ways, the task of linguistic assessment.

There is always the temptation to bring archaeological data to bear at once upon linguistic issues, and perhaps to invoke also the data available from molecular genetics for the reconstruction of population histories. But such an interdisciplinary approach carries with it certain dangers, of which the most evident is circularity. If one is not very careful one may find oneself using rather inconclusive archaeological information with the hope of supporting (or of negating) a hypothesis from historical linguistics which has not yet found resolution within its own field (see McMahon & McMahon 1995). Such a procedure may simply amount to the compounding of uncertainties (a point made by Campbell (1986) in relation to an interdisciplinary paper (Greenberg *et al.* 1986) utilizing linguistic, genetic and dental evidence). The interdisciplinary approach has undoubted value, but I would argue that the conclusions from each discipline should first be formulated independently, and evaluated and assessed by competent specialists within the discipline before anyone seeks to apply them elsewhere. That is why there were no archaeological papers, and no papers by molecular geneticists at the Symposium. The Nostratic hypothesis is a linguistic hypothesis, and it must first be argued and assessed by competent linguists. Only at a later stage would it be appropriate to bring other disciplines to bear.

It is clear already that there remain wide divergences of view about the Nostratic theory and about various approaches to its scrutiny and assessment. Of course the organizers are deeply grateful to Aharon Dolgopolsky for agreeing to produce the short monograph (Dolgopolsky 1998) which we used to set our proceedings going, and indeed it stimulated some very interesting papers. I should explain, however, that he was not invited to give there a full outline of the Nostratic theory in its various aspects, nor indeed was his objective to set out the most basic or persuasive Nostratic vocabulary. An earlier version which he made available to us at an archaeological seminar at the McDonald Institute proved particularly relevant to our interests as prehistorians, with its use of linguistic palaeontology in an endeavour to reconstruct the material world for the period in question. He kindly agreed to expand it to provide a short volume for our Symposium. I should point out, however, that its very aptness for its original archaeological audience, with its emphasis on the specific material culture of the time, led to the exclusion of many central elements of vocabulary, such as body parts, numbers, pronouns and so forth, whose semantic universality would make them archaeologically uninteresting. Yet it is precisely words such as these which find their place in vocabulary word lists used for comparative purposes, such as those of Swadesh, which would form an important part of any comprehensive presentation of a Nostratic core vocabulary.

The Symposium proved, I believe, to be a very interesting one, as the papers which follow make clear. We are very grateful to all those scholars who participated so effectively and energetically. I should add that we have invited Aharon Dolgopolsky to publish his forthcoming *Nostratic Dictionary* with the McDonald Institute within the framework of the 'Prehistory of Languages' Project, supported by the Alfred P. Sloan Foundation. For it is already clear that controversies will continue and that several issues remain unresolved. The publication of the *Nostratic Dictionary* will be a significant step in making the relevant evidence available for critical scrutiny.

Many of the papers which follow undertake the task, in their different ways, of making explicit what is implied, in linguistic terms, when a genetic relationship is claimed, and of applying such criteria to the Nostratic case. As R.M.W. Dixon (who was not able to be present at our Symposium) has concisely stated in relation to linguistic familial relationships:

> Any hypothesis of relationship must be proved — by reconstructing a good deal of the linguistic system of the proto-language, and by detailing the systematic changes by which modern languages developed from this. (Dixon 1997, 34)

For the case of Proto-Nostratic with a claimed *macrofamilial* relationship (a case which Dixon himself does not accept) there is presumably the two-fold task of first reconstructing the proto-languages for the individual families — a task already at least in part accomplished and indeed for Proto-Indo-European largely complete — and then turning to the linguistic system of Proto-Nostratic and proceeding to detail the systematic changes by which the individual proto-languages of the various families developed from it. In a sense there is a hierarchical system proposed here, and Proto-Nostratic should stand in the same relationship to the various proto-languages of the constituent language families as does each proto-language to the family-member languages which descend from it. That is one of the central themes of the papers which follow.

Many of these papers stress that the consideration of lexicon alone is not enough. At the same time, however, lexical comparisons between languages have proved more open to direct quantification than comparisons in terms of phonology or morphology or other aspects of the linguistic systems of the languages under review. And quantification seems an indispensable approach if it is to be shown that the resemblances between two languages for which a genetic relationship is claimed are more numerous than could be expected from chance equivalencies alone between unrelated languages. But probabilistic methods present their own difficulties of procedure. One of their leading advocates Donald Ringe (who again was not able to be present at the Symposium) has considered the Nostratic case and concludes (Ringe 1995, 74):

> The resemblances between recognized language families on which the
> Nostratic hypothesis is based have never been demonstrated to be greater-
> than-chance — unlike the resemblances between languages of the Indo-
> European family, or within any other generally recognized language family.

That, since it is based upon a systematic quantitative study, is an important
statement, but it cannot yet be taken to close the matter definitively. For what it
is in effect saying is that the methods of inter-language comparison which have
hitherto been used have not shown more numerous indications of genetic relationship than could have arisen by stochastic processes. But it is the experience
of scientific workers in every discipline that there are sometimes patterns among
the data which require quite subtle methods of analysis to be made manifest.
Such has, for instance, been the case with the analysis of DNA sequences from
human mitochondrial DNA where increasingly refined methods of data handling have had to be devised. The 'Out of Africa' hypothesis for human origins
was at first approached through the construction of maximum parsimony trees
to order the DNA data, a method which ran into interpretative difficulties
(Maddison 1991; Templeton 1992) even though the underlying principles were
no doubt sound enough. The application to the same sequence data of network
analysis has led to much more finely-structured conclusions (e.g. Watson *et al.*
1997). In the case of prehistoric Europe it seemed at first that the mtDNA data
were not capable of yielding historically interesting results. Now it is clear that
a whole chapter concerning the population history of Europe in Palaeolithic
times, over a time frame of some 50,000 years, is currently being written
(Richards *et al.* 1998). That example does not of course necessarily imply that
there will be some comparable success in finding new analytical methods in the
field of historical linguistics, although the rather remarkable claims in this respect of Johanna Nichols (1992) have yet to be examined with the careful and
sceptical scrutiny which they merit.

Such reflections may lead one, however, to approach the somewhat po-
lemical conclusions of Ringe (1995, 72) in more interrogative mood:

> In any discipline that deals with real-world phenomena, empirical proof is
> basic to everything else. If after ten millennia (or twelve, or whatever the
> threshold is exactly) the similarities between diverging languages of com-
> mon origin become indistinguishable from similarities that could easily
> have arisen by random chance, language relationships at that and greater
> time depths *simply cannot be posited by scientific linguists*; no other con-
> clusion can be accepted.

There, I think, one encounters the underlying problem which we were beginning to address at our Symposium. What precisely is 'the threshold' of which Ringe writes? How is it established (see Dixon 1997, 48–9)? Where has it been documented, or even discussed, by 'scientific linguists'? What precisely are the methods most suited to detecting and evaluating relationships between languages at great time depth, taking due account of the workings of 'random chance'? These are the questions which begin to emerge in the papers which follow. Until we have more systematic and convincing answers to them it is likely that the Nostratic hypothesis will retain its current somewhat enigmatic status.

References

Barbujani, G.A. & A. Pilastro, 1993. Genetic evidence on origin and dispersal of human populations speaking languages of the Nostratic macrofamily. *Proceedings of the National Academy of Sciences of the USA* 90, 4670–73.

Barbujani, G.A., A. Pilastro, S. de Domenico & C. Renfrew, 1994. Genetic variation in North Africa and Eurasia: Neolithic demic diffusion vs palaeolithic colonisation. *American Journal of Physical Anthropology* 95, 137–54.

Bellwood, P., 1996. The origins and spread of agriculture in the Indo-Pacific region: gradualism and diffusion or revolution and colonisation, in *The Origins and Spread of Agriculture and Pastoralism in Eurasia*, ed. D.R. Harris. London: UCL Press, 465–98.

Bomhard, A.R., 1984. *Towards Proto-Nostratic: a New Approach to the Comparison of Proto-Indo-European and Proto-Afroasiatic*. Amsterdam: John Benjamins.

Bomhard, A.R., 1996. *Indo-European and the Nostratic Hypothesis*. Charleston (SC): Signum.

Brugmann, K., 1897–1916. *Grundriss der vergleichenden Grammatik der indogermanischen Sprachen*. 2 vols. Strasbourg: Karl J. Trubner.

Bulatova, R., 1989. Illič-Svityč: a biographical sketch, in *Reconstructing Languages and Cultures*, ed. V. Shevoroshkin. Bochum: Brockmeyer, 14–28.

Campbell, L., 1986. Comments on 'The settlement of the Americas: a comparison of the linguistic, dental and genetic evidence', by J.H. Greenberg, C.G. Turner & S.L. Zegura. *Current Anthropology* 27, 488.

Cauvin, J., 1994. *Naissance des divinités, naissance de l'agriculture*. Paris: Éditions CRNS.

Cauvin, J., M.-C. Cauvin, D. Helmer & G. Willcox, 1997. L'homme et son environnement au Levant nord entre 30,000 et 7500 BP. *Paléorient* 23(2), 51–69.

Cavalli-Sforza, L.L & F. Cavalli-Sforza, 1995. *The Great Human Diasporas*. Reading (MA): Addison-Wesley.

Diamond, J., 1997. *Guns, Germs and Steel: the Fates of Human Societies*. New York (NY): Norton.

Dixon, R.W., 1997. *The Rise and Fall of Languages*. Cambridge: Cambridge University Press.

Dolgopolsky, A.B., 1973. Boreisch - Ursprache Eurasiens? *Ideen des exacten Wissens, Wissenschaft und Technik in der Sowjetunion* 73(1), 19–30.

Dolgopolsky, A.B., 1987. The Indo-European homeland and lexical contacts of Proto-Indo-European with other languages. *Mediterranean Archaeological Review* 3, 7–31.

Dolgopolsky, A.B., 1993. More about the Indo-European homeland problem. *Mediterranean Archaeological Review* 6–7, 251–72.

Dolgopolsky, A.B., 1998. *The Nostratic Macrofamily and Linguistic Palaeontology*. (Papers in the Prehistory of Languages.) Cambridge: McDonald Institute for Archaeological Research.

Greenberg, J.H., 1963. *The Languages of Africa*. Stanford (CA): Stanford University Press.

Greenberg, J.H., 1987. *Languages in the Americas*. Stanford (CA): Stanford University Press.

Greenberg, J.H., C.G. Turner & S.L. Zegura, 1986. The settlement of the Americas: a comparison of the linguistic, dental and genetic evidence. *Current Anthropology* 27, 477–97.

Kaiser, M. & V. Shevoroshkin, 1988. Nostratic. *Annual Review of Anthropology* 17, 309–29.

McMahon, A.M.S. & R. McMahon, 1995. Linguistics, genetics and archaeology: internal and external evidence in the Amerind controversy. *Transactions of the Philological Society* 93, 125–226.

Maddison, D.R., 1991. African origin of human mitochondrial DNA re-examined. *Systematic Zoology* 40, 355–63.

Militiarev, A.Y. & V.A. Shnirelman, 1988. The problem of Indo-European home and culture. *12th International Congress of Anthropological and Ethnological Sciences, Zagreb, Yugoslavia, July 24–31, 1988*. Moscow: Central Department of Oriental Literature.

Miller, R.A., 1991. Genetic connections among the Altaic languages, in *Sprung from some Common Source: Investigations into the Prehistory of Languages*, eds. S.M. Lamb & E.D. Mitchell. Stanford (CA): Stanford University Press, 293–327.

Nichols, J., 1992. *Linguistic Diversity in Space and Time*. Chicago (IL): Chicago University Press.

Otte, M., 1990. The northwestern European plain around 18,000 BP, in *The World at 18,000 BP*, vol. 1, eds. O. Soffer & C. Gamble. London: Unwin Hyman, 54–68.

Pedersen, H., 1931. *The Discovery of Language: Linguistic Science in the Nineteenth Century*. (1972 reprint. Original Danish edition 1924.) Bloomington (IN): Indiana University Press.

Renfrew, C., 1973. Problems in the general correlation of archaeological and linguistic strata in prehistoric Greece: the model of autochthonous origin, in *Bronze Age Migrations in the Aegean: Archaeological and Linguistic Problems in Greek Prehistory*, eds. R.A. Crossland & A. Birchall. London: Duckworth, 263–75.

Renfrew, C., 1987. *Archaeology and Language: the Puzzle of Indo-European Origins*. London: Jonathan Cape.

Renfrew, C., 1991. Before Babel: speculations on the origins of linguistic diversity. *Cambridge Archaeological Journal* 1(1), 3–23.

Renfrew, C., 1992. World languages and human dispersals: a minimalist view, in *Transition to Modernity: Essays on Power, Wealth and Belief*, eds. J.A. Hal & I.C. Jarvie. Cambridge: Cambridge University Press, 11–68.

Renfrew, C., 1996. Language families and the spread of farming, in *The Origins and Spread of Agriculture and Pastoralism in Eurasia*, ed. D.R. Harris. London: UCL Press, 70–92.

Renfrew, C., 1998. Introduction: the Nostratic hypothesis, linguistic macrofamilies and prehistoric studies, in *The Nostratic Macrofamily and Linguistic Palaeontology*, by A. Dolgopolsky. Cambridge: McDonald Institute for Archaeological Research, vii–xxii.

Richards, M.B., V.A. Macaulay, H.-J. Bandelt & B.C. Sykes, 1998. Phylogeography of mitochondrial DNA in western Europe. *Annual of Human Genetics* 62, 241–60.

Ringe, D.A., 1995. 'Nostratic' and the factor of chance. *Diachronica* 12(1), 55–74.

Ruhlen, M., 1992. An overview of genetic classification, in *The Evolution of Human Languages*, eds. J.A. Hawkins & M. Gell-Mann. Santa Fe (CA): Santa Fe Institute; Redwood City (CA): Addison Wesley, 159–89.

Ruhlen, M., 1994. *On the Origin of Languages: Studies in Linguistic Taxonomy*. Stanford (CA): Stanford University Press.

Shevoroshkin, V. (ed.), 1989. *Reconstructing Languages and Cultures*. Bochum: Brockmeyer.

Shevoroshkin, V. (ed.), 1990. *Proto-Languages and Proto-Cultures*. Bochum: Brockmeyer.

Sturtevant, F.H., 1962. The Indo-Hittite hypothesis. *Language* 38, 105–10.

Templeton, A.R., 1992. Human origins and analysis of mitochondrial DNA sequences. *Science* 255, 737.

Torroni, A., H.-J. Bandelt, L. D'Urbano, P. Lahermo *et al.*, 1998. mtDNA analysis reveals a major late Paleolithic population expansion from southwestern to northeastern Europe. *American Journal of Human Genetics* 62, 1137–52.

Warnow, T., 1997. Mathematical approaches to comparative linguistics. *Proceedings of the National Academy of Sciences of the USA* 94, 6585–90.

Watson, E., P. Forster, M. Richards & H.-J. Bandelt, 1997. Mitochondrial footprints of human expansions in Africa. *American Journal of Human Genetics* 61, 691–704.

Zvelebil, M., 1995. Indo-European origins and the agricultural transition in Europe. *Journal of European Archaeology* 3(1), 33–70.

Chapter 1

The Nostratic macrofamily: a short introduction

Aharon Dolgopolsky

1. The Nostratic macrofamily

This is a hypothetic macrofamily of languages, including Indo-European [**IE**], Hamito-Semitic [**HS**] [= Afroasiatic] (comprising Semitic [**S**], Egyptian [**Eg**], Berber [**B**], Cushitic [**C**], Omotic [**Om**] and Chadic [**Ch**]), Kartvelian [**K**], Uralic [**U**] (= Finno-Ugric [**FU**], Samoyed [**Sm**] and Yukaghir [**Y**]), Altaic [**A**] (= Turkic [**T**], Mongolic [**M**], Tungusic [**Tg**], Korean [**Ko**], and Japanese [**J**]), and Dravidian [**D**]. The hypothesis is based on a large number of common roots (more than 2300) and many common grammatical morphemes, in which regular sound correspondences have been established (cf. Illič-Svityč 1967; 1968; 1971; 1974; 1984; Dolgopolsky 1964; 1969; 1972; 1984; 1989; 1992; 1995). Among the most important resemblances is that of personal pronouns and inflectional person-markers of the 1st and 2nd persons (*mi for "I" in IE, U, A and K, *ṭü (> *ṭi, *śü) for "thou" in IE, HS, U and M, etc.), that of interrogative pronouns (originally *ḳo for "who" and *mi for "what", surviving entirely or partially in IE, HS, K, U and A), basic lexical roots such as *ʔeśo "stay" (> "be") preserved in IE (*es-), HS, U and K, *ʔitä "to eat" (IE, HS, M), *bari "to take" (all branches except U), *wetV "water" (all branches except K), *nimʔV "name, to name" (IE, HS, U, A), as well as words connected with the culture of the final Palaeolithic age, such as *kälu "woman of another moiety" > words for "daughter-in-law", "sister-in-law" and "bride" in IE (Latin glos, Greek γάλως, Slavic *zolv-), S, U, A and D. The original Nostratic phonology (as reconstructed by V. Illič-Svityč and A. Dolgopolsky) had a rich consonant system (opposition of voiced - voiceless - emphatic [= ejectives or fortes], three series of sibilants and affricates, lateral obstruents, laryngeal, pharyngeal and uvular consonants) and seven vowels. The grammatical structure was, most probably, analytic with a rigid word order (a sentence-final verb, the attributive precedes its head, pronominal subject follows its verb) and with grammatical meanings expressed by word order, postpositions (*nu for genitive, *ma for marked accusative, and others) and grammatical pronouns.

2. Phonology

2.1. Consonants

According to the extant comparative evidence, proto-Nostratic had a rich consonant system and seven vowels.

Nostratic consonant chart

Stops and affricates			Fricatives		Central approxi- mants	Nasals	Lateral sonants	Vib- rants
Voiced	Voice- less	Emph. less	Voiced	Voice- less				
b	p	p̣			w	m		
d	t	ṭ				n	1	
						ṅ = ŋ	]	r
ʒ	c	ç	z	s				
ǯ	č	č̣	ž	š				
ʒ́	ć	ć̣	ź	ś	y	ń	ĺ	ŕ
ʒ̂	ĉ	ĉ̣	ẑ	ŝ				
g̗	k	ḳ				ŋ		
g	q	g̣	ɣ	X				
		ʔ		ħ (= ḥ) .	ʕ			
				h				

Symbols in the chart: affricates: ʒ = d͡z, c = t͡s, ǯ = d͡ž, č = t͡š, ʒ́ = d͡zʸ, ć = t͡sʸ; lateral obstruents: ʒ̂, ĉ, ĉ̣, ẑ, ŝ - lateralized ʒ, c, ç, z, s; palatalized consonants: ʒ́, ć, ć̣, ź, ś, ń, ĺ, ŕ = palatalized ʒ, c, ç, z, s, n, 1, r; uvular stops: g̗, q, g̣ = uvular g, k, ḳ; uvular fricatives: X = Spanish j, ɣ = Arabic غ; epiglottal (pharyngeal) consonant: voiceless ħ (= ḥ = Arabic ح), voiced ʕ (= Arabic ع).

In proto-Nostratic, as it is reconstructed on the basis of extant data, there are three series of stops and affricated: voiced (*d, *g, *ʒ, etc.), voiceless (*t, *k, *c, etc.), and "emphatic" (*ṭ, *ḳ, *ç, etc.). The exact phonetic realization of the "emphatic" consonants is not yet clear. Illič-Svityč and I (until recently) interpreted them as glottalized ejectives. But today I do not insist on this particular interpretation. In fact, the emphatic stops are represented in K as glottalized, in HS as glottalized or plain voiceless (the distribution being probably owing to prosodic factors), in U (in the intervocalic position) as geminated voiceless stops, in A as fortes, in IE (in its traditional interpretation) as voiceless. The common denominator of their K, HS, U and A reflexes is an additional effort (if compared to the reflexes of N plain voiceless stops). One cannot determine the original phonetic realization of this additional effort (glottalization, aspiration, fortis articulation?). I prefer to denote them as "emphatic" and to use the traditional Orientalistic underdot as their symbol.

In the following table of sound correspondences the symbol "–" denotes zero. The sign ":" symbolizes the lengthening of the preceding vowel, "⊥:" denotes lengthening of the consonant. The sign "⊥" denotes glottalization of an adjacent consonant, "⊥" is its uvularization, "⊥ᶜ" is its tensification (transformation of a lax consonant into a tense one [fortis]), "⊥" is its devoicing, "ì" is its retroflexivization, "⊥ʸ" is its palatalization. The symbol ° denotes here labialization of the adjacent vowel, the sign ¨ denotes its palatalization. Within conditioning formulas, "_U" means "before a labial vowel", "_E" means "before a palatal vowel". IE +*(s)- denotes the addition of the initial IE *s mobile as a reflex of N word-middle palatal elements. The symbol "**" is used for working hypotheses: in cases where we have sufficient factual confirmation for a group of N phonemes only rather than for each individual N phoneme, e.g. in the case of *n and *ṅ, where a distinction is possible only if the phoneme is represented in Ostyak, so that in daughter languages where there are no *n‖ṅ-roots common with Ostyak we cannot find formal proof of representation of N *n and N *ṅ separately, but only representation of unspecified *n‖ṅ. In such cases we suppose (as a working hypothesis) that both phonemes (in the case described *n and *ṅ) are reflected in the same way, which is symbolized by "**". The letter "N" symbolizes an unspecified non-labial nasal consonant, "L" is an unspecified lateral sonorant. IE *G = *g‖gʷ‖ǵ, *Gʰ = *gʰ‖gʰwʰ‖ǵʰ. M *G = *g‖*g, *K = *k‖q.

N	S	Eg	B	K	IE	U	T	M	Tg	D
*b-	*b	b	*b	*b	*bʰ	*p	*b	*b	*b	*p
*-b-	*b	b	*b, *β	*b	*bʰ	*w, ⊥_/*p	*b	*b	*b	*v
*p-	*p	f	*f	*p	*p, *b	*p	*p, *b	*φ	*p	*p
*-p-	*p̦	f	*f	*p	*p, *b	*p, √	*p	*b, *β>*ɣ	*p	*v
*ṗ-	*p	ṗ	*f	*p, *ṗ	*p	*p	*h>*–	*φ	*p	*p
*-ṗ-	*p	ṗ	*f	*p, *ṗ	*p	*pp	*p	*b	*p	*pp
*d-	*d	d	*d	*d	*dʰ	*t	*j	*d, _i/ *ʒ	*d	*t
*-d-	*d	d	*d	*d	*d	*δ	*δ	*d	*d	*t/tt
*t-	*t	t	*t	*t	*d	*t	*ť	*d, _i/*c	*d	*t

N	S	Eg	B	K	IE	U	T	M	Tg	D
*-t-	*t	t	*t	*t	*d	*t	*t	*d	*d	*t/tt, *t/tt
*ṭ-	*ṭ,*t	d	*ḍ	*ṭ	*t	*t	*t‘	*t,*t i/ *c		*t
*-ṭ-	*ṭ,*t	d,t	*ḍ,*t	*ṭ	*t	*tt	*t	*t	*t	*tt/t
*g-	*g	g,ȝ	*g	*g	*gh, *ĝh, *gʷh	*k	*k̄,*k‘	*g,*g	*g	*k
*-g-	*g	g,ȝ	*g	*g	*gh, *ĝh, *gʷh	*ɣ	*g	*g	*g	*:-
*k-	*k	k,c	*k,*g?	*k	*g,*ĝ, *gʷ	*k	*k̄	*k,*q	*k	*k
*-k-	*k	k,c		*k	*g,*ĝ, *gʷ	*k	*g,*k	*g,*g	*g	*k
*ḳ-	*ḳ,*k	ḳ,k	*ɣ	*ḳ	*k,*k̂, *kʷ	*k	*k‘,*k̄	*k,*q	*x	*k
*-ḳ-	*ḳ	ḳ	*ɣ,*k	*ḳ	*k,*k̂, *kʷ	*kk	*k	*k,*q	*k	*kk
*ɣ-	*ɣ	ʕ?		*ɣ	*x, *xʷ, [*ʁ?]	*-	*-	*-	*-	*-
*-ɣ-	*ɣ	H		*ɣ	*X, ?*h	*-, ?*ɣ	*-	*-	*-, ?*g	*-
*q-	*χ	χ	*H	*q	*x, *xʷ, [*ʁ?]	*-	*-	*-	*-	*-
*-q-	*χ	χ	?*H	*q	*H	*-	*-	*-,*g, ?*g	*-	*-
*ɋ-	*ḳ,*χ	ḳ, χ	*ɣ	*q	*k,*k̂, *kʷ	*k	*k‘,*k̄	*k,*q	*x	*k
*-ɋ-	*ḳ	ḳ	?*ɣ	*q	*k,*k̂, *kʷ	*k, *kk	*k	*k,*q	*k	*k, *kk
*ʒ-	*z	ʒ?		*ʒ̂=*ʒ₁	*s	*s	*ȷ	*ʒ?	*ȷ	*c
*-ʒ-	*z	ʒ?		*ʒ̂=*ʒ₁	*s	?*ć		*ʒ?	*ȷ?	*ṭ?
*c-	*s			*č=*c₁	?*(s)K	*ć	*c	*c?	*c	*c
*-c-	*s	?c	?*s	*č=*c₁	*s	*ć	*c?	*c?		
*ç-	*ç			*ç̂=*ç₁	?*(s)K	*ć	*c	*c	*c	*c
*-ç-	*ç, *s	?ȝ		*ç̂=*ç₁	*s	?*ć	*c	*c		*c
*s-	*š	s	*s	*ŝ=*s₁	*s	*s	*s	*s	*s	*c
*-s-	*š	s	?*s	*ŝ=*s₁	*s	*s	*s	*s	*s	*c
*z-	*z			*ẑ=*z₁	*H	*s	*ȷ	?*s	*s	*c
¿*-z-		z?	?*z	*ẑ=*z₁	?*H	*s		?*s,*y		
*ʒ́-	*z	z?		*ʒ	*s	*ć	*ȷ	*ʒ?	*ȷ?	
*-ʒ́-	*z			*ʒ,*z	*s	*ć		*ʒ		*c
*ć-	*s		*s	*c	*sK	*ć	*c		*c	*c
*-ć-	*s			*c	*s	*ć	*c?	*c?		*c
*ḉ-	*ç			*ç	*sK	*ć	*c		*c	*c
*ḉ-	*ç, *s	?ȝ	?*s	*ç	?*s	*ć(ć)	*c	*c?		?*c(c)

N	S	Eg	B	K	IE	U	T	M	Tg	D
*ś-	*š	s	*s	*s	*s	*ś	*s	*s	*s	*c
*-ś-	*š	s	*s	*s	*s	*ś	?*s	*s	*s	*c
*ź-	*z			*z	*H	*ś	*ȷ	?*s	*s	*c
*-ź-	*z	z?, ś?	*z?	*z	*H	*ś		*ʒ?		*c
*ǯ-	*ð	z?		*ǯ	*s	*č, ?*y ?*š	*ȷ	*ʒ	*ȷ	*c, ?*ṭ
*-ǯ-	*ð	ʒd		*ǯ	*s, *d, *sd?	*ð	*ð	*ʒ, ?*d	*ȷ?	
*č-	*θ			*č	*(s)t-	*č	*c	*c	*c	*c
?*t̆	??*d	?*ȷ								
*-č-	*θ	?c	*s	*č	*s	*č	*c	*c	*c?	*c
*č̣-	*θ̣			*č̣	*(s)t	*č	*c	*c	*c	*c
*-č̣-	*θ̣	ʒ̇		*č̣	*tʰ, *sT	*č	*c	*c	*c	*c
*š-	*š	s	?*s	*š	*s	*š	*s	*s	*s	*c
*-š-	*š	s	*s	*š	*s	*š	*s	*s	*s	*c
*ž-	*š	?z		*z	*H	*š			*s ?	
*-ž-	*š, ?*z	??ʒ	*z	*ž, *z	*H	*š			*ȷ ?	
*ǯ̂-	*ŝ	?s		*ǯ̀	*l	*λ	? *ȷ	*ʒ	*ȷ ?	*c
¿*-ǯ̂-			*s	*ž̀	*l	*ẑ	*l			*ṭ, *ṭṭ
*ĉ-	*ŝ	š	?*s	*c̀	*s	*ć	*c	*c	*c	*c
*-ĉ-	*ŝ	š		?*c̀	*s	*ć	*c	*c	?*c	*c
*ĉ̣-	*ṣ̂	?ʒ	?*ʒ	*c̣̀		*ŝ	*c	*c	*c	*c
*-ĉ̣-	*ṣ̂	ʒ		*c	*s	*ć	*c	*c	*c	*c
*ŝ-	*ŝ	š		*s̀=*s₁	*s, *k͡s	*ŝ	*s	*s	*s, *š	*c
*-ŝ-	*ŝ	š		*s̀=*s₁	*s	*ŝ	*s	*s	*s, ?*l	*c
*ẑ-	*ŝ	š		?*l	*l	*l, *ŝ	*ȷ	*s	*s	*n
*-ẑ-	*ŝ	??n	?*s	*l	*l	*ẑ	*l	*l	*l	*l
*ɣ-	*ʕ	ʕ		*ɣ	*X	*_	*_	*_	*_	*_
*-ɣ-	*ʕ	?ʕ	*H	?*ɣ, ⊥_/*χ	?*X, *_	*_, ?*ɣ	*_	*_	*_	*_, *:
*χ-	*ħ	ħ	*H	*χ	*X	*_	*_	*_	*_	*_
*-χ-	*ħ	ħ	?*H|-	*χ	*X	*_	*_, *:	*_	*_, *:	*_
*ʕ-	*ʕ	ʕ	?*H|-	*_	*H	*_	*_	*_	*_	*_
*-ʕ-	*ʕ	ʕ	?*H|-	*_	*H	*_, *:	*_, *:	*_	*_, *:	*_
*ħ-	*ħ	ħ, x́	*H	*_	*H	?*_	*_	*_		*_
*-ħ-	*ħ	ħ	*H|-	*_	*H	*_	*_, *:	*_		*_
*h-	*h	?h		*_	*X	*_	*_	*_	*_	*_
*-h-	*h, *_	h, -	?*_	*_	*X	*_	*_, *:	*_	*_	*_, *:
*ʔ-	*ʔ	i̊, ȝ	*ʔ-, *H	*_	*ʔ = *_	*_	*_	*_	*_	*_
*-ʔ-	*ʔ	ȝ, y, -	*_, *ʔ	*_, *⊥̓	*_, *:	*ʔ = *_	*_, *:	*_	*_, *:	*_
*m-	*m		*m	*m	*m	*m	*b|m	*m, _#/*b	*m, _#/*b	*m
*-m-	*m	m	*m	*m	*m	*m	*m	*m	*m	*m
*n-	*n	n	**n	**n	*n	*n	**ȷ	*n	**n	*n

N	S	Eg	B	K	IE	U	T	M	Tg	D
*-n-	*n	n	**n	*n	*n	*n	**n	*n	*n	*ń
*ń-	*n	n	**n	**n	*n, ??*kn	*ń	*ʝ	*n	**n, ?*ŋ	*n
*-ń-	*n	n	*n	**n	*n	*n	*n	*n	**n	*-ṇ-, t/n
*ń-	*n	n		*n	*į̂	*ń	*ʝ(<*ń)	*n	*ń	*n
*-ń-	*n			*n	*į̂,?*n	*ń	*ń>*y	?*n	*N	*N
?*ŋ-	*n ?				*n	*n,?*-	*-,*ʝ	*-,*n	*ŋ	?*n
*-ŋ-	*n, *m	n	*n	*n	*n, *ngʰ, *n̄gʰ, *ngʷʰ	*ŋ	*ŋ	*ŋ, *ng, *ng, *ŋK	*ŋ	*ŋk
*ḷ-	*ḷ	?į̂	*ḷ		*ḷ	*ḷ	*ʝ	*n	?*ḷ	??*t
*-ḷ-	*ḷ	r?,3	*ḷ	*ḷ	*ḷ	*ḷ	*ḷ	*ḷ	*ḷ	*ḷ
*ḷ̣-	*ḷ	?n	*ḷ	*ḷ	*ḷ	*ḷ	*ʝ	*n	*ḷ	*n
*-ḷ̣-	*ḷ		*ḷ	*ḷ	*ḷ	*ḷ	*ḷ	*ḷ	*ḷ	*ḷ
*ḷ̂-	*ḷ		?*ḷ	*ḷ	*ḷ	*ḷ̂	?*ʝ	?*ḷ, ?*n	?*ḷ	*ń, **n
*-ḷ̂-	*ḷ	r,3	*ḷ	*ḷ	*ḷ	*ḷ̂	*ḷ̂	*ḷ	*ḷ	*ḷ
*r-	*r	r	?*r	*r	*r	*r	*ʝ	?*n	*ḷ, *n	*n
*-r-	*r	r,3	*r	*r	*r	*r	*r	*r	*r	*ṛ; *r (< *rḷ)
*-ŕ-	*r	r,3	*r	*r	*r	*r	*ŕ; _⊥/*r	*r	*r	*ṛ̂
*w-	*w	ɯ	*w	*w	*u̯	*w	*b,*ᵽ	*b	*b, ?*ᵽ	*v, _U/*-
*-w- /V_V	*w	ɯ₃	?*w	*w,*-	*u̯	*w	*b,*-	*β,*b	*b	*v
*-w- /⊥_V	*w,*-	??-, ɥ	??*w	*w,*-	*u̯,*-	*w,*-		*b,*-	*b,*-	*-
*-w-_⊥ /a,E ?*V	*w,*-		*w	*u̯	*w,*ᵽ	?*ᵽ	*-,*ᵽ	*-	*-,
*-w- /u_⊥	*:		?*:	*-,*w	*:,*-	*-	*:	*-		*:
*y-	*y	į̂	?*y,*i	*-,?*y	*į̂,*ei̯	*y	*ʝ	*y	?*y	*··
*-y- /V_V	*y	ɥ-	*y	*-	*į̂/*i	*y	*y	*y	*y, *-	*y,*-
*-y- /⊥_V	*y,*-	?-	*-	*-	*-,*į̂, +*(S)-	*y,*⊥ʸ	*⊥ʸ, *-,*	*-,*y	*⊥ʸ, *į̂	*-, *į̂
*-y- /V_⊥	*y,*-	ɥ-	?*y	*-	*į̂,*-	*y,*⊥ʸ	*-,*⊥ʸ	*-,*y	*-, *į̂	*-,*y

This chart needs comment and additional explanations. But in this short introduction I cannot afford to go into detail. Some of the problems have been discussed by V. Dybo in his "Editor's Introduction" ("Ot redaktora") of Illič-

Svityč 1971, in Illič-Svityč 1968, Dolgopolsky 1992 and 1997. I may add here a short remark about the origin of the Dravidian intervocalic r-consonants. According to the extant data, D *-ř- (= *-r̞- of the traditional notation, retroflex vibrant/fricative) goes back to N *-ř- or *-ry-, D *-ṛ- (= *-r̞- or *-ṭ- of the traditional notation, a trill, becoming a stop if geminated) goes back to intervocalic N *-r-, while D *-r- goes back to N consonant clusters with *r.

2.2. Structure of words (roots)

The roots (words) have the structure CV (auxiliary words and pronouns only), CVCV, CVCCV, CV(C)CVCV, and CVCVCCV.

2.3. Vowels

The original system of vowels, as reconstructed by Illič-Svityč and accepted by the present author, is as follows:

*i   *u   *ü

    *e   *o

      *ä   *a

The original vowels of the first syllable survive in proto-Uralic, partially in proto-Dravidian (where both *a and *ä have yielded *a) and partially in the Altaic languages (with mutual assimilation of the vowels within a word). The vowels in those languages are stable, i.e. do not undergo alternation (except for quantitative alternation of short and long vowels in Dravidian). In Indo-European, Hamito-Semitic and Kartvelian there is apophony, i.e. a morphologized alternation of vowels (as well as of simple and geminated consonants) that diminishes the importance of vowels for lexical distinction. This apophony is based on phonologization of former allophones [of accentual origin] and subsequent morphologization of the phonemic alternation. Another source of apophony (especially in Hamito-Semitic) is the incorporation of affixes (prefixes → infixes) within word stems, e.g. the prefix *w (passive and non-active verbs) turned into Semitic *u ~ *ū as marker of the passive voice within the stem, the prefix *-an- (< auxiliary verb used in periphrastic constructions of imperfect) turned into the infixes -n-, -a- and into gemination of the stem-internal consonant in Semitic, Berber, branches of Cushitic and possibly Chadic. Due to the apophony the vocalic distinction between roots has been partially lost in IE, HS and K, but indirectly preserved in the prevocalic velar and laryngeal consonants. Thus, the N consonants *g, *k, *k̂ and *q, when followed by N *o, yield IE *gʷʰ, *gʷ and *kʷ; if followed by N *e and *ä, they yield IE palatalized consonants *ĝʰ, *ĝ and *k̂; if followed by *a or consonant, they yield plain velar $*g^h$, $*g$ and $*k$. But the N vowels $*i$, $*u$ and $*ü$ have been preserved better — as IE "sonants" (i.e. high vowels and glides) $*i/*i̯$ and $*u /*u̯$ (see examples in my book *The Nostratic Macrofamily and Linguistic Palaeontology*, in the "Essay of comparison of Nostratic languages" by Illič-Svityč and in my forthcoming dictionary).

3. Grammar

The proto-Nostratic language was analytic. Its grammar was based on a rigid word order, auxiliary words and pronouns.

All words belonged to one of three classes: [1] lexical words, [2] pronouns, [3] auxiliary words. These classes differ in their syntactical functioning. But some pronouns may follow syntactical rules of lexical words, too.

A. The word order may be described by the following rules:
1. The predicate is the final lexical word of a sentence. It may be followed by personal and demonstrative pronouns (*ʔite mi "I eat"), but not by other lexical words.
2. Attributive (expressed by a lexical word) precedes its head.
3. Direct object immediately precedes its verb. Other objects also precede the verb.
4. Pronominal subject follows the predicate.
5. Pronominal attributive ("my", "this") may follow the noun.
6. Case markers follow the noun.
Where is the place of the (non-pronominal) subject? The only place left for it (and for adverbial modifiers) is before the verb with its objects.

This word order survives in U, T, M, Tg, Ko, J, D, K, C as word order and in all daughter-languages as the order of morphemes within words. It was preserved in proto-IE (and its most ancient descendants) as the unmarked word-order, but when the IE words became syntactically autonomous (marking their syntactic function by their morphological form [obligatory cases, etc.]), the former rigid word order disappeared, so that the word order began functioning as a means of focalization. In S, B and Eg the old word order was displaced by a new one (originally emphatic, e.g. attributives following their head).

B. There was a very rich system of pronouns, among them:
[1]   personal pronouns: $*mi$ "I" and $*t̯ü \sim *śü$ "thou" in the direct case, other pronouns in oblique cases ($*Hou̯\nabla$ "by me, my", $*k\nabla \sim *g\nabla$ "thee, thy"),

as well as pronominals [i.e. lexical words replacing the pronouns, e.g. *ʔakE functioning as lexical replacement for *mi "I", whence IE *eĝoH ~ *eĝH-, Semitic *-āku, etc.], pers. pronouns of 1 pl. excl. (*n|n̄∇, *gU), as well as compound pronouns: *mi Ha "we", *ṭ⸢ü⸣ Ha "ye" (with the collectiveness marker *Ha)

[2]   interrogative pronouns: *Ḳo "who?", *mi "what?", *y∇ "which?"

[3]   deictic particles *ʔi, *ʔa, *ʔu indicating the degree of proximity to the interlocutors (hic-deixis, iste-deixis, ille-deixis, etc.), demonstrative pronouns for active (animate and the like) beings\objects and for inanimate objects: *sE "he, she" for animate [active] and *ṭ∇ "it" for inanimate, etc., for collectivity (*Ha, *ʇA), collectivity-plurality (*n|n̄⸢ä⸣, *⸢g∇), plurality (*śA and *ʔ|yi for animate beings; *t∇), duality (*n⸢i⸣ "they [two]", *⸢h⸣u for animate beings, *yi for inanimate objects), individualization based on relation (*y∇ "that which, belonging to") etc. In the descendant languages these pronouns were transformed into personal endings of the verb (1st and 2nd persons from personal pronouns, 3rd person from demonstratives), pronominal possessive suffixes, markers of the nominative case (e.g. IE nominative *-s [for nouns of the active gender] from the demonstrative active *sE), affixes of plural, dual and collectivity. In some languages (IE, S, K) the genitive case marker, too, is based on pronouns (e.g. IE *-oi̯os, K *-is < *y∇ sE, originally "that which X").

C. Auxiliary words: [1] postpositions (in many cases functioning also as preverbs): *nu "of, from", *ma - formative of marked accusative, *Ḳ∇ "towards, to", *ś∇ "to, towards", *tA "from", as well as lexical words transformed into postpositions/preverbs: *ʔin|n̄⸢A⸣ "place" (→ "in"), *do⸢ʔ⸣a "place (within, below)" (→ locative particle *da "in"); [2] auxiliary words of other meanings: *d⸢i⸣, marker of imperfective (< an auxiliary verb?), *ni "no, not", etc.

4. Grammatical typology

As we can see, proto-Nostratic was a highly analytic language. Concerning this point there is a certain disagreement between Illič-Svityč and myself. Illič-Svityč, albeit recognizing the analytic status of many grammatical elements in N, still believed that some of them were agglutinated affixes: the marker of oblique cases *-n (= my *nu "of, from"), the formative of marked accusative *-m (= my *ma), the plural marker *-NA (= my *n|n̄ä of collectiveness and plurality), and several others. This interpretation is hardly acceptable because the N etyma in question still preserve traces of their former analytic status: mobility within the sentence (a feature of separate words rather than affixes), several pN particles are still analytic in some descendant languages.

Thus, the element *nu "of, from" functions in the daughter-languages not only as a case suffix (genitive in U, T, M, Tg, formative of the stem of oblique case in the IE heteroclitic nouns, part of the ablative case ending in T, K and in IE adverbs), but also as a preverb of separation/withdrawal in IE (Baltic), as a prenominal *nota genitivi* in several branches of HS, as an analytic marker of separation/withdrawal (ablative) in B (functioning in postverbal and other positions). The element *ma is still analytic in Manchu (bᴇ, postposition of the direct object, cf. Harlez 1884: 35, 74–5) and Japanese (Old Japanese wɔ > Jap. o as a focalizer, "emphatic object referent particle" [Bernard Bloch]). The element *nǁn̄ä functions not only as a postnominal and postverbal marker of pl. (> pl. suffix of nouns in K, HS and A, ending of 3 pl. of verbs in K, part of the IE ending *-nti ~ *-nt of 3 pl.), but also as the *initial* marker of pl. in U and Eg pronouns: Finnish nuo pl. "those" ↔ tuo sg. "that", nᴇ pl. "those" ↔ sᴇ sg. "that", Eg nꜫ "these things" (and abstract "this") ↔ pꜫ "this" m. ↔ tꜫ f. The animate plural deictic element *ʔǁyi "these, they" functions not only as the postnominal marker of plural (> plural ending in IE, U, A and C), but also as a prenominal and prepronominal plural marker (in B, Beja and Old Eg).

In the descendant languages most of these grammatical auxiliary words and some pronouns turned into synthetic affixes (agglutinative in Early U and A, inflectional [fusional] in IE and to a certain extent in HS and K).

5. Derivation

Less clear is the original status of the N etyma underlying derivational affixes of the daughter-languages. For some of them the analytic origin is obvious. Thus, the etymon *m∇ that underlies affixes of *nomina actionis* and *nomina actoris* in the descendant languages, was a separate word, which is evidenced by its position: in HS and K it is found both in front of the verb and after it (while in IE, U, D and A its position in the word is always final). The same is true of the etyma *ʔa and *ṭ∇ (> suffixes and prefixes of verb; affixes of nouns, infinitives, participles, etc. in the daughter-languages). The affix forming causative verbs in HS may both precede the verbal root and follow it (e.g. in deverbal nouns), which points to an original analytic status of the corresponding N etymon. The adjectival particle *baǁä forming animal names and other names of quality bearers (IE *elη̥-bʰo-s "deer", S *θaʕla-b- "fox", U *ora-pa "squirrel", Tg *kȫr-bᴇ "male reindeer", Manchu oŋgo-ba "forgetful") is interpreted as analytic on the evidence of its phonetic behaviour: the regular reflex of the intervocal *-b- in U is *-w-, but in the word *orapa "squirrel" (> Finnish orava) we find *p, which is regular in the word-initial position only. But for many other etyma of this sort we are not yet able to draw conclusions.

6. Place of Hamito-Semitic

In modern long-range comparative linguistics there are two opinions as to the place of Hamito-Semitic (Afro-Asiatic) among the languages of the world: (1). The traditional view among the long-range-comparativists (H. Pedersen, V. Illič-Svityč, the present author, etc.) is that HS belongs to the Nostratic macro-family as a branch. (2) Recently several scholars have expressed another opinion: HS is coordinate with N rather than subordinate to it. Joseph Greenberg (according to the papers of his pupil M. Ruhlen) believes that HS, Kartvelian and Dravidian do not belong to "Eurasiatic" (his term for N) as its branches but are coordinate with it. Recently Sergei Starostin has also expressed an opinion about the coordinate relationship between HS and "N proper".

   J. Greenberg's opinion (to judge from Ruhlen's accounts) is based on comparison of words of different families within a list of arbitrarily chosen items. Ruhlen published a short list of these items and words for the "Eurasiatic" languages (Ruhlen 1994, 16–17). It is a list of 30 lexical items. It is not free from mistakes and very subjective conjectures. The main IE word for "eat" is not *tap (found in Tokharian only, but registered as the representative of IE in Greenberg & Ruhlen's list), but *ed- (found in almost all branches of IE: Latin edo, Germanic *it-, Sanskrit at-, Hittite it-, etc.), which is related both to Altaic (Mongolian ide "eat") and to HS *ʔit- "to eat" (in East Cushitic and West Chadic). The ancient word for "what?" is not that represented by IE *jo-~*je-, Uralic *jo-, etc. (which is an ancient N root, but it means "which"), but *mi, which is represented not only in Uralic, Altaic (Chuvash), but also in HS (all branches), Kartvelian and probably in Dravidian (cf. Illič-Svityč 1976, 66–8). IE *tek- "to touch" (adduced in the list in the item "arrive") corresponds exactly to HS *√tḳ (in Cushitic and in Semitic, cf. Dolgopolsky 1973, 276). If this list is corrected, enlarged and compared with roots of different branches of HS (as well as Kartvelian and Dravidian), we will see that all these languages are much nearer to "Eurasiatic" than believed by Greenberg and Ruhlen (see Table 1.1):

Table 1.1. *'Eurasiatic cognates' (Ruhlen 1994, 16–17) and their cognates in Hamito-Semitic, Kartvelian and Dravidian.*

Meaning	'Eurasiatic cognate'	Ham.-Sem.	Kartv.	Drav.
I	IE *mē-, U *m, etc.	Highland East Cush. *-m	*me	
I	IE *-x 1 sg. marker in verbs	? *ʔ- id.	*χw- id.	
thou	[1] IE *tu-~te, Ur. *t-, etc., [2] IE *-s, Turk. *sän	*t-	*si-	
pronoun base (actually "I","ego")	IE *eĝʰo-m "ego"	S *-āku "I" & cognates in B, Eg.		
who?	IE *kʷo-, Ur. *ku, etc.	preserved in Om, Beja and Ch, but replaced by *m- "what?" elsewhere	*min (< N *mi "what?")	replaced by *y∇ "which?"
what?	Ur. *mi, Chv. mən, etc.	*m-		replaced by *y∇ "which?"
which?	IE *yo-/*ye-, Ur. *yo-, etc.	? S *ʔayy-		*y∇
this	IE *k̂-, etc.	Cush. *k-		
that	IE *to-, etc.	*t, fem. & inanim. demonstr.		*-t inanim.
not	IE *ne-, etc.	Eg. n	*nu "do not!'"	

Meaning	'Eurasiatic cognate'	Ham.-Sem.	Kartv.	Drav.
not, do not	Ur. *äla "do not"	S *ʔal "do not"		*all- "not to be"
plural	Ur., Turk. *-t, etc.	S *-āt pl.	*-ta	
two	IE *dwō, etc.	S *tuʔm- "twin"	*ṭqu-m- "twin", ṭqu-č̣- "double"	
eye	IE *okʷ-	Agaw *√ʕk̟ʷ- "see", Geez *ʕuk- id.		
see (not "eye")	Yukaghir nuɡie "have seen", etc.			*nik- "be seen"
bark	Ur. *kopa, Turkic *kāp-, etc.	Cush. *k̟app, Ch. *√k̟Hp	Georg. k̟ep̣- "sheet of paper"	
bark, skin	IE *ker-, FU *kere-, Tung. *xere-	S *√k̟rm	Georg. kerk-	
feather	Ur. *tulka, Turk. **däl∇k̔- > *jäläk̔-	Glavda (Ch.) dlākʷà	*bur-ṭq̊l-	
star	IE *Hastēr	*ʕaθtar- "Venus"		
moon	Korean tal (-l < *-r)	Ch. *√tr		
fish	Ur. *kala, Tung. *xol-sa, etc.	Ch. *√klp	Svan k̟almax	*kol(l)-
wolf	Ur. *loka "fox", Mong. *noqa "dog"		*lek̟w- "dog"	*nakka "jackal, fox"

Meaning	'Eurasiatic cognate'	Ham.-Sem.	Kartv.	Drav.
elder brother	Turkic *āka, etc.	S *ʔaχ- < **ʔaq-		
edge	Ur. *käćä, etc.	S *ḳiçç-	Svan ḳäcχ	
wet	Ur. *ńōre, etc.	?S *√nhr "river"		*nīr "water"
dark	[1] Ur. *poḷ▽, etc.			*puḷ(1)- "brown"
	[2] FU *rüm▽	Ch. *rim-	*rum-	
speak	IE *keḷ-, etc.	Arb qāla "say", etc.	Sv. qul- "say"	
sleep	Ur *uni-, etc.	S *ʕūn-		
eat	IE *ed-, Mong.ide-	Cush. *ʔit-, Ron *ʔet-		
arrive	FUr. *tule	S *√dχ1, Ch. *ḍ▽1		
take, grasp	IE *kap-, etc.	Cush. *ḳab-		*kap(p)-
wash	Ht. arra	Arab. √ʔry "pour"		? *ur-
wash		S *rḥṣ̂	*rc₁χ-	

Starostin's hypothesis on HS as a sister-language rather than a daughter-language of N is based on his measurement of shared and replaced vocabulary (of Semitic, IE, Uralic, Turkic, etc.) within Swadesh's list of 100 words (the so-called "basic vocabulary"). Starostin concluded that Semitic (taken as a representative of HS) diverged from N earlier than the "Strictly-N" daughter-families from one another. As it is known, the glottochronological method of measuring linguistic relationship is based on the unproved assumption that languages replace words of the "basic vocabulary" at a constant rate. But glottochronology cannot serve as a reliable instrument of genetic classification of related languages for two reasons: (1) It fails to distinguish between cladistic proximity (German and Swedish are nearer to each other than to Italian and Spanish, because the former go back to Proto-Germanic, while the latter are descendants of Latin, hence German is a "sister-language" of Swedish, but a "cousin-language" of Italian) and dialectal areal proximity (adjacent dialects of a language share innovations without going back to a special intermediate proto-language, e.g. Czech is nearer to Polish than to Bulgarian, but there was no Proto-West-Slavic, i.e. it cannot be claimed that Polish diverged from Czech **later** than from Russian, Bulgarian or Slovene and that it is **genetically nearer** to Czech than to Bulgarian; on the other hand, Russian is nearer to Polish than to Czech, but there was no Proto-Russian-Polish). (2) It fails to take account of major structural (phonological and morphological) factors encouraging word replacement in some languages. For instance, in French some phonological factors (loss of many intervocalic consonants and of the post-tonic syllables) encouraged homonymy and replacement of lexical units (even belonging to the sacrosanct "basic vocabulary" of 100 words): N *ʔeyⱽ "to go, come" is preserved in Proto-IE *ei- "to go" and in Latin ī- "to go", but is lost in French, because the phonetic laws in the history of French do not allow this verb to exist: it would have yielded *ɒi [wa] "goes" indistinguishable from many other ancient verbs which would have merged in *ɒi [wa] unless the language had expelled these potential homonyms. The same is true of N *ʔite "to eat" > IE *ed- > Latin ɛd-, which would have yielded the same *ɒi [wa], unless it had been lost in the prehistory of French. Now, let us take just the same N roots and see what happened to them in HS and in Semitic: N *ʔeyⱽ "go, come" yielded HS *ʔiy- "come" (preserved in Egyptian and Cushitic), but could not survive in Semitic: due to Semitic historical phonology and morphology, "he went" would have been **ʔā in Arabic and **ʔā in Hebrew (because Semitic verbal roots were devocalized and the intervocalic *-y- was lost); N *ʔite "eat" survives in HS (namely in Cushitic and Chadic), but because of the devocalization of verbal roots it was lost in Semitic (otherwise it would have been undistinguishable from other verbs with the same historical consonants, such as *ʔatⱽ "to come"). The alleged constant rate of lexical replacement is a hypothesis at variance with the structure of languages. If in Swadesh's list the percentage of words shared by Semitic and IE, Semitic and Uralic, Semitic and Turkic, etc. is indeed lower than that shared by IE and Uralic, IE and Turkic, etc. (as Starostin claims), it may be due to the structural history of Semitic rather than to the date of separation of HS from other daughter-families of Nostratic.

If Proto-"Nostratic proper" (without HS) had ever existed, it would have lead to the creation of a specific "Strictly-N" word stock, not found in HS (just as there is a Proto-Germanic word stock clearly distinguishable from Proto-Slavic or Proto-Indo-Iranian). But among the 2300 N roots forming the file of my *Nostratic Dictionary* (in prep.) most (about 1600) do appear in HS. The N words found in several daughter-families but not in HS (which could have justified a hypothesis of "N proper") are even fewer than those found in several branches but not in IE, but nobody will exclude IE from N! *Therefore the traditional Nostraticist view considering HS as a branch of N is still valid.*

7. The conference, the remarks of my colleagues and the methodology

This conference, the discussion and the remarks of my colleagues are very helpful in improving the quality and the exact formulation of the etymologies in the *Nostratic Dictionary* in preparation. This is true not only about the remarks with which I agree (and which will be taken into account), but also about those with which I disagree. They are important because they suggest the necessity of explicit and more precise formulation of the ideas concerned with etymologies. One example: in my book *The Nostratic Macrofamily and Linguistic Palaeontology* (hereafter *NM*), I state that "milk as food exists only in societies with husbandry". I meant, in this case, milk as food for adults rather than mother's milk for babies. I supposed that this is obvious. But now I see that there may be misunderstanding, so that a more explicit statement is needed. A further example is the use of capital letters to denote unspecified phonemes of a certain class. They are used not in order to conceal conflicting evidence in daughter-languages (as one colleague suggested), but to refer to cases when the extant evidence is not enough for identifying a phoneme (see below). Here also explicit formulation of the usage will help to avoid misunderstanding.

Therefore it will be useful now to dwell on some questions of methodology:

7.1 The purpose of NM

The book was not intended to be a proof of the relationship between the Nostratic languages. Alexander Vovin is quite right in stressing that "Dolgopolsky's goal in the book is to reconstruct Nostratic homeland and habitat and not to prove the hypothesis itself". The hypothesis was proved more than 30 years ago by V. Illič-Svityč in his "Essay of comparison of the Nostratic languages".

In order to prove genetic relationship, one must compare words of the basic vocabulary and grammatical morphemes. That is what Illič-Svityč did (Illič-Svityč 1971, 3–37). But in a paper concerning linguistic palaeontology the basic vocabulary and the grammatical morphemes are of no use. If I find that IE *ed- "to eat" is cognate with Mongolian ide "to eat", East Cushitic *ʔit- and Ron Chadic *ʔet "to eat" and I reconstruct N *ʔite "to eat", this will add nothing to the study of the life, habitat, homeland and culture of the speakers of proto-Nostratic. The same is true of reconstructing proto-Nostratic pronouns for "I", "thou", "who?", "this" and the Nostratic markers of genitive and accusative. Even without comparative linguistics one expects that the speakers of that ancient language had concepts for "to eat", for "I", "thou", "what?", etc., and had syntactic means to build a sentence. In linguistic palaeontology we work with words and roots belonging to culture and to geographically bound natural phenomena, which is not a basis for proving genetical connections between languages. Usually what is important for the demonstration of genetic relationship of languages is irrelevant for linguistic palaeontology, and vice versa.

Unfortunately, some of my colleagues ignored the goal of *NM* and tried to draw conclusions about the validity of the Nostratic theory on the basis of the etymologies quoted in *NM*. This is like trying to check the existence of the Indo-European linguistic family by analyzing the etymologies found in *Le vocabulaire des institutions indo-européennes* by Émile Benveniste (1969), which is a study in IE linguistic palaeontology.

7.2. Morphology

Some of my distinguished colleagues stressed the crucial importance of morphology for the demonstration of genetic kinship of languages. This is an old idea, expressed already by Antoine Meillet. I am ready to accept the idea, but with reservation: the concept "morphology" must include both synthetic and analytic grammatical morphemes. Actually, the same morpheme may be analytic earlier and synthetic later. One of the essential parts of IE morphology is the personal conjugation of verbs such as Old Indian 1 sg. bharāmi - 2 sg. bharasi - 3 sg. bharati and Greek 1 sg. δίδομι - 2 sg. δίδος - 3 sg. δίδοσι. But already Franz Bopp, one of the founders of IE comparative linguistics, paid attention to the fact that the marker of 1 sg. *-mi in the IE verbs is etymologically identical to the stem of the 1 sg. pronoun (in the oblique cases: cp. Latin mē, Sanskrit mā, English me). It is obvious that the IE personal endings go back to personal pronouns of the 1st and 2nd person and to a demonstrative pronoun (for 3 sg.). What happened in the prehistory of IE happened also in some Mongolic languages - not in the prehistory, but almost before our eyes, in recent centuries: in proto-Mongolic and in Classical

Mongolian there is no synthetic personal conjugation, but in Buryat, Kalmuck, Dagur and Moghol it has been formed from a predicative word + personal pronoun (Buryat ɥereхe-b "I shall come", Kalmuck ɥoβ-na-β "I go", Dagur ičim-bē "ich fahre, werde fahren", Moghol rȧ-nȧn-bi "I come, am coming" with -b, -β, -bē and -bi < proto-Mongolic *bi "I"; Kalmuck ɡarβ-č, Buryat ɡarba-š "you [sg.] went out", Moghol irȧn-či "you come", Dagur ɥawbei̯-ši "you will go" with -č, -š, -či and -ši < Mongolic *či "thou" < *ti).

But if we define morphology as a system of synthetic morphemes only, it is wrong to claim that "morphological correspondences provide the key to the reconstruction of any proto-language" (as Prof. Sinor said here). Shall we exclude Sino-Tibetan and other languages without synthetic morphology from comparative linguistics? Prof. Sinor believes that "a comparative dictionary of Nostratic languages will never bring proof of their genetic relationship, a task that only comparative morphology could accomplish" (Sinor 1998, 8). In the case of Nostratic (an analytic language with grammatical particles and pronouns changing into synthetic morphemes in daughter-languages) the term "comparative morphology" is valid only if it means analysis of the system of these grammatical particles and pronouns with their subsequent transformation into synthetic morphemes. Such comparative morphological analysis was begun by Illič-Svityč, especially in the introductory part of his "Essay of comparison" (Illič-Svityč 1971, 10–18), although his position as to the status of some grammatical morphemes was different from mine (see above section 4).

7.3. Capital letters

Prof. Comrie suspects that the capital letters (used in Nostratic reconstructions as signs of unspecified phonemes of certain classes) are a refuge for cases with conflicting evidence provided by different daughter-languages. He quotes (with indignation) the Nostratic etymon *ḲER∇ for leguminous plants (NM, p. 54), where all letters are capital! In fact what stands behind the capital letters is lack of specific information indispensable for distinguishing between certain phonemes. The symbol *Ḳ means "*ḳ or *q". The distinction between the velar *ḳ and the uvular *q has survived in Kartvelian only and has been lost in all other branches of Nostratic. Hence, if a word is not attested in Kartvelian, we have to use the capital letter Ḳ (or to write explicitly "*ḳ or *q"). In the entry in question the Kartvelian reflex is unknown, therefore we use *Ḳ. The unspecified R means "*r or *ř" (and not "all kinds of rh-sounds", as Comrie erroneously believes). The distinction between the reflexes of *r or *ř has survived in Turkic and Dravidian only. If the word (as *ḲERᐁ) is not attested either in Turkic or in Dravidian, we have to use the capital letter *R. The symbol *E is used here instead of *e|ä because both Indo-European and Hamito-Semitic (the only languages where this word is attested) have lost the former phonological distinction between N *e and *ä. Here I admit that it would have been more accurate to symbolize the reconstruction as *Ḳe|äRᐁ (in order to rule out *i and *ü). The symbol *ᐁ (for unspecified vowel) is used here because no information for identifying the final vowel is available. The use of capital letters is not a refuge but rather a convenient method for distinguishing between the known and the unknown.

7.4. Merger of homonyms

One of my colleagues has indicated cases of overlapping etymologies and has even considered them "a common error in purposes of distant linguistic relationships" (Campbell 1998, 11). The distinguished scholar has not paid attention to the extremely typical phenomenon of homonymic merger in the history of languages. Every new speaker of a language reconstitutes the language on the basis of utterances he heard (and read). It is true of any speaker and of any generation of speakers of any language. If a language has inherited (or borrowed, derived) several homonyms and if it is possible to bridge between their meanings (according to the typical patterns of polysemy - like metonymy, metaphore, ellipsis, broadening or narrowing of meanings, etc.), the homonyms will inevitably merge into one word. I shall cite only several examples (from hundreds and thousands found in the history of languages).

In Russian there is a word сало "lard, tallow, animal fat" and a corresponding adjective сальный "made of tallow, of animal fat". In the nineteenth century Russian borrowed from French the adjective sale "dirty", that according to the laws of Russian morphology turned into сальный (sale souris "dirty smile" > сальная улыбка). But for any speaker of Russian (including those knowing French, like myself) сальный in both meanings is the same word. If in Russian we hear сальная улыбка (as of a man looking at a woman with indecent thoughts), we imagine a face stained with dirty fat.

In Georgian there is a word ḳuli "slave" (an old loan from Turkic ḳul; -i is a suffix of nominative). In the nineteenth century Russian borrowed the word кули from English coolie (of Dravidian origin). The word won popularity in Russian (probably due to the translation of the English novel "Coolie" by the Indian writer Mulk Raj Anand), and in the famous song "От края до края" ("From border to border", by the poet Lebedev-Kumach) there are words: Поют эту песню и рикши и кули, поёт эту песню китайский солдат 'This song [about Stalin] is sung by rikishas and coolies, this song is sung by a Chinese soldier". From Russian the word penetrated Georgian. But in Georgian it coalesced with ǧuli "slave". For speakers of Georgian this is obviously the same word, because the meanings "slave" and "coolie" are very near. A formal proof of this coalescence is the uvular consonant ǧ- in ǧuli "coolie" rather than the velar ḳ- (that usually renders Russian к-).

The Spanish subjunctive sea (of the verb for "to be") goes back both to siat and sedeat (subjunctive forms of the Latin verbs for "to be" and "to sit"), while the Spanish infinitive ser "to be" is from Latin sedēre "to sit" without homonymic merger.

In IE there is a verb *bʰer- that means both "carry, take, bring" (> Latin fer-ō, Greek φέρ-ω, Old Indian bharā-mi "I carry", Slavonic ber-ǫ "I take", Armenian berem "I carry, bring") and "give birth to" (Gothic baíran, English bear "to give birth to", Albanian mberat "pregnant"). It goes back to two different Nostratic words: (1) *bari "to hold, take" [> Mongolian bari- "hold"], (2) *ber∇ "to give birth to; child" [> Dravidian *peṟ- v. "beget, bear (a young)"], as well as possibly to (3) *bär?∇ "to give" [> Turkic bēr- "give", proto-Tamil *paric- "gift"]. In IE, due to the apophony (ablaut), the vocalic distinction between roots with *a, *ä and *e was lost (see above section 2.3), so that the two or three Nostratic etyma lost the phonetic difference between them. The semantic distance between "hold, take" and "give" was small ("give" can be interpreted as metonymy from "hold" → "bring"), but even "give birth to" could be understood as metonymy from "hold, carry", so that the three (or two) Nostratic roots merged into one. In many Indo-European languages the root preserved the original meanings as polysemic variants (such as Gothic baíran "carry, bring, give birth", Old Irish breth "fait de porter/emporter, fait de porter un enfant").

As mentioned in *NM*, Dravidian *civ∇ŋki "leopard" (or sim.) goes back to N *Siw∇ŋgE "leopard", but N *ĉib∇ɣ|ʕ∇ "hyena" merged with it (because in Dravidian in the word-initial position voiceless sibilants and emphatic affricates coalesced, and so did the intervocalic *-w- and *-b-).

Hence overlapping etymologies is not an error but an inevitable result of merger of homonyms — which is a universal law.

7.5. 'Isolated cognates' and the amount of preserved phonological information
Sergei Starostin's comments on my book (Starostin, this volume pp. 137–56) are a brilliant contribution to long-range comparative linguistics. In these comments, together with some other papers, he found Sino-Caucasian parallels to Nostratic etyma, which are the first step for establishing a Macro-Eurasian super-family covering both Nostratic and Sino-Caucasian (as well as probably

some other families). But I have some methodological reservations as to his approach and results.

One reservation (shared by A. Vovin, this volume, pp. 367–86) concerns "isolated cognates", i.e. words represented in only one of many (three or more) branches of a family. According to Starostin, "in families like this the probability of a common root being preserved in only one branch is quite small, so that a root present only in Turkic or Japanese has a very little chance to be actually Common Altaic [i.e. going back to proto-Altaic - A.D.]" (Starostin, this volume, p. 138). Practical application of this principle (not applied by Starostin himself - e.g. in his book on Altaic and Japanese [Starostin 1991]) will bring about disastrous results to etymological research.

The Nostratic etymon *kälu|ü "woman of the other exogamous moiety (of the same age or younger than ego)" is represented in Semitic *kall-at- "bride, daughter-in-law" (*NM*, pp. 84–7), but is not attested by certain cognates elsewhere in Hamito-Semitic. Shall we dismiss this Semitic cognate or find it unreliable only because it is not known in Omotic or Chadic? Shall we share Starostin's strange opinion that such a root "has a very little chance to be" proto-Hamito-Semitic? Let us not forget that all other branches of HS (except Egyptian) are represented by modern languages only, so that a word which might have existed in proto-Omotic or proto-Libyan-Berber was lost several thousand years ago (just as it has been lost in all modern Indo-European languages outside the Slavic sub-branch). By the way, recently possible (but not certain) cognates of this word have been found in Chadic and East Cushitic (cf. the entry *kälu|ü in my forthcoming dictionary).

The Nostratic word *qanṭ∇ "forehead, front" was reconstructed by Illič-Svityč (1967, 354; 1968, 336) on the basis of IE, Altaic and Egyptian. The Semitic reflex of the word was not known to Illič-Svityč because the languages preserving it had not been described then. But according to the laws of Nostratic comparative phonology (discovered by Illič-Svityč) the Semitic reflex has to be *χanṭ-. Today, due to the late Prof. Johnstone's research, we know that in Jibbali (a Semitic language in southwestern Oman) there is a word χanṭi "front, front part of anything" (Johnstone 1981, 303). Both the sound and the meaning of the word correspond exactly to what was predicted by Illič-Svityč. Actually it resembles Leverrier's prediction of the existence of Neptune long before it was actually discovered, or Saussure's hypothesis of the proto-IE "sonantic coefficients" predicting the laryngeals long before they were discovered in Hittite. Shall we neglect or underestimate this extremely important cognate and deny its Proto-Semitic origin only because it is absent in the Semitic languages outside the Southeastern branch (Jibbali, Mehri and

Harsusi)?

The IE word *memso- "meat" is known to have survived in Gothic mimz "meat", but not in any other Germanic languages. Shall we deny the proto-Germanic origin of this Gothic word? Shall we deny the proto-Germanic antiquity of the Gothic verb hlifan "to steal" (obviously from IE *klep- "steal, hide") only because it has been lost by all other Germanic languages?

"A root present only in Turkic and Japanese has a very little chance to be actually Common Altaic" (Starostin). By "Common Altaic" Starostin means "proto-Altaic". Is this statement true? When he speaks about Japanese, I can understand it — but for other reasons: the Japanese language has lost very much of the proto-Altaic phonological information, so that the probability of chance coincidence is rather high here. With Turkic the situation is different: Turkic preserves much of the phonological information of proto-Altaic, so that proto-Turkic *tolu "hail" is a legitimate cognate of IE *del- "rain, dew" and probably of FU *tälwä "winter", in spite of its absence in all other branches of Altaic, and hence it must have existed in proto-Altaic. If a root is preserved in Tungusic (a phonologically conservative branch with *ꭓ- going back to N *ḳ- and *g̣- only) and has extra-Altaic cognate in other Nostratic languages, is has much more than "a very little chance" of being proto-Altaic: Tungusic *ꭓodi- "to finish, stop" (a cognate of Dravidian *kōṭo/*koṭṭ- "end, summit, top", IE *kʷe(:)d-/*kʷo(:)d- "sharp point", Semitic *°√ḳtw|y ~ *ḳuṭṭ- > Geez ḳʷaṭṭ, ḳʷaṭṭa "butt end of spear", etc.) is very likely to have existed in proto-Altaic, though we find no traces of this root in the other branches of Altaic.

Of course, at the initial stage of research of a possible genetic connection between languages we are justifiably recommended to be careful with such "isolates" as the only argument of the common origin of language families. But later, when the genetic connection has been proved beyond reasonable doubt and we know the basic phonological correspondences between the languages in question, we may and should use the isolates (especially if they are rich enough in phonological information) to elucidate etymology of words.

I have already mentioned the preservation of phonological information as an important factor in evaluating attested words as sources of etymology. Words that preserve much phonological information (Spanish tiempo "time" - with *all* information of phonemes of Latin tĕmpus, except for the final -us) are more important than those with little information (as French [tã] spelled as temps). Words with loss of phonological information may go back to different alternative etymons (as French [tã] going back to several Latin words: tempus "time", tantum "so much", tendit "[he] stretches", etc.) and hence cannot prove much. This linguistic factor is much more important than the mechanical factor of "isolatedness".

Starostin's statistical conclusion based on the principle of "isolatedness" and aimed at determining the taxonomic place of Hamito-Semitic (Starostin, this volume, pp. 155–6) has no real value, because the principle of "isolatedness" is wrong.

7.6. *Etymological doublets*

In the extremely interesting remarks of Alexander Vovin there is one theoretical postulate that cannot be accepted. For Vovin it is methodologically impossible that two different roots of a language go back to the same Nostratic etymon (cf. Vovin, this volume, pp. 369, 374). In my opinion, the postulate is wrong. Etymological doublets do exist in languages, if a root is found in different phonetic conditions (incl. phonetic influence of adjacent morphemes), undergoes lexical attraction, analogy, etc. - cf. English off and of, life [laif] and live [liv], wife [waif] and woman ['wu-man] / pl. women['wɩ-mɩn], French homme and on, Hebrew 'leḇ "heart" and la'ḇaḇ id. - both from *'libab-um.

7.7. *External comparative evidence and 'teleological reconstruction'*

On several occasions Vovin mentions "teleological reconstruction" as an illegitimate procedure (Vovin, this volume, pp. 378, 382). By "teleological reconstruction" he means reconstruction of elements (in an intermediate proto-language) that cannot be proved by direct evidence of the descendant languages, but are suggested by external comparison. An example: in M *qoruβ|γu "film, cataract" I prefer the variant *qoruβu which is in regular correspondence with Tung., Kartv., HS and IE, though the attested M languages have lost the phonetic distinction between earlier *-β- and *-γ-. Another example is *K in proto-Tungusian *ɟiₗKⱼ-kte "berries". The element *-kta/e is a suffix of *nomina collectiva*, but there is no direct evidence for the preceding *K. If the Altaic word goes back to N *dik∇ "edible cereals or fruit" (reflected in Kartvelian *dik̇- and in Hamito-Semitic *d∇k̇-), we have to expect in Tungusian *ɟiₗKⱼ-kte > *ɟikte. I cannot share Vovin's attitude to external comparative evidence. The procedure labeled by him "teleological reconstruction" is well known in comparative linguistics and is entirely legitimate. In the proto-Slavic noun *sъnъ "sleep, dream" there is no *p before *n, but we must suppose its existence in the prehistory of Slavic (and its subsequent loss due to the Slavic law of open syllables) on the external comparative evidence of other Indo-European languages: Greek ὕπνος, Old Indian svapnaḥ, etc. In proto-Italic we reconstruct *pes-ni-s (> Latin pēnis "tail, penis"), though the preconsonantic *s has not been attested in any Italic language, but its presence (and subsequent loss due to phonetic laws) is suggested by the external comparative evidence of Old Indian pasas-, Greek πέος "penis". If a proto-language lost phonemes in certain environments (e.g. consonant clusters) without leaving traces in descendant languages, we sometimes may suppose their former existence by analyzing the ancient cognate languages ("sisters" of the proto-language). In reconstructing the history of languages we cannot afford to neglect evidence of any source.

7.8. Trisyllabic etymons

In Illič-Svityč's reconstruction most lexical etymons (but not pronouns or grammatical morphemes) are disyllabic. But even Illič-Svityč recognized the existence of some N trisyllabic words: *Ḳawing∇ "arm-pit" (Illič-Svityč 1971, 344), *pʿaliHma "palm of hand" (Illič-Svityč 1984, 93–5) and probably *purč∇(g∇) ~ *pülč∇(g∇) "flea" (Illič-Svityč 1976, 99–100). In my forthcoming dictionary trisyllabic etyma are more numerous: *ʔin|n̂Aše|i "person, man", *ʔ|hi|üśUt̪∇ "to sweep, to rake", *ʔeẑekU "thorn, hook" (> "tooth"), *ʕ|ɣ∇P∇r∇ "bank (of a river)", *ʕ|ɣEw∇S∇ "(a species of) grass", *ħ|χ⸢iʼ⸣ˌLˌt∇R∇ "vein, sinew, root", *χako|aR∇ ≈ "top part, tip, extremity", *g|ɣ∇Rg|ɣ∇VHT∇ "waterfowl", *qUb∇ź∇ "food made of ground cereals", *q⸢oʼ⸣LP∇ħ∇ or *q⸢oʼ⸣LuPħ∇ "to gulp, swallow", *ḳUˌyˌm∇ĉ∇ "(≈) shin, thigh", *ḳiruʕ∇ "to strike, hit", *ḳ⸢uʼ⸣R⸢ʕ∇ʼ⸣d∇ or *ḳuRt̪∇ʕ∇ "stinging insect", *Ḳ∇R∇Hp̣|p∇ "piece of leather (used esp. as footwear)", *ḳaRup∇ "bark of a tree, skin", *ḳ⸢ü⸣ry∇p∇ "sack, wicker basket", *Ḳa|UˌRˌḲub|p∇ "top, summit, crown of the head", *ḲäRus|š∇ "to congeal", *ḳERH∇ʒ|ʒ́∇ "hornet, wasp", *ḳUR∇ċ|ĉ∇ "hard, to dry up, to harden", *Ḳ⸢oʼ⸣yaŕ̩wˌi (or *ḲE⸢wʼ⸣aŕ̩wˌi) "fat, tallow", *Ḳe|ä⸢hʼ⸣uy∇ "to heat, singe, burn" (trans.), *Ḳ⸢ä⸣ʼyap̣∇ "sharp stone\rock\cliff", *künü|iʕa "a joint in a limb (knee, elbow), to bend in a joint", *kenˌ∇ˌc|ĉ∇d∇ "joint (articulation), shoulder joint", *kiRuHgE "to gnaw", *gurand∇ "log, trunk of a tree", *gor∇b|p∇ "to scratch, scrape", *g⸢ä⸣ʼyŝ∇ʔa "to be frightened, sorrowful, to worry", *ge⸢ʒ́⸣üŝ∇ "late, evening", *ĉä⸢ʕ|ɣU⸣R∇ "calf of the leg, shank", *ĉoyp∇ʕ|ɣ⸢aʼ⸣ "clay, mud, slush", *sa⸢hʼ⸣ida "to throw, cast; take aim, direct (e.g. a weapon) straight to the aim", *ś∇lχit̪|d∇ "to slip", *Siw∇ŋgE "leopard", *šiŋ∇r∇ "mouse", *š⸢aʼq⸣∇R∇ "coal, soot", *š⸢ayuʼ⸣t∇ ~ *šat̪Uy∇ "twig, rod", *ŝäɣUŕ∇ "hair", *ŝitaw∇ "cold weather", *źig⸢oʼ⸣d∇ "stake, peg", *ZEgut∇ "thigh, leg", *źaguí∇ or *źugaí∇ "to flow, pour", *ʒaʕ|ɣid∇ "to cut", *ẑäʼḲi⸢ʼ⸣d∇ "to move, go", *ẑeh⸢aʼ⸣Ra "moon", *ʒ|ʒ́∇1|⸢ʼi⸣KE "to slip, to slide", *ʒuw∇⸢n̂ʼ⸣∇ "to copulate, fornicate", *dagur∇ "shoulder-blade as part of the back", *daRug∇ "to tremble, shake", *de|äRH∇k∇ ~ *de|äRH∇ga "to walk, run; road", *tawigE "insect, vermin" (→ 'mouse'), *toqUz∇ "to plait, wattle", *ṭuHib∇ "reed, stick", *ʳṭˀuˀ̣ˀiˤ̣ɣE "to come, enter", *ṭEɪˤUˀɣE "breast, female breast", *ṭoHury∇ "dirt, be dirty", *bukEɣ̣ˤ∇ "billy goat, ram", *boruˤ̣ɣ∇ "trunk" (→ "log"), *buruH∇ "eyebrow, eyelash", *baˤ̣ɣ̣gut∇ "to kick, push", *ʳpˀaʟqaṭ∇ ~ *ʳpˀaʟṭ∇q∇ "broad and flat", *poqEžˇ∇ ~ *pož∇q∇ "thigh, haunch", *p̣p∇R∇ćˌχˌ∇ "fingernail, claw", *p̣poriˤU "summit, tip", *mariʔ∇ "young man, young male", *meʔiŝ∇ "ram\sheep, hide", *ṇñigES∇ "to butt, pierce", *naher∇ "day, sun, daylight", *ṇñ∇yäR∇ "man, male animal", etc.

In my opinion, trisyllabic words (> roots) are not an exception, but one of the existing types of syllabic structure. Hence I cannot accept the rejection of trisyllabic words as an argument against some of my reconstructions (see Michalove & Manaster Ramer, this volume, p. 240 about *dˀoTˀgiHU "fish"). I suppose that contraction of trisyllabic words into disyllabic is a common phenomenon in the later history (daughter-families of Nostratic), which explains the loss of *-ˀoTˀ- (originally in an unstressed syllable?) in HS, IE and A. Compare similar phenomena in the history of many languages, such as the fate of Latin *digitus, cubitum, calidus* and *frigidus* in the Romance languages.

Note

I should appreciate it if the readers of *NM* will take note of my poor English style and replace my inappropriate (actually Russian traditional) expression *subtropical climate* (for the Mediterranean and the Near East) with *warm temperate climate*, and *water body* with *body of water*.

References

Benveniste, É., 1969. *Le vocabulaire des institutions indo-européennes*, vols. I–II. Paris: Les Éditions de Minuit.

Campbell, L., 1998. Is it Believable?: Nostratic and Linguistic Palaeontology in Methodological Perspective. Pre-circulated paper submitted to the Symposium on the Nostratic Macrofamily at the McDonald Institute for Archaeological Research, Cambridge, July 17–18, 1998.

Dolgopolsky, A., 1964. *A Long-Range Comparison of Some Languages of Northern Eurasia*. (VII Intern. Congress of Anthropological and Ethnographical Sciences.) Moscow: Nauka.

Dolgopolsky, A., 1969. Nostraticheskije osnovy s sochetanijem shumnyx soglasnyx, in *Etimologija 1967*, ed. O. Trubachev. Moscow: Nauka, 296–313.

Dolgopolsky, A., 1972. Nostraticheskije korni s sochetanijem lateral'nogo i zvonkogo laringala, in *Etimologija 1970*, ed. O. Trubachev. Moscow: Nauka, 356–69.

Dolgopolsky, A., 1973. *Sravnitel'naja fonetika kushitskix jazykov*. Moscow: Nauka.

Dolgopolsky A., 1984. On personal pronouns in the Nostratic languages, in *Linguistica et Philologica: Gedenkschrift für Björn Collinder*, eds. O. Gschwantler, K. Rédei & H. Reichert. Vienna: Braumüller, 65–112.

Dolgopolsky, A., 1989. Problems of Nostratic comparative phonology (preliminary report), in *Reconstruction of Languages and Cultures*, ed. V. Shevoroshkin. Bochum: Brockmeyer, 90–98.

Dolgopolsky, A., 1992 [written in 1976]. The Nostratic vowels in Indo-European, in *Nostratic, Dene-Caucasian, Austric and Amerind*, ed. V. Shevoroshkin. Bochum: Brockmeyer, 298–331.

Dolgopolsky, A., 1995. Sud'ba nostraticheskix glasnyx v indojevropejskom jazyke. *Moskovskij Lingvisticheskij Zhurnal* 1, 14–33.

Dolgopolsky, A., 1997. The Indo-European stops in the light of the long range relationship of Indo-European with Afroasiatic and some language families of Northern and Eastern Asia, in *IV Mezhdunarodnaja konferencija po jazykam Dal'nego Vostoka, Jugo-Vostochnoj Azii i Zapadnoj Afriki. Tezisy dokladov*, vol. II, ed. M. Kaplun. Moscow: [Moscow University], 109–12.

Dolgopolsky, A., 1998. *The Nostratic Macrofamily and Linguistic Palaeontology*. (Papers in the Prehistory of Languages.) Cambridge: McDonald Institute for Archaeological Research.

Harlez, H. de, 1884. *Manuel de la langue mandchoue: grammaire, anthologie et lexique*. Paris: Maisonneuve & Leclerc.

Illič-Svityč, V.M., 1967. Materialy k sravnitel'nomu slovarju nostraticheskix jazykov, in *Etimologija 1965*, ed. O. Trubachev. Moscow: Nauka, 321–73.

Illič-Svityč, V.M., 1968. Sootvetstvija smychnyx v nostraticheskix jazykax, in *Etimologija 1966*, ed. O. Trubachëv. Moscow: Nauka, 304–55 & 401–4.

Illič-Svityč, V.M., 1971. *Opyt sravnenija nostraticheskix jazykov. Vvedenije. Sravnitel'nyj slovar' (b - Ķ)*. Moscow: Nauka.

Illič-Svityč, V.M., 1974b. *Opyt sravnenija nostraticheskix jazykov. Sravnitel'nyj slovar' (l - ʒ́). Ukazateli*. Moscow: Nauka.

Illič-Svityč, V.M., 1984. *Opyt sravnenija nostraticheskix jazykov. Sravnitel'nyj slovar' (p - q)*. Moscow: Nauka.

Johnstone, T.M., 1981. *Jibbāli Lexicon*. Oxford: Oxford University Press.

Ruhlen, M., 1994. *On the Origin of Languages*. Stanford (CA): Stanford University Press.

Sinor, D., 1998. Personal Remarks on the Nostratic Theory Prepared for a Symposium to be held on the Subject. Pre-circulated paper submitted to the Symposium on the Nostratic Macrofamily at the McDonald Institute for Archaeological Research, Cambridge, July 17–18, 1998.

Starostin, S.A., 1991. *Altajskaja problema i proisxozhdenije japonskogo jazyka*. Moscow: Nauka.

Part II
The Composition and Reconstruction of Nostratic

Chapter 2

Review of Dolgopolsky's *The Nostratic Macrofamily and Linguistic Palaeontology*

Allan R. Bomhard

Aharon Dolgopolsky's *The Nostratic Macrofamily and Linguistic Palaeontology* (hereafter *NM*) begins with an introduction by the well-known British archaeologist Colin Renfrew. Renfrew does an excellent job in tracing the history of the Nostratic Hypothesis, though the names of several contemporary scholars who have made important contributions to Nostratic studies are conspicuous by their absence (Václav Blažek and Allan Bomhard, for example). Renfrew then presents a very balanced summary of the problems and pitfalls involved in attempting to demonstrate distant linguistic relationship, and he quite rightly points out that this kind of work.is still looked upon with disapproval, if not outright hostility, by most mainstream linguists. However, the very fact that Dolgopolsky's work has been published and that a symposium has been devoted to discussing this work and its implications indicates that the Nostratic Hypothesis has gained both recognition and a modicum of respectability, if not general acceptance.

In *NM*, Dolgopolsky is mainly concerned with linguistic palaeontology, and the focus of his attention, therefore, is on putative etyma pertaining to habitat, social organization, and material culture. Dolgopolsky's conclusions are supported by a sample of 124 proposed cognate sets. The book ends with a reconstruction of the Proto-Nostratic phonological system and the reflexes of the consonants (but not the vowels) in the major branches of Nostratic.

So, what then is Dolgopolsky trying to establish? The fact is, he never explicitly says, at least not in one place — we have to infer what his thesis is from the introduction to the book written by Renfrew and from the introductory sections that Dolgopolsky provides to each of the topic areas he is discussing. It would have been helpful if Dolgopolsky had laid out his conclusions in detail in an introduction or in a summation at the end of the book. What I have in mind here is something similar to what Calvert Watkins prepared for the introduction to the *American Heritage Dictionary of Indo-European Roots* (1985). Basically, what he is saying is that there is a group of languages, stretching across Northern and Central Eurasia, the Near East and North Africa, and the Indian subcontinent, and belonging to several well-established language families, which, upon closer investigation, appear to belong a larger grouping, and which, following the name proposed in 1903 by Holger Pedersen (cf. Pedersen 1931, 335–9 for details), has come to be known as the Nostratic macrofamily. Furthermore, by applying the techniques of linguistic palaeontology, it is possible to come up with a possible date when the parent language (so-called 'Proto-Nostratic') of this macrofamily was spoken, namely, somewhere between 15,000 to 12,000 BCE, to locate its place of origin or 'homeland', namely, in Southwest Asia, that is to say, in the Near East in the vicinity of the Fertile Crescent, and to get a rough idea about the social organization and material culture (late Upper Palaeolithic ~ early Mesolithic) of the speakers of the parent language. The conclusions reached by Dolgopolsky, it may be noted, concur fairly closely with those I reached in Chapter 6 of my 1996 book entitled *Indo-European and the Nostratic Hypothesis*.

Two considerations need to be kept in mind when evaluating the cognate sets proposed by Dolgopolsky. The first of these is the question of semantic plausibility. Has Dolgopolsky established recurrent sound-meaning correspondences for a reasonably large sample of lexical material, using the oldest forms available from as many languages as possible? Has he selected lexical forms for comparison from the daughter languages that have identical or similar meanings? If, on the other hand, the material he is comparing contains forms that are divergent in meaning, can they convincingly be derived, through widely-attested semantic shifts, from earlier forms with identical or similar meaning? Finally, has he proposed semantic structures for Proto-Nostratic that reflect the habitat, social organization, and material culture of the late Upper Palaeolithic and early Mesolithic periods as known from other disciplines such as archaeology? The second consideration concerns sound correspondences. Has Dolgopolsky established regular sound correspondences (that is, those that occur consistently and systematically)? When exceptions to the regular sound correspondences occur, has he explained them? Has he reconstructed proto-forms that reflect what is actually attested in the daughter languages, or are his reconstructions *ad hoc* or based upon theoretical considerations that do not necessarily reflect what is actually attested? Finally, has he formulated the sound laws leading to the forms in the descendant languages, identifying the laws that have produced the regular sound correspondences as well as the exceptions?

Let us look at the sound correspondences first. Dolgopolsky's reconstruction of the Proto-Nostratic phonological system appears at the end of the book on page 101, though only the consonants are given. This is followed by a table of sound correspondences, beginning on page 102. Though Dolgopolsky uses slightly different symbols than I use, the phonological system he posits for Proto-Nostratic is quite close to what I posit, namely:

Stops and affricates:

p^h	t^h	c^h	$č^h$	t^{yh}	$tł^h$	k^h	k^{wh}	q^h
b	d	3	ǯ	d^y		g	g^w	G
p'	t'	c'	č'	t'^y	tł'	k'	k'^w	q'	q'^w	ʔ

Fricatives:

s	š	s^y		h	ħ
z	ž (?)	z^y (?)			ʕ

Glides:

w	y

Nasals and Liquids:

m	n	n^y	ŋ
	l	l^y	
	r	r^y	

Vowels:

i ~ e		u ~ o
	ə ~ a	

Also the sequences:

iy ~ ey	uy ~ oy	əy ~ ay
iw ~ ew	uw ~ ow	əw ~ aw

Unlike Dolgopolsky, I reconstruct a series of labialized velars (= 'labiovelars'). In place of Dolgopolsky's *ʒ́, *ć, *ć', I set up a series of palatalized alveolars *d^y, *t^y, *t'^y, respectively. There are several other disagreements between my reconstruction and Dolgopolsky's, but all of these differences are relatively minor.

The major disagreement I have with Dolgopolsky (and, it goes without saying, with Illič-Svityč as well) concerns the sound correspondences. Let me repeat here the objections I have raised repeatedly in the past.

In 1972 and 1973, the Georgian scholar Thomas V. Gamkrelidze and the Russian scholar Vjačeslav V. Ivanov jointly proposed a radical reinterpretation of the Proto-Indo-European stop system. According to their reinterpretation, the Proto-Indo-European stop system was characterized by the three-way contrast glottalized ~ voiceless (aspirated) ~ voiced (aspirated). In this revised interpretation, aspiration is viewed as a redundant feature, and the phonemes in question could also be realized as allophonic variants without aspiration. Paul

J. Hopper made a similar proposal at about the same time. I should point out here that, even though I support the revisions proposed by Gamkrelidze, Hopper, and Ivanov, my views are not dependent upon any particular reconstruction of the Indo-European stop system — the sound correspondences I have proposed can be maintained using the traditional reconstruction as well. What the new views of Indo-European consonantism did was bring into light the implausibility of certain Nostratic sound correspondences established by Dolgopolsky and Illič-Svityč (see below for details).

This new interpretation opens new possibilities for comparing Proto-Indo-European with the other Nostratic daughter languages, especially Proto-Kartvelian and Proto-Afrasian, each of which had a similar three-way contrast. The most straightforward assumption would be that the glottalized stops posited by Gamkrelidze and Ivanov for Proto-Indo-European would correspond to glottalized stops in Proto-Kartvelian and Proto-Afrasian, while the voiceless stops would correspond to voiceless stops and voiced stops to voiced stops. This, however, is quite different from the correspondences proposed by Dolgopolsky and Illič-Svityč. They see the glottalized stops of Proto-Kartvelian and Proto-Afrasian as corresponding to the traditional plain voiceless stops of Proto-Indo-European, while the voiceless stops in the former two branches are seen as corresponding to the traditional plain voiced stops of Proto-Indo-European, and, finally, the voiced stops to the traditional voiced aspirates of Proto-Indo-European. Dolgopolsky and Illič-Svityč then reconstruct the Proto-Nostratic phonological system on the model of Kartvelian and Afrasian, with the three-way contrast glottalized ~ voiceless ~ voiced in the series of stops and affricates.

The mistake that Dolgopolsky and Illič-Svityč have made is in trying to equate the glottalized stops of Proto-Kartvelian and Proto-Afrasian with the traditional plain voiceless stops of Proto-Indo-European. This reconstruction would make the glottalized stops the least marked members of the Proto-Nostratic stop system. Dolgopolsky's and Illič-Svityč's reconstruction is thus in contradiction to typological evidence, according to which glottalized stops are uniformly the most highly marked members of a hierarchy. The reason that Dolgopolsky's and Illič-Svityč's reconstruction would make the glottalized stops the least marked members is as follows: Dolgopolsky and Illič-Svityč posit glottalics for Proto-Nostratic on the basis of one or two seemingly solid examples in which glottalics in Proto-Afrasian and/or Proto-Kartvelian appear to correspond to traditional plain voiceless stops in Proto-Indo-European. On the basis of these examples, they assume that, whenever there is a voiceless stop in the Proto-Indo-European examples they cite, a glottalic is to be reconstructed for Proto-Nostratic, even when there are no glottalics in the corresponding Kartvelian and Afrasian forms! This means that the Proto-Nostratic glottalics have the same frequency distribution as the Proto-Indo-European plain voiceless stops. Clearly, this cannot be correct. The main consequence of the mistaken comparison of the glottalized stops of Proto-Kartvelian and Proto-Afrasian with the traditional plain voiceless stops of Proto-Indo-European is that Dolgopolsky and Illič-Svityč are led to posit forms for Proto-Nostratic on the basis of theoretical considerations but for which there is absolutely no evidence in any of the Nostratic daughter languages. Let us look at one or two examples to illustrate the *ad hoc* nature of these reconstructions:

1. On page 17, Dolgopolsky reconstructs a second singular personal pronoun *ṭü > *ṭi 'thou', with an initial glottalized dental, on the basis of data from Indo-European, Afrasian (Dolgopolsky uses the term 'Hamito-Semitic' for this language family), Uralic, and Mongolian. When one looks at the attested forms in the daughter languages, one cannot find a single form anywhere that begins with a glottalized consonant. Indeed, in natural languages having glottalized consonants, these sounds tend to be underrepresented in pronoun stems and inflectional affixes. What, then, is the basis for the reconstruction *ṭü? — nothing more than an *ad hoc* rule set up by Illič-Svityč.
2. Also on page 17, Dolgopolsky reconstructs an interrogative stem *ḳo- 'who?'. As in the preceding example, there is no evidence to support the reconstruction of an initial glottalized velar in this stem.
3. On page 79, no. 100, Dolgopolsky sets up a Proto-Nostratic *ḳVRVHṗ/pV 'piece of leather (used esp. as footwear)'. Again, we find an initial glottalized velar in the reconstructed form, without a shred of evidence in the cited material to back up this reconstruction. Apparently, the basis for this reconstruction is the assumption that a plain voiceless stop in Proto-Indo-European always implies a glottalic in Proto-Nostratic.

Do these criticisms invalidate *in toto* the cognate sets proposed by Dolgopolsky and Illič-Svityč in which glottalics in Kartvelian and Afrasian appear to correspond to plain voiceless stops in Indo-European? Well, no, not exactly — it is not quite that simple. In some cases, the etymologies are correct, but the Proto-Nostratic reconstructions are wrong. This applies to all of the examples cited above — for the second person personal pronoun, I would reconstruct Proto-Nostratic *tʰi, in place of *ḳo- 'who?', I would reconstruct Proto-Nostratic *kʷʰa-, and in place of *ḳVRVHṗ/pV 'piece of leather (used esp. as footwear)', I would reconstruct Proto-Nostratic *kʰVr-Vpʰ-. Other examples adduced by Dolgopolsky and Illič-Svityč admit alternative explanations, while still others are questionable from a semantic point of view and should be abandoned. Once the questionable examples are removed, there is an extremely small number (no more than a handful) left over that appear to support their position. However, compared to the massive counter-evidence in which glottalized stops in Kartvelian and Afrasian correspond to similar sounds (the traditional plain voiced stops) in Proto-Indo-European, even these residual examples become suspect (they may be borrowings or simply false cognates). Finally, there are even some examples where Dolgopolsky's and Illič-Svityč's comparison of glottalized stops in Proto-Kartvelian and Proto-Afrasian with plain voiceless stops in Proto-Indo-European is correct. This occurs in the cases where two glottalics originally appeared in a Proto-Nostratic root: *C'VC'-. Such roots are preserved without change in Proto-Kartvelian and Proto-Afrasian, while in Proto-Indo-European, they have been subject to a rule of regressive deglottalization: *C'VC'- > *CVC'-.

These disagreements, however, are not serious, and they in no way undermine or even diminish the work done by Dolgopolsky and Illič-Svityč, nor do the disagreements in any way invalidate the existence of the Nostratic macrofamily. Very few linguists doubt the existence of an Afrasian (also called Afroasiatic, Hamito-Semitic, or Semito-Hamitic) language family. And yet, there are three separate reconstructions of the Proto-Afrasian phonological system. First, there is the system of Vladimir Orël and Olga Stolbova (1995, xxi–xxiv); next, that of Christopher Ehret (1995, 55–67); and, last, that of Igor M. Diakonoff (1992, 65–97). In some cases, such as in the sibilants and affricates, each of these scholars establishes very different sound correspondences. Diakonoff and Ehret reconstruct labialized velars, but Orël & Stolbova do not. Diakonoff sets up a vertical vowel system consisting of *ə and *a, while Orël & Stolbova posit the vowels *a, *e, *i, *o, *u, and *ü and Ehret sets up five short vowels and five long vowels: *a, *aa, *e, *ee, *i, *ii, *o, *oo, *u, *uu. Sometimes these scholars arrive at different reconstructions even though they cite the same data from the daughter languages. I view the disagreements between Dolgopolsky and Illič-Svityč, on the one hand, and myself, on the other hand, as no more serious than the disagreements regarding the reconstruction of the Proto-Afrasian phonological system.

I would like to make one last point concerning the table of correspondences: Dolgopolsky compares the reconstructed phonological systems of Proto-Kartvelian, Proto-Indo-European, Proto-Uralic, and Proto-Dravidian, but he does not include Proto-Afrasian or Proto-Altaic. In the case of Afrasian, he lists Semitic, Egyptian, and Berber separately (presumably, Proto-Semitic, Proto- or pre-Egyptian, and Proto-Berber since the sounds are preceded by an asterisk), but not Cushitic, Omotic, or Chadic. In the case of Altaic, he treats Turkic, Tungus, and Mongolian separately in the table of correspondences. However, in the examples, he usually gives Proto-Altaic reconstructions, though not Proto-Afrasian. Why is there not more consistency here or at least an explanation?

Now let us turn to the heart of Dolgopolsky's book, namely, the sections on habitat (where and when?), social organization (kinship), and material culture. We will begin by examining each of the etymologies proposed by Dolgopolsky:

1. *ʔibrE 'fig tree': though the semantics are acceptable, the phonology is not plausible. Therefore, this etymology must be rejected.

2. *ĉ[i]bVɣV (or *ĉ[i]bVʕV) 'hyena': this etymology is plausible. I would reconstruct a Proto-Nostratic root *ƛʼib- 'hyena', to which Afrasian, Dravidian, and Altaic have added different suffixes — it is very important to understand Proto-Nostratic root structure patterning and to be able to distinguish between roots and affixes and to explain what has happened in each of the daughter languages. In this regard, Afrasian is particularly important since it is clearly the most ancient branch of Nostratic — it was the earliest branch to split off from the rest of the Nostratic speech community. Thus, Afrasian may be presumed to have preserved some very archaic features, and indeed it does, root structure patterning being one of them.

3. *ʔ[ü]řVwV 'large feline': though the semantics are acceptable, the phonology is not plausible. Therefore, this etymology must be rejected.

4. *SiwVŋgE 'leopard': this etymology is not convincing.

5. *ʔoř[u] 'antelope (male), deer': the Proto-Afrasian stem is *ʔar- 'ram, goat' (cf. Orël & Stolbova 1995, 68, no. 694) and should, therefore, be removed from this etymology. On the basis of the Dravidian and Altaic material cited by Dolgopolsky, I would reconstruct Proto-Nostratic *ʔurʸ-/*ʔorʸ- 'deer'.

6. *maŋ[g]V or *maN[i][g]V 'monkey': this etymology is plausible. I would reconstruct Proto-Nostratic *maŋ-g- 'monkey'.

7. *šüŋU 'snow': this etymology is possible, though highly speculative. A Proto-Nostratic *šiŋ- (or possibly *šuŋ-) may be reconstructed, to which Indo-European has added the suffix *-gʷ- > *šiŋ-gʷ- > *šŋi-gʷ- (through metathesis, as proposed by Dolgopolsky), which, in turn, > *sne̯igʷʰ- (using traditional transcription).

8. *ĉaĺ[U]gV 'snow, hoarfrost': this etymology is plausible. Note also the following Dravidian cognates: Tamil caḷi 'cold, chilliness'; Kannaḍa caḷi, cali,

sali 'coldness, cold, coolness, chill, frost, snow'; etc. (cf. Burrow & Emeneau 1984, 211, no. 2408). I would reconstruct Proto-Nostratic *t^{yh}al^y- 'snow, frost'.

9. *č[a]RʔV 'hoarfrost' > 'frozen snow': this etymology is plausible. I would reconstruct Proto-Nostratic *t'^{y}ar- 'hoarfrost'.

10. *k̩ir[u]qa 'ice, hoarfrost; to freeze': the Indo-European forms should be removed — they are probably ultimately related to other Indo-European words meaning 'hard, hard surface, crust' (cf. Buck 1949, §1.77 ice). On the other hand, the following Dravidian forms can be added: Parji girgira 'cold'; Kurux kīrnā 'to be cold, to feel cold'; etc. (cf. Burrow & Emeneau 1984, 144, no. 1568). I would reconstruct Proto-Nostratic *k'ir- '(vb.) to freeze, to make cold; (n.) ice, frost'.

11. *Sah[i]bV 'saline earth, desert': neither the semantics nor the phonology is plausible, and, therefore, this etymology must be rejected.

12. *tälwA or *talwä 'cold season, rain': Proto-Indo-European *del- probably meant something like 'to drip, to fall in drops, to sprinkle, to wet, to moisten' and not 'to rain', though this is the semantic development in Armenian. This is the source of English tallow. The Indo-European forms have no connection with 'winter'. This etymology must be rejected.

13. *yamV 'water body, water': this is a plausible etymology. I would reconstruct Proto-Nostratic *yam- 'body of water'.

14. *morE 'water body': this is a plausible etymology. I would reconstruct Proto-Nostratic *mar- 'any body of water: lake, sea'.

15. *qaRp/p̣V 'to harvest cereal': Hittite ḫar-pa-aš appears to be an Akkadian loan (cf. Puhvel 1984, vol. 3, 183–4). This etymology is not convincing.

16. *ʒükV or *ʒukE 'edible cereals, harvest (of wild plants)': this etymology is not convincing.

17. *galV 'cereals': the Indo-European forms cited by Dolgopolsky probably do not go back to Proto-Indo-European (cf. Puhvel 1984, vol. 3, 35–9). The semantics are weak. Therefore, this etymology must be rejected.

18. *χäntV 'kernel, grain': the only Hittite form I can find in Puhvel (1984, vol. 3, 263–5) that comes close to what Dolgopolsky cites, namely, ḫattara-, means 'prick, awl'. The form cited by Dolgopolsky is listed, however, by Tischler (1977, vol. 2, 220). In spite of attempts to come up with an Indo-European etymology for ḫattar, it is more likely to be a borrowing from a non-Indo-European language. The Dravidian forms cited by Dolgopolsky go back to pre-Dravidian *andi not *antV. This etymology must be rejected.

19. *mälge 'breast, female breast': this etymology is plausible, but the Proto-

Nostratic root is *mal- 'to draw (out), to pull (out), to suck (out)' (cf. Bomhard & Kerns 1994, 672–3, no. 552).

20. *halbV (or *χalbV) 'white': Dolgopolsky is correct in questioning Hittite alpaš 'cloud' — it probably is not related to the other Indo-European forms cited by Dolgopolsky (cf. Puhvel 1984, vol. 1, 37–8). I would remove the Dravidian material and reconstruct a Proto-Nostratic *hal-b- 'white'.

21. *mayȝ̂V 'tasty beverage': neither the semantics nor the phonology is plausible, and, therefore, this etymology must be rejected. Proto-Indo-European *mel-i-t 'honey' is to be compared with Proto-Afrasian *mal(ab)- 'honey, mead' (cf. Bomhard & Kerns 1994, 657, no. 535).

22. *ḳadV 'to wicker, wattle' ('wall, building'): Dolgopolsky's etymology is better, at least in part, than what I proposed in Bomhard & Kerns 1994, 496–7, no. 344. There is a problem, however — Dolgopolsky has lumped together two separate roots, though it is fairly easy to sort them out. The first root is Proto-Nostratic *k'ad- 'to form, to fashion, to build', which is the source of the Afrasian, Kartvelian, and Dravidian forms cited by Dolgopolsky. The second root is Proto-Nostratic *kʰatʰ- 'to plait, to weave, to twist', which is the source of the Indo-European and Turkic forms, plus the following forms from Dravidian: Gondi kaṭṭĭ, ketti 'mat', (?) kaṭṭī 'palmleaf mat'; Konḍa kati 'wall'; Kuwi katti 'mat-wall', kati 'wall' (cf. Burrow & Emeneau 1984, 113, no. 1205). The following Semitic forms probably belong with this second root as well: Arabic katafa 'to fetter, to shackle, to tie up'; Geez katafa 'to bind firmly, to tie up'; Soqoṭri kə́tof 'to tie (to the top of the back)'; metathesis in Mandaic kpt 'to tie, to bind' and Aramaic kəφaθ 'to tie, to bind'.

23. *ḳoʔć/cV 'basket': so many different stems are mixed up here that this etymology cannot stand as written.

24. *p̣/pat[a] 'basket, box': only the Uralic and Dravidian forms belong together — the Afrasian and Indo-European forms should be removed. The original meaning can then be narrowed to 'cauldron, pot'. I doubt that this goes back to Proto-Nostratic.

25. *ʕ/γařḲ[u] 'sinew': this etymology is not convincing. In Bomhard & Kerns 1994, 532, no. 384, I derived the Indo-European forms for 'bow, arrow' from a Proto-Nostratic stem meaning 'to move, to set in motion' (cf. Buck 1949, §20.25 arrow — Buck notes: 'A few of the words for "arrow" are derivs. of those for "bow", either through the medium of a verb "shoot with the bow, shoot arrows", or directly as "belonging with the bow"'. Also note Buck (1949, §20.24 bow), where he says: 'The derivation of the

words for "bow" from verbs for "bend" is, as to be expected, widespread. Other connections are for "stretch, draw" or names of kinds of wood furnishing the material'). The semantic connections proposed by Dolgopolsky in this and in some of the following etymologies are a little too shaky for my taste.

26. *yaŋ[y]V 'sinew, tendon', 'bow (weapon)': this etymology is not convincing.

27. loŋḲa 'to bend': this is a plausible etymology, though I am not entirely satisfied with some of the material cited by Dolgopolsky nor with the phonology. The Afrasian forms are suspect — the Egyptian form should unequivocally be removed, while the Hausa form appears to be isolated. There are also problems with the Uralic forms. Most Uralicists would reconstruct initial *l and not *ḷ. The Uralic forms, if native, are probably derived from the stem that Rédei (1986–88, 256) reconstructs as *lɣŋk₃ 'to split, to crack'. Finally, there may be loanwords involved here.

28. *ńoγ/ʕlE (or *ńaγ/ʕlE) 'sinew; to tie together': this etymology is not convincing.

29. *p/ṗešqE ~ *p/ṗeqšE 'spear': though the semantics are acceptable, the phonology is not plausible. Therefore, this etymology must be rejected.

30. *ṭul[i][g]V 'to spread like a veil/net, cover with a veil/net, catch with a net': this etymology is not convincing.

31. *goki 'track' ('way'): the Uralic and Altaic forms may be related, but the Afrasian forms should be removed. This is not a strong etymology.

32. *[d]EʕSV or *[d]Eγ/χSV 'to follow the tracks': this etymology is not convincing.

33. *šubyV 'spike, spear; to pierce': Arabic sabba 'to cut, to wound' probably is related to sabal 'spear'. We can set up an earlier biconsonantal root *šab-, which, in turn, has been extended to create two different roots in Arabic: *šab-ab- (reduplication of the second consonant) and *šab-al- (-al- suffix). See Orël & Stolbova (1995, 456, no. 2159), for additional Afrasian cognates. Though Orël & Stolbova reconstruct an *a in the first syllable of the Proto-Afrasian stem, the original vowel is not certain. For the time being, Dolgopolsky's etymology can be accepted, though I seriously doubt that the Altaic forms belong. I would reconstruct a Proto-Nostratic *šub- '(vb.) to pierce; (n.) spike, spear'.

34. *ṭaṗV 'to hit (the target)': only the Uralic and Altaic forms cited by Dolgopolsky have any chance of being cognates, though loanwords are also possible here.

35. *menṭV 'to miss one's aim': though the semantics are weak, this etymology may tentatively be accepted. Note that there is no evidence to support reconstructing a glottalized dental in the Proto-Nostratic form.

36. *gurHa 'antelope, male antelope': this is a plausible etymology, though I would reconstruct an initial voiced labialized velar and the vowel *a on the basis of the Southern Cushitic forms cited by Dolgopolsky: Proto-Nostratic *gʷar(H)- 'antelope'. Note that Orël & Stolbova (1995, 203, no. 898) reconstruct Proto-Afrasian *gar-/*gawar- 'antelope' (Orël & Stolbova do not reconstruct labialized velars for Proto-Afrasian). The following Dravidian forms should be added to this etymology: Kolami kori 'antelope'; Parji kuri 'antelope'; Gondi kurs 'deer, antelope'; etc. (cf. Burrow & Emeneau 1984, 161, no. 1785).

37. *ʔEl/ḷi 'deer': the Afrasian forms should be removed. The rest of the etymology can stand as it is. I would reconstruct Proto-Nostratic *ʔil- 'hoofed, cud-chewing animal'.

38. *boča 'young deer': this etymology is plausible, though the Afrasian material cited by Dolgopolsky must be removed.

39. *buḲa 'bovine(s)': the original meaning here is probably something like 'male of small, hoofed animals: he-goat, buck'. Note that Orël & Stolbova (1995, 75, no. 310) reconstruct Proto-Afrasian *boḳar- 'cattle', which, in turn, they derive from *boḳ- 'goat'. The Proto-Indo-European cognate is *bhŭĝo-s 'buck' (cf. Pokorny 1959, 174), which Gamkrelidze & Ivanov (1995, vol. I, 501) reconstruct as *bʰuk̂'o-s 'goat' (with glottalized palato-velar!). The Slavic forms cited by Dolgopolsky are either loanwords or have an imitative origin (cf. Buck 1949, §3.21 bull). I would reconstruct Proto-Nostratic *buk'-(/*bok'-) 'male of small, hoofed animals: he-goat, buck'. There is some confusion here with forms listed below under no. 45, *bukEɣ/ʕ- 'billy goat, ram'.

40. *čoma 'aurochs, wild bovine': this etymology is plausible.

41. *č[a]w[V]rV (or *čurV) 'bull, calf': this etymology is plausible, though not without problems. First, Dolgopolsky is surely correct in seeing Proto-Indo-European *tau̯ro-s as a borrowing. It is difficult to reconstruct the Proto-Indo-European antecedent of the other Indo-European forms cited by Dolgopolsky, though *steu̯ros 'steer' or something very similar is probably the best that we can do. If this word is ancient in Indo-European and not a derivative of the root *tēu̯- 'to swell', as some have maintained, then Dolgopolsky's etymology can be accepted. In my opinion, *steu̯ros is not a derivative of *tēu̯-. I would reconstruct Proto-Nostratic *tʸʰaw-r-'bull, steer'.

The Altaic forms should be removed.

42. *γ/gawV 'wild sheep/goats': this etymology is plausible, but the Altaic forms are questionable. I would remove the Altaic forms and reconstruct Proto-Nostratic *ʕuw-(/*ʕow-) 'flock or herd of small animals: sheep and goats', and I would add Proto-Finno-Ugrian *u-če (< *uwi-če) 'sheep' (cf. Rédei 1986–88, 541).

43. *diqa 'goat': this etymology cannot stand as written and needs to be re-worked. According to Fähnrich & Sardshweladse (1995, 102), the Proto-Kartvelian form is to be reconstructed as *daq- 'goat'. This can be compared with the following Dravidian forms: Tamil takar 'sheep, ram, goat, male of certain animals'; Kannaḍa tagar 'ram'; Tuḷu tagaru 'ram'; etc. (cf. Burrow & Emeneau 1984, 259, no. 3000). I would reconstruct Proto-Nostratic *daqʰ- 'male of certain animals: billy goat, ram'. The remaining material cited by Dolgopolsky from other languages must be removed.

44. *k[ä]ʗV 'wild goat': though the semantics are acceptable, the phonology is not plausible. Therefore, this etymology must be rejected.

45. *bukEγ/ʕ- 'billy goat, ram': this etymology is not convincing. See comments under no. 39 above.

46. *ʕVp̣VrV 'wild boar': this is a plausible etymology, though, once again, there is no basis for reconstructing a glottalized labial in the Proto-Nostratic form. The Balto-Slavic forms should be removed. I would reconstruct Proto-Nostratic *ʕVpʰ-r- 'wild boar'.

47. *ʕir[i] '(male, young) artiodactyl': only the Kartvelian and Dravidian forms can possibly be cognates — the Afrasian and Indo-European forms are too divergent semantically to be given serious consideration. I would reconstruct Proto-Nostratic *Hir- 'deer, stag'.

48. *p̣oḲü 'pack, wild cattle': there are too many uncertainties about the Indo-European side of this comparison for me to be comfortable with this etymology. The Proto-Indo-European stem may originally have meant 'sheep' (cf. Buck 1949, §3.15 livestock), in which case this etymology would be far less attractive. The semantic development may have been 'sheep' > 'any small domestic animal owned as property' (it was at this stage of semantic development that 'cattle' began to figure in the equation) > 'property (in general)' (cf. Lehmann 1986, 102–3 for argumentation both for and against this position). In any case, glottalics should not be reconstructed for the Proto-Nostratic form.

49. *gadi (or *gati ?) 'kid, young goat': the Afrasian and Dravidian comparison seems solid, but the Indo-European forms can only be made to fit by throw-

ing sound laws out the window. I would reconstruct Proto-Nostratic *gad-y/i- 'kid, young (of any small, hoofed animal)'.

50. *buyẑV 'fur-bearing animal': this etymology is not convincing.

51. *ʔ/hUrV(-ba) 'squirrel or a similar animal': this etymology is not convincing.

52. *ḳun/ŋV(ŕV) 'small carnivore (marten, polecat, wild cat or sim.)': while the semantics are attractive, the phonology is not plausible. Consequently, this etymology must be rejected. The Proto-Kartvelian form implies an original labialized velar: Proto-Kartvelian *k'wenr- < Proto-Nostratic *k'ʷan-r-/*k'ʷən-r-. A labialized velar would have been preserved in Proto-Indo-European and Southern Cushitic. I suspect that we may be dealing with a Wanderwort here.

53. *diḳ- 'edible cereals or fruits': though the semantics could be tighter, this etymology is plausible. I would reconstruct Proto-Nostratic *dik'- 'edible cereals or fruits'.

54. *ʒ/ǯugbV '(a kind of) fig tree': the semantics are strong, but the phonology is weak. Therefore, this etymology must be rejected.

55. *b[i]ŕ[uw]q̇a '(a kind of) edible fruit': Fähnrich & Sardshweladse (1995, 51) reconstruct Proto-Kartvelian *berq̇en- 'wild pear' or 'wild plum'. Phonologically, this is a perfect match with Arabic burḳūḳ, birḳūḳ 'apricot, yellow plum' (note also birḳarūḳ 'plum'), which are related to Akkadian barraḳītu 'a plant', Hebrew *barḳōn- 'thorny plant, brier', and Jewish Palestinian Aramaic barḳānayyā 'thorny plant'. The Dravidian material cited by Dolgopolsky is difficult to fit in both semantically and phonologically — I would leave it out. On the basis of the Afrasian and Kartvelian material alone, I would reconstruct Proto-Nostratic *bVr-q'- 'a plant and its fruit'. If the Indo-European forms truly belong here, they are derived from the same root (that is, *bVr-), but with different extensions: Proto-Indo-European *bhrūĝ- (< *bhr-u̯ə-ĝ-) 'fruit'.

56. *ḲuSV 'nut': this is a solid etymology, but it may just be Eurasiatic (as defined by Greenberg) and not Nostratic. I would not reconstruct an initial glottalic.

57. *LVǯV (or *LVwǯV) '(a kind of) nut': this etymology is not convincing.

58. *buṭV 'pistachio tree/nut': this etymology is plausible. I would reconstruct Proto-Nostratic *but'- 'pistachio tree/nut'.

59. *mar[y]V '(mul-, black-)berries': I like this etymology better than what I proposed in Bomhard & Kerns (1994, 655, no. 532). I would reconstruct Proto-Nostratic *mar-(y-) 'mulberry, blackberry; mulberry bush'.

60. *m[o][y]ʒ́V '(a kind of) berry': this etymology is not convincing.

61. *ḲERV 'fruit of a leguminous plant': this etymology is not convincing.

62. *m[u]rḳV(-ŋḲV) 'root, root-crops, edible roots': this etymology is not convincing.

63. *mol/ḷV 'to pound, gnaw/smash into pieces': this is a solid etymology. I would reconstruct Proto-Nostratic *mul-(/*mol-) 'to rub, to crush, to grind'.

64. *ʔäPHi 'to bake, to prepare food on hot stones': this is a plausible etymology. I would reconstruct Proto-Nostratic *ʔapʰ- 'to burn, to be hot, to cook, to boil, to bake'.

65. *qubʒ́V (< *qupʒ́V) 'food made of ground cereals', 'flour': this etymology is not convincing.

66. *[ʔ]omśa 'meat': though the semantics are acceptable, the phonology is not plausible. Therefore, this etymology must be rejected.

67. *q̇[u]ʒV 'intestines; pluck (as food)': this etymology is not convincing.

68. *ʔayŋo 'marrow, brain, soft fat of animals' ('to smear, anoint'): this etymology is not convincing.

69. *mag[i]za 'liver': this etymology is not convincing.

70. *ń[a]ḲU 'soft parts of an animal's body (liver, marrow, suet)': this etymology is not convincing.

71. *muŋa(-t/dV) 'egg': this is a good etymology. Note, however, that the Proto-Uralic form is to be reconstructed as *muna 'egg, testicle' and not *muŋa (cf. Rédei 1986–88, 285–6). I would reconstruct Proto-Nostratic *mun- 'egg, testicle'.

72. *ʔ[a/o]h/χi or *ʔuh/χi 'egg' (or 'white of egg'): this is a very attractive etymology. However, it must be noted that Arabic ʔawḥ- 'white of egg' is isolated within Semitic (cf. Cohen 1970, 12). Moreover, even though the Proto-Indo-European form is traditionally reconstructed as *ōu̯i̯om 'egg', no single reconstruction can account for all of the forms found in the daughter languages. So there are difficulties with this etymology. I would hesitatingly reconstruct Proto-Nostratic *ʔaw-h- 'egg' (or 'white of egg'). If this is a valid etymology, it would imply that the Proto-Indo-European form is to be reconstructed as *ə₁ōu̯ə₂i̯om 'egg'. The Old Japanese form should be removed.

73. *ḲolV '(large) fish': this is a plausible etymology. The material from the Indo-European daughter languages requires that an initial labialized velar be reconstructed at both the Proto-Indo-European and Proto-Nostratic level. As usual, there is nothing to support reconstructing an initial glottalic. I would reconstruct Proto-Nostratic *kʷʰal- '(large) fish'. I would also

substitute the following Dravidian forms for those cited by Dolgopolsky: Tuḷu kalkorè 'a kind of fish'; Kuṛux xalxō 'a kind of fish, shad fish' (cf. Burrow & Emeneau 1984, 123, no. 1314).

74. *doTgiHU 'fish': this is a plausible etymology. The Uralic form does not fit phonologically — perhaps it is to be analyzed as a reduplicated stem: *totke < *to-tke < pre-Uralic *to-toke (??). I would reconstruct Proto-Nostratic *dug-(/*dog-) 'fish'. The following developments may be assumed for Mongolian: *dug-i- > *dügi- > *digi- > *dʸiga- > *ǯiga- (> *ǯaga-).

75. *men/ṇi '(a kind of) fish': this is a plausible etymology. The Proto-Indo-European stem may have contained a laryngeal: *mṇǝ-i- '(a kind of) fish'. Assuming a laryngeal in pre-Dravidian would also account for the long vowel in the Dravidian forms: *mīṇ- < *minH-. I would reconstruct Proto-Nostratic *min-H- '(a kind of) fish'. The Uralic forms do not belong here.

76. *p/ṗayV '(a kind of) fish': this is a plausible etymology. I would reconstruct Proto-Nostratic *pʰay- '(a kind of) fish'.

77. *ṭüRV 'hard-roe': this is a plausible etymology. An initial glottalic is not warranted on the basis of the data cited by Dolgopolsky. I would reconstruct Proto-Nostratic *tʰur-(y/i-) 'hard-roe'.

78. *[ḳ]ür[w]v or *[ḳ]ur[w]E 'hard-roe, spawn': this is a plausible etymology. The Georgian form implies an initial labialized velar in Proto-Nostratic, and there may have been an initial labialized velar in Proto-Indo-European as well, though it is difficult to tell on the basis of the forms found in the daughter languages. In my opinion, the lack of glottalization in the initial consonant in Georgian is regular. I also take the Georgian vowel to represent the original vocalism of this stem. I would reconstruct Proto-Nostratic *kʷʰir-(w-) 'hard-roe, spawn'.

79. *madu 'honey': this is a solid etymology. I would reconstruct Proto-Nostratic *mad-w/u- 'honey, mead'. The absence of Uralic *mete 'honey' from this etymology is too glaring to be an oversight. Does Dolgopolsky consider it to be a borrowing (from Indo-European perhaps)?

80. *č[ü]rV 'flint-stone, knife': this is a plausible etymology. Note that Orël & Stolbova (1995, 120, no. 514) reconstruct Proto-Afrasian *čur- 'flint, flint knife'. I would reconstruct Proto-Nostratic *t'ʸur- 'flint, flint knife'.

81. ? *buRV 'flint': this is a possible etymology. However, Orël & Stolbova (1995, 67, no. 266) reconstruct Proto-Afrasian *ber- 'to cut' as the source of the Afrasian forms cited by Dolgopolsky. I would compare this with Proto-Indo-European *bher- 'to work with a sharp tool, to cut, to split' (cf. Pokorny 1959, 133–5) and Proto-Uralic *parɜ- 'to scrape, to cut, to carve'

(cf. Rédei 1986–88, 357). On this basis, I would reconstruct Proto-Nostratic *bar- 'to cut, to cut off, to cut down; to carve, to scrape'.

82. *ti/e[ʔa]ĺo (or *tü[ʔa]ĺV) 'stone, heap of stone': this etymology is not convincing.

83. *kiw[V]hE 'stone': this is a plausible etymology. I would reconstruct Proto-Nostratic *kʰiw- 'stone'.

84. *boruʕ/γV 'trunk' ('log'): this etymology is not convincing.

85. *ćUlV 'stalk, stick': the Finno-Ugrian and Dravidian forms may be related but not the others. I would cautiously reconstruct Proto-Nostratic *t'ʸulʸ- 'stalk, stick'.

86. *ḳožʕV 'tree trunk': though the semantics are acceptable, the phonology is not plausible. Therefore, this etymology must be rejected.

87. *kaŋV(-bV) 'stalk, trunk' ('log'): the Indo-European forms are too divergent semantically to be given serious consideration, and, therefore, they should be removed. Perhaps better Indo-European cognates would be *ḱent- 'prick, point, spike' and *ḱentrom 'point, spike, spur' (cf. Mann 1984–87, 609; Walde 1927–32, vol. I, 402). In any case, on the basis of the remaining material cited by Dolgopolsky, I would reconstruct Proto-Nostratic *kʰanʸ- 'stalk, stick'.

88. *žyRV 'pole, long piece of wood': this etymology is not convincing.

89. *ȝirγu/ü 'vein, sinew': though the semantics are acceptable, the phonology is not plausible. Therefore, this etymology must be rejected.

90. *ʔeẑekU 'thorn, hook' (< 'tooth'): this etymology is not convincing.

91. *ḳ[a]k[w]V 'tooth, claw', 'hook': it appears to me that two separate stems need to be recognized here. The Proto-Kartvelian form finds an exact match in Indo-European. I would reconstruct Proto-Nostratic *k'ak'- 'hook', which would have been preserved intact in Kartvelian (Fähnrich & Sardshweladse 1995, 182 reconstruct Proto-Kartvelian *ḳaḳ-), but which would have yielded Proto-Indo-European *kʰak'- (> *kʰok'- [traditional *kog-]; cf. Pokorny 1959, 537–8 *keg- 'hook, peg') through a rule of regressive deglottalization. The remaining forms cited by Dolgopolsky go back to a parallel stem *kok(k)V 'hook', using Dolgopolsky's notation (I would write *kʰukʰ-/*kʰokʰ-).

92. *toŕV 'bark; to bark (remove the bark), to peel': though the semantics are acceptable, the phonology is not plausible. Therefore, this etymology must be rejected. Proto-Indo-European *der- 'to tear, to rend, to flay' (= *t'er- according to Gamkrelidze & Ivanov's reinterpretation) is related to the following Dravidian forms: Tamil taṛi 'to lop, to chop off, to cut off'; Kannaḍa

taṛi, taṛe 'to strip off, to cut off, to cut'; Kuṛux tārnā 'to fell (tree), to lop off (bough)'; etc. (cf. Burrow & Emeneau 1984, 273, no. 3140). On the basis of the Indo-European and Dravidian material, I would reconstruct Proto-Nostratic *t'ar- 'to tear, to rend, to cut, to sever'.

93. *Ḳa[pʔ/ʕ][E] 'bark': this is a possible etymology, though the phonology is a little too lax for my taste.

94. *ḲayerV 'bark, film': the Altaic forms do not fit phonologically and must, therefore, be removed. Setting up a pre-Uralic *kayerV is purely *ad hoc*. I also doubt that Finno-Ugrian *kerV belongs here. The remaining forms cited by Dolgopolsky can be derived from Proto-Nostratic *kʰar- 'skin, hide; bark, rind' (no initial glottalized velar).

95. *ṭo[w]q̇a or *ṭoq̇-wV 'hide, skin': in Bomhard & Kerns (1994, 315–16, no. 135), I derived the Kartvelian forms from Proto-Nostratic *t'aq'- '(vb.) to cover, to hide; (n.) covering' and included Proto-Indo-European *(s)t(h)eg- 'to cover' and Proto-Afrasian *t'ak'- 'to cover, to obscure'. The Proto-Indo-European form would be *(s)tʰek'- in Gamkrelidze & Ivanov's notation. Proto-Indo-European *(s)tʰek'- can be derived from earlier *(s)t'ek'- through a rule of regressive deglottalization. On the basis of this alternative proposal, I cannot accept Dolgopolsky's etymology.

96. *ṭal[U]ya 'skin, pelt': this is a possible etymology, though there is nothing in the material cited by Dolgopolsky to warrant reconstructing an initial glottalized dental. I would reconstruct Proto-Nostratic *tʰal- 'skin, hide'.

97. *Ḳaʃ[ü] 'skin, film, bark': this is a possible etymology, though, once again, there is nothing in the material cited by Dolgopolsky to warrant reconstructing an initial glottalized velar. I would reconstruct Proto-Nostratic *kʰalʸ- 'skin, hide'.

98. *ḳoRuṗV '(kind of) bark, skin': Orël & Stolbova (1995, 349) reconstruct Proto-Afrasian *ḳur- 'skin, bark'. Note also Ehret (1995, 239, no. 426): *-k'ûur-/*-k'âar- 'to be covered, to go under cover', source of Oyda k'uːro 'bark' and Male k'urubi 'skin' (both Omotic). As in no. 10 above, the Indo-European forms should be removed — their underlying meaning is 'hard, hard surface, crust'. Finally, the Altaic forms should be removed as well — the semantics do not match. We are thus left with a rather shaky etymology based on the comparison of a single form from Kartvelian and several forms from Afrasian.

99. *Ḳoẑ̌V 'to skin, to bark': though the semantics are acceptable, the phonology is not plausible. Therefore, this etymology must be rejected.

100. *ḲVRVHṗ/pV 'piece of leather (used esp. as footwear)': this is a possible

etymology. The Afrasian and Dravidian forms do not point to a laryngeal in Proto-Nostratic, but the Indo-European forms do: Proto-Indo-European *kerəp-/*krep- < *kerə̣p-/*kreə̣p-. On the basis of the evidence from Afrasian and Dravidian, I would reconstruct Proto-Nostratic *kʰVr-Vpʰ- 'piece of leather (used especially as footwear)' (no initial glottalized velar). Different extensions are found in the Proto-Indo-European form: *kerəp-/*krep- < *kerə̣p-/*kreə̣p- < *kʰVr-VH-pʰ-.

101. *p̌iχ/γγA 'sharp bone, sharp tool': this etymology is not convincing.

102. *pišV 'bile': this is a plausible etymology. I would reconstruct Proto-Nostratic *p'iš- 'bile', with initial glottalized labial on the basis of the Proto-Indo-European form.

103. *[t]äχl/ḷa ~ *[t]äl/ḷχa or *[t]aχl/ḷE ~ *[ṭ]al/ḷχE 'spleen': this is a possible etymology, though I seriously doubt that the Kartvelian forms belong. On the basis of the Afrasian and Altaic material, I would reconstruct Proto-Nostratic *tʰaȟl- 'spleen'.

104. *l[ä/e]p̌A 'spleen': in the Nostratic daughter languages, there are two different stems for 'spleen' that may ultimately be related. In Afrasian, there is *lap- 'spleen' (cf. Orël & Stolbova 1995, 358, no. 1651), and this matches Proto-Finno-Ugrian *läppɜ 'spleen, milt' (cf. Rédei 1986–88, 242). In Indo-European, on the other hand, we find a stem that has been variously reconstructed as *sp(h)elĝh(en, -ā), *splenĝh-, *splě̆ĝh- 'spleen' (cf. Pokorny 1959, 987). These stems appear ultimately to be based on a root *(s)pel- 'spleen', to which various extensions have been added. This matches Proto-Dravidian *palla 'spleen' (cf. Burrow & Emeneau 1984, 355, no. 3995). We can unite these into a single etymology by assuming metathesis in one of the sets. Given that Highland East Cushitic, within Afrasian, has a stem that matches Indo-European and Dravidian (Proto-Highland East Cushitic *hi-fella 'spleen' — *hi- is a prefix, and *-e- is secondary), I suspect that it was the order of the consonants in Indo-European and Dravidian that was original and that metathesis took place in Uralic and, in part, in Afrasian. On this basis, I would reconstruct Proto-Nostratic *pʰal- 'spleen'. This means that Dolgopolsky's etymology needs to be reworked.

105. *ṭEqme 'sinciput, crown of the head': though the semantics are acceptable, the phonology is not plausible. Therefore, this etymology must be rejected.

106. *[g]edi 'occiput, hind part': this is a possible etymology, though the phonology is a bit shaky.

107. *go/atK̲E 'popliteal space (back of the knee), armpit': though the semantics

are acceptable, the phonology is not plausible. Therefore, this etymology must be rejected.

108. *ŋiḲa 'jugular vertebra, neck, nape of the neck': this is a possible etymology, but it is only attested in Eurasiatic. The Indo-European forms are difficult to fit in phonologically, and, therefore, they should be removed. I would reconstruct Proto-Eurasiatic *nʸikʰa 'jugular vertebra, neck, nape of the neck'.

109. *kälu/ü 'a woman of the other exogamous moiety': this is a strong etymology. I would reconstruct Proto-Nostratic *kʰal-w/u- 'female relative'. The initial *ĝ- in the Proto-Indo-European form is irregular — I would expect *ǵ- instead. This may mean that the Indo-European form is a false cognate. In Bomhard & Kerns (1994, 438–9, no. 283), I attempted to show that Proto-Indo-European *ĝ(ₑ)lōu̯- 'husband's sister' (cf. Pokorny 1959, 367–8; Mallory & Adams 1997, 521–2 *ĝl̥h₃-u̯os- 'husband's sister') is to be derived from the same root found in Greek γάλα 'milk', Latin lac 'milk', and Hittite galattar, galaktar 'soothing substance, balm, nutriment', gala(n)k- 'to soothe, to satiate, to satisfy' (cf. Puhvel 1984, vol. 4, 18–20), all ultimately from an unattested *(ĝel-)/*ĝl̥-/*ĝ(ₑ)l- 'to suckle, to nourish'. I assumed the same semantic development as in Greek τηθίς 'father's or mother's sister, aunt' and Sanskrit dhénā 'female', both of which are derived from Proto-Indo-European *dhē(i̯)- 'to suck, to suckle' (cf. Pokorny 1959, 241–2). I then compared the Indo-European forms with the following Semitic forms: Amharic ḳälläbä 'to feed, to provide support, to nourish', ḳälläb 'food, supplies, rations, stipend'; Tigrinya ḳälläbä 'to feed'; Argobba ḳälläba 'to feed'; Gurage ḳälläbä 'to support by providing food, to feed'.

110. *kuda 'a man of the other moiety' (> 'male relative-in-law'): this is a possible etymology, though the sound correspondences are a bit irregular — Proto-Uralic *δ is not equal to IPA [ð]. Rather, it appears to have been some sort of lateral, most likely a fricative lateral [ɬ] or a lateralized affricate [tɬ] — my own research indicates that Proto-Nostratic *tɬʰ- became *ś- (Dolgopolsky writes *ŝ-) initially in Proto-Uralic but *-δ- (= [tɬ]) medially. Finally, I would remove the Kartvelian forms from this etymology.

111. *śeʒA 'a relative of the other moiety' ('father/son-in-law, mother's brother, and sim.'): this is a possible etymology, though the Afrasian forms are too divergent phonologically to be given serious consideration. My interpretation of the sound laws involved here is a little different than Dolgopolsky's interpretation — consequently, I would reconstruct Proto-Nostratic *siʒ-

(/*seǯ-) 'a relative of the other moiety' ('father/son-in-law, mother's brother, and sim.').

112. *[h/χV]wäń/nV 'relative (of a younger/the same generation)': this is a possible etymology, though the Egyptian forms do not appear to belong here either semantically or phonologically. I would reconstruct Proto-Nostratic *wan- 'relative through marriage, in-law (male or female)'. In my 1996 book (Bomhard 1996, 217, no. 621), I set up a slightly different etymology on the basis of some of the same forms cited by Dolgopolsky: Proto-Nostratic *wan-/*wǝn- 'first, first-born, eldest': (A) Afrasian: Proto-Highland East Cushitic *wanaa 'first' > Burji wanáy 'first-born', wanawwa 'eldest sister', wanay, wonáy 'eldest brother'; Kambata wana(a) beetu 'first-born' (beetu = 'child'), wanabii 'first'; (B) Uralic: Proto-Finno-Permian *wanša 'old' > Finnish vanha 'old', vanhemmat 'parents'; Estonian vana 'old'; Votyak/Udmurt vuž 'old'; Zyrian/Komi važ 'old'; (?) Proto-Finno-Ugrian *wɪ̈nɜ 'old' > Zyrian/Komi vener 'old'; Hungarian vén 'old'; and (C) Dravidian: Kolami vanna 'brother's wife'; Naikṛi vanna 'older brother's wife'; (?) Konḍa oni 'older brother's wife, maternal uncle's daughter (older than person concerned)'; (?) Pengo oni 'older brother's wife'.

113. *n/ŋu/üśV or *n/ŋu/üsyV 'woman (general term)', 'woman of the other moiety': Orël & Stolbova (1995, 406, no. 1887) reconstruct Proto-Afrasian *nüs- 'woman', but the very next entry (1995, 407, no. 1888) is *nüs- 'man'. The meaning 'woman' appears to be secondary, which throws doubt on the validity of this etymology. The Kartvelian form is indeed a loan from Indo-European, and Indo-European loans are also found in North-west Caucasian (cf. Bžedux nǝsa '[father's] brother's wife, daughter-in-law').

114. *Hić/cχV or *-ć/ç-, *-γ/g/h- 'father, head of a family': though the semantics are acceptable, the phonology is not plausible. Therefore, this etymology must be rejected.

115. *ʔediNV 'pater familias' (or 'owner'): this is a possible etymology. I would reconstruct Proto-Nostratic *ʔid-in-/*ʔed-in- 'father, head of family' (or 'owner').

116. *ʔemA 'mother': this is a good etymology. I would reconstruct Proto-Nostratic *ʔima/*ʔema 'mother'.

117. *ʔ[ä]yV (or *h[ä]yV) 'mother' (originally a nursery word): this is a good etymology. Note also Proto-Inuit *ayak 'maternal aunt'. I would reconstruct Proto-Nostratic *ʔay(y)- 'mother, female relative'.

118. ?? *ʔaba ~ *ʔaṗa 'daddy, father' (a nursery word): this is a good etymology.

Note also Proto-Eskimo *ap(p)a 'grandfather'. I would reconstruct Proto-Nostratic *ʔaba 'daddy, father'.

119. *ʕoᶐul/ḷV 'child, one's child; to beget, to bear a child': this etymology is not convincing. Note that Orël & Stolbova (1995, 247, no. 1110) reconstruct Proto-Afrasian *ʕigal- 'cow, calf'. In Bomhard & Kerns (1994, 518, no. 365), I compared the Afrasian forms with the following Indo-European forms: Avestan azí 'with young (of cows or mares)'; Sanskrit ahī́ 'cow'; Middle Irish ag 'ox, cow', ál (< *aglo-) 'litter, brood'; perhaps also Armenian ezn (with e-vocalism) 'ox' — all from Proto-Indo-European *ₐ₂eĝh-'with young (of animals)' (cf. Pokorny 1959, 7 *aĝh- 'pregnant animal'; Mann 1984–87, 233 *eĝhis 'ox, cow').

120. *ʔarV 'member of the clan': this is a good etymology. I would reconstruct Proto-Nostratic *ʔar- 'member of one's clan, kinsman'.

121. *ʔarba 'to make magic, to cast spells': this is a possible etymology, though the Afrasian material probably does not belong here. On the basis of the Uralic and Altaic material, I would reconstruct Proto-Eurasiatic *ʔarba 'to make magic, to cast spells'.

122. *ʕ[a]lV 'to burn (esp. sacrifices), use magic means (sacrifices, magic formulae, etc.) to produce a particular result': it appears that two different stems are mixed together here. The Afrasian and Indo-European forms go together well, and the Uralic and Altaic forms go together well, but the Afrasian and Indo-European forms, on the one hand, do not match the Uralic and Altaic forms, on the other. On the basis of Afrasian and Indo-European, I would reconstruct Proto-Nostratic *ʕal- 'to make a fire, to light, to ignite, to kindle, to burn'.

123. *ŝoṭV 'to exercise magic force' (> 'to curse, to bless'): on page 116, this is listed as etymology no. 124, while no. 123, *ʕ/γal/ḷV 'device (esp. a dishonourable one) for doing something', is nowhere explained. *ŝoṭV 'to exercise magic force' (> 'to curse, to bless') is a possible etymology. I would reconstruct Proto-Nostratic *tʰut'-(/*tʰot'-) 'to cast spells, to bewitch, to hex, to curse'.

124. *tulV 'to tell (a story), to pronounce magic/ritual texts': this is not a convincing etymology.

This completes our examination of the etyma proposed by Dolgopolsky. Unfortunately, I have had to be very succinct in my comments — in many cases, I would have liked to have given extensive explanations about why particular etymologies are not convincing. To have done so, however, would have meant that this paper would have greatly exceeded the size limitations set by the organizers of this symposium.

Now let us summarize our findings, section by section.

1. Where and when?

The first 30 etymologies are devoted to answering this question. Our examination indicates, however, that half of the proposed etymologies in this section are either not convincing or must be rejected for various reasons. Fortunately, enough good etymologies remain to support some of Dolgopolsky's conclusions. But we must be very careful here in drawing conclusions here — the climate in the Near East (and in the rest of the world, for that matter) was different at the end of the last Ice Age from what we find at the present time, which means that we cannot judge what existed then on the basis of what exists now. Nevertheless, there is nothing in the etyma cited by Dolgopolsky to contradict his claim that Proto-Nostratic was spoken in 'Southwestern Asia' (= the Near East). That the speakers of Proto-Nostratic were not familiar with agriculture, animal husbandry and pottery can be reasonably inferred as well, and, it goes without saying, this is precisely what we would expect on the basis of archaeological evidence. However, the claim that the speakers of Proto-Nostratic used bows, arrows and fishing nets cannot be supported by the lexical evidence presented by Dolgopolsky, though the archaeological evidence indicates that bows and arrows have been in use since Palaeolithic times.

2. Hunter-gatherers

Etymologies 31 through 62 are devoted to this topic, about a third of which are not convincing or must be rejected for various reasons. Here, Dolgopolsky has done a fairly good job at identifying some of the fauna that were known to the speakers of Proto-Nostratic, as well as some of the grains, nuts, berries, and fruits that constituted part of their diet.

3. Foods

Etymologies 63 through 79 discuss various foods (above and beyond those already identified in the previous section), along with the fact that the speakers of Proto-Nostratic knew how to pound grains and how to bake (on hot stones). Nearly half of the etymologies in this section were found to be less than convincing or were rejected outright. From what remains, it is clear that fish, eggs, and honey were part of their diet and that they knew how to pound grains and how to bake (on hot stones).

4. Technological activities

Etymologies 80 through 101 are devoted to technological activities, about a quarter of which are not convincing or must be rejected. The remaining etymologies show that the speakers of Proto-Nostratic had flint knives, hooks, poles, and leather footwear. They used animal skins and the bark of trees.

5. Anatomy

Etymologies 102 through 108 are devoted to anatomy. The valid etymologies include those for bile, the spleen, and the (nape of the) neck.

6. Kinship

Etymologies 109 through 119 discuss kinship terminology. Nearly half of these etymologies are not convincing or must be rejected. Among the convincing etymologies, are those for 'a woman of the other exogamous moiety', 'a relative of the other moiety', 'relative through marriage, in-law (male or female)', 'father, head of family', 'daddy, father', 'mother', and 'member of the clan'. Unfortunately, these kinship terms tell us relatively little about the family structure of the speakers of Proto-Nostratic.

7. The realm of the supernatural

Etymologies 120 through 124 discuss words denoting magic activities. One of these etymologies is not convincing, while another cannot stand as written. The remaining etymologies do indeed point to casting of spells and use of magic.

Even though some of his conclusions cannot be supported on the basis of the evidence he presents, Dolgopolsky's has, nevertheless, made a good start in identifying the world in which the speakers of Proto-Nostratic found themselves. No one would deny that the picture is far from complete or even without controversy, but it is more than what we had before, and, for that, we should be thankful.

I would like to close by presenting my own views on where and when Proto-Nostratic was spoken (this is a slightly modified version of what appears in Chapter 6 of my 1996 book *Indo-European and the Nostratic Hypothesis*). It will then be clear how closely Dolgopolsky and I are in agreement on these issues.

In my opinion, John C. Kerns has hit the nail on the head (Bomhard & Kerns 1994, 155): 'I believe that the Mesolithic culture, with its Nostratic language, had its beginning in or near the Fertile Crescent just south of the Caucasus'. Let us now re-examine the evidence from the Nostratic daughter languages and see how it leads to this conclusion.

The Indo-European homeland was most likely to the north of and between the Black and Caspian Seas (this is the view of Marija Gimbutas and many others — it differs from the views of Renfrew, Dolgopolsky, and Gamkrelidze and Ivanov, who posit an Anatolian homeland for Indo-European). However, Johanna Nichols (1997, 122–48) has convincingly argued that Pre-Indo-European originated in Central Asia and later spread westward to the North Pontic/Steppe zone that was the geographical location where Proto-Indo-European proper developed, where it began to split up into different dialect groups, and from which its descendants spread into Europe, the Iranian plateau, and northern India. Likewise, again as argued by Nichols, Pre-Uralic may be presumed to have originated in Central Asia and to have spread westward, following a more northerly route than Pre-Indo-European. Thus, it is likely that the Eurasiatic parent language (as defined by Greenberg forthcoming) was located in Central Asia and that it is to be dated roughly at about 9000 BCE. This would mean that the eastern Eurasiatic languages (Altaic, Chukchi-Kamchatkan, Gilyak, and Eskimo-Aleut) must have spread eastward from Central Asia (more specifically, the area traditionally called 'Western Turkestan') to their prehistoric homelands. Nichols has also speculated that Pre-Kartvelian may have originally been located in Central Asia, from which it spread westward along a southern route below the Caspian Sea to the Caucasus Mountains. The Elamo-Dravidian homeland may be placed roughly in western and central modern-day Iran and dated at about 8000 BCE. Finally, the homeland of Afrasian may be placed in the Middle East in the Levant and dated at about 10,000 BCE. Working backwards geographically and chronologically, we arrive at the only possible homeland for Proto-Nostratic, namely, 'the Fertile Crescent just south of the Caucasus' (= Dolgopolsky's 'Southwestern Asia').

Thus, the following scenario emerges: The unified Nostratic parent language may be dated to between 15,000 to 12,000 BCE, that is, at the end of the last Ice Age — it was located in the Fertile Crescent just south of the Caucasus. Beginning around 12,000 BCE, Nostratic began to expand, and, by 10,000 BCE, several distinct dialect groups had appeared. The first to split off was Afrasian. One dialect group spread from the Fertile Crescent to the northeast, eventually reaching Central Asia sometime before 9000 BCE — this was Eurasiatic. Another dialect group spread eastward into western and central Iran, where it developed into Elamo-Dravidian at about 8000 BCE. If Nichols is correct in seeing Pre-Kartvelian as having migrated from Central Asia westward below the Caspian Sea to the Caucasus, this would seem to imply that Pre-Kartvelian had first migrated northeastward from the Fertile Crescent along with or as part of Pre-Eurasiatic, that it stopped somewhere along the way, and that it then returned to the Middle East.

Analysis of the linguistic evidence has enabled us to determine the most likely homeland of the Nostratic parent language, to establish a time-frame during which Proto-Nostratic might have been spoken, to date the disintegration of Nostratic, and to trace the early dispersal of the daughter languages. To round out the picture, let us now correlate the linguistic data with archaeological data. During the last Ice Age (the so-called 'Würm glaciation'), which reached its zenith about 18,000 to 20,000 years ago, the whole of northern Eurasia was covered by huge sheets of ice, while treeless steppe tundra stretched all the way from the westernmost fringes of Europe eastward to well beyond the Ural Mountains. It was not until about 15,000 years ago that the ice sheets began to retreat in earnest. When the ice sheets began melting, sea levels rose dramatically, and major climatic changes took place — temperatures rose, rainfall became more abundant, all sorts of animals (gazelles, deer, cattle, wild sheep, wild goats, wild asses, wolves, jackals, and many smaller species) became plentiful, and vegetation flourished. Areas that had formerly been inhospitable to human habitation now became inviting. Human population increased and spread outward in all directions, exploiting the opportunities created by the receding ice sheets. New technologies came into being — toward the end of the last Ice Age, hunter-gatherers had inhabited the Middle East, living either in caves or temporary campsites. As the Ice Age began coming to an end, more permanent settlements started to appear, and there was a gradual transition from an economy based on hunting and gathering to one based on cultivation and stock breeding. This was the setting in which Nostratic arose. Nostratic was indeed at the right place and at the right time. The disintegration of the Nostratic parent language coincided with the dramatic changes in environment described above, and Nostratic-speaking people took full advantage of the new opportunities.

References

Barbujani, G., A. Pilastro, S. de Domenico & C. Renfrew, 1994. Genetic variation in North Africa and Eurasia: Neolithic demic diffusion vs Paleolithic colonisation. *American Journal of Physical Anthropology* 95, 137–54.

Bomhard, A.R., 1984. *Toward Proto-Nostratic: a New Approach to the Comparison of Proto-Indo-European and Proto-Afroasiatic*. (Current Issues in Linguistic Theory 27.) Amsterdam: John Benjamins.

Bomhard, A.R., 1996. *Indo-European and the Nostratic Hypothesis*. Charleston (SC): Signum Desktop Publishing.

Bomhard, A.R. & J.C. Kerns, 1994. *The Nostratic Macrofamily: a Study in Distant Linguistic Relationship*. Berlin, New York (NY) & Amsterdam: Mouton de Gruyter.

Buck, C.D., 1949. *A Dictionary of Selected Synonyms in the Principal Indo-European Languages*. Chicago (IL): University of Chicago Press.

Burrow, T. & M.B. Emeneau, 1984. *Dravidian Etymological Dictionary*. 2nd edition. Oxford: Oxford University Press.

Cavalli-Sforza, L.L. & F. Cavalli-Sforza, 1995. *The Great Human Diasporas: the History of Diversity and Evolution*. Reading (MA): Addison-Wesley.

Cavalli-Sforza, L.L., P. Menozzi & A. Piazza, 1994. *History and Geography of Human Genes*. Princeton (NJ): Princeton University Press.

Cohen, D., 1970–. *Dictionnaire des Racines Sémitiques*. The Hague: Mouton; Leuven: Peeters.

Diakonoff, I.M., 1965. *Semito-Hamitic Languages*. Moscow: Nauka.

Diakonoff, I.M., 1988. *Afrasian Languages*. Moscow: Nauka.

Diakonoff, I.M., 1990. Language contacts in the Caucasus and the Near East, in *When Worlds Collide: Indo-European and Pre-Indo-Europeans: the Bellagio Papers*, eds. T.L. Markey & J.A.C. Greppin. Ann Arbor (MI): Karoma, 53–65.

Diakonoff, I.M., 1992. *Proto-Afrasian and Old Akkadian: a Study in Historical Phonetics*. (= *Journal of Afroasiatic Languages* 4:1/2.) Princeton (NJ): Institute of Semitic Studies.

Dolgopolsky, A., 1984. On personal pronouns in the Nostratic languages, in *Linguistica et Philologica. Gedenkschrift für Björn Collinder (1894–1983)*, eds. O. Gschwantler, K. Rédei & H. Reichert. Vienna: Wilhelm Braumüller, 65–112.

Dolgopolsky, A., 1989. Problems of Nostratic comparative phonology (preliminary report), in *Reconstructing Languages and Cultures*, ed. V. Shevoroshkin. Bochum: Brockmeyer, 90–98.

Dolgopolsky, A., 1992. The Nostratic vowels in Indo-European, in *Nostratic, Dene-Caucasian, Austric and Amerind*, ed. V. Shevoroshkin. Bochum: Brockmeyer, 298–331.

Dolgopolsky, A., 1993. Nostratic, in *The Encyclopedia of Language and Linguistics*, vol. 5, ed. R.E. Asher. Oxford: Pergamon Press, 2838.

Dolgopolsky, A., 1998. *The Nostratic Macrofamily and Linguistic Palaeontology*. (Papers in the Prehistory of Languages.) Cambridge: The McDonald Institute for Archaeological Research.

Ehret, C., 1995. *Reconstructing Proto-Afroasiatic (Proto-Afrasian): Vowels, Tone, Consonants, and Vocabulary*. Berkeley & Los Angeles (CA): University of California Press.

Fähnrich, H. & S. Sardshweladse, 1995. *Etymologisches Wörterbuch der Kartwel-Sprachen*. Leiden: E.J. Brill.

Gamkrelidze, T.V. & V.V. Ivanov, 1972. Lingvističeskaja tipologija i rekonstrukcija sistemy indoevropejskix smyčnyx [Linguistic typology and the reconstruction of the Indo-European occlusives], in *Konferencija po sravnitel'no-istoričeskoj grammatike indoevropejskix jaykov, pradvaritel'nye materialy*

[*Working Papers of the Conference on the Comparative-Historical Grammar of the Indo-European Languages (12–14) December 1972)*]. Moscow: Nauka, 15–18.

Gamkrelidze, T.V. & V.V. Ivanov, 1973. Sprachtypologie und die Rekonstruktion der gemeinindogermanischen Verschlüsse [Linguistic typology and the reconstruction of the Indo-European occlusives.] *Phonetica* 27, 150–56.

Gamkrelidze, T.V. & V.V. Ivanov, 1995. *Indo-European and the Indo-Europeans: a Reconstruction and Historical Typological Analysis of a Protolanguage and a Proto-Culture.* 2 vols. English translation by J. Nichols. Berlin, New York (NY) & Amsterdam: Mouton de Gruyter.

Greenberg, J.H., forthcoming. *Indo-European and its Closest Relatives: the Eurasiatic Language Family.* 2 vols. Stanford (CA): Stanford University Press.

Hegedűs, I., 1992. *Bibliographia Nostratica 1960–1990 (A List of Publications on, or Relevant for Nostratic Studies).* Szombathely: Seminar für uralische Philologie der Berzsenyi-Hochschule.

Hegedűs, I., P.A. Michalove & A.M. Ramer (eds.), 1997. *Indo-European, Nostratic, and Beyond: Festschrift for Vitalij V. Shevoroshkin.* Washington (DC): Institute for the Study of Man.

Illič-Svityč, V.M., 1965. Materialy k sravnitel'nomu slovarju nostratičeskix jazykov (indoevropejskij, altajskij, ural'skij, dravidskij, kartvel'skij, semito-xamitskij) [Materials for a comparative dictionary of the Nostratic languages (Indo-European, Altaic, Uralic, Dravidian, Kartvelian, Hamito-Semitic)]. *Etimologija* 1965, 321–73.

Illič-Svityč, V.M., 1971–. *Opyt sravnenija nostratičeskix jazykov (semitoxamitskij, kartvel'skij, indoevropejskij, ural'skij, dravidskij, altajskij)* [An Attempt at a Comparison of the Nostratic Languages (Hamito-Semitic, Kartvelian, Indo-European, Uralic, Dravidian, Altaic)]. 3 vols. Moscow: Nauka.

Joseph, B. & J. Salmons (eds.), 1998. *Nostratic: Sifting the Evidence.* Amsterdam & New York (NY): John Benjamins.

Klimov, G.A., 1964. *Etimologičeskij slovar' kartvel'skix jazykov* [*Etymological Dictionary of the Kartvelian Languages*]. Moscow: Nauka.

Klimov, G.A., 1998. *Etymological Dictionary of the Kartvelian Languages.* Berlin & New York (NY): Mouton de Gruyter.

Lamb, S.M. & E.D. Mitchell (eds.), 1991. *Sprung from Some Common Source: Investigations into the Prehistory of Languages.* Stanford (CA): Stanford University Press.

Lehmann, W.P., 1986. *A Gothic Etymological Dictionary.* Leiden: E.J. Brill.

Mallory, J.P. & D.Q. Adams, 1997. *Encyclopedia of Indo-European Culture.* London & Chicago (IL): Fitzroy Dearborn Publishers.

Mann, S.E., 1984–87. *An Indo-European Comparative Dictionary.* Hamburg: Helmut Buske Verlag.

Nichols, J., 1997. The epicentre of Indo-European linguistic spread, in *Archaeology and Language*, vol. I: *Theoretical and Methodological Orientations*, eds. R. Blench & M. Spriggs. London & New York (NY): Routledge, 122–48.

Orël, V.E. & O.V. Stolbova, 1995. *Hamito-Semitic Etymological Dictionary: Materials for a Reconstruction.* Leiden: E.J. Brill.

Pedersen, H., 1931. *The Discovery of Language: Linguistic Science in the Nineteenth Century.* English translation by John Webster Spargo. (Midland book edition 1962.) Bloomington (IN): Indiana University Press.

Pokorny, J., 1959. *Indogermanisches etymologisches Wörterbuch* [*Indo-European Etymological Dictionary*]. Bern: Francke Verlag.

Puhvel, J., 1984–. *Hittite Etymological Dictionary.* Berlin, New York (NY) & Amsterdam: Mouton de Gruyter.

Rédei, K. (ed.), 1986–88. *Uralisches etymologisches Wörterbuch* [*Uralic Etymological Dictionary*]. Wiesbaden: Otto Harrassowitz.

Shevoroshkin, V. (ed.), 1989a. *Explorations in Language Macrofamilies.* Bochum: Brockmeyer.

Shevoroshkin, V., 1989b. *Reconstructing Languages and Cultures.* Bochum: Brockmeyer.

Shevoroshkin, V., 1990. *Proto-Languages and Proto-Cultures*. Bochum: Brockmeyer.

Shevoroshkin, V., 1991. *Dene-Sino-Caucasian Languages*. Bochum: Brockmeyer.

Shevoroshkin, V. & T.L. Markey (eds.), 1986. *Typology, Relationship, and Time*. Ann Arbor (MI): Karoma Publishers.

Sinor, D. (ed.), 1988. *The Uralic Languages: Description, History and Foreign Influences*. Leiden: E.J. Brill.

Tischler, J., 1977–. *Hethitisches etymologisches Wörterbuch* [*Hittite Etymological Dictionary*]. Innsbruck: Innsbrucker Beiträge zur Sprachwissenschaft.

Walde, A., 1927–32. *Vergleichendes Wörterbuch der indogermanischen Sprachen* [*Comparative Dictionary of the Indo-European Languages*]. Revised and edited by J. Pokorny. 3 vols. Reprinted 1973. Berlin: Walter de Gruyter.

Watkins, C., 1985. *The American Heritage Dictionary of Indo-European Roots*. Boston (MA): Houghton Mifflin Company.

Chapter 3

Nostratic languages: internal and external relationship

Vitaly Shevoroshkin

Over the last three decades, there have been many meetings on Nostratic in Moscow, and a few conferences on Nostratic in the United States. The 1998 Nostratic Symposium in Cambridge — aptly organized by Professor Renfrew and his associates — seems to be the first meeting on Nostratic in Western Europe.

At each conference on Nostratic outside Russia, a few attending colleagues happen not to be Nostraticists but linguists who know something about Nostratic research (which, in itself, is commendable). Such colleagues may be divided into two groups — namely, those who are Cautious but Curious, and those who are Prejudiced. This latter category seems to be hopeless: they simply never learn (though they may be knowledgeable experts in their own fields).

Curious but Cautious colleagues usually would like to learn more, and more than one would join the Nostratic club and contribute valuable papers to the field (as has happened in the United States over the last two decades).

As far as I can judge, our Symposium has several (not always easily compatible) aims — to introduce scholars to the reconstructed Nostratic proto-language; to discuss reconstructed Nostratic words in relation to the people who spoke this language some fifteen to fourteen thousand years ago, etc. But Dolgopolsky's book is not an introduction to the field: the author is discussing words which do not belong to the basic lexicon. For an elementary introduction, one should take semi-popular papers (see material published in Shevoroshkin 1989a) written by A. Dolgopolsky, V. Dybo, E. Helimski, I. Peiros *et al.*: see, for instance, English translation of these papers, along with more special work, in the 'red books', or 'Bochum books', which have appeared in W. Koch's *Bochum Publications in Evolutionary Cultural Semiotics* (Shevoroshkin 1989a,b; 1990) in the years 1988–92; three or four more volumes are expected to be published in 1999 by P. Sidwell of the Department of Linguistics and Applied Linguistics at Melbourne University, Australia. Actually, one may start with R.L. Trask's *Historical Linguistics* which includes a few well-chosen data on Nostratic (Trask 1996, 381–4, 390–91, 404–6).

The founder of modern Nostratic, V. Illič-Svityč, reconstructed about 750 roots; in Dolgoposky's forthcoming dictionary there will be about 2300 roots, this figure being the highest reasonable figure of word roots (plus grammatical elements) in any spoken language. We may expect some slight changes in Dolgopolsky's reconstruction of the Nostratic lexicon, but, as a whole, I think, it will remain, along with V. Illič-Svityč's Nostratic dictionary, a highly important achievement of twentieth-century scholarship. (And soon we shall have on our desks the first ever *Altaic Etymological Dictionary* by S. Starostin, A. Dybo, and O. Mudrak).

Still, even now a few questions and objections may be formulated which cover different aspects of the Nostratic linguistics — phonetics, semantics, reconstruction of some lexemes, borrowings into and from Nostratic languages, relationship between five Nostratic daughter languages (IE, Kartvelian, Uralic, Altaic, Dravidian) and Hamito-Semitic; chronology of Nostratic and its daughter-languages, etc.

1. Phonetic correspondences between Nostratic langauges

Nostraticists argue among themselves about the phonetic reality behind the reconstruction of Nostratic glottalized stops *p' – * t' – *k' – *q' (V. Illič-Svityč, A. Dolgopolsky, *et al.*).

Starostin proposes Nostr. *ph – *th – *kh instead, regarding Altaic aspirated stops *p' – *t' – k' as phonetically identical to Nostratic. As for Kartvelian (which has the above four glottalized stops), Starostin is inclined to explain them as a kind of a borrowing from neighbouring Hurri-Caucasian (Dolgopolsky's term; Starostin prefers North-Caucasian). Typologically, such a borrowing/re-interpretation of a phonetic sub-system is possible. As for Hamito-Semitic (HS) which shows *p' (?) – *t' – *k', both Militarev and Starostin prefer to consider this latter proto-language as a sister (and not as a daughter) of Nostratic: the proto-HS was much older than any of the five remaining Nostratic daughter-languages (see above); Bomhard considers HS as the first split from Nostratic which, as a result, turned into two branches — HS vs the rest — with this latter splitting eventually into five other daughter-languages. This scenario, if correct, would be comparable with the split of proto-Indo-Hittite into Anatolian and West-Indo-European, with this latter eventually splitting into many IE daughter languages — without laryngeals, but with a newly-developed opposition between masculine and feminine gender: cf. Lehrman 1998.

*   *   *

In Dolgopolsky's as yet unpublished *List of Nostratic Roots* (1861 items) we find:

108 roots in *t-' (Star.: *th-) reflected in: 81 Altaic; 53 IE; 38 Kartvelian roots

78	*t-	55	44	34
59	*d-	43	37	31

These data may confirm Starostin's interpretation of the Nostratic T'-series as Th (this latter being the unmarked member of the triad Th – T – D).

Accordingly, the following Kartvelian data (listed after Klimov 1964):

55 roots in *k'- (underlying *kh- ?) vs 25 roots in *k- vs 37 roots in *g-

may support the underlying reconstruction of the system as Th – T – D (instead of T' – T – D). As for *k- being the most marked member of the phonetic-phonemic triad *k' – *k – *g, it may mean that the phonetic realization of T- was a tense voiceless dental stop [T:]; see below.

Still, the traditional reconstruction of Nostr. T' – T – D might be supported by the identical reconstruction of the related Hamito-Semitic (be it a sister or a daughter of Nostratic), as well as by the reconstruction of the proto-Hurri-Caucasian language — apparently a sister of Nostratic; Hurri-Caucasian shows both *k' and *q', as Kartvelian does, which may be an indication of a Nostratic archaism in Kartvelian and not an innovation.

In their independent studies published over a decade ago, several linguists concluded that proto-IE (or proto-Indo-Hittite, for that matter) was closer to proto-Armenian and proto-Germanic (probably also to proto-Anatolian) than to other IE languages. IE system of stops was re-interpreted as Th – T – D [instead of the traditional reconstruction T – D – Dh, or, for that matter, of the 'glottalic' reconstruction T(h) – T' – D(h)].

In my part of the introduction to the book *Typology, Relationship, and Time* (Shevoroshkin 1986, xxxix) the transition of the underlying Nostr. stops T' – T – D to the appropriate IE stops has been explained as follows:

> It seems possible that IE *T was *Th, *D was *T, and *Dh was *D, as in Altaic, so that we have Nostr. *T', *T, *D > IE *Th, *T, *D respectively (as in Armenian) with a 'strong' *Th and a very breathy *D. Certainly, the second IE stop was not glottalized.

When compared with the statistical data based of Pokorny's *Indogermanisches Etymologisches Wörterbuch*, the new interpretation happens to be confirmed; the set:

94 roots in *th- (tradit. *t-) vs 57 in *t- (tradit. *d-) vs 67 in *d- (tradit. *dh-)

indicates that the underlying phonetic system was a routine [Th] – [T:] – [D] where [Th] is the unmarked, natural realization of voiceless stops; [D] is a natural, marked (= voiced), counterpart of [Th] — but [T:] represents the 'difficult' plain-voiceless-stop realization, the strongly marked, tense, series [p:] – [t:] – [k:].

Such interpretation shows, by the way, why Slavic *d may have been marked by a lengthening of the preceding stressed vowel (a wide-spread phenomenon in some Anatolian languages which show -add- from *-éd-): this was a reflection of the underlying [ét:] (with the tense voiceless IE stop [t:], not a 'glottalic' [t']).

Both Hittite and Luwian intervocalic writing of the type -tt- seems to reflect the underlying PIE *th (traditional transcription *t does not explain the doubling).

If we reconstruct the proto-IE system of stops as Th – T – D it would match the Altaic system, on the one hand (as well as proto-Nostr., according to Starostin), and the proto-Armenian system, on the other hand. As for proto-Germanic, the system þ (voiceless fricative) – T – Ð (voiced fricative) represents a 'weakening' of the underlying PIE triad Th – T – D (this latter being a 'breathy' [Dh]).

Taking the above into consideration, we would not need the 'classical Nostratic/classical IE' explanation of Nostr. *wete becoming IE *wed- becoming Germanic *wet-; it was a plain (*)wet- [wet] in all three languages (Nostr. *wet-, not *wete, is based on Helimski's interpretation of the appropriate Uralic root as *wet-).

As for Greek obstruents of the type th – t – d, they seem to reflect a 'circular' shift (which becomes feasible as soon as we use our new notation of PIE):

PIE *th yields Greek t; PIE *t yields Greek d; PIE *d ([dh] ?) yields Greek th.

In this way, we conclude that a Grimm's-Law-like circular shift was realized in Greek, not in Germanic (albeit into the opposite direction: Th > T, not T > Th, etc.).

*   *   *

Those associated with the Moscow school of historical Linguistics (Dolgopolsky, Starostin, Nikolaev, Lehrman *et al.*) do not accept the so-called mainstream laryngeal theory, according to which a PIE *Hent- 'front' turned to hant- in Hittite-Luwian, and to [ant-] in other IE daughter-languages since the laryngeal *H was a-colouring (cf. also Hitt. pahs- : WIE *pās-). An o-colouring laryngeal would be responsible for the colour of the vowel in post-laryngeal roots WIE *owi- 'sheep' *dō- 'give', whereas an e-colouring (or e-preserving) laryngeal would be responsible for the colour of the vowel of *es- 'be' or *dhē- 'put'. This traditional interpretation presupposes that there was only one PIE vowel *e, and that, by some mysterious 'adding' (by whom ?) of two or three mysterious vowel-colouring laryngeals to non-specified IE proto-roots (something like /ent/,

/pe()s/; /ewi/, /de/; /es/, /dhe/, respectively [and how else ?]), IE laryngeal-containing roots were created with laryngeal-determined vowels /a/, /o/, /e/ (respectively), leading to *ant-, *pās-; *owi-, *dō-; es-, *dhē-.

As Lehrman wrote (1998, 258-9), 'Those who believed that **h$_3$ was a labiovelar . . . have to explain why there is no trace of the labial element in its Anatolian continuation, while the labial element is so well preserved in other labiovelars . . . continued in Hittite (Hitt. kuis 'who': Lat. quis . . . Hitt. nekumanza 'naked': Ved. nagná-, Hitt. kuenzi 'slays': Ved. hanti). . . . There is in fact no shortage of genuine labiovelar spirants in Hittite: the frequent occurrence of h and hh before u(w) closely parallels that of k and kk before u(w), and as good a case could be made for the Hittite labiovelar 'laryngeals' hh^w and h^w . . . as for kk^w and k^w'. Cf. my remarks in Bammesberger (1988, 542):

> As I have noticed at the beginning of this article, a IE labiovelar 'laryngeal' *x^w or x̱^{w} would yield Hittite hw- (as in huis-) and [w] in other languages. Indeed, some facts allow us to reconstruct this laryngeal, and not the mysterious 'H$_3$,' which allegedly coloured the neighbouring vowels into *o/*ō. With deep satisfaction, I find a welcome confirmation of this conception in S. Nikolaev's independent study on the historical morphology of Greek . . .; he writes here as follows: '. . . the auslauting stem cluster *wə proposed by V.A. Dybo has to be re-interpreted as *-H^{w}V where *H^w is not the abstract 'labialized laryngeal' which allegedly disappeared in most IE languages after having coloured e to o, but a real IE *H^w appearing as hw in Hittite and giving more or less the same reflexes as IE *w in other IE languages. Thus, H^w must be reconstructed in the anlaut of *H^{w}es- 'live' (cf. Hitt. hweszi) . . . *H^{w}ak-/g- 'beat, kill' (Hitt. hwek-, Gr. Fag-, Lith. vógti), . . . *H^{w}arg- 'wheel' (Hitt. hurki-) [etc.].

His examples include Hittite stems beginning with hwe/iC- and huC- only, but it is possible to identify *X^w- . . . also in some stems beginning with huwa(C)-: cf. *k^w- in Hitt. stems beginning with kue/i(C)- / kuwa(C)-.

I have argued (Shevoroshkin 1986, xxix) against Illič-Svityč's theory about Nostratic roots of the type *qant'- 'front' turning to PIE *hent- first, and to (h)ant- in Anatolian and other IE languages later (after the appropriate PIE laryngeal has coloured the underlying PIE *e to [a]):

> To explain, say, Nostr. *qant'- as having first resulted in IE *hent- . . . which then became *ant- in the various IE dialects, seemed highly artificial. Why, indeed, must one reconstruct Nostr. *a > PIE *e > *a . . ., rather then Nostr. *a > IE *a, when all dialects reflect a and not e? The answer is obvious. Classical Nostratic Theory required that all Nostratic vowels first become *e, *ye, *we in Indo-European. After Indo-European laryngeals, however, the quality of the three types of Nostratic vowels seemed to be preserved.

This is valid for initial laryngeals as well.

We may briefly summarize our conception about PIE laryngeals as follows. The existence of laryngeals in PIE (or, in Sturtevant, Cowgill, & Lehrman's terminology, proto-Indo-Hittite = PIH) is confirmed not only by Anatolian data, but also by Nostratic: as per Dolgopolsky (cf. his phonetic tables in *NM*), both Nostr. uvular stops *q and *9, and fricatives *x, *γ, *h yielded PIE fricatives of the type *X, *Xʷ.

There is no reconstruction yet of Nostr. vowel length and stress, though IE accentuation is being reconstructed and several ancient IE languages contain long vowel phonemes. It is important that Lehrman (1998) insists on the reconstruction of PIE vowel length in many cases where mainstream research identifies reflexes of lost laryngeals of various types. We may also note that the reconstructed Proto-North-Caucasian (a 'sister' of the Nostratic proto-language) differentiates between reduced, regular, and long vowels.

It also seems clear enough that, sooner or later, Nostratic subsystems of stops (types K, T) and 'laryngeals' (types X / H) will be re-reconstructed into K, Kʷ, T, Tʷ (see below) vs X, Xʷ, H, Hʷ, etc.

*   *   *

An important re-interpretation of the Nostratic consonantism was recently proposed by Starostin who explains the hitherto unexplained Nostratic (Alt.–Kartv.–IE) correspondences of the type

Alt. *t' – Kartv. *dw-	– PIE *t(w) [tradit. *d(w)]
Alt. *k' – Kartv. *gw (or *g before *o)	– PIE *kʷ [tradit. *gʷ]

as a reflection of a specific Nostr. labial consonants *dʷ and *gʷ. These complex consonants changed into the only complex consonants *t' and *k' in Altaic; they were reflected as tense [t:(w)], [k:ʷ] in PIE, but preserved as *dw and *gw (or *g before *o) in Kartvelian.

Starostin provides nine examples of the above correspondences in a paper *Nostratic Stops Revisited* (to appear in one of the Melbourne books in 1999); I am listing here two of his examples:

1. Alt. *t'ioŕe 'tree, pole' : Kartv. *dwir- : PIE *terw- (tradit. *derw-).
2. Alt. *k'ori 'mountain' : Kartv. *gora : PIE *kʷer- (tradit. *gʷer-).

The reconstruction of Nostratic labiodentals and labiovelars is supported both by typological and genetic data (as for the latter, cf. PIE labiovelars, as well as labial series in Hurri-Caucasian and other languages, remotely related to Nostratic).

2. Phonetic correspondences between Nostratic and other languages

As Starostin has shown (Starostin 1989), a genetic relationship exists between Nostratic and Sino-Caucasian (this latter being reconstructed on the material of North-Caucasian (= Hurri-Caucasian), Yeniseian, and Sino-Tibetan.

It is clear by now that many languages of the Americas are either a part of the Sino-Caucasian phylum, or genetically related to Sino-Caucasian (= Dene-Caucasian; Nikolaev's term). These languages are: Na-Dene/Athapaskan, Algonquian-Wiyot-Yurok, Salishan-Wakashan (+ Kutenai), Siouan, as well as many others (wrongly considered by J. Greenberg and M. Ruhlen as Amerind, though they do not show Amerind-type personal pronouns and other, very stable, grammatical and lexical elements; note that almost all languages from Greenberg's Almosan-Keresiouan phylum are Sino-Caucasian, not Amerind).

By comparing some, phonetically stable, languages of North America which are related to Sino-Caucasian (such as Salishan) to the reconstructed Proto-North-Caucasian (NC), Proto-Sino-Caucasian (SC), and Proto-Nostratic (Ns.), one may notice that the most stable elements of Salishan grammar and lexics are, practically, identical to those of NC / SC, showing also some ancient ties to Ns.

I am going to briefly compare a few living Salishan languages with the reconstructed Proto-North-Caucasian (see Nikolaev & Starostin 1994) and proto-Sino-Caucasian (see Starostin 1989). It seems to me that the relationship between NC and Salishan languages is quite obvious, even if we do not use the existing proto-Salishan reconstruction (which is quite shallow; note that many existing Salishan languages are very similar to each other both phonetically and grammatically).

Sal[ishan] languages are represented below by appropriate dictionaries:
MC = Moses-Columbia (Kinkade 1981).
Se. = Sechelt (Timmers 1977).
Sp. = Spokane (Carlson & Flett 1989).
UC = Upper Chehalis (Kinkade 1991).
Wak[ashan] languages (Lincoln & Rath 1980).

Examples 3–19 represent several very stable roots of Sal., NC/SC, and Ns.:

3. I, ME: Sal. (*)ca : SC *zō (cf. synonymous Sal. and NC *nV).
4. THOU, THEE: Sal. (*)ʔaxw- : NEC *ʔaɣ, *ɣu (syn.: Sal. *wV, NC *wo).

5. TWO: MC t-q'aw?- : SC *t'-?q'wE [Borrowing: Kartv. *t'q'ub 'twins' ?].
6. BONE: MC s-c'ám', Sp. c'om' : NC *Hc̣'wēymš̌ 'leg-bone'.
7. EYEBROW: UC cúm- : NC *c'fiwĕme [Note typical simplification in Sal.].
8. EAR: UC q'ʷal- : Ns. *q'ewlE (: NC *?i-kVl- vs Sal.: UC k'wal- 'hear').
9. HEAD: UC mátin: NC *mət'i 'face' : Ns. *mEt(')ha 'head, top'.
10. FOREHEAD: UC λ'óxʷ- : NC *λ'arq'wĕ [Cf. NC -rC(C)-: ex. 11, 26, 32].
11. HORN: MC qəx̣-mín : NC *qwírHV (<SC *qwVrHV) : Ns. *k'irV 'top, horn'.
12. ELBOW/KNEE: UC q'ʷə́m-xʷ- 'elbow-joint' : NC *q'am-q'(w)a 'knee, leg-bone'.
13. MEAT/FLESH: Se. s-łiqʷ 'flesh' : NC *x̣wǐł?i 'meat' : Ns. *Laɣ/ɣwV or *liw?V-.
14. HIDE (noun): MC pkʷú-t : NC *bākwV.
15. HAND; TAKE: MC, Sp. kʷúł- 'borrow' : NC *kwĭl?i- 'hand'.
16. GREASE/FAT: UC kʷíxʷ- 'greasy' : Ns. *koyHV 'fat' [Structurally similar: ex. 30].
17. ROT(TEN): UC nó?-, nu?ú-; MC ná?q' 'rotten food' : NEC *nĕwq'u 'pus'.
18. DIE: MC túxʷ- (: UC tíxʷ- 'kill') : Ns. *diwHV > IE *dhweiH- (?); cf. HS.
19. LEAF: UC λ'ə́c'- 'grow (about plants)' : NC *λ'acă 'leaf'.

Example 12 reflects an old reduplication, as seen in NWC *q'ʷa-q'ʷa 'hip-bones'. Modern Sal. languages preserve the ancient root *q'wVm- better than the reconstructed NC (the original meaning may be *'lump' may be old: cf. 'lump of the hip' in Se. which is homophonous to UC). As frequently in compounded stems, fricatives replace stops: cf. -xʷ- in ex. 10, and x̣ʷ- in example 29.

Example 7 shows deglottalized root in UC; note the underlying compound ca-cum-an in Se. which can be explained by comparison with a related NC compound (but Sal. data support the meaning 'eye', not 'eyebrow', for the 1st stem in NC): example 21.

See examples 22–3 for two more archaic compounds (body parts as well) which look simplified in Sal. languages when compared with more archaic NC/SC and Ns.

20. ELBOW/HIP: UC x̣ʷúm-ač'a 'elbow' [č(') <*k(')], x̣ʷúm-nč 'hips'; NC in ex. 12.
21. EYEBROW(S)/EYELASH: Se. ca-cum-an : NC *c'ĭlV-c'fiwĕme: Lezgi *çil-ç̌ʷem 'eye-lash' : Nakh ça-ç?Vm; cf. UC có:-qʷa 'tear'; Se. c'il- 'look' : NC *c'ĭlV 'eye'.
22. UC kʷanā-məl-ən 'claw' : NC *mħā̆λă/ĕ 'nail' : Ns.: IE *mél-os 'knuckle, member'.
23. UC kʷana-pəl-ən 'wrist' : SC *b/pArV 'claws, paw' : Ns. *pArÄ 'nail, claw, finger'.

Consider an additional set of rather stable roots from Sal., NC/SC, and Ns.:

24. DRINK: UC q^wő? : SC: NC *?V-qV : Ns.: IE *eg^wh- (as in Hitt. [egu-], etc.).
25. (BE) AFRAID: UC q^wanú- : NC *-Hä-ǥwVn- [Sal. q(^w) reflects pre-Sal. *q(w)/*ǥ(w)].
26. BREAK: MC lóq'^w- : NC *-irq'wĚ(r) 'split' [cf. ex. 10 for NC *-rq'w-; cf. ex. 11].
27. BRAID: Sp. q'ic' 'braided' : Ns. *k'o?cV 'basket'.
28. GRAY: UC (reduced stem ? Cf. -məl-, ex. 22) q^wáx̣^w : NC *q'VhwVrV.
29. SEW: MC lóx̣^w- : NC *-ilq'wVn [cf. Sal. -x^w- vs NC *-q'w- in ex. 16].
30. DAWN: Se. k^wíy : Ns. *ǥoHyV 'sunshine, dawn' [Ns. *ǥ^w-, as Ns. *k^w-, ex. 10?].
31. EARTH, CLAY: Sal. (*)tiq^w 'mud(dy)' : NWak. tqwá, tq'a : SC *dVqV : Ns. *diqV.
32. CHILD: MC tw'í-t 'boy', Puget táwix^w- : NC *dwirx̣E (Sal t < pre-Sal. *t/*d).
33. KINDLE: UC p'ač'- (č' from *k') : Ns. p'äk'U 'heat'.
34. COVER: UC λ'íp- : NC *λVpV (cf. HS *λ'VpV).

*   *   *

There are many more systemic ties between Sal. languages and NC than between Sal. and Ns. or, for that matter, between NC/SC and Ns. Sal. languages either show consonants, identical to those in NC (l, ł, n, m, w, k(w), q(w), q'(w), p, p', λ'), or expected reflexes (l for NC *r, ex. 23 and 26; q^w for *ǥ^w, ex. 25 [cf. ex. 13 for Ns.]; p for *b, ex. 14 [and 23?]; t for *d, ex. 31; t(a)w- for *dw-, ex. 32; c for *z, ex. 3; x for *γ, ex. 4; x̣ for *rH, ex. 11; m for *mh, ex. 22; q' for *q'H, ex. 28; c' for *c̣'w, ex. 6)

Loss of glottalization in Sal. (as compared to glottalized consonants in NC) seems highly unusual: t : NC *t' (ex. 5, 9); c : *c'ɦ (ex. 7 = 21); c in compounds : *c̣' (ex. 21). More frequent is spirantization of underlying uvular stops in Sal.: x^w : NC *(r)q'w (ex. 10); x̣^w : *q'w, ex. 29).

A tendency to simplify sometimes rather complex underlying stems into CVC- in Sal. languages seems to characterize examples 6, 7, 10, 11, 13, 15, 17, 19, 21, 22, 23, 26, 27, 28, 29, 34; cf. examples 16, 18, 30. Cf. also 'stretching' some underlying clusters (CC, CCC) into the familiar pattern CVC-: examples 5, 26, 29.

There seems to be auslauting glottalization due to the loss of pre-Sal. sounds which succeeded the consonant in question: examples 6, 19, 27, 32 (MC).

Sal. may preserve the underlying stem structure, where NC shows a metathesis: ex. 13 (note Ns. cognate). Sal. may have preserved labial uvular stop where NC may show delabialization: ex. 12. Sal. stops may be more archaic than NC fricatives in the appropriate cognate in ex. 13.

The above stable roots show only sporadically possible cases of sound-symbolism (cf. ex. 8: UC shows an inherited uvular for 'ear' vs a velar for 'hear').

Ns. cognates are present in examples 8, 9, 11, 13, 16, 18, 22, 23, 27, 28. 29, 31.

3. Volatility of Nostratic etymologies with doubtful Anatolian links

There are at least two groups of words which tend to show a considerable volatility as far as their interpretation is concerned.

A) Words from languages which recently became subject to a very intense historico-phonetic and etymological research — such as Anatolian (= Hittite-Luwian) languages.

B) Words which represent cultural notions, and thus may be borrowings. There are many such words, interpreted as a part of Common Nostratic lexicon, in Dolgopolsky's *NM*.

Let us consider four entries in *NM*, namely, entry 24 *p'/pat[a] 'basket, box'; 15 *qaRp/p'a 'to harvest'; 17 *ǥaLV 'cereals'; 18 *xänt'V 'kernel, grain'. All four entries include Anatolian lexical items.

35. Dolgopolsky's entry 24 *p'/pat[a] 'basket, box' shows alleged IE cognate *pod-'box, vessel, pot', but why Ns. *a has turned IE *o is unclear. Moreover, this IE reconstruction (*pod-) contradicts Anatolian material, used by Dolgopolsky since IE *pod- would neither yield Hitt. pattar (: Lyc. patár-a 'basket' as shown by Greek versions) nor Hitt. paddur 'basket' (by the way, this latter does not exist).

There might have been a Luw. *paddur 'tray', reconstructed on the material of existing derivatives from paddun- in Hittite texts, to Luw. *padd- 'carry' which reflects Anat. *péd-. This latter yields Hitt. pēd-a- 'bring'. (As for the alleged IE *pod-, it would turn to Hitt. [pād-]. Note also that Luwian — not Hittite — *paddur/n- may have existed in Milyan padr-e-/pdur-a- 'bring; establish').

What Hittite does show, is a word combination peran pedunnas (in the meaning 'tray', lit.: 'that of bringing forth': *The Hittite Dictionary*, Chicago Oriental Institute, 1997, vol. P, fasc. 3, p. 611) where the second word is a hittitized version of Luw. *paddunas. There is an even stronger hittitized version of the above phrase, namely, peran pēdunas, — as well as a plain Hittite construction peran pēdunas (Hitt. peran matches Luw. parran 'before, in front').

We are left with isolated Hitt. pattar and Lyc. (in Gr.) patára: they can be tied neither to Hitt. pēd- nor to Luw. *padd-. An IE root **pat- which could accommodate Hitt pattar does not exist. Hitt. pattar is comparable, though, with other Hitt. vessel-words in *-r (this suffix is Anatolian) — mostly without any acceptable etymology (cf. data in Neumann 1994, 166; cf. also Furnée 1972, 150: 'offensichtlich voridg. Sprachgut').

The most plausible interpretation of Hitt. pattar (and its Lycian match) may be a comparison with a NC vessel-word *phǎt'V (Starostin proposes to compare it to the above Ns. *p'/pat[a] 'basket, box' — see his paper in this volume — but this Ns. word may be fictitious). There is no support for a Ns. *p'/pat[a] in IE; HS support is very weak (Starostin, this volume), so what we have is Uralic *pata and a suspicious Dravidian pāt(t)alV 'pot'. It remains to be seen if the above Ns. root can be salvaged as East-Ns. *pata 'pot'. It is quite possible, though, that, in the East as well, we are dealing with one of many migratory terms (cf. *pott-).

36. Entry 15 *qaRp/p'a 'to harvest' equals in meaning only HS *xrp — but this meaning has been reconstructed on the basis of only one Arabic word: xrf 'to pluck fruit'. Another possible Semitic cognate is Akkadian xarpū 'early autumn'.

As for IE, alleged root *Ha/orP- is postulated only on the basis of a Hittite noun harp(iy)as which means 'feast of harvest'; but it is certain that this latter word is a borrowing from Semitic. As Puhvel states in his *Hittite Etymological Dictionary* (1991, 183), 'EZEN ŠE$_{12}$ harpiya . . . can be interpreted as EZEN ŠE$_{12}$ HARPI-ya "feast of winter and summer", with *HARPI* from Assyr. harpū "summer"'.

It is clear that we can not consider Hitt. harp(iy)a- as an inherited IE word, which makes the IE gloss disappear from the list of possible cognates in our entry 15 (cf. also Starostin, this volume). What remains beside HS, is Altaic *arp'a 'barley'.

37. Entry 17 *ɢaLV 'cereals' is based on one Arabic word (γall-at- 'cereals') representing the entire HS phylum; on one Georgian word (γalva 'ripe grain') representing, possibly, along with γala 'rich crop', the whole Kartvelian family. This leaves us with three IE words (Hittite, Greek, and Latin) which clearly represent borrowings from one non-IE source.

The entire IE entry *xel[V]K-, without a determined meaning and with an unfounded reconstruction *-e-, shall be considered non-existent since it is based on borrowings only:

A) Hittite noun of non-IE origin halki- 'grain' (genetically identical to the name of Hurrian grain-god Halki- as suggested by Sommer and recently supported by offner, Puhvel *et al.*: see Hoffner 1974, 82–4; Puhvel 1991, 38).

B) Greek word hálik(a) 'spelt' — probably borrowed from the same source as Hitt. halki- 'grain' (above).

C) Lat. halica 'spelt' (later alica) borrowed from the above Gr. hálika. There is also an Etruscan word, halx 'beer made with barley', which is usually associated with our noun [hal(i)ka]: see Puhvel 1991, 38–9; we may well assume that the primary meaning of our word was 'barley'.

As for the original source of Gr. hálik(a), etc., it may be proto-Nakh-Daghestanian *HV̆lk̆V (a kind of grain) as suggested by Nikolaev 1985, 61, no. 7.

38. Entry 18 *xänt'V 'kernel, grain' includes Sem. *hi/unt'-at- 'wheat'; IE *x́et(e)n- — as seen in Hitt. hattar (a kind of grain), Middle Irish eitne 'kernel' — and Drav. *anṭi 'kernel'.

A putative relation between the above Semitic, IE and Dravidian forms is based on one, highly doubtful, assumption that IE shows a metathesis. But Hitt. hattar is an isolated word (as many other Hittite 'grain words': almost all of them borrowings) — it is not even discussed in Puhvel's dictionary. It will be excluded from the list of possible cognates. This leaves us with three, phonetically different, culture words from three geographically distant language families: not the ideal material for comparison and reconstruction.

4. Nostratic etymologies with doubtful Indo-European links

When reconstructing the Nostratic proto-language, V. Illič-Svityč compiled a list of some thirty IE words which he considered borrowings from proto-Semitic; these cultural terms showed, on many occasions, unusual phonetic shape. The borrowing from Semitic into IE occured at the time when IE-speaking people were neighbours of the Semites somewhere in the Near East.

After having accomplished, in essence, his reconstruction of Proto-North-Caucasian, Starostin published several papers (the most complete one 1988) where he discussed IE–NC word pairs which represented borrowings either from IE into NC or vice versa. His word-list in the 1988 paper contains 82 items; the vast majority of 82 word sets include NC borrowings into IE.

Starostin maintains (p. 154 of the above paper) that there are no Indo-Europeanisms in the reconstructed Proto-NC lexicon, but there are many North-Caucasianisms in the reconstructed PIE lexics; therefore, the direction of the borrowing process was, essentially, from NC to IE. This might have happened in the fifth to fourth millennium BC, when Indo-Europeans were located on the territory inhabited by North-Caucasians (= Hurri-Caucasians) somewhere to the

South of the Caucasus. Starostin says also that there are no grounds to ascribe to the Proto-North-Caucasians a higher cultural level when compared to that of the Proto-Indo-Europeans.

This latter statement is questionable. Since we have so many borrowings from PNC to PIE (and none from PIE to PNC), why not conclude that the North-Caucasians stood at that time (and somewhat later, when many borrowings occured from ENC to IE) on a much higher cultural level than the Indo-Europeans (cf. part 5 of the present paper)? Besides, Starostin himself ascribes to Proto-North-Caucasians a much earlier date (sixth to fifth millennium BC) than to Proto-Indo-Europeans. The Proto-North-Caucasians were slow-moving, essentially sedentary, people who only managed to migrate as far as the Northern Caucasus from their southern homeland; as for the Proto-Indo-Europeans, they just started their long migration, namely, to Asia Minor where they split into Anatolians and West-Indo-Europeans; the latter continued their movement to the west, until they temporarily settled in the Balkan area.

Starostin's interpretation of many (P)IE words as borrowings from (P)NC represents a highly important progress in the study of the Near Eastern populations, their languages and their cultures. One of the words, borrowed from NC into PIE (and not vice versa), is PIE *eḱwo-s 'horse' (note unusual phonetic structure; see Starostin 1988, 114–15: to NC *hĭnčwV) which has cognates in all major WIE languages, as well as in EIA, i.e. Anatolian (Luw. azzuwa- [with -zz- < *-ḱ-], Hierogl. Luw. azúwa-, Lycian esbe- [Cb < *Cw]; the appropriate Hittite word, hidden behind ideograms, may have been [akkwa-]. Note that both Luwian and Lycian have preserved the reflexes of all three types of PIE guttural stops: velars, palatals, and labiovelars, whereas Hittite is a plain *centum*-language)

*   *   *

What follows is a critical analysis of three doubtful entries from *NM* which seem to include IE borrowings from North-Caucasian (= Hurri-Caucasian). Since these words are being discussed by Starostin as well (Starostin, this volume), I limit myself to very short notes. I consider it important to underline a high probability of many IE reconstructed words as being borrowings, which effectively excludes their presence in a Nostratic dictionary.

39. Dolgopolsky's entry 79 *madu 'honey' may be fictitious: PIE *medhu- may well be a borrowing from EC *hw-mĭʒū 'honey' (see Starostin, this volume). There is Luw. word madduwiya- 'of wine', related to Russian medv'anyj 'made of honey'; the underlying Luw. root should match Hitt. *médu-. This latter does not exist, but it may indicate phonetic similarity between EC i-vowel and Hitt. ē-vowel (very narrow, also spelled i).

After removing IE, we are left with a suspicious Sem., as well as with Drav. *matt- 'honey, sweet juice' which rather originates from *mayȝV (Starostin, this volume).

40. Entry 43 *diq'a 'goat' seems to include a IE borrowing *dik-/*digh- from NEC *dV(r)q'wV 'goat'; this may be also the source of Kartv. borrowing (*dqa- 'goat'). Starostin (this volume) also mentions irregular IE phonology (note, by the way, a precise match to IE *k/*gh [better: *kh/*g] in HS: Omotic *dVk'-/*dVg- 'capricorn, lamb').

41. Entry 76 *p/p'ayV (a kind of fish) may represent a genuine ENs. set of roots (Uralic *payV and Drav. *payy-) which has nothing to do with IE *peisk-. This latter may well be borrowed from NC *bV̄s̰wA 'fish'; *-k- may be IE diminutive suffix (cf. Starostin 1988; for the suffix, see Starostin 1989, 116, no. 1.10).

5. Dating of Nostratic and its daughter-languages

Dolgopolsky's list of Nostratic words for grain, nuts, berries, fruit, edible roots (see *NM* entries 16–17 and 53–62), as well as reconstructed words for containers and food-processing, seem to indicate a relatively shallow dating of the Nostratic proto-language and its speakers (scarcely older than twelfth millennium BC), when these latter were able not only to gather edible parts of plants but also to store them for use in winter.

This thesis may be considered as a confirmation of a 'sisterhood' of both Proto-Nostratic and Proto-Hamito-Semitic (= Afro-Asiatic), this latter being not much older than Proto-Nostratic. Both proto-languages existed at an age which immediately preceded the appearance of agriculture and cattle-breeding. According to Militarev *et al.*, the most ancient speakers of Hamito-Semitic (this latter being some twelve thousand years old) were Natufians, the most cultured people at their time. The stage of Hamito-Semitic people, which immediately preceded the Natufian era, was that of hunters-gatherers with a developed system of food processing and conservation — which is close to the stage of the Nostratic people as described in *NM*.

If the Proto-Indo-Europeans inhabited a part of the predominantly Hurri-Caucasian territory not earlier than seven thousand years ago, then the former were not the people who had developed the high urban culture of Asia Minor at a much older age. It is more likely that (Pre-)Proto-Hurri-Caucasians developed this culture. In any case, the Proto-Hurri-Caucasians can be considered as being one millennium older than Proto-Indo-Europeans; the former may have inhabited a much broader territory than Proto-Indo-Europeans several hundred years later and, even if the earliest possible age of the Proto-Hurri-Caucasians was eight thousand years ago, their close relatives may have been dwelling in South-Central Asia Minor as early as 9000–8500 years ago. After all, Hurri-Caucasian languages seem to have been spread over extremely vast territories.

Hurri-Caucasian peoples and languages inhabited Europe and the Near East way before the Indo-Europeans started to expand. We may consider the historical Hurri-Caucasians (North-Caucasians, Hurrians, Hatti people, probably also Sumerians and Basques) as 'islands' in the Indo-European 'sea'. Besides the historically documented Hurri-Caucasian languages, we have strong Hurri-Caucasian substrata all over Europe and Western Asia. We may also notice an exceedingly high cultural level of Hurri-Caucasian people (Hatti, Hurrians, Sumerians) when compared with the level of their neighbours.

When turning to the Nostratic people — the ancestors of the Indo-Europeans, and to the Sino-Caucasian people — the ancestors of the Hurri-Caucasians, we may be looking at a similar picture: the older, predominantly Sino-Caucasian territories (Northern Caucasus, Yeniseian settlements, Sino-Tibetan regions) are 'islands' in the Nostratic 'sea'. Being older than the Nostratic people, the Sino-Caucasians have come not only to the Far East; they also have spread all over America some twelve thousand years ago; their offsprings speak Na-Dene-Athapaskan, Algic, Salishan, Wakashan, Siouan, and many other American Indian languages (whereas Nostratic is represented only by a relatively recent wave of Altaic, namely Eskimo-Aleutian).

*   *   *

In conclusion, I would like to underline that I consider many entries in *NM* with a substantial dose of scepticism: these entries may rather represent migratory terms (Wanderwörter). It is not by chance that certain reconstructions in such entries are frequently based on just one word, sometimes representing a whole language family. It is also not by chance that many reconstructions, or documented words, included into these entries have unusual phonetic shape (sometimes being represented by two or more phonetic variants).

But there are many other reconstructions in *NM* which may be safely considered as correct. It is important to underline that such reconstructions reveal the same phonetic correspondences which have been established by Illič-Svityč — for instance, Nostr. glottal stops (Starostin's aspirated stops) matching Alt. aspirated stops, IE voiceless [better: aspirated voiceless] stops, Kartvelian glottal stops, etc.

Dolgopolsky has further developed Illič-Svityč's conception of Nostratic phonetics, adding a subsystem of lateral obstruents. Starostin now proposes one more re-interpretation, showing that Nostratic had a series of labialized stops (to which labiolaryngeals may now be added) with a specific phonetic correspondence in Nostratic daughter-languages (Nostr. voiced labialized stops being preserved in Kartvelian, but yielding aspirated stops in Altaic, and voiced stops [better: voiceless stops] in Indo-European).

There is one more important thing in the recent development of historical phonetics: instead of sticking to illogical rules of the type '*t > *d > *t', '*a > *e > *a', we may consider a much stronger language stability when *t was not changing over millennia and still remains t in many languages, or when *a remained *a all the way, staying as a in many modern languages. This latter aspect (stability of vowels) may be used as the basis for the reconstruction of IE laryngeals: just accept a stable laryngeal (as documented in Anatolian texts) before or after any vowel, and you do not need anything else.

It is not excluded that Illyč-Svityč's and Dolgopolsky's conception of the Nostratic proto-language as having split into six daughter-languages will be changed, following Militarev's and Starostin's proposal to regard the old and complex Hamito-Semitic phylum as Nostratic's sister (this won't change much in the Nostratic reconstructions, probably resulting in a few simplifications). If so, we will have three sister proto-languages: Hamito-Semitic (or Afro-Asiatic), Nostratic, and Sino-Caucasian.

This latter is considered by Starostin (who has been working on a comparison of Ns. and SC for more than a decade now) as more archaic and more complex than Nostratic. We may have many language families in America which either are daughters of Sino-Caucasian, or represent special branches, closely related to Sino-Caucasian, and remotely related to Nostratic (cf. part 2 of the present paper). It may happen that future linguo-historical studies will concentrate not only on further work in the fields of HS, Ns., and SC, but also on reconstructions of Sino-Caucasian-type macro-families on American soil.

NM is especially important since it combines linguistic with ethnological research. The book supplies us with a better understanding of the life of our remote ancestors. Hopefully, further studies in comparison and deep reconstruction of languages will take in consideration both linguistic and ethnological data — as envisioned by Professor Renfrew.

References

Bammesberger, A., 1988. *Die Laryngaltheorie*. Heidelberg: C. Winter.

Carlson, B. & P. Flett, 1989. *Spokane Dictionary*. Missoula (MT): University of Montana.

Dolgopolsky, A., 1998. *The Nostratic Macrofamily and Linguistic Palaeontology*. (Papers in the Prehistory of Languages.) Cambridge: The McDonald Institute for Archaeological Research.

Dolgopolsky, A., 1991. *List of Nostratic Roots*. Haifa. (Manuscript)

Furnée, E., 1972. *Die wichtigsten konsonantischen Erscheinungen des Vorgriechischen*. The Hague: Mouton.

Güterbock, H., 1980–. *The Hittite Dictionary*. Chicago (IL): The Oriental Institute.

Hoffner, H., 1974. *Alimenta Hethaetorum*. New Haven (CT): Yale University Press.

Kinkade, M.D., 1981. *Dictionary of the Moses-Columbia Language*. Nespelem: Colville Confederate Tribes.

Kinkade, M.D., 1991. *Upper Chehalis Dictionary*. Missoula (MT): University of Montana.

Klimov, G.V., 1964. *Ètimologicheskij slovar' kartvel'skix jazykov [Etymological Dictionary of the Kartvelian Languages]*. Moscow: Nauka.

Lehrman, A., 1998. *Indo-Hittite Redux*. Moscow: Paleograph.

Lincoln, N. & J. Rath, 1980. *North Wakashan Comparative Root List*. Ottawa: National Museums of Canada.

Neumann, G., 1994. *Ausgewählte Kleine Schriften*. Innsbruck: Institut für Sprachurssenschaft.

Nikolaev, S., 1985. Severokavkazskie zaimstvovanija v xettskom i drevnegrecheskom. *Drevn'aya Anatoliya*, 60–73.

Nikolaev S. & S. Starostin, 1994. *North Caucasian Etymological Dictionary*. Moscow: Nauka.

Pokorny, J., 1959. *Indogermanisches Etymologisches Wörterbuch*, Band I. Bern & München: A. Franke.

Puhvel, J., 1991. *Hittite Etymological Dictionary*, vol. 3. Berlin & New York: Mouton.

Shevoroshkin, V., 1986. Introduction, in *Typology, Relationship and Time*, eds. V. Shevoroshkin & T. Markey. Ann Arbor (MI): Karoma.

Shevoroshkin, V. (ed.), 1989a. *Reconstructing Languages and Cultures*. Bochum: Brockmeyer.

Shevoroshkin, V. (ed.), 1989b. *Explorations in Language Macrofamilies*. Bochum: Brockmeyer.

Shevoroshkin, V. (ed.), 1990. *Proto-Languages and Cultures.*, Bochum: Brockmeyer.

Shevoroshkin, V. (ed.), 1991. *Dene-Sino-Caucasian Languages*. Bochum: Brockmeyer.

Starostin, S., 1988. Indoevropejsko - severnokavkazskie izoglossy. *Drevnij vostok* 1988, 112–63.

Starostin S., 1989. Nostratic and Sino-Caucasian, in *Explorations in Language Macrofamilies*, ed. V. Shevoroshkin. Bochum: Brockmeyer, 42–66.

Timmers J., 1977. *A Classified English-Sechelt Word List*. Lisse: de Ridder.

Trask R.L., 1996. *Historical Linguistics*. London: Edward Arnold.

Chapter 4

Nostratic — or proto-human?

Christopher Ehret

Deep-time comparative reconstruction

To subject the Nostratic hypothesis to serious scholarly debate is to engage oneself with what I take to be the next great challenge for historical linguistics — to extend the comparative method to the establishing of deep-time language relationships. How we face that challenge, of pushing back the reach of historical linguistic reconstruction to earlier periods of human history, will have much to do with whether historical linguistics in the future pursues bold and invigorating new directions of research or bogs down in a kind of latter-day scholasticism.

Whether Nostratic itself is a valid grouping as presently constituted by its proponents is not the real issue. The issue that hinders advance is an attitudinal one. We can hardly spend much time in our field of endeavour without encountering a peculiar and not very scientific kind of thinking. In this mode scholars may declare, as a kind of *a priori* assertion, that systematic historical reconstruction will never be possible for more than 6000 years ago. Or they may even construct theoretical frameworks for claiming that it *should* be impossible to do such work. This is rather as if the seventeenth- and eighteenth-century astronomers had decided that telescopes and our ability to use them would never improve, and that the only extraterrestrial object we would ever be able to know much about was the near side of the moon. One can only wonder at what could possibly motivate such a self-defeating attitude toward one's own field of contribution to human knowledge.

In any case, the work of historical linguists and archaeologists in Africa already provides practical refutations of this attitude. (By the way, there is almost no serious dissent among those historical linguists who have worked closely on the African families as to their overall validity, but only on their details of subclassification and reconstruction. The one exception is Khoisan, where the inclusion of Hadza and Sandawe is sometimes a contentious issue.) So let me present two examples from Africa.

The Bantu languages, it is now generally agreed among both linguists and historians of the continent, trace back to a Proto-Bantu language spoken around the fourth millennium BC (Ehret 1982; Vansina 1990). The establishment of this group across a third of Africa can be successively correlated with a variety of archaeological manifestations, appearing first in the northwestern areas of the equatorial rainforest before 3000 BC (Klieman 1997), reaching the Western Rift Valley system in the heart of the continent at no later than the tenth century BC, and then widely occupying the eastern and southeastern parts of the continent between about the third century BC and the second century AD (Ehret 1998). In other words, the Bantu languages reflect a history almost as deep, in most scholars' reckonings, as that of the Indo-European family.

Yet the Bantu languages form just one sub-sub-sub-sub-branch of a sub-sub-sub-branch of a sub-sub-branch of a sub-branch of a branch of the whole Niger-Congo family. The stage of language expansion, Benue-Kwa, immediately preceding the Proto-Bantu era of the fourth millennium BC can quite reasonably be correlated with the expansion of peoples with polished stone axes into the central and eastern parts of the West African rainforest at around 1500–2000 years earlier, so our correlation of Niger-Congo languages with archaeology can already be taken back to probably 7000 years ago. But we still have four earlier stages of Niger-Congo history yet to be accounted for, and these can hardly have taken less than several more thousand years to eventuate.

A second deep-time case is that of the Nilo-Saharan family. A detailed, rigorous, and systematic historical reconstruction of the phonology and morphology, along with an etymological dictionary, exists now for this family. Like Dolgopolsky's work on Nostratic, it is currently in the process of publication, so the linguistic palaeontology that I will refer to leaves us in the same kind of scholarly limbo. Nevertheless, here is what appears to be the situation.

At the third, fourth, and fifth stages of the differentiation of Nilo-Saharan into daughter languages, the first evidence of a shift over to food production appears in the lexical data. According to the lexical stratigraphy, at the first of these three periods only the raising of cattle can be identified; at the second period, large complex homesteads, including granaries, are attested, and cultivation, apparently of African grains, is added; and at the third period sheep and goat raising are indicated. Exactly these three successive stages in the establishment of food production and of more complex settlements (with some disputed findings on particular bones and seeds) have been discovered in just the areas that linguistic geographical reasonings would best locate the Nilo-Saharan peoples who belonged to these three stages of prehistory — namely, in the true tropical side of the eastern Sahara. The stages date from 8000 to 5500 BC, which if we could calibrate them would surely give us calendrical dates beginning well before 8000 BC. Nilo-Saharan history extends two stages further back in time than these archaeologically attested periods. In this case, we have evidence that systematic phonological reconstruction is quite possible for a language family whose proto-language must surely date significantly earlier than 10,000 years ago (see Ehret 1993 for further discussion).

What does this tell us about Nostratic? Most basically it says that we cannot reject Nostratic out of hand; the evidence must be subjected to serious scholarly scrutiny, and it deserves that scrutiny. With the documentation at hand, we are not in a position right now to move to that level of analysis, and we have not been allowed the span of time needed to give this task its proper due, even if we did have the materials we need. So our evaluations must of necessity be based on a partial view of the evidence.

On the validity of Nostratic

Nonetheless, it is possible to raise some very interesting issues with respect to Nostratic, but not the ones that might be expected. These issues cast doubt not on the reality of deep-time language families and not on our ability to apply the comparative method to them, but on our ability at present to successfully define the limits of such macro-groupings. We launch this inquiry with a comparison of claimed Nostratic materials with data drawn from the systematic historical reconstructions of other language families not claimed to be part of the family, and to show the results such a comparison produces. For this comparison, I have chosen the Nilo-Saharan and Niger-Congo families of sub-Saharan Africa.

Because we lack as yet the promised etymological dictionary of Aharon Dolgopolsky, the Nostratic data has been taken from the careful work of Alan Bomhard and J.C. Kerns (1994). For the non-Nostratic side of the comparison, the evidence comes from my own etymological dictionary of 1602 Nilo-Saharan roots (in press) and from Malcolm Guthrie's dictionary of Bantu roots found in his *Comparative Bantu*, volumes 3 and 4 (1970). In the Nilo-Saharan work, I have been rigorous in demanding near Neogrammarian regularity of sound correspondences (there remain issues in the histories of the vowels and tone, however, that are still to be resolved), and I have applied more narrow and demanding criteria of semantic relation between acceptable cognates than has been typical of Nostratic work (or than often are applied, for that matter, in Indo-European studies). The Bantu division of Niger-Congo was chosen to represent its family, both because we lack as yet a comparable etymological dictionary of the family as a whole and because Bantu by itself is a grouping with a time depth on the order of that of Indo-European.

Materials from each of these dictionaries has been extensively compared with evidence from Bomhard & Kerns (1994). I have simplified the phonetic representation of the proposed Nostratic roots and sometimes their definitions, but their forms and their range of meanings should still be clear. In several cases, I have treated one root of theirs as two roots. These were instances in which Bomhard & Kerns gave two constellations of meanings to a supposed single root, whereas the Nilo-Saharan or Niger-Congo comparisons gave two roots, one that went with one of the sets of meanings and the other that linked up with the second set of meanings. The overall results make just as strong a case for the inclusion of Nilo-Saharan and of Niger-Congo in Nostratic as of several other language groups long presumed to belong to it.

We begin our survey with the comparison of Nostratic and Nilo-Saharan (ṭ, ṯ, and ḍ represent a proto-Nilo-Saharan series of stops of uncertain but probably prepalatal articulation):

Nostratic		Nilo-Saharan	
*balʸ-	'to shine, be bright'	*beːḷ	'to shine brightly'
*bar-	'to be kind, do good'	*ɓoːr	'to be good'
*bar-	'to bear, carry'	*mbar	'to catch'
*bi	'with'	*bɛː	'of, having'
*bur-	'to bore, pierce'	*ɓuːr	'pit, hole'
*buw-	'to go, come, proceed'	*bwɔ	'to approach'
*pal	'stone'	*p'ɛl	'grindstone'
*pal	'to fill' (but outside IE, usually 'much, many')	*pol	'much; of large quantity or size'
*palʸ-	'to burn, be warm'	*peḷ	'to burn' (Nilotic)
*par-	'to fly, flee; move swiftly'	*pɛr	'to fly'
		*pʰor	'to flee'
*par-	'to precede, surpass, overtake'	*pʰaːr	'to run'
*par-	'to spread, scatter'	*poːr	'to come apart, fall apart'
*pasʸ-	'to split, break, shatter'	*pwaːθ	'to break'
*paʔ-	'to swell, fatten'	*pʰe	'fat'
*paʕw-	'fire, flame, spark'	*poːw	'bright'
*pid-	'to seize, hold, capture'	*pʰed	'to pluck out'
*pilʸ-	'to split, cleave'	*p'iḷ	'to tear, break (off)'
*pinʸ-	'to watch (over)'	*pʰɛŋ	'to hear, notice, sense'
*pir-	'to turn, twist'	*pʰir	'to spin'

Nostratic		Nilo-Saharan	
*pir-	'to tremble, shake'	*piːr	'to shake'
*puw-	'to blow'	*pʰu	'to blow'
*da	'along with, together with'	*nda	'and'
*dab-	'to make fast, fit together, fasten'	*ndob or *ndop	'to bend around, fold around'
*day-	'to look at, consider, examine'	*di	'to look at' (V ≠ ?)
*dur-	'spot, dirt, blemish'	*ɗur	'dark'
*ta-	'this'	*tʰa	'that nearby'
*tu-	'that'	*tʰi	'here (direction?)'
*tak-	'to form, make, create'	*tʰaːkʰ	'to intend, have in mind to do'
*tak'-	'to touch, push, strike'	*tʰoːk'	'to pound lightly'
*tar-	'to spread out'	*ṭer or *ṭ'ɛr	'to spread apart'
*tar-	'to pull, drag'	*ter	'to pick up'
*tal-	'head, top, end'	*tʰɔːtʰɔːl	'blister'
*tam-	'to cover over'	*tʰim	'to cover' (V ≠)
*tanʸ-	'to extend, spread out, stretch'	*tʰaŋ	'to stretch out'
*tar-	'to scratch, scrape'	*tʰwɛr	'to tear off, scrape off'
*tum-	'to complete, end'	*ṭiwm	'to finish, complete'
*t'ah-	'to split'	*t'ɔh	'to break into small pieces'
*t'ar-	'to tear, cut, sever'	*t'or	'to snap, break, cut'
*t'ar-ap-	'to tear, rend, pluck'	*t'or-up	'to cut ends off'
*t'arʸ-	'to grasp, embrace'	*ṭ'ir	'to grab, seize and hold tightly'
*t'aw-	'to leave, let go'	*ṭ'ɔw	'to cease, leave off, not function'
*t'ay-	'to shine, gleam, glow'	*ṭ'a	'to kindle, make burn'
*t'um-	'to twist, turn, wind'	*t'amp	'to turn around' (NS *p is a verb suff. of extended action; V ≠)
*t'uw-	'to give, put, place'	*ṭ'i	'to set down'
*dʸi-	demonstrative stem	*ḍ-	demonstrative stem ('there'?)
*dʸar-	'to hold firmly'	*ḍwar	'to restrain'
*t'ʸak-	'to cut into small pieces, chop, chip'	*ṭ'waːkʰ	'to rap, tap, peck at'

Nostratic		Nilo-Saharan	
*t'ʸul-	'to overshadow, make dark'	*t̠'iːl	'to die (of fire), be extinguished'
*sʸaw-	'to be dry, arid, withered'	*θwa	'to dry (tr.)'
		*θwaw	'to stiffen, harden'
*sʸir-	'to twist, turn, tie, bind'	*ṣiːd̠	'to twist (tr.)'
*sʸul-	'to be safe, well, sound'	*ṣɔːl	'to arrange, put in order' (V ≠ ?)
*sʸur-	'to surge, gush, flow, spring forth'	*ṣul̠	'to leak out' ? (l̠ ≠)
*dᶻaʔ-	'to waste away, become weak'	*zaː	'young, weak, immature' (expected *zah ?)
*tˢuk-	'to bend, turn, wind, twist'	*sukʰ	'to bend'
*tˢ'ab-	'to press, tie, or join firmly together'	*saːʼw	'to put (several) together'
*sa-	'this, that'	*si	'this one' (stem with *i nearness marker)
*sag-	'to reach, attain, get' (IE 'hold fast; overcome; might; firm')	*sɛɟ	'to be strong' (see IE meanings)
*saw-	'to sleep, rest'	*saːy	'to become lower'
*saw-al-	'to wet; to flow'	*saʼy	'to spill out'
*sin-	'sinew, tendon'	*siːl	'strip' (expected *siːn, however)
*t̠ˡar-	'to cause harm, injure: harm, injury'	*l̠aːwr	'harm' (Saharo-Sahelian branch)
*t̠ˡar-	'to cut, cut into'	*l̠er	'to cut apart'
*t̠ˡay-	'to advance, go on, grow old'	*l̠aːw	'to rise, go higher'
*t̠ˡim-	'to enclose, wrap, contain'	*l̠im	'to darken' (wide African semantics: 'dark' < earlier 'cover')
*gab-	'to cook, roast, boil, burn'	*ɟweːb or *ɟweːɓ	'to burn (tr.)'
*gasʸ-	'to touch, feel, handle'	*gwaːθ	'to scratch (surface)'
*gat'-	'to grasp'	*ŋgaːT	'to grasp' (*T = *t' or *tʰ or *t̠ʰ)
*gaʔ-	'to be empty, void, lacking'	*gah or *ɟah	'to not do'

Nostratic		Nilo-Saharan	
*gir-	'to scratch'	*gir or *ɠir	'to scratch, scrape'
*gud-	'to throw, toss'	*gwinḍ	'to toss'
*gub-	'highest point, top'	*gobar or *goɓar	'crested crane' (characteristic feature of this bird is a very noticeable *crest*; *-ar is a common NS noun suffix, i.e, one characterized by a crest)
*gun-	'to perceive, notice, be aware of'	*ɠwɔɲ	'to observe'
*gur-	'to stand out, jut out, project'	*ŋgwiːr	'horned or tusked herbivore'
		*ɠwor	'to puncture, pierce with point'
*gur-	'to turn, twist, wind, wrap, roll'	*ŋguːr	'to bend'
*gur-	'to rumble, roar, growl, gurgle'	*ɲuːr	'to growl' (expected *ŋguːr ?)
*gʸab-	'to bestow upon, give'	*gaːb or *gaːɓ	'to grip, hold in the hand'
*gʷan-	'to swell, abound'	*gɔŋg	'to swell up'
*ɢar-	'to cry (out), yell, shout'	*ɲaːr	'to make a deep sound'
*ka-	demonstrative pronoun stem	*ka, *ki	'that/this'
*kad-	'to twist, wind, wrap, bend'	*kʰuḍ	'to turn (tr.)' (expected *a?)
*kal-	'to make a noise, sound'	*kʰaḷ	'to shout, call out'
*kal-	'to hold (back)'	*kʰɔḷ	'to take hold of'
*kalʸ-	'to rob, steal, hide'	*kʰwaḷ	'to grasp and take'
*kam-	'to seize, grasp; gather together'	*kʰamp	'to press together' (NS *p is a verb suff. of extended action)
*kan-	'to do in proper manner; to set straight, make right'	*kʰaːn	'to direct, guide, send'
*kap-	'to take, seize; hand'	*kap	'to grab'
*kar-	'to cut'	*kʰoːr	'to tear off, rip off, cut off'
*kar-	'hard, strong; rough, coarse'	*k'wakʰar	'tough, hard'?
*kay-	'to scoop out'	*kʰay	'to break off, tear off (tr.)'

Nostratic		Nilo-Saharan	
*kum-	'to heap up'	*kʰom	'hump, mound'
*kuŋ-	'fat, fatty part of body'	*kʰwiɲ	'entrails'
*k'ab-	'to seize with the teeth, bite'	*k'ap	'to eat' (expected *k'ab, though)
*k'al-	'to suckle'	*k'ol	'to chew'
*k'al-	'highest point, top; to lift, raise up, make high'	*k'eyl	'horn'
*k'ar-	'to twist, turn, bend'	*k'er	'to twist'
*k'il-	'to decrease, diminish'	*k'il	'to sink, go down'
*kʷar-	'to scratch, scrape'	*kʰar	'to be cracked (of skin)'
		(*k'wɛr	'to scrape': but C ≠)
*kʷul-	'to bend, curve, revolve'	*kʰul	'to bend'
*kʷur-	'body, belly'	*kʰuːr	'skin, hide'
*k'ʷur-	'to crush, grind'	*k'uːr	'to scrape'
*q'ʷal-	'to swell, expand'	*k'uːl	'to swell'
*ʕab-	'to grasp, seize'	*hab or *haɓ	'to take'
*ʕan-C-	'to breathe' (IE)	*haːŋ	'to breathe'
*ʕuw-	'flock of small animals'	*hɛw	'to gather, place together'
*yiw-	'grain'	*yih	'grass' (w/h ≠ ?)
*han-aɢ-	'to press or squeeze together'	*han	'to grasp'
*ħaw-	'to shine'	*haʼw	'to be hot'
*ħay-aw-	'to live'	*hayṭ	'person' (*ṭ is NS noun-forming suffix)
*haŋ-	'to split apart, open'	*aŋ	'to open' (expected *haŋ ?)
*har-	'to set free, become free'	*har	'to be lacking' (i.e. free of) ?
*ʔab-	'to become strong, mighty'	*bo	'big'
*ʔap-	'to burn, be hot, bake, cook'	*pʰaːy	'to burn (intr.)'
*ʔar-	'to cut (off, apart)'	*re	'to cut in two'
*ʔay-	'to come, to go'	*ya,*yɛ,*yɔ	'to go/come'
*ʔay-	'mother'	*ya, *aya	'mother'
*ʔay-	interrogative pronoun	*y-	interrogative particle
*ʔa-	1st person singular pronoun stem	*ah, *a-	1st person singular pronoun stem
*ʔa	distant demonstrative particle	*-a	element commonly found in NS non-near demonstratives

Nostratic		Nilo-Saharan	
*ʔi	proximate demonstrative particle	*-i	element commonly found in NS near demonstratives
*ʔi	'to, toward, near to, hither, here'	*-i	ventive (UDUK i 'in, to, at')
*ʔul-	demonstrative pronoun stem	*-l-	demonstrative pronoun base
*wa-	1st person pronoun stem	*wah	'me'
		*wa(h)iʾy	'we, us'
*wa-	'to call, cry out, sound'	*'we	'to tell'
		*'wiː	'to cry out' (V ≠)
*wal-	'to be or become strong'	*'waːl	'to grow'
*wal-	'to cry out, call out, shout'	*wel	'to speak loudly'
*wal-	'to set fire to, burn, heat up'	*wal or *'wal	'to light, set afire'
*wal-	'to flow, well up, flow forth'	*'wel	'to pour, spill (intr.)'
*wal-	'to strike, wound, destroy'	*'wel	'to bruise, wound'
*walʸ-	'to blaze, shine, be bright'	*weːl	'to shine, burn' (expected *ḷ ?)
*waŋ-	'to bend'	*went	'to go round' (stem plus apparent verb extension in *t)
*war-	'to raise; to grow'	*war	'to rise, go up'
*wir-	'to stretch, extend, expand'	*wer	'to increase in size or amount'
*wur-	'to burn'	*'wir	'to shine (of sun, etc.)'
*wurʸ-	'to scratch, incise, dig up'	*wɛyr	'to dig out, dig up'
*ma-	relative pronoun stem	*ma	relative pronoun
*ma-,	demonstrative stem	*ma,	demonstrative stem
*mu-		*ama	(also UDUK mu-n 'there')
*ma-	1st person pl. inclusive stem	*am	'we (excl.)'
*mi-	interrogative pronoun stem	*mi, *ma	interrogative pronoun stem
*ma(ʔ)	negative/prohibitive particle	*ma	negative of irreal aspects/ modes
*mah-	'to increase, swell, be great'	*mɔːh	'to become fat, swell in size'
*mal-	'to fill, become full, increase'	*mɛl	'to increase'
*man-	'to divide, apportion'	*mentʰ	'to pull off pieces (of)' (*tʰ is NS v. suff. of continued action)
*mun-	'to suckle'	*moːɲ-	'to eat soft foot'
*mar-	'young man, young animal'	*maːwr	'ox' (Southern Nilotic 'calf')

Nostratic		Nilo-Saharan	
*mar-	'to soil, stain; spot, stain'	*merih	'leopard' (*-ih is NS noun-deriving suff.; i.e. spotted animal)
*mat-	'to set in motion; to flourish, be fruitful, vigorous, strong'	*mɛːt	'to rise'
*mat'-	'to become wet, moist'	*mant̪' or *mant̪	'to wet'
*maw-	'water, liquid, fluid'	*ma	'to rain'
*na, *ni, *nu	negative/prohibitive particle	*(a)neː	negative particle ('not yet')
*na-, *ni-, *nu-	demonstrative stem	*ne	demonstrative stem ('here'?)
*na-	1st person pronoun stem	*ana	'we (incl.)'
		*na-	1st person sing. subj. marker
*naw-	'to sound, call'	*neh	'to utter'
*naʕ-	'to come, go, arrive'	*na or *nah	'to reach, catch up with'
*nʸaʕ-ar-	'to appear, rise, sprout, grow up'	*ɲa	'to expand'
*nʸam-	'to press, squeeze'	*ɲom	'to squeeze'
*nʸim-	'to stretch, extend, increase'	*ŋam	'to extend, stretch out' (V ≠)
*lab-	'to take hold of, grasp'	*laːɓ or *laːb or *laːp	'to pat, touch, grope'
*lah-	'to make flow, pour, wet'	*leh	'to seep' (intensive: *lih 'to moisten, wet down')
*lak-	'to lick, lap up'	*lakʰ	'to eat soft food'
*luk'-	'to lick, lap up, gulp down, swallow'	*liːŋk'	'to swallow' (V ≠)
*rak-	'to twist, turn, bind'	*rik	'to tie up' (V ≠)
*rak-	'to put together'	*raːk or *raːkʰ	'to put together'
		*rokʰ	'to put together, join (two things)'
*rak-	'to put in order, arrange'	*rɛkʰ	'to match, fit'

Note the recurrent consonant and vowel correlations evident in this array of comparisons:

Nilo-Saharan	Nostratic	Nilo-Saharan	Nostratic
*b, *ɓ, and *mb	*b	*l	*l
*p, *p', and *pʰ	*p	*ḷ and *tˡ	*lʸ
*ḍ, *d, *ɗ, *nd, and *nḍ	*d	*r (and *ḍ /V_)	*r
*t, *tʰ, and *ṭ	*t	*m	*m
*t' and *ṭ'	*t'	*ɲ and *ŋ	*nʸ ~ *ŋ
*ṭ'	*t'ʸ	*a, *aː, o, *oː, *ɛ, *e,	
*æ and *ṣ	*sy	*eː, *aːw, *ey /_C	*a
*dᶻ	*z	*e, *ɛː /_#	*i
*s, *tˢ, and *tˢ'	*s	*ɔ, *ɛw /_#	*u
*g, *ɠ, and *ŋg	*g	*o /[+velar/	*u
		+obstr]_m,b	
*k, *kʰ	*k	*u, *uː	*u
*k'	*k'	*i, *iː	*i
*y	*y ~ w/_#	*wi, *wɛy, *wey, *iw	*wu; *u /C_C
*w	*w; *w~*y/_#	*wo, *wɔ /C_C	*u
*'w	*w; *b/_#	*Cwɔɲ, *Cwoɲ	*Cun

Some of the individual sound correlations occur just once in these data but fit into a wider pattern that includes other sounds with the same position of articulation. Two other singly attested match-ups lack this kind of backup but are phonologically plausible (see above Nostratic *wir- = NS *wer, with /e/ instead of the usual /i/, and Nostratic *G /#_ = NS *ŋ). No special linkage of the hypothesized Nostratic labial velars or palatal velars with the reconstructed Nilo-Saharan sequences of velar plus labial glide is evident.

The comparison of Bomhard & Kerns' Nostratic with the Bantu division of Niger-Congo presents a similar array of plausible comparisons. In these data, a hyphen separates a demonstrable Bantu verb extension from the stem so as to clarify what is being compared. Proto-Bantu considerably contracted its inherited Niger-Congo consonant phonology, most notably collapsing all voiced alveolars to a sound represented in Guthrie's reconstruction as *d (but probably articulated as a lateral of some kind).

Nostratic		Bantu (Niger-Congo)	
*bad-	'to split, cleave, divide'	*-bad-	'to split'
*bak'-	'to cleave, split, break open'	*-baka	'knife'
*balʸ-	'to shine, be bright'	*-bad-	'to shine'
*bar-	'to shine, be bright'		
*bar-	'to make a sound, utter a noise'	*-bad-	'to count'
*bar-	'to scrape, carve, whittle, trim'	*-bada	'baldness'
*bar-	'projection, bristle, point'	*-bodo	'penis'
*bar-	'to bear, carry, bring forth'	*-bed-ik-	'to bear (child); to carry (child)'
*bul-	'to overflow'	*-buḍa	'rain'
*bul-	'to swell, expand'	*-bud-	'to become plentiful, many'
*bul-	'to become worn out, weak, tired, old'	*-bud-	'to get lost, be lacking, lack'
*bur-	'to strike, hit, smash'	*-bud-	'to break, smash, hit, kill'
*bur-	'to whirl'	*-bud-ung-	'to become round'
*buw-	'to become, come into being' (*bi-w- ?)	*-bi-	'to become, be'
*pal-	'flat of hand, palm'	*-padi̧	'sole (of foot)'
*par-	'to precede, surpass, overtake'	*-ped-ik-id-	'to accompany'
*pasʸ-	'to split, cleave, break, shatter'	*-pac-	'to split'
*patˢ'-	'to part, split open, split apart'		
*pat-	'to flutter, quiver, palpitate'	*-pet-	'to winnow'
*pat-	'to open; to be open, wide, spacious'	*-pata	'valley'
*paʕw-	'fire, flame; to warm, heat'	*-pi-	'to become burnt, hot, cooked' (V ≠ ?)
*pinʸ-	'to watch (over), protect, nurture'	*-pingo	'charm (to protect from harm)'
*pir-	'to turn, twist'	*-pid-	'to turn'
*puw-	'to blow, exhale, puff up'	*-puup-	'to blow (as wind)' (redup.)
*dab-	'to make fast, join together'	*-dob-	'to fish (with hook and line)'
*daɢ-	'to glitter, shine, burn brightly'	*-daŋg-	'to shine'
*dal-	'to cut, prick, pierce, gash'	*-dad-	'to crack'
*dan-	'to flow'	*-dand-	'to crawl, spread (as vine)'
*daw-	'to become exhausted, die'	*-du-ad-	'to become ill'

Nostratic		Bantu (Niger-Congo)	
*dilʸ-	'to shine, be or become bright'	*-dido	'fire'
*diq-	'earth, ground, soil, clay'	*-diko	'country'
*tal-	'head, top, end'	*-tada	'platform'
*talʸ-	'to lift, raise, make high'		
*talʸ-	'to stretch, spread, extend'		
*tar-	'to spread, stretch, strew'	*-tadi	'long; length'
*t'al-	'to stretch out, extend'		
*tam-	'to cover over, hide'	*-tomb-	'to copulate' (cf. English term 'to cover (animal)' as euphemism for animal copulation)
*tanʸ-	'to extend, spread, stretch'	*-tand-	'to spread'
*tar-	'to draw, pull, drag'	*-tood-	'to pick up, take, carry'
*t'arʸ-	'to grasp, embrace'		
*tar-	'to scratch, scrape'	*-ted-id-	'to slip, slide'
*ta-	'this'	*-ti	'that, namely'
*tu-	'that'		
*tur-	'to cram, push in, thrust in'	*-tud-	'to pierce'
*t'ak-	'to take, seize, grasp, obtain'	*-tek-	'to draw (water)'
*t'ar-	'to tear, cut, sever'	*-tad-	'to cut open'
*t'aw-	'to strike'	*-tu-	'to pound'
*t'ay-	'to shine, glow, burn brightly'	*-tue	'ashes'
*t'uw-	'to give, put, place'	*-tu-ad-	'to carry'
*t'ʸur-	'to run, flow'	*-cudo	'stream'
*sʸur-	'to surge, gush, flow (forth)'		
*t'ʸak-	'to cut into small pieces, chop, chip'	*-ceke	'sand, grains, small particles'
*dᶻar-	'to gush forth, spirt'	*-jade	'river'
*tsʼar-	'to become visible, clear'	*-ced-	'to clean'
*sag-	'to reach, attain, get'	*-caag-ud-	'to choose'
*gad-	'to force, drive or press together, gather, collect'	*-good-	'to pull'
*kal-	'to make a noise, to sound'	*-kod-um-	'to growl'
		*-kood-, *-kod-ud-	'to cough'

Nostratic		Bantu (Niger-Congo)	
*kam-	'to seize, grasp, grip, clutch'	*-kam-	'to squeeze'
		*-kam-at-	'to seize'
*kam-	'to work; to do, make'	*-kom-	'to hit with a hammer'
*kap-	'to take, seize'	*-kap-	'to bale out (water)'
*kar-	'to cut'	*-ked-	'to cut'
*kar-	'skin, hide; bark, rind'	*-kada	'crab' (i.e. shelled animal)
*kar-	'firm, hard, strong'	*-kod-	'to become strong'
*kas-	'to cut'	*-kec-	'to cut'
*kaw-	'to swell, grow, increase'	*-ku-ed-	'to go up'
*kay-	'to put, place, lay; to be placed, lie'	*-ki-ed-	'to stay'
*kum-	'to heap up, pile up, accumulate'	*-kumba	'load'
		*-kumb-at-	'to hold in arm, hand'
*kur-	'blood'	*-kuda	'red colour'
*k'ak'-	'to cackle, chatter'	*-kok-ud-	'to cackle'
*k'al-	'to burn, warm, cook, roast'	*-kada	'embers; charcoal'
		*-kad-aŋg-	'to fry, roast'
*k'am-	'to weep, moan, lament'	*-kem-	'to cry out'
*k'ar-	'to cut into, cut off, cut in two'	*-kad-	'to tear'
(*qal-	'to strike, split, cut, wound' ?)		
*gʸab-	'to bestow upon, give'	*-gab-	'to give, bestow'
*kʸil-	'to rise, ascend, raise up'	*-kid-	'to pass, surpass, cross over'
		*-kid-uk-	'to jump over'
*kʷar-	'to scrape, scratch'	*-kod-ud-	'to scrape'
*kʷa-	interrogative pronoun stem	*ki	'what?'
*kʷi-	relative pronoun stem		
*kʼʷul-	'to bend, curve, turn, revolve'	*-kud-uŋg-	'to make smooth and round'
*kʼʷan-	'to suckle, nurse; to suck'	*-ken-	'to show the teeth'
*kʼʷat'-	'to cut'	*-ket-	'to cut'
*kʼʷur-	'to crush, grind'	*-kud-	'to scrape'
*kʼʷurʸ-	'to be heavy, weighty, bulky'	*-kud-	'to grow (up), become big'
		*-kudu	'big; mature'
*kʼʷutʸ-	'to say, speak, call'	*-kuut-	'to shout'
*Gub-	'to bend, twist'	*-goob-	'to bend'

Nostratic		Bantu (Niger-Congo)	
*qam-	'to cover, conceal'	*-kamba	'shelled animal'
*qar-	'neck, throat'	*-kodo	'throat, gullet'
*q'al-	'neck, throat'		
*ʕir-	'to descend, set (sun), become dark'	*-ị̄d-	'to get dark'
*halʸ-	'to grow, be strong'	*-adi	'young woman at puberty'
*hak'-	'field'	*-ika	'grassland, savanna'
*hat'-	'to scratch, scrape, cut into'	*-at-	'to split'
*han-	'to bend, curve, twist'	*-in-/*-ịn-	'to bend'
*hag-	'to cover over, hide, obscure'	*-ig-	'to close'
*haŋ-	'to lift, raise, rise'	*-aŋg-	'to hang up'
*ʔal-	'to purify, cleanse (> sift, clean grain)'	*-ed-	'to winnow'
*ʔap-	'to burn, cook, boil, bake'	*-ịp-ik-	'to cook, boil'
*ʔar-	'earth'	*-ado	'land'
*ʔi	'to, toward, near to, hither, here'	*-i	locative marker (in, at, to)
*ʔim-	'to seize, grasp, take'	*-ịm-	'to refuse to give'
*ʔul-	demonstrative pronoun stem	*-da, *-de, *-dia	'that/this'
*hap-	'to turn, turn away, turn back'	*-ep-	'to avoid, get out of way'
*hal-	'to light up, shine'	*-ed-	'to shine'
*walʸ-	'to blaze, shine, be bright'		
*wal-	'to pull (out)'	*-od-	'to gather up'
*wal-	'to flow, wet, well up, flow forth'	*-ed-	'to float'
*war-	'to look, watch out for, observe'	*-ed-	'to try, measure'
*wat'-	'to moisten, wet'	*-ịt-	'to pour' (V ≠ ?)
*man-	'to count, reckon, consider, think'	*-man-	'to know'
*mat'-	'to become wet, moist'	*-mat-	'to daub (plaster, mud)'
*na-, *ni-, *nu-	demonstrative stem	*-na, *-ne, *-nia	'that'
*ʕin-im-	'to say, speak, name; name (n.)'	*-yịna	'name'

Nostratic		Bantu (Niger-Congo)	
*lak-	'to lick, lap up'	*-daka	'tongue, throat'
*law-	'to bend, twist, turn'	*-du̧i	'knee'
*mi	1st person sing. pronoun stem	*mi	'I, me'
(IE) *iw-	'you'	*-u-	2nd person sing. pronoun stem

Again there are recurrent consonant and vowel correlations between the reconstructed roots of the African Language family and the proposed Nostratic roots:

Bantu (Niger-Congo)	Nostratic
*b	*b
*p	*p
*d	*d, *l, *lʸ, *r, *rʸ
*t	*t, t', tʸ
*c	*s, *sʸ, *tˢ, *tˢ'
*j	*dʸ
*g	*g, *gʸ
*k	*k, *k', *q, *q', *kʷ, *k'ʷ
*Ø /#_V	*ʕ, *ħ, *h, *ʔ, *w
*m, *mb	*m
*n, *nd	*n
*a, *e, *o	*a
*u, *u̧	*u
*u ~ *u̧	*Vw
*i	*Vy

The vowels in the proposed Nostratic roots that begin with *ʕ, *ħ, or *h, with one exception, are all *a, whatever the vowel may be in the comparison form taken from Bantu. There also are two single correlations that fit into a potential wider pattern once the Nilo-Saharan examples above are considered: (1) Nostratic *G = Bantu *ŋg /V_ (compare the Nilo-Saharan example above in which *G = NS *ŋ) and (2) Bantu *o(o) /g_b = Nostratic *gub- (the two Nilo-Saharan/Nostratic comparisons with a parallel environment show the same vowel match-up). Conflicting matchings of proposed Nostratic *nʸ with Bantu *ŋg and *nd appear in the data as well.

Rethinking deep-time historical reconstruction

Do these results mean that we seriously should include Nilo-Saharan or Niger-Congo in Nostratic? No, they do not. Do they mean that the whole effort is useless, that we can always find many words in distant human language families that look alike and have the same or closely similar meanings, but have no historical significance? No, they do not support that view either.

The resemblances charted here seem to me, for the most part, too sharp and too specific to be all simply chance. What I think we will discover with wider research through the languages of the world is that these are very ancient and very widespread human root words. This is not really a very daring claim, if we take a moment to think about the how vocabulary would have been transmitted down to us from remote times.

Let us engage in a thought experiment. In this experiment we hypothesize the existence of an original 'proto-human' language. The usual history of vocabulary in real languages consists principally of the remorphologizing of existing stems, reshaping of the semantic scope of existing words of the language, dropping of words from use, and adoption of words from time to time from other languages (word borrowing). We begin, then, with an original human language, having an initial lexicon of perhaps 10,000–20,000 words, as is characteristic of the spoken vocabularies typical of the world's languages in more recent ages. That vocabulary would provide the majority of the materials to be reshuffled and morphologically modified in various ways over the rest of the history of humankind. It would provide the words retained in any particular language; it would also be the ultimate source of words borrowed at later times from language to language. Occasionally, new words might still be created completely anew, and over the long run of language history the body of words thus created might become relatively numerous. But even including onomatopoeic coinages, this element would not likely overwhelm the contributions that came from the original stock of words.

An essential feature to understand in carrying out this thought experiment is just how narrow and circumscribed the range of possible semantic shift usually is. What I have found in doing reconstruction in both the Nilo-Saharan and Afroasiatic families is that there are a very great number of narrow semantic fields in a typical language within which the meanings of particular roots circulate. Over the long run of language history, if a word is preserved in the spoken language, its changes in meaning stay within one of those narrow and self-evident ranges. If a word has something to do with holding or carrying, it will continue nearly always to be used in a meaning that belongs in obvious and overt ways to that semantic category. If it has to do with turning, the most far-out shift it might make is to the meanings 'change' or 'bend', and after the latter shift perhaps it might be drafted as the basis for the construction of a noun meaning 'snake' or 'knee'. Every time I am tempted to make a creative semantic connection between a pair of words in two related languages, sooner or later I discover that all along there was a much better and more straightforward semantic link between a different pairing of words, a pairing that I had overlooked before.

Let me suggest a second way of looking at this matter. Now, what I am about to propose goes against an unexamined habit of thought imbibed like mother's milk by historical linguists, so I must adjure the reader to think before reacting. We in this field of scholarship often, in fact we generally, say that *the farther we work back into the past*, the fewer data we will have from which to reconstruct earlier proto-languages. But that idea rests on upside-down logic. The fact of the matter is instead this: *the nearer we move toward the present*, the more the languages we study *lose* what they once possessed. The more we move *forward* in time, the more *different* the individual related languages become from each other — the more they discard older features and add new materials and processes that obscure their relationships. In contrast, each time we recess farther into the past, each time we reconstruct an earlier stage in language history, we peel away more and more of the layerings of historical change, and we reach successively earlier periods when these languages would have been more and more alike. If we return to the basic hypothesis of our thought experiment — that the languages we study have a common ancestor — we should expect that at each stage of historical reconstruction farther back in time, slowly more and more of the same ancient root words should emerge out of our work. Similarly, more and more of the same morphological markers should appear, and phonological systems should become more and more alike.

What obscures this logic from us is that we focus on the individual language. Yes, each particular language preserves only a part of its earlier inheritance, and the longer the span of time, the less that language maintains of its earlier content. A single language like Basque, far distant in relationship from any other language, is indeed exceedingly difficult to classify. But when the language belongs to a wider genetic group, each language of that group preserves a different portion of the common inheritance, and its portion partially overlaps in different ways with each of the portions preserved in each of its sisters. Comparative method in this typical situation necessarily reconstructs more root morphemes of the proto-language than are preserved in any of its daughters. We have only to look to Proto-Indo-European to recognize the truth of this insight.

The larger the language family we study, the more numerous are the individual sources of data available to us, and the more we can therefore reconstruct of the morphemes, both stem and affixal, of its proto-language. When we move still another stage back into the past and compare several reconstructed proto-languages with one other, we essentially engage in the same process. We increase the number of our sources of evidence, because each proto-language adds another set of languages to our data base. Each proto-language was, as well, a language spoken at an earlier time, with the layerings of later historical change, represented by its daughters, peeled away by the comparative method. If related, they provide data from earlier times when they were far more alike than their modern-day descendants.

In this light, it should not be surprising to find, in distant parts of the world, what appear to be the same words with their meanings fitting within the same narrow semantic ranges. This finding does not necessarily show a closer relation between the languages that have the words; it does not show that borrowing has somehow been more massive and common than we thought; and it does not show, either, that vocabulary is a suspect tool for classification and reconstruction. Rather, what we have to face is the possibility that we really may be dealing with very ancient human vocabulary.

But what is more important for us here is that these data throw into sharp relief the essential problem we all face in trying to push the frontiers of linguistic reconstruction back in time. And that is the problem of comparative perspective. Our perspectives have to be exceedingly wide, eventually of world scope, if we are to build viable results.

Once we turn our attention wider, we find that we simply do not have the basis as yet for defining the boundaries of a hypothesized macrofamily like Nostratic. How can we say something is truly unique to whatever macrofamily we hypothesize to exist, and therefore diagnostic of that family? We need to be able to answer this question, and we can answer it only if we take on our research in the proper order. We must reconstruct the intermediate stages. We must possess sufficient reconstructed vocabulary of both stem and affixal morphemes from families all over the world, if we are to distinguish what is pan-human from what is limited to whichever macrofamily we are seeking to demonstrate. Nostratic work does build on intermediate reconstructions, but it lacks the critical perspective that a wider comparison with families elsewhere in the world would bring.

To sum up, I find good reason to doubt the composition of the Nostratic family as presently offered by *any* of its proponents. A significant proportion of data cited in its favour turn out to be data of wider human occurrence, as we see from the Nilo-Saharan and Niger-Congo comparisons. Faced with this problem, we are hardly in a position to evaluate the human historical implications of Nostratic culture vocabulary, since we may or may not be dealing with a chimera.

On the other hand, we do already have systematic reconstructions of deep African families, whose reach is as far back as 12,000–15,000 BP. Our experience in African research is that the tools of historical linguistics indeed have the power to track language reconstruction very, very far into the past. What this meeting can do, if nothing else, is serve as an affirmation that the time for deep-time linguistic reconstruction has come. We ought to get about the task in the right order, however, and that means getting to work, with no more doubt than is heuristically useful, on reconstructing lower-level families all over the world.

References

Bomhard, A. & J.C. Kerns, 1994. *The Nostratic Macrofamily: a Study in Distant Linguistic Relationship*. Berlin & New York (NY): Mouton de Gruyter.

Ehret, C., 1993. Nilo-Saharans and the Saharo-Sudanese Neolithic, in *The Archaeology of Africa: Foods, Metals and Towns*, eds. T. Shaw, P. Sinclair, B. Andah & A. Okpoko. London & New York (NY): Routledge, 104–21.

Ehret, C., 1998. *An African Classical Age: Eastern and Southern Africa in World History, 1000 BC to AD 400*. Charlottesville (VA): University Press of Virginia.

Ehret, C., in press. *A Historical-Comparative Reconstruction of Nilo-Saharan*. Köln: Koeppe.

Guthrie, M., 1970. *Comparative Bantu*, vols. 3 & 4. Farnborough: Gregg International Press.

Klieman, K., 1997. Peoples of the Western Equatorial Rain Forest: a History of Society and Economy, from *c*. 3000 BC to 1890. Unpublished Ph.D. dissertation, University of California at Los Angeles.

Vansina, J., 1990. *Paths in the Rainforests*. Madison (WI): University of Wisconsin Press.

Chapter 5

Reflections on a distant prospect of Nostratic

Robert Coleman

1.1   The first task of comparative linguists is to compare languages and establish systematic correspondences among them in phonology and morphology and thereafter lexis and syntax. On the basis of these correspondences, which secure relationship among the languages, they may then, if they wish, go on to reconstruct a proto-language, if not ancestral to the languages thus analyzed at least summarizing the comparative relationships.

1.2   Phonological correspondences come first, and the semantic connections between the words exhibiting them are of much less importance. The precise meaning of a word and especially the directions and degrees of change in its history are far more difficult to establish. Some dissimilar cognates are close in meaning, like Fr. faire and Eng. do, Fr. venir and Germ. kommen; others more remote, like Mo. Gk adelfé 'sister' and Dardic Pashayi sagabbhā 'pregnant'; some similar cognates are close in meaning, like Eng. bear and Arm. berem, Umbr. pir and Toch.A poṛ 'fire', others more remote, like Gk légō 'I say' and Lat. legō 'I read'. Incidentally it is worth noting the PIE etyma for each of these pairs, to illustrate the divergences required: *dheə$_1$-, *g^{u}m̥-, *sm̥-g^{u}olbh-ā, *bher-,*pūr. To take account of all the cognates *pūr must be further derived from *peəur, peuər/puər, which illustrates that a mass of secure cognates can reflect an indeterminate etymon, even in a relatively accessible linguistic family.

2.1   The reconstruction of proto-forms from data that are themselves proto-forms of language families, though it has sometimes excited disapproval, is not in principle unreasonable. Proto-Indo-European (PIE) is after all built up on a system of proto-forms in Germanic, Celtic, Italic, etc., which already reveal indeterminacies of their own, and in isolates like Albanian and Armenian, which may or may not be survivors of lost families. It is possible that Linear B and later Greek may be separate languages of an Hellenic family (like Occitan and French) rather than dialects of a single language.

2.2   The advantage that comparativists have in Indo-European, as in Semitic, is the diachronic spread of material. Hittite and Tocharian survive from early dates, Indic and Iranian languages, Greek and Latin (including Romance) have a continuous recorded history over long periods to the present, Celtic, Germanic, Slavic and Armenian over shorter periods, Albanian and Lithuanian relatively recent attestation. We can thus form a picture of the diachrony of Indo-European (IE), which would not be possible if all the data we had were contemporary with Hittite or Albanian. If we had only, say, Hittite, Tocharian, Albanian and Lithuanian, IE comparison would be full of question marks and PIE a poor fragmentary thing.

3.1   In fact the best model for comparative reconstruction is Proto-Romance (PR). For most of the surviving languages we have material going back for almost a millennium, so that individual diachronies can be analyzed. We have independent historical knowledge of the various communities concerned, to confirm the general appropriateness of the divergency model, and we can support conjectures about convergence from the history of population movements or bilingual interaction in sometimes shifting border areas. More important, there is a time-scale for the divergences. The Sardinian vowel system does not make a qualitative distinction between ĕ and ē, ŏ and ō, so must date from the pre-Classical period, before 100 BC. It is appropriate to note that proto-Romance is already built upon asterisked forms — Proto-Sardinian, Proto-Italian, etc. All the proto-forms of language families are built in turn on the proto-forms of individual languages.

3.2   Abundant documents in Latin, including textual evidence for its Vulgar forms, which are not to be equated with the abstract reconstruction of PR, provide valuable material for comparison with PR, enabling us to recover, for instance, the older forms of PR *kapu, *biβerȩ, *bȯve in Lat. caput 'head', bibere 'drink', bouem (acc.) 'ox'; the Latin sources of Sp. hablar, It. parlare in fabulārī, and the Greek loanword parabolāre, replacing loquī (without certain IE etymology) 'speak'; and the Latin sources of Sp. comer and Log. man(d)igare in comedere and mandūcāre, replacing edere (with abundant IE cognates) 'eat'. Sometimes the presence of Latin enables otherwise indeterminate reconstructions to be settled conclusively and morphological and syntactic developments in PR to be understood. In phonology final consonants can be recovered, also h and ae, which unlike au was probably lost completely in Vulgar Latin before the divergences reconstructed for PR took place.

3.3   Many Italic phenomena not preserved in Latin would have remained irrecoverable if PR were our only representation of Italic. For instance Paelignian and Oscan have puklos, an inherited word for 'son' (cf. Ved. putrás and probably Lat. puer) in contrast to the innovative Lat. fīlius; Faliscan and Volscian (or whatever language is represented by the Satricum inscription of *c.* 500 BC) have -osio, unique examples of the PIE etymon for the Greek and Indo-Iranian the-

matic genitive singular, beside the Italo-Celtic -ī found in Latin. In some instances we should be left with incomparable items in PR. Thus *fǫku the etymon
for fuoco, feu etc. reflects the accusative of Lat. focus 'hearth', which has no
cognates and replaces both the PIE roots reflected in Lat. ignis, Umbr. pir. Without the latter evidence we might be tempted to conjecture a third 'fire' word for
PIE.

3.4   Nevertheless, if PR were our only representative from Italic, we should
still have evidence for reconstructing a lot of the lexicon and phonology of
Proto-Italic (very much less of the morphology and syntax, but that is not unique
in comparative studies) on which to build PIE reconstructions. Asterisked forms
can of course be hazardous starting points for the reconstruction of further
asterisked forms, as this example clearly shows, but the check provided here,
uniquely, by Latin indicates that, when the attested data are abundant and
diverse and the time-scale relatively short, the hazard is not too serious to nul-
lify totally a cautious application of the method. What is clear is that PR draws
up definitively the limits of possible reconstruction in any language family.

4.1   One of the disquieting features of Nostratic studies is the scepticism that
is continually being expressed by specialists in the relevant language families
or individual component languages within them, not so much towards the concept of Nostratic itself as to the ways in which data from their own field are
being interpreted and used. In itself this is not altogether surprising. Specialists
usually have intimate first-hand knowledge of continuous texts in their chosen
languages, whether oral or written, and are therefore sensitive to the inevitable
simplifications that have to be made in even authoritative descriptions of the
phonology, grammar or lexicon of these languages. For many of the languages
the relevant reference works are very summary, if they exist at all. There is
nothing comparable to the standard historical accounts of most IE languages
and the etymological lexica and comparative accounts of particular IE language
families. But these IE accounts have been going for more than 180 years.

4.2   Even for Indo-European the situation is far from ideal. Brugmann's mighty
Grundriss has not been revised for eighty years, Delbruck's contribution to it
on comparative syntax not for well over a century. The new *Indogermanische
Grammatik* begun by Kuryłowicz proceeds fitfully and seems to be trained on a
somewhat different target. Few scholars working in IE would cite Pokorny's etymological dictionary (1959) without qualification. It is a magnificent compila-
tion of data, inevitably short on Anatolian and Iranian, but less pardonably it
takes no account of laryngeals or of most of the research on root structure and

gradation patterns published since the *Grundriss*. Monstrous lemmata parading *del-, *delēgh-, *(d)longho-, *dḹghó- 'lang' and the like may summarize the data cited but cannot reflect a real protolanguage, since they bring together, typically, variants that are structurally incoherent, and could only belong to different dialectal areas or different chronological levels. Watkins, in his valuable index of PIE roots in the *American Heritage Dictionary*, tactfully cites the relevant pages of Pokorny, leaving curious readers to discover for themselves the wide discrepancies between the two accounts. It is alarming to find non-Indo-Europeanists citing Pokorny as if it were definitive while attacking Nostratic reconstructions for the same faults, unmindful of the fact that Nostratic etymology is still a very young discipline. There has not yet been time enough for the infrastructures referred to in §4.1 to be properly in place or for the tidying up at each asterisked stage that would prevent what is irrelevant to an earlier period from being swept back into the macro-reconstruction.

4.3   Pokorny lists over eighty different items, including suffixed variants, with the generic meaning 'cut'. They range from the familiar *bher-, *(s)ker-, *sek-, *tem- to weirdies like *bhrondho- and *(s)kerībh-. Dolgopolsky claims two dozen roots with this meaning (*The Nostratic Macrofamily and Linguisitic Palaeontology*, hereafter *NM*, p. 64). It is not clear in either instance whether these were thought to be semantically distinct in the proto-language, to be separated from one another, at least in theory, by componential analysis, or whether some belonged to a particular dialect or period. It is rarely that we can answer such a question. The cognates of Eng. apple occur in a restricted group of IE languages — Celtic, Germanic, Baltic and Slavonic, maybe Italic — and should probably not be accorded PIE status. The cognates of Eng. sheep are confined to Western Germanic, where they replace PIE *$ə_3$eu̯is (> Ved. avis, Lat. ouis etc.), which also survives there, e.g. Eng. ewe. Both apple and sheep are likely, the latter especially so, to reflect loanwords from outside IE, from communities that, like the immigrant IE-speakers, already knew and presumably farmed sheep and introduced the newcomers to the apple.

4.4   The self-confident optimism that inspired Schleicher in the mid-nineteenth century to compose a folk tale in PIE has long since evaporated. Nowadays hardly any self-respecting Indo-Europeanist would venture to put even two whole words of PIE together to make a proto-sentence. Yet we know much more than Schleicher did about the system of correspondences on which reconstruction depends and about the rules that governed phonological combinations, word formation, paradigms and even basic syntactic structures in PIE. What we cannot be sure about is the diachronic and dialectal placing of these rules in relation to one another.

4.5 For instance, what was the relation between the forms reflected by Gk stégō and Lat. tegō 'cover' and other pairs exhibiting 'mobile' s-? At what point in reconstruction should we introduce laryngeals, substituting ə₂egros for agros etc.? What was the paradigmatic vocalism of *$q^uetur̥$-, *$q^utu̯%_er$- 'four'? What was the relation between the three forms of thematic genitive singular -osio (> Ved. ájrasya), -oso (> Gk agroû) and -ī (> Lat. agrī; cf. §3.3)? We know that the variation between *$leiq^u$-, *$loiq^u$-, *liq^u and *$lineq^u$, *$linq^u$ was grammatically, not lexically, significant, but what determined the choice between *$leiq^u$- (> Gk leípei) and *$lineq^u$- (> Ved. riṇákti) in the present tense? Or between the stative verbal adjectives *plə₁-nó- (> Ved. pūrṇás, Lat. plēnus) and plə₁-tó- (> Ved. prātás, Lat. plētus). Particularly relevant here are the indeterminacies in the lexical etyma exemplified in §4.3, since these make a shaky foundation for Nostratic comparison.

5.1 The phonological inventory of PIE is in fact much smaller now than it was in Brugmann's *Grundriss*, thanks to the systematic distinctions since established between phoneme and positional allophone. Sound change operates at the allophonic level and it is allophones that we reconstruct in the first instance; so a sorting procedure is needed at each stage of reconstruction.

5.2 It is not easy to see whether the large phonological inventory attributed to Proto-Nostratic in *NM* is due to a failure to do this sorting or to the impossibility of making precise distinctions at such a remote period. Thus ŋ is frequently set up before velar consonants, e.g. in *maŋ[g]V 'monkey' (*NM* 6: In using throughout a single form of square bracketing for all the various brackets employed by Dolgopolsky I hope not to have misrepresented his analyses seriously). However, in *šüŋU 'snow' (*NM* 7) it appears to be a distinct phoneme. We are familiar of course with the dual functional status of ŋ in Eng. thin, thing and think. But the reason for ŋ here is not clear. Moreover the steps proposed to reach PIE *$sneig^uh$ seem very *ad hoc* — loss of rounding in ü, metathesis of iŋg to nig, with change of the final high back vowel to voiced labio-velar plus aspiration. It might not appear so arbitrary if the changes could be set in a context of systematic historical phonology. But they are not.

5.3 The derivation of PIE *medhu- 'honey' from Proto-Nostratic (PN) *madu (*NM* 79) is incompatible with the table of reflexes (*NM* p. 102), which indicates PN initial d > PIE dh, but medial d > d. A systematic historical phonology would eliminate this inconsistency, though one suspects at the price of removing an important family attestation. The other 'honey' etymon is *mai̯ʒV (*NM* 21) 'a tasty beverage'. This meaning looks as if it has been adopted in order to accommodate the Finno-Ugrian and Kartvelian words glossed as 'milk, birch-sap, cream'. The sound change that produces PIE *melit-/meln- might again look less awkward if we had an historical phonology to place it in. Both roots are indeed used of 'honey' in IE and the *mel- roots seem never to have been used of 'mead' or 'wine', but *methu is certainly so used in Greek and Old Irish, which both reflect *melit for 'honey', and in W. Gmc, which has the non-IE loanword *χunaŋ for honey. So the semantics in IE generally point to *medhu 'sweet drink, liquid honey' and *melit 'solid honey' as the original PIE distribution, whatever may be the case in other families.

5.4   The doubts acknowledged in the text (*NM* 41) about the 'bull' etymon *č[a]w[V]rV or *čurV are more than justified. The change of č- to PIE (s)t- needs supporting evidence, and the appeal to *tauro- beside *steuro- 'steer' merely contributes to the mobile s- problem, as well as reviving an etymological connection nowadays generally rejected. Nor do the Altaic reflexes look very convincing to a non-specialist. Altaicists please pronounce. The aw/u variation implicit in the PN etymon looks like some sort of gradation pattern; but what? And the vagueness and uncertainty of the reconstruction, with only č and u/w firm, inspires little confidence. As so often, we are also left puzzled as to how we should analyze the word into root + suffix. But then what *is* a root in PN? It seems on the whole better to stay with the old derivation of Gk taûros etc. (the word is not attested in Eastern IE languages) from $*tea_2$-u- reflected in Ved. tāuti, tavīti 'swell, be strong' and in Greek (cf. Hesychius' taũs · mégas, polús) and the Ved. tavāgām of Indra the Bull. The latter etymology incidentally favours the view that the similar forms in Semitic are borrowed from, not to, IE.

5.5   The question of lexical morphology arises also with *ḳVRVHṗ/pV 'piece of leather (used especially as footwear)' (*NM* 100), where the distinction between root and suffix is again unclear. Nostratic etymology is still in its early days, but a glance at etymological dictionaries in language areas that have already been long researched — Pokorny is typical — reveals a large number of homophonous roots (hardly surprising with a basic CVC root-structure), which are only differentiated by affixation of various classifiable kinds. Now the amount of phonological vagueness in *NM* is enormous (capitals denote classes, not precise phonemes of course): here we have indeterminate vowels, resonants and laryngeal, an ambiguous unvoiced labial stop and an initial ejective velar, which is not at all guaranteed by the cited reflexes except for PIE, and then only if we adopt the controversial Gamkrelidze-Ivanov version of the occlusive system. We may not like Pokorny's PIE *kerəp-, *krēp, where the additional p suffix to $*ker-ə_1$, $*kr-ə_1$ is unexplained though not unparalleled; but at least we know precisely what we are being invited to accept.

5.6 These examples, selected casually from the 124 etymologies offered in *NM*, illustrate some of the criticisms that can be made of many PN etymologies. Work along the lines adumbrated in §§4.1–3 should meet some of these criticisms, but it will take time, and the observations on PIE made in §§4.3–5 are a warning that disappointments lie in store.

5.7 To end this section on a less carping note, sometimes a Nostratic etymology raises interesting possibilities for IE. Italic (Latin), Celtic, Germanic, Baltic and Slavonic all reflect an etymon *mari 'sea'. If this is not to be given PIE status, then the isogloss must represent an innovation shared by the group, perhaps borrowed from outside IE. If it does reflect a PIE etymon, then the isogloss represents a shared conservation and is of little importance as a piece of lexical convergence. This is also the case, obviously, if the PIE root in turn is a reflex of PN *morE (*NM* 14). However, if *mari does not go back through PIE to Nostratic but was a loanword, for example from Altaic or Kartvelian, into one of the IE families listed, subsequently spreading through the rest, then the isogloss is important and has implications for population movements. This is by itself too hypothetical to take us very far, but there may well be other evidence with which it is congruent, so it should not be put aside and forgotten.

6.1 In pursuit of macro-reconstruction scholars sometimes extend the range of their data by drawing a word from the only language in a family that actually attests it. To 'reach down' and find a single item to represent a whole family is a procedure used in reconstructing all proto-languages, PR and PIE as well as PN. There is a case for censure here only if the word fails to show the systematic correspondences characteristic of the family concerned and so cannot be taken back through an asterisked proto-form for the family.

6.2 For instance Osc. feíhúss (acc.pl.) 'walls' is unique in Italic but has cognates in Ved. dehī, Gk teîkhos, as well as the semantically more distant Lat. fingere 'to mould', Goth daigs 'dough'. The form reflects the appropriate correspondences between Italic and the families of all the cognates, something we cannot say for the Latin synonyms mūrus, moenia, which have no agreed etymology. Moreover the reaching down process is simply the reverse of the method by which we are able to identify feíhúss as a cognate of the other words in the first place. Which reminds us that reconstructions from one group of languages can be used to elucidate obscurities in another related group. For feíhúss and daigs provide the means of explaining the anomalous correspondence of Ved. d- with Gk t- by supporting a PIE reconstruction *dheigh- (Grassmann's Law).

6.3   An instance where reaching down is more hazardous is the citation of Gothic aiþei 'mother' as an IE reflex of PN *ʔ[ä]iV, *h[ä]iV (*NM* 117). The root is apparently reflected in proto-Dravidian *āi- and in Hamito-Semitic, where forms like Somali āyo 'stepmother' also look very much like the fruits of reaching well down into Cushitic. Now the IE cognates are peculiar to Germanic: OHG fuotar-eidī 'nurse' occurs beside the panIE mother-word muotar; MLG eide and ON aeþei are both minor synonyms respectively of mōdar and mōdir. In Gothic however aeþei appears to have replaced the panIE word, as atta, a form attested also in Latin, Greek, Turkish, Elamite etc., has almost wholly replaced PIE *pəₜtḗr.

6.4   If aiþei and atta are indeed colloquial words, maybe originating in the nursery, as PN *ʔemA (*NM* 116) presumably is also, then we have parallels for Welsh mam, tad, replacing the PIE forms reflected in Irish athair, máthair, and the colloquial English use of dad, mum/mam, derived from the specifics Dad, Mum/Mam in place of the more formal father, mother. The conventional view, rejected in *NM*, that aiþei etc. are loans from Finno-Ugric (cf. Nor. Lapp. æide, Eston. eit, Finn. äiti) at a date early enough to have undergone the Germanic occlusive sound shift seems on the whole more plausible. But we do not have the detailed patterns of correspondence for the relevant non-IE languages to be confident, and the conventional view does deprive Nostraticists of an IE representative for this etymon, which is unfortunate. Each instance of reaching down has to be treated on its merits, not damned or nodded through on purely *a priori* grounds.

7.1   The time-span back to PN remains highly speculative, as to a lesser degree it is for PIE, and for most of the proto-languages of the IE families (for the one exception see §§3.1–4). Lexico-statistics, which enables assessment of degrees of relationship to be made between languages at arbitrary points in the history of each (see Coleman 1994, 359–77), has not been very successful in actual diachronic explorations. Indeed the absurd results arrived at by glotto-chronologists in assessing divergency dates in Germanic and Romance have brought discredit on the whole enterprise.

7.2   To begin with, the proposition that a lexicon changes at a constant rate if one takes long enough units of time, not in itself an obvious one, is extremely difficult to test. The number of languages for which we have continuous data over a long enough period is very small: within IE for more than 2000 years, beside the Indic group there are only Hellenic, Persian and Latin (with its Romance descendants).

7.3   Moreover we cannot trawl total lexicons: for dead languages and older stages of living languages they are not there. Indeed *total* lexicons are not available even for living languages. A basic lexicon, whose size and composition is specified (and can be debated, though it seldom is) tends to be relatively stable over long periods — all, drink, fire are typical of survivors from Old English — and it is often accessible even when the total available lexical stock is small. There are still problems of course. Do we choose for English small or little, broad or wide, big or large (both incidentally loanwords)? *NM* has three 'father' etyma, *Hiḉ/ cχV with alternatives in — ḉ/ç- and γ/g/h (*NM* 114), *ʔediNV (*NM* 115), both having apparently the biological sense and the socio-legal sense of 'master, owner', and *ʔaba ~ ʔap̉a (*NM* 118), a less secure etymon and probably a nursery formation. We have already noted the numerous 'cut' etyma (§4.3). The problem of distinguishing between major and minor synonyms, hyponyms and plesionyms is often simply insoluble, in a dead language or in an earlier stage of a living one, especially at any great distance in time. In such cases it is perhaps best to omit the semantic item altogether.

7.4   When basic lexemes are replaced, they are often not lost from the language, and conversely their successors often come from the existing lexicon. Thus OE fugol has been replaced by its hyponym brid 'chick', becoming in its turn, as MoE fowl, a hyponym to bird; OE bearn (> dial. bairn) replaced by its minor synonym cild (> child); OE wīf (> wife) by its compound form wīfman(n), becoming in its turn a hyponym to woman; scūfan (> shove) by the loanword push (< Fr. pousser), surviving as a minor synonym in MoE. By contrast OE swegel was replaced by Scand. ský 'cloud' and has no known survivor. In general such recycling is a characteristic of basic vocabulary, with individual items drawn from the native stock of semantically close material and, when demoted, returned thereto. Lexical mortality is in fact quite rare.

7.5   On the most rigorous criteria of exact semantic and morpho-phonological correspondence it has been shown (see Coleman 1990, 69–86) that only 65.2 per cent of an OE basic vocabulary of 224 items is retained in the MoE basic vocabulary. However, only 4 per cent of the OE basic stock has been totally lost; e.g. rīman 'to count', replaced by Fr. conter (now compter). Conversely 14.7 per cent of the MoE basic vocabulary, a much higher proportion, is not found in OE; e.g. animal (from French/Latin), replacing dēor (> deer), big (from Scandinavian; cf. Norw. bugge 'strong'), replacing mycel (> much, dial. muckle). These are typical of the great majority of imports, reflecting the period of Scandinavian immigration along the East coast, the Norman Conquest and the period of political and cultural contact between France and Britain that followed. The Latin–French input to the English lexicon generally is enormous (see §8.1–3). Most of the basic vocabulary imports became established by 1400 AD. Since then their only successor has been split, a seventeenth-century loan from Dutch splitten, replacing cleave (< OE clēofan), now an obsolescent hyponym.

7.6   The figure of 65.2 per cent for full retention is much lower than Swadesh's 85 per cent per millennium, but his 15 per cent loss figure is close to the 14.7 per cent of MoE basic vocabulary absent from OE! The real mortality rate of 4 per cent means that a basic vocabulary would take many millennia to disappear totally from the lexicon. As for the rate of change too many local variables need to be reckoned with. For instance are the last 500 years, when foreign influences, though great, have not been reinforced by anything like the Scandinavian immigrations or the Norman Conquest and have hardly affected the basic vocabulary, more typical of a language's lexical history than the preceding 300 years when these special factors were present and the changes in the basic vocabulary considerable? The remarkably small changes in the basic vocabularies of Polynesian languages in the last 800–900 years, for most of which individual linguistic communities have been racially homogeneous (see §8.5) and in minimal bilingual contact with others, indicate that more case studies are needed before we hastily settle on a statistical norm.

7.7   Care is needed therefore in quantifying the lexical history of any language. But the use of lexico-statistics to compute the time-span for divergence between two or more related languages bristles with further difficulties. Not only would the rates of change, even if only a little uneven, not necessarily synchronize, but they would also affect different groups of lexemes. Whether each language replaced the same x per cent for example or a quite separate x per cent in each period would result in enormous variation in the rate of divergence over two or three millennia, and this takes no account of differences in their recycling of demoted items.

7.8   If lexico-statistics offers a very defective tool then for establishing absolute or even relative chronologies, systematic lexical comparison on a large scale is at least able to deliver handsomely in the reconstruction of a proto-lexicon. By gathering together loanwords that phonological criteria have distinguished from cognates it can also contribute to our knowledge of the relative chronology both of sound changes in the languages concerned and of the contacts between them. A typical example is the replacement of OE blōstm, reflected in MoE blossom, by MiE flur, flour (< Fr. flour, flor, cognate with blōstm, from PIE *bhlō-s) and comparison with the pronunciations of the modern forms Fr. fleur and MoE flower. Finally, where there is, as here, the material for diachronic analysis, there is some possibility of distinguishing between semantic fields that belong to the historical development of the individual languages and those that can be taken back into the proto-lexicon itself. Before anything of this sort can be done for Nostratic many historical dictionaries need to be compiled from the languages concerned and etymological dictionaries for the families to which they belong.

8.1 Loanwords are of course the most obvious examples of convergence between languages, and the possibility that some of the similarities between IE and other 'Nostratic' lexical items are not due to systematic correspondence but to lexical borrowing is very tempting. PN *tulV (*NM* 124) may well unite Arabic tuwal- 'witchcraft' with Hungarian táltos 'sorcerer, shaman', but the IE representation is somewhat fragile. Only Hittite and Germanic are cited. In the former talliṣazi 'he invokes, implores' need not reflect PIE *d-, said to go back to PN *t-, which unlike the u, which is sparsely attested in the reflexes cited, seems to survive with suspect tenacity as far away as Somali and other Cushitic languages. The semantics are favourable, but the word may equally well be a loan from Semitic or Uralic. Germanic reflexes of proto-Germanic *taljan abound, except in Gothic. They are united in combining the meanings 'tell' and 'count' (cf. the semantics of Eng. recount and teller), without any trace of religion or magic. The IE presence of *taljan need not go back beyond Germanic and could again be a loanword, but not obviously from a reflex of *tulV.

8.2 Convergence produces similarities rather than correspondences; which is why we are able to distinguish loanwords from cognates and diffusion phenomena in phonology, unless they have initiated a major restructuring in the host system or have themselves been incorporated into a characteristic change in the host system like the Germanic occlusive sound shifts. Usually a long period of bilingual interaction is necessary — as between communities settled on either side of a linguistic boundary or in immigrant communities retaining their language along with the host language. In the latter situation some convergences may arise quite rapidly, where the host language is transmitted to the next generation of immigrants by speakers whose use of the host language is marked by foreign 'accent', idioms and vocabulary. Where the immigrant language continues to be spoken, it will of course itself be subject to convergent pressures from the host language and may influence in various ways its use by native speakers. Loanwords in particular can spread rapidly: a new commodity or concept is imported along with its linguistic label and the two are diffused together. Words may travel rapidly and widely, but not phonology or grammar.

8.3 Generally convergence is easier between languages that are already closely related, like Occitan and French as against German and French. It can affect all levels of language. In phonology the diffusion of uvular r, lenition and palatization through bilingualism is well documented. Secure examples in grammar are harder to find; but the often quoted emergence of volitive phrases as exponents of futurity in the distantly related but contiguous Balkan languages, Greek, Slavonic and Rumanian, can hardly be coincidental.

8.4   Convergence of the kind mentioned in the preceding paragraphs is very unlikely to occur between populations on the move, unless they are nomads moving perpetually on the same circuits and regularly renewing contacts with the same language communities, as in the traditional pattern of life among the Aboriginal Australians. However, bilingual contacts or population movements are almost impossible to recover for the prehistoric period in which Nostratic must have spread over its three continents and the speakers of the various languages occupied very different regions from those where they subsequently came to settle.

8.5   Another possible source of convergences, both close and distant, was canvassed a generation ago by the geneticist Darlington and the linguist Brosnahan, who noted that certain phonetic phenomena like aspiration of initial voiceless occlusives, affrication and rounded front vowels showed a high correlation with blood groups. This work has not been specifically followed up since DNA analysis arrived to provide a much more powerful tool for the recovery of genetic relationships among past populations. The genetic code could in principle account for parallel developments in languages totally unrelated, spoken by populations far apart from each other and occurring at different periods in their history. The influence on Latin from the Celtic speaking populations of North Italy, Gaul and Iberia or from the later Germanic invaders — Lombards in Italy, Franks in Gaul and Goths in Iberia — would then have been two-pronged: firstly the linguistic interaction of a relatively short period of bilingualism, secondly the substrate laid down in the genetic codes of the mixed populations and capable of surfacing in their language at any time. Nor would phonetics and phonology alone be affected: the tendency to create or avoid lexical compounding, the choice between agglutinative and fusional morphology, the organization of the verb system, the choice of word order — nothing would in principle be excluded. Divergence will remain the chief hypothesis in diachronic and comparative linguistics, but convergences between widely separated languages that are divergences within their own respective families may at last find their cause.

9.1   Meanwhile there is no shortage of purely linguistic research to be done.

About the account of Nostratic that we are offered at present I remain somewhat sceptical. That there was a macro-family to which PIE belonged (and other proto-languages too — proto-Semitic has long had its supporters as a sister-family to PIE) is a probable enough hypothesis. My scepticism is based on two considerations.

9.2 The first is an awareness of the limitations that have steadily emerged (see §§4.4–5) in the reconstruction of PIE. If this is true of PIE, where the relevant data are abundantly attested over a significant part of the total time-scale (see §2.2) and research has been intense over a long period, then it is *a fortiori* true of PN, where data are far more widely scattered over three continents, the time-scale is much longer and far less research has been done on the diachrony and immediate relationships of many of the relevant languages.

9.3 My second ground for scepticism is a suspicion that indeterminacies at various stages of the reconstruction are often resolved in favour of what the Nostratic hypothesis seems to require rather than on intrinsic linguistic probabilities. The fact that many of the phonemes in the living reflexes are identical with those attributed to a language spoken thousands of years ago is not in itself impossible. MoGk patéras reflects PIE *p_2tḗr 'father', Lith. sniẽgas PIE *$snóig^who$s 'snow', Sp. pleno PIE *$plə_1nós$ 'full' and It. mente 'mind' PIE m̥tís 'thought' (all the English glosses except the last are also reflexes). The real difference is that we are able to give comprehensive accounts of the IE correspondences and diachronies which lie behind every one of these pairs of similarities.

9.4 A further point arises here. The close working relations that exist between Indo-Europeanists and their colleagues whose research on the systematic descriptions of the languages ensure a basis of the larger reconstructions. Many scholars work concurrently in the two fields. The great achievement of IE linguistics has been to establish the method for discovering the systems of correspondence and changes that bind these languages together and to shed light upon their prehistory. Some of the important contributions in the latter field have been the reconstruction, primarily from Greek and Vedic data, of the pattern of PIE accentuation, which led to Verner's Law in Proto-Germanic, and more recently the reconstruction of laryngeals in PIE, again based in the first instance on Vedic and Greek data (as analyzed by the young Saussure) and subsequently on data from Hittite, which has enabled better understanding of the early morphophonology of a number of other IE languages. This valuable sense of co-operation between the two groups of researchers and the mutual trust that goes with it is not always in evidence in Nostratic studies (see §4.1).

9.5 For IE we may well have to be content with the firm conviction that there was a PIE language which is no longer recoverable as a language; there are simply too many asterisked forms based on asterisked forms along the way. This must be even truer of PN, where we shall have to settle for no more than shadowy fragments of a language. Nor is it just a matter of finding, so to speak, a radio telescope to replace the optical instruments we have been using so far. It is rather that whatever one reconstructs will be so indeterminate and fragile that it cannot be integrated into a firm and coherent linguistic system and may even dissolve altogether under closer scrutiny.

9.6   That some of the specific faults I have mentioned in Nostratic research can and will be overcome need not be doubted. What is urgently required is more intensive work on the daughter families of PN and their constituent languages and on the comparative studies and etymological dictionaries which must support the broader investigation. The touchstone of progress will be a rise in the degree of confidence that the specialist linguists have in Nostratic reconstruction and its account of the diachrony linking PN to their own families.

References

Brugmann, K. & B. Delbrück, 1893–1916. *Grundriss der vergleichenden Grammatik der Indogermanischen Sprachen*. Strassbourg: Karl J. Trübner.

Coleman, R., 1990. The assessment of lexical mortality and replacement between Old and Modern English, in *Papers from the Fifth International Conference on English Historical Linguistics*, eds. S. Adamson, V. Law, N. Vincent & S. Wright. Amsterdam: John Benjamins, 69–86.

Coleman, R., 1994. The lexical relationships of Latin in Indo-European, in *Linguistic Studies in Latin*, ed. J. Hermen. Amsterdam: John Benjamins, 359–77.

Kuryłowicz, J. & M. Meyrhofer, 1968–. *Indogermanische Grammatik*. Heidelberg: Carl Winter.

Pokorny, J., 1959. *Indogermanisches etymologisches Wörtebuch*, I. Bern: Francke.

Watkins, C., 1981. *American Heritage Dictionary*. Boston (MA): Houghton Misslin, 1496–1550.

Chapter 6

Beyond Nostratic in time and space

Gyula Décsy

Nostratic studies are, in spite of the sceptical views of traditional comparativists (Matthews 1997, 247), a serious business. Palaeolinguists and language origins researchers (LOR) owe admiration to Dolgopolsky and other preprotolinguists (their names are listed on p. 110 of *The Nostratic Macrofamily and Linguistic Palaeontology* hereafter *NM*) who put together an imposing collection of sound sequences (words, lexical units) with similar sound-shape and semantics ('lookalikes', German '*Gleichklänge*') from the languages of this huge area which played a major role in shaping the modern human race and its global culture (Northern Asia, the entire European continent, Near East, North Africa). In my estimate, about four billion people speak Nostratic languages (Décsy 1986a,b; 1988) out of the six billion inhabitants of our planet (as of the year 2000).

The relationship of the Nostratic languages ensues by deduction based on the following tenets:

1.   All languages of the world are related. All people of the world produce sounds the same way. The *monogenetic* origin of *sound production* in the languages of the world is generally accepted today. All languages have basically the same vowels and consonants. This is in itself already an irrefutable proof of their common origin and their *close* genetic relationship. All human individuals produce vowels and consonants biologically-anatomically the same way (minor articulatory differences can be disregarded here). The phonology of the languages of the world is *mutatis mutandis uniform.*

2.   It is obvious that contiguous (geographically adjacent) languages of a given area must be even more (closely) related (prehistorically) to each other than the languages of the world generally. Dolgopolsky's Nostratic units consist only of languages which are spoken within a geographically well-defined area (Eurasia, Near East and North Africa). There are other concepts of Nostratics too (Durjalan, see Décsy 1998b).

3.   As the sounds of the languages of the world are basically similar everywhere on our planet, the sound sequences (words, lexical units) denoting even primitive concepts (accordings to Wierbiczka: *primes)* are *quite different* even in the Nostratic family. This can be explained so that the different smaller or larger groups of humans (clans) set up the sound sequences *relatively late* independently from each other. As the non-timbric (pre-timbric, unarticulated) sounds (consonantic and vocalic laryngeals universally present even today in crying, laughing, coughing, snoring, new-born babies sounds, etc.) are very old in humans (several hundred thousand years old), the timbric sounds (such as a, i, u, w, ng, k, t, etc.,) are much younger (*c.* 15,000 years, see Appendix) developed by Anatomically Modern Humans (Neanderthal could not speak them, as generally accepted). This means that the languages of the world are, with regard to the sound sequence (word, lexical unit) production, *polygenetic* (and not monogenetic as with regard to the phoneme production).

4. If the sound sequence (word, lexical unit) production is polygenetic, then it is natural that the words in the different languages cannot be of the same origin: they cannot go back to common forms. If they are similar in different well-established language families (phyla), then this similarity is accidental (we speak about lookalikes, *Gleichklänge*). As the phoneme inventory of early languages was simpler and in their use more restrictive than the one of modern languages, the individual sound combinations in the thousands of different clans must have led to similar forms in different prehistoric language communities (clans). Such ancient similarities (called by Mrs Key *Red Marble Bloc* units) cannot be cited as proof of genetic relationship. They are not genemes, nor aremes, nor typemes but tychemes (gamblemes, hazardemes, cf. Décsy 1983, 41, # 007).

5. I suppose that the largest part of the Nostratic similarities listed in Dolgopolsky's collection (*NM* and projected publication with 2200 or so entries, as well as in Bomhard, this volume) are mainly gamblemes: accidental similarities. Such similarites can be put together by a skillful linguist within several days from any given two, three, four, or any number of languages.

6. This does not mean that the work of Dolgopolsky and of other Nostraticists is futile. The opposite is true. In a modern computerized world everything has to be compared with everything. The point is that the similarity does not prove, *without further evidence,* a genetic relationship. It stands only for the experience that two forms in two (or more) languages are similar — and nothing else. The problem with interphyletic comparison is not that the word forms are not similar; they are similar but they are similar by accident.

7.   A serious problem in Dolgopolsky's Nostratic word collection is the transcription. It is not phonemic; he uses the eccentric denotation of the individual philologist of the particular phyla. The forms are rendered with signs which cannot be read and interpreted even by well-trained linguists of the area in question. I quote here the Uralic forms with which Nostraticists are quite well acquainted. On p. 34 the Uralic protoforms are correctly jäntä 'tendon, sinew' and jongsa 'bow' (Décsy 1990, 99, simplified phonematic denotation). If we accept those protoforms, it is not necessary to cite the numerous data from the individual languages (c. thirty different Uralic languages taking up almost one full page in *NM*). Data from individual languages should not be quoted if the correct protoform is easily available. This is mostly the case in conection with Uralic, Indo-European and Turkic (Décsy 1990; 1991; 1998a,b).

8.   This leads to the principle that only protoforms should be included in interphyletic word and form comparison. The problem is that only Indo-European, Uralic, Turkic and Semitic are reconstructed in a proper way (Décsy 1990; 1991; 1998a,b). Mongolic, Tungusic or Japanese protoforms can be reconstructed easily. But what should be done with the denotationally extremely complicated, inconsistent and eccentric Hamitic or Korean data? Who takes the responsibility for a correct phonemic reconstruction? What we get here from the Nostraticist is mostly *filius ante patrem;* they put the cart before the horse.

9.   In connection with the reconstruction of the Nostratic phoneme system we are driven into a precarious situation. The principle of the evolutionary theory is: the older, the simpler. Dolgopolsky assumes seven vowels for Proto-Nostratic (p. 17, however, he does not name them) and c. 50 consonants (p. 101), among them a large number of affricates. Affricates and, e.g. r/l, are new everywhere (*mutatis mutandis*). Palatality correlation (nj, cj, etc. see *NM* 101) is phonemically completely improbable for the time 15,000 BC. We can paraphrase Jakobson's famous saying (he referred to the traditional Indo-European phoneme system): no human being can/could speak with such a complicated phoneme system. Not today and not around 15,000 BC. In my opinion, in this time depth (15,000–17,000 years) a maximum of three timbric vowels could exist (*a, i, u,* the big invention of Anatomically Modern Humans) and c. 8–10 simple consonants (ng, j, w, m, t, k, perhaps s and p). This problem is a much discussed item in Language Origins Research (LOR), and we can regret that Dolgopolsky ignored the particular views brought up in these disputes (see Décsy 1997a).

10. Laryngeals, intonation, duration and accent are pre-timbric phenomena. They may have played a larger role in Nostratic times than today. They can change and can be reinstated in different phases of the development of individual languages or linguistic phyla. These constituents have never been denoted in a clear way in any traditional script; nevertheless, the apparently archaic Semitic-Hamitic spoken forms compared with the other languages could allow here some conclusions or at least guesses.

11. Personally, I do not accept an Altaic linguistic unity. But this is not of importance in Dolgopolsky's work: the 'down-reaching' concept often mentioned in this volume is quite common in phyla with well-reconstructed protoforms. Most professional Uralists also reject a Uralic-Yukagir unity. I do not understand how this idea became common place in American interphyletic comparison. Ruhlen (1987, 328) may have made the decision lightheartedly which then spread like bushfire among the uninitiated.

12. Out of six billion people of the world, about four billion speak Nostratic languages (see also 1 above). Will this concept not rise to a term of white racial supremacy? If we divide the world population in Nostratic and 'Vestratic' (my humorous term, see Décsy 1983, 83), will this not lead to a discrimination of the minority Vestratic group? Note that almost all of China, the huge phylum Austro-Tai, the Amerindian languages and the majority of the African languages will be regarded as somehow alien and excluded from the global human community. Ehret's list (this volume) shows that it would be extremely easy to extend Nostratic to South (Subsaharan) Africa. As a persiflage, I put together within several days almost 100 lookalikes from Thai, Finnish and Hungarian. Hungarian *ház* and English *house* have almost the same sound form and meaning. Nevertheless, English goes back to Germanic *husum*, and Hungarian *ház* to Finno-Ugric *kota* (in Finnish today *kota* 'shelter, Lapp hut'). Trained linguists know that Uralic and Finno-Ugric k became h before back vowels in Hungarian; and the ancient intervocalic t is rendered there as z. And o > a (á) is a regular sound change in Old Hungarian carried out in the first syllable around AD 1350 (as the old documents show). What a coincident, convincing convergence! He who does not know these details might rush to the conclusion that English *house* and Hungarian *ház* prove a genetic relationship between these two languages. How many such cases may occur in Dolgopolsky's and Bomhard's collections?

13. The homeland of the Nostratic protolanguage can be placed anywhere in

the large area between Japan and North Africa. Nevertheless, the most probable area is Anatolia, the 'railroad-turn-table' (*Drehscheibe*) of the world population in the Late Palaeolithic. For migrations at this time, geotectonic changes were perhaps more responsible than was the wave-like spread of agriculture in the sense used by Renfrew. It is well-known that around 15,000 BC the earth's axis may have changed its position so that the North Pole moved suddenly from South Greenland (its earlier position) to its present-day location. The result: the Big Flood, Northern Europe became ice free, Siberia's fauna became deep frozen, the Sahara (originally good farmland) became desert (its population moved to the Nile creating a brainpower accumulation of enormous measure), Scandinavia emerged from the sea, the White Bridge between Alaska and Northwest Siberia sank into the water and below ice. Subsequently, the population explosion of the Near East catapulted the people to the new forest and steppe zones of the western parts of Eurasia which became inhabitable. *Europe was born* as a result of brainpower accumulation. Is this not a convincing scenario? I have never understood why archaeologists and palaeoclimatologists disregard this possible factor of migration (scenario detailed in Décsy 1977, 30–31).

14. The action radius of classical comparison is a maximum of 6000 years. Its method cannot be used before 4000 or maximum 5000 BC. This was clear, among others, to Holger Pedersen (Décsy 1983, 82), the linguist who coined the word Nostratic. Linguists do not trust archaeologists: culture and language borders cannot be synchronized historically *a posteriori*. This means that everything is possible with regard to the linguistic scenarios in the times before 4000 or 5000 BC. We can also place the homeland of the ancestral Nostratic phylum in the Near East. As a guess, it may convince. In any case, it cannot be disputed that the primordial home of the Nostratic group was somewhere within the territory of their present-day area.

15. Most linguistic comparativists suppose that Eurasia (Europe + Northern Asia) around 4000 to 5000 BC accommodated five primordial homes of Nostratic phyla ('phyla' used here in the plural!):

Indo-European: between Weser and Vistula (Thieme's evidence);
Uralic: between Wolga-Knie and Ural (eventually as far as Ob-Irtysh);
Turkic: in Semirechie (northeast of Almaty, close to the continental divide);
Mongolic: east of the Baikal;
Tungusic: inland, west of the Pacific Rim of northern Eurasia.

These were imperial/conqueror languages of ancient times probably absorbing thousands of clan languages except Basque, the Caucasus languages and the Palaeosiberian group (conveniently disregarded by Nostraticists). Eurasia became unique among the continents of our planet: the normal-regular high number of languages was reduced to a practicable minumum already in the seventh–eighth millennia BC. The five conqueror languages covered large areas with coherent verbal communication. The pre-conqueror (Pre-Indo-European, Pre-Uralic, etc.) languages could survive only in remote areas (the Caucasus, Basque country, Yenissei area and northern Siberia).

16. The discussion in Cambridge strengthened the view that a Nostratic reconstruction can proceed step by step from low order protolanguage to a higher order protolanguage. Protolinguistics has to precede preprotolinguistics (concepts: Décsy 1983, passim). A comparative dictionary of a language family (such as Pokorny 1959; Tsintsius 1975–77) does not mean that the particular protolanguage is reconstructed. Reconstructive protolinguistics has a special method based on interphyletic experience. My three books tried to demonstrate this (Décsy 1990; 1991; 1998a,b).

17. Nostratic is basically a segment of Global Linguistics; an important segment, but nothing more than a segment. And it is also a part of preprotolinguistics and Language Origins Research. Its structure can be almost better approached descendently from the earliest (prototypical) language forms of mankind than by the classical comparative method applied by Dolgopolsky and his companions.

18. And as the ultimate annoyance a question to our Russian friends ('*zu guter Letzt*'). Is their immense enthusiasm for Nostratic not motivated by the almost atavistic need for Russians to embrace (and eventually to lead) from Moscow the entire Western world which has been the target of political and eventually military conquest since late medieval times by the Romanovs and then by their successors Lenin and Stalin? This hidden design may explain the theories of the Eurasists (Prince Troubetzkoy and the young Roman Jakobson shortly after the First World War in Western emigration in Bulgaria, Vienna and Prague) and the Marxist oriented infamous Japhetic ideas of Nikolai Jakovlevich Marr (1865–1934), a Caucasist of Irish origin in St Petersburg. Both Eurasist and Iaphetic (a term of biblical origin like Hamitic and Semitic) were outlawed in communist Russia for political reasons. Nostratic may be a kind of modernized and accommodable renewal of the theories of the Eurasists and of the Japhetists. A little psychological checkup (German '*Seelenforschung*') could establish connections between the three Russian idea-groups.

Appendix. Paris Diagram No. 1.

Chronological frame
Improved version of a diagram prepared by Décsy and accepted as working paper in a Round Table in the *XVI Congress of Linguists in Paris,* July 22, 1997. (Original version printed in Décsy 1997.)

Universe: 12–15 billion years old;
Earth: 4 billion years;
Life: 2 billion years;
Noise production by nature: as old as air and motion (pre-pulmonary noises/ sounds;
Mammal pulmonary sounds: 60,000,000 (sixty million) years; phonemically H/ E(ʔ/ə); quantity, accent, pitch, register ancient variable;
Humans: 4 or 5 million years;
Bipedality: 3.6 million years; causes sinking of Larynx;
Unarticulated single-sound production with targeted call semantics (G. Révész) in imperative mood and quick indicativization of human (Neanderthal) communication: 200,000 years ago. Imperative older than indicative. Original sense of verbal communication: command. Self-referentiality does not exist;
Soundsequentialization (birth of syllable, probably CV): *non-timbric* soundsequences/ syllables 100,000; (H/E; quantity, stress/intensity, pitch, register still main variables). These were the main speech communicative elements of Neanderthal Man;
Instinct-based reasoning: 70,000–80,000 years; time (tense) and modality;
Intensive sinking of Larynx: 35,000 years (Cro-Magnon).

Birth of modern human soundsequential language
Timbric sounds (oldest: u, i, a, j, w + nasal/nasalized velar consonants such as ng) 25,000 years ago. Chances for real iconicity given from this time on;
Perfection of pharyngovelar closure (anatomically, human [Cro-Magnon] only!): 20,000 years. Before this time, all sounds were nasalized;
/w/ —> [w/m/p/b] —> phonologization of labials and stops becomes possible; t > s, 15,000 years ago;

Bifurcation of voiceless media: (p/b, t/d, k/g) 12,000 years ago;

Monosyllablic units (CV) in large number with clear lexical semantics: 11,000 years;

Red Marble Block prime products: (I/you [my/yours], light/dark, here/there, stay/go, good/bad [God/devil] 10,000 years. Note: concepts now *reasoning-based;* however, as instinctively-subhuman, they may be more ancient (70,000–80,000 years, see above);

Beginning of abstraction ability on a broad base mainly by introducing the 3rd person: 9000 years; lexical units with high frequency became grammatical elements.

Multilingualism begins

Unfolding individualized-separate soundsequence production in local isolated clans in very large number: 8500 years (thousands of clan languages, originally secretcodes);

Multisyllabicity (Polysyllabicity). Little professor at the campfire (inventionalism): 8000 years (explained: Décsy 1986b). Note that inventionalism is not the same as creationism;

Proto-languages (Indo-European, Uralic, Turkic, Mongolic, Afroasiatic (Semitic), Austro-Tai, etc. established in their final shape: 8000–7000 years;

Syntax and then Morphology as complicated systems: 7000–6000 BC. (Syntax is older than Morphology). Synthetic type is born;

Abstract vocabulary: 4000–1500 BC. Demythization of thinking;

Linguistic sophistication 500 BC.

References

Décsy, G., 1977. *Sprachherkunftsforschung*, Band I: *Einleitung und Phonogenese/Paläophonetik*. (Bibliotheca Nostratica 2:1.) Wiesbaden: Otto Harrassowitz.

Décsy, G., 1981. *Sprachherkunftsforschung*, Band II: *Semogenese/Paläosemiotik*. (Bibliotheca Nostratica 2:2.) Bloomington (IN): Eurasian Linguistic Association.

Décsy, G., 1983. *Global Linguistic Connections*. (Contributors R. Anttila, G. Décsy, C.T. Hodge, J.R. Krueger, J. Lotz, A. Makkai, M. Ruhlen & T.A. Sebeok.) (Bibliotheca Nostratica 5.) Bloomington (IN): Eurolingua.

Décsy, G., 1986a. *Statistical Report on the Languages of the World*, part 2. (Bibliotheca Nostratica 6:2.) Bloomington (IN): Eurolingua.

Décsy, G., 1986b. Paris reassertion versus Paris prohibition: the 1981 Language Origins Research Symposium in the capital city of France. *Reviews in Anthropology* 12(1985), 264–71.

Décsy, G., 1988. *Statistical Report on the Languages of the World*, part 4. (Bibliotheca Nostratica 6:4.) Bloomington (IN): Eurolingua.

Décsy, G., 1990. *The Uralic Protolanguage: a Comprehensive Reconstruction*. (Bibliotheca Nostratica 9.) Bloomington (IN): Eurolingua.

Décsy, G., 1991. *The Indo-European Protolanguage: a Computational Reconstruction.* (Bibliotheca Nostratica 10.) Bloomington (IN): Eurolingua.

Décsy, G., 1997a. Language origins research: state of the art as of 1997. XVIème Congrès International des Linguistes, Paris, France, July 20–25, 1997. *Occasional Papers of the International Paleolinguistic Society* 1.

Décsy, G., 1997b. *Carleton T. Hodge as Language Origins Researcher: Carleton T. Hodge Bibliography 1944–1997.* (Arcadia Bibliographica Virorum Eruditorum 16.) Bloomington (IN): Eurolingua.

Décsy, G., 1998a. *The Turkic Protolanguage: a Computational Reconstruction.* (Bibliotheca Nostratica 11.) Bloomington (IN): Eurolingua.

Décsy, G., 1998b. Durjalan as a Nostratic unit. Short review of the book by H.P.A. Hakola. *Eurasian Studies Yearbook* 70, 236.

Dolgopolsky, A., 1998. *The Nostratic Macrofamily and Linguistic Palaeontology.* (Papers in the Prehistory of Languages.) Cambridge: The McDonald Institute for Archaeological Research.

Matthews, P.H., 1997. *Oxford Concise Dictionary of Linguistics.* Oxford & New York (NY): Oxford University Press.

Pokorny, J., 1959. *Indogermanisches Etymologisches Wörterbuch.* Bern & Munich: Frauke Verlag.

Ruhlen, M., 1987. *A Guide to the World's Languages*, vol. I. Stanford (CA): Stanford University Press.

Tsintsius, V.I., 1975–77. *Sravnitel'nyi slovar' tunguzo-,man'chzhirskikh jazykov*, vols. I–II. Leningrad: Nauka.

Chapter 7

Subgrouping of Nostratic: comments on Aharon Dolgopolsky's *The Nostratic Macrofamily and Linguistic Palaeontology*

S.A. Starostin

Dolgopolsky's book (hereafter *NM*) is an excellent introduction to the Nostratic theory, which I completely support. Most of the lexical material that he presents is valid and reflects, to my opinion, a deep genetic unity of the languages involved — Indo-European, Kartvelian, Altaic, Uralic, Dravidian and Hamito-Semitic. However, before we proceed with 'linguistic palaeontology', we must first decide a couple of rather urgent linguistic questions.

I omit here a section that could be very large — the discussion of whether long-range comparison is theoretically possible and admissible. The book that we are discussing is the best proof of the validity of traditional comparative method and its applicability to distantly related genetic units.

There is, however, a problem that can not be left without discussion: the problem of Nostratic taxonomy. I had, almost ten years ago, already expressed my position on the classification of Nostratic languages based primarily on lexicostatistics and considerations of time depth (see Starostin 1989). The crucial point here is the position of Hamito-Semitic within Nostratic. If I am right (and some scholars — for example, Joseph Greenberg — share this point of view) in separating Hamito-Semitic from the rest of Nostratic families, this will certainly have impact on our debates around the time of Nostratic split and the homeland of Nostratic.

At the first glance, Dolgopolsky's book is an overwhelming proof of Hamito-Semitic belonging to Nostratic — in fact, occupying a central position within Nostratic. Among 124 lexical items included in the book, 106 have reflexes in Hamito-Semitic — as against, for example only 75 having reflexes in Indo-European or 91 in Altaic. I shall, however, attempt to show that this is a very superficial evaluation.

Below I shall combine the evidence from Dolgopolsky's book with the material of three other families of the Old World — namely, North Caucasian, Sino-Tibetan and Yenissean. I have written a number of papers where I proposed to unite these three families within a single macrofamily called 'Sino-Caucasian', and there are a number of scholars who now support this hypothesis. Several authors have added some other linguistic units (Na-Dene, Basque,

Burushaski), but I myself have studied only the three families above and shall confine myself here to their evidence. A preliminary list of phonetic correspondences was given in my 1989 paper ('Nostratic and Sino-Caucasian'), where I tried to demonstrate a possibility of distant genetic relationship between these two macrofamilies.

A chart of all Nostratic roots from Dolgopolsky's book with their proposed Sino-Caucasian cognates is given below. In this paper I would not like to get involved into a detailed discussion of technicalities — comparative phonology, lexicostatistical and grammatical considerations, etc. This all should be the subject of a much larger work which I hope to produce. I shall only attempt to propose a simple statistical procedure which will help us in the classification of linguistic families involved.

The eight families participating in our test (Indo-European, Hamito-Semitic, Uralic, Altaic, Kartvelian, Dravidian, North Caucasian, Sino-Tibetan, Yenissean) are subdivided into three types:

I.   Kartvelian, Yenissean: these are very small linguistic units (only 4 languages in Kartvelian, and only 4 languages in Yenissean — and of those only one is still living and more or less well recorded). It is therefore not surprising that the overall number of reconstructed Proto-Kartvelian and Proto-Yenissean roots is rather small (about 1000 roots in each family). In families like this even a word attested in a single language (e.g. Georgian or Ket) has a good chance of reflecting a common root.

II. Uralic, Dravidian, North Caucasian. These are larger families, but they all share a common feature: a dichotomic split. Uralic consists of Fenno-Ugric vs Samoyedic; Dravidian consists of North Dravidian vs South-Central Dravidian; North Caucasian consists of East Caucasian vs West Caucasian. For families like this the probability of a common root being preserved within only one branch is rather high, so that, for example a root present only in Fenno-Ugric has a good chance of being Common Uralic, even though it is absent in Samoyedic.

III. Indo-European, Hamito-Semitic, Altaic, Sino-Tibetan. These are very large families, with multiple branching. In families like this the probability of a common root being preserved within only one branch is quite small, so that a root present only in Turkic or Japanese has a very little chance of actually being Common Altaic. A great number of roots isolated within one branch may be explained as later loans. Certainly there must be exceptions, and not every root like this should be just thrown away, but one should certainly apply caution while dealing with etymological isolates within large genetic families.

With all that in mind, I shall proceed with the analysis of the data in *NM*. The chart given below has six columns:

1. number of the Nostratic root according to *NM*;
2. the root itself;
3. the distribution of the root within Nostratic. I regard the root as reflected in a family of type III only when it is present in at least two of its subbranches (e.g. in Semitic and Egyptian; in Slavic and Germanic; in Turkic and Tungus etc.). Otherwise I regard the reflex as insecure and demanding some further evaluation. In families of type I and type II no such restriction is possible, and a root may be withdrawn from the comparison only if it can be shown to be irregular in phonology, dubious in semantics or borrowed from some other known source;
4. etymological comments;
5. Sino-Caucasian evidence. This section is necessarily short (only reconstructions are included). I hope to provide soon a larger paper (or book) on the Sino-Caucasian comparison;
6. the distribution of the root within Sino-Caucasian.

Abbreviations used in the table below

Comp. = Illič-Svityč 1971–84, vols. 1–3

HSED = Orël & Stolbova 1995

Mat. = Illič-Svityč 1967

NSC = Starostin 1989

No.	Root	Distri-bution	Comments	Sino-Caucasian evidence	Sino-Caucasian distribution
1	*ʔibrE 'fig tree'	2: HS,D			
2	*ĉ[i]bVɣV 'hyena'	0	HS: only Semitic; A: only Ewenki Ayan, and very probably — a loan from Turk. Alt. čepke 'wolverine' (< Turk. *jepken); D: the Dravidian root is actually the same as in 4. *SiwVŋgE		
3	*ʔ[ü]řVwV 'large feline'	2: HS, D	In Altaic: only Old Turk. irbiš ~ irbič, cf. Chag. ilbirs — possibly a tabooistically corrupted form of Common Turkic *jolbars 'leopard' (which in its turn is a compound of *jolb- = TM *dolbi 'fox' and the borrowed *bars).	ST *wăr 'a beast of prey'.	ST

No.	Root	Distri-bution	Comments	Sino-Caucasian evidence	Sino-Caucasian distribution
4	*SiwVŋgE 'leopard'	3: IE, D, A	TM *sibige = Turk. *jebke-n 'wolverine' (Mong. ǯeɣeken 'wolverine' is a contamination of this root and another one, represented by TM *ǯaga-ri 'bear') < Alt. *zibke (~ *zipge).	NC *čǟnq̇V 'lynx, panther', ST *chi(ə)k 'leopard'	NC, ST
5	*ʔoŕ[u] 'antelope, deer'	3: HS, A, D	A: besides the listed forms cf. also Turk. *ar-kun 'cross-bred horse', *ar-ga-mak 'stallion')		
6	*maŋ[g]V 'monkey'	1: D?	In HS: only East Chadic. Otherwise: only Drav. *maŋk- 'monkey'; Manchu mońo is actually a variant form, the basic one being bońo (also reflected in Church. bonen < PTM *bońa 'monkey'). The phonetic match between Drav. *maŋk- and Manchu *bońa is impossible. On the other hand, Drav. *maŋk- could go back to *malVk- and be compared (as a loanword?) with Sino-Tib. *mlŭk 'monkey'. On the whole, a very dubious case.	ST *mlŭk 'monkey'	ST?
7	*šüŋU 'snow'	3: IE, U, A	In HS: only an uncertain Eg. word. See Mat. 366 (IE,U,A).	ST *ś(r)iǟŋ (= *r-śiǟŋ) 'cold, frost'. See NSC 121.	ST
8	*čaĺ[U]gV 'snow, hoar-frost'	3: HS, U, A			
9	*č[a]RʔV 'hoar-frost'	5: IE, K, A, U, D	The analysis presented here raises many doubts. In HS we have only an isolated Arabic form. The dialectal Georg. čχar- 'hoarfrost' may have a NC source: cf. NC *čowqı̇ 'drizzle, rain; snow-storm, cold' (or else Nakh *tχir- 'hoarfrost'). The Altaic form given probably has the original meaning 'crust, hard cover': besides the Turk. and Mong. forms presented cf. Ewk. čerī 'excrescence (on birch bark)' < Alt. *č'era. This all rather favours the original etymology of Illič-Svityč, who compared the Altaic form with IE *sker- 'crust, hard cover', Ural. *ćarV 'film; to harden', Drav. *carV- 'coarse, brushy' and Kartv. (Chan.) cara 'hard earth', reconstructing Nostr. *ĆarV 'hard crust' (see Comp. 1, 205).	NC *č̣ĥōrV 'skin, shell', PY *tər-ap- 'crust'. See NSC 113.	NC, ST, Y
10	*ḳir(u)qa 'ice, hoar-	5: HS, K, IE, U, A	See Comp. 1, 353 (HS, IE, U, A).	NC *=irG̣wVr 'to freeze, get cold', ST *kră-ŋ/*kră-k 'cold'.	NC, ST

No.	Root	Distri-bution	Comments	Sino-Caucasian evidence	Sino-Caucasian distribution
	frost, to freeze'				
11	*Sah(i)bV 'saline earth, desert'	2: D, U	HS: an Arabic–East Cush. match with irregular correspondences. A: Turk. *saj (not *sāj) actually goes back to PA *sajV 'stony or shallow place' (besides Turk., cf. also Mong. sajir 'stony riverbed, pebbles', PTM *saj-'sandbank' and OJap se 'shallow place'), and can not be compared with forms containing -b-. We are left with the comparison of Drav. *cava 'brackish/saline earth' and Uralic *ś/šojwa 'clay' — which actually reflects a different Nostratic root (*śab[ʔ]V 'soil, clay', quoted *ibid.*).		
12	*tälwA 'cold season, rain'	3: IE?, U, A	IE *del- is somewhat dubious (a not quite secure Armeno-Celtic isogloss). A: *tōlu (besides Turk. *dōlu [not *tolu] one could also compare OJap. turara 'icicle').		
13	*yamV 'water body'	3: HS, U, D	Illič-Svityč compares also Drav. (North Drav.) *am- 'water', which seems quite plausible. See Comp. 1, 279 (HS, U, D).		
14	*moRE 'water body'	5: HS, D, IE, K, A	The root actually means 'water, moisture'. HS: the distinction of HS *mar- 'drop, rain' and *mir-'river' (HSED) is hardly plausible — the two roots are perfectly well unitable. D: *maṛai- 'rain, cloud'. K: besides Megr. 'lake' cf. Svan. mare 'cloud'. A: *mǖri 'water' (besides Mong. forms, certainly MKor. mir 'water', OJap. mi-du and PTM *mū). Such was the analysis of Illič-Svityč, and I see hardly any reason to modify it. See Comp. 2, 60 (HS, D, IE, K, A).	NC *mărλÅ 'cloud, rain cloud'; Y *pVr (< *mVr) 'cloud'; ST *mrǯw 'fog, mist' (I earlier compared ST *mūk, but this has different Cauc. parallels). See NSC 118.	NC, Y, ST
15	*qaRp/pV 'to harvest'	1: A	HS: only Semitic. IE: only Hittite (possibly < Sem.?). Corrections for PA *arp'a 'barley': for Turk. *arpa, Mong. *arbaj cf. OJap. apa: Manchu arfa is most probably borrowed from Mong.		
16	*ʒükV 'edible cereals'	1: U	HS: only Arabic; the Eg. word is usually given a different etymology (Berb. *sVk- 'plough, till' etc.).		
17	*GalV	1: K?	HS: only Arabic. IE: Greek áliks is		

No.	Root	Distri-bution	Comments	Sino-Caucasian evidence	Sino-Caucasian distribution
	'cereals'		usually derived from aléō 'to grind', the relationship of which to Hitt. halki- 'grain, crops' is not at all clear.		
18	*χäntV 'kernel, grain'	3: HS, IE, D		NC *fiwăṭi 'a cereal; flour, dough'; ST *wāt 'grass roots; flower'.	NC, ST
19	*mälgc 'breast'	3: IE, HS, U	See Comp. 2, 57 (IE, HS, U).	NC *nhĕλ̌V 'milk'. See NSC 118.	NC
20	*ħalbV 'white'	3: HS, IE, D			
21	*mayʒ̂V 'tasty beverage'	4: U, IE, D, A	HS: only East Cushitic. A: besides Turk. *bal 'honey' cf. TM *mala 'sesame oil'. K: Laz mža 'milk' is not quite clear (it is usually considered to be derived from PKartv. *(s)ʒé-, but Manaster-Ramer reconstructs Proto-Kartvelian as *mlʒe, deriving it rather from Nostr. *mälgc, see above). Note that Dolgopolsky excludes from the comparison the traditionally linked Drav. *maṭṭ- 'honey, sweet juice' (to compare it with IE *medhu, see below) — although it belongs here quite plausibly. See Comp. 2, 38 (U, IE, D, A).	NC *mǐʒV 'sweet', *hwmǐʒū 'honey' (probably borrowed in IE as *medhu). ST: OChin. mit 'honey' is usually regarded as an Indo-Europeanism, although it may well be genuine.	NC, ST?
22	*ḳadV 'to wicker, wattle'	4: K, HS, IE, D	A: the basic meaning of the Turk. root *kat- is rather 'to mix', and it goes back, together with Mong. qudqu- and OJap. kata-, to PAlt. *kat'V (*k'-) 'to mix'). See Comp. 1, 316 (K, HS, IE, D).	PNC *ḳwɔ̌dV 'a big vessel, jar', *kŭdwV 'basket, receptacle', ST *k(h)ŏt 'a k. of basket'.	NC, ST
23	*ḳoʔc̓|cV 'basket'	6: HS, IE, K, U, D, A	A: Besides Tung. forms, cf. also Turk. *ḳača 'a k. of vessel' < Alt. *k'ač'V. See Comp. 1, 365 (with much less evidence: HS, IE, U).	NC *q̓HečwV 'a k. of vessel, jar' (cf. also *q̓wečV 'wineskin, leather sack' and *q̓wicVrV id.); Y *(x)ǐʒ̂ 'vessel made of birch bark'.	NC, Y
24	*p̓|pat[a] 'basket, box'	3: IE, U, D	HS: only Akk. See Mat. 366 (IE, U, D).	NC *pħǎṭV 'a k. of vessel', ST *Put 'basket'. See NSC 119.	NC, ST
25	*ʕ|γaŕ̌K[u] 'sinew'	3: IE, D, K	Here Dolgopolsky modifies the traditional etymology, within which IE *arkʷ- 'bow, curve' was compared with Kartv. *γrek(w)- 'to bend, bow' (see Comp. 1, 240: K, IE). While the addition of Drav. *eŕVt- 'bow' may be plausible (if *eŕVt- < *erkVt-), Alt. *ark'a 'to bind, rope', as well as the isolated Sem. (only	Cf. NC *=ig(w)Vr (or *=irg(w)V-r) 'to bend, fold'; ST *kuar 'bent, crooked'; PY *kǝr(~-l-) 'crooked, bent'. See NSC 114.	NC, ST, Y

No.	Root	Distri-bution	Comments	Sino-Caucasian evidence	Sino-Caucasian distribution
			Arabic) ʕirq- 'root, sinew' probably have nothing in common with the other forms.		
26	*yaŋ[y]V 'sinew, tendon'	1: U	HS: only an isolated Eg. form. The reconstruction relies on a dubious match of Turk. *jāń 'bow' with Ural. *jäntä 'sinew, tendon' or *joŋ(k)se 'bow'. The two Uralic forms are hardly related to each other (the former being derived from *jäntV- 'to stretch, strain', and compared by Illič-Svityč with Drav. *ēnt- 'to stretch (arms)', Turk. *jēt- 'to lead, pull', see Comp. 1, 147). The match between *joŋ(k)se and Turk. *jāń is hardly more reliable: the Turkic form goes fairly well with Tung. *žeje-n 'sharp point' and OJap. ja 'arrow' < Alt. *žēja.		
27	*łoŋḲa 'to bend'	3: IE, U, D?	HS: only Hausa-Eg. with irregular correspondence. A: only TM (the Mong. parallel toŋga- given by Illič-Svityč is dubious). Illič-Svityč draws here also Drav. *toŋk- 'to bow, bend; dangle', which is possible if the correspondence *ł- = Drav. *t- is justified. See Comp. 2, 27 (IE, U, D, A).		
28	*ńoγ|ʕIE 'sinew, to tie together'	1: U	HS: only Sem., with the meaning 'shoe, sandal; (shoe) strap', thus hardly comparable with Ur. *ńōle 'arrow'. A: an isolated Ewk. form.		
29	*p|p̓ešqE 'spear'	2: HS, U			
30	*ṭul(i)[G]V 'to spread like a net, catch with a net'	4: K, U, A, D	HS: only Sem. ('spread') with a highly dubious Eg. match.	ST *t(h)ol 'net, trap'. See NSC 122.	ST
31	*goki 'track'	3: HS, U, A	See Comp. 1, 309 (U, A).	NC *q̓əq̓ə 'street; canyon'; PY *χiχ 'road'; PST *kɔ̄ŋ id.	NC, Y, ST
32	*[d]eʕSV 'to follow the tracks'	1: K	Neither Georg. ʒi- 'search, look for', nor Georg. ʒγ(w)-/ʒeχ- 'to follow' can be satisfactorily compared with IE *des- 'to find, meet'. Mong. des 'following' does not have exact parallels in other Altaic languages; it should be perhaps analyzed as a suffixed form de-s- < *di-se-, with an early vocalic assimilation, where		

No.	Root	Distri-bution	Comments	Sino-Caucasian evidence	Sino-Caucasian distribution
			the root *di- is the same as in Old Mong. ǯi-rin 'two' (< PAlt. *tiuwa, reflecting a quite different Nostratic root). HS: a different etymology for Arab. dʕs- see HSED (HS *diʕas- 'to walk'). The comparison in general is very shaky.		
33	*šubyV 'spike, spear, to pierce'	2: U, A	HS: only Arabic. The comparison of PFU *šuye 'spear, spike' with Mong. sojuɣa and Manchu sujfun (also sujχun, sojχon) seems quite probable. Besides the mentioned forms in Altaic cf. Ewk. čije 'needle of a coniferous tree' (pointing, together with the Manchu form, to PTM *šüje), Turk. *sojaɣu 'cock's spur; pine needle', OJap. soja 'arrow', MKor. sāi 'straw'. However, Georg. šub 'spear' can hardly belong here, being rather related to Alt. *sũbi '(sharp) edge'.		
34	*ṭapV 'to hit (the target)'	4: IE, U, A, D	HS: only Semitic. See Mat. 356 (IE, U, A, D; different, but also unreliable HS reflexes).	ST *tūp 'answer, correspond, fit', Y *tVPV 'hear, perceive'. See NSC 121.	ST, Y
35	*menṭV 'to miss one's aim'	3: U, IE, A	HS: only West Chadic. I would also add Alt. *umVŋ[t]o 'to forget' (Turk. *umnit-, Mong. umta-, TM *omŋa-), although the initial u- is not quite clear; Illič-Svityč provides a different (and less reliable) Altaic parallel, uniting several different Altaic roots. See Comp. 3, 52 (U, IE, A, HS).		
36	*gurHa 'antelope'	3: HS, A, IE, D	A: Dolgopolsky apparently makes the same division between Nostr. *gurHa 'antelope' and *gUjrä 'wild animal' as Illič-Svityč (Comp. 1, 234, 237: HS, A, IE, D), based on the distinction in Mong. between gura(n) 'a k. of antelope' and görüɣe 'wild animal'. However, Mong. gura(n) means actually 'roe-buck, male wild goat' and should be rather compared with PTM *ŋur 'male (of small wild animals' and probably OTurk. uri 'male child, son'< Alt. *ŋurV (with a regular development *ŋ- g-). It is thus quite safe to compare MKor. korani 'deer' with Mong. görüɣe 'wild animal' (cf. perhaps also PTM *gur-ma/*gur-na 'hare; squirrel') and reconstruct Alt. *gurI (~ *gorI) 'deer, wild	ST *khij 'barking deer', Y *gəʔj 'deer, game'. See NSC 114.	ST, Y

No.	Root	Distri-bution	Comments	Sino-Caucasian evidence	Sino-Caucasian distribution
			animal' — which can be very satisfactorily compared with IE *g'hwēr- 'wild animal' and Drav. *kūr- 'deer, antelope' < Nostr. *gujrV.		
37	*ʔElħi 'deer'	4: IE, A, K, D	HS: only Semitic. U: only Yukagir. See Comp. 1, 272-3 (IE, A, K, D).	ST *lă 'musk-deer'. See NSC 115.	ST
38	*boča 'young deer'	2: K, U	A: The Tungus forms cited (Neg. bočan, Ulch. bočan etc.) go back actually to Manchu *bugu-čan (bučin), with *bugu (also attested in Manchu as buɣu, buχu) being most probably borrowed from Mong. buɣu 'deer, aurochs'. HS: only Arabic with a very unsecure East Chad. (Lele) parallel.		
39	*buḲa 'bovine(s)'	1: A	Despite superficial resemblance, IE *bŭk- 'bull' (if such a form really existed, which is doubted by many scholars) can hardly be compared with Turk. *būka 'bull' (certainly borrowed in Mong. as buqa). The latter is quite plausibly explained from Alt. *mūk'u 'male' (whence also Mong. *mok- 'one- or two-year-old deer; penis'; PTM *muka-/muke- 'male; man'; OJap. mukwo 'bridegroom').	The Altaic *mūk'u 'male, young man' can be perhaps compared with: NC *mVχwa 'fiancé, son-in-law', ST *māk 'son-in-law', Y *-mVχV/*pVχV 'nephew'.	NC, ST, Y
40	*čoma 'aurochs, wild bovine'	2: D, K		NC *ćimV 'goat'	NC
41	*č[a]w(V)RV 'bull, calf'	2: IE, A	HS: only Semitic.		
42	*ɣ\GawV 'wild sheep\goats'	2: IE, HS	Dolgopolsky compares Turk. *āb 'wild game, hunt' with Mong. aba 'chase, hunt' (quite correctly); however, he adds TM *abdu(n) 'cattle, flock' which actually means 'herd (of deer or horses)' and is quite transparently related to Mong. aduɣu(n) 'herd (of horses); horse', and further — to Turk. *at 'horse' < Alt. *at-bu(n) 'herd, horse herd'. The actual TM parallel for Turk. *āb and Mong. *aba 'hunt, chase' is TM *wā- 'to hunt, kill' (where the quite exceptional initial *w- points to a vowel reduction: *wā- < *awā-) < Alt. *āba (*āwa) 'hunt, kill' — most probably related to IE *əwā- 'to wound, hurt'.	Y *χV̄j 'deer', ST *ɣŭ 'deer, sheep'.	ST, Y

No.	Root	Distri-bution	Comments	Sino-Caucasian evidence	Sino-Caucasian distribution
43	*diqa 'goat'	2: K?, HS	Irregular phonology and distribution in IE may suggest a loan: the source, both for Kartv. and IE, could be East Cauc. *dV(r)q̇wV 'goat'.	NC *dV(r)q̇wV 'goat'; ST: OC *dhə̄k 'male animal, bull'.	NC, ST
44	*k[ä]ćV 'wild goat'	2: K?, HS	A: only Turk. *geči 'goat'.	NC *k̇īʒV̆/ *ʒīkV̆ (~ -ä̆-) 'goat, kid'.	NC
45	*bukEɣ|ʕV 'billy goat, ram'	2: HS, A	For Alt. *pUkV should be reconstructed (besides Turk. *bugu and Mong. *bugu cf. also Ewk. heglen, hewlen 'young of elk'		
46	*ʕVp̌VrV 'wild boar'	1: IE	HS: only Arabic.	? Cf. OCh *prā 'pig'.	
47	*ʕir[i] '(male, young) artiodactyl'	3: K, IE, D	HS: only Semitic.	ST *ra 'goat'.	ST
48	*p̌oKü 'pack, wild cattle'	2: IE, A	HS: only one East Chad. language (Ndam). See Comp. 3, 126 (IE, A, HS?).		NC, ST
49	*gadi 'kid, young goat'	3: HS, IE, D			
50	*buyẑV 'fur-bearing animal'	4: IE, U, A, D		NC *bȟěrčǐ 'wolf, jackal'; ST: OCh *prāts 'a mythical predatory animal'; Y *pes-tap 'glutton, wolverine'.	NC, Y
51	*ʔ|hUrV 'squirrel or a similar animal'	3: IE, U, D, A	HS: only a very unsecure Akk. form. A: from Alt. I would add *Uri-k'V 'ground-squirrel' (Turk. *örke, TM *urike).	ST *ru (~-iw) 'a k. of small animal (flying squirrel, bamboo rat)'.	ST
52	*k̇un|ȟV 'small carnivore'	4: K, IE, HS, A	See Mat. 346 (IE, A, K).	NC *fiq̇wə̄nə̄ (~ *finə̄q̇wə̄) 'mouse, rat'; Y *kūń (~g-) 'wolverine'. NC, Y	
53	*dik̇V 'edible cereals or fruit'	2: K?, D	HS: only Berber with a questionable Eg. parallel. Altaic *diK-ktä 'edible berries' does not exist: Tungus forms like Ewk. ǯikte etc. are most probably borrowed from Mong. ǯedege(ne) 'berry', the latter being itself borrowed from Turk. *jigde — for which genuine matches are Mong. ǯeɣe-rgene 'a k. of berry' and TM *ǯüksi(-kte) 'blueberry'	NC *dik̇wi 'a k. of cereal (millet, rice)'.	NC
54	*ʒ/ǯugbV 'a k. of fig tree'	3: HS, D, A	I would add here Alt. *ǯiugV 'berry' (see under *dik̇V).	*ǯägV 'a k. of berry (cherry, raspberry)'.	NC

No.	Root	Distri-bution	Comments	Sino-Caucasian evidence	Sino-Caucasian distribution
55	*b[i]ř[uw]q́ 'a k. of edible fruit'	3: K, IE, D	HS: only a very dubious Arabic form.	NC *pĩrqwÅ 'a k. of fruit'; ST *phrŭŋ (/*phrŭm) 'grain; fruit'.	NC, ST
56	*Ḳ̣uSV 'nut'	2: IE, A	The match looks fine, but IE *k- (instead of the expected *gʷ-) is not quite clear. [Note that Dolgopolsky here confuses two Altaic roots: Turk. *Kusik 'nut', Mong. *kusi-gan 'nut', TM *koši-kta 'nut' (also OJap. kusi 'a k. of nut) < Alt. *kušu, and Mong. kusi 'cedar, thuja', TM *xusi-kta 'acorn, oak-tree', OJap. kasi 'Quercus acuta' < Alt. *k'usa 'a k. of tree, oak-tree').		
57	*LVǯV 'a k. of nut'	2: K, IE	HS: only Semitic.		
58	*buṭV 'pistachio'	0	HS: only Semitic. A: only Turk., with an unclear variation of *butur-gak 'a thorn tree' and *bitrik 'pistachio nut'.		
59	*mar(y)V 'berries'	4: IE, K, U, A	A: instead of Azer. müri 'strawberry' — which is borrowed from Lezghian — one should cite Turk. *bürü-lgen 'a k. of berry'. See Comp. 2, 43 (IE, K, U, A).	NC *mer(ʔ)V 'a k. of berry'; Y *bar₁in 'bird-cherry'. See NSC 118.	NC
60	*m[o](y)ẑV 'a k. of berry'	2: U, A	HS: only a very unsecure Arabic parallel. Alt.: besides TM *mile-kte, cf. also Turk. *beleʃ 'ashberry'). IE: *māl- 'apple' is more probably = *(a)mas-l- and hardly belongs here.	NC *ʕwmãrço̧ 'rowan, a k. of berry'; Y *puʔs 'bilberry'.	NC
61	*ḲERV 'fruit of a leguminous plant'	2: HS, IE		NC *qǒrʔā (~-rfi-) 'pea(s)'.	NC
62	*m[u]rḳV 'root, sinew'	3: K, IE, D	HS: only East Cushitic. A: Ewk. muɲi 'tendon' hardly belongs here, being related to Turk. *büŋüř 'horn', Mong. möɣe(r)-sün 'cartilage, gristle' and MKor. (nis)-mii(ŋ)im 'gums' < Alt. *mujŋe 'horn, cartilage, tendon').	NC *mĭrqwǎ 'root'; ST *mrēk 'vein, root'.	NC, ST
63	*mol|łV 'to pound, smash, gnaw'	3: IE, U, A	HS: only Semitic. Alt.: Alt. *muʃe (besides Mong. mölʒi- 'to gnaw into pieces' cf. also Manchu muʃa- 'to swallow', muʃan 'jaw', MKor. mir- 'to bite', OJap. musir- 'to pluck out, pick out'). See Comp. 2, 69 (IE, U, A, HS).	ST *mjal 'cut into little pieces'. See NSC 118.	ST

No.	Root	Distri-bution	Comments	Sino-Caucasian evidence	Sino-Caucasian distribution
64	*ʔäPHi 'to bake'	4: HS, A, D, IE?	Alt. *ep'e (besides Turk. *ep-mek 'bread' cf. also TM *epe- 'cake', OJap. opo-mono 'food')	NC *=HēwχV(n) 'to bake, warm'; ST *kǎŋ 'to roast'; PY *(h)əqan 'to boil'	NC, ST, Y
65	*qUbźV 'food made of ground cereals'	1: K	HS: only Semitic. Kartv. *qweza- 'loaf' can hardly be compared with TM *upa 'flour' — especially since the latter goes back to Alt. *op'V 'powder' (whence also Turk. *opa 'white powder, white lead', Mong. oγo 'white lead').		
66	*[ʔ]omśa 'meat'	4: U, IE, HS, D	HS: the evidence can be perhaps strengthened if we take into account Cush. *HVmS-/*HmVS- 'cow' (Illič-Svityč). D: Dolgopolsky does not list Drav. *ūñ(c)- 'meat', compared by Illič-Svityč. See Comp. 1, 252 (U, IE, HS, D).	NC *jōmcō 'bull, ox'; ST *chǔ (~-o,-ăw) 'cow, bull'; PY *ʔise 'meat'. See NSC 114.	NC, ST, Y
67	*q̇[u]ʒV 'intestines'	3: K, IE, D		NC *k̠wĭc̠Ě/*čĭk̠wĚ 'spleen; intestines' (also *q̇wičV/ *čiq̇wV (~-ä-)); Y *kic (~-g-,-č) 'meat, carcass'.	NC, Y
68	*ʔayŋo 'marrow, brain'	2: HS, U	Here PIE *ongʷ- 'to smear' is compared with Ural. *ajŋe 'brain, marrow' (?), and, even less convincingly, with Turk. *eŋ 'cheek' (for the latter cf. also Manchu eŋge 'beak' < Alt. *eŋgV). I think, however, that the match between HS *Hangʷ- 'brain' and Ural. *ayŋe (*ayŋo) id. is quite acceptable.		
69	*mag(i)za 'liver'	2: HS, U	HS *mayz- presupposes rather Nostr. *mayzV (Ural. *maksa < *mas-k(s)a?)	NC *wĕmçŬ (~-ŏ-) 'liver, spleen'.	NC
70	*ń[a]K̠u 'soft parts of the animal's body'	2: IE, U	HS: only Arabic. Altaic: only Old Turkic.	NC *hwnĕrq̇ǔ 'meat soup'; ST *nuk 'meat; roe'.	NC?, ST?
71	*muńa 'egg'	3: U, D, A	HS: an isolated Musgu form. IE: only Slavic. In Alt. we can compare *mVŋe/*ŋVme 'testicle' (TM *ŋāma/ *māŋa, Mong. nim/im 'testicle'). See Comp. 2, 72 (U, D, HS, IE).		
72	*ʔ[a|o]h|χi 'egg'	1: IE	HS: only a dialectal Arabic form. The Old Japanese u 'egg', cited according to my own personal communication in 1976, is unfortunately a misunderstanding: I must have confused the character		

No.	Root	Distri-bution	Comments	Sino-Caucasian evidence	Sino-Caucasian distribution
			for 'egg' with a similar character used for the 4th cyclic sign of the 12-sign cycle, 'hare' (actually u is an artificially shortened form of OJap. usagi 'hare'). Therefore the traditional etymology, deriving IE *ōwio- from *əwi- 'bird' seems preferable (the latter, in fact, has a very good match in Alt. *āwi 'a k. of water-bird').		
73	*ḲolV 'large fish'	6: HS, U, A, IE, D, K	Alt. *k'ula (the Kor.-Jap. *kurV-ra 'whale' also belongs here). K: Illič-Svityč compares also Svan. ḳalmax- 'fish'. See Mat. 362 (HS, U, A, IE, K).	Y *kol(a) 'a k. of big fish' (eel, sterlet).	Y
74	*doTgiHu 'fish'	3: IE, U, A	HS: only Semitic. See Comp. 1, 219 (IE, HS, A).	Y *tə?G 'perch'.	Y
75	*mEn|ǹi 'a k. of fish'	3: IE, D, U?, A	I would also add Alt. *mańu-kV 'a k. of fish' (reflected in Turk. Yak. majaɣas 'white-fish', Mong. muniɣ, man-ǯaɣ 'different sp. of fish', TM *māń-gu, *mań-ma id., MKor. məijuki 'trout', OJap. munagi 'eel').	ST *mā̀ 'eel; shark'; Y *boŋ- 'herring'.	ST, Y
76	*p|ṗayV 'a k. of fish'	2: U?, ?D	I would prefer to regard IE *peisk- as a borrowing from North Caucasian *bV̄s̱wA 'fish'.		
77	*ṭüRV 'hard-roe'	2: U, A			
78	*[ḳ]ür(w)V 'hard-roe, span'	1: IE	The Alt. forms here are questionable: Azer. kürü 'hard-roe' is quite isolated within Turkic and most probably has a Lezghian source: cf. Lezgh., Tab. kür id. < Proto-Lezg. *k̇ʷir. A good West Caucasian match is Abkh. a-kʷər-t (presupposing North Cauc. *kʷirV), which is no doubt the source of Georg. kvirita. We are left thus only with a not quite clear parallel between IE *krek- 'fish eggs' and Alt. *k'iurpe 'young (of animal, fish)' (besides the cited TM *xürbe- 'spawn' cf. Turk. *körpe 'newborn; newborn lamb'; Mong. körbe id.).		
79	*madu 'honey'	0	HS: only Omotic, with quite obscure second consonant. Otherwise IE *medhu 'honey' is compared with Drav. *maṭṭ- — the latter, however, can be quite plausibly derived from *mayȝ̌V q.v. A very probable		

No.	Root	Distri-bution	Comments	Sino-Caucasian evidence	Sino-Caucasian distribution
			source for the isolated IE *medhu is North Caucas. *hwmĭʒūV 'honey' (derived from the adjective *mĭʒV 'sweet').		
80	*č̣[ü]rV 'flint-stone, knife'	3: HS, A, D	Alt. *č̣'iora: besides Tungus forms cf. Turk. *čar 'whetstone'.	ST *ćVr(H) ~ ǯ- 'hoe, pick-axe'.	ST
81	*buRV 'flint, cut/carve with a flint'	4: HS, A, IE, D	Although Dolgopolsky places a question mark here, the root seems rather reliable — although it tends to contaminate with Nostr. *p'urV 'to dig, hole' (the two roots are also confused by Illič-Svityč in his *bura 'to bore', see Comp. 1, 186–7). In Altaic, besides TM *burV 'flint', we have Ewk. burbe- 'to pierce, bore through', Turk. *buragu 'drill', Mong. burgui 'wire (for cleaning pipes)', OJap. por- 'to bore, engrave' < Alt. *burV. This root can be quite plausibly compared with IE *bherə- 'to cut with a sharp instrument', Ural. *pura 'drill, to drill' and Drav. *pōr̠- 'to split, chisel, bore'.		
82	*ti|e(ʔa)ʕo 'stone'	3: A, K, D	HS: only Semitic. Cf. Mat. 343 (A, K).	NC *λ̌äƚŭ 'stone'. See NSC 121.	NC
83	*kiw(V)hE 'stone'	3: HS?, K, U	Cf. Comp. 1, 298 (HS, K, U).	NC *ʔäwqV 'mountain slope'; ST *khʷi 'hill, mound'; Y *qäʔj 'mountain'.	NC, ST, Y
84	*boruʕ|γV 'trunk, log'	3: IE, U, D	HS: only Semitic, with the meaning 'reed', hardly corresponding to 'log, board' in other languages. See Mat. 332 (IE, U).		
85	*ćUƚV 'stalk, stick'	4: K, HS, U, D	A: only an isolated Tung. (Solon) form.	NC *č̣hwiƚū (~ -ʕ-) 'beam, girder'; ST *ćeƚ 'a k. of bamboo (used for arrows)'.	NC, ST
86	*ḳoǯʕV 'tree trunk'	2: HS, K	A: only an isolated Mong. form which may be actually derived from qoǯi-(γa)- 'to be naked, bald': 'the bared part of tree').		
87	*kaǹV(-bV)	4: IE, HS, D, U, A	There must be at least 3 different roots here: a) IE *gen(ə)bh- 'peg, stalk': Drav. *kāmp- 'stem, stalk'; b) HS *kann-: Drav. *kaǹǹ-; c) Ural. *kanta 'ground, base', for which cf. Alt. *kɛnt'a 'floor, threshhold'.	NC *ĥq.wīnV̆ 'nail, peg'; Y *(x)īńi- 'nail, finger-nail'; ST *kūŋ 'plant, branch'	NC, Y, ST
88	*ǯRV 'pole, long piece'	3: HS, IE, K	A: Mong. ǯoruγa 'arrow with a horn head' can not be parted from Alt.		

No.	Root	Distri-bution	Comments	Sino-Caucasian evidence	Sino-Caucasian distribution
	of wood'		*ńóra 'blade, edge' (whence, e.g. TM *ńuru 'arrow') and thus does not belong here.		
89	*ǯiryulü 'vein, sinew'	4: K, IE?, A, D	HS: only a very unsecure Cush. (Iraqw) form. Illič-Svityč had also added Drav. *cir- 'root', and I see no reason to separate it from the etymology. Cf. Mat. 341 (IE, A, D; Illič-Svityč also lists Ural. and HS forms, which are — probably correctly — moved by Dolgopolsky to a different Nostratic root).	NC *r̓ʔēč̓V̓/*ç̌wVrʔV 'string, bow-string'; ST *sVr 'thread'	NC, ST
90	*ʔeʒ̇ekU 'thorn, hook?'	1: A	Here Alt. *ŏlke 'hang on a hook' is compared with HS *šikk- 'thorn, pin, tooth' — a very dubious comparison.		
91	*k̲[a]k(w)V 'tooth, fang, hook'	5: K, IE, U, A, D	HS: only Semitic. A: Dolgopolsky compares Tung. *xŭkte 'tooth', but this goes back to Alt. *k'iūk'i 'tooth; root', and perhaps a better match would be Common Altaic *gek'o 'hook'.	ST *kŭk 'bend', *khjŏk 'bend, crooked'	ST
92	*toŕV 'bark'	1: A	HS: only Chadic. IE: *der- goes back to Nostr. *teri 'to tear, burst'. The Altaic form alone is unsufficient for reconstructing a special Nostr. root.		
93	*Ḳa[pʔ\ʕE] 'bark'	4: HS, U, A, K	Cf. Mat. 344 (A, U, with a different Kartv. parallel — quite correctly transferred by Dolgopolsky to a different root, *ṭo(w)q̇a).		
94	*ḲayerV 'bark, film'	4: A, I, K?, U	K: Kartv. *kerk- has a somewhat unclear *k- instead of *ḳ-: perhaps it would be better to compare Georg. ḳr-ol- (cited under *Ḳaĺ[ü]). U: FU *körV has a different Altaic parallel: *k'iuru 'bark, shell, and should be regarded as a different root. Cf. Comp. 1, 341–3 (IE, U, A, K, with addition of Semitic *ḳrm).	NC *k̲həri (~ -ʕ-) 'bark, skin'; ST *khrǝ̄w (~ gh-, qh-, Gh-) 'shell, bark'.	NC, ST
95	*ṭo(w)q̇a 'hide, skin'	5: K, IE, U, A, D	HS: only Chadic. A: *t'uk'i (the PTM form is not *tiki-, but *tüki-, cf. besides the cited forms Manchu tuku 'fur-coat cover'; cf. further Turk. *tük/*tüg 'fur, hair (on body)', Mong. toqum 'cover of saddle, saddle blanket').		
96	*ṭal(u)ya 'skin, fell'	3: U, D, A	HS: only Chadic. A: besides TM *talu 'birch bark' cf. Turk. *tul-gak	ST *[t]ałH 'membrane, pellicle'.	ST

No.	Root	Distri-bution	Comments	Sino-Caucasian evidence	Sino-Caucasian distribution
			(*tol-gak) 'bared skin; leather sack', perhaps also Mong. tulum id. < Alt. *t'alo.		
97	*K̓al̥[ü] 'skin, film, bark'	4: IE, U, A, D	Cf. a somewhat different analysis in Comp. 1, 289, where this root is confused with *kal̥V 'bare, naked'; however, Drav. *kaḷ- 'to skin' should still be kept here (it can not be regarded as a reflex of *K̓ožV 'to peel, skin').	NC *q̓wăłV 'bark, crust'.	NC
98	*k̓oRupV 'bark, skin'	2: HS, IE	A: only Mongolian (and rather dubious semantically).	NC *q̄ārp̓V/*p̄ārqV 'fur-coat'; ST *qruap 'scale, shell'	NC, ST
99	*K̓ožV 'to skin'	2: U, A	HS: only Arabic. A: *k'Ul̓V 'bark, scales' (besides the cited Mong. form qoltu- 'bark; peel off' cf. also TM *xolda-ksa 'bark; board' and possibly Turk. (Osm.) kuš a hairless spot (on horse's skin)'.		
100	*K̓VRVHp̓|pV 'piece of leather'	2: IE, D	HS: only Chadic (with an irregular initial consonant). One wonders if this is not in fact the same root as no. 98 *k̓oRupV.		
101	*p̓iχ|γγA 'sharp bone, sharp tool'	5: K, IE, U, A, HS?	A: Alt. *p'egV 'to cut, mow, tear' (besides Manch. fe- 'mow' cf. also the TM derivate *pegde- 'to tear, tear off'). Cf. Mat. 352-3 (K, IE, U, A).	ST *ph(j)ăj 'to divide, split'.	ST
102	*pišV 'bile'	3: IE, U, D	Cf. Mat. 340 (IE, U).		
103	*[ṭ]äχ|l̓a 'spleen'	2: A, K	HS: only Semitic. A: Alt. *tiāle (besides the forms cited, cf. also TM *dilba 'diaphragm' and Kor. čira, čirä 'spleen').	NC *Hl̥älV (/*Hlal̥V) 'liver'.	NC
104	*l[ä|e]p̓A 'spleen'	4: HS, U, A, IE	The somewhat feeble match of Ural. *läppV (or *leppV) 'spleen' with the isolated Orok word lipče 'spleen' can be perhaps strengthened. In Altaic cf. also Mong. naγalta, niγalta, Khalkh. nält 'spleen', allowing, together with the Orok form, to reconstruct *lip'a (or *liap'a) 'spleen'. Cf. also the isolated Germanic *libara- 'liver' and Armenian leard id. (which are very hard to trace back to Common IE *iekʷr-). See Comp. 2, 17 (HS, U, IE).		
105	*ṭeqmE 'sinciput, crown of	3: K, A	IE: only Slavic. HS: a very disputable comparison of Arab. ʔaṭχam- 'anterioris pars nasi' with Awngi		

No.	Root	Distri-bution	Comments	Sino-Caucasian evidence	Sino-Caucasian distribution
	head'		dūmī 'top' and Oromo ḍuma 'end'. A: Alt. *t'úmu (Mong. teme-sü 'edges of a net' hardly belongs here, though; one should rather compare Tung. *tumŋu- 'sinciput' with Turk. *tumak 'hat', Mong. tomi-la- 'chief', tumur-liɣ 'hat', OJap. tumuri, tuburi 'head, top').		
106	*[g]edi 'occiput, hind part'	4: A, IE, K, HS	A: Alt. *gedi (cf. also OJap. kita 'North'). Cf. also IE *g'hed- 'behind, hind part' (traditionally compared, but for some reason omitted by Dolgopolsky). See Mat. 342, Comp. 1, 227–8 (A, IE, K, HS).		
107	*Go|atḲE 'popliteal space, armpit'	2: A, I	HS: only Semitic, with a quite irregular Eg. parallel. The Altaic and IE forms point rather to *Ho|aḲE.		
108	*ǹiḲa 'jugular vertebra, nape'	3: IE, U, A	Cf. Mat. 355, Comp. 2, 92 (IE, U, A).	NC *nVqV 'behind'; ST *nŏk 'cervical vertebra; back'. See NSC 119.	NC, ST
109	*kälulü 'a woman of the other moiety'	5: K, IE, U, A, D	HS: only Semitic. Cf. Comp. 1, 295–6 (K, IE, U, A, D, HS).		
110	*küda 'a man of the other moiety'	3: U, A, K	Cf. Comp. 1, 302–4 (U, A, K).		NC, Y
111	*šeʒA 'a relative of the other moiety'	2: K, U	HS: only East Cushitic, with a dubious Eg. parallel.	Cf. Proto-Lezgian *sič:V 'relative-in-law'.	
112	*[ħ|χV]wän| nV 'relative of the other moiety'	2: U, D	HS: only Egyptian. A: TM *bene- 'wife's sibling' can hardly belong here — both because initial *b- is unclear (Nostr. *w- normally yields Alt. *0-) and because TM *bener very probably goes back to *bere-n, cf. Mong. beri, ber-gen.		
113	*n|ǹu|üśV 'woman of the other moiety'	2: HS, K?	Besides HS, we are presented with a comparison of Kartv. *nusa 'son's wife' with IE *snuso- id. (note that Hitt. nasarti 'concubine' is a transparent loan from Hurrian našardə and does not reflect IE *snuso-). However, the IE form is	NC *nŭsA (~ -ŏ-) 'daughter-in-law'; ST *nŏ 'female relative'.	ST, NC

No.	Root	Distri-bution	Comments	Sino-Caucasian evidence	Sino-Caucasian distribution
			much better explained as a loanword from North Caucasian: cf. North Cauc. *nŭsA id. Borrowing allows also to explain the enigmatic *s- in IE: cf. forms like Khin. çi-nas 'bride, son's wife' — actually a compound *çăn-nusA lit. 'new bride'. For Kartvelian borrowing from North Caucasian also can not be ruled out.		
114	*Hić|cχV 'father, head of a family'	3: IE, U, A	HS: only a dubious Ge'ez form. IE: *esHo- 'master, lord' (besides Hittite, also Lat. erus): In Altaic Dolgopolsky cites dubious forms (Saró-Yugh. ise goes back to *edi-si and Mong. ežen to *edi-n: the latter form is listed as a reflex of two roots simultaneously, see no. 115). There are, however, some forms that can be related to IE *esHo- and Ural. *ićä: cf. Turk. *eči (*ečü) 'ancestor, elder relative', TM *ačV 'ancestor; father'.	ST *ćɨH 'govern, rule, lord'.	ST
115	*?ediNV 'pater familias'	2: HS, A	The reconstruction is rather *?edi (the -n, occurring in some Altaic forms, is certainly a frequent nominal suffix).	NC *dājV/*?ādājV 'father'.	
116	*?emA 'mother'	5: HS, U, A, IE, D	Cf. also *mā- in IE *mā-tēr id. A Lallwort, but no doubt archaic.	ST *māH 'mother, woman'; Y *?ama 'mother'.	ST, Y
117	*?[ä]yV 'mother'	2: U, D	HS: only Cushitic. IE: only a somewhat dubious Germanic form.	NC *jājV 'mother, grandmother'.	NC
118	*?aba ~ *?apa 'father'	4: HS, A, IE, D	I would also add *pə- in IE *pə-tēr. Certainly a Lallwort, but archaic.	NC *?ŏbV̄(jV) 'father'; ST *p(h)aH 'father'; H *?ob 'father'.	NC, ST, Y
119	*[?|h]oₒl|łV 'child'	3: K, A, D	HS: only Cushitic. Svan. ɋlaw- 'child, boy' should be perhaps compared not with Alt. *uka(lV) 'child, son' (besides Turk. *ogul 'son' cf. also MKor. àhăi 'child', and possibly Mong. uɣal-ǯa 'male mountain goat'), but with Alt. *kūlV 'slave, servant'. A possible Drav. match is D *kūli 'hired labourer, servant'.	NC *ɋVlē (~ ɋ̣-,-i) 'child, young one'; ST *kʷāł 'servant'.	NC, ST
120	*?arV 'member of the clan'	3: HS, IE?, U?	IE *ar- (*arìo-, cf. perhaps also Hitt. arawa- 'free') could be regarded as a borrowing from North Caucasian.	NC *?wŏhri (~ -e) 'troop, army'; ST *raH 'troop, enemy'; Y *(h)ar- 'servant; Arin (ethnonum)'.	NC, Y, ST
121	*?arba 'to make magic'	1: U	HS: only Semitic (and rather dubious semantically); A: only Turkic. Cf. Comp. 1, 261-2 (U, A, HS).		

No.	Root	Distri- bution	Comments	Sino- Caucasian evidence	Sino- Caucasian distribution
122	*ʕ[a]lV 'to burn (sacrifices)'	3: IE, K, U	HS: only Semitic. The Altaic parallels are somewhat unsecure: Turk. *alka- 'to bless, sacrifice' goes back to *p'iolko, cf. TM *pulgu-, Mong. *hörgil and can not belong here, while a comparison with Alt. *āli 'deceit, cunning' raises semantic doubts. Cf. Comp. 1, 276 (IE, K, HS).		
123	*šoṭV 'to exercise magic force'	5: HS, U, D, K, A	A: cf. Alt. *sVtV 'to curse' (Turk. *satga-; Mong. sadur 'treacherous').	NC *sVrdV 'curse, to curse'.	NC
124	*tulV 'to tell, pronounce magic texts'	3: HS, IE, U		ST *tiə̄lH 'scold, rebuke'.	ST

In the statistics below I shall take into account only those Nostratic roots that are (according to the rules formulated above) represented in more than one Nostratic branch — that is, the roots that we are actually able to call Nostratic. It is clear that Alt. *tōr̄V 'birch bark' (under no. 92) can have a Nostratic origin, but since IE *der- compared with it has a different origin (Nostr. *ter[i] 'to tear, burst'), and the Hamito-Semitic match for it is only attested in one subbranch (Chadic), the Nostratic etymology as such is rather weak. The number of valid roots among Dolgopolsky's evidence is rather high — 106 out of 124. Within that subset we have the following distribution of reflexes:

IE	A	U	D	NC	HS	ST	K	Y
63	61	60	56	47	47	46	42	22

The low figures for Kartvelian and Yenissean are easily explained by the fact that both of the families belong to group I (very small families with insufficient lexical material). Other evidence — basically lexicostatistical and morphological — proves beyond doubt their affiliation with respectively Nostratic and Sino-Caucasian.

Among other families, however, there is a very clear division between Indo-European, Altaic, Uralic and Dravidian, on one hand (with more than 56 reflexes in each family), and North Caucasian, Hamito-Semitic and Sino-Tibetan, on the other hand (with less than 47 reflexes in each family). This does not mean, of course, that North Caucasian and Hamito-Semitic are closer to each other — they are just equally distant from Nostratic proper. The fact that Hamito-Semitic roots are so abundant within Dolgopolsky's material is explained by a —

probably unvoluntary — violation of the 'rules of the game'. The huge number of Hamito-Semitic languages and, unfortunately, a not very good state of comparative Hamito-Semitic linguistics allows to find matches for almost any root — in some Hamito-Semitic subbranch or even in a single isolated Hamito-Semitic language.

The fact that Proto-Nostratic and Proto-Hamito-Semitic reveal a system of regular phonetic correspondences does not change the situation: regular correspondences are observed between, for example Russian and German, although the former belongs to Slavic, and the latter to Germanic. It just suggests a relationship on a deeper taxonomic level.

These statistics, of course, are very preliminary — being based on very restricted material consisting of A. Dolgopolsky's 124 Nostratic roots. It would be highly desirable to make a large-scale investigation on the whole volume of Nostratic etymologies in A. Dolgopolsky's forthcoming (and long awaited) *Nostratic Etymological Dictionary*. The evidence available until now, however, seems to favour the following conclusions:

1. Three macrofamilies of the Old World — Hamito-Semitic, Nostratic and Sino-Caucasian — are quite possibly related on a deeper level. I would call the super-family uniting them all Eurasiatic (not to be confused with Greenberg's 'Eurasiatic' — which is actually a subset of Nostratic proper). Although we still are nowhere near a reconstruction of the hypothetical Austric (Austronesian-Thai-Austroasiatic) protolanguage, there are some hints that it could belong there, too.

2. Nostratic proper includes Dravidian (probably the first family to split off) and a core of more closely related families: Indo-European, Uralic, Altaic, Kartvelian. The inclusion of Eskimo-Aleut and Chukchee-Kamchatkan languages into Nostratic also seems quite probable to me, although their exact position within the Nostratic genealogy is not clear yet.

References

Illič-Svityč, V.M., 1967. Materials for a comparative dictionary of Nostratic languages. *Etnologiya* 1965, 321–73.
Illič-Svityč, V.M., 1971–84. *Comparative Dictionary of Nostratic Languages*, vols. 1–3. Moscow: Nauka.
Orël, V.E. & O.V. Stolbova, 1995. *Hamito-Semitic Etymological Dictionary: Materials for a Reconstruction*. Leiden & New York (NY): Köln.
Starostin, S.A., 1989. Nostratic and Sino-Caucasian, in *Explorations in Language Macrofamilies*, ed. V. Shevoroshkin. Bochum: Universitaetsverlag, 42–66.

Chapter 8

Why should a language have any relatives?

R.L. Trask

Why should a language have any relatives? Like many historical linguists, I was trained in the tacit assumption that languages belong in families. Large families were seen as 'normal'; tiny families were problems requiring further work; and isolates were a positive embarrassment: Basque and Burushaski were regarded with some amazement, if not with consternation. How could such things exist?

But things are not like that, not at all. In this paper, I want to argue that isolates and tiny families are to be *expected*, that they represent the norm. The real question, in my view, is not why isolates exist, but why *families* exist — and above all large families. Why should there be huge families like Indo-European and Austronesian? Or, to restate my title, why should a language have any relatives? Naturally, in the present forum, my question will be directed specifically toward the Nostratic hypothesis. Why should Nostratic exist? How *could* it exist? And, furthermore, even if it somehow does exist, how can it have the properties ascribed to it?

The rise of language families

Modern human beings (*Homo sapiens*) have existed on this planet for 100,000 years or more. Most linguists and anthropologists believe that our species has been able to speak from the beginning. Admittedly, a minority of specialists prefer to place the origin of full-blown language no more than 50,000 years in the past, but then again there are anthropologists who argue that some of our hominid ancestors could speak. In any case, for my purposes, it matters little which of these dates we prefer: even 50,000 years is enough.

During the overwhelming majority of our presence on the planet, human beings existed only in the form of small foraging bands. The available technology did not permit high population densities, and each band required a sizeable chunk of territory in order to feed itself. This conclusion is not in doubt: at the time of the European expansion several centuries ago, such foraging bands still occupied significant parts of the earth's surface, and a few still survive even today in New Guinea and elsewhere.

Now: what would be the linguistic consequences of tens of millennia of such an existence for the entire human population? Regrettably, we have little in the way of hard data with which to approach this question, apart from what we can glean from observations of surviving foragers in recent centuries. But I want to argue that the likeliest linguistic outcome is *diversity.*

In circumstances in which everybody belongs to a small band, and in which technological advances are rare and in any case do not permit significantly higher population densities, just how could one language manage to impose itself over a sufficiently large area to give rise, over time, to a large and far-flung language family? By what mechanism could this be achieved?

After all, a language does not spread into surrounding populated areas because it has a particularly nice verbal system. It can only spread because its speakers have some kind of material advantage over neighbouring speakers. This is true regardless of whether a language spreads by displacement or absorption of neighbouring peoples or whether it merely diffuses into neighbouring populations. Nobody in Wales has ever learned English because of the agreeable linguistic features of that language: Welsh-speakers learn English because those who can speak English have a clear material advantage over those who cannot. And why should it ever have been different in the remote past?

Of course, our host Professor Renfrew has in recent years been championing precisely this view (Renfrew 1992; 1994; 1995). Save only for the special case of expansion into previously uninhabited territory (which itself may require technological advances, as in the Polynesian case), Renfrew argues forcefully that languages spread because their speakers possess some kind of clear economic or technological advantage. And I agree with him. Like many linguists, I have a few problems with some of his specifics — notably the dating of Proto-Indo-European — but, on the whole, I am persuaded that his view of language spread is the correct one. In fact, he is not the first person to advance such views: the archaeologist Peter Bellwood, who holds the same views, has drawn attention to similar arguments in the literature preceding Renfrew's work by a few years (Bellwood 1997). But it is Renfrew's case which is best articulated and best known.

Renfrew concludes that the established great language families are rather recent developments in human affairs: scarcely more than 10,000 years old, and often much younger than that. Indo-European, Afro-Asiatic, Bantu and others — all, in Renfrew's view, result from the obtaining, by some group of people, of an economic or technological advantage which enabled their languages, by one means or another, to spread at the expense of other languages, which were accordingly displaced or obliterated. And I agree.

But what, then, was the linguistic map of the world like 20,000 years ago, or even 10,000 years ago, before these great expansions? Was much of the world already occupied by still earlier vast families resulting from still more ancient expansions? I very much doubt it. Recall that we are speaking of a world without metalworking, without agriculture, without animal husbandry, and even without pottery, a world dominated by stone, bone, wood, animal hides and vegetable fibres. In such a world, what innovation could have permitted one language to spread out over most of a large continent?

My knowledge of Eurasian prehistory is, to be blunt, sketchy. However, the sole event — if 'event' is the right word — singled out by the reference books I have consulted before the rise of agriculture is the advent of the Mesolithic, with its associated microlithic technology. Just how significant this was, I do not know. The advent of the Neolithic is commonly trumpeted as a great leap forward, and the venerable phrase 'the Neolithic revolution' is still in use. But no one ever seems to speak of a 'Mesolithic revolution', and indeed the Mesolithic is commonly presented as a kind of late appendage to the Palaeolithic. Still, I find it interesting that Professor Dolgopolsky, in *The Nostratic Macrofamily and Linguistic Palaeontology* (hereafter *NM*), places his Proto-Nostratic construct approximately on the boundary between the Palaeolithic and Mesolithic periods. In this connection, I might also note that Nicholas Evans and Rhys Jones have recently argued, or perhaps better suggested, that the deeply puzzling spread of the Pama-Nyungan languages in Australia might have resulted from Australia's very own 'Mesolithic revolution', the introduction of microlithic technology only a few thousand years ago, probably in the northeast of the continent, in the form of the 'Australian small-tool tradition' (Evans & Jones 1997). Consequently, I will be interested to hear whether the archaeologists can provide any support for a Mesolithic dispersion that could plausibly be identified with Dolgopolsky's language — though, given our great difficulties with the seemingly much simpler case of Indo-European, I am not holding my breath.

In any case, my central point here is the following: if Nostratic is real, and if Proto-Nostratic actually existed, then somebody had better be able to provide a plausible account of how a single language, spoken something like 15,000 or 20,000 years ago, could have succeeded in imposing itself over such a large area of the Old World as to give rise ultimately to most of the languages of Europe, of northern Africa, and of the larger part of Asia.

However, with this little discursus into archaeology, I am exceeding my competence, so let me return to the linguistic issues.

Outside the territory of the great families, the linguistic picture is the very opposite. Where the huge families are absent, we do not in general find merely moderate-sized families. Instead, we find great diversity: tiny families and numerous isolates, with only the occasional larger family, like Algonquian or northeast Caucasian — and most of these middle-sized families appear to be of no great time-depth. In Siberia, in New Guinea, in northern Australia, in southeast Asia, in pre-Roman Spain and Italy, and elsewhere, we find tiny families and isolates in substantial numbers. New Guinea alone, an island not much bigger than Texas, has over sixty families, in spite of the early development of agriculture in its highlands. Indeed, over half of the world's 300 or so known families are tiny, with only one to six members — and more often one. Following Bright (1992), Crystal (1997, 289) counts no fewer than 296 isolates; this figure includes some dead languages like Sumerian, but excludes other possible candidates, such as Ket (whose known relatives are all extinct) and Japanese (counted as a family of more than one language).

In fact, our standard handbooks undoubtedly underestimate the degree of diversity. For example, the Nilo-Saharan and Khoisan families proposed by Greenberg (1963) are routinely cited as secure families almost everywhere — and yet they are no such thing. Neither has ever been shown to be valid; neither has even been supported by a substantial body of evidence; and both are now being seriously questioned. There is reason to believe that both may be no more than 'dustbin' groupings — mere areal groupings sweeping up all the leftover languages that can not be fitted into the large language families adjoining them. Khoisan in particular looks uncomfortably like a collection of detritus, the miscellaneous residues of the former linguistic diversity of southern Africa, before the Bantu expansion of the last two millennia.

Nowhere is this diversity more evident than in the Americas, where specialists have so far been unable to reduce the number of established families below about 150 — and even this figure necessarily excludes an unknown number of indigenous languages which were obliterated by European settlement before they could be recorded. In spite of their comparatively recent settlement, the Americas exhibit only a few largish families like Mayan and Oto-Manguean: the overwhelming picture is one of isolates and tiny families with two, three or four members. (Here I disregard the ambitious but speculative far-flung proposals of Sapir, Greenberg and others as unsubstantiated.)

What we see in the Americas, in New Guinea, in Siberia and elsewhere satisfies that most rigorous of all academic criteria: it confirms my prejudices. I believe that, before the comparatively recent economic and technological events stressed by Renfrew, most or all of the planet must have been a crazy-quilt of thousands of isolates and tiny families, with even a middle-sized family being a rarity at best. That appears to me to be the almost inevitable outcome of many millennia of a foraging existence. In the last few thousand years, non-linguistic advantages have increasingly enabled some languages to spread and to grow into huge families, in the process obliterating the earlier diversity. Where this has not happened, we can still see that earlier diversity much as it formerly was. It is not Indo-European, but the immense diversity of the Pacific coast of North America, which best represents our linguistic past.

The problem of convergence

In fact, it is quite possible that our current picture of the world's languages significantly underestimates the degree of historical diversity. The reason for this is the existence of convergence phenomena, and above all of diffusion. It has long been known that linguistic features — words, sounds and grammatical forms — can diffuse across language boundaries, but, once again, the linguists of the past were often inclined to see diffusion as only an annoying but tractable nuisance, and not as something which could seriously disrupt the construction of family trees. But again things have changed. In recent years, and perhaps especially since the publication of Thomason & Kaufman (1988), the study of convergence phenomena has become steadily more prominent in my field. A series of astonishing examples of massive diffusion has been uncovered, and the venerable term *mixed language* has been fleshed out with indisputable instances, while my colleagues are coining a battery of new terms to label newly discovered phenomena: *metatypy*, *non-genetic language*, *portmanteau language*, and others. Models of linguistic descent based upon convergence, rather than upon the traditional divergence, have been dusted off or newly created, such as the *rhizotic model*, the *crystallization model* and the *social-network model* (Trask forthcoming). More and more linguists are arguing not only that languages can be massively affected by diffusion but even that languages need not descend from single ancestors at all.

Very prominent here is Bob Dixon's (1997) argument that Pama-Nyungan is not a language family at all, but only the result of tens of millennia of diffusion across language boundaries, but even linguists who are not prepared to scrap family trees altogether are now frequently prepared to be suspicious of proposed groupings which have already won a wide degree of acceptance. A case in point is the connection between Tlingit and Athabaskan, which was proposed by Sapir in 1915 and has recently been widely accepted, and yet some specialists are now seriously querying this proposal on the ground that the obvious resemblances are perhaps more likely to be the result of areal diffusion than of common inheritance (Campbell 1997, 286).

Convergence, of course, need not be an insuperable obstacle. In southeast Asia, for example, specialists have enjoyed some success in extracting a genetic signal from the large amount of diffusional noise: the assignment of Vietnamese to Austro-Asiatic is a good example. (See Clark 1992, 139 and Nguyên 1987, 777–8, but note also the cautious position of Schiller 1994, 2522.) Even so, we cannot hope to succeed in this without limit, and southeast Asia must be very close to the limits of what we can hope to achieve in distinguishing common ancestry from diffusion. Unless we want to claim that cases more difficult than Vietnamese cannot exist, we are forced to confront the possibility that some of our accepted groupings are chimaeras resulting from massive diffusion.

Of course, to some extent the effects of convergence conflict with the picture of almost limitless divergence and diversity that I sketched out above. But the conflict is probably more apparent than real. I have argued for a world, in the not-so-distant past, occupied by a vast number of tiny linguistic group-ings which were not, in general, discoverably related. Convergence muddies that picture, but does not destroy it. When unrelated languages converge strongly, the result may be an illusory 'family', and if, as a few of my colleagues are suggesting, convergence can actually give rise to new languages with no single ancestor, our attempts at constructing family trees must be in deep trou-ble indeed.

As I read the work now being produced by my colleagues in linguistics, together with the contributions of the archaeologists and the anthropologists, I am increasingly impressed by the direction that work is taking. We now know that language change is vastly more complex and variable in nature than was ever suspected in my student days, a quarter of a century ago, and a growing number of linguists are arguing that the relationships among speech varieties are correspondingly complex and variable. The exceptionless sound laws of the Neogrammarians have been overtaken by our direct observations of the messy ways in which languages can and do change. Today it seems a minor miracle that the Neogrammarians were as successful as they were, or that proto-lan-guages could be reconstructed in considerable detail. Clearly our venerable models of language change must possess some considerable validity, or none of this would have been possible, but more and more of us are persuaded that those models cannot represent the whole truth, or perhaps even anything close to it.

Today we can see a shift of direction in historical linguistics. Attempts at constructing ever larger family trees are still being carried out, and in some cases with success. At the same time, however, some of us are beginning to wonder whether such activity represents the best use of our time, and even whether these investigations are plausible undertakings at all. If our understanding of convergence phenomena is severely limited, we may be in danger of mistaking areal groupings for genetic families, and of reconstructing proto-languages which never existed. That is precisely the concern which worries me and some of my colleagues.

Given our limited but growing appreciation of the nature and importance of convergence, and given also my own beliefs about the almost irreducible linguistic diversity of the not-so-remote past, I can see a degree of irony in the fact that Professor Dolgopolsky has chosen this moment to present his preliminary account of the most ambitious proposal of deep genetic unity that I have ever seen — apart, of course, from those based purely upon inspection and/or speculation. To his Nostratic proposal I now turn.

The Proto-Nostratic phonological system

The set of phonemes proposed by Dolgopolsky for his Proto-Nostratic consists of fifty consonants and at least seven vowels. This is a moderately large system: for comparison, Proto-Indo-European is commonly reconstructed with 22 or 25 consonants plus a maximum of five vowels (plus vowel length). I should like to begin by comparing this Proto-Nostratic system with those recorded in the UPSID database published in Maddieson (1984), containing a sample of 317 languages.

In the UPSID data base, the largest number of consonant phonemes recorded is 95, in the Khoisan language !Xũ, of which 48 are clicks, leaving only 47 non-click consonants. The next largest totals are 60 for the North Caucasian language Lak, 56 for an unidentified variety of Arabic, and 49 for Panjabi — but all three of these totals are achieved because geminate consonants are treated as separate phonemes. If the geminates are excluded, the Lak inventory is somewhat reduced (though still prodigious), while the other two fall dramatically. The only other languages with 40 or more consonants are Kabardian (48), Haida (46), Mazahua (45), Shilha (45), Irish (44), Igbo (43), Tlingit (43), Sui (42), Otomi (41) and Hindi/Urdu (40). In every one of these languages except Irish (and also in Lak), these large totals are achieved by the systematic use as distinctive features of at least two of aspiration, glottalization, labialization and breathy voice. The Irish total results from the pervasive pairing of palatalized and non-palatalized consonants.

So, out of 317 languages, only 14 have as many as 40 consonants, representing just over 4 per cent. Only three languages have as many as 50 consonants, and all three depend either on clicks or on geminates to achieve this total: no language in the sample has 50 non-click, non-geminate consonants except perhaps for Lak, whose system appears to present some puzzles of analysis. The mean number of consonants per language in the sample is 22.8.

The principal reason for the large size of the Proto-Nostratic inventory is the presence of no fewer than twenty coronal affricates and fricatives — a startling total. For comparison, modern Georgian has just ten of these things (Catford 1991, 242), while Proto-Indo-European (PIE) had only one, the sibilant */s/ (Beekes 1995, 124). In Dolgopolsky's table of correspondences, about fifteen of these twenty merge in PIE as */s/ (or occasionally as a cluster containing */s/), while the rest mostly become */l/ or a laryngeal.

Now a total of twenty coronal affricates and fricatives is by no means inconceivable. Some of the modern North Caucasian languages (not included in the Nostratic hypothesis) have this many or more: the Bzyb dialect of Abkhaz, for example, has 27 (Catford 1991, 243), and the extinct Ubykh had 30 (Catford 1994, 487). But the posited system of twenty does not seem to have survived with any robustness in the various daughter languages recognized: as far as I can make out from the table of correspondences, the twenty were reduced to nine in Semitic, to seven in Egyptian, to two or three in Berber, to one (of course) in PIE, to nine in Uralic, to two in Turkic, to three in Mongolic, to two in Tungusic, and to one in Dravidian. (Proto-Dravidian, according to Sharpe 1994, 1064, had no sibilant consonants at all.) Only Kartvelian, with fifteen, exhibits anything close to the posited original set. (Naturally, some of these sounds in some of these languages are listed with additional *reflexes* (descendant sounds) than counted here, but these other reflexes, which in any case are not numerous, are not coronal friction sounds.)

Moreover, languages with such rich sets of coronal friction sounds are, at best, rare in the UPSID sample. The Caucasian language Lak has 20, while !Xũ has 18 (not counting the ones with click articulations). Otherwise, we find Arabic with 14 (of which 6 are mere geminates), Tlingit with 13, Kabardian and Mazahua with 12, and scarcely any other language with as many as 10. Even consonant-rich Haida has only seven.

Therefore, taking the UPSID sample as a guide, I conclude that the posited Proto-Nostratic system of 50 consonants, including 20 coronal affricates and fricatives, is at best very unusual. It appears that only North Caucasian languages and Khoisan languages even approach such figures — and neither grouping is included in the Nostratic hypothesis.

Let us now compare the Proto-Nostratic total with those found in the daughter languages. Apart from the 22 or 25 consonants of PIE, I find that Proto-Dravidian had 16 or 17 consonants (Krishnamurti 1992, 374; Steever 1998, 14), that Proto-Uralic had 17 consonants (Janhunen 1992, 208), and that a proposed version of Proto-Altaic had 18 consonants (Tekin 1994, 83). I can find no data for Proto-Kartvelian, though the modern Kartvelian languages have between 28 and 30 consonants (Catford 1994, 486). We have no accepted reconstruction for Proto-Afro-Asiatic. Still, it appears clear that the Nostratic hypothesis, as presented here, requires a very high degree of system collapse for the proto-consonants in all the daughter languages (possibly excepting the unknown Proto-Afro-Asiatic); indeed, apart perhaps from Kartvelian, we might speak of the 'meltdown' of the posited ancestral consonant system.

Now, I do not consider that a reconstructed phoneme system which is much larger than the system found in any daughter language is a fatal objection: such a state of affairs is perfectly possible. But it is not appealing, and it opens the door to an obvious question: can we, simply by multiplying proto-segments as required, obtain spurious 'systematic correspondences' wherever we require them? After all, if you will allow me to posit additional proto-segments without limit, I can probably establish spurious correspondences between any languages at all — though naturally each one of these spurious correspondences is going to be instantiated only in very few cases. Let us consider this.

The instantiation of posited correspondences

Dolgopolsky's book presents only 124 proposed cognate sets (or 125, counting the extra one listed on page 116 but absent from the body of the text; something has gone wrong with the numbering.) Of these 124 etyma (reconstructed forms), very few contain more than three consonants, and most contain no more than two. Further, quite a few of the consonants reconstructed in particular cases are generic or of uncertain phonetic quality. Consequently, it inevitably follows that very many of the fifty reconstructed consonants appear only rarely in the reconstructions. Just to pick two examples at random, Proto-Nostratic */ŝ/ appears in only one etymon (number 123 in the text, but number 124 in the final list), while */ś/ appears in only two, numbers 66 and 111. Many other consonants are similarly rare. The upshot of this paucity of occurrence is that I find it next to impossible to judge whether the reflexes claimed for the several daughter languages are actually instantiated by the data.

Since */ŝ/ occurs only once, it could be matched with any segments at all in any of the daughter languages without producing the slightest difficulty.

With */ś/, things are marginally better, with two etyma, but now we encounter the problem that the languages reported as continuing this proto-segment in entry 66 are almost entirely different from those reported in entry 111. Only Uralic occurs in both — but here we at once encounter yet another difficulty, and an even more worrying one. While the Uralic reflex given under 66 does indeed match the Uralic continuation listed for */ś/ in the table of correspondences, the Uralic reflex given in 111 does not: instead of the claimed Uralic */ś/, we find */ć/ given. To be fair, Dolgopolsky notes this problem and suggests a solution, but that solution involves both a hypothetical assimilation and a hypothetical dissimilation — not impossible, but certainly not encouraging.

Before I am accused of deliberate obstructivism, let me stress that I did indeed pluck these two segments from the inventory essentially at random, subject only to the constraint that I wanted characters that I could easily print. Naturally, I was expecting that the unmarked consonants, the ones that are most frequent in the world's languages, would prove to be far more frequent in the etyma, but here I received a surprise. The next segment I checked was */s/. Now /s/ is the least marked of all fricatives, and Maddieson (1984, 44) reports that 83 per cent of the languages in the UPSID database possess an /s/, and further that /s/ is present in 88.5 per cent of all languages that have any fricatives at all. Moreover, while I have no data, I am impressionistically persuaded that /s/ is usually a consonant of high frequency of occurrence in those languages that have it. Yet, in the 124 Proto-Nostratic etyma listed, */s/ occurs in *none at all*, save only in a possible variant form of number 113. I find this astonishing. It would appear that Proto-Nostratic */s/ was vanishingly rare, and certainly rarer than the more highly marked friction sounds reconstructed, such as the various ejectives and voiceless laterals. Proto-Nostratic is beginning to look like a language with a very odd phonological system indeed.

However, I am possibly in danger of focusing too narrowly on peripheral details. To counterbalance this, I propose in the next section to undertake an examination of what I hope will be a representative sample of the comparisons on offer.

The etyma containing */m/

The consonant /m/ is one of the least marked of all consonants, and, unsurprisingly, it is comparatively frequent in the Proto-Nostratic etyma, occurring in 18 of the 124. Here I propose to look at these 18.

6.   'monkey', really consists of a Dravidian word for 'monkey' plus some names for particular species of monkey in Tungusic and one Chadic language. I do not consider this substantial.

13.   'water body', involves only Afro-Asiatic and Samoyedic — too small a set to be persuasive.

14.   'water body', includes watery words from Indo-European, Egyptian, one Chadic language, Kartvelian and Mongolic. This is a little better, though the Chadic witness should probably be disregarded, but the range of senses permitted — 'sea', 'lake', 'pool, channel', 'haven', 'river' — makes the possibility of chance resemblances not insignificant, especially since the reconstructed form, */moRE/, involves just one unmarked consonant and one generic consonant.

19.   '(female) breast', strongly overlaps with the global etymology proposed by Greenberg & Ruhlen (1992, 64–5), which embraces a number of languages in North and South America. The languages cited are Indo-European, Arabic, Egyptian, Somali and Finno-Ugric. The phonological matches, apart from Egyptian, are reasonably good, and the semantic range — 'milk', 'suck', 'female breast', 'chest, breast' — is not outrageous, though still generous.

21.   'tasty beverage', involves Finno-Ugric, Turkic, Laz, East Cushitic and Indo-European. The semantics is troubling: 'tree sap' or 'milk' in Finno-Ugric, 'honey' in Indo-European, '(butter)milk' in Laz. Given that Greek /meli/ 'honey' is cited here, I cannot resist mischievously noting Hawaiian /meli/ 'honey'.

35.   'miss one's aim', involves Finno-Ugric, Indo-European and West Chadic. The forms are fine, but the semantics is deeply disturbing: 'miss one's mark, be mistaken' versus '(in) vain, liar, deceit' versus 'forget'. This is too much semantic latitude.

40.   'aurochs, wild bovine', involves only Dravidian and a word from one dialect of Georgian. This is insubstantial.

59.   'mulberries, blackberries', involves a larger number of languages: Indo-

European, Egyptian (though the word is described by Dolgopolsky as of 'questionable' reality), Kartvelian, Finno-Ugric, Turkic and Korean. The semantics is better than average, as all the words denote berries except for the Korean word, which means 'grapes' — and grapes were formerly called 'wineberries' in English. Again, though, */mar[y]V/ is not a very distinctive form.

60. 'a kind of berry', involves Finno-Ugric, Tungusic, Arabic and Indo-European, of which the last two are marked as deeply questionable. Given the doubtful semantics and the unexplained extra material in Tungusic, this looks very much like a collection of miscellaneous resemblances.

62. 'root, root-crops, edible roots', involves Indo-European and Dravidian, more or less representing the cited sense, but with phonological problems, and East Cushitic and Tungusic representing the sense of 'tendon' or something similar. This is far too much semantic leeway.

63. 'pound, crumble, gnaw/smash into pieces', involves Indo-European, Semitic, Uralic and Mongolic. The matches are respectable, though the 'gnaw' senses are troubling.

66. 'meat', compares Uralic with Indo-European and Egyptian items of the wrong form and a doubtful Arabic word. Here the forms require a good deal of special pleading.

69. 'liver', involves only Egyptian, North Omotic and Uralic, of which Dolgopolsky acknowledges that the first two have the wrong forms.

71. 'egg', cites Uralic, some very dubious Chadic data, Dravidian and Slavonic. The semantic variation between 'egg' and 'testicle' is quite acceptable, but suitable comparanda apparently occur nowhere in Indo-European except in Slavonic, which has long been in contact with Uralic.

75. '(a kind of) fish', features only Indo-European and Dravidian, plus a very questionable addition from Finno-Ugric. The difficulty here is the citation of a variety of words for particular varieties of fish: there must be enough named varieties of fish to provide plenty of scope for chance resemblances.

79. 'honey', features Indo-European, Dravidian, Omotic and a single East Chadic language. This looks a little better than some of the other comparisons.

105. 'sinciput, crown of the head, top, tip', involves Arabic, Cushitic, Georgian, Slavonic, Mongolic and Tungusic, among which the Mongolic is semantically deviant. The remaining forms look respectable, but are extracted from low-ranking branches of their families.

116. 'mother', featuring Afro-Asiatic, Uralic and all three branches of Altaic, looks far too much like a nursery word: something like /ama/ for 'mother' is found all over the planet. Surely such words should not be used as comparanda.

In sum, then, my evaluation of this small and unscientific, but perhaps not unrepresentative, sample of the comparisons on offer is that they may be consistent with a remote genetic link among the languages cited but that they are also consistent with a set of chance resemblances supplemented by a few ancient loans and one obvious nursery word.

Before I sum up, I would like to turn to another point.

Identical correspondences

Above I drew attention to the seeming collapse of the posited Proto-Nostratic coronal friction contrasts in the various daughter languages. Here I want to point to a very different feature of Dolgopolsky's reconstructions, one which also troubles me: the pervasive occurrence, apart from those coronal friction sounds, of identical correspondences.

The posited Proto-Nostratic labial, coronal and velar plosives overwhelmingly remain unchanged in the table of correspondences. Apart from a few lenitions in medial position, and the odd shift of voicing, we seem to find */p/ continued almost everywhere as /p/, */b/ as /b/, */k/ as /k/, and so on. And these failures to do anything much, recall, occupied a time-period of many millennia. In a much shorter period, PIE */p/ changed to /f/ in Germanic, to /h/, /w/ or /v/ in Armenian, and to zero in Celtic, while the PIE velars underwent fairly dramatic changes in Germanic, Slavonic, Romance and elsewhere, quite apart from the assibilation in the satem languages of the inherited plosives sometimes reconstructed as */k' g' gh'/.

Similarly, the posited */m/ just remains /m/ everywhere, apart from the occasional fortition to /b/, and /n/ appears to do almost nothing at all except to remain /n/. The posited */s/ remains /s/ almost everywhere except in Dravidian, or occasionally shifts to another sibilant. Those labile consonants, the liquids, exhibit only a modest tendency to shift to anything else, and even the glides */w/ and */j/ (= */y/) seem to be outstandingly stable in the majority of the daughter languages. Apart from the back consonants, which frequently disappear, there are very few instances of the conversion of anything to zero.

This troubles me. Over the time-depth we are supposedly dealing with here, I would expect to see complex and sometimes dramatic phonological changes affecting most of the daughter languages. In Indo-European and elsewhere, over a much shorter time-scale, we are presented with numerous examples of changes like /p/ > /h/ > zero (Celtic, Japanese, some Dravidian languages), /s/ or /ʃ/ > /h/ > zero (Hawaiian, Greek, Costanoan), /k/ > /x/ > /h/ > zero (Germanic), /g/ > /j/ (= /y/) (English), /n/ > zero (Portuguese, Basque), /w/ > zero (Greek), /t/ > /k/ (some Austronesian languages, some Athabaskan languages), /kʷ/ > /p/ or /b/ (Brythonic, Greek, Muskogean), /r/ > /t/, /tʃ/ or /j/ (some Mayan languages), and so on, either categorically or in some positions. Why do we find so few examples of such changes in the table of correspondences? Are we supposed to believe that phonological change was vastly slower in the Mesolithic than what we can observe in the last few thousand years? If so, I am not happy. Our linguistic version of the scientists' Uniformitarian Principle requires that ancient languages should not be different from modern ones, and a much lower rate of change looks to me like a violation of that principle.

Just to cite one familiar example, English in the last 1000 years alone has undergone the lenition or loss of the inherited velars /k g x/ in many positions, as well as lenition or loss in some positions of /b f l/ (and in some varieties of /r/). At the same time, English has acquired, by various means, eight new consonant phonemes which were absent in Pre-Old English (/tʃ dʒ ʃ ʒ ð v z ŋ/). Nor is English exceptional: in the last 1500 or 2000 years, the changes in the consonant systems of French, German, Swedish, Russian, Greek and other languages have been comparably substantial.

Especially to the non-linguists, it may look as though I am being a little perverse here, by complaining that the phonological matches are too good. But my experience has been that, except in the case of a very shallow family, we should routinely expect to see a substantial proportion of non-obvious correspondences like those illustrated by English fish, Spanish pez 'fish' and Irish iasg 'fish', all of which are cognate, or by Greek ikhthys 'fish', Lithuanian žuvis 'fish', Old Prussian suckis 'fish' and Armenian jukn 'fish', which are also cognate, according to Buck (1949, table 3.65) and Pokorny (1959: I, 416). The really good-looking matches, like Latin piscis 'fish' and Cornish pisc 'fish', result as often as not from borrowing, as in this case, or from chance, as with Malay ikan 'fish', Hixkaryana (Brazil) kana 'fish', and Japanese sakana 'fish'.

A sideways glance at Basque

While working through the book, I was occasionally startled to encounter a posited Proto-Nostratic etymon that bore a striking resemblance to a word in my own favourite language, Basque. Now Basque is not included in the Nostratic hypothesis, and by rights it ought not to show more than the occasional vague resemblance to anything in Nostratic. Moreover, Basque is, on the face of it, a most implausible language for exhibiting many chance resemblances to the Nostratic etyma on offer: native Basque words do not normally begin with any of /p t k d r/; they do not normally contain /m/ at all except when that /m/ is secondary; the permitted word-initial consonants are few, and about half of native words begin with vowels; and Basque has no post-velar consonants except where these are of very recent origin. Since the Nostratic etyma proposed are invariably consonant-initial, and since the majority of them begin with a voiceless plosive, /m/ or a post-velar consonant, good-looking chance resemblances should be exceedingly few. On top of this, a number of the Nostratic etyma involve things like 'leopard', 'hyena', 'monkey', 'frozen soil', 'salty desert', 'aurochs' and 'pistachio', none of which is relevant to the region in which Basque is spoken. Finally, Basque has been in intense contact with Latin and Romance for 2000 years; its lexicon has been very heavily affected as a result, and doubtless very many indigenous words have disappeared. Still and all, I have decided that listing the resemblances that leap out at me is worth doing. Here they are.

[5]   */ʔoɾ[u]/ 'antelope (male), deer': Basque /oɾein/ 'deer' looks a splendid match, better then some of the comparanda cited.

[17]   */gaL∇/ 'cereals': Basque /gaɾi/ 'wheat' is a perfect match, especially since we know that it derives from earlier */gali/ (intervocalic */l/ categorically changed to /ɾ/ in the early medieval period).

[24]   */pat[a]/ 'box': regional Basque /pataʃa/ 'bottle' constitutes a weak match.

[51]   */ʔlhUr∇/ 'squirrel': Basque /urtʃintʃa/ 'squirrel' looks a decent match, given that /tʃintʃa/ is a common imitative form applied to various noises from blowing one's nose to jingling a small bell — possibly here to the animal's chattering?

[59]   */mar[y]∇/ 'mulberries, blackberries': Basque /marrubi/ 'strawberry' and eastern Basque /marruga/ 'blackberry' seem excellent matches.

[68]   */ʔayŋo/ 'marrow, brain, soft fat of animals': Basque /huiɲ/ ~ /hun/ ~ /un/ 'pith, marrow, brain' looks a very decent match.

[81]   ?*/buR∇/ 'flint, cut with a flint': Basque /burtsi/ 'spear', whose formation is opaque, would not seem out of place here.

[84]   */boruʕlɣ∇/ 'trunk (of tree)': Basque /enbor/ 'tree-trunk' is not the worst match imaginable.

[91]   */k[a]k[w]∇/ 'tooth, claw', 'hook': Basque /kako/ ~ /gako/ 'hook' is a fine match.

[101] */piχlɣyA/ 'sharp bone, sharp tool': Basque /pika/ 'pick' (a pointed tool) is, of course, a loan word from Romance, though the Romance source is not here connected with the Nostratic etymon.

[111] */śeʒA/ 'a relative from the other moiety': Basque /śuhi/ 'son-in-law' provides a fairly decent match.

[114] */Hićlcχ∇/ 'father, head of a family': Basque /aita/ 'father' matches about as well as some of the other comparanda.

[116] */ʔemA/ 'mother': Both Basque /ama/ 'mother' and /eme/ 'female' (which are unrelated) constitute magnificent matches.

[118] ??*/ʔaba/ 'daddy, father': Amusingly, many Basque dictionaries list the word /aba/ 'father', but this word is a nineteenth-century invention.

[122] */ʕ[a]l∇/ 'burn, use magic means to produce a particular result': Given that the claimed reflexes of this include items meaning 'pray, promise,

devote, curse, scold', I might mention Basque /ala/, a word used in swearing allegiance, as in /ala jainkoa/ 'by God!/. There is also a noun /ala/ 'torment'.

So, out of just 124 etyma, I have noticed no fewer than fifteen Basque resemblances which look surprisingly good to me. Given the difficulties explained above, this strikes me as rather more than I might have expected. Now, I certainly do not want to be known as the person who introduced Basque into the Nostratic hypothesis: I am doing no such thing. But this amusing little exercise does suggest to me that chance resemblances between arbitrary languages are by no means so difficult to find as is sometimes suggested. And note that I have only cited the cases that leapt off the page at me: I have not scoured a large Basque dictionary looking for possible matches, and I am confident that, especially with a little more semantic generosity, a dogged search would turn up a number of further plausible-looking matches, at least as good as many of those cited by Dolgopolsky for modern languages.

Conclusions

Like many linguists, I am deeply skeptical of the very possibility of identifying genetic links at the kind of time-depth envisaged here: my prejudice, based upon decades of experience, is that language change is just too rapid and too remorseless. Moreover, like some of my colleagues, I am beginning to have a few doubts about the general validity of our venerable family-tree model of linguistic descent, and I am beginning to suspect that we have underestimated the importance of diffusion across language boundaries. In addition, as I explained above, I have some difficulty with the idea of a vast language family spreading across much of Eurasia some 15,000 or 20,000 years ago, as apparently required by the Nostratic hypothesis.

Nevertheless, I do not consider the Nostratic hypothesis to be *a priori* out of court. This hypothesis deserves the most careful scrutiny from the rest of us. Unlike so many self-styled 'long-rangers', Professor Dolgopolsky and his colleagues have rejected the mere assembly of miscellaneous lookalikes — an activity which is little better than a waste of time, in my view — in favour of the more rigorous methods which are the only ones that have ever brought us success in these enterprises.

I am also aware that the Nostratic enterprise consists of something larger than what is contained in *NM*. Still, that book is what is in front of us, and we have been asked to base our remarks directly upon it.

And I am not persuaded. We do indeed have a lengthy table of proposed systematic correspondences in sound linking most of the posited daughter languages. But those involving the unmarked consonants like /p/, /s/ and /m/ exhibit an extraordinarily large number of identical correspondences across many, many thousands of years, and suggest a distressing lack of ordinary phonological change of the type which so commonly makes our lives difficult even in well-established families. At the same time, the very large set of reconstructed coronal affricates and fricatives, which collapses into a much smaller set in almost all the daughters, looks worryingly like a device for forcing refractory segments into correspondences which may not exist, especially since each of them is instantiated so rarely in any given set of daughters.

In fact, I am altogether troubled by the paucity of instances of any given set of correspondences in the present book, a consequence which is perhaps inevitable when we have only 124 lexical sets to look out, but made worse when so few daughters are cited as witnesses in any given set. And I am further troubled by the practice of 'reaching down' within a family, so that, for example, Afro-Asiatic is represented only by Arabic, or only by Omotic plus one solitary Chadic language, or Indo-European is represented only by Slavonic, or Kartvelian is represented only by a single dialect of Georgian. As comparanda, I would much prefer to see Proto-Kartvelian forms reconstructed by specialists in Kartvelian with no stake in the Nostratic hypothesis, and PIE forms reconstructed in a comparable way. Reaching down just provides far too many opportunities for obtaining spurious matches.

Also complicating any scrutiny of proposed correspondences is the large measure of phonetic blur in the etyma: the frequent presence of generic segments like *R and *K, the presence of segments of uncertain phonetic quality like *l/ḷ, and the existence of segments whose very presence is uncertain, like *[w]. Doubtless such blur is unavoidable in this kind of work, but it also has the effect of making matches easier to find: something like */Sah[i]bV/ (number 11) is easier to match than a more explicit form like */sahibe/ would be.

Nor am I happy with the semantics. I have already drawn attention to one or two cases of unacceptable semantic latitude, but there's another problem: some of the comparisons, including a few of the best-looking ones, involve remarkably specific senses like 'leopard', 'monkey', 'pistachio' and 'fig tree', which are not exactly the kinds of words I would expect to be most resistant to replacement, more so than items of basic vocabulary like 'eye' or 'two'. I have to wonder if we are not looking at a few loan words here.

Consequently, I am not persuaded. In my view, the linguistic evidence in front of us here does not add up to a substantial case for the reality of a Proto-Nostratic parent language which gave rise to a vast family of languages. Naturally, I am not yet flatly rejecting the Nostratic proposal. When further evidence becomes available for Professor Dolgopolsky's proposal, I will try to evaluate it as fairly as I can. For now, though, I must remain a sceptic.

References

Asher, R.E. & J.M.Y. Simpson (eds.), 1994. *The Encyclopedia of Language and Linguistics.* 10 vols. Oxford: Pergamon.

Beekes, R.S.P., 1995. *Comparative Indo-European Linguistics: an Introduction.* Amsterdam: John Benjamins.

Bellwood, P., 1997. Prehistoric cultural explanations for widespread language families, in McConvell & Evans (eds.), 123–34.

Bright, W. (ed.), 1992. *International Encyclopedia of Linguistics.* 4 vols. Oxford: Oxford University Press.

Buck, C.D., 1949. *A Dictionary of Selected Synonyms in the Principal Indo-European Languages.* Chicago (IL): University of Chicago Press.

Campbell, L., 1997. *American Indian Languages: the Historical Linguistics of Native America.* New York (NY): Oxford University Press.

Catford, J.C., 1991. The classification of Caucasian languages, in *Sprung from Some Common Source: Investigations into the Prehistory of Languages*, eds. S.M. Lamb & E.D. Mitchell. Stanford (CA): Stanford University Press, 232–68.

Catford, J.C., 1994. 'Caucasian languages', in Asher & Simpson (eds.), 486–9.

Clark, R., 1992. Austro-Asiatic languages, in Bright (ed.), vol. 1, 137–45.

Crystal, D., 1997. *The Cambridge Encyclopedia of Language.* 2nd edition. Cambridge: Cambridge University Press.

Dixon, R.M.W., 1997. *The Rise and Fall of Languages.* Cambridge: Cambridge University Press.

Dolgopolsky, A., 1998. *The Nostratic Macrofamily and Linguistic Palaeontology.* (Papers in the Prehistory of Languages.) Cambridge: The McDonald Institute for Archaeological Research.

Evans, N. & R. Jones, 1997. The cradle of the Pama-Nyungans: archaeological and linguistic speculations, in McConvell & Evans (eds.), 385–417.

Greenberg, J., 1963. *The Languages of Africa.* Bloomington (IN): Indiana University Press.

Greenberg, J. & M. Ruhlen, 1992. Linguistic origins of native Americans. *Scientific American* 267 (November), 60–65.

Janhunen, J., 1992. Uralic languages, in Bright (ed.), vol. 4, 205–10.

Krishnamurti, B., 1992. Dravidian languages, in Bright (ed.), vol. 1, 373–8.

McConvell, P. & N. Evans (eds.), 1997. *Archaeology and Linguistics: Aboriginal Australia in Global Perspective.* Melbourne: Oxford University Press.

Maddieson, I., 1984. *Patterns of Sounds.* Cambridge: Cambridge University Press.

Nguyên, D-ình-Hoà, 1987. Vietnamese, in *The World's Major Languages*, ed. B. Comrie. London: Croom Helm, 777–96.

Pokorny, J., 1959. *Indogermanisches Etymologisches Wörterbuch.* 2 vols. Bern: Francke.

Renfrew, C., 1992. World languages and human dispersals: a minimalist view, in *Transition to Modernity: Essays on Power, Wealth and Belief*, eds. J.A. Hall & I.C. Jarvie. Cambridge: Cambridge University Press, 11–68.

Renfrew, C., 1994. World linguistic diversity. *Scientific American* 270 (January), 104–10.

Renfrew, C., 1995. Language families as evidence of human dispersals, in *The Origin and Past of Modern Humans as Viewed from DNA*, eds. S. Brenner & K. Hanihara. Singapore: World Scientific, 285–306.

Sapir, E., 1915. The Na-Dene languages, a preliminary report. *American Anthropologist* 17, 534–58.

Schiller, E., 1994. Mon-Khmer languages, in Asher & Simpson (eds.), 2522–3.

Sharpe, R., 1994. Dravidian languages, in Asher & Simpson (eds.), 1063–5.

Steever, S.B., 1998. Introduction to the Dravidian languages, in *The Dravidian Languages*, ed. S.B. Steever. London: Routledge, 1–39.

Tekin, T., 1994. Altaic languages, in Asher & Simpson (eds.), 82–5.

Thomason, S.G. & T. Kaufman, 1988. *Language Contact, Creolization, and Genetic Linguistics*. Berkeley (CA): University of California Press.

Trask, R.L., forthcoming. *The Dictionary of Historical and Comparative Linguistics*. Edinburgh: Edinburgh University Press.

Part III
Methodological Reflections

Chapter 9

Nostratic and linguistic palaeontology in methodological perspective

Lyle Campbell

In this paper I attempt to assess the evidence Dolgopolsky (1998) has presented for his Nostratic hypothesis and associated claims involving linguistic palaeontology from a methodological perspective. In doing this, I hope to show why the vast majority of historical linguists do not accept the Nostratic proposal. Nearly all of Dolgopolsky's 124 Nostratic lexical sets exhibit serious problems from the point of view of methodology, meaning the hypothesis of genetic relationship among the language families involved is not adequately supported and provides no adequate foundation for inferences about prehistory. There are lessons to be derived from such a methodological assessment for both research on proposed 'macrofamilies' and linguistic palaeontology.

1. Introduction

Both believers in Nostratic and non-believers agree on the importance of methodology and, importantly, both hold faith in the same methodological principles. That is, there is general agreement upon the methods, principles, and criteria involved in research on distant genetic relationships (proposed 'macrofamilies'). Methodology is important also in another sense, because others do not always understand how we linguists practise our craft. Renfrew (1998, viii) reports that 'the discipline of historical linguistics has had some difficulty, or so it would seem, in evaluating the claims of those who have proposed the existence of various macrofamilies'. This, however, only appears so to non-linguists. In fact, historical linguists have little difficulty in evaluating proposed macrofamilies — the methodological principles are tried and true, and accepted by all (with the exception of Greenberg, whose 'multilateral comparison' has been rejected by nearly all practising historical linguists). Where linguists part company is over how these methods are employed in actual practice. The goal of this paper is to attempt to assess Dolgopolsky's (1998, henceforth *NM*) Nostratic hypothesis and associated linguistic palaeontology from the perspective of methodology. I begin with an overview of how *NM*'s 124 proposed Nostratic cognate sets fare in the light of general methodological criteria. (Naturally, as other participants in the symposium also pointed out, it would be better if the 'more than 2300' sets in Dolgopolsky's forthcoming Nostratic etymological dictionary were available for evaluation, but the task assigned here is to address those currently available in *NM*.) Following this, I discuss typological and areal linguistic considerations, and then finally *NM*'s linguistic palaeontology.

A proposed distant genetic relationship (macrofamily) is a hypothesized family relationship among groups of languages not yet demonstrated to be related. How claims about remote linguistic kinship are evaluated is the topic of this paper. Linguistic classification is about the relationships among languages. A language family is a group of genetically related languages, i.e. languages which share a linguistic kinship by virtue of having developed from a common ancestor. A number of terms have also been used for postulated but unproven higher order, more inclusive putative families (proposed distant genetic relationships), *stock, phylum,* and the compounding element '*macro-*' (as in *Macro-Mayan, Macro-Penutian,* or *macrofamily*) — what Lass (1997) calls *hypertaxa.* These terms have proven confusing and controversial, as might be expected when names are at stake for entities that are not fully agreed to exist. If the postulated relationship were confirmed, it would simply become a language family, and the families which make up its constituents would become subgroups of the more inclusive family. Since 'stocks', 'phyla', and 'macrofamilies' would be *bona fide* language families if they were could be demonstrated (and they will not be families if they do not hold up), it is better to avoid the confusing terms and to refer to these putative but unsubstantiated relationships as just 'proposed distant genetic relationships'.

Dolgopolsky's version of the 'Nostratic macrofamily' classifies together as its branches (constituent families): Indo-European, Hamito-Semitic (Afroasiatic), Uralic (including also Yukagir), Altaic (including Turkic, Mongolic, Tungusic, Korean, and Japanese), and Dravidian (and at least in [119] also Gilyak as an additional branch). There are several difficulties for *NM* which have to do with questions of sheer classification. There is dispute over what the postulated Nostratic family's members might be and how they are to be classified. First, there is dispute over the status of some of the entities ascribed to Nostratic; for example, the validity of Altaic, a proposed macrofamily itself, is contested (see below); the classification of Yukagir with Uralic is rejected by most leading Uralicists; and some of the members of Afroasiatic are controversial. Second, there are a number of competing proposals for Nostratic which disagree concerning what languages and families should be assigned to it. For example, does Afroasiatic belong in Nostratic, or is it outside of Nostratic but related as a sister to it, or is it just unrelated to the other proposed Nostratic languages (cf. Starostin 1989, 42; this volume; Shevoroshkin, this volume)? Dolgopolsky's earlier work on Nostratic excluded Dravidian but was sympathetic to the possibility of 'Chuckchi-Kamchatkan' also being included. Starostin (1989, 43, 44; this volume) excludes Afroasiatic, but includes Eskimo-Aleut and 'Chuckchee-Kamchatkan' as quite probably included in Nostratic. Bomhard & Kerns' (1994, 2, 34) and Bomhard's (this volume) version of Nostratic includes Indo-European, Uralic-Yukaghir, Elamo-Dravidian, and Altaic, with Sumerian also as a possibility, but equivocates over whether Afroasiatic really belongs in Nostratic or may be a parallel sister to Nostratic. Other proposals would add several other groups in one of two ways, either by placing the new languages directly within Nostratic, or by assuming that they are not actually part of Nostratic itself but rather are related to it as sister branches of some higher-order macrofamily which would also include Nostratic as one of its branches. The groups involved in these expanded proposals include Eskimo-Aleut, various American Indian groups, Yeniseian, Gilyak (Nivkh), Sumerian, Elamite (with Dravidian), Sino-Tibetan, North-Caucasian, among others (cf. Bomhard & Kerns 1994, 3, 34; Shevoroshkin 1989; this volume; Starostin 1989, 43; 1991; this volume). Greenberg's (1990; 1991; forthcoming) Eurasiatic hypothesis was not intended to be equated with Nostratic (but see Dolgopolsky this volume), since the languages he includes coincide only in part with those of Nostratic. Eurasiatic overlaps Nostratic by including Indo-European, Uralic, Yukaghir, Altaic, Korean, and Japanese; it differs by excluding Dravidian, Kartvelian, and Afroasiatic, and by further including Ainu, Nivkh (Gilyak), Chukotian, and Eskimo-Aleut. Still, Greenberg holds that these Eurasiatic languages and the other putative Nostratic languages are related, but more distantly (Greenberg 1990, 88). Third, even among competing Nostratic hypotheses that are more consistent with one another with respect to language membership there are disagreements about what the sound correspondences among these languages are and, consequently, about what words may be considered cognates. For Dolgopolsky, Indo-European $*b$, $*d$, $*g$ < Nostratic p, t, k respectively, and Indo-European $*p$, $*t$, $*k$ < Nostratic p', t', k' (glottalized), but for Bomhard (traditional) Indo-European $*b$, $*d$, $*g$ < his Nostratic p', t', k', and Indo-European $*p$, $*t$, $*k$ < his Nostratic p, t, k. That is, Bomhard accepts the glottalic theory for Indo-European, but the glottalic and traditional views of Indo-European phonology require entirely different sound correspondences, found in different proposed cognate sets (cf. Bomhard & Kerns 1994; Kaiser & Shevoroshkin 1987). These are serious disagreements. Fourth, numerous other 'macrofamilies' have been proposed which overlap partially with Nostratic by assigning to radically different classifications one or more of the entities *NM* places in Nostratic. For example, different proposed distant genetic relationships would relate Japanese variously with Altaic, Austronesian, Thai, Austric, Dravidian, Papuan, and others (cf. Benedict 1975; 1990). Other proposals would link Dravidian with Elamite, Uralic, Altaic, Japanese, Austric, Sumerian, and various African families (not to mention a full contingent of truly fringe proposals) (Zvelebil 1990, 99–123). There are similar lists of variously proposed remote relationships for all the language groups in *NM*. As Janhunen (1996a, 246) points out, 'there exist other hypotheses which, by objective criteria, have to be regarded as equally well, or equally poorly, justified'. These comparable but contradictory groupings cannot all be correct, and Nostraticists need to face this problem, but so far have not. I agree with Janhunen (1996a, 246) that 'all this makes it impossible for the neutral observer to make a final choice between the alternative comparative frameworks [competing macrofamily proposals] . . . the fundamental *lack* of a consensus in the . . . comparisons suggests that there may be no scientifically recoverable truth at all' (see Campbell 1998a for discussion).

A misconception outside of linguistics is that a family relationship might be established just by amassing a bunch of shared similarities among the languages compared. However, for the historical linguist, this assembling of shared similarities is just the beginning, since similarities can be due also to borrowing, chance, onomatopoeia, and other factors (see Campbell 1998b). This being the case, the principles and criteria linguists rely on have to do with attempting to eliminate any other factor that might explain particular shared similarities, leaving inheritance from a common ancestor the most likely explanation for why the languages share the elements in question. Unfortunately, for some proposals of distant genetic relationship, the alternative explanations appear just as strong or stronger than the possibility of shared inheritance. It is the belief of those who do not accept the Nostratic hypothesis that the evidence amassed for it does not succeed in showing that other possible explanations do not account for the assembly of forms offered in support. In this paper, I will address some, not all, of the standard criteria in an effort to show why many of the 124 'Nostratic' sets offered in *NM* are not accepted by other historical linguists. In this context, I end this introduction with the definition of 'Nostratic' given in Matthews' (1997, 247) dictionary:

> **Nostratic**: Conjectural family of languages whose branches are usually said to include at least Indo-European, Afro-Asiatic, Altaic, Dravidian, Kartvelian, and Uralic. Divers others are added by divers enthusiasts . . . An old con-

> jecture, but despite continuing attempts to give substance to it, still the
> kind of hypothesis one believes to the extent that one believes in that kind
> of hypothesis.

This reflects the caution with which most historical linguists approach the Nostratic hypothesis. In this paper, I attempt to show why they doubt the hypothesis and why this caution is appropriate.

2. General methodological evaluation

In this section, I look at *NM*'s 124 lexical comparison sets from the perspective of the standard principles for investigating proposed 'macrofamilies'. The data do not hold up well when looked at in this way, in spite of the fact that these criteria are accepted by almost all linguists, including Nostraticists (cf. Campbell 1998a).

Proposals of distant genetic relationship usually begin with assembled similarities among the compared languages. However, similarities can be due not only to inheritance from a common ancestor (from Proto-Nostratic in this claim), but also to several other factors, including borrowing, accident, onomatopoeia, sound symbolism, nursery formations, and so on. The standard method for assessing proposed 'macrofamilies' which are not yet established requires the investigation of these similarities to eliminate those which have plausible non-genetic explanations, so that those which survive may potentially represent inheritance from an earlier ancestor and constitute support for the proposed family relationship. To the extent that the similarity among forms presented as evidence is potentially explained by factors other than inheritance from a common ancestor, it will not be considered persuasive. Unfortunately, the large majority of Dolgopolsky's data do not eliminate other possible explanations, leaving historical linguists to doubt the proposal. In the following consideration of some of the standard criteria for investigating 'macrofamily' claims, I attempt to show why this doubt is justified.

2.1. *'Regular sound correspondences'*
Problems with sound correspondences are perhaps the most serious for Dolgopolsky's thesis. Most scholars, including Nostraticists, insist that regular sound correspondences are necessary (or at least very helpful) for the demonstration of linguistic affinity. While sound correspondences are of fundamental importance, they can be misused, and it is important to understand how this can be in order to see why most historical linguists reject Nostratic, in spite of its claimed adherence to this principle.

There are a number of ways in which the criterion of sound correspondences can be misapplied and misinterpreted. Sometimes corresponding sounds can be found in loanwords. For example, by Grimm's law real French–English cognates exhibit the correspondence p : f, as in père/father, pied/foot, pour/for. However, French and English appear to exhibit also the correspondence p : p where English has borrowed from French or Latin, as in paternel/paternal, piédestal/pedestal, per/per. Since English has many such loans, examples illustrating this bogus p : p sound correspondence abound. In comparing languages not yet known to be related, we must avoid the problem of undetected loans and the illegitimate sound correspondences they can offer. Generally, sound correspondences found in basic vocabulary are legitimate, not found just in loans, since basic vocabulary is borrowed only infrequently. However, even basic vocabulary can be borrowed, though more rarely. For example, Finnish äiti 'mother' and tytär 'daughter' are borrowed from Indo-European languages; if these loans were not recognized, one would suspect a sound correspondence of t : d involving the medial consonant of äiti (cf. Old High German eidī) and the initial consonant of tytär (cf. Germanic *dohtēr) based on these basic vocabulary items (found also in other loans). Below we see that borrowing is a serious problem for many of *NM* sets, one source of doubts about the proposed Nostratic sound correspondences.

Another source of some non-genuine sound correspondences is accidentally similar words. Languages can share some similar vocabulary by sheer accident, e.g. Proto-Je *niw 'new'/English new; Kaqchikel mes 'mess, garbage'/English mess; Zuni nas 'wet'/German nass 'wet', and the famous examples of Persian bad/English bad, and Malay mata 'eye'/Modern Greek mati 'eye', to mention just a few examples which illustrate this. Other cases of unreal sound correspondences turn up when semantic latitude in proposed cognates is permitted, where phonetically similar but semantically disparate forms are equated. For example, in Pipil (Uto-Aztecan) teki 'to cut' : Finnish teki 'made', teːn 'mouth' : teen 'of the tea', tukat 'spider': tukat 'hairs', tilaːn 'pulled': tilaan 'into the space', tuːlin 'cattails, reeds': tuulin 'by the wind', etc., we notice a t : t correspondence (and these forms also show k : k, n : n, and l : l recurrent correspondences, not to mention the vowel correspondences). However, the sound correspondence in these compared words is accidental, since it is always possible to find phonetically similar words among languages if their meanings are ignored, as in these sets. With semantic permissiveness it is easy to come up with spurious correspondences such as the Pipil-Finnish t : t. Unfortunately, wide semantic latitude is another serious problem for Nostratic (see below). Other non-inherited phonetic similarities crop up when onomatopoetic, sound-symbolic, and nursery forms are compared (Nostratic examples below). A set of proposed cognates involving a combination of loans, accidental similarity enhanced by semantic latitude, onomatopoeia, and such factors may exhibit false sound correspondences. For this reason, some proposed remote relationships which purportedly are based on regular sound correspondences nevertheless fail to be convincing. This appears to be what is behind the proposed Nostratic sound correspondences and is a principal reason why most historical linguists doubt the hypothesis.

Dolgopolsky's treatment of his forms raises other problems with regard to sound correspondences. He has 15 different notational devices which he calls 'uncertainty signs' (NM, 15–16). These include the use of 'I', as in 'aIe', to mean either a or e, but uncertainty as to which; capital letters to denote uncertainty in a class of sounds, e.g. 'S', an unspecified sibilant or lateral obstruent; ∇ or V is an unspecified vowel; [], as [a], 'uncertainty brackets' (Dolgopolsky uses two kinds of half brackets, the upper half in some cases and the lower half in others, but since my fonts do not have these notations, I use [] for both) ; ** 'a questionable reconstruction'; *° 'a reconstruction based on one daughter- or grand-daughter-language' (a practice not licensed in standard historical linguistic procedures, called 'reaching down' by Larry Trask, a term also used by others in the symposium, see below); ? 'a questionable Nostratic etymology or questionable cognate' (Dolgopolsky on occasion lists forms with as many as three question marks; Kaye (this volume), with focus on Afroasiatic forms, counts 23 question-marked Proto-Berber and 27 Egyptian forms); etc.

Many of these 'uncertainty' devices clearly involve violations of expected sound correspondences or doubtful cognates. Others merely relate to ambiguities, involving cases where the particular languages from which forms are compared in a particular proposed cognate set do not preserve distinct reflexes of certain Nostratic sounds which Dolgopolsky reconstructs. For example, in the sound correspondence charts (NM, 102–5), Indo-European has *k, *k̂, *kʷ as the reflexes of both Nostratic *k' and *q', with the assumption that these originally distinct Nostratic sounds merged in Proto-Indo-European; therefore, Nostratic forms attested only in languages such as Indo-European, which preserve no indication of the original difference, are given by Dolgopolsky with uncertainty device K', a cover symbol to mean that it could go back to either Nostratic *k' or *q'. This use of an uncertainty sign, unlike many of the others which involve sounds not behaving as expected in the correspondence sets, reflects not irregular correspondences so much as ambiguous ones. In principle this is not an illegitimate practice; however, it presents a problem of a different sort.

Dolgopolsky's reconstruction of Proto-Nostratic has over 50 consonants, although each of the putative daughter languages has far fewer consonants than this (cf. Trask this volume). This greatly increases the possibility of finding accidentally matching forms which nevertheless fit into one or another assumed correspondence set. Thus, for example, where Dravidian *k is assumed to reflect any of Nostratic *g, *k, *k', or *q', a Dravidian form with k can be compared with forms in other languages exhibiting any of these four patterns, greatly increasing the number of targets with which to compare a Dravidian word and the likelihood of finding an accidental match. The upshot of having many consonants in the proto-language and many different correspondence sets is that it is easier to find seemingly conforming lexical comparisons, though each correspondence will in fact have a much smaller number of examples which fits it than is the case when fewer proto segments are postulated (cf. Comrie this volume). Of course, it may well be that a particular proto-language did indeed have a rich consonant inventory; nevertheless, confidence in such a reconstruction requires a sufficiently large number of supporting cognate sets supporting each correspondence which are not otherwise challenged on standard criteria of comparison. This is not clearly the case with Dolgopolsky's lexical material.

The matter becomes even more serious. The number of 'uncertainty' devices rises when we add Dolgopolsky's others which are not listed among those on pp. 15–16. These include: (1) 'or' used to slip in multiple possibilities. (2) ~ with the same 'or' function, as in [103] *[t']axlǁa ~ *[t']alǁxa or *[t']axlǁE ~ *[t']alǁxE 'spleen'. (3) 'By assimilation', frequently invoked when the sequence of sounds does not fit the expected sound correspondences, e.g. [26] with Uralic 1. *yäntä 'sinew, tendon' and 2. *yoŋse *yoŋkse 'bow (weapon)', where to make the first fit expectations it is necessary to speculate that 'the vowel *ä in the first syllable of Ural. *yänte [note the different final vowel from that of the form as presented first] is due to assimilation (vowel harmony)', and for the second, that 'the labialization of the first vowel in *yoŋ(k)se is obscure' [NM, 35]; in [111] *śeʒA 'father-in-law, son-in-law', 'mother's brother', Uralic *ćećä 'uncle', Dolgopolsky tells us that 'in the prehistory of Uralic we may suppose an assimilation and dissimilation of sibilants: ≈ *śeʒA > **ćećä > *ćećä' (p. 88). (4) 'Metathesis' (e.g. [18]); and (5) by 'popular etymology' for others whose phonological correspondences are not right (e.g. [2]).

How these are distributed in the forms presented as evidence is eye-opening. In sum, of the 124 Nostratic reconstructions, 116 exhibit one (or usually more than one) of these 'uncertainty signs'. That is, only 9 sets (19, 31, 38, 40,

43, 68, 79, 110, 121) do not contain some 'uncertainty sign'. Moreover, of these, 6 clearly involve diffusion (38, 40, 43, 79, 110, 121, see below); that is, the forms which ought to be the best evidence, because they do not involve notations which reveal that they are ambiguous or do not conform to the requirement of regular sound correspondence, turn out mostly to be borrowings. However, the story is even grimmer: in addition to the 'uncertainty' devices found throughout the forms, some 25 sets contain additional comments, special stories, about problems involving lack of phonological correspondences (1, 20, 22, 26, 32, 38, 43, 47, 49, 60, 61, 65, 73, 82, 89, 91, 92, 93, 96, 97, 104, 107, 110, 111, 113).

Very serious, given Nostraticists' professed dedication to regular sound correspondences, is the fact that not infrequently *NM* sets involve forms which violate the expected sound correspondences in further ways, e.g. 1, 3, 6, 7, 8, 10, 12, 24, 26, 31, 43, 89, 91, 94, 104, to mention a few. (I did not have time to attempt to check the fit of the sounds in the forms presented with the sound correspondences of Dolgopolsky's charts; rather, these are a few of the exceptional forms which came to my attention while looking for other things; I have little doubt that a thorough investigation would find many more violations.) For example, for [43] *diq'a 'goat', with Indo-European *dig^h-, Dolgopolsky comments that 'IE *-k- is a regular reflex of the consonant *-q'-; the origin of the voiced *-g^h- is not clear' (p. 45). (Dolgopolsky gives as an alternative for Indo-European *dik, but the *k is not supported by the Indo-Euorpean cognates.) (See Comrie, Kaye, Shevoroshkin, Sinor, Starostin, Vovin, and Zvelebil all in this volume for other examples or discussion of some of these examples.)

Finally, about correspondences, it should be pointed out that while we speak informally of 'similarity' and much research on proposed macrofamilies is aimed at identifying similarities, in fact it is systematic correspondences that the historical linguist really seeks, and true historical correspondences do not necessarily involve similarity. In fact, a much repeated criticism of Nostratic is that the proposed sound correspondences on the whole involve near identities, which is unrealistically different from what is seen in the history of most documented language families, where various sound changes typically leave a number of sound correspondences which are not phonetically very similar, for example the different reflexes of Proto-Indo-European *k^w in various Indo-European languages in particular contexts as: k^w, p, t, č, h, š, w, etc.

In sum, numerous sets list forms which do not match the expected sound correspondences in some way. The extent of the problems involving non-corresponding sounds alone is enough to prevent the majority of historical linguists from accepting this Nostratic hypothesis.

2.2. *Borrowing*

Borrowing is an extremely serious problem for proposals of distant genetic relationship, and for *NM* forms in particular. It should be kept in mind, in this context, that the 124 Nostratic 'lexical items' (sets of words compared from putative Nostratic languages which Dolgopolsky presents as potential cognates) were selected for their potential cultural and geographical relevance to *NM*'s goal of looking towards linguistic palaeontology, from the much broader, yet unpublished set of some 2300 putative Nostratic cognates. It is frequently recommended that 'the borrowing factor can be held down to a very small percentage by sticking to non-cultural words' (Swadesh 1954, 313). That is, in cases of doubt about whether an item in question is borrowed or not, more credit is due basic vocabulary, non-cultural forms, because they are less likely to be borrowed. Unfortunately, however, the very cultural content of these 124 items — not from basic vocabulary — increases the likelihood that some of the words in question are loanwords. Some 76 of *NM*'s 124 sets involve actual or potential loans; however, the postulated Nostratic sets which are yet to appear may not be of this sort, whose semantic content suggests such a high percentage of borrowings. For *NM*, Shevoroshkin (this volume), closely associated with the Nostratic hypothesis, confronts 'many Ns [Nostratic] entries in Dolgopolsky's book with a substantial dose of scepticism . . . these entries may represent migratory term[s]'. It is clear that borrowing is a serious but mostly unaddressed problem for numerous Nostratic cognate sets (Campbell 1998a).

Given the extent of the territory of putative Nostratic languages, we might not suspect much contact or borrowing among presumed Nostratic constituent families. However, wide geographical distribution is no more an obstacle to borrowing than it is to a possible genetic relationship. If the languages are genetically related, regardless of their attested locations, in the past there would have been a single proto-language spoken in a particular geographical location from which the daughter languages departed to reach their current locations. The postulation of such a proto-language requires the supposition of movement after the break up of a proto-language, to accommodate current geographical distribution of daughter languages, and such movement is no more likely nor unlikely in the case of a postulated but as yet undemonstrated 'macrofamily' than the parallel assumption that the languages were once geographically close enough to borrow from each other but later shifted their locations to reflect their present-day distribution. In both scenarios, that of related languages or that of former neighbouring but not necessarily related languages, it is necessary to postulate movements not yet demonstrated actually to have occurred. If earlier geographical proximity because of genetic relationship is plausible, then closer proximity of unrelated languages that could result in borrowing is equally plausible. In either case, we would be assuming that the languages share some things, either by inheritance or by borrowing, due to a different earlier geographical arrangement of the languages. Given the known history of central Eurasia and its contacts, with wave after wave of conquest, expansion, migration, trade and exchange, of multilingual and multi-ethnic states, it is not at all surprising that some of the linguistic forms do turn out to be borrowed among languages found in this broad area, which are no longer neighbours. For example, a number of words of precisely this sort, which include several forms cited by Dolgopolsky as evidence for Nostratic, have been identified as loans (Häkkinen 1996, 129–42; Janhunen 1983; Joki 1973; Koivulehto 1994; 1995; Rédei 1986). Considerable early borrowing among Uralic, Indo-European, and also so-called Altaic languages has been identified (Campbell 1990; 1998a; Gamkrelidze & Ivanov 1984.1, 224, 295; 1984.2, 941–2; 1985, 14–21; Janhunen 1983; 1996a,b; Joki 1973; Koivulehto 1984; 1991; Manaster Ramer 1993, 224; Rozycki 1994; among others). To cite a specific semantic domain, the numerous borrowings among tree names show the kind of early language contact which could lead to such loanwords (Campbell 1990; 1997c; Friedrich 1970; Hajdú 1975; Róna-Tas 1988, 745–6; Suhonen 1988, 605–6).

Here, I single out a few of *NM*'s 124 sets for discussion, to show the nature and extent of the borrowing problem. Some involve clear borrowings; others represent instances where borrowing is suspected because of their semantic content. These sets should be set aside, since they have an equally plausible alternative explanation for why they are shared among the languages involved. I list *NM*'s Nostratic reconstruction and concentrate on the Uralic forms (listed only as Finno-Ugric if the Uralic representative involves only the Finno-Ugric branch of the Uralic family), but do not repeat all the forms given in the individual sets; rather I mention other forms only as relevant to the discussion. I list loans from non-Uralic languages that others have identified when I am aware of these. I begin with a case of borrowing which illustrates one of the major problems with the Altaic hypothesis, set [48].

[48] *p'oKʼü 'wild cattle, pack' (Indo-European *peḱu/*peḱwe- 'cattle'; Altaic *p'ok'üŕ- 'bovine animal, bull'). This set clearly involves borrowing. In

effect the set involves only two Nostratic subfamilies, Indo-European and Altaic; *NM* lists Ndam (East Chadic, in Hamito-Semitic) pàgàr 'antelope' also, but as highly dubious (with three question marks, ???). The Altaic *p'ok'üř-, represented only by Turkic, is a clear example of a documented loan, involving one of the strong points among the arguments of those who oppose the Altaic hypothesis. Proto-Turkic *s split into s and z, and *š into š and ž in specific environments (involving roots of two syllables and with long vowels), and then in the highly influential Bulgaric (Chuvash) branch of the family z > r, and ž > l. As a result, words in Mongolian (and Tungusic) which have an r or l corresponding to s, z, š, or ž in other Turkic languages can only be borrowings from this branch of Turkic, not true cognates to other Altaic languages (or they are accidental similarities). There is a sizeable number of these in the *NM* putative Altaic lexical comparisons. In this case, in set [48], the word involved is Proto-Turkic *pöküs 'bovine', borrowed from Bulgaric into Mongolian and from there on into Tungusic (Janhunen 1996a, 240–41, 255). This set would be questionable in any case, given the important role of cattle in the prehistoric cultures from the area of the Proto-Indo-European homeland and in the territory of the various so-called Altaic languages. Janhunen (1996a, 256) argues that even the Proto-Turkic *pöküs (< *peküs) is probably borrowed from Indo-European (cf. Latin pecus 'cattle'), connecting it with the corpus of Indo-European loanwords in Turkic from Pre-Proto-Tocharian; Shevoroshkin (1998, 8) believes the Indo-European form may be borrowed from Hurri-Caucasian. (For other problems with the Altaic forms in [48], see Clauson 1956, 186; Sinor, this volume p. 390; Starostin, this volume p. 146). The Turkic word (cf. Old Turkish öküz — note that Nostratic *p' is reflected by Turkic *h or Ø) has also been claimed to be an loan from Indo-European *ukʷs-en- 'bull, ox' (cf. English ox) (Janhunen pers. comm.).

Other sets which have r or l in other so-called Altaic languages and in Turkic which reflect forms with original Turkic *s and therefore are loanwords among 'Altaic' languages are: [30] 'to spread like a veil/net', [52] 'small carnivore (marten, polecat)', [82] 'stone, heap of stones' (perhaps only accidental word associations in this set), and [92] 'bark' (Altaic 'birch bark'), and probably a few others. That is, since the Altaic forms in sets 30, 52, 82, and 92 involve loanwords, they are illegitimate as evidence for the Nostratic hypothesis.

I should add here that Starostin and Dolgopolsky (in discussion in the symposium) disputed this interpretation of the Turkic facts, preferring reconstructions of Proto-Turkic which reflect the liquids rather than the sibilants and in this way they deny that borrowing is a problem for these 'Altaic' forms. This interpretation would require assuming that the liquids (l/r) were original and changed to sibilants in certain of the Turkic languages, a kind of sound change seldom seen in the world's languages, though changes in the other direction are common (as in rhotacism). There is considerable literature precisely on this topic. Among Turkologists, those who believe in the Altaic hypothesis (as well as Doerfer, who opposes Altaic, though he holds Mongolian forms in these comparisons to be Turkic loans) postulate original liquids (which then would make the sibilants of other Turkic languages the results of later sound changes); those who oppose the Altaic hypothesis (with the exception of Doerfer) hold the sibilants to be original (which makes the liquids the results of later sound changes). Put differently, those with a grasp of phonological systems and phonetic plausibility all postulate a change of *s > z > r and *š > ž > l, where the steps in the change are seen as incremental, intimately interrelated, and natural. No one with a sense of phonology postulates the reverse, the unnatural and implausible changes of *r > z/s and *l > ž/š, which are almost unknown in languages elsewhere (Ščerbak 1986b; Janhunen pers. comm.).

[10]   *k'ir[u]qa 'ice, hoarfrost; to freeze'. Finno-Ugric (1) *kir∇ 'snow-crust', (2) *kirte ~ *kerte 'snow-crust, frozen soil'. The Finnish form kirsi 'frost on the ground, ice-crust' of the second Finno-Ugric set is identified as a Baltic loan (cf. Lithuanian skiřsti 'to be covered, apskiřsti 'to freeze') (Itkonen & Kulonen 1992, 372; Häkkinen 1996, 153). (Note the problem of listing two separate Finno-Ugric etyma in a single set, discussed below.)

[13]   'water body' (Appleyard, this volume).

[15]   'to harvest (cereal)' (Sinor, this volume; Starostin, this volume).

[17]   'cereals' (Shevoroshkin, this volume).

[20]   ?'white' ('milk') (Appleyard, this volume).

[21]   *mayɜ̂∇ 'tasty beverage'. In support of Finno-Ugric *mayɜ̂∇ 'sap of trees', NM (p. 29) lists only Finnish maito 'milk' and Votyak meḷ 'sweet tree sap', but this is not an accepted Finno-Ugric etymology. The Finnish word is identified by some as a loan from Germanic *smaitō 'a mix pre-

pared with milk, beat, throw, mushy mass, dough', and the Votyak comparison is 'especially uncertain' (Kulonen 1995, 139) (cf. also Vovin, this volume).

[**23**] 'basket' ('vessel') (Appleyard, this volume).

[**24**] *p'/pat[a] 'basket, box'. Indo-European *pod- 'vessel, pot, box'. Finno-Ugric *pata 'cauldron, pot'. Finnish pata 'pot, kettle'. Dravidian *patalV 'pot'. This set is generally considered to involve an ancient loan; in particular the Indo-European and Uralic forms have been seen as indicative of early contacts; indeed this set has been linked with the inception and spread of ceramic culture across Europe beginning as early as the sixth millennium BC. (Häkkinen 1996, 132; 1997, 192; Kulonen 1995, 322; Joki 1973, 301; cf. Shevoroshkin, this volume p. 84, who suggests the possibility of borrowing in Indo-European from Hurri-Caucasian). Janhunen (1977, 123) includes this in a 'group of Eurasian Wanderwörter' which includes 'names for various types of containers (vessels, bags). He points out that the Samoyed forms (e.g. Nenets pad 'sack, bundle') are borrowed from Tungusic *puta(-). Notice for the Dravidian form in *NM*, there is no account given of the lV, while the *t of Nostratic has four apparently unpredictable possible outcomes in Dravidian (*t/*tt/*/*ṭ/*ṭṭ), not legitimate by the demands of regular (predictable) sound change that all practitioners accept. (It is to be assumed that these are conditioned variants, different outcomes in different phonetic contexts, but this is not specified in *NM*.)

[**26**] *jaŋ[y]V 'sinew, tendon', 'bow (weapon)'. *NM* offers two Uralic etyma in this set: (1) *jäntä 'sinew, tendon' and (2) *yoŋse/*yoŋkse 'bow (weapon)'. This is compared with Turkic *jáń (> *jāy/*jā) 'bow', but the actually occurring Turkic forms reflect only *jā or *jāy. Since this is short, it could be just accidental, but could also reflect ancient borrowings in Eurasia. In particular, this set contains only representatives from Uralic and Altaic (where only Turkic is present), plus the not very convincing Egyptian ỉwn.t 'a kind of weapon (bow)' (there is no real account of the w nor the t, two of the four segments in this form).

[**27**] *ńoɣ/ʕIE (or *ńaɣ/ʕIE) 'sinew', 'to tie together'. Uralic *ńōle 'arrow' (cf. Sammallahti 1988 Proto-Uralic *ńixlɨ 'arrow'). Except for the Hamito-Semitic forms, this set is represented only by Evenki (in Tungusic in Altaic)

ńulga/julga/yulga 'arrow'. Janhunen (1977, 127–8) shows, based on phonological evidence, that the Samoyed forms cited in the Uralic set (e.g. Nenets luki 'blunt arrow') are recent loans from Tungusic (cf. Evenki lukī).

[29] *p/p'ešqE ~ *p/p'eqšE 'spear'. Uralic *pekše 'arrow' may well be diffused; its status within Uralic or Finno-Ugric is not clear (Rédei 1986–88, 369).

[30] *t'ul[i][g]∇ 'to spread like a veil/net, cover with a veil/net, catch with a net'. Finno-Ugric *tulk∇ 'seine, drag-net'. This form is clearly not reconstructible within Finno-Ugric (cf. Rédei 1986–88, 536) and may well be a borrowing. Notice that the Altaic forms mean 'hobble' and the Dravidian form (illustrated only in Parji) means 'weaver', and thus seem too far-fetched semantically.

[34] *t'ap'∇ 'to hit (the target)'. Finno-Ugric *tap(p)∇- 'to find, succeed, fit', Finnish tapaa-/tavata 'to find, meet, come across'. This Finnish form is now known to be a Germanic borrowing (Häkkinen 1997, 222, 252); the Votyak tupa- 'to find, hit the target, guess', the only other Finno-Ugric form *NM* presents, is not considered cognate.

[37] *ʔEl/ḷi 'deer'. Uralic is represented only by Yukaghir (not a Uralic language, but thought related by some) ile 'deer', which may well be a borrowing from Turkic *elälik 'roe-buck' (*NM*, 42).

[38] *boča '(young) deer'. Georgian boč-ik'-i 'one-year old deer'. Uralic *poča 'reindeer, reindeer fawn'. Tungusic *buCan '(a kind of) deer'. The Uralic form is reconstructible only back to Finno-Permic (Sammallahti 1988, 553) and almost certainly involves borrowing in northern Eurasia as part of reindeer culture. *NM* also compares (with a question mark) some Samoyed forms, e.g. Kamassian po/du 'goat', Koibal podo 'goat', pooto '*Cervus*' [i.e. '*Capreolus*']. These Samoyed forms and perhaps all those in this set are better seen, as Joki (1973, 304) does, as loans, involving also Votyak pudo 'cattle', Tajik (Iranian) poda 'herd (of cows, sheep)', Yaghnobi poda, Ormuri pâda 'cattle'. Róna-Tas (1983, 243) shows that some 'Altaic' languages have clearly borrowed the form from other putative 'Altaic' languages and that there is also internal borrowing among some of the Finno-Ugric languages, and that 'the Votyak or Permian word was borrowed by Tatar, Bashkir, Tobol Tatar, and Russian'.

Interestingly, for the Nostratic sets involving the non-deer, meat animals, Uralic has no representatives, suggesting some of the other languages in these sets may involve borrowing (for if they were true cognates, we would expect some examples throughout the putative family, including in Uralic). Thus, [39] 'bovines', [40] 'aurochs, wild bovine', [41] 'bull, calf', [42] 'wild sheep/goats', [43] goat', [44] 'wild goat', [45] 'billy goat, ram', [46] 'wild boar', [47] '(male, young) artiodactyl' ('ass'), and [48] 'pack, wild cattle', are suggestive of borrowing, and indeed borrowing is documented for some of these.

[**39**]   'bovine' (Starostin this volume).

[**41**]   ?*č[a]w[∇]R∇ 'bull, calf'. Semitic *θawar- 'bull', Indo-European *stewr-/ *stowr- 'bull' (Latin tauru-) has frequently been identified as involving loanwords. This form is generally identified as a borrowing into Indo-European. Gamkrelidze & Ivanov (1985, 15) list the forms here as Indo-European *t/^{h}/auro- 'ox', borrowed from Semitic *tawru 'ox' (cf. Appleyard, this volume p. 304).

[**45**]   *bukEɣlʕ∇ 'billy goat, ram' is widely borrowed, explaining the similarity among many of the forms in this set.

The forms involving 'fig trees' ([1] 'fig tree' and [54] '(a kind of) fig tree') involve only Hamito-Semitic and Dravidian representatives and as such are suspicious; they may involve borrowings if they are not merely accidentally similar. (These were challenged by several other papers in this symposium.)

[**59**]   'berries' (Starostin, this volume p. 147).

[**65**]   The forms with upa, ufa, opa 'flour, bread' in various Tungusic languages, Manchu, Jurchen, etc. are almost certainly diffused. This may include some of the Semitic forms (for example Arabic xubz- 'bread').

[**68**]   'marrow, brain' (Appleyard, this volume).

[**79**]   *madu 'honey' (cf. 'mead'). Indo-European *med^{h}u- 'honey'. Dravidian *maṭṭ꜇ 'honey'. Various Hamito-Semitic representatives. This form has frequently been identified as involving loanwords in Eurasian languages (Hajdú 1975,

33; Joki 1973, 281–5; 1988; Shevoroshkin, this volume; Sinor, this volume), including multiple forms within Finno-Ugric languages, not listed by *NM* (e.g. Finno-Ugric *meti 'honey' (Sammallahti 1988, 545), Finnish mehu 'juice' (from *mekši 'bee, honey', thought to involve Indo-Iranian and Finno-Ugric loans).

[84]   *boruʕ|ɤ∇ 'trunk' ('log'). Finno-Ugric *pora 'logs used as a raft or a bridge'. This may well involve an Iranian loan (*)pr̥tu- 'bridge' (generally assumed to be involved in early contact between Iranian and Samoyed, Joki 1973, 304; Janhunen 1983, 122; Rédei [1986–88, 395] cites several problems with the proposed Finno-Ugric cognates).

[94]   *K'ayer∇ 'bark, film'. Uralic *kār∇, Finno-Ugric *kōr∇ 'skin, bark', Finnish kuori 'skin, peel, bark, crust, shell'. Finnish kuori has been explained as a loan from Indo-European, where proposed cognates elsewhere in Uralic are questionable (Häkkinen 1996, 208; Itkonen & Kulonen 1992, 442).

[97]   *K'aʃ[ü] 'skin, film, bark'. Uralic *kaʃw∇ 'film, thin skin', Finnish kalvo 'film, membrane'. Many of the forms listed under Finno-Ugric have been considered to involve a loanword from early Proto-Germanic *kalƀon, Proto-Germanic *kalƀan 'sack-like end of a seine, womb' (Itkonen & Kulonen 1992, 292; Häkkinen 1996, 161).

[98]   ?'bark, skin' (Appleyard, this volume).

[109]   *kälulü 'female relative-in-law'. Uralic *kälü (*käl∇-w∇). Rédei (1986–88, 135) reconstructs this to Proto-Finno-Permic (with ?Proto-Uralic) *kälɜ, ?*kälɜ-wɜ 'sister-in-law', but considers the whole set uncertain. This form is generally thought to involve borrowing (Joki 1973, 267–8). While initially the phonetic and semantic similarities between this Uralic form and those from other languages might seem attractive, there are problems. These phonetically quite similar forms for affinal kin may easily represent old borrowings. At least some of the Uralic languages are known to have borrowed this word from Turkic (e.g. Permiak Zyrien and Votyak ken- 'sister-in-law' < Old Chuvash ken < Proto-Turkic *kelin, Róna-Tas 1988, 762). The similarities seen in a number of non-Uralic languages are thought to be the result of an old *Wanderwort* whose origin may be impossible to determine (Itkonen & Kulonen 1992, 471).

[110] *küda 'male relative-in-law'. This set should be eliminated for the same reason. It is represented by only Uralic *küðü 'wife's husband, husband's or wife's brother' (Finnish kyty) and in Altaic, by Turkic k̄üðä-gü 'younger sister's husband, wife's sister' and by Mongolian *quda 'father of one's son-in-law or daughter-in-law' (plus a Kartvelian form which Dolgopolsky doubts, listed with ?). However, these forms involve known loanwords. This is what is behind Mordvin kuda 'go-between (in wedding ceremonies)', which is a Tatar loanword (Tatar qoda, ultimately from Mongolian into Tatar) (Róna-Tas 1988, 767). This Uralic form is not reconstructed by Sammallahti or Rédei. Votyak kir- 'brother-in-law', borrowed from Chuvash kürü, is ultimately from Proto-Turkic *küdeg(ü); and Cheremis oń 'father-in-law', borrowed from Chuvash xoń, is ultimately from Proto-Turkic *qaðin (Róna-Tas 1988, 764, 767, 770). Possible loans involving Indo-European languages have also been proposed (cf. Joki 1973, 267–8). One need but recall that Finnish has borrowed its terms for 'mother', 'daughter', 'sister', and 'bride' from Indo-European sources, and that Votyak (Finno-Ugric) borrowed 'mother', 'father', 'grandmother', 'grandfather', 'husband', 'older brother', 'older sister', and 'uncle' from Tatar (Turkic), to be convinced of the possibility of kinship terms, particularly affinal ones, being borrowed (Csúcs 1990, 69).

[112] 'relative of the other moiety' (Kaye, this volume).

[120] *ʔar∇ 'member of the clan'. ?Ugric (in Uralic) *ar∇ 'relative belonging to one's mother's clan', Hungarian ara 'bride'. This has sometimes been identified as an Indo-Iranian loan (Joki 1973, 74).

[121] *ʔarba 'to make magic, cast spells'. Finno-Ugric *arpa, Finnish arpa 'lot, magic stick, soothsaying, tool for prediction', Proto-Lapp vōrpē 'luck, lot'. Altaic arba- (plus some Semitic forms listed in NM as questionable). These are almost certainly loans. In Finno-Ugric they do not reconstruct beyond the Finnic languages. Borrowing of such a term among the shamanistic peoples of northern Eurasia is not unlikely. It has also been argued that the Finnic forms are borrowed form Germanic (*arb̄a-z 'inheritance, inherited land') or Indo-Aryan (Itkonen & Kulonen 1992, 83; Joki 1973, 156, 252); the Lapp form is identified as a Germanic loan (Korhonen 1981, 35). The Balto-Finnic form was borrowed into Old Russian and from there into Cheremis (Toivonen et al. 1955–81, 24).

[**123**] *ŝot'∇ 'to exercise magic force'. Finno-Ugric *ŝot[a] '(magic) force', 'curse', 'bless' > ? Finnish sota 'war'. Finnish sota and its cognates have been argued to be the result of loans from Indo-European languages (see Joki 1973, 117, 119, 121, 123, 124, 161, 232–3 for details).

[**124**] *tul∇ 'to tell (a story), pronounce magic\ritual texts'. Finno-Ugric *tult∇ 'witchcraft'. This in not a Uralic or Finno-Ugric reconstruction, but is found only in the Ugric branch of the family, where it means also 'heat, fever' and 'trance', and so the gloss of the reconstructed form is uncertain (Rédei 1986–88, 895); it may involve borrowing.

(**p. 17**) *nimʔV 'name' (said to be represented in Indo-European, Hamito-Semitic, Uralic, and Altaic) (cf. Proto-Uralic *nimi). The forms in this set involve well-known loanwords (Abondolo 1998, 35; Joki 1973, 291; 1988, 586; Rédei 1986–88, 641, 652). 'Name' is, in fact, a cultural concept, and the term is borrowed also in other areas of the world.

(**p. 17**) *wet∇ 'water' (said to be represented in all constituent families except Kartvelian). Arguments that this set involves borrowing have been presented (Abondolo 1998, 36; Gamkrelidze & Ivanov 1984.2, 942; Joki 1973, 344; Koivulehto 1983; Rédei 1988, 641, 654; Salminen 1989, 19). While we might not expect 'water', as a basic vocabulary item, to be borrowed, there are several other attested cases where the word for 'water' has been borrowed, e.g. among different Quechua languages and others of the Andes, from Cushitic to some South Ethiopic (Semitic) languages (Appleyard this volume), etc. For example, though some reconstruct Proto-Uralic *weti 'water', others point out that it is not truly a Common Uralic word, since a cognate is not found in Lapp and Ostyak. They argue that the true Proto-Uralic word for 'water' was *šäčä (cf. Northern Lappish čáhci 'water', Ostyak seč 'tide, flood'), replaced by the Indo-European word for 'water' in the other Uralic languages (Salminen 1989, 19; Koivulehto 1983; Abondolo 1998, 36).

2.3. Excessive semantic latitude

It is dangerous to present phonetically similar forms with different meanings as potential evidence of 'macrofamily' relationship under the assumption that semantic shifts have taken place. Of course meaning can shift, but in hypotheses of remote relationship the assumed semantic shifts cannot be proven, and the greater the semantic latitude permitted, the easier it is to find phonetically similar forms which have no historical connection (e.g. the Pipil-Finnish examples, above). When semantically non-equivalent forms are compared, the possibility that chance accounts for the phonetic similarity is greatly increased. 'Admitting comparisons between non-synonyms cannot make it easier to demonstrate the relationship of two languages . . . it can only make it more difficult to do so' (Ringe 1992, 67). Swadesh's (1954, 314) advice is sound: 'count only exact equivalences'. Even etymology within families where the languages are known to be related still requires an explicit account of any assumed semantic changes. The problem of excessive semantic permissiveness is one of the most serious in proposals of distant genetic relationship.

Of *NM*'s 124 Nostratic sets, even allowing semantic matches fairly liberally, 56 exhibit such semantic latitude as to call them seriously into question as potential cognates, e.g.:

[15]   'to harvest (cereal)': 'to pluck, harvest', 'to gather (fruit)', 'autumn and winter', 'early autumn', 'winter'; 'harvest feast'; 'barley', 'oats';

[16]   'edible cereals, harvest (of wild plants?)': 'to grow (of a plant)'; 'to plough, cultivate a field'; 'autumn';

[20]   'white': 'milk', 'white (of an egg)'; 'white'; 'clear (of liquids)';

[30]   'to spread like a veil/net, cover with a veil/net, catch with a net': 'to spread, stretch, spread like a veil, veil, cover with a veil, 'to catch (fish)'; 'to fish by net', 'to look for, hunt'; 'seine, drag-net'; to hobble (a horse)', 'hobble'; 'weaver';

[34]   'to hit (the target)': *wohin gelangen*, 'place', 'tolerate', 'become', 'to know, be informed', *habile, savant*, 'find, fit, meet', 'hit the target, guess', 'appointed time, chance';

[42]   'wild sheep/goats': 'sheep', 'wild', 'goat', 'game, hunt', 'hunt, chase', 'cattle, flock';

[62]   'root', root-crops, edible roots': 'sinew': 'stump of cabbage'; 'edible root, carrot, parsnip'; 'tendon, nerve', 'tip of nose', 'muscle'; Indian horse-radish tree'; 'tendon';

[68]   'marrow, brain, soft fat of animals' ('to smear, anoint'): 'fat, grease', 'smear,

anoint', 'melted butter', 'marrow', 'brain', 'cheek', 'the sides of the lower jaw', etc.;

[84]   'trunk' ('log'): 'reed', 'bridge', 'trunk, log', 'raft', 'hilt of sword'.

2.4. Short forms

How long proposed cognates are and the number of matched sounds (segments) within them are important, since the more matching segments in a proposed cognate set, the less likely that accident accounts for the similarity (Meillet 1958, 89–90). Monosyllabic forms (V, CV, VC) may be true cognates, but they are so short that their similarity to forms in other languages could also easily be due to chance. (See Ringe 1992 for mathematical proof.) Some 14 of *NM*'s 124 sets involve such short forms (1, 5, 20, 37, 47, 51, 64, 68, 72, 116, 117, 118, 120, 122).

2.5. Erroneous morphological analysis

In proposals of long-range relationships, where compared words are etymologized into assumed constituent morphemes, it is necessary to show that the segmented morphemes (roots and affixes) in fact exist in the grammatical system. Unfortunately, unmotivated morphological segmentation is found very frequently in proposals of remote relationship. Also, undetected morpheme divisions cause difficulties and are a frequent problem. Both of these can make the compared languages seem to have more in common than they actually do. Some examples of this sort in *NM*'s sets are: 10, 19, 26, 35, 53, 61, 65, 107, 108, 113. For example, in [26] *jaŋ[y]V 'sinew, tendon', 'bow (weapon)', *NM* (pp. 24–5) offers two Uralic etyma, (1) *jäntä 'sinew, tendon' and (2) *yoŋse/*yoŋkse 'bow (weapon)', but to get these to fit the expected sound correspondences, he must assume an otherwise unmotivated morphological analysis of each: 'Ural. *-tä and *-[k]se probably go back to suffixes of derivation.' (See Appleyard for [19], Kaye for [65], Vovin, and Sinor, this volume.)

2.6. Sets represented by only two constituent families

Since Meillet, it has been accepted that the likelihood of forms being cognate is stronger (and therefore provides better evidence of potential genetic relationship) if the forms of the set are found in several branches of a putative family than if illustrated only in one or two branches. Illič-Svityč (1989) established as one of his criteria that only cognate sets with representatives from at least three of the six putative Nostratic families would be considered supportive of the hypothesis:

> Clearly, a special proof is necessary to show that the similarities found
> between compared languages are not accidental, but rather point to a dis-
> tant linguistic relationship . . . Toward this end, we propose the following
> method of evaluation the character of the similarities collected . . . We will
> take the similarities between three pairs, made up of any three of the six
> proto-languages being compared . . . (Illič-Svityč 1989, 112)

Nevertheless, this was a serious problem for Illič-Svityč, since 134 sets from his 378 involved forms found in only two of the member families (Campbell 1998a), and this is a problem for 19 of *NM*'s 124 sets: 1, 11?, 13, 16, 16, 29, 36, 40, 46, 48, 54, 56, 58, 61, 69, 77, 81?, 90, 104.

There are good logical (and statistical) reasons why Meillet's principle concerning distribution of putative cognates across members of a family is important. If a lexical matching for a particular word from some specific language is sought from any of six Nostratic constituent families as targets, it is vastly easier to find a look-alike than it would be if it were necessary for the matching to be distributed across, say, a majority of the six. That is, it is much easier to find accidental similarities if a matching is required from only one or two of the languages compared. In the case of *NM*, it is even worse, in that the number of targets is often not just six, but, rather, comparisons of the 'reaching down' sort occur where some form can be selected from any of a large number of target languages within the constituent families of Nostratic (cf. Janhunen 1996a, 247).

2.7. Limited scope comparisons ('reaching down')

Without doubt, forms that have clearly established etymologies in their own families by virtue of having cognates in a number of sister languages stand a better chance of having even more remote associations with languages that may be even more distantly related than some isolated form in some language which has no known cognates elsewhere within its own family and hence no prima facie evidence of potential older age. Meillet's (1925, 38) principle helps to reduce the likelihood of chance accounting for similarities among words in different languages which have no know cognates in sister languages of their own language families:

> When an initial 'proto language' is to be reconstructed, the number of witnesses
> which a word has should be taken into account. An agreement of two languages,
> if it is not total, risks being fortuitous. But, if the agreement extends to three,
> four or five very distinct languages, chance becomes less probable.

Of Dolgopolsky's sets, 44 are of the limited scope (reaching down) sort, where the form given to illustrate some particular constituent family is taken from a particular language (or few languages from) within the particular constituent family, but is not shown to be related to the other languages of that particular family: 2, 6, 9, 13?, 14, 15, 17, 21, 25, 26, 31, 34, 36, 37, 40, 41, 44, 46, 48, 53, 60, 72, 78, 82, 84, 85, 86, 88, 89, 93, 94, 95, 98, 99, 100, 104, 105, 112, 114, 119, 120, 121, 122, 124. One example is [108] *ñiK'a 'jugular vertebra, neck, nape of the neck'. Uralic *ñika 'vertebra, joint, neck', Finnish nikama 'vertebra, node of a stalk'. In fact, for the Finnish form 'it has not been possible to present a believable Proto-Finnic or pre-Finnish etymology' (Häkkinen 1997, 225); the form has no cognates beyond Finnic and it has been suggested that it is a 'descriptive' word in origin (Kulonen 1995, 220; Toivonen *et al.* 1955–81.2, 379). Appleyard (this volume) points out that of 102 sets which include Afroasiatic forms, '36 consist of items occurring only in Semitic, and not an insubstantial number of these consist of attestations from a single branch of Semitic only . . .' (nos. 16, 17, 24, 25, 30, 33, 46, 51, 60, 66, 70, 72, 85, 99, 107)'.

The seriousness of the problem is seen in clear relief when we contrast Dolgopolsky's claim for 2300 reconstructible Proto-Nostratic forms with the fact that, for example, only about 140 words are reconstructible to Proto-Uralic (Sammallahti 1988, 479). That is, it is clear in virtually all reconstructions that the more time depth involved, the more vocabulary replacement takes place in the languages compared and the fewer lexical items can be reconstructed to various proto-languages. If only some 140 forms can reliably be reconstructed in Proto-Uralic, clearly the vast majority of Dolgopolsky's 2300 Nostratic sets which involve Uralic comparisons must be of the 'reaching down' sort. Standard methods do not permit this on such a wholesale basis. Starostin argues (at the symposium) that within Uralic, it is possible that Finno-Ugric forms which do not have cognates in the Samoyed branch could still represent Proto-Uralic forms and therefore are legitimate for comparisons with other Nostratic languages. It is true, of course, that it is possible that Samoyed replaced Uralic vocabulary which may be preserved only in the Finno-Ugric branch; Starostin takes this to mean that little vocabulary is ever lost if we have several branches to compare. Taking this analogy further, we might say that it is possible that Finnish or Hungarian vocabulary may preserve Proto-Uralic forms lost in the other languages, justifying the 'reaching down' strategy of comparing forms from individual languages broadly in Nostratic even when they lack cognates within their own families. This would mean, in essence, that any form in any language might legitimately be compared with others in attempts to get at broader possible macro-family relationships — hence Starostin's assertion that vocabulary is rarely lost when seen in a broader family context. But it is also possible that the individual words, say in Finno-Ugric without Samoyed cognates, or in Finnish or

Hungarian without other Finno-Ugric cognates, have other histories which do not extend back to Proto-Uralic and on to Nostratic. It is the fact that their histories are unknown that lies behind Meillet's principle requiring broader distribution and avoidance of 'reaching down' — it is just as possible that these forms do not come from Uralic (or Nostratic), but rather came into the language later in its history. It is the distributional criterion which makes it more likely that a form has an older history within its own language family and hence conceivably an even older history in more remote comparisons. Without this, the likelihood is greatly increased that the 'reaching down' forms compared have no older status and are only accidentally similar to forms in other languages. This 'reaching down' greatly increases the number of targets one has to aim at and hence vastly increases the probability of encountering similarities with forms from other families which are only accidentally similar, not true cognates.

2.8. Overlapping sets

A common problem in proposals of distant genetic relationship is the presentation of a word from some language as evidence for more than one proposed cognate set. A single form in one language cannot be cognate simultaneously with multiple forms in another language (unless the cognates are derived from a common root, meaning that ultimately only one cognate set is involved). Some 21 sets of Dolgopolsky's 124 exhibit this problem: 2, 4, 10, 32, 37, 39, 42, 45, 47, 48, 51, 59, 60, 94, 97, 98, 99, 109, 110, 114, 115.

2.9. Onomatopoeia

Onomatopoeic forms may be similar in different languages due to the fact that they have independently approximated the sounds of nature rather than because they may share a common ancestor. Therefore, such forms are to be eliminated from proposals of distant genetic relationship. Swadesh's (1954, 313) sensible proposal was:

> A simple way to reduce the sound-imitative factor to a negligible minimum is to omit from consideration all such words as 'blow, breathe, suck, laugh' and the like, that is all words which are known to lean toward sound imitation.

Naturally, the determination of what words reflect onomatopoeia is often subjective, but there is general agreement that forms which are suggestive of imitation and which turn up in similar phonetic form widely in languages all over the world should be avoided. The following appear to involve onomatopoeia in one way or another in *NM*'s sets: 3, 19, 38?, 42?, 51, 78, 91, 116.

2.10. Nursery forms

It has been recognized for centuries that nursery formations (the mama-nana-papa-dada-caca sort of words) should be avoided in proposals of relationship, since these words typically share a high degree of similarity in languages through-out the world which is not due to common ancestry. The terms involved typi-cally have glosses of 'mother', 'father', 'grandmother', 'grandfather', and often 'brother' 'sister', 'aunt', and 'uncle'. Murdock (1959) investigated 'the tendency of unrelated languages 'to develop similar words for father and mother on the basis of nursery forms' (Jakobson 1960, 538); his investigation included 531 terms for 'mother' and 541 for 'father', which 'confirm the hypothesis under test' — a striking convergence in the structure of these parental kin terms throughout historically unrelated languages' (Jakobson 1960, 538). Jakobson explained the non-genetic similarity among such nursery forms. He observed that stops and nasals predominate, that labials and dentals predominate over velars and palatals, and that the vowel a is preponderant. Murdock's data showed that nasals dominate for 'mother', while they are in less than 15 per cent for terms denoting 'father'. Jakobson explains this:

> Often the sucking activities of a child are accompanied by a slight nasal murmur, the only phonation which can be produced when the lips are pressed to mother's breast or to feeding bottle and the mouth is full. Later, this phonatory reaction to nursing is reproduced as an anticipatory signal at the mere sight of food and finally as a manifestation of a desire to eat, or more generally, as an expression of discontent and impatient longing for missing food or absent nurser, and any ungranted wish . . . Since the mother is, in Grégoire's parlance, *la grande dispensatrice*, most of the in-fant's longings are addressed to her, and children . . . gradually turn the nasal interjection into a parental term, and adapt its expressive make-up to their regular phonemic pattern. (Jakobson 1960, 542–3.)

Jakobson (1960, 544) also explained why among familial terms the nursery forms are not confined to parental designations. Added to Jakobson's explana-tion is the frequent spontaneous development of such terms for affective rea-sons (e.g. English ma, mama, mamma, mammy, mommy, mom, mummy, mum, and father compared with pa, papa, pappy, pop, poppy, da, dad, dada, daddy).

Of *NM*'s sets, 6 involve such nursery forms: 111, 114, 116, 117, 118, 119. (Dolgopolsky acknowledges the problem in several of these.)

2.11. Two-in-one: non-cognates

Another problem is that of non-cognate forms (or forms from more than one cognate set) within one family being compared in the same proposed cognate set for a broader proposed 'macrofamily'. Often unrelated forms from related languages, joined together in the belief that they may be historically connected in some way, are compared with forms from other language families as evidence for even more distant relationships. However, if the forms are not even cognates within their own family, any further comparison with forms from languages outside the family is called into doubt. Among *NM*'s 124 sets, 16 sets involve more than one cognate set in the forms presented as representing a single constituent family: 4, 10, 21, 26, 41, 58, 61, 68, 80, 82, 87, 92, 94, 98, 101, 108. Several of these openly cite multiple cognates within constituent families. (See Appleyard, this volume p. 310 for [98]; Starostin, this volume p. 150 for [87].)

2.12. Erroneous reconstructions

Another problem occurs when false reconstructions enter into more remote comparisons. Some inaccurate reconstructions can make forms misleadingly appear to be more similar to forms compared from other language groups than would be the case if true cognates with accurate reconstructions had been compared. I have not attempted to survey all such cases among *NM*'s forms, but it is clearly a problem. Several examples are mentioned below in the borrowed material. To cite just one example here, in set [7] *šüŋU 'snow', Uralic *šüŋe 'wet snow' is said to be supported by Finnish hyy 'ice, slush' and Lapp *sōvē 'snow with ice and water'. However, the Balto-Finnic comparisons do not extend to Finno-Ugric. As Itkonen & Kulonen (1992, 201) report, the comparisons with non-Finnic relatives in Uralic have problems both with sound correspondences and meanings, and 'uncertain comparisons have also been presented from Altaic languages'. (For other problems with this set, particularly with the Egyptian comparison, see Hegedűs, this volume pp. 262–3.)

2.13. Summary for consideration of standard criteria

In summary of section 2, nearly all of Dolgopolsky's (1998) proposed Nostratic sets exhibit serious problems from the perspective of the standard criteria surveyed here. It is for this reason that the overwhelming majority of historical linguists do not accept the Nostratic hypothesis — the evidence is just too flawed and inconclusive to warrant the confidence Nostratic supporters have for the hypothesis.

3. Typology, genetic relationship, and 'Altaic'

In this section I look briefly at typological problems of the Nostratic hypothesis and at the role typology has played in the proposal of distant genetic relationships, in particular the Altaic hypothesis.

Problems of how well Nostratic, as reconstructed by Illič-Svityč and Dolgopolsky, fits expectations from general typology and universals have been pointed out numerously. Bomhard & Kerns (1994, 13) and Bomhard (this volume) point out that in Dolgopolsky's version of Nostratic, glottalized stops (p', t', k') have the same as or a greater frequency of occurrence than plain voiceless stops (p, t, k) in Proto-Indo-European (where Proto-Indo-European plain voiceless stops are assumed to reflect Nostratic glottalics), but typology requires universally across languages that the marked glottalized stops have a less frequent occurrence in a language than the plain voiceless counterparts, and hence the major difference between. Manaster Ramer (1993, 211) showed that counter to typological expectations, there are 'very few cases of roots containing two voiceless stops' (where 'in almost all of these the second voiceless stop is clustered with a preceding sonorant'). Given that voiceless stops are less marked, they should occur more freely and with greater frequency than is the case in the Nostratic reconstructions. (For other arguments involving the typological deficiencies of Nostratic as proposed, see Campbell 1998a; Doerfer 1973; and Manaster Ramer 1993; 1994.)

Typology has played an important role in the framing of some proposed 'macrofamilies', including some involved in Nostratic. A frequent misapplication of typology in the framing of hypothesized macrofamilies is the reliance on shared traits which are the sort which develop easily and independently in languages, regardless of their genetic classifications. Typological traits which are commonplace and show up frequently in unrelated languages are not reliable evidence of genetic relationship. Nevertheless, some well-known proposals of remote linguistic kinship got their start precisely on the basis of this sort of commonplace typological traits. Since some of these enter into proposals involving Nostratic, it is instructive to consider examples, and I will illustrate the problems by considering 'Altaic'.

Dolgopolsky considers 'Altaic' a valid family and a branch of Nostratic. For him, Altaic includes Turkic, Mongolic, Tungusic (Manchu-Tungus), Korean, and Japanese (NM, 7–8). However, many of the leading 'Altaicists' have rejected Altaic, arguing that the evidence does not support the genetic affinity among the groups usually identified as 'Altaic' (Austerlitz 1983; 1991; Clauson 1956; Doerfer 1973; 1984; Janhunen 1996a; Róna-Tas 1983; Sinor 1988; Unger 1990; Abondolo 1998, 8, 28). Even some Nostraticists do not accept Altaic (though they may still believe Turkic, Mongolian, and Tungusic, and sometimes also Korean, Japanese, and Ainu, to be independent branches of a broader Nostratic superfamily; see Markey & Shevoroshkin 1986, xviii–xix; Starostin 1986; 1989,

42). The problems for Altaic include extensive borrowing, lack of clear cognates, and the sort of typological problems that are the focus of this section (cf. Campbell 1997b; Comrie 1992, 50; Janhunen 1996a, 237–56).

The original motivation for 'Altaic' was a certain number of shared typological traits: vowel harmony, simple phoneme inventories, agglutination, suffixing, (S)OV [Subject-Object-Verb] word order, and non-main clauses which are in form non-finite (participial). However, none of these typological traits, the original basis for postulating a genetic relationship, is good evidence; they are of the commonplace sort that are easily found independently in languages. Moreover, some of these are not independent of one another. For example, suffixing, SOV word order, and non-finite subordinate clauses are correlated and tend to co-occur in languages which have them, and such languages are found not just among the so-called Altaic languages, but on all continents of the world. The presence of this set of typological traits in two languages is no strong indication that they are related. Moreover, some of these typological traits have been diffused areally among some of the 'Altaic' languages.

The Altaic hypothesis has a long history, controversial from the beginning (see Campbell & Poser 1998). Not only was Altaic originally based on commonplace historically non-diagnostic typological traits, but lying behind it was the ethnocentric assumption that the typology of the language a people spoke both reflected and was determined by the level of social evolution the speakers had attained in evolutionary 'progress'. Thus, isolating languages were equated with savagery, agglutinating [as in 'Altaic' groups] with barbarism, and 'flexional' [Indo-European] with civilization. The first classifications of languages associated with 'Altaic' sometimes included more and sometimes fewer languages, called variously 'Tatar languages', 'Scythian' languages, and 'Turanian' languages, but they were not based on the comparative method at all, but rather represented the non-Indo-European, non-Semitic languages which shared agglutinative structure, associated with a particular stage of social evolution of society, which, for example, Müller (1855) called 'nomadic languages'.

Typological considerations make the Altaic hypothesis seem unlikely, since the traits that were suggested as evidence can easily develop in independent languages with no necessary historical connection. As pointed out frequently, it is not the commonplace which shows linguistic kinship, it is the unusual. Moreover, several of the typological traits upon which Altaic was based have been considered areal linguistic traits, shared by borrowing, not by inheritance from an earlier common ancestor (see below).

Classifications based on such commonplace typological features are called into question by the important linguistic principle advocated by Meillet and now generally accepted which permits only comparisons that involve both sound and meaning together, strongly promoted also by Greenberg (1957; 1963). Similarities in sound alone (e.g. tonal systems, or vowel harmony) or in meaning alone (e.g. grammatical gender, of suffixing) are not reliable, since they often appear in different languages independently of genetic relationship, due to diffusion, accident, or general typological tendencies. In Meillet's (1958, 90) words:

> Chinese and a language of Sudan or Dahomey such as Ewe, for example, may both use short and generally monosyllabic words, make contrastive use of tone, and base their grammar on word order and the use of auxiliary words, but it does not follow from this that Chinese and Ewe are related, since the concrete detail of their forms does not coincide; only coincidence of the material means of expression is probative.

In the case of the typological traits once thought supportive of 'Altaic', there is unfortunately a continuum in the distribution of these traits across northern Eurasia. This is what lies behind the now fully discredited and abandoned Ural-Altaic hypothesis, but these features are better explained as a combination of commonplace typological traits and areal diffusion (cf. Janhunen 1996a, 244). Given this, it is perhaps not surprising that Dolgopolsky posits similar traits for the grammar of Proto-Nostratic, principally: Object-Verb word order, post-positions, case markers following the noun, and attributes preceding their heads (*NM*, 17; Dolgopolsky, this volume). These are all consistent with SOV typology, where these features are expected to co-occur in a language of this type. Also, these broad, commonplace typological traits are widely distributed in several of the linguistic areas involving languages in the Nostratic complex (in the South Asian (Indian subcontinent) area, central and eastern Eurasian areas, and so on). That is, whatever other function the postulated grammatical traits of Nostratic might fulfill, they do not constitute any significant support for the proposal, since other explanations can account for why the languages involved share these traits. Appleyard (this volume) reports this grammatical 'evidence' as 'too diffuse' to be convincing; he finds 'the Afroasiatic "evidence" for some of these [grammatical morpheme reconstructions] is either easily contestable or highly suspect, however, and what is marginally more convincing is very little indeed'.

4. Areal linguistics and typology

Let us turn to areal linguistic problems for Nostratic and for proposed macrofamilies in general. Much of the evidence for relationship among so-called 'Altaic' languages and for broader connections with Nostratic is compromised by vocabulary and typological traits that are the result of areal diffusion among the languages involved. To date, work in Nostratic has avoided areal linguistics, but it is necessary in questions of remote linguistic kinship to take areal linguistics carefully into account. Areal linguistics involves the borrowing of structural traits across languages in a particular geographical region. Areal linguistic issues must be taken seriously in the discussion of Nostratic since a number of well-known language areas involve a range of 'Nostratic' languages (e.g. the Baltic area, South Asian (Indian subcontinent) area (with Dravidian and Indo-European), Ethiopian Highlands (Ferguson 1976; Heine 1992, 33), and the central and northeastern Eurasian areas (Janhunen 1996a, 240–44, 250–51, 253–6; Sinor 1990). As Sinor (1990, 16) puts it in his discussion of Inner Asia:

> While there are those scholars who aver that some or even all of them [Uralic and 'Altaic (or Turkic, Mongolian, and Tungusic)] are genetically related — that is, that they descend from a common, ancestral *Ursprache* — others, including myself, believe that the elements which they unquestionably have in common are due to constant interaction over the centuries if not millennia, and that they result from convergent rather than divergent development. Beyond purely linguistic arguments . . . the historically documented absorption by either Uralic or Altaic languages of many of the so-called Paleoasiatic tongues would support such a theory.

(For some works on areal linguistics involving putative Nostratic languages, see Abondolo 1998, 4–5; Adamović 1983; Campbell 1990; Doerfer 1984; Futaky 1983; Häkkinen 1996, 127–66; Haspelmath 1998; Jakobson 1931; Janhunen 1983; 1989; 1996a; Johanson 1998; Koivulehto 1984; Kuteva 1998; Masica 1976; Nedjalkov 1998; Nurse 1994; Östman & Raukko 1993; 1995; Raukko & Östman 1994; Róna-Tas 1983; Starostin 1989, 43; Suhonen 1995; Thomason & Kaufman 1988; Ureland 1987; Wiik 1995; Zeps 1962.)

As pointed out above, the principal motivation for proposing the Altaic hypothesis in the first place was certain shared typological traits among Turkic, Mongolian, and Tungusic (and later also Korean and Japanese); however, the areal diffusion of these typological traits may seem to call the whole construct into question. As Janhunen (1996a, 237) says, 'in view of their structural Altaicization, the Mandarin dialects of Chinese are also close to being an Altaic language'. Not only are many of those typological traits diffused areally, the vocabulary which has been presented in favour of the hypothesis also turns out mostly to be borrowed as a result of extensive and far-reaching language contacts. It is hardly surprising, then, that the hypothesis has been abandoned by many and is at best highly disputed (see Clauson 1956; 1969; Doerfer 1966;

1974; 1981a,b; Ščerbak 1966; 1986a,b; Janhunen 1992; 1994; 1996a, in addition to those cited above).

The typological traits shared among the three core Altaic families, Turkic, Mongolian, and Tungusic, have been shown to be due to areal linguistic diffusion and the shared vocabulary, which is mostly confined to semantic domains that are not basic, e.g. social structure, cultural items, which are suggestive of borrowing. Most of this vocabulary is not shared by all three, and much of it is demonstrably borrowed. Sinor (this volume) reports that 'many, if not most, of the posited Proto-Altaic forms suffer from the fatal flaw that they are attested in only one of the three Altaic groups and, even worse, there is often one single word that stands for the whole family'. The distribution of this borrowed vocabulary is connected with particular ethnic and political events:

> Much of the shared vocabulary between Turkic and Mongolic is . . . the result of Xiongnu cultural impact on the Xianbei. Only part of this shared vocabulary was further transmitted from Mongolic into Tungusic, while many of the other lexical items shared by Mongolic and Tungusic seem to be due to early contacts between Para-Mongolic and Jurchenic. Thus the absence of direct parallels between Turkic and Tungusic is a simple and irrefutable piece of evidence of the areal nature of the Altaic lexical relations. (Janhunen 1996a, 239–40)

Altaic vocabulary in general fails on Meillet's distribution criterion (above), which is why many reject the Altaic hypothesis; there are no items of basic vocabulary shared by all or most Altaic groups of languages. The amount of borrowing between Turkic and Mongolian, but also involving Tungusic, is extensive. Janhunen (1996a, 248) summarizes the Altaic evidence:

> The Anti-Altaists . . . have shown that the corpus presented *so far* in support of the Altaic Hypothesis is the result of areal contacts. In this sense, the Altaic Hypothesis has been seriously discredited, no matter how much influence it may still possess as a personal conviction among the Pro-Altaists. Any attempt to rescue the Altaic Hypothesis would have to be based on some essentially new evidence.

Even a supporter of the Altaic hypothesis, Vovin (this volume), accepts only 26 of the 80 Altaic etymologies among Dolgopolsky's 124 in the book. This highlights the difficulty with the Altaic lexical material.

As with Altaic, areal linguistics also presents serious problems for Afroasiatic. In particular the Semitic, Cushitic, and Omotic languages of Ethiopia contain 'a large body of shared vocabulary' and many linguistic features shared due to diffusion in the linguistic area, traits not shared by Afroasiatic languages outside the area (Appleyard, this volume; Ferguson 1976). For example, Appleyard reports that Amharic (Ethiopian Semitic) has borrowed the following basic vocabulary items from various neighbouring Cushitic languages: 'tongue', 'brain', 'knee', 'ear', 'lung', 'hair', 'moon', 'cloud', 'stone', 'day(time)', and 'water'. Others postulate a linguistic area in Western Asia in which Indo-European and languages of Eastern Anatolia and the Caucasus influenced one another and borrowed lexical items and structural properties (cf. Appleyard, this volume; Shevoroshkin, this volume pp. 88–9).

5. Africa and Afroasiatic

Altaic and Afroasiatic (Hamito-Semitic) are constituents of the Nostratic hypothesis but are themselves proposed macrofamilies which owe their beginnings largely to typological considerations of a questionable sort. Altaic has been discussed above; in this section Afroasiatic and its background are taken up briefly. Dolgopolsky's Hamito-Semitic (Afroasiatic) includes Semitic, Egyptian, Berber, Cushitic, Omotic, and Chadic. Afroasiatic is accepted by many (Renfrew 1998, xi), but also remains controversial for some scholars. In particular, Omotic (a disputed proposal) is doubted by some, and Chadic is held uncertain by others. Typology and areal linguistic complications loom large in these doubts. Here, I will look briefly at the background of Afroasiatic and then consider some problems not so much about whether it is a legitimate genetic grouping, but having to do with how Afroasiatic material has been deployed in Nostratic works.

Greenberg's classification of African languages (Greenberg 1963) is pivotal to discussion of Afroasiatic. Greenberg (1949–54) classified 321 African languages into 16 families, reduced to 12 in Greenberg (1955), and Greenberg (1963) grouped all these in 4 large-scale 'families' now known as Niger-Kordofanian, Nilo-Saharan, Afroasiatic, and Khoisan. Though it is often asserted that Greenberg's classification is generally accepted (cf. Renfrew 1998, xvii), it is *not* as generally accepted as asserted, and is less accepted now than formerly. As Winston (1966, 160) put it, Greenberg's African classification 'now require[s] considerable refinement, both in specific points of the classification, and in the underlying conceptual scheme' (see also Heine 1972, 7). Heine's (1992, 32) characterization of it represents the view that is now becoming more general:

> [Greenberg's] approach is largely inadequate for the PROOF of genetic relationship; it can do little more than offer initial hypotheses, to be substantiated by more reliable techniques like the comparative method. In a number of instances, languages or language groups have been placed in a given

family solely on the basis of a handful of 'look-alikes' . . . The Nilo-Saharan family, in particular, must be regarded as a tentative grouping.

Ringe (1992, 104), like many others now, urges re-examination:

> I would suggest that parts of Greenberg's famous classification of African languages, which was posited on the basis of multilateral comparison and more or less achieved the status of orthodoxy . . ., urgently needs to be reinvestigated by reliable methods.

Some of Greenberg's African hypotheses involve such assumed time depth and internal diversity that they remain unproven and probably can never be demonstrated (Bender 1987; Welmers 1973, 16–19). As frequently noted, many of the successful parts of Greenberg's African classification simply repeat classifications of earlier scholars (Gregersen 1977; Nurse 1997, 367–8; Welmers 1973), and Greenberg's methods have been heavily criticized in their African application (e.g. Winston 1966; Fodor 1966). Leading Africanists consider several aspects of Greenberg's African classification to be mistaken and others still undetermined (undemonstrable?). Fleming's (1987) description of Greenberg's African work is telling, since Fleming is a strong supporter of Greenberg, a recognized Africanist authority, and an enthusiastic booster of distant genetic proposals:

> It [Nilo-Saharan] has also been called 'Greenberg's waste basket', hence a collection of hard-to-classify languages and a very unreliable entity as a phylum. Vis-a-vis AA [Afro-Asiatic] or N-K [Niger-Kordofanian], N-S [Nilo-Saharan] is widely viewed as the more shaky of the three, but it no longer gets the kind of stubborn opposition that Khoisan receives in South Africa and Britain. When Greenberg finished his first classificatory sweep of Africa, he ended up with fourteen phyla. Of those, one was AA. One was N-C [Niger-Congo], which then had Kordofanian joined to it. The fourth was Khoisan. All the rest, or 10 phyla of the first classification, were put together as Nilo-Saharan. It represents far less consensus, far less agreement on sub-grouping, and very little progress on reconstruction. (Fleming 1987, 168–9; cf. also Bender 1991; 1993)

As Fleming indicates, two of Greenberg's big four African groups, Khoisan and Nilo-Saharan, are widely contested, denied by many. (For an assessment of Khoisan which leaves little doubt of its serious flaws, see Sands 1995; Nurse 1997, 269.)

M. Lionel Bender (1989, 1), also sympathetic to Greenberg's classification and a well-known African specialist reports 'controversies remain in the case of all four phyla established by Greenberg'. Bender's (pers. comm.) more recent assessment cites serious problems. He says Khoisan 'may well be two or three phyla rather than a single one . . . the evidence is minimal and maybe insufficient to answer this'. He views Niger-Kordofanian as 'a vast phylum for which there are problems about sub-grouping, some marginal members which seem to be possible overlaps with Nilo-Saharan or something else, plus a major problem of the status of the Mande family'. Regarding Nilo-Saharan, where Bender has worked extensively, he believes some major modifications in membership from those proposed by Greenberg are necessary. Of Afrasian (Afroasiatic), he writes, 'are Cushitic and Omotic (Greenberg's West Cushitic) really part of the same family? . . . Is Cushitic really five separate families (Beja, Agaw, etc.)?; Is there a special genetic grouping of Egyptian, Berber, and Semitic (or some other such arrangement . . .)?' He also criticizes Greenberg's methods, his 'extremely careless documentation (forms wrongly cited in many ways)'.

It should also be pointed out that areal linguistics has not played a significant role in African linguistics, though clearly serious areal linguistic problems complicate the classification (cf. Appleyard, this volume; Heine 1972, 7; 1992, 33; Ferguson 1976; Sasse 1986). To mention just one example, in the Ethiopian language area, 'Cushitic, Omotic, and Ethiopian Semitic show a number of features which are virtually absent from Afro-Asiatic languages outside the area, but which are shared by non-Afro-Asiatic languages within it, e.g. the presence of ejective consonants and of Subject-Object-Verb syntax' [both claimed to be properties of Proto-Nostratic, *NM*, pp. 17, 101] (Heine 1992, 33). For discussion of several cases of Cushitic and Bantu languages which have converged so extensively that accurate classification is made very difficult, see Mous 1994; Nurse 1991; 1994; Thomason & Kaufman 1988, 202–4, 223–8.

As noted, Greenberg's classification relied heavily on earlier classifications, and some of the typological consideration upon which these classifications were based still underlie Greenberg's groupings to a certain extent (e.g. clicks as diagnostic of 'Khoisan' languages). Those families which are clearly established and are not in dispute in Africa have relied on standard criteria; those proposals which remain controversial have relied on questionable criteria, typological traits or unreliable methods such as multilateral comparison. Not even Niger-Congo, though generally accepted by Africanists, has been established by standard methods. As Nurse (1997, 368) points out, it is on the basis of general similarities and the noun class system that most accept Niger-Congo, and yet 'the fact remains that no one has yet attempted a rigorous demonstration of the genetic unity of Niger-Congo by means of the Comparative Method'. This well-known noun class system (noun-classification concord), said to be found 'in a well-preserved, reduced or purely vestigial form . . . in every branch of the [Niger-Congo, in Niger-Kordofanian] family' (Williamson 1989,

31), was the main characteristic upon which many linguists have relied for classifying West African languages. However, these morphemes are prefixed in some language groups, suffixed in others, and barely visible at all in still others, and in any case the noun-class markers are thought to originate from grammaticalized independent demonstratives (Greenberg 1977; 1978). It appears that this feature so persistently present in African classifications is much overrated. If it were reconstructible to Proto-Niger-Congo, it would have to be as independent demonstrative words or particles, which became attached as suffixes in some languages and prefixes in others, after the break up of the proto language (Williamson 1989, 31–40). This trait reflects a typological feature (of meaning without sound) which can evolve independently or result from diffusion, the sort against which Greenberg (1963) himself warns — only comparisons involving both sound and meaning (not merely a trait like the presence of gender or of noun classification alone) can be considered reliable!

It is in the context of Greenberg's classification, typological considerations, and areal linguistics that Afroasiatic must be understood (see Campbell & Poser 1998 for fuller discussion). While Egyptian, Berber, and Semitic may be related, and Cushitic may be more remotely connected with these, doubts still surround Omotic and Chadic. For example, Porkhomovsky (1988, 102) has characterized them as follows:

> Chadic and Cushitic languages are extemely diverse. As a matter of fact, it would be correct to consider these language groups up to the second half of the 20th century, as areal, but not genetic communities, viz.: Chadic as non-Berber and non-Semitic Afrasian languages of the Western and Central Sudan, and Cushitic as a similar group in North-East Africa south of Sahara.

Comparison is complicated by long-term language contacts and borrowing, where Berber and Chadic have influenced one another; Omotic and Cushitic share areal traits; Egyptian influenced Semitic and was itself influenced; Cushitic has influenced Semitic; and Semitic, especially through Arabic in the last millennium, has influenced many others. There is no reconstruction of Proto-Afroasiatic comparable to that of Indo-European, Uralic, or Dravidian, and this results in Afroasiatic linguistic material being treated differently from that of the other putative Nostratic daughter languages. Unlike the forms listed from the other Nostratic families, *NM* does not present reconstructions for Afroasiatic in the putative cognate sets, but rather lists examples from different branches within this grouping. Important methodologically is the fact that because Nostraticists do not always obey Meillet's prohibition against limited scope ('reaching down') comparisons, it is hard for them to miss coming up some word they find similar to forms in other 'Nostratic' languages when shooting into Afroasiatic territory. With some 250 languages to choose words from (with *c.* 150 in Chadic alone, *c.* 50 in Cushitic; Zaborski 1992, 36), each with a large vocabulary and with no strict constraints on semantic equivalence which permits a large range of potential targets to look at, it is hard not to find forms which match in some way or another forms from other putative Nostratic languages. This is, of course, a problem in the treatment of all the Nostratic families; speaking of Altaic and Uralic, Sinor (this volume) recounts the procedure: 'most of the posited forms listed in *NM* rest on a handful of haphazardly collected words, fished out from the virtually limitless vocabulary of perhaps a hundred or more languages'. (For example, in [48], of the *c.* 250 Afroasiatic languages to choose from, *NM* finds a lexical match in only one, Ndam [East Chadic].) Finally, the quality and quantity of the data available from individual languages (especially Chadic, Cushitic, Omotic, and Berber) is uneven, often of questionable reliability (cf. Appleyard, this volume).

The main criterion upon which Hamito-Semitic has relied has been morphological agreements, in particular matchings in pronominal paradigms and a masculine-feminine gender distinction. This evidence is attractive, but not compelling. With respect to grammatical evidence for Afroasiatic in Nostratic, Appleyard (this volume) reports: 'The Afroasiatic "evidence" for some of these [grammatical morphemes which Dolgopolsky reconstructs for Nostratic] is either easily contestable or highly suspect, however, and what is marginally more convincing is very little indeed.' And, for the lexical comparisons, Afroasiatic scholars (except perhaps Greenberg) are in general agreement that the findings have been more limited and harder to interpret. In 1980 Newman reported 'the lists of supposedly cognate lexical items between Chadic and other Afroasiatic languages presented in the past have on the whole been less reliable' (1980, 13), and this still holds today.

Regardless of how much morphological and lexical evidence for Afroasiatic there may be, there is a methodological lesson to be gained in examining one flawed argument which has been considered among the strongest for Afroasiatic, i.e. Newman's (1980). Newman (1980, 19) argued that in

> a range of Afroasiatic languages from whatever branch, one finds that the words for 'blood', 'moon', 'mouth', 'name', and 'nose', for example, tend to be masculine; 'eye', 'fire', and 'sun', feminine; and 'water', grammatically plural' . . . where the overall consistency in gender assignment contrasts strikingly with the considerable diversity in form.

He compared 14 words which have the same gender across the branches of Afroasiatic and assumed this coincidence proves the genetic relationship. (His table has 15, but 'egg' is listed as doubtful, and in any case, there may be a real-world gender connection between females and eggs.) There are several problems with this account. First, it violates the principle of permitting only comparisons which involve both sound and meaning; Newman's comparisons involve only meaning (gender) and are not for the most part phonetically similar. Second, it assumes that the choice of gender marking is equally arbitrary for each of the forms compared, but this is not clearly the case. For example, 'sun' and 'moon' tend to be paired cross-linguistically in a set where the two have opposite genders, one masculine, the other feminine (e.g. Newman's 'Afroasiatic' masculine 'moon' and feminine 'sun' parallels German and many other languages). When feminine also signals 'diminutive' (as it does here and in many languages elsewhere), this may lie behind the masculine gender of the larger animals 'crocodile' and 'monkey' (cf., for example, the tendency for some English speakers to equate 'cat' with feminine). 'Sun' and 'fire', both feminine, may be associated in some way, affecting their shared gender. In any case, only 4 of the 14 are feminine, so perhaps masculine is unmarked, the gender most commonly found unless there is some reason for a word to be assigned to the feminine class. As for 'water' being plural, in three of the groups masculine and plural have the same form, so that it would be as accurate in these to say that 'water' is masculine. Also, plurality and mass-noun may be associated in some non-arbitrary way. Finally, the most serious problem is that of probability. As Nichols (1996) points out, even if there were an equal probability for any word in the set to show up as either masculine or feminine (and as just argued, this is not the case), for Newman's argument to have force, it would need a closed set with exactly these words and no others being tested for gender parallels. As Nichols shows, the probability of finding this number of forms with identical gender across the 6 branches of Afroasiatic if an open sample of basic nouns is searched comes out to be roughly equivalent to the 14 in Newman's table. The number he found is about what should be expected. The argument does not work.

In short the Afroasiatic hypothesis is not without problems of its own, and the way examples from the wide range of Afroasiatic languages are used in Nostratic violates standard principles.

6. Linguistic prehistory (which includes linguistic palaeontology)

In this section I address two issues: (1) can non-linguistic evidence help to determine linguistic classifications, and (2) how do *NM* linguistic palaeontological interpretations hold up in closer methodological scrutiny?

6.1. Non-linguistic evidence

It is important to understand the limitations of non-linguistic evidence in considerations of proposed macrofamilies, in particular because non-linguistic considerations often lead to erroneous linguistic classifications. This is not always understood well outside of linguistics. For example, Renfrew (1998, xvii) suggests 'there is the hope that evidence from molecular genetics will cast more light upon population histories which may in turn have a bearing upon language history also'. However, a valid principle, universally accepted among linguists, permits only linguistic information, and no non-linguistic considerations, as evidence for linguistic family relationships (Greenberg 1957; 1963). Shared cultural traits, mythology, folklore, technologies, human biology, and the like must be eliminated from arguments for linguistic kinship. The wisdom of this principle is seen from the many outlandish proposals which have been based on non-linguistic evidence. For example, some African classifications proposed that Ari (Omotic) belonged to either Nilo-Saharan or Sudanic 'because the Ari people are Negroes', that Moru and Madi belong to Sudanic because they are located in central Africa, or that Fula is Hamitic because the Fulani herd cattle, are Moslems, and are tall and Caucasoid (Fleming 1987, 207). Clearly, speakers of various languages can have different material cultural traits or biological genetic features in common with no necessary implication for the classification of their languages — these are independent variables, as demonstrated long ago by Boas and reconfirmed over and over since then.

Greenberg (1963) reaffirmed that only linguistic evidence is justified in considerations of linguistic relationship. Nevertheless, it has been suggested that Greenberg's (1987) classification of Native American languages into three groups has non-linguistic support. As Newman (1991, 454) indicates, there is an irony in this appeal to non-linguistic evidence, since Greenberg (1963) himself forcefully affirmed the principle that external non-linguistic evidence is irrelevant and often misleading in linguistic classifications. Attempts to correlate language classifications with human genetic information face grave difficulties. A single language can be spoken by a genetically diverse population, and a genetically homogeneous group may speak more than one language, i.e. both multilingualism and language shift are facts of life; genes neither cause these phenomena nor cater to them. This being the case, it is not surprising that claims of linguistic–human genetic correlations in support of the three-way classification of Native American languages have been heavily criticized by non-linguist geneticists (for details, see Campbell 1997a, 100–106; McMahon & McMahon 1995; Meltzer 1993a,b, 1). (As for other claims which attempt to correlate human genetic and linguistic histories on a grand, global scale, e.g. Cavalli-Sforza *et al.* 1988; 1989, the interpretations are so flawed on both sides of the equation, linguistic and genetic, both methodologically and substantively, that they command little serious attention. For the Americas, they uncritically accept Greenberg's three groups and base their schemes on them. For criticism, see Bateman *et al.* 1990a,b; McMahon & McMahon 1995, among many others.) More to the point, potential correlations with non-linguistic evidence (from dentition, human genetics, and archaeology) are ultimately irrelevant to issues of remote linguistic affinities, given the principle of linguistic classification which permits only linguistic (and no non-linguistic) evidence. This is not to discount non-linguistic evidence in the resolution of many issues in prehistory, nor to deny the many contributions to prehistory that linguistics in correlation with other sources of prehistoric information can make. It only reaffirms the principle that genetic relationships among languages are exclusively a linguistic matter and therefore cannot be determined by or based on any non-linguistic considerations.

6.2. Linguistic prehistory and Nostratic claims
Linguistic prehistory can be exciting, but the way the Nostratic 'macrofamily' hypothesis is talked about seems to cry out for greater caution. Consider the following from Renfrew's introduction to *NM*:

> The significance to the understanding of human history and prehistory, if the validity of such macrofamilies were accepted, is enormous (p. vii).

> If the Nostratic hypothesis is accepted, the *Nostratic Dictionary* . . . will clearly be a fundamental and pioneering contribution to our understanding of the prehistory of Europe and Western Asia and of the principal languages of these regions (p. viii).

> If the initial hypothesis (of the validity of the proposed macrofamilial relationships and equivalences) is accepted, then it throws a flood of light upon the world of the Upper Palaeolithic and perhaps even the Early Neolithic of a vast segment of the earth (pp. viii–ix).

> There is no doubt that the Nostratic hypothesis, if considered valid, is of the highest interest to prehistorians, and indeed to those concerned with population history, as well as to historical linguists (p. xx [in the concluding paragraph]).

The 'if' in these quotations seems to encourage readers to want to believe and accept, rather than the more typical use of 'if' to call upon readers to exercise caution until the hypothetical, conditional statement may be more solidly substantiated and to assess the evidence carefully in hopes of establishing the truth one way or the other. It is true that if the condition in these 'if' clauses could be substantiated, there would be wonderful spin off for prehistory. However, this is precisely what is at issue, and, as I argue here, there is stronger reason to withhold belief in the Nostratic hypothesis than to embrace it. So — and pardon the mixed metaphor — if the 'if' clause doesn't hold water, then the Nostratic boat with its prehistory cargo won't float.

This enthusiasm for the possible contributions to prehistory from a questionable linguistic construct gives me an uncomfortable sense of *déja vu*, of non-linguistic prehistorians becoming disenchanted with contributions from linguistics (Sinor, this volume, already expresses this sentiment). There are precedents. A number of archaeologists who put faith in glottochronology felt taken in by linguists when they found out that glottochronology did not work and that most linguists reject it. Similarly, some archaeologists based certain interpretations on proposed macrofamilies only to feel taken in by linguists when it became clear that some of these proposals were never taken that seriously by most linguists. In some of these instances, the archaeologists concluded that linguistics had nothing to offer archaeology at all. This is truly unfortunate, since historical linguistics can and does contribute successfully and significantly in many ways to a fuller picture of prehistory (for examples, see Campbell 1998c, 339–73).

This leads me to caution non-linguists from embracing Nostratic prematurely, which, as I try to show in this paper, is not generally accepted by historical linguists for good reasons. It matters not that 'Dolgopolsky's paper gives rich food for speculation [about prehistory]' (Renfrew 1998, xiii). Rather, the methods of linguistic palaeontology are rather exacting, permitting inferences where warranted by the evidence, but not encouraging raw 'speculation'. Until such time as the Nostratic hypothesis may, if ever, pass muster with the standard, legitimate, and accepted methods of historical linguistics, there can be no trustworthy non-linguistic inferences based on it.

The linguistic palaeontological inferences drawn in any given instance are only as reliable as the evidence upon which they are based. Unfortunately, even when applied to false classifications of languages and erroneous reconstructions of proto vocabulary, the methods of linguistic prehistory still render outcomes. For example, the method of searching for the linguistic homeland based on the distribution of the related languages and the centre of gravity (involving maximum diversification and minimal moves), even if applied to totally unrelated languages, will still render as output a location where these languages, if they had been related, would have once been and from where they would have spread out to reach their current geographical locations. In the cultural interpretation of reconstructed vocabulary, if we erroneously reconstruct for a proto language, say, terms for automobile, airplane, and personal computer, an investigation of the cultural contents of the proto lexicon will tell us that the speakers of this proto language had cars, planes, and computers in their cultural inventory. More to the point, if Dolgopolsky's sets [1] 'fig tree' and [6] 'monkey' are erroneous (and both were challenged by several of the participants in the symposium), then inferences about a Nostratic homeland and cultural inventory which takes 'fig tree' and 'monkey' as correct will produce a very different picture of these from one which eliminates these two sets from consideration. If 'Dolgopolsky's paper gives rich food for speculation', this does not make the inferences derived from it reliable. If the language families in the Nostratic hypothesis cannot be shown to be related, then the homeland exercise is no more reliable than it would be applied to any other arbitrary assembly of several different unrelated language families. If the sets Dolgopolsky has assembled as putative Nostratic etymologies are not true cognates, then they provide no evidence at all of any value for the interpretation of the culture history of the various groups involved. (Documented loanwords do provide valuable information for prehistory, but that is not what *NM* is about.)

The correlation of findings in Indo-European historical linguistics and in archaeology shows how productive linguistic prehistory can be and the sorts of contributions it can make to a fuller picture of prehistory in general. Renfrew (1998, xiii) reports that earlier scholars

> argued that the Proto-Indo-Europeans must have been pastoralists rather than agriculturalists, on the grounds that very few words for domesticated food plants are reconstructed into the protolexikon. But more recently archaeologists have come to realise that early Eurasian pastoralists must have been familiar with the crop plants of their agricultural contemporaries. So the absence of such terms from the protolexikon must be viewed as unexplained happenstance rather than as the absence of such elements from the original environment of the Proto-Indo-Europeans.

However, the earlier scholars to whom he refers were mistaken, and the more reliable linguistic reconstruction reveals positive evidence for the hypothesis that speakers of Proto-Indo-European were pastoralists who had knowledge of agricultural plant terms, e.g.:

*ekwo- 'horse' (it is argued that the expansion and migration of Indo-Europeans in the later third and early second millennia BC are bound with the horse)

*gʷou- 'bull, ox, cow' (English cow)

*owi- 'sheep' (see English ewe)

*ag^wh-no- 'lamb'

*aig- 'goat' (see English aegis)

*ghaido- 'goat' (English goat)

*uk^ws-en- 'bull, ox' (English ox)

*peku- 'wealth, movable property, livestock' (see German Vieh 'cattle'; see English fee, fief); suffixed *peku-n- gives Latin pecūnia 'property, wealth' (see the borrowing in English pecuniary)

*wegh- 'to go, transport in a vehicle') (see English way)

*wogh-no- 'vehicle (wagon)' (derived from *wegh- 'to go, transport in a vehicle') (English wagon, wain)

*k^w(e)k^wl-o- 'circle, wheel' (derived from *k^wel- 'to revolve, move around') (see English wheel)

*aks-lo- 'axle' (see *aks- 'axis')

Herein lies a whole cultural complex associated with pastoralism, a complex some argue is confirmed in the archaeological record. These pastoralists also had knowledge of agriculture:

*gr̥ə-no- 'grain' (see English corn, kernel)

*jewo- 'grain'

*pūro- 'grain'

*wrughjo- 'rye'

*bhares, *bhars- 'barley'

*al- 'to grind'

*melə-, *mel- 'to grind, crush' (seen in English mill, meal)

*sē- 'to sow' (the suffixed from *sē-ti- Germanic *sēdiz 'seed') (see English sow, seed)

*arə- 'to plough', *arə-trom- 'plough' (compare the loanword arable in English)

*pr̥k- 'furrow, trench' (seen in English furrow), derived from *perk- 'to dig out, tear out'

*solk-o- seen in Latin sulcus 'furrow, groove' (derived from *selk- 'to draw, pull')

*wog^wh-ini- 'ploughshare, wedge'

*jug-o- 'yoke' (derived from *jeug- 'to join')

*serp- 'sickle, hook'

*kerp- 'to harvest, gather, pluck'

*g^werə-nā- 'millstone, quern' (derived from *g^werə- 'heavy ') (see English quern)

*agro- 'field, fallow land on which cattle were driven' (from *ag- 'to drive') (see English acre) (Campbell 1998c, 341–5).

In this instance, the linguistic evidence appears to bear independent witness to the interpretation the archaeologists came to, that the Proto-Indo-Europeans were pastoralists who know agriculture. The two independent sources help to confirm each other's conclusions.

Caution about arguments based on negative information (which Renfrew and several others stressed in the symposium) would seem to raise questions for the interpretation which correlates the distribution of the constituent families of the putative Nostratic macrofamily with agricultural dispersals (cf. Renfrew 1998, xiv–xv). The model (cf. Renfrew 1998, fig. 3, p. xiv) holds that the consequence of agricultural dispersal is likely to be a series of linguistic replacements in adjoining areas, and this is supported by the suggestion 'that a number of the world's language families may be explained in terms of agricultural dispersals' (Renfrew 1998, xiv; cf. Bellwood 1996, 886). This, however, would appear at best a weak correlation, neither necessary nor sufficient for language distributions or replacements. For example, there is no evidence in Mesoamerica, highland South America, eastern North America, or the American Southwest for agriculturalists dispersing and replacing other languages along with the spread of agriculture. One could argue just the opposite: the inception of agriculture seems to provide the stability for some groups in some areas to settle in and to undergo more internal linguistic diversification locally than was possible before agriculture. There is evidence in a number of cases of non-agriculturalists acquiring agriculture from their neighbours while maintaining their linguistic (and ethnic) identity, as for example is documented by both linguistic and archaeological evidence in the case of the Apachean speakers in the American Southwest and Xincan speakers in Guatemala (Sapir 1936; Campbell 1998c), to mention just a couple. Mesoamerica, with its intense agriculture, has extremely dense linguistic diversity, and yet the relatively rich linguistic and archaeological documentation shows no linguistic expansions with agriculture. Rather, in fact, it reveals just the opposite; namely, loanword evidence reveals from whom small isolated linguistic-ethnic groups acquired their knowledge of agriculture. For example, in the small, marginal Xincan family of four languages in southeastern Guatemala, virtually all the terms for agriculture and cultigens are borrowed from neighbouring Mayan and Mixe-Zoquean languages, showing that Xincan speakers acquired agriculture from their neighbours, yet Xincan territory and languages survived intact until modern times. Internal linguistic evidence shows that Apachean speakers in the American Southwest acquired agriculture from their neighbours, but all groups continue to survive. The fact that the areas of the world with the oldest and most intensive agriculture typically have the greatest linguistic diversity (Mesoamerica, southeast Asia, central Africa, western South America, and Mesopotamia) show clearly that there can be no expectation of agriculture expansion correlating closely with linguistic expansion which takes over other languages. Ethnic and linguistic maintenance and shift are clearly influenced by many factors, but the gross acquisition of agriculture does not necessarily play a deterministic role.

More to the point, concerning Nostratic, a practitioner of linguistic palaeontology would find the association postulated between Nostratic divergence and dispersal of agriculture strange indeed, for it relies on — or better said, must face but ignore — negative evidence of the sort about which caution is generally called for. That is, as Dolgopolsky (1998, 26) says, 'the Nostratic vocabulary (as reconstructed in the extant two thousand etymological entries) has no words that can be unequivocally connected with Neolithic culture'. 'It has no words for sowing or ploughing, but has words for harvesting.' Moreover, the four reconstructed words connected with harvest and cereals are not at all persuasive. The postulated etymological set [15] is glossed 'to harvest' ('cereal'), but contains only Hamito-Semitic forms meaning variously 'to pluck and gather (fruit)', 'autumn and winter', 'winter'; Indo-European represented only by a Hittite form meaning 'feast of harvest' (involving borrowing); and Altaic forms for 'barley, oats' diffused among these languages across this part of central Eurasia (also involving borrowing) (Sinor, this volume; Starostin, this volume). Set [16] is glossed 'edible cereals, harvest (of wild plants?)', but is represented only by Hamito-Semitic ('to grow [of a plant]', 'to plough, cultivate a field') and Uralic ('autumn'). This semantic latitude and lack of representation in any but two branches of putative Nostratic call this form seriously into question. Set [17] is a weak set; it is represented by only three of the Nostratic families, but is not actually reconstructible to the proto-language in any of the three constituent families. In Hamito-Semitic it is represented only by Arabic 'cereal'; Kartvelian has only Georgian 'zu mähendes reifes Korn'; and in Indo-European a form meaning 'grain' is found only in Hittite and Greek (and borrowed into Latin) — which are not attested cognates and are possibly borrowed (Shevoroshkin, this volume p. 86). Set [18] 'kernel, grain' is represented in three branches of Nostratic, Hamito-Semitic, Indo-European, and Dravidian. However, to get the Indo-European forms to fit, it is necessary to call upon otherwise unmotivated metathesis (Nostratic *Xänt'∇/Semitic *hint-at- 'wheat'/Indo-European *x̂et(e)n 'kind of cereal'). Borrowing is possible in this case. Not only are all four sets problematic, but even if some merit could be found for them, just based on the semantic associations of the languages involved in the various sets, it is not at all clear that the 'harvest' and 'cereal' meanings should be chosen to represent their original meanings. Thus, the evidence upon which the notion of Nostratic knowledge of agriculture is based is challenged. In short, the linguistic evidence does not offer any support for correlating Nostratic dispersal with spread of agriculture.

All specialists agree that Proto-Uralic speakers had no knowledge of agriculture, and evidence even for later Finno-Ugric speakers' involvement with agriculture is limited (Campbell 1997c; Häkkinen 1996, 117–26). Given that there is no evidence of agriculture in Uralic, any argument which attempts to account for the location of the Uralic with respect to other Nostratic families on the basis of diversity in Nostratic correlated with the expansion of agriculture can be nothing more than sheer speculation.

To reiterate, unless Nostratic can be supported with more compelling linguistic evidence, any interpretations of non-linguistic prehistory based on it remain sheer speculation.

7. Conclusions

It is hoped that this brief methodological look at the evidence presented illustrates well why the vast majority of historical linguists do not accept the Nostratic hypothesis. There are good reasons for this: as argued here, it does not hold up even on the basis of the historical linguistic principles and criteria that Nostraticists themselves believe in. Because nearly all of *NM*'s 124 sets exhibit serious problems from a methodological perspective, the hypothesis is not well founded and therefore no non-linguistic culture historical interpretations based on these forms can be embraced.

References

Abondolo, D., 1998. Introduction, in *The Uralic languages*, ed. D. Abondolo. London: Routledge, 1–42.

Adamović, A., 1983. Das Tchuwaschische im Lichte der Substrattheorie, in *Symposium Saecularle Societatis Fenno-Ugricae*. (Mémoires de la Société Finno-Ougrienne 185.) Helsinki: Suomalais-Ugrilainen Seura, 9–24.

Austerlitz, R., 1983. Genetic affilation among proto-languages, in *Symposium Saecularle Societatis Fenno-Ugricae*. (Mémoires de la Société Finno-Ougrienne 185.) Helsinki: Suomalais-Ugrilainen Seura, 51–8.

Austerlitz, R., 1991. Alternatives to long-range comparison, in Lamb & Mitchell (eds.), 353–64.

Bakker, P. & M. Mous (eds.), 1994. *Mixed Languages: 15 Case Studies in Language Intertwining*. Amsterdam: Institute for Functional Research into Language and Language Use.

Bateman, R.M., I. Goddard, R. O'Grady, V.A. Fund, R. Mooi, W.J. Kress & P. Cannell, 1990a. The feasibility of reconciling human phylogeny and the history of language. *Current Anthropology* 31, 1–24.

Bateman, R.M., I. Goddard, R. O'Grady, V.A. Fund, R. Mooi, W.J. Kress & P. Cannell, 1990b. On human phylogeny and linguistic history: reply to comments. *Current Anthropology* 31, 177–82.

Bellwood, P., 1996. Phylogeny vs reticulation in prehistory. *Antiquity* 70, 881–90.

Bender, M.L., 1987. First steps towards Proto-Omotic, in *Current Approaches to African Linguistics*, vol. 4, ed. D. Odden. Dordrecht: Foris Publications, 21–35.

Bender, M.L., 1989. Nilo-Saharan pronouns/demonstratives, in *Topics in Nilo-Saharan Linguistics,* ed. M.L. Bender. (Nilo-Saharan linguistic analyses and documentation 3.) Hamburg: Buske, 1–34.

Bender, M.L., 1991. Sub-classification of Nilo-Saharan, in *Proceedings of the Fourth Nilo-Saharan Linguistics Colloquium,* ed. M.L. Bender. (Nilo-Saharan: Linguistic Analyses and Documentation 7.) Hamburg: Buske, 1–35.

Bender, M.L., 1993. Is Nilo-Saharan really a phylum? Paper presented at the 24th African Linguistics Conference, July 23–5, Columbus, Ohio.

Benedict, P.K., 1975. *Austro-Thai Language and Culture, with a Glossary of Roots.* New Haven (CT): Human Relations Area Files.

Benedict, P.K., 1990. *Japanese/Austro-Tai.* (Linguistica Extranea, Studia 20.) Ann Arbor (MI): Karoma Press.

Bengtson, J., 1991. Notes on Sino-Caucasian, in *Dene-Sino-Caucasian Languages: Materials from the First International Interdisciplinary Symposium on Language and Prehistory,* ed. V. Shevoroshkin. Bochum: Brockmeyer, 67–157.

Biggs, B., 1965. Direct and indirect inheritance in Rotuman. *Lingua* 14, 383–415.

Bomhard, A.R. & J.C. Kerns, 1994. *The Nostratic Macrofamily: a Study in Distant Linguistic Relationship.* Berlin: Mouton de Gruyter.

Bright, W. (ed.), 1992. *International Encyclopedia of Linguistics.* Oxford: Oxford University Press.

Campbell, L., 1990. Indo-European and Uralic trees. *Diachronica* 7, 149–80.

Campbell, L., 1997a. *American Indian languages: the Historical Linguistics of Native America.* Oxford: Oxford University Press.

Campbell, L., 1997b. Genetic classification, typology, areal linguistics, language endangerment, and languages of the north Pacific rim, in *Languages of the North Pacific Rim*, vol. 2, eds. O. Miyaoka & M. Oshima, 179–242.

Campbell, L., 1997c. On the linguistic prehistory of Finno-Ugric, in *Language History and Linguistic Modelling: a Festschrift for Jacek Fisiak*, eds. R. Hickey & S. Puppel. Berlin: Mouton de Gruyter, 830–61.

Campbell, L., 1998a. Nostratic: a personal assessment, in *Nostratic: Sifting the Evidence*, eds. B. Joseph & J. Salmons. Amsterdam: John Benjamins, 107–52.

Campbell, L., 1998b [In press]. How to show languages are related: methods for distant genetic relationship, in *Handbook of Historical Linguistics*, eds. R.D. Janda & B.D. Joseph. London: Blackwell.

Campbell, L., 1998c. *Historical Linguistics: an Introduction.* Edinburgh: Edinburgh University Press; Cambridge (MA): MIT Press.

Campbell, L. & W. Poser, 1998 [manuscript]. *How to Show that Languages are Related: a Historical and Methodological Review of Linguistic Classification.* [Monograph in preparation.]

Cavalli-Sforza, L.L., A. Piazza, P. Menozzi & J. Mountain, 1988. Reconstruction of human evolution: bringing together genetic, archaeological, and linguistic data. *Proceedings of the National Academy of Science of the USA* 85, 6002–6.

Cavalli-Sforza, L.L., A. Piazza, P. Menozzi & J. Mountain, 1989. Genetic and linguistic evolution. *Science* 244, 1128–9.

Clauson, G., 1956. The case against the Altaic theory. *Central Asiatic Journal* 2, 181–7.

Clauson, G., 1969. A lexicostatistical appraisal of the Altaic theory. *Central Asiatic Journal* 13, 1–13.

Cohen, M., 1947. *Essai comparatif sur le vocabulaire et la phonétique du chamito-sémitique.* Paris: H. Champion.

Comrie, B., 1992. Altaic languages, in Bright (ed.), 48–51.

Csúcs, S., 1990. *Die tatarischen Lehnwörter des Wotjakischen.* Budapest: Akadémiai Kiadó.

Doerfer, G., 1966. Zur Verwandtschaft der altaischen Sprachen. *Indogermanische Forschungen* 71, 81–123.

Doerfer, G., 1973. *Lautgesetz und Zufall.* (Betrachtungen zum Omnikomparatismus. Innsbrucker Beiträge zur Sprachwissenschaft, vol. 10, ed. by Wolfgang Meid.) Innsbruck: Innsbrucker Beiträge zur Sprachwissenschaft.

Doerfer, G., 1974. Ist das Japanische mit den altaischen Sprachen verwandt? *Zeitschrift der Deutschen Morgenländischen Gesellschaft* 124, 103–42.

Doerfer, G., 1981a. The conditions for proving the genetic relationship of languages. *The Bulletin of the International Institute for Linguistic Sciences* 2(4), 38–58.

Doerfer, G., 1981b. Bazisnaya leksika i altaiskaya problema. *Voprosy yazykoznaniya* 4, 35–44.

Doerfer, G., 1984. Prolegomena zu einer Untersuchung der dem Tungusischen und Mongolischen gemeinsamen Wörter. *Journal de la Société Finno-Ougrienne* 79, 65–85.

Dolgopolsky, A., 1998. *The Nostratic Macrofamily and Linguistic Palaeontology.* (Papers in the Prehistory of Languages.) Cambridge: The McDonald Institute for Archaeological Research.

Ferguson, C.A., 1976. The Ethiopian language area, in *Language in Ethiopia,* eds. M.L. Bender, J.D. Bowen, R.L. Cooper & C.A. Ferguson. London: Oxford University Press, 63–76.

Fleming, H.C., 1987. Review article: Towards a definitive classification of the world's languages (review of *A Guide to the World's Languages,* by Merritt Ruhlen). *Diachronica* 4, 159–223.

Fodor, I., 1966. *The Problems in the Classification of the African Languages: Methodological and Theoretical Conclusions Concerning the Classification System of Joseph H. Greenberg.* Budapest: Center for Afro-Asian Research of the Hungarian Academy of Sciences.

Friedrich, P., 1970. *Proto-Indo-European Trees: the Arboreal System of a Prehistoric People.* Chicago (IL): University of Chicago Press.

Futaky, I., 1983. Die Frage der uralisch-tungusischen Sprachbeziehungen, in *Symposium Saecularle Societatis Fenno-Ugricae.* (Mémoires de la Société Finno-Ougrienne 185.) Helsinki: Suomalais-Ugrilainen Seura, 89–104.

Gamkrelidze, T.V. & V.V. Ivanov, 1984. *Indoevropejskij jazyk i indoevropejtsy.* (2 volumes.) Tbilisi: Tbilisi State University.

Gamkrelidze, T.V. & V.V. Ivanov, 1985. The ancient Near East and the Indo-European question: temporal and territorial characteristics of Proto-Indo-European based on linguistic and historico-cultural data. *The Journal of Indo-European Studies* 13, 3–48.

Golla, V. (ed.), 1984. *The Sapir-Kroeber Correspondence.* (Survey of California and Other Indian Languages, report 6.) Berkeley (CA): University of California, Department of Linguistics.

Greenberg, J.H., 1949, 1950, 1954. Studies in African linguistic classification. *Southwestern Journal of Anthropology* 5, 79–100; 6; 10.

Greenberg, J.H., 1955. *Studies in African Linguistic Classification.* New Haven (CT): Compass Publishing Company.

Greenberg, J.H., 1957. Genetic relationship among languages, in *Essays in Linguistics.* Chicago (IL): University of Chicago Press, 35–45.

Greenberg, J.H., 1963. *Languages of Africa.* (Publications of the Indiana University Research Center in Anthropology, Folklore, and Linguistics, 25.) Bloomington (IN): Indiana University Press.

Greenberg, J.H., 1977. Niger-Congo noun class markers: prefixes, suffixes, both or neither. *Studies in African Linguistics* (Supplement 7), 94–104.

Greenberg, J.H., 1978. How does a language acquire gender markers?, in *Universals of Human Language,* vol. 3, eds. J.H. Greenberg, C. Turner II & S. Zegura. Stanford (CA): Stanford University Press, 47–82.

Greenberg, J.H., 1987. *Language in the Americas.* Stanford (CA): Stanford University Press.

Greenberg, J.H., 1990. The prehistory of the Indo-European vowel system in comparative and typological perspective, in *Proto-languages and Proto-cultures: Materials from the First International Interdisciplinary Symposium on Language and Prehistory,* ed. V. Shevoroshkin. Bochum: Universitätsverlag Dr. N. Brockmeyer, 77–136.

Greenberg, J.H., 1991. Some problems of Indo-European in historical perspective, in Lamb & Mitchell (eds.), 125–40.

Greenberg, J.H., forthcoming. *Indo-European and its Closest Relatives: the Eurasiatic Language Family.* Stanford (CA): Stanford University Press.

Greenberg, J.H., C. Turner II & S. Zegura, 1986. The settlement of the Americas: a comparison of the linguistic, dental, and genetic evidence. *Current Anthropology* 27, 477–97.

Gregersen, E.A., 1977. *Language in Africa: an Introductory Survey.* New York (NY): Gordon & Breach.

Häkkinen, K., 1996. *Suomalaisten esihistoria kielitieteen valossa* [*The Prehistory of the Finns in the Light of Linguistics*]. Helsinki: Suomalaisen Kirjallisuuden Seura.

Häkkinen, K., 1997. *Mistä sanat tulevat: Suomalaista etymologiaa* [*Where do Words Come From?: Finnish Etymology*]. Helsinki: Suomalaisen Kirjallisuuden Seura.

Hajdú, P., 1975. *Finno-Ugrian Languages and Peoples.* London: André Deutsch.

Haspelmath, M., 1998. How young is Standard Average European? *Language Sciences* 20, 271–87.

Hegedűs, I., 1992. Reconstructing Nostratic morphology: derivational elements, in *Nostratic, Dene-Caucasian, Austric and Amerind*, ed. V. Shevoroshkin. Bochum: Brockmeyer, 34–47.

Heine, B., 1972. Historical linguistics and lexicostatistics in Africa. *Journal of African languages* 2, 7–20.

Heine, B., 1992. African languages, in Bright (ed.), 31–5.

Illič-Svityč, V.M., 1989. The relationship of the Nostratic family languages: a probablistic evaluation of the similarities in question, in *Explorations in Language Macrofamilies: Materials from the First International Interdisciplinary Symposium on Language and Prehistory*, ed. V. Shevoroshkin. Bochum: Universitätsverlag Dr N. Brockmeyer, 111–21. [English translation of the introduction to Opyt sravneniia nostraticheskikh iazykov (semitokhamitskii, karvel'skii, indoevropeiskii, ural'skii, dravidiiskii, altaiskii). 1971. Moscow: Nauka.]

Itkonen, E. & U.-M. Kulonen, 1992. *Suomen sanojen alkuperä: etymologinen sanakirja*, vol. 1: *A–K* [*The Origin of Finnish Words: Etymological Dictionary*, vol. 1: A–K]. Helsinki: Suomalaisen Kirjallisuuden Seura.

Jakobson, R., 1931. Über die phonologischen Sprachbünde. *Travaux du Cercle Linguistique de Prague* 4, 234–40.

Jakobson, R., 1960. Why 'mama' and 'papa'?, in *Perspectives in Psychological Theory*, eds. B. Kaplan & S. Wapner. New York (NY): International Universities Press, 21–9. (Reprinted in 1962, in *Roman Jakoson Selected Writings*, vol. 1: *Phonological Studies*. The Hague: Mouton, 538–45.)

Janhunen, J., 1977. *Samoyed–Altaic Contacts: Present State of Research.* (Mémoires de la Société Finno-Ougrienne, 158.) Helsinki: Suomalais-Ugrilainen Seura.

Janhunen, J., 1983. On early Indo-European-Samoyed contasts, in *Symposium saeculare Societatis Fenno-Ugricae.* (Mémoires de la Société Finno-Ougrienne 185.) Helsinki: Suomalais-Ugrilaisen Seura, 115–27.

Janhunen, J., 1989. On the interaction of Mator with Turkic, Mongolic, and Tungusic. *Journal de la Société Finno-Ougrienne* 82, 287–97.

Janhunen, J., 1992. Das Japanische in vergleichender Sicht. *Journal de la Société Finno-Ougrienne* 84, 145–61.

Janhunen, J., 1994. Additional notes on Japanese and Altaic (1–2). *Journal de la Société Finno-Ougrienne* 8, 236–40, 256–60.

Janhunen, J., 1996a. *Manchuria: an Ethnic History.* (Mémoires de la Société Finno-Ougrienne 222.) Helsinki: The Finno-Ugrian Society.

Janhunen, J., 1996b. Prolegomena to a comparative analysis of Mongolic and Tungusic, in *Proceedings of the 38th Permanent International Ataistic Conference*, ed. G. Stary. Wiesbaden: Harrassowitz, 209–18.

Joki, A.J., 1973. *Uralier und Indogermanen: Die älteren Berührungen zwischen den uralischen und indogermanischen Sprachen.* (Mémoires de la Société Finno-Ougrienne 151.) Helsinki: Suomalais-Ugrilaisen Seura.

Joki, A.J., 1988. Zur Geschichte der uralischen Sprachgemeinschaft unter besonderer Berücksichtigung des Ostfinnischen, in *The Uralic Languages: Description, History, and Foreign Influences*, ed. D. Sinor. Leiden: E.J. Brill, 575–95.

Johanson, L., 1998. Code-copying in Irano-Turkic. *Language Sciences* 20, 325–37.

Kaiser, M. & V. Shevoroshkin, 1987. On recent comparisons between language families: the case of Indo-European and Afro-Asiatic. *General Linguistics* 27, 34–546.

Koivulehto, J., 1983. Suomalaisten maahanmuutto indoeurooppalaisten lainojen valossa [The immigration of the Finns in light of Indo-European loans]. *Journal de la Société Finno-Ougrienne* 77, 107–31.

Koivulehto, J., 1984. Itämerensuomalais-germaaniset kosketukset [Summary: The early contacts between Germanic and Finnic], in *Suomen väestön esihistorialliset juuret.* (Bidrag till kännedom av Finlands natur och folk 131.) Helsinki: Finnish Academy of Sciences, 191–205.

Koivulehto, J., 1991. *Uralische Evidenz für die Laryngaltheorie.* (Österreichische Akademie der Wissenschaften, philosophisch-historische Klasse, Sitzungsberichte 566.) Vienna: Der Österreichischen Akademie der Wissenschaft.

Koivulehto, J., 1994. Indogermanisch-Uralisch: Lehnbeziehungen oder (auch) Urverwandtschaft, in *Bopp-Symposium 1992 der Humboldt-Universität zu Berlin,* ed. R. Sternemann. Heidelberg: Winter.

Koivulehto, J., 1995. Zur indogermanisch-germanischen Kontinuität in der Nachbarschaft der Finnougrier, in *Der Ginkgo Baum.* (Germanistisches Jahrbuch für Nordeuropa 13.) Helsinki.

Korhonen, M., 1981. *Johdatus lapin kielen historiaan* [Introduction to the History of the Lapp Language]. Helsinki: Suomalaisen Kirjallisuuden Seura.

Kulonen, U.-M., 1995. *Suomen sanojen alkuperä: etymologinen sanakirja,* vol. 2: *L–P* [The Origin of Finnish Words: Etymological Dictionary, vol. 2: *L–P*]. Helsinki: Suomalaisen Kirjallisuuden Seura.

Kuteva, T., 1998. Large linguistic areas in grammaticalization: auxiliation in Europe. *Language Sciences* 20, 289–311.

Lamb, S.M. & E.D. Mitchell (eds.), 1991. *Sprung from Some Common Source: Investigations into the Prehistory of Languages.* Stanford (CA): Stanford University Press.

Lass, R., 1997. *Historical Linguistics and Language Change.* Cambridge: Cambridge University Press.

Lepsius, C.R., 1863. *Standard Alphabet.* (2nd ed.) London: Williams & Norgate.

Lynch, J., 1998. *Pacific Languages: an Introduction.* Honolulu (HI): University of Hawaii Press.

McMahon, A. & R. McMahon, 1995. Linguistics, genetics, and archaeology: internal and external evidence in the Amerind controversy. *Transactions of the Philological Society* 93, 125–225.

Manaster Ramer, A., 1993. On Illič-Svityč's Nostratic theory. *Studies in Language* 17, 205–50.

Manaster Ramer, A., 1994. Clusters or affricates in Kartvelian and Nostratic? *Diachronica* 11, 157–70.

Markey, T.L. & V.V. Shevoroshkin, 1986. Foreword, in *Typology, Relationship and Time: a Collection of Papers on Language Change and Relationship by Soviet Linguists,* ed. and trans. with a critical foreword by V.V. Shevoroshkin & T.L. Markey. Ann Arbor (MI): Karoma Publishers, vii–xliv.

Masica, C.P., 1976. *Defining a Linguistic Area: South Asia.* Chicago (IL): University of Chicago Press.

Matthews, P., 1997. *The Concise Oxford Dictionary of Linguistics.* Oxford: Oxford University Press.

Meillet, A., 1925. *La méthode comparative en linguistique historique.* Paris: Champion. (Translation 1967: *The Comparative Method in Historical Linguistics.* Paris: Champion.)

Meillet, A., 1958. *Linguistique historique et linguistique générale.* (Société Linguistique de Paris, Collection Linguistique 8.) Paris: Champion.

Meinhof, C., 1912. *Die Sprachen der Hamiten.* Hamburg: L. Friederichsen.

Meltzer, D.J., 1993a. *Search for the First Americans.* Washington (DC): Smithsonian Books.

Meltzer, D.J., 1993b. Pleistocene peopling of the Americas. *Evolutionary Anthropology* 1, 157–69.

Müller, M., 1855. *The Languages of the Seat of War in the East: with a Survey of Three Families of Languages, Semitic, Arian, and Turanian.* London: Longmans, Green & Co.

Mous, M., 1994. Ma'a or Mbugu, in Bakker & Mous (eds.), 175–200.

Mudrak, O. & S. Nikolaev, 1989. Gilyak and Chukchi-Kamchatkan as Almosan-Keresiouan languages: lexical evidence, in *Explorations in Language Macrofamilies: Materials from the First International Interdisciplinary Symposium on Language and Prehistory,* ed. V. Shevoroshkin. Bochum: Universitätsverlag Dr N. Brockmeyer, 67–87.

Murdock, G.P., 1959. Cross-language parallels in parental kin terms. *Anthropological Linguistics* 1(9), 1–5.

Nedjalkov, I., 1998. Converbs in the languages of eastern Siberia. *Language Sciences* 20, 339–51.

Newman, P., 1980. *The Classification of Chadic within Afroasiatic*. Leiden: Universitaire Pers.

Newman, P., 1991. An interview with Joseph Greenberg. *Current Anthropology* 32, 453–67.

Nichols, J., 1996. The comparative method as heuristic, in *The Comparative Method Reviewed: Regularity and Irregularity in Language Change*, eds. M. Durie & M. Ross. New York (NY): Oxford University Press, 39–71.

Nikolaev, S., 1991. Sino-Caucasian languages in America, in *Dene-Sino-Caucasian Languages: Materials from the First International Interdisciplinary Symposium on Language and Prehistory*, ed. V. Shevoroshkin. Bochum: Universitätsverlag Dr N. Brockmeyer, 42–66.

NM = Dolgopolsky 1998.

Nurse, D., 1991. Language contact, creolization, and genetic linguistics: the case of Mwiini. *Berkeley Linguistic Society* 17, 177–87.

Nurse, D., 1994. South meets North: Ilwana = Bantu + Cushitic on Kenya's Tana river, in Bakker & Mous (eds.), 213–22.

Nurse, D., 1997. The contributions of linguistics to the study of history in Africa. *Journal of African History* 38, 359–91.

Östman, J.-O. & J. Raukko, 1993. Extending the domain of areal linguistics: a pragmatic visit to Baltic Europe, in *Proceedings of the XVth International Congress of Linguists*, vol. 3, eds. A. Crochetière, J.-C. Boulanger & C. Ouellon. Quebec: Les Presses de l'Université Laval, 233–6.

Östman, J.-O. & J. Raukko, 1995. The 'pragmareal' challenge to genetic language tree models, in *The Fenno-Baltic Cultural Area*, ed. Seppo Suhonen. (Castrenianumin toimittteita 49.) Helsinki: Vammala, 31–66.

Porkhomovsky, V.Y., 1988. On methodological problems of the genetic classification of the Afrasian (Hamito-Semitic) languages, in *Proceedings of the Ninth International Congress of Ethiopian Studies*. Moscow: USSR Academy of Sciences Africa Institute, 99–103.

Raukko, J. & J.-O. Östman, 1994. *Pragmaattinen näkökulma Itämeren kielialueeseen [A Pragmatic View of the Baltic Linguistic Area]*. (Publications of the Department of General Linguistics 25.) Helsinki: University of Helsinki.

Rédei, K., 1986. *Zu den indogermanisch-uralischen Sprachkontakten*. (Österreichische Akademie der Wissenschaften. Philosophisch-historische Klasse. Sitzungsberichte 468.) Vienna: Veröffentlichungen der Kommission für Linguistik und Kommunkationsforschung.

Rédei, K., 1986–88. *Uralisches etymologisches Wörterbuch*. (7 fascicles.) Budapest: Akadémiai Kiadó.

Rédei, K., 1988. Die ältesten indogermanischen Lehnwörter der uralischen Sprachen, in *The Uralic Languages: Description, History, and Foreign Influences*, ed. D. Sinor. Leiden: E.J. Brill, 638–64.

Renfrew, C., 1998. Introduction: the Nostratic hypothesis, linguistic macrofamillies, and prehistoric studies, in *The Nostratic Macrofamily and Linguistic Palaeontology*, by A. Dolgopolsky. Cambridge: The McDonald Institute for Archaeological Research, vii–xxii.

Ringe, D.A., Jr, 1992. On calculating the factor of chance in language comparison. *Transactions of the American Philolsophical Society* 82(1), 1–110.

Ringe, D.A., Jr, 1993. A reply to Professor Greenberg. *Proceedings of the American Philosophical Society* 137, 91–109.

Róna-Tas, A., 1983. De hypothesi Uralo-Altaica, in *Symposium Saecularle Societatis Fenno-Ugricae*. (Mémoires de la Société Finno-Ougrienne 185.) Helsinki: Suomalais-Ugrilainen Seura, 235–52.

Róna-Tas, A., 1988. Turkic influence on the Uralic languages, in *The Uralic Languages: Description, History, and Foreign Influences*, ed. D. Sinor. Leiden: E.J. Brill, 742–80.

Rozycki, W., 1994. *Mongol Elements in Manchu*. (Indiana University Uralic and Altaic Series 157.) Bloomington (IN): Indiana University.

Ruhlen, M., 1994a. *On the Origin of Languages: Studies in Linguistic Taxonomy.* Stanford (CA): Stanford University Press.

Ruhlen, M., 1994b. Linguistic evidence for the peopling of the Americas, in *Method and Theory for Investigating the Peopling of the Americas*, ed. R. Bonnichsen & D.G. Steele. Corvallis (OR): Oregon State University, Center for the Study of Americans, 177–88.

Salminen, T., 1989. Classification of the Uralic languages, in *Proceedings of the Fifth International Finno-Ugrist Students' Conference*, eds. R. Grünthal, S. Penttinen & T. Salminen. (Castrenianumin toimitteita 35.) Helsinki: University of Helsinki, 15–24.

Sammallahti, P., 1988. Historical phonology of the Uralic languages, in *The Uralic Languages: Description, History, and Foreign Influences*, ed. D. Sinor. Leiden: E.J. Brill, 478–554.

Sands, B.E., 1995. Evaluating Claims of Distant Linguistic Relationship: the Case of Khoisan. Unpublished Ph.D. dissertation, UCLA, Los Angeles, CA.

Sapir, E., 1925. The similarity of Chinese and Indian languages. *Science* 62 (October 16), 12.

Sapir, E., 1929. Central and North American languages. *Encyclopaedia Britannica*, 14th edition, 5, 138–41.

Sapir, E., 1936. Internal linguistic evidence suggestive of the Northern origin of the Navajo. *American Anthropologist* 38, 224–5.

Sasse, H.-J., 1986. A southwest Ethiopian language area and its cultural background, in *The Fergusonian Impact*, vol. 1: *From Phonology to Society*, ed. J.A. Fishman. Berlin: Mouton de Gruyter, 327–42.

Shevoroshkin, V., 1989. A symposium on the deep reconstruction of languages and cultures, in *Reconstructing Languages and Cultures: Materials from the First International Interdisciplinary Symposium on Language and Prehistory*, ed. V. Shevoroshkin. Bochum: Universitätsverlag Dr N. Brockmeyer, 6–8.

Shevoroshkin, V., 1990. Introduction, in *Proto-languages and Proto-cultures: Materials from the First International Interdisciplinary Symposium on Language and Prehistory*, ed. V. Shevoroshkin. Bochum: Universitätsverlag Dr N. Brockmeyer, 8–12.

Shevoroshkin, V., 1991. Introduction, in *Dene-Sino-Caucasian Languages: Materials from the First International Interdisciplinary Symposium on Language and Prehistory*, ed. V. Shevoroshkin. Bochum: Universitätsverlag Dr N. Brockmeyer.

Shevoroshkin, V., 1998. Nostratic languages: 1) inner kinship vs external links; 2) inheritance vs borrowing in daughter languages, in *Symposium on the Nostratic Macrofamily*. Precirculated papers for a symposium on the Nostratic macrofamily held at the McDonald Institute for Archaeological Research, Cambridge, July 17–18 1998.

Ščerbak, A.M., 1966. O xaraktere leksicheskix vzaimosvyazei tyurkskix, mongol'skix i tunguso-man'chzhurskix yazykov. *Voprosy yazykoznaniya* 3, 21–35.

Ščerbak, A.M., 1986a. Tyurksko-mongol'skie yazykovye svyazi. (K probleme vzaïmodeistviya i smesheniya yazykov.) *Voprosy yazykoznaniya* 4, 47–59.

Ščerbak, A.M., 1986b. Problema rotacizma i perspektivy dal'neishego izucheniya tyurksko-mongol'skix yazykovyx svyazei, in *Istoriko-kul'turnye kontakty narodov altaiskoi yazykovoi obshhnosti*, vol. 2: *Tezisy dokladov XXIX sessiï Postoyannoi Mezhdunarodnoi Altaïsticheskoi Konferenciï [Tashkent 1986]. Lingvistika.* Moscow: AN SSSR.

Sinor, D., 1988. The problem of the Ural-Altaic relationship, in *The Uralic Languages: Description, History and Foreign Influences*, ed. D. Sinor. (Handbuch der Orientalistik, Achte abteilung.) Leiden: E.-J. Brill, 706–41.

Sinor, D., 1990. Introduction: the concept of Inner Asia, in *The Cambridge History of Early Inner Asia*, ed. D. Sinor. Cambridge: Cambridge University Press, 1–18.

Starostin, S.A., 1984. Gipoteza o genetičeskix sv'az'ax sinotibetskix jazykov s enisejskimi i severnokavkazskimi jazykami, in *Lingvističeskaja rekonstruktsija i drevnejsaja istorija vostoka*, vol. 4. Moscow: Nauka, 19–38. [Translation by W.H. Baxter, III, in *Genetic Classification of Languages*, ed. V. Shevoroshkin.]

Starostin, S.A., 1986. Problema genetičeskoi obščnosti altaiskikh jazykov. Istoriko-kul'turnye kontakty narodov altaiskoi jazykovoi obščnosti. *Tezisy doklodow XXIX sessii Postoiannoi Meždunarodnoi Altaističeskoi konferencii* [PIAC]. Moscow: Nauka, 94–112.

Starostin, S.A., 1989. Nostratic and Sino-Caucasian, in *Explorations in Language Macrofamilies: Materials from the First International Interdisciplinary Symposium on Language and Prehistory*, ed. V. Shevoroshkin. Bochum: Universitätsverlag Dr N. Brockmeyer, 42–65.

Starostin, S.A., 1991. On the hypothesis of a genetic connection between the Sino-Tibetan languages and the Yeniseian and North-Caucasian languages, in *Dene-Sino-Caucasian Languages: Materials from the First International Interdisciplinary Symposium on Language and Prehistory*, ed. V. Shevoroshkin. Bochum: Universitätsverlag Dr N. Brockmeyer, 12–41.

Suhonen, S., 1988. Die baltischen Lehnwörter der Finnisch-Ugrischen Sprachen, in *The Uralic Languages: Description, History, and Foreign Influences*, ed. D. Sinor. Leiden: E.J. Brill, 596–615.

Suhonen, S., (ed.), 1995. *The Fenno-Baltic Cultural Area/Itämerensuomalainen kultturialue.* (Castrenianumin toimitteita 49.) Helsinki: Vammala.

Swadesh, M., 1953a. Mosan I: a problem of remote common origin. *International Journal of American Linguistics* 19, 26–44.

Swadesh, M., 1953b. Mosan II: comparative vocabulary. *International Journal of American Linguistics* 19, 223–36.

Swadesh, M., 1954. Perspectives and problems of Amerindian comparative linguistics. *Word* 10, 306–32.

Thomason, S.G. & T. Kaufman, 1988. *Language Contact, Creolization, and Genetic Linguistics.* Berkeley & Los Angeles (CA): University of California Press.

Toivonen, Y.H., E. Itkonen, A.J. Joki, R. Peltola, S. Tanner & M. Cronstedt, 1955–81. *Suomen Kielen Etymologinen Sanakirja* [*Etymological Dictionary of the Finnish Language*]. Helsinki: Suomalais-Ugrilainen Seura.

Unger, J.M., 1990. Summary report of the Altaic panel, in *Linguistic Change and Reconstruction Methodology*, ed. P. Baldi. Berlin: Mouton de Gruyter, 479–82.

Ureland, S. (ed.), 1987. *Sprachkontakt in der Hanse.* Tübingen: Niemeyer.

Welmers, W.E., 1973. *African Language Sstructures.* Berkeley & Los Angeles (CA): University of California Press.

Wiik, K., 1995. The Baltic sea prosodic area revisited, in Suhonen (ed.), 75–90.

Williamson, K., 1989. Niger-Congo overview, in *The Niger-Congo Languages: a Classification and Description of Africa's Largest Language Family*, ed. J. Bendor-Samuel. Lanham: University Press of America, 3–45.

Winston, F.D.D., 1966. Greenberg's classification of African languages. *African Language Studies* 7, 160–69.

Zaborski, A., 1992. Afro-Asiatic languages, in Bright (ed.), 36–7.

Zeps, V., 1962. *Latvian and Finnic Linguistic Convergence.* (Uralic and Altaic Series 9.) Bloomington (IN): Indiana University Press.

Zvelebil, K.V., 1990. *Dravidian Linguistics: an Introduction.* Pondicherry: Pondicherry Institute of Linguistics and Culture.

Chapter 10

The use of reconstructed forms in Nostratic studies

Peter A. Michalove & Alexis Manaster Ramer

The Nostratic hypothesis, like most attempts to establish a genetic affiliation among a set of established language families, makes use of second-order reconstructions, that is reconstructions reached by comparing reconstructed forms of the proposed daughter families. This chapter examines the significance and reliability of using reconstructed forms as input to a deeper reconstruction, both as a general principle, and in the specific case of Nostratic. By considering sample Nostratic reconstructions, in this case two of the proposed Nostratic forms for 'fish', we see how changes in our knowledge and analysis of the daughter languages since the work of Illič-Svityč in the 1960s affect the higher-level reconstructions of Dolgopolsky and will inevitably continue to affect further work in Nostratic. At the same time, changes to reconstructed forms do not necessarily change our view of the geneticity of a set of languages.

1. Professor Dolgopolsky's new book, *The Nostratic Macrofamily and Linguistic Paleontology* (hereafter *NM*) has given us all ample food for thought. Dolgopolsky presents us with a sampling of the roughly 2000 reconstructions he attributes to Nostratic, and he gives a glimpse of the habitat and economy suggested by the vocabulary of these reconstructions. While we will have to wait for his forthcoming *Nostratic Dictionary* to have a more complete view of the proposed Nostratic reconstruction, we would like to use this paper to discuss one particular aspect of Dolgopolsky's work: the use of reconstructed forms to establish higher-level reconstructions.

Dolgopolsky, like Illič-Svityč (e.g. 1967 & 1971–84) and others before him, has attempted to reconstruct a common language prior to Afroasiatic, Indo-European, Uralic and other languages by comparing reconstructed proto-Afroasiatic, proto-Indo-European, etc. Illič-Svityč's, Dolgopolsky's and others' purpose in using reconstructed forms is to make use of the earliest possible forms and screen out as much secondary development as possible. To the extent that reconstructions are built up from attested forms, they contain much that may be considered reliable. Some scholars, such as Ivanov (1980) have explicitly defended the use of reconstructed forms as input for higher-level reconstructions, as indicated in the title of his paper, 'Proto-languages as objects of scientific description', to use the English translation of Shevoroshkin and Markey.

At the same time, reconstructions are inherently imperfect, reflecting our incomplete knowledge of the parent language. They are always subject to change as new data on the descendent languages are discovered, or known data are subjected to new analysis. Such changes in reconstructed forms may undermine the deeper level reconstructions into which they in turn feed. To take the classic example, the discovery of Anatolian texts with retained reflexes of the laryngeals profoundly changed our view of proto-Indo-European and, even today, there is controversy about exactly how to reconstruct proto-Indo-European, the language family which has been subject to deeper historical study than any other in the world.

Thus, writers such as Dixon (1997) have denied the reliability of reconstructed forms for building higher-level reconstructions. Dixon's rejection of the use of reconstructed forms as input for deeper reconstructions stems partly from our lack of detailed information about the reconstructed forms (1997, 45–6), as we have discussed above. Dixon's other concern is that the reconstructed proto-languages may never have existed in the first place, but may represent areal convergence, which he takes to be a step in a process of punctuated equilibrium (1997, 97–102 and passim). He further considers punctuated equilibrium to be the normal course of language history. However, there are many serious problems with Dixon's vision of language development which we cannot pursue further in this paper. Suffice it to say that, if we accept the principle of genealogical relationships among languages we consider related to be a valid one, that such languages have 'sprung from some common source', as Sir William Jones so memorably phrased it, then it is only Dixon's first objection that need concern us here.

In fact, as is often the case when scholars assume extreme positions, the reality to the working historical linguist is not as black and white as the partisans on either side would suggest. To begin with, the use of higher-level reconstructions based on lower level constructs is nothing new. Indo-Europeanists have always worked in this manner at relatively shallow time depths. Since proto-Germanic, proto-Celtic, proto-Slavic, etc. are not attested, the input of these branches necessarily represents reconstructed forms. Even what we call classical Greek, which has traditionally been used as a crucial element in Indo-European studies, represents a group of dialects, and our knowledge of Mycenean Greek is quite limited. Our knowledge of some Indo-European branches (such as Venetic or Phrygian) is very scant, and we have no idea what other branches may have disappeared over time, leaving no traces for us whatsoever.

While forms from Gothic, Old Irish, or Old Church Slavonic are frequently cited as surrogates for proto-Germanic, proto-Celtic, or proto-Slavic, in practice Indo-Europeanists make use of the whole range of attested forms in these branches as part of their input to a deeper reconstruction. To take a well-known example, when we consider the Old Church Slavonic form gradŭ 'city', we must also look at the other Slavic forms, such as Russian gorod 'id.', Ukrainian (archaic) horod 'id.', Polish gród 'town, (fortified) castle', Czech and Slovak hrad 'castle', Polabian gord 'city', Slovincian and Kashubian gard 'id.', Serbo-Croatian grâd 'id.', Slovene grâd 'castle', and Bulgarian grad 'town, city' in order to reconstruct the common Slavic form, *gordŭ. Only through comparison and reconstruction from the entire range of attested Slavic languages can we see the metathesis of vowel plus tautosyllabic liquid, and the attendant vowel lengthening in the southern dialects that led to the attested Church Slavonic form, gradŭ. And it is only at this point that a comparison with forms like Latin hortus 'garden', Lithuanian gãrdas 'pen', Gothic gards 'house', Sanskrit gr̥há 'house', etc. can reveal developments of an earlier time-depth in Slavic, such as the loss of aspiration, the loss of word-final consonants, and the raising of the stem vowel /o/ to /u/. It is also only at this point that the Slavic data can help us to understand the developments in the other branches and allow us to reconstruct a still earlier Indo-European form, *gʰordʰ-o-s 'an enclosed area'.

If, then, our reconstructions, even of widely accepted etymologies, rely on what we may call second-order reconstructions, and Nostratic work must necessarily represent even deeper orders of reconstructions, we may reasonably ask how reliable our reconstructed forms really are. In this, we may take some encouragement from the fact that a reconstruction is by definition a set of correspondences among attested languages, and the exact phonetic realization of a reconstructed form is not nearly as important to historical linguists as the fact of the attested correspondences. Even with the addition of new data, we still work from the fact that a set of correspondences in one group of languages regularly corresponds to a similar or different set of correspondences in another group. As we have mentioned, after the development of the laryngeal theory (or theories) in the twentieth century, views of Proto-Indo-European phonology were subjected to profound modification. But the geniticity of Indo-European was not affected by the inclusion of laryngeals in reconstruction work, and most the previously accepted cognate relationships still held; a new set of correspondences simply took the place of some earlier reconstructions. Similarly, the use of the glottalic theory by some Indo-Europeanists is an attempt to explain phonetic realizations, but still relies on the same set of correspondences.

At the same time, there are cases, even in well-established families, but especially in cases like Nostratic, where there is so much that is uncertain at this time, when we do not know whether certain forms really are cognate, or are loans, or are merely chance similarities. In such cases, modifications in lower-level reconstructions can indeed affect our view of a proposed cognate set, or even of what phonological reflexes to expect in a given language. For example, Indo-European forms for 'star', such as Latin stēlla, Greek ἀστήρ, Armenian astł, Gothic staírnō, etc. were once thought by some to be derived from similar forms for 'strew', such as Greek στόρνῡμι, Latin sternō, Old Irish sernim, Old Church Slavonic pro-stĭr-ǫ, etc., stars being seen as 'the scattered ones'. (See Buck 1949, 56 for references, if not approval.)

Today, however, most scholars treat 'star' as $*H_2ster-$, and 'strew' as $*sterH_3$. Here, attested forms that were earlier believed to be cognate turned out to be two entirely separate forms. As our knowledge of the various daughter languages proposed for Nostratic is refined, we will inevitably have to discard many, possibly even most of the originally proposed cognate sets, and perhaps find new ones, but in any case we will inevitably learn more about the history of the various languages involved, which is, of course, the goal of the enterprise.

2. At this point it may be useful to recall the set of languages with which Dolgopolsky works. Afroasiatic, Indo-European, Kartvelian, Uralic, Altaic, and Dravidian are the same six families that Illič-Svityč compared in the 1960s. But consider has happened to our knowledge of each of these families in the 30 years since Illič-Svityč 's work.

In the 1960s Afroasiatic had only recently been established beyond question by Greenberg (1955; 1963), and there was not a reconstruction *per se* which could neatly be used as input for higher-level reconstruction. There had been extensive work on Semitic, but little on formal reconstructions integrating the Semitic forms with the other branches of Afroasiatic. The family had been proposed at least as early as Meillet & Cohen (1924), but Cohen (1947), which was one of Illič-Svityč 's main sources on the family, dealt primarily with the lexicon, and included only scant references to Chadic.

Since that time, there has been extensive work on the lexicon and phonology of Afroasiatic. In addition, the field has developed from a perspective primarily emphasizing the Semitic group to one that takes fuller account of the other languages as well, resulting in a better understanding of Cushitic and Omotic in particular. Therefore, Dolgopolsky (and we) now have the somewhat differing visions of Diakonoff (1988), Orël & Stolbova (1994), and Ehret (1995) from which to work. And despite the merits in each of these, none of them is likely to be the last word on the subject.

For Indo-European, the textbook example of a language family, Illič-Svityč relied primarily on Pokorny (1959) as input, with many modifications of his own, and there has not been a satisfying alternative reconstruction published since then. But Indo-Europeanists today are keenly aware of Pokorny's weaknesses, particularly the absence of any attention to the role of the laryngeals. Thus, the Indo-European input to any deeper reconstruction must differ from that which Illič-Svityč used.

Illič-Svityč based his Kartvelian input on Klimov (1964), and now we have Fähnrich & Sardshweladse (1995), which presents a slightly, if not radically, new perspective. But even in Illič-Svityč's time, there was controversy over whether some of the sibilants reconstructed by Klimov, as well as Machavariani (1960), might represent proto-Kartvelian consonant clusters, as advocated by Schmidt (1961; 1962), and this question remains controversial today (see Testelec 1995). Manaster Ramer (1994) showed how the interpretation of these forms can affect our view of Nostratic, and Michalove (1997) has applied similar arguments to Altaic (and possibly Uralic and Afroasiatic).

For Uralic, Rédei (1986–88) has supplanted and revised much of the picture from Collinder's (1955; 1960) work, which Illič-Svityč used, while Janhunen (1981a,b) provides an even more contrasting approach from Collinder's work. But perhaps more significantly, Dolgopolsky and some other scholars now see Yukaghir as closely related to Uralic or even, as we believe Dolgopolsky correctly puts it, part of Uralic. If we are to take Yukaghir into account, surely it will further inform our reconstruction of Uralic as a whole. Integrating Yukaghir into traditional Uralic is a major task facing Uralists today, and the result of that work will inevitably affect the Uralic input with which Nostraticists must reckon.

Dolgopolsky takes Starostin (1991) as his input for Altaic, and this work makes major revisions to Poppe's (1960) formulation, which was the basis for Illič-Svityč's treatment of Altaic (along with a number of important modifications of Illič-Svityč's own). Starostin's inclusion of Japanese, his greater integration of Korean into the picture, and the different treatment of a number of phonological issues make the work in our view a substantial advance over Poppe's work (for which we have the greatest respect). Nonetheless, Starostin (1991) leaves many problems unanswered, and is far from the last word on the subject.

And finally, for Dravidian, Burrow & Emeneau (1961), which Illič-Svityč used, has been supplemented by Burrow & Emeneau (1984) and Andronov (1978), which add a number of new etymologies, but do not substantially change the view of Dravidian reconstruction.

Thus, each of the six widely recognized families with which Illič-Svityč and Dolgopolsky worked has seen significant changes in the material that the Nostraticist must use as input for further reconstructions. And here, we have only reviewed the definitive etymological dictionaries and comparative grammars. There is also a host of journal articles addressing smaller individual points of reconstruction within each of these families and, as we indicated, further work is inevitable in each of them.

Except in the case of Altaic, where the controversy has continued unabated, none of the revisions to the reconstructed forms of these families has generated the slightest question of the genetic affiliation of the families. Thus, a simple answer to how Nostratic can survive changes in the reconstructed input on which it is based is that the principle is the same as for lower-level entities: while views frequently change on the interpretation or phonetic realization of correspondences in the attested languages, it is the set correspondences that is the basis for our work. Scholars can speak of a 'new sound of Indo-European' (Vennemann 1989), or confront three different reconstructions of Afroasiatic (as discussed in Greenberg 1996), or two of Uralic (Janhunen vs the Collinder/Rédei tradition), but no one is talking of dismantling Indo-European, Afroasiatic or Uralic.

Since so much new work was done between Illič-Svityč's efforts of the 1960s and Dolgopolsky's *NM*, it is not surprising that the details of Dolgopolsky's reconstructions differ in almost every case from those of Illič-Svityč. In this paper we will examine two of the reconstructions Dolgopolsky proposes for the semantic field of 'fish', and consider how they differ from Illič-Svityč's work, largely because of revised ideas on the input from lower-level reconstructions.

3. Dolgopolsky's no. 73 (*NM*, 61), *k'olV, corresponds to Illič-Svityč's no. 155, *kalV (1971–84.I, 288–9). The reconstructed forms differ in two features: the phonation of the initial velar, and the quality of the first-syllable vowel. Illič-Svityč bases the phonation type on a reconstructed Afroasiatic root *kl- 'fish', attested in Semitic, East Cushitic, and Chadic; as well as an Altaic reconstruction, *kali-ma 'whale', based on Tungusic forms, with a Korean cognate indicated as questionable. The Uralic proto-form *kala does not give us any indication of the original phonation.

Dolgopolsky reconstructs a glottalized initial velar based largely on the same Afroasiatic forms (although marking the Semitic as questionable), and a different Tungusic form, *xol-sa, (Ewenki ollo, Ewen olra, Negidal olo, Orochi okto, Udehe olo^{h}o, Ulcha xolto(n-), Nanai xolto), as well as Mongolic *qoli-sun 'fish-skin' (Classical Mongolian qolisun). However, the Mongolian form appears to be derived from qalisu(n) 'the outer layer of something, such as skin, hide, membrane, bark, etc.', and thus semantically not connected to the Tungusic forms. Ralf-Stefan Georg has suggested that the labial feature of qolisun came about by analogy to körisü, a word for 'skin' with about the same range of meanings. In the *Secret History of the Mongols*, the form qalisu(n) is used only once (§111; Rachewiltz 1972, 45, 287), and then adjacent to körisu, in the combination qalisu körisü 'scraps of skin', which could have given rise to the analogical rounding of qalisu(n) > qolisu(n) in the more specialized sense we see here, while qalisu(n) remained as the more common form with the broader meaning.

Dolgopolsky also introduces Indo-European *k^{w}olal- '(a kind of) large fish', based on Iranian (Khotan Saka, Young Avestan kara, Sogdian krw kry 'a monster fish'), Germanic (Old Norse hvalr, Old High German wal, German Walfisch, English whale, etc.), and Baltic (Old Prussian kalis 'sheet fish'), and possibly Italic (Latin squalus 'shark') and Hellenic (Hesychius ἄσπαλος 'fish') forms, which suggests a glottalized velar at the Nostratic level. Dolgopolsky repeats Illič-Svityč's Uralic *kala (Finnish and Estonian kala 'fish', Hungarian hal 'id.', Tundra Nenets xal'a 'id.', Taz Selkup qɜlı 'id.', and others); and introduces Malayalam kolli '(a kind of) fish' and Tulu koleji 'id.' to reconstruct a proto-Dravidian form *koll- '(a kind of) fish'. It is not clear whether this is related to Tamil kōlā 'flying fish' and Malayalam kōlān, kōlā-min, kōli 'needle fish', cited in Burrow & Emeneau (1984 as no. 2241, 200; essentially unchanged from Burrow & Emeneau 1961, no. 1856, 148), or if so, what the origin of the long vowel might be. Neither the Uralic nor the Dravidian forms tell us about the original phonation. Except for the Dravidian forms, we are now essentially back to the proposal of Illič-Svityč (1967, 288), who originally reconstructed *K'olV, as does Dolgopolsky now.

Dolgopolsky considers Tungusic *kali-ma, cited here by Illič-Svityč on the basis of forms like Manchu kalimu, Nanai kalima, Orochi, Udehe, Negidal, Ewenki, Ewen kalim 'whale', to be unrelated to the other forms cited here. He and Illič-Svityč suspect that Classical Mongolian qalim is a loan from this Tungusic form. Ralf-Stefan Georg has infomed us that the Tungusic form is a borrowing from Gilyak qalm 'small whale', so the -m is part of the root, and any attempt to treat the Gilyak form as cognate to the other forms in a root *kal-, without the -m, must take this into account.

The issue of the vowel quality in the initial syllable is more difficult, as Dolgopolsky's *NM* does not give a set of vocalic correspondences, and the development of the comparative vocalism presents a number of problems. Illič-Svityč posited a Nostratic */a/ for this form based on the Uralic forms and the Tungusic *kali-ma that he equated with the form, while the Afroasiatic root was not conclusive for the vocalic quality.

Dolgopolsky proposes an */o/ vocalism on the basis of the different Altaic forms he cites, as well as his use of Dravidian, and notes that the Uralic vocalism is unexplained. While the development o > a is unremarkable in itself, and might have occurred in some environments in the development of Uralic, the difference in vocalism here is significant because we do not see the correspondence on a recurring basis between Uralic and the other families. Some of the modern Uralic forms have a rounding feature (e.g. Norwegian Lapp guolle, Cheremis kol, Tavda Vogul kōl, Vakh Ostyak kul, Nganasan kolı, Kamassian k'ōlǎ), but this is the regular reflex of Uralic */a/ in these languages. The Uralic reconstruction of Dolgopolsky agrees with that of Rédei (1986–88, 119).

The Indo-European forms, however, deserve closer inspection. The Iranian, Germanic, and Baltic forms in -a- could go back to either short */o/ or */a/. (While Pokorny 1959, 958 points out that Avestan kara- is a borrowing from Uralic because the /o/ here cannot be original, Dolgopolsky cites other Iranian forms, including younger Avestan kara.) But what is telling here is Dolgopolsky's suggestion that Latin squalus 'shark' and Greek (Hesychius) ἄσπαλος 'fish' may represent an original compounded form, *Hs-kʷal-. If the laryngeal here is *H₂, this would account for the /a/-vocalism from a prior *Hs-kʷol- in these forms, and would not be inconsistent with the other Indo-European forms adduced here. The colouring effect of the laryngeals at some stage of Indo-European would have rendered earlier vocalic distinctions allophonic.

But what would be inconsistent is the Afroasiatic result. The Afroasiatic forms are already suspicious because a Nostratic *K'- should yield Afroasiatic *K'-, not the k- we find attested in Semitic (South Arabic Shari kāl 'whale', Mehri kell 'id.'); East Cushitic (Afar kúllum 'fish', Somali kallūn 'id.' and kallūm- 'to catch fish'); and Chadic (Hausa kúlmā̃ '(a kind of) large fish'). If we assume an initial laryngeal in the Indo-European form, the Afroasiatic results are again inconsistent, since they should also reflect the laryngeal in some form.

Thus, the two problems in these forms, that of the phonation of the initial velar stop, and the vocalism of the initial syllable, may lead us to consider two separate forms. One set of forms must begin with a glottalized stop, on the basis of Tungusic *x- and Indo-European *(s)k-. If we associate the Altaic and Indo-European forms, the vocalism with *-o- suggested by Altaic *xol-sa is not inconsistent with Indo-European, which, as we noted, would have been subject to the colouring effect of the laryngeal. The Dravidian forms, Malayalam kolli and

Tulu koleji (and possibly Tamil kōlā and Malayalam kōlān, kōlā-min, and kōli, if we can explain the vocalic length) may be associated with this group as well, yielding a reconstructed Nostratic form *K'olV.

Afroasiatic, as we noted is inconsistent with these forms, and is inconclusive in its vocalism. Uralic, which clearly goes back to a vowel *-a- in the initial syllable is not inconsistent with the phonation of Afroasiatic, so these two may be combined for a proto-form *kalV. We thus may be dealing with two separate forms, each of which is internally consistent, and is consistent with the correspondences we expect from other examples involving these phonemes.

4. Dolgopolsky's other form for 'fish', *doTgiHU (*NM*, 61–2) corresponds to Illič-Svityč's *diga (1971–84.I, 219). Despite the superficially different reconstructions, both scholars have used almost the same material. The primary difference is Dolgopolsky's inclusion of Uralic, which, as we will see below, is questionable.

Illič-Svityč began with the Afroasiatic forms from Semitic (Ugaritic dg 'fish') and Egyptian dāg̲ (masc.), dā̰g̲ā̰ (fem.). Dolgopolsky includes only the Semitic, adding Hebrew ˈdāg̲, for a proto-Semitic *ˈdag- or *daˈwag- 'fish'. For Indo-European, both authors cite Armenian ju-kn 'fish', Greek ἰχθῦς, 'id.', and Baltic forms like Lithuanian žuvìs and Old Prussian suckis 'id.' for an Indo-European form *dĝʰū- 'id.', following fairly closely Pokorny's (1959, 416–17) *ĝʰdū or *ĝʰi̯ū, although most Indo-Europeanists now would probably use a following laryngeal to account for the long *ū, yielding a reconstructed form, *dĝʰuH- (e.g. Beekes 1995, 35).

For Altaic, Illič-Svityč cites only Mongolian, as in Written Mongolian ǰigasun < *diga-sun, questioning Poppe's (1960, 57) reconstruction, *ǰïrka-sun. Dolgopolsky reconstructs a proto-Altaic *dŏgi ~ dŏki, adding Tungusic *ǯogi or *ǯoyi 'a species of fish' on the basis of Negidal ǯoyo 'salmonid fish', Nanai ǯoi 'id.', and Udehe ǯüi-so 'id.'; and proto-Japanese *(d)íwuá 'fish' > Old Japanese iwo. The Japanese form is possible if it reflects an original *(d)í(g)-wuá. The loss of the voiced stops, *d in this environment, and *g in all cases, is regular, while *-wuá reflects a nominal suffix.

The Tungusic forms here are possible, but they must be treated with some caution for two reasons. First, they occur only in a geographically limited area of Tungusic-speaking territory, in the lower Amur basin and some of its tributaries. And second, they assume the development of *gi > yi, which is characteristic of Nanai, but not normally of Negidal and Udehe. Therefore, we may be dealing with this form as native to only one Tungusic language, Nanai, with borrowings into Negidal and Udehe.

In any case, we find Starostin's (1991, 275) *diogV ~ *diokV more plausible for proto-Altaic than *dőgi ~ dőki, as there is no evidence in the attested forms for an original *-ö-. The front vowel that led to the development of Mongolic and Tungusic *d > ʒ- and to the loss of a preceeding *d in Japanese would have to be */i/. If we exclude the Tungusic forms, the vocalism of the initial syllable is greatly simplified to */i/.

Where Dolgopolsky departs most clearly from his predecessor is by including Uralic *totke 'a fish of the genus *Cyprinus*' (following Rédei 1986–88, 352), on the basis of forms such as Estonian tõtkes 'Schleie, *Cyprinus tinca*' Erzya Mordvin tutko 'id.', Moksha Mordvin tutka 'id.', Taz Selkup tutı '*Cyprinus carassius*' with similar foms in other Selkup dialects. Hungarian has an interesting compound of the two forms treated by Illič-Svityč and Dolgopolsky: tat-hal 'a worthless fish, *Cyprinus tinca*, *Tinca vulgaris*'.

Although Dolgopolsky has proposed this reconstruction, making use of the Uralic forms at least since Dolgopolsky (1969), we see serious difficulties in attempting to connect the Uralic forms with the others cited here. On the basis of Uralic, Dolgopolsky augments Illič-Svityč's *diga to *d[oT]giHU. While Dolgopolsky's analysis of the final laryngeal and vocalism appear justified, we have noted the additional *-oT- in brackets here as questionable. To explain this portion of the form as a reduplication of the initial dental would be uncharacteristic of Uralic and, of course, Dolgopolsky does not suggest such an explanation. But if we consider the *-oT- as part of the original form, then we face two problems. First, we have a root form that is excessively complex for the root structure we usually attribute to Nostratic (typically (C)V(C)CV). And second, we find no motivation for the loss of the *-oT- in Afroasiatic, Indo-European and Altaic. Thus while Dolgopolsky has provided a better reconstruction of the final *-HU, and has benefited from using the additional Altaic forms from Starostin (1991), we feel this reconstruction, as *digHU, is more persuasive without the inclusion of the Uralic forms.

5. Our consideration of these two sample forms from the *NM* has shown how dependent more distant reconstructions are on lower-level reconstructions, and how further information and analysis at the lower level inevitably affects the form of higher-level reconstructions. This effect may take the form of confirmation, revision, or even rejection of earlier ideas contributing to a reconstruction. In any of these outcomes, the information from lower-level reconstructions has made a positive contribution to our understanding of the higher-level form.

That Dolgopolsky's findings differ in many respects from Illič-Svityč's work of the 1960s, and that our views differ somewhat from Dolgopolsky's is inevitable; it would be hard to imagine that research in the various languages associated with Nostratic in the past generation did not affect current work in Nostratic. It is significant in this regard that Illič-Svityč did not limit his work to Nostratic, but made important contributions to some of the daughter languages, such as Indo-European and Altaic, as Dolgopolsky has to Afroasiatic. Just as all living languages are continuously in a process of change, so all viable reconstructions are continuously subject to revision. This dynamic does not invalidate work on higher-level reconstructions; it is a healthy process that, in the long run, will refine and deepen our understanding of the history of the various attested languages.

Acknowledgements

We greatly appreciate the thoughtful comments provided by Ralf-Stefan Georg to this paper.

References

Andronov, M.S., 1978. *Sravnitel'naja grammatika dravidskix jazykov*. Moscow: Nauka.

Beekes, R.S.P., 1995. *Comparative Indo-European Linguistics: an Introduction*. Amsterdam & Philadelphia (PA): Benjamins.

Buck, C.D., 1949. *A Dictionary of Selected Synonyms in the Principal Indo-European Languages*. Chicago (IL) & London: University of Chicago Press.

Burrow, T. & M. Emeneau, 1961. *A Dravidian Etymological Dictionary*. Oxford: Clarendon Press.

Burrow, T. & M. Emeneau, 1984. *A Dravidian Etymological Dictionary*. Second edition. Oxford: Clarendon Press.

Cohen, M., 1947. *Essai comparatif sur le vocabulaire et la phonétique du chamito-sémitique*. Paris: Champion.

Collinder, B., 1955. *Fenno-Ugric Vocabulary*. Stockholm: Almqvist & Wiksell.

Collinder, B., 1960. *Comparative Grammar of the Uralic Languages*. Stockholm: Almqvist & Wiksell.

Collinder, B., 1977. *Fenno-Ugric Vocabulary*. Second revised edition. Stockholm: Almqvist & Wiksell.

Diakonoff, I., 1988. *Afrasian Languages*. Moscow: Nauka.

Dixon, R.M.W., 1997. *The Rise and Fall of Languages*. Cambridge, New York (NY) & Melbourne: Cambridge University Press.

Dolgopolsky, A., 1969. Nostratičeskije osnovy s sočetanijem šumnyx soglasnyx, in *Etimologija 1967*, ed. O. Trubachev. Moscow: Nauka, 296–313.

Dolgopolsky, A., 1998. *The Nostratic Macrofamily and Linguistic Paleontology*. (Papers in the Prehistory of Languages.) Cambridge: The McDonald Institute for Archaeological Research.

Ehret, C., 1995. *Reconstructing Proto-Afroasiatic (Proto-Afraisian: Vowels, Tone, Consonants and Vocabulary)*. Berkeley (CA): University of California Press.

Fähnrich, H. & S. Sardshweladse, 1995. *Etymologisches Wörterbuch der Kartwel-Sprachen*. (Handbuch der Orientalistik, Abt. I, Band 24.) Leiden: E.J. Brill.

Greenberg, J.H., 1955. *Studies in African Linguistic Classification*. New Haven (CT): Compass.

Greenberg, J.H., 1963. *The Languages of Africa*. Bloomington (IN): Indiana University.

Greenberg, J.H., 1996. Review of Orël & Stolbova 1994. *Anthropological Linguistics* 38(3), 550–56.

Illič-Svityč, V.M., 1967. Materialy k sravnitel'nomu slovarju nostratičeskix jazykov, in *Etimologija 1965*, ed. O. Trubašev. Moscow: Nauka, 321–73.

Illič-Svityč, V.M., 1971–84. *Opyt sravnenija nostratičeskix jazykov*. 3 vols. Moscow: Nauka.

Ivanov, V.V., 1980. Prajazyki kak objekty opisanija, in *Teoretičeskie osnovy klassifikacii jazykov mira v izdanii 'Jazyki mira'*. Moscow: Nauka, 181–207. [Translated in 1986 as Proto-languages as objects of scientific description, in *Typology, Relationship and Time*, eds. V.V. Shevoroshkin & T.L. Markey. Ann Arbor (MI): Karoma Press, 1–26.]

Janhunen, J., 1981a. On the structure of Proto-Uralic. *Finnisch-ugrische Forschungen* 44, 23–42.

Janhunen, J., 1981b. Uralilaisen kantakielen sanastoa. *Journal de la Société Finno-Ougrienne* 77, 219–74.

Klimov, G.A., 1964. *Etimologicheskij slovar' kartvel'skix jazykov*. Moscow: Akademija nauk SSSR.

Machavariani, G.I., 1960. O trëx rjadax sibiljantyx, spirantov i affrikat v kartvel'skix jazykax, in *XXV Meždunarodnyj kongress vostokovedov: Doklady delegacii SSSR*. Moscow: Izd. vostočnoj literatury.

Manaster Ramer, A., 1994. Clusters or affricates in Kartvelian and Nostratic. *Diachronica* XI(2), 157–70.

Meillet, A. & M. Cohen (eds.), 1924. *Les Langues du monde, par un groupe de linguistes sous la direction de A. Meillet et Marcel Cohen*. Paris: Champion.

Michalove, P.A., 1997. Altaic evidence for clusters in Nostratic, in *Indo-European, Nostratic, and Beyond: Festschrift for Vitalij V. Shevoroshkin*, eds. I. Hegedűs, P.A. Michalove & A. Manaster Ramer. (*Journal of Indo-European Studies* Monograph 22.) Washington (DC): Institute for the Study of Man, 243–56.

NM = Dolgopolsky 1998.

Orël, V.E. & O.V. Stolbova, 1994. *Hamito-Semitic Etymological Dictionary: Materials for a Reconstruction*. Leiden: E.J. Brill.

Pokorny, J., 1959. *Indogermanisches etymologisches Wörterbuch*. Berne: Franke.

Poppe, N., 1960. *Vergleichende Grammatik der altaischen Sprachen*, Teil I: *Lautlehre*. Wiesbaden: Otto Harrassowitz.

Rachewiltz, I. de, 1972. *Index to the Secret History of the Mongols*. (Uralic and Altaic Series 121.) Bloomington (IN): Indiana University.

Rédei, K., 1986–88. *Uralisches etymologisches Wörterbuch*. Budapest: Akadémiai Kiadó.

Schmidt, K.H., 1961. Sibilanten und Affrikaten-korrespondenzen in den Kartwelsprachen. *Bedi Kartlisa* 11/12, 149–73.

Schmidt, K.H., 1962. *Studien zur Rekonstruction des Lautstandes der südkaukasischen Grundsprache*. Wiesbaden: Franz Steiner.

Starostin, S.A., 1991. *Altai'skaja problema i proisxoždenie japonskogo jazyka*. Moscow: Nauka.

Testelec, Y.G., 1995. Sibilanty ili kompleksy v prakartvel'skom? *Voprosy jazykoznanija* 1995(2), 10–28.

Vennemann, T., 1989. *The New Sound of Indo-European: Essays in Phonological Reconstruction*. Berlin & New York (NY): Mouton de Gruyter.

Chapter 11

Nostratic language and culture: some methodological reflections

Bernard Comrie

I consider Aharon Dolgopolsky's book The Nostratic Macrofamily and Linguistic Palaeontology *(hereafter* NM*) from two aspects, the first essentially internal to linguistics, namely the testability of the Proto-Nostratic reconstruction in primarily phonological terms, the second relating to linguistic palaeontology, namely the validity of the reconstruction of the kinship system. With respect to the validity of the reconstruction, I suggest that a number of characteristics of the reconstruction make it less than optimally testable, in particular unexplained irregular developments, the use of unspecified segments, the size of the reconstructed phoneme inventory, and the positing of synonyms. I suggest a criterion of 'openness' to make such problems explicit, thus facilitating the dialogue between scholars advocating and rejecting the Nostratic hypothesis. In my discussion of the reconstructed kinship system, I accept for the sake of argument the bulk of the reconstructions proposed in NM, but question whether they provide any evidence for a moiety system. In a final remark I consider the integration of Nostratic and Eurasiatic hypotheses.*

1. Some reflections on proto-forms

In recent work that has attempted to establish far-reaching genetic groupings by comparing the forms of morphemes with comparable semantics, two main trends can be discerned. On the one hand, scholars like Joseph H. Greenberg and his followers have made use of multilateral comparisons without relying on regularities of sound correspondences, which would be the synchronic-comparative reflexes of regular (à la Neo-Grammarian hypothesis) sound changes. On the other hand, other scholars, including those of the Moscow comparative school like Aharon Dolgopolsky, have insisted on the importance of regular correspondences in establishing valid cognates, much as is done in practice in such well-established sub-disciplines as comparative Indo-European linguistics. It is not my intention here to go into all the details of the differences between these two approaches, although some preliminary remarks are in order before I turn to more specific details. Let me emphasize that certain preliminaries are necessary in the following discussion before I turn to the specific consideration of *NM.*

In the historical-comparative study of most well-established language families, there is a residue of problematic cases where the regularity of sound change seems to be violated. To take a rather trivial example, it is generally accepted that the Modern English third person singular feminine nominative pronoun ʃiː derives from Old English seːo, although no combination of the regular sound changes that relate Old English to Modern English will derive the Modern English form from its apparent etymon. One can, of course, come up with plausible reasons why there might be an irregular phonetic development here, but crucially these go beyond both regular sound change and the usually accepted list of specific factors that can affect the regularity of sound change (such as analogy). The longer the time period with which one is dealing, the more likely it is that the number of such perturbations will approach and even cross the threshold beyond which it is impossible to establish regular correspondences even among forms that do in fact descend from the same etymon. In other words, given enough time-depth, the search for phonologically regularly related cognates may simply be inapplicable. If this is so, and if one assumes that regularly related cognates are essential to establishing genetic relatedness of languages — as is done by the Moscow school of comparative linguistics — then it follows that beyond a certain limit the method is inapplicable.

Certain clarifications are necessary to the foregoing. Although I have spoken about elapsed time (time-depth) separating the ancestor language from its descendant(s), I do not literally mean that a certain number of years can be specified beyond which the comparative method is inapplicable. I do not believe in a constant rate of linguistic change. Nor do I believe that all linguistic changes lead to the same degree of likelihood of retrieving the ancestral system. Thus I would certainly not exclude the possibility that it might be possible to establish regular correspondences within one pair of languages separated from their common ancestor by a time-depth of 10,000 years and yet impossible to do the same for another pair of languages separated from their common ancestor by 7500 years. And I agree with a point made repeatedly by wide-ranging comparativists, namely that the reconstruction of a proto-system becomes more likely to succeed the more branches of the proto-language we have available for comparison.

But the crucial point remains that given enough changes, and in particular enough incidence of perturbations, it is in principle the case that it will be impossible to establish regular correspondences between languages that do in fact descend from a single common ancestor. Of course, one might object that in practice human language has not been around long enough for such cases to arise, and thus that the genetic relatedness of all attested human languages is feasible (à la Greenberg) — I take no stand on this, although my best guess would be that human language has indeed been around long enough for this to happen. And one might object more specifically that the Nostratic macrofamily falls this side of the threshold; certainly *NM*, and even more so the forthcoming *Nostratic Dictionary*, assume that this is the case, since they present regular sound changes that derive the individual branches of the Nostratic macrofamily from the reconstructed ancestor language, Proto-Nostratic. Given these preliminaries, I can now turn to specific reactions on the reconstructions proposed in *NM*.

If one maintains that regularity of sound correspondences is crucial to the establishment of cognate forms, as *NM* does, then I think there is an important criterion that I will call 'openness'. What I mean by this is that the attested forms should indeed be derivable from the reconstructed ancestral form by means of regular sound changes; or, what amounts to the same thing, the attested forms should be relatable to one another by means of regular sound correspondences. That this is not always the case in work from the Moscow comparative school is something that I have noted in, for instance, my review in *Language* of Starostin (1991). I feel that if the commitment to regularity of sound correspondences is to be taken seriously, then those using this criterion in establishing far-reaching genetic affiliations absolutely must apply the commitment literally, or at the very least discuss explicitly each example where a cognate set departs from the set of regular sound correspondences that has been established. Now, this is a matter that relates not so much to *NM* as to the forthcoming *Nostratic Dictionary*, and I recognize after discussions with Professor Dolgopolsky that I should refrain from specific criticisms until I have seen this work. However, I do note that other scholars who are either committed Nostraticists or are at least more convinced by wide-ranging comparisons than I am voice similar concerns about a number of items. Thus, in his contribution to this volume Allan Bomhard characterizes a number of the reconstructions in *NM* with the evaluation 'the phonology is not plausible', while Alexander Vovin likewise identifies a number of 'correspondence problems'. Only if Nostratic etymologies avoid such problems, or explicitly note their existence, can linguists not yet convinced of the validity of the overall hypothesis or of specific etymologies evaluate them objectively.

A more general problem inherent in constraining the reconstruction of

Proto-Nostratic is that the language is reconstructed with a large consonant inventory: 50 consonantal phonemes in the table on page 101. *NM* actually describes the consonant inventory of Proto-Nostratic as 'rich' (p. 17), but there is a danger of this being interpreted as a positive value judgement, when in fact quite the opposite is the case. A larger number of phonemes in the proto-language simply reflects a larger number of correspondence sets among the descendant languages. Indeed, it is trivially true that if one allows the set of proto-phonemes to grow sufficiently — though admittedly this would have to go several magnitudes beyond the 50 consonants and 7 vowels (p. 17) proposed in *NM* for Nostratic — then one can establish cognate sets between any randomly selected languages, the only problem being that ultimately each putative proto-phoneme is represented by only a single correspondence set. I emphasize that a consonant inventory of the size proposed by *NM* is by no means typologically implausible, nor are there any other aprioristic reasons why it should be excluded, especially since the reflexes in the individual branches of Nostratic are related to the proto-phonemes in a phonetically plausible manner. But it does remain the case that positing a new proto-phoneme can be an illicitly facile way of making exceptions disappear. I remain methodologically suspicious, for instance, of the distinction between Proto-Nostratic *n and *ṇ (*NM*'s n-grave), which seems, from pages 104–5, to show up only questionably in initial position in Indo-European and Tungusic, and medially in Dravidian; a distinct retroflex nasal in the absence of retroflex stops also seems typologically questionable.

A final problem that makes the testing of Proto-Nostratic reconstructions problematic is that often several different etyma are proposed with the same, or at least indistinguishable, meaning. We have, for instance, two words for 'water body' (items 13, 14), several words in the 'sheep/goat' area (items 42–5), three words for 'bark' (items 92–4) and four for 'skin' (items 95–8, some of which also cover bark), two words for 'spleen' (items 103, 104). There are further examples where this phenomenon is less clearly set out in *NM*, as with items 3 and 4, both of which cover 'leopard' and 'lion'. In addition, some items are given such wide-ranging semantic definitions that they cannot in practice be distinguished semantically from other items, e.g. different fish-words given as items 73–6. The reason why this reduces the testability of proposed cognate sets is that as the number of such sets increases, the easier it is for some word quite by chance to fit one or other of the sets; instead of having to fit a word into a particular set, one has a choice of sets. Perhaps the most striking example is on page 64, where we are told: '. . . we know two dozen words for "cutting", but . . . we have no idea about the original semantic difference between them. The precious information about different ways, directions and aims of cutting has not been preserved . . .'. The passage continues by noting that there are also many words for 'bending', 'twisting', 'boring/drilling', 'barking/flaying/peeling', 'rubbing', 'scratching', 'but the specific meaning of each one has been lost'. With two dozen cutting words to choose from, especially given the factors discussed in previous paragraphs of this section, it might actually be difficult to come up with a random form for 'cut' with appropriate morpheme structure that would not be assignable to one or other of these cognate sets.

Before leaving the problems that I have suggested for the evaluation of Proto-Nostratic reconstructions or Nostratic cognate sets, I do need to consider one possible objection, namely that the various objections I have made in the case of Nostratic can be matched by similar phenomena in well-established genetic groupings of languages, such as Indo-European, or even Germanic, or even Romance; as it was once put to me: 'If you reject this example, you'd have to reject Indo-European.' I do not deny that there are problem cases in these groupings, and other parallels, such as doublets, to the objections I have raised to Nostratic. Indeed, I started this section with the irregular development of the English third person singular feminine nominative pronoun over a time-depth of about a single millennium. But there is a substantial difference. The claim that Modern English is descended from Old English does not depend on the assumed irregular development of the third person singular feminine nominative pronoun. Should someone come up with incontrovertible evidence that this development is incorrect, for instance that the Modern English form is in fact a loan, this would not affect the vast array of evidence that the bulk of the core morpheme stock of Modern English (and much beyond that) can be regularly derived from Old English. Likewise, if we are required to reject what might at first look like plausible cognates among Indo-European languages (such as Latin deus, Greek tʰeós 'god'), this does not substantially affect the mass of lexical and, even more convincingly, morphological evidence that speaks in favour of genetic relatedness. By contrast, the incidence of problems in Nostratic reconstructions is sufficiently great at least to call into question their validity. Of course, we should not be surprised, as we go further back in time, that the validity of reconstructions, other things being equal, should decrease, since the greater relative time-depth means that a greater number of perturbing factors have had the opportunity to be at play. But this really does mean that there may come a point at which we will be unable to distinguish between common ancestry on the one hand and borrowing or chance similarity on the other.

Indeed, there are traces of this realization in *NM*. In several cases, forms that might plausibly have been treated as etyma are identified as at least possible loans; I discuss some in section 3. In other cases, a form in a particular language or branch is said to reflect a conflation of two proto-forms, as when items 2 and 4 coalesce in Dravidian (pp. 20–21).

To conclude this section, my concern with the reconstruction of Proto-Nostratic forms (or equivalently, with the cognate sets established for Nostratic) is their testability. A number of features that characterize this reconstruction conspire to reduce its empirical testability, to a degree that is quite different from what is found with well-established language families.

2. The kinship system

One of the sections in *NM* that interested me most personally was that on kinship (84–95). According to *NM* (84) the kinship terms reconstructed for Proto-Nostratic 'reflect exogamy, the division of the society into two exogamous moieties. Among the kinship terms we can see a clear-cut distinction between those referring to ego's own moiety and those of the other moiety.' This picture, with terms for both male and female ego's kin from the other moiety, is interestingly different from the picture for Proto-Indo-European that is usually derived from the reconstruction of Proto-Indo-European kin terms, where the possibility of reconstructing words for ego's husband's kin but not for ego's wife's kin presents a significant asymmetry that can be interpreted in terms of virilocality: if the wife lives with the husband's family, then she is more likely to need terms for her in-laws than he is for his. Under the scenario presented in *NM*, the shift from Proto-Nostratic to Proto-Indo-European would thus reflect not only linguistic but also social changes in the kinship system. In this section of my paper, I will begin and end with some general considerations relating to kin terms, while the central part of this section will be concerned with some specific aspects of the reconstruction presented in *NM*.

One of the problems with working with kin terms and kinship systems is that they form an aspect of social and linguistic interrelationships that is particularly subject to outside influence. A clear example of this is provided, for instance, by Modern English kin terms (compare *NM*, pp. 18–19). Essentially, the Modern English kin terms that can be traced back, in form and meaning, to Old English and beyond are those relating to the nuclear family: *husband, wife, son, daughter, brother, sister*. Once we go beyond this, we are dealing either with loanwords (*uncle, aunt, nephew, niece, cousin*), loan constructions (e.g. all the *grand-* words, with the *grand-* element itself borrowed from French), or neologistic constructions (e.g. all the *-in-law* terms). If we had not known the details of the historical background, we might well have been led to patently false conclusions, for instance that English-speaking society is one where the extended family is becoming more important than the nuclear family. But the general lesson is clear: kin terms are quite likely to be borrowed when languages are in contact, so that great caution is needed in their use for purposes of establishment of genetic affiliation, whence also for their use in reconstructing proto-lexical items and proto-kinship systems.

But let us assume, for the sake of argument, that the Nostratic cognates presented in *NM* are, at least for the most part, correct. Do the reconstructions provide evidence specifically for the kind of kinship system proposed in *NM*, namely one where there are terms for kin in ego's moiety contrasting with terms with kin in the other moiety? The items that come into question are numbers 109–13 (pp. 85–90), since the other kin terms are equally compatible, in terms of the meanings reconstructed by Dolgopolsky, with either an in-law or a moiety system. In fact, none of these terms from attested languages suggests a division of the whole society into moieties. Rather, the terms distinguish blood relatives from relatives by marriage. The difference between what I will call a moiety system and an in-law system is, of course, far-reaching. In a moiety system, every member of the society must belong to one moiety or the other, so that every member of the society is classifiable as a member of ego's moiety or as a member of the other moiety. In an in-law system, there are those who are related to ego by blood (extending as far as the society chooses to apply kinship by blood), those who are related to ego by marriage, and those who are related by neither (and conceivably those who are related by both, if for instance 'cousin' is a recognized blood relationship and cousin marriages are permitted). I emphasize that all of the relevant terms from attested languages point to an in-law system rather than to a moiety system, with the proviso that brides and bridegrooms may be treated as in-laws. Indeed from the very first item on page 84, *NM* explicitly notes the shift (given his reconstruction of Proto-Nostratic kinship) from, for instance, 'a woman of the other moiety (of the same age or younger than ego)' to 'a bride, or a female relative-in-law, or both'.

But are there other indications that would suggest that *NM* is correct in assuming such a shift, or at least indications that would support the plausibility of this shift? The fact that the in-law words sometimes include 'bride' and 'bridegroom' is not a strong indication in this direction. A bride or bridegroom is someone who is about to become a wife or husband, and thus to contract in-law relationships. This is very different from someone who is a potential marriage partner, as would be the case in a moiety system. Assuming that *NM*'s translations using *bride* and *bridegroom* are correct — and I have no reason to doubt them — then a kin term translatable as 'X's bride' denotes the specific woman that X is about to marry, and thus a future in-law of X's blood relatives, and not any woman that would be available in principle as a marriage partner for X.

To be more specific: In number 109, all items denote relatives by marriage, with the exception of Kartvelian with a general term for 'young woman, maid' (which thus provides no evidence for a moiety distinction), and one Dravidian item, namely Malto qali 'mother's sister'; one Dravidian item does not seem enough on which to build the whole edifice of exogamous moieties, and even Dolgopolsky glosses the Proto-North Dravidian form as 'female relative-in-law'. In number 110, all items denote in-laws. In number 111, while the Kartvelian and Afroasiatic items denote in-laws, the Uralic ones do not. However, these Uralic items cannot all denote individuals belonging to the same exogamous moiety; thus, 'father's brother' and 'mother's brother' cannot belong to the same exogamous moiety, nor can 'mother's mother' and 'mother's father'.

In items 112 and 113 on pages 89–90, most of the languages indeed restrict the reflexes to in-law semantics, but at least one putative branch of Nostratic does not. In the case of item 112, for which the Proto-Nostratic semantics is reconstructed as 'relative [of a younger/the same generation] of the other moiety', Ancient Egyptian, as the sole Afroasiatic language with reflexes of this Proto-Nostratic item, shows the semantic range 'boy, young man; (one's) child, son', 'girl, virgin', 'become young'. The hypothesis would be that the word originally referred to a younger (or same-age) relative of the other moiety; that in most branches this underwent the expected shift from moiety to in-law semantics; but that in the development leading to Ancient Egyptian it extended its semantic range, losing the restriction to the other moiety. Thus, while no attested language shows the precise meaning element 'of the other moiety', one might argue that such a meaning element is a plausible ancestor to the more extended semantics found in Ancient Egyptian and to the more restricted semantics found in the other branches. But even if one were to accept this by no means compelling evidence, there remain problems with item 112. In-law reflexes are given for Uralic, Altaic (in fact, all citations are more narrowly from Tungusic), and Dravidian, though it is acknowledged that the Dravidian items might be loans from Prakrit, the Prakrit item not being derivable from this Proto-Nostratic etymon. Thus overall, *NM* cites forms with confidence from three branches of Nostratic — Afroasiatic, Uralic, Altaic — the minimum taken as providing a reasonably good basis for reconstruction back to a proto-language. However, the semantics of the Ancient Egyptian items remains problematic. If the translation '(one's) child, son' is correct, then not only has the semantic component 'other moiety' been lost, but the word has actually come to take on the semantic component of 'blood relative'. Given this, one really begins to wonder whether there is a sufficiently strong semantic motivation for grouping the Ancient Egyptian root, isolated as it apparently is within Afroasiatic, together with the forms from the other languages. And even if one considers the Uralic and Tungusic forms to be cognate, their semantics is specifically in-law, thus providing no evidence in favour of a moiety system.

Similar considerations apply to item 113, where *NM* proposes reflexes in Afroasiatic (all with the meaning 'woman') and in Kartvelian and Indo-European (all denoting a female in-law). For reasons that are not clear to me, *NM* actually proposes that the Proto-Nostratic etymon already covered 'woman' (general term), 'woman of the other moiety', although there seems to be no reason to pinpoint the time at which the meaning extended to 'woman (in general)' other than to date it before the split-up of Proto-Afroasiatic. *NM* acknowledges (p. 90) that the Kartvelian words might be a loan from Indo-European, so we may be down to only two branches reflecting the putative etymon, namely Afroasiatic and Indo-European. And the initial s of the Proto-Indo-European root *snusos is, as *NM* acknowledges, 'unexpected'. *NM* suggests that the initial s may reflect metanalysis from the final s of a preceding genitive, i.e. *...-(o)s nusos becoming *...(o)s snusos; but the need to make such an assumption only serves to weaken further an etymology that does not in any case belong to the strongest. (Note that if Kartvelian *nusa is a loan from Indo-European, this is not necessarily relevant to determining the development of the initial *s in Indo-European, since Kartvelian could have borrowed the word from one of the several branches of Indo-European that would by regular sound change have lost all traces of the sibilant in Proto-Indo-European initial *sn; compare, for instance, Armenian nu 'son's wife'.)

To conclude this part of the discussion, even accepting as valid the bulk of the reconstructions of kin terms proposed for Nostratic by *NM*, I see no reason to accept the conclusion that Proto-Nostratic society was characterized by a moiety system.

I wish now to turn to another more general principle of reconstruction that manifests itself perhaps particularly clearly, within the lexical range considered by *NM*, in kin terms. For basic kin terms, especially those for 'mother' and 'father', it has often been noted that there are remarkable similarities that seem to have nothing to do with common genetic linguistic origin, but rather with universals of sound imitation and of nursery words. *NM* shows clear awareness of this. For instance, on pages 91–4 we are told that each of the Highland Cushitic, Chadic, and Indo-European possible cognates of item 116 'mother' might be an independent nursery word rather than their being cognates; that all of the items cited for item 118 'father' might be branch-specific independent nursery word creations; and that item 117 'mother' might be in origin a nursery word. Indeed, it is not clear to me why *NM* stops at this point, and why all of the words in items 116–18 should not be dismissed as valid Proto-Nostratic etyma on the basis of the high plausibility of independent creation of nursery words in the individual branches or even lower in the family tree. Of course, if one has a large number of branches or languages showing the same, cross-linguistically rare nursery word, then this is less likely to reflect independent creation in each language, rather than either common genetic descent or widespread diffusion. Unfortunately, this is not the case here, where the cross-linguistically unusual form for 'mother', item 117 *ʔäy∇, is given as reliably attested only in Cushitic (within Afroasiatic) and Dravidian, as doubtfully attested in Germanic (within Indo-European) and as doubly doubtfully attested in Samoyedic (within Uralic).

This should not, however, be taken to mean that one can do nothing historically with words that are patently or possibly of onomatopoetic or nursery word origin. A classical example involves the Ancient and Modern Greek words denoting the cry of a sheep. The Ancient Greek form bɛ: is presumably imitative of the cry of a sheep, and I doubt if any linguist would try to build a case of genetic relatedness using this and similar sounding items in other languages. The Modern Greek correspondent is vi. The Modern Greek form is clearly not imitative, but turns out to be the expected development of the Ancient Greek form given the regular sound changes that separate the modern from the ancient language, namely the regular shift of Ancient Greek b to Modern Greek v and of Ancient Greek ɛ: to Modern Greek i. Thus Modern Greek vi must be treated as the regular reflex of Ancient Greek bɛ:; and, indeed, if Modern Greek had continued to use the sound sequence bɛ:, we would have been obliged to treat this as non-cognate with the phonetically identical or almost identical Ancient Greek form. This same technique can be used in assessing kin terms, namely looking for aspects of the form of kin terms that are not explainable in terms of nursery word formation. The Proto-Indo-European etyma reflected in Latin pater 'father' and ma:ter 'mother' may contain initial elements that are nursery words. But the second syllable, which is well attested across the branches of Indo-European, cannot be treated as a nursery creation, and is thus a good piece of evidence for the genetic relatedness of the words in the various individual languages and branches. Moreover, we find across the Indo-European languages the regular correspondences that we would expect to find, for instance the initial *p of the word for 'father' shows up as f in Germanic (e.g. English fɑ:ðə(r)), as h in Armenian (hajɹ), and as zero in Celtic (e.g. Irish ɑhər), giving rise to forms that are quite far removed from what might be expected as the product of nursery word creation.

To summarize this section, kin terms provide a number of specific problems, although this does not mean that it is impossible to work with them in linguistic reconstruction — only that one has to be aware of the problems and of ways of accommodating them. On a more specific point, I do not see strong evidence in the materials provided by *NM* for reconstructing a Proto-Nostratic kinship system based on moieties; even if one accepts the formal reconstructions, their semantic content is better captured in terms of the in-law relationship.

3. Broader perspectives

One further point that occurred to me in working through *NM* is the relationship between the Nostratic hypothesis and the Eurasiatic hypothesis, as proposed for instance in Greenberg (in prep.); see Renfrew's introduction to *NM* (p. xii) for the importance of this question. I am concerned here not so much with families that are included in Nostratic but not in Eurasiatic (Afroasiatic, Kartvelian, Dravidian), but rather with those that are included in Eurasiatic but not in Nostratic, in particular Chukotko-Kamchatkan and Eskimo-Aleut. (I would note that while *NM* does not assign Nivkh (Gilyak) to Nostratic, whereas Greenberg does assign it to Eurasiatic, one Nivkh form does creep into *NM* without further comment, namely Amur Nivkh oɣla 'son' (item 119, p. 94).) *NM* is necessarily — given its emphasis on linguistic evidence for Proto-Nostratic society — concerned primarily with vocabulary (specifically: lexical morphemes) rather than with grammar (specifically: grammatical morphemes — but see *NM*, p. 17). Nonetheless, grammatical morphemes, such as personal pronouns and corresponding inflectional affixes, do seem to provide some of the strongest evidence in favour of macro-groupings including but going beyond Indo-European. (Of course, to the extent that the pronominal inflectional affixes are derived historically from personal pronouns, they do not provide evidence independent of the personal pronouns.) Moreover, evidence from the personal pronoun system is more strongly in favour of linking Chukotko-Kamchatkan and Eskimo-Aleut to Indo-European than of linking Afroasiatic, Kartvelian, or Dravidian. Indeed, some precirculated extracts from Greenberg (in prep.) suggest that the parallelisms go well beyond such general similarities between Chukotko-Kamchatkan and Indo-European or Uralic as first person m versus second person t, but include more specific aspects of the formation of personal pronouns when forms from documented but extinct or older varieties of Chukotko-Kamchatkan are taken into account.

There are of course problems in integrating Chukotko-Kamchatkan and Eskimo-Aleut into the kind of picture that is built up by *NM*. Until recently, one would have bemoaned the absence of etymological dictionaries for Chukotko-Kamchatkan and Eskimo-Aleut, but Fortescue *et al.* (1994) and ongoing work by such scholars as Michael Fortescue and O.A. Mudrak on Chukotko-Kamchatkan are rapidly filling the gap. More significantly, one would note that even if Chukotko-Kamchatkan and Eskimo-Aleut are branches of Nostratic, their speakers' move to Arctic and sub-Arctic regions would have involved such a shift in social, especially economic, life that little would have been left that might be germane to the main task of *NM*, namely the use of linguistic evidence for the reconstruction of Proto-Nostratic society, simply because so much of Proto-Nostratic social life would have changed in the move to regions with a radically different climate. Clearly, any attempt to retrieve Nostratic parallels from the Chukotko-Kamchatkan and Eskimo-Aleut material should involve detailed comparison and reconstruction of the kind that underlies *NM*. But that there might be parallels that would justify further investigation — and I make no stronger claim than this — is suggested by such facts as the striking similarity of Chukchi qora-ŋə 'reindeer' to item 36 (*NM*, p. 41) *gurHa 'antelope, male antelope'; compare in particular forms like Middle Korean kòrání 'deer'. (In the Chukchi form, -ŋə is, at least synchronically, an absolute singular suffix. The shift in semantics would, of course, be expected on the basis of the change in ecosystem involved in the northward migration; compare the similar shift in meaning to 'reindeer' in Uralic proposed by *NM* in item 38 (pp. 42–3).) I note, however, that Vovin (this volume), in addition to correcting the Middle Korean form to kwòlání and the gloss to 'elk', suggests that the Korean word may be a loan.

4. Conclusions

In my paper, I have questioned the validity of the relations among the individual families assigned by *NM* to Nostratic and, even assuming the validity of the assumed genetic grouping, I have questioned the implications that *NM* draws concerning the Proto-Nostratic kinship system. I suppose this might be qualified as a negative assessment. But this would be a one-sided characterization of my qualitative evaluation. I have found it valuable to work through *NM*, in part because it has helped me to clarify my own positions on various issues, and indeed I would hope that my remarks would also encourage Nostraticists to clarify their own formulations. Progress can only be made by setting up hypotheses whose viability cannot be guaranteed in advance, and then subjecting those hypotheses to testing. Although I have expressed reservations about the degree of testability of Nostratic as presented in *NM*, it is clearly a more testable hypothesis than some of its rivals, and I would hope that more systematic attention to my criterion of 'openness' would improve its testability, in which case only the particular improvements suggested by Nostraticists will tell whether or not their hypothesis survives these tests.

References

Comrie, B., 1993. Review of Starostin (1991). *Language* 69, 828–32.

Fortescue, M., S. Jacobson & L. Kaplan, 1994. *Comparative Eskimo Dictionary with Aleut Cognates*. Fairbanks: Alaska Native Language Center.

Greenberg, J.H., in prep. *Eurasiatic: Indo-European and its Closest Relatives*. Stanford (CA): Stanford University Press.

Starostin, S.A., 1991. *Altajskaja problema i proisxoo(zh)denie japonskogo jazyka*. Moscow: Nauka.

Chapter 12

Linguistic palaeontology: for and against

Irén Hegedűs

Linguistic palaeontology has been received with serious reservations ever since its foundation by Kuhn (1845) and further development by Pictet (1859-63). Aharon Dolgopolsky's book The Nostratic Macrofamily and Linguistic Palaeontology *(hereafter NM) discusses the linguistic palaeontological aspects of Nostratic reconstructions. Since the hypothesis of the Nostratic macrofamily does not (yet) enjoy widespread acceptance, we are faced with a fragile situation in which a much debated hypothesis is paired with a controversial method. This situation calls for an assessment of both content and method though this paper will concentrate on methodological issues with a discussion of some etyma only.*

1. Introduction

NM covers a special group of reconstructed Nostratic lexemes. The sample concentrates on etyma which may provide a basis for making conclusions about the natural, economic and social conditions prevailing at the time of existence of the Nostratic protolanguage. Some experts might want to see the Nostratic hypothesis proven first and only after that would they proceed with the palaeontological interpretation of the reconstructed Nostratic vocabulary. Moreover, some of them would not make a further step to draw palaeontological conclusions, even if the idea of Nostratic turns out to be principally correct, because linguistic palaeontology has been judged extremely frail and unreliable. The primary task of those involved in the evaluation of *NM*, however, is to examine the validity of Dolgopolsky's palaeontological conclusions rather than the feasibility of the Nostratic hypothesis itself. Thus we are dealing with a situation in which a debated hypothesis is combined with a controversial method. Starting with the assumption that the Nostratic hypothesis is accepted, let us consider then the possible pitfalls of linguistic palaeontology.

2. The notion of linguistic palaeontology

Linguistic palaeontology has been received with serious reservations ever since its introduction (for a discussion see Polomé 1990; Diebold 1994). There are various definitions of what linguistic palaeontology is by different authors. Each of the definitions seems to emphasize slightly different aspects of the notion, so it may be worthwhile to survey them.

2.1. Linguistic palaeontology in the general sense

Raimo Anttila defines linguistic palaeontology as 'the whole doctrine of making cultural inferences from linguistic evidence' (Anttila 1989, 373). A similar formulation is given by Winfred Lehmann: the 'use of language for determining culture' (Lehmann 1992, 297), or a later definition by the same author: 'the procedure of deriving cultural information from the language is known as palaeontology' (Lehmann 1993, 16). A clear and succinct definition is provided by Larry Trask, who has earned a reputation for clarifying and defining linguistic concepts by editing dictionaries of linguistics, as follows: 'the technique of drawing conclusions about the material and non-material cultures of ancient peoples by extracting evidence from their languages' (Trask 1996, 354). Anthony Fox points out the potentials of linguistic palaeontology by saying that it can make us 'able to recover something of the culture and society of the speakers of a reconstructed language from the study of the language itself, . . . the nature and structure of this proto-lexicon . . . will provide information about the material and intellectual framework of the speakers' of a protolanguage (Fox 1995, 306). Richard Diebold adds the aspect of areal or genetic relationship to the definition when he says that linguistic palaeontology is 'an approach and an attitude toward the use of diachronic and diatopic data for elucidating the external history and/or prehistory of a language or of several languages that are areally and/or genetically related' (Diebold 1994, 2909). In *NM* Dolgopolsky defines linguistic palaeontology as a field of linguistics which by 'the analysis of meaning of the words present in a proto-language (the common ancestor of languages in a family) casts some light on the way of life, geographical, historical and cultural parameters of the corresponding linguistic community' (*NM*, p. 18).

These definitions converge on the point that linguistic palaeontology entails a process leading from linguistic facts to conjectures about extralinguistic factors. This is a relevant circumstance that we have to bear in mind when trying to relate linguistic and archaeological results. Furthermore, it is also inherent in the above definitions that the conclusions made on the basis of reconstructed etyma about the cultural background of a protolanguage will relate not only to objects known by the speakers of a protolanguage but also to abstract phenomena that may not be traced by material remnants accessible by archaeological investigations. Relating the results of linguistic reconstruction to external (non-linguistic) systems of archaeological, palaeontological, etc. evidence was sought with an eye to supporting the realism of linguistically reconstructed items. Attempts at connecting linguistic results to the realia of prehistoric conditions came as a natural necessity: it was needed for confirming the feasibility of reconstructions by embedding them in a physical setting, which process was described by Paul Friedrich as 'disambiguation through contextualization' (Friedrich 1970, 3). There seems to be nothing wrong with this aspiration of historical comparative linguists; they just try to be pragmatic about the highly theoretical issue of linguistic reconstruction.

To synthesize the above said we can state that linguistic palaeontology can be considered the interface between historical comparative linguistics and archaeology; it aims at and is thought to be capable of correlating the results of linguistic reconstruction with historical cultures identified in space and time by archaeology. By establishing a bridge between historical-comparative reconstruction and archaeology, linguistic palaeontology can take us closer to a fuller picture of a reconstructed protolanguage because it may provide a cultural embedding for linguistic reconstruction, thus it can eliminate the sterility and increase the reality of reconstructed etyma. Linguistic palaeontology emerged as a 'by-product' of linguistic reconstruction because the reconstruction of the protolexicon provides clues about the protoculture and gives impetus to extralinguistic reconstruction.

2.2. Linguistic palaeontology in a narrower sense

Linguistic palaeontology can be especially crucial in the quest for the geographical seat of an ancient community associated with a reconstructed protolanguage because lexical reconstruction can be used for recovering 'information pertaining to prehistoric culture, society, perhaps even to geographical facts' (Hock 1991, 573). The reconstruction of plant and animal names is relevant for homeland localization theories since the geographical area in which the botanical and zoological species were spread at the estimated time of existence of a protolanguage may be equated with the original seat of the ancestor of a language family. By establishing the time-depth of a protolanguage we can set the temporal limits, while the ancient spread-zone of the fauna and flora known from reconstructed terms defines the spatial limits of the centre of language dispersal. Unfortunately, the correct establishment of both the temporal and spatial limits in itself can be a very difficult task; and if one of them is incorrect, the other is rendered invalid and we miss the target of the identification of a homeland. Since linguistic palaeontology has been first and most extensively applied in the field of Indo-European studies, especially in trying to solve the homeland problem, it seems justified that there is also a narrower interpretation of linguistic palaeontology as 'one of the most widely recognized techniques for delimiting the Indo-European homeland' (Mallory 1989, 158).

The necessity for cooperation between historical linguists and archaeologists is also obvious both in the general and in the narrower definitions, as Raimo Anttila says: 'collaboration between archaeologists and linguists is desirable, because each side tends to apply the findings of the other too simplistically' (Anttila 1989, 372). Yet linguistic palaeontology has 'rarely enjoyed particularly high repute' (Anttila 1989, 373) and it is often harshly criticized or even 'discredited' (Lehmann 1993, 16).

3. Reconsidering the criticism of linguistic palaeontology

Why linguistic palaeontology has been disavowed is due to three factors according to Richard Diebold (1994, 2909). First he mentions the 'racial determinism of the 19th century', which — to my mind — has been surpassed and forgotten by now and therefore does not constitute a 'serious deficiency'.

Second, he refers to Colin Renfrew's dismissal (Renfrew 1989) of linguistic palaeontology. My understanding of Colin Renfrew's argumentation, however, is quite different: what Colin Renfrew has repeatedly called our attention to is the vicious circle of the mutual support between archaeological and linguistic evidence (Renfrew 1987, 18; 1989; 1998, xiii), rather than a rejection of linguistic palaeontology on the whole. Indeed, both linguists and archaeologists have to exercise more caution in making linguistic palaeontological conclusions.

Circularity in reasoning has also been held against the comparative method itself. It has been indicated that the comparative method as used in historical linguistics involves circular reasoning. This claim argues that in the process of establishing genetic relationship between languages we proceed from comparing presumably related languages with an eye to find regular sound correspondences and once we have been able to establish regular sound correspondences we go on to comparing further lexical items from the languages under scrutiny with the aim of corroborating the regular ('ausnahmslos' = 'exceptionless') correspondences established in the first approach.

This is not a real circularity phenomenon however. In the first approach we formulate tentative rules about sound correspondences on the basis of a relatively small section of the data available (usually starting with basic vocabulary which is judged to be more stable than the rest of the vocabulary), then with the tentatively established rules in hand we return to comparison and start testing the validity of our rules against the bulk of data. As a result of the test we either confirm the tentative rules or correct them. So our logic moves not in a circle but rather along a spiral, recurring to the same position but on a higher level. The recurrence to basic points, i.e. the reevaluation of our initially established rules and reconstructions seems inevitable (e.g. in the case of re-constructing the PIE stop system or that of the laryngeals). Constant reevaluation is the guarantee of increasing precision in linguistic reconstruction. Only by permanent reconsideration can we reach a higher degree of reliability and real-ity in our reconstructions.

The third deficiency is mentioned as the absence of a 'principled method-ology for making inferences about the extralinguistic world of a reconstructed language and its speakers' which also includes the drawback that 'semantic re-construction lacks rigor' (Diebold 1994, 2909). This third deficiency is taking us closer to the heart of the problem.

3.1. Semantic reconstruction
Semantic reconstruction is often imperfect and vague due to a variety of possi-ble hindrances such as:

3.1.1. It is difficult to correlate the reconstructed meaning with the signified (note the classical example of the ambiguities surrounding the 'beech argu-ment'). 'A reconstructed meaning does not necessarily mirror the exact refer-ence in the protolanguage' (Anttila 1989, 373; cf. also Lehmann 1993, 16). This difficulty is present also in *NM*, e.g. when it comes to the identification of cereal names, it is hard to say whether the signified was the wild or the already domes-ticated version of the plant (cf. NM, p. 28). The problem is not quite precisely formulated by A. Fox when he states that 'we are not necessarily able to estab-lish unambiguously the original meaning of a particular word in the protolanguage, since meaning, as well as phonological form, are subject to change' (Fox 1995, 307), because, although phonemes are subject to change, sound change is regular and therefore recoverable as far as we can establish the laws governing sound changes; semantic changes, however, are more elusive and semantic reconstruction as a result is not always as reliable as phonological reconstruction. There are no 'laws' established for semantic developments, thus linguists may clash on points like whether it is correct to ascribe such meanings as 'eye' and 'to see' to one and the same reconstructed etymon, or whether we can justify a semantic reconstruction like 'dog/wolf' for PNostr. *K'üjnA (cf.

Manaster Ramer 1992, 135-7; 1997, 90-91). Frequently we can see that some linguists would be uncritical in their attitude to semantic reconstruction, while others are unreasonably squeamish. We cannot expect full semantic congruity of an etymon in descendant languages, just as we do not expect a protoform to come down to daughter languages without phonological alterations. There are cases when semantic congruity is perfect between the reconstructed protoform and the attested words, just as the phonological shape of a word may not necessarily change over centuries or even millennia; but then there have to be extreme cases when the semantic content becomes so 'distorted' that cognacy is difficult (yet not impossible) to prove, like phonological identity is so 'absurd' (yet explicable) between e.g. Latin duo and Armenian erku.

Recent (mostly cognitive) linguistic research has been quite efficient in establishing universal tendencies and patterns of semantic change that are applicable in reconstructing the meaning of etyma. The task is now to 'identify crosslinguistically regular tendencies of semantic association, where they exist, and then use these natural tendencies to justify and/or to search for plausible cognates' (Wilkins 1996, 266).

3.1.2. There are 'linguistic indeterminacies and archaeological gaps', therefore the matching of animal and plant names against palaeobotanical and palaeozoological results cannot be expected to solve automatically the problem of homeland localization (cf. Anttila 1989, 373; Renfrew 1989).

3.1.3. Another possible and serious trap that is difficult to avoid is 'overestimating the probative value of the available evidence' (Hock 1991, 573). Such a possible overestimation and indeterminacy of the available evidence may be exemplified by the following two cases in *NM*:

• No. 7. PN *šüŋU 'snow'
The initial consonant is reconstructed on the basis of the distinctive evidence of PFU and Egyptian. The Egyptian evidence (šnj.t 'haily weather') is not reliable unless there is supporting data from other Afroasiatic branches; besides the Egyptian word could be a derivation from *šly.t 'hail' (Gábor Takács pers. comm.).

Instead of the Proto-Finno-Ugric evidence *šüŋe 'wet snow' I find another etymon better matching. A word form *suŋe is reconstructed for Proto-Uralic (PU) with high plausibility (cf. Rédei 1986-91, 451), because it has attested forms not only in FU but also in Samoyedic languages. The semantic reconstruction at first sight, however, may seem to be a misfit for the Nostratic comparison.

The meaning of this etymon is reconstructed for PU as 'summer' but an earlier semantic change is postulated to have taken place so the original meaning of the etymon is 'eine milde Jahreszeit, Tauwetter; tauen (Schnee)' = 'mild season, thawing weather; to thaw (of snow)' (cf. Rédei 1986–91, 451). If this Uralic parallel is acceptable then we have a correspondence of PIE s: PU s: Mongolian, Turkic, Tungusic, Japanese s, which points to a PN s. So I would modify no. 7 as PNostr. *suŋe 'melting snow', where vocalism is established on the basis of Proto-Uralic because Altaic languages show an extensive tendency to assimilate the vowels, perhaps under the pressure of establishing vowel harmony of the syllables.

It seems indeed plausible that the speakers of the hypothetical Proto-Nostratic language lived in a climatic zone where cold seasons were known. We could also mention another PN etymon here *burV 'snow (sand) storm' with widespread reflexes in Afroasiatic, Indo-European, Uralic and Altaic languages (cf. Illič-Svityč 1971.I, 188–90, no. 23).

- No. 14. PN *moRE 'water body'

The evidence does not necessarily mean that Nostratic speakers 'did not distinguish the sea from other relatively large water bodies' (*NM*, p. 25). The distinction may have existed in Proto-Nostratic but later this distinction could have become redundant for the speakers of the descendant languages who migrated to continental areas and lost direct contact with the sea. I assume that PIE and Proto-Afroasiatic (PAA) speakers remained in territories near a sea, while other Nostratic descendants specialized the word, e.g. Kartvelians moved to a mountainous area (-> 'lake'), Mongolians retain this element with the meaning 'river' possibly from an earlier meaning of 'river falling into a sea/lake'. I suspect that the Proto-Mongolian reconstructed meaning as 'sea' is incorrect but this is not within my competence to judge.

3.1.4. The validity of a reconstructed form and meaning is sometimes undermined by scarcity of attestation, so 'the presence of cognate words in the daughter languages does not necessarily imply their presence in the protolanguage' (Fox 1995, 306). However, if a word has cognates in daughter languages that have not been in contact with each other or with one and the same non-related language, we have a relatively safe basis for postulating the archaic nature of that lexical item and for deriving it from the ancestral protolinguistic stage.

NM has three entries for the gloss 'sinew': nos. 25, 26 and 28. If we make a distributional analysis for the three Nostratic etyma, what emerges is seen in Table 1. There is no evidence available from Kartvelian for any of the three

	no. 25 'sinew'	no. 26 'sinew, tendon' > 'bow'	no. 28 'sinew', 'tie together'
West Nostratic K	–	–	–
IE	+	–	–
HS	[+] (only Arabic)	[+] (only Egyp.)	+ (only Semitic)
East Nostratic U	–	+	+ ('arrow')
A	+ (only Turkic)	+ (only Turkic)	+ ('arrow' (only Tung.)
D	+	–	–

Table 1. *Distributional semantic analysis of the gloss 'sinew'.*

etyma. The distribution is balanced between East and West Nostratic only for no. 25, so it seems to be a feasible Nostratic etymology. Etymon 26 seems to be East Nostratic (Ural-Altaic) only. The fact that Uralic and Altaic languages have been in long-lasting areal contact weakens the proof value of the attested forms. The word may have been borrowed by Turkic. The possibility of an opposite direction of borrowing is certainly discarded because Uralic has evidence both from FU and from Samoyedic, so this must be an ancient Uralic word. The same situation holds for no. 28, where Tungusic 'arrow' may be a borrowing from Uralic. The specialized meaning ('arrow') appears to be a semantic isogloss connecting Uralic and Tungusic only, it is not attested in Semitic.

4. Perspectives

A relevant argument for maintaining attempts at the application of linguistic palaeontology is that linguistic palaeontology 'may exceed the reconstructive powers of prehistoric archaeology, obviously so in instances where ancient sociocultural traits are more cognitively rather than artifactually encoded' (Diebold 1994, 2910). The 1990s saw the birth of cognitive archaeology, which 'seeks to draw upon the cognitive, and the mathematical and computer sciences' (Renfrew & Zubrow 1994, xiii), at the same time in the field of linguistics there is a similar tendency to examine language phenomena with an eye to uncovering mechanisms of human cognition. One of the merits of cognitive linguistics is that it ascribes a far more relevant role to historical comparative linguistic research than did generative linguistics.

Increasing the feasibility of correlating results of linguistic reconstruction and archaeology can be achieved. Linguistic palaeontological conclusions based on Nostratic reconstructions, as exemplified by *NM*, would obtain a safer grounding if we could strengthen the validity of the Nostratic hypothesis itself, i.e. if we can eliminate incorrect details in the adduced materials and can provide further proof for the hypothesis. For eliminating inconsistencies it is crucial that linguists working on reconstructing the Nostratic protolanguage receive constructive criticism and work with a self-critical attitude. Proof of the Nostratic hypothesis cannot emerge from linguistic palaeontological studies; this can only provide a 'three dimensional picture' of our hypothetical protolanguage and the notions related to it such as material or spiritual culture, speakers or homeland.

Morphological reconstruction rather than lexical reconstruction could be the cutting edge in further research because it seems to provide qualitative proof rather than merely accumulate evidence for Nostratic quantitatively. Most critics of Nostratic linguistic research would tame their antagonistic attitude if Nostratic shaped up grammatically. If we could finally demonstrate cases in which Proto-Nostratic derivational elements surface as thematic consonants in PIE as perhaps the PN derivational suffix *-l- in PIE thematic adjectives (cf. Vine 1991, 19), or if in the r/n heteroclisis of PIE we could identify a PNostr. morpheme, these would provide hardcore arguments for the hypothesis. Attempts in this direction have been made but little attention has been paid to them (e.g. Ivanov 1979; 1990). My own efforts revising and updating the evidence in Illič-Svityč's *Nostratic Dictionary* have been concentrated on morphological elements (mostly derivational elements rather than inflectional) (cf. Hegedűs 1988; 1992; 1997).

I agree with Anttila saying that 'linguistic paleontology very neatly provides assumptions to be tested' (Anttila 1989, 373). The importance of the Cambridge symposium and the present volume is the initiation of this testing. Since the time frame of our investigation is 'deeper than usual' and we are dealing with a macrofamily, testing our assumptions is more complex and difficult but not impossible. Cooperation of experts in the subfields of language families involved in Nostratic studies complemented by an interdisciplinary approach that includes — among others — archaeological considerations is a necessary requirement for a satisfactory solution.

The publication of Aharon Dolgopolsky's *The Nostratic Macrofamily and Linguistic Palaeontology* and the subsequent meeting devoted to its discussion took place 10 years after the 1st International Symposium on Language and Prehistory that was organized at the University of Michigan in Ann Arbor by

Vitaly Shevoroshkin and was attended by several of those involved in the present evaluation. That symposium was a significant milestone in the study of long-range linguistic comparison because it brought together experts of conflicting opinion. A similar symposium — though with fewer participants — took place at the Eastern Michigan University, Ypsilanti in 1993 (materials published in Joseph & Salmons 1998). The Cambridge meeting was an equally important event and hopefully it will act as a catalyst in the development of Nostratic studies. One obvious merit of the meeting was that eminent scholars whose main interest does not otherwise cover the Nostratic hypothesis have temporarily suspended their disbelief and cared to evaluate the most recently published results of Aharon Dolgopolsky's research. The Nostratic hypothesis — no matter how strongly debated or fiercely rejected by a lot of linguists — has grown out of material correspondences observable in languages of Eurasia and its supporters work in accordance with the principles and established practice of historical linguistic comparison and reconstruction. The process of proving this hypothesis is long and difficult but has already provoked meaningful discussions, it attracts more and more attention and is gaining a more objective critical treatment than earlier. Progress is possible only by maintaining this objective critical attitude whether we argue for or against the Nostratic hypothesis.

References

Anttila, R., 1989. *Historical and Comparative Linguistics.* Amsterdam & New York (NY): Benjamins.

Diebold, R.E., Jr, 1994. Linguistic paleontology, in *The Encyclopedia of Language and Linguistics*, vol. 6, eds. R.E. Asher & J.M.Y. Simpson. Oxford: Pergamon Press, 2906–13.

Dolgopolsky, A., 1998. *The Nostratic Macrofamily and Linguistic Palaeontology.* (Papers in the Prehistory of Languages.) Cambridge: The McDonald Institute for Archaeological Research.

Fox, A., 1995. *Linguistic Reconstruction: an Introduction to Theory and Method.* Oxford: Oxford University Press.

Friedrich, P., 1970. *Proto-Indo-European Tree Names: the Arboreal System of a Prehistoric People.* Chicago (IL) & London: The University of Chicago Press.

Hegedűs, I., 1988. Morphologische Übereinstimmungen in den uralischen, altaischen und einigen paläosibirischen Sprachen. *Specimina Sibirica* 1, 71–86.

Hegedűs, I., 1992. Reconstructing Nostratic morphology: derivational elements, in *Nostratic, Dene-Caucasian, Austric and Amerind*, ed. V. Shevoroshkin. Bochum: Universitätsverlag Brockmeyer, 34–47.

Hegedűs, I., 1997. On grammaticalization in Nostratic, in *Indo-European, Nostratic, and Beyond. Festschrift für V. Shevoroshkin*, eds. I. Hegedűs, P. Michalove & A. Manaster Ramer. (*Journal of Indo-European Studies* Monograph 22.) Washington (DC): Institute for the Study of Man, 106–15.

Hock, H.H., 1991. *Principles of Historical Linguistics.* Berlin & New York (NY): Mouton de Gruyter.

Illič-Svityč, V.M., 1971. *Opyt sravnenija nostratičeskih jazykov*, vol. 1. Moscow: Nauka.

Ivanov, V.V., 1979. Sravnitel'no-istoričeskij analiz kategorii opredelennosti-neopredelennosti v slavjanskih, baltijskih i drevnebalkanskih jazykah v svete indoevropeistiki i nostratiki [A historical-comparative analysis of the category of definite-indefinite in Slavic, Baltic and Palaeobalkanic languages in the light of Indo-European and Nostratic studies], in *Kategorija opredelennosti-neopredelennosti v slavjanskih i balkanskih jazykah*. Moscow: Nauka, 11–63.

Ivanov, V.V., 1990. Ob otdalennom rodstve v predelah sem'i: anatolijskij i indoevropejskij, jukagirskij i ural'skij [On distant relationship within a family: Anatolian and Indo-European, Yukaghir and Uralic], in *Uralo-Indogermanica*, vol. 2, eds. V.V. Ivanov, T.M. Sudnik & E.A. Helimsky. Moscow: Akademija nauk SSSR, 84.

Joseph, B. & J. Salmons, 1998. *Nostratic: Sifting the Evidence*. Amsterdam: Benjamins.

Kuhn, A., 1845. *Zur ältesten Geschichte der indogermanischen Völker*. Berlin: Nauck.

Lehmann, W.P., 1992. *Historical Linguistics*. London: Routledge.

Lehmann, W.P., 1993. *Theoretical Bases of Indo-European Linguistics*. London: Routledge.

Mallory, J.P., 1989. *In Search of Indo-Europeans: Language, Archaeology and Myth*. London: Thames & Hudson.

Manaster Ramer, A., 1992. On anecdotal universals in historical linguistics. *Diachronica* 9, 135–7.

Manaster Ramer, A., 1997. Nostratic from a typological point of view. *Journal of Indo-European Studies* 25(1–2), 79–104.

Pictet, A., 1859–63. *Les origines indoeuropéennes, ou les Aryas primitifs. Essay de paléontologie linguistique* I–II. Paris: Cherbuliez.

Polomé, E.C., 1990. Linguistic paleontology: migration theory, prehistory, and archeology correlated with linguistic data, in *Research Guide on Language Change*, ed. E.C. Polomé. Berlin: Mouton de Gruyter, 137–59.

Rédei, K (ed.), 1986–91. *Uralisches etymologisches Wörterbuch*, vols. 1–3. Budapest: Akadémiai Kiadó.

Renfrew, C., 1987. *Archaeology and Language: the Puzzle of Indo-European Origins*. London: Jonathan Cape.

Renfrew, C., 1989. They ride horses, don't they?: Mallory on the Indo-Europeans. *Antiquity* 63, 843–7.

Renfrew, C., 1998. Introduction: the Nostratic hypothesis, linguistic macrofamilies and prehistoric studies, in Dolgopolsky, vii–xxii.

Renfrew, C. & E.B.W. Zubrow, 1994. Preface, in *The Ancient Mind: Elements of Cognitive Archaeology*, eds. C. Renfrew & E.B.W. Zubrow. Cambridge: Cambridge University Press, xiii–xiv.

Trask, L., 1996. *Historical Linguistics*. London: Arnold.

Vine, B., 1991. Indo-European and Nostratic. *Indogermanische Forschungen* 96, 9–35.

Wilkins, D.P., 1996. Natural tendencies of semantic change and the search for cognates, in *The Comparative Method Reviewed: Regularity and Irregularity in Language Change*, eds. M. Durie & M. Ross. New York (NY) & Oxford: Oxford University Press, 264–304.

Chapter 13

Family trees and favourite daughters

April McMahon, Marisa Lohr & Robert McMahon

In recent research, we have applied computational models designed to assess biological relatedness to linguistic data. We show that, using data derived from Swadesh-type wordlists, the programs construct robust family trees strongly resembling those generally assumed for Indo-European internal relationships. A second data set based on phonological similarity (but including safeguards to reduce contamination due to borrowing or chance resemblances) produces similar trees; non-Indo-European languages are also correctly identified as forming distinct groups. However, data from earlier language states produce interesting and unexpected results with the second data set, in that reconstructed Proto-Indo-European is robustly positioned within Romance, rather than being near the root of the Indo-European tree, where a computer simulation suggests we should expect to find it. Further simulations indicate that one explanation might be a skewing of Proto-Indo-European phonology towards Latin. We argue that our methods may allow for the detection of apparent bias in other reconstructions; such bias will be of considerable relevance in longer-range comparisons of the Nostratic type, as it may introduce cumulative effects in higher-order family trees. Our tree-drawing methods may also provide a useful initial diagnostic of family groupings, of relative retentiveness of family members, and of deeper connections between recognized language groups.

Biological methodology and linguistic data

Tree diagrams in biology and linguistics have much the same purpose: that is, the representation of inherited relationships between entities and groups. The entities at issue vary, of course, being subspecies, species and higher-order groupings of species in biology, and dialects, languages and language families in linguistics, but trees are central to the historical subdisciplines of both: as Lass (1997, 113) puts it, 'the lineage historian is Arborifex, regardless of what species of trees he happens to make'.

Nonetheless, there is one fundamental difference between tree-drawing in biology and linguistics. While biologists typically treat classification as a quantitative discipline, using computer programs to establish the most parsimonious trees, and calculating standard deviations for the various contenders, linguists have typically worked intuitively. The best guide for a linguist to the acceptability of a particular linguistic grouping is therefore not the statistical robustness or mathematical fit of the tree, but the agreement of his or her colleagues that the classification is correct beyond reasonable doubt. Unfortunately, as the families posited become larger and older, as is the case for the proposed Nostratic macrofamily, consensus becomes more elusive.

The introduction of quantitative methods in other areas of linguistics has undoubtedly been beneficial: we need think only of the possibilities made available by corpus linguistics and concordances, or the advances in sociolinguistics predicated on detailed statistical analysis of data. There have also been limited attempts at quantification in comparative linguistics, notably the development of lexicostatistics (Swadesh 1950). Methodologically, lexicostatistics is similar to numerical taxonomy in biology (Sokal & Sneath 1963): both base their classifications on quantifiable similarities, using a matrix of 'distances' between all pairs of species or languages under comparison. In lexicostatistics, wordlists are drawn up for each language, typically 100 or 200 items in length; a matrix of pairwise cognacy scores is then produced, as shown in Figure 13.1, where = indicates cognacy.

English		German		French		Italian
tree		Baum		arbre	=	albero
one	=	ein	=	un	=	uno
hand	=	Hand		main	=	mano
you		du	=	tu	=	tu
mouse	=	Maus		souris		topo
son	=	Sohn		fils	=	figlio
foot	=	Fuss	=	pied	=	piede

	German	French	Italian
English	5	2	2
German		3	3
French			6

Figure 13.1. *Wordlists and cognacy scores.*

Higher values here indicate greater similarity; typically, lexicostatisticians first link the pair of languages with the highest shared score, which would mean French and Italian in this case. The mean of the scores of these languages with every other language is then taken, and the next highest-scoring pair is linked; here, this next connection would be between English and German. The process is then repeated for the whole matrix. This method is also popular in biology, where it is known as UPGMA, or Unweighted Pair-Group Method using arithmetic Averages.

However, other clustering methods are also possible. Ruvolo (1987) suggests using biological methods for linguistic classification, but very much from the biological point-of-view and without linguistic detail. In previous work (Lohr *et al.* 1998a,b) we have attempted to put Ruvolo's advice into practice, arguing that one technique which may be particularly applicable to the linguistic situation is the least-squares method (Fitch & Margoliash 1967). This is a special case of maximum likelihood, which generates a large number of trees from a distance matrix, and for each tree calculates a value using the equation:

$$\sum_i \sum_j \frac{(D_{ij} - d_{ij})^2}{D_{ij}^2} \tag{1}$$

Here, D is the observed distance between species i and j in the matrix, and d is the expected distance, computed as the sum of lengths of the segments of the tree from species i to species j. The best tree is taken to be the one with the lowest value for this sum of lengths; this can be tested by calculating average percentage standard deviations, again with the lowest being favoured.

The UPGMA method discussed earlier necessarily assumes a constant rate of change. While a molecular clock may be relatively uncontroversial in biology, its linguistic analogue, the glottochronological constant, is responsible for much of the scepticism historical linguists feel towards lexicostatistics. It is therefore important to note that classification under the least-squares method does not depend on the assumption of a constant rate of change; without this assumption, the resulting trees will simply be unrooted. To clarify this point, Figure 13.2 shows on the left an unrooted topology which can be rooted, in theory, at any point, giving rise to the four rooted trees on the right. To estab-

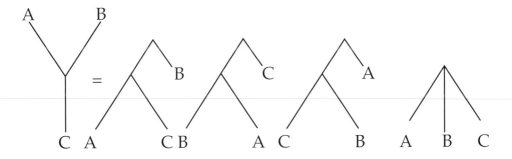

Figure 13.2. *Unrooted topology and corresponding rooted trees.*

lish the true position of the root, biologists rely on fossil data, outgroups, and archaeological evidence (Cavalli-Sforza *et al.* 1994, 33–4); and linguists can use the appropriate analogues of these (Lohr *et al.* 1998a,b).

Computational methods and Indo-European data

To test the hypothesis of a constant rate of change, and as an initial demonstration of the value of the computational method, we used wordlists similar to Swadesh's basic vocabulary lists for twelve Indo-European languages (for details of how these lists were compiled, and of other statistical tests and programs employed, see Lohr (in prep.)). A matrix of pairwise cognacy scores was produced, and the scores subtracted from the total number of words on the lists, to give a crude measure of distances between languages. The resulting matrix was then run through a variety of tree-drawing programs in the PHYLIP package written by Joseph Felsenstein.

The first tree, given in Figure 13.3, is the output of the KITSCH program, which is based on the Fitch-Margoliash least-squares method and assumes a constant rate of change: consequently, branch-lengths are not relevant in this tree, although order of branching is.

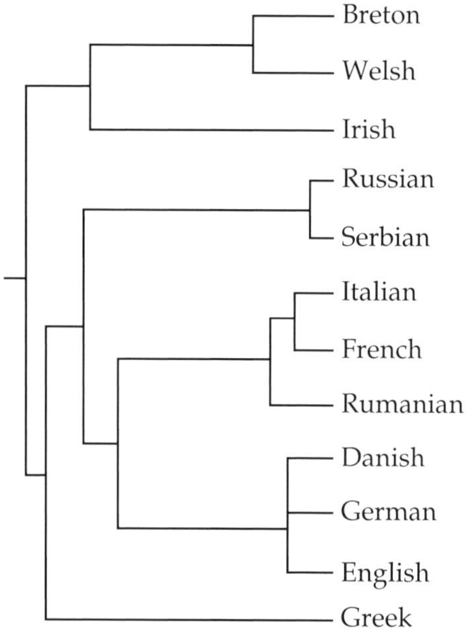

This tree compares well with the classification usually accepted for Indo-European internal relationships, with a number of relatively minor exceptions. PHYLIP programs generally favour binary branching, whereas the traditional Indo-European family tree has all first-order daughters branching directly from the root. In addition, the closer relationship of English and German vis-à-vis Danish is not reflected in the KITSCH tree. The average percentage standard deviation of the tree in Figure 13.3 is 7.62. However, this can be compared with Figure 13.4, the best tree produced by the FITCH program, which does not assume a constant rate of change: branch length here is therefore mean-

Figure 13.3. *Best KITSCH Indo-European tree.*

ingful, and indicates degree of change from the common ancestor.

This tree is unrooted (that is, the root has been assigned arbitrarily), but it reflects accurately the greater rate of change in Celtic and Greek compared with the other Indo-European groups included, and the relative retentiveness of Danish, Serbian and Italian, compared with English, Russian and Rumanian. The internal organization of the Germanic group is also more familiar than in the KITSCH tree. For clarification, the topology of the FITCH tree is shown in Figure 13.5. Note that in the remainder of this chapter, we shall generally use the term 'tree' to refer to topologies of this type: these give a truer representation of the data, since no root need be artificially assigned, as would be the case to derive a more familiar tree-diagram structure.

The average percentage standard deviation of this tree, at 2.56, means that the FITCH tree fits the distance matrix significantly better (at P < 0.001) than the KITSCH tree; we may therefore reject the assumption of a constant rate of change, at least for the data set at issue. To reiterate, however, the unrooted nature of the best fitting trees is no obstacle to classification, linguistic or biological; and the rejection of a glottochronological constant, or any other expression of the putatively constant rate of linguistic change, does not undermine the use of lexicostatistical

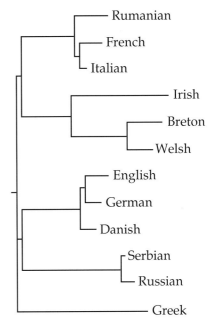

Figure 13.4. *Best FITCH Indo-European tree.*

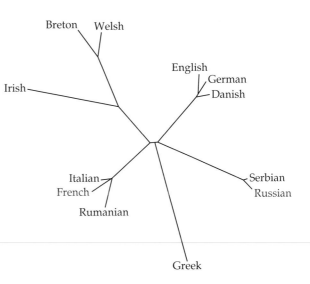

Figure 13.5. *Unrooted topology of FITCH Indo-European tree.*

data in applications of these computational methods.

Finally, it should be noted that in an analysis involving as many as twelve languages, it is not feasible for the program to search through all possible trees: there are 6.55×10^8 unrooted trees, and 1.37×10^{10} rooted ones, but only 4141 unrooted and 6698 rooted trees were actually considered. It is therefore possible that an even better fitting tree exists, but was missed. The robustness of a tree can, however, be checked by bootstrapping, which involves resampling the data used, and repeating the test as many times as is thought necessary. For this purpose, a second wordlist was used, somewhat longer than the first, and omitting some items on the first wordlist: the resulting FITCH tree was markedly similar to Figure 13.5, and we conclude that the classification is robust.

Since the lexicostatistical matrices were arrived at using knowledge of contributory sound changes and therefore of cognacy, a further investigation was made of the potential value of this method if phonetic similarity of words alone was considered in producing pairwise distance scores. That is, the lexicostatistical method would regard English 'four' and French 'quatre' as cognate, but English 'measure' and French 'mesurer', from which the English form is borrowed, as non-cognate. However, the similarity method, which simply searches for phonetic identity, would find no similarity between the phonetic forms of 'four' and 'quatre', but one-fifth similarity between 'measure' and 'mesurer'. It is therefore possible that borrowing could skew the results given the similarity method, as could chance resemblances between phonological systems. In order to minimize the latter problem, the similarity data were modified for each language pairing tested by removing the expected amount of similarity due to accidental congruence of the sound systems concerned (method described in Lohr (in prep.)): these modified values are used below. To reiterate, the great advantage of this method is that it is entirely blind to the hypothesis being tested, since it is not based on prior decisions as to which forms are cognate, but involves a purely computational assessment of phonetic similarity. This makes the similarity method both unusual and useful in comparative linguistics.

For this test, several non-Indo-European languages, namely Finnish, Hungarian, Basque and Mandarin, were included. The first three of these have been in contact with various Indo-European languages for centuries; this should therefore provide evidence of resistance of the method to admixture. The resulting tree is shown in Figure 13.6. Note that the program, being designed for biological classification, assumes ultimate monogenesis: no significance should therefore be attached to the fact that all languages considered form part of a single tree. The important point is the branching and groupings under this common root.

The Indo-European languages here emerge as a single group. Of the other languages considered, Finnish and Hungarian are correctly diagnosed as forming a group of their own. Basque does not attach itself to Romance, the source of the bulk of its Indo-European borrowings, or indeed even appear within Indo-European, suggesting a certain resistance of the model to admixture. As far as statistical significances are concerned, we have not tested this

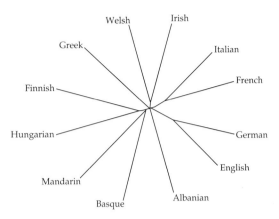

Figure 13.6. *Similarity topology including non-Indo-European languages.*

tree by bootstrapping, but have tested all language pairings. All within-Indo-European pairings show 99 per cent significant similarity, as do Finnish and Hungarian to one another. In addition, several pairings of Indo-European languages with Finnish or Hungarian are significantly similar at the 95 per cent level, and others at 99 per cent, which might support some connection of Indo-European and Uralic, although the similarity data cannot determine whether this reflects contact or deep genetic relationship.

Including earlier attested and reconstructed data

The next stage in our investigation is to include data from earlier language states within Indo-European: initially, these comprised attested Latin and Classical Greek, and reconstructed Proto-Indo-European. The programs are designed to place entities preferentially at branch tips rather than nodes, and it is consequently unclear how one might expect these non-contemporaneous systems to behave. One method of addressing this issue is to construct simulated data sets with essentially the same properties as the languages compared. This might allow us to establish 'normal' behaviour for an ancestral language, and ideally to discover the factor or factors responsible for any deviation from this prediction in the real data.

First simulation
Our initial simulation involved the construction of a data set based on one hundred points of comparison (which might be thought of as a virtual 100-word

list, or as 100 sounds), with the following assumptions:
• the nine 'languages' consisted of one parent, with the score 100 indicating its status as common ancestor, and eight daughters;
• for each daughter, random numbers were generated to indicate the 'items' which have undergone change from the common ancestor;
• all changes are assumed to result in non-identity between that item and all others; that is, changes are non-convergent. This is, of course, a gross simplification when compared to the real data and methods;
• different rates of change, that is different numbers of changes, occur in different branches.

A diagram showing the output of these processes appears in Figure 13.7, along with the distance matrix derived from the simulated data.

A topology derived from these data is given in Figure 13.8. The additional 'language' O is taken to be unrelated, and shares 3 per cent homology with all the related 'languages' A to I: the inclusion of this outgroup material permits location of the root, where O joins the cluster: as might be predicted, F, the common ancestor of the family excluding O is located precisely at that root.

This topology for the related languages alone, excluding the outgroup O, can also be converted to a conventional tree, as shown in Figure 13.9. As it turns out, the program handles the common ancestor differently here, locating it on the baseline rather than as a first-order branch. The same pattern can be

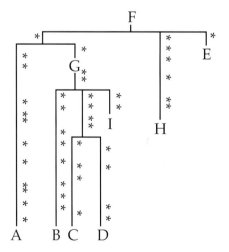

* = alterations from ancestral forms

Figure 13.7a. *Simulated language family history.*

	A	B	C	D	E	F	G	H	I
A	0	22	22	22	13	12	13	18	16
B		0	16	16	13	12	10	18	10
C			0	8	13	12	10	18	10
D				0	13	12	10	18	10
E					0	1	3	7	7
F						0	2	6	6
G							0	8	4
H								0	12
I									0

Distance matrix calculated by counting differences between 'twigs'

Figure 13.7b. *Distance matrix calculated from first simulation data.*

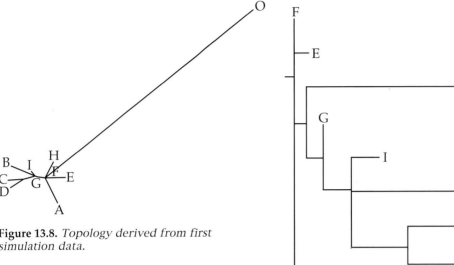

Figure 13.8. *Topology derived from first simulation data.*

Figure 13.9. *Tree derived from first simulation data, excluding outgroup O.*

seen for daughter G, which is the common ancestor for languages B, C, D and I, and similarly appears on an embedded baseline for that group, indicating that G has not itself changed since the initial split of its daughters. There is an apparent contradiction here with our earlier observation that languages typically appear only at branch tips: it would appear that when the drawing package is faced with a branch length of zero, indicating no change from an earlier stage, the language concerned will appear effectively at a node.

In short, this initial simulation establishes that the tree-drawing package can deal with common ancestral languages in a sensible fashion, and that such common ancestor systems might be expected to appear, in the unmarked case, at the roots of their family trees and distinct from their daughter groups.

Results from the two data sets
When data from Latin, Classical Greek and reconstructed Proto-Indo-European are included in the lexicostatistical set, the resulting tree (Fig. 13.10) conforms to the predictions arising from the simulation reported above.

However, these predictions are not borne out so clearly with the modified similarity data. In this case, as can be seen from the tree in Figure 13.11, an apparent anomaly emerges: Indo-European appears robustly in the Romance group.

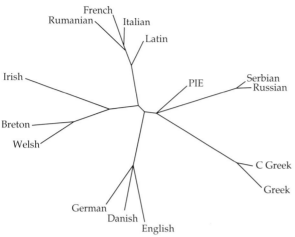

Figure 13.10. *Tree from lexicostatistical data, including Latin, Classical Greek and Proto-Indo-European.*

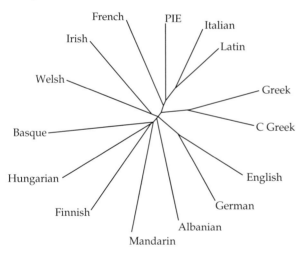

Figure 13.11. *Tree from modified similarity data, including Latin, Classical Greek and Proto-Indo-European.*

Second simulation

Our second simulation seeks to address the apparent misplacement of Proto-Indo-European within Romance which is evident from the similarity data. In this case, the data used were derived from the distance matrix generated by the similarity method in the section on computational methods and Indo-European data above, for the Indo-European languages shown in Figure 13.11. Classical Greek was excluded purely for simplicity; however, to test any possible significance of this exclusion, a further tree was generated from the similarity data minus Classical Greek: this was not significantly different from Figure 13.11, but if anything, the position of Proto-Indo-European was marginally closer to Latin in the absence of Classical Greek.

Initially, a simulated tree was constructed without Latin or Proto-Indo-European. Distance matrix data were transformed by averaging the values for the remaining four pairs of languages, namely French and Italian, English and German, Irish and Welsh, and Greek and Albanian, to give identical branch lengths for the members of the pairs. Note that this does not involve classifying Greek and Albanian as a subgroup: they will simply be assumed to have diverged by the same amount from the root. The purpose of this averaging is solely to remove perturbations relating to individual language histories, and to allow straightforward calculation of values for the simulated common ancestor. This value is then assigned to the analogue of Proto-Indo-European; however, this protolanguage is not placed directly on the baseline, but is arbitrarily assigned 30 per cent divergence to account for the contribution of daughter languages (like Sanskrit, Hittite, and so on) which are not included in the language inventory considered here.

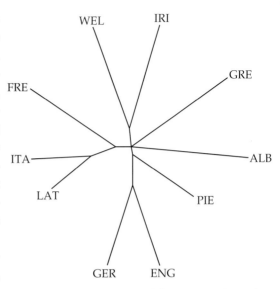

Figure 13.12. *Tree derived from second simulation data.*

A distance matrix was then calculated on the basis of these smoothed branch-lengths, with the addition of values for Latin derived from the average for French and Italian. However, the position of Latin relative to Italian and French was maintained from the original distance matrix: that is, Latin appears as skewed towards Italian in the Romance group. This synthetic distance matrix was then used to generate the tree in Figure 13.12.

In this tree (with all language names reduced to three letter strings to indicate that the data involved are synthetic, though ultimately based on real values), the common ancestor, PIE, joins at the root as in the first simulation and the real lexicostatistical data. In repeated runs of the program, PIE is consistently non-significantly different from root position, although it appears to join in various sectors of the topology in different repetitions. Why, then, did our real, reconstructed Proto-Indo-European attach so robustly to Romance on the similarity data?

One possibility, and surely the obvious one, is that Proto-Indo-European phonological reconstructions have an especially strong influence from Latin. To test this hypothesis, we progressively modified the synthetic data set for the second simulation to model increasing levels of 'borrowing' from LAT into PIE, without altering the relationship of PIE to the non-Romance languages. At 5 per cent 'borrowing', the resulting tree is indistinguishable from Figure 13.12. With 10 per cent, PIE consistently joins the tree at the root of Romance, as shown in

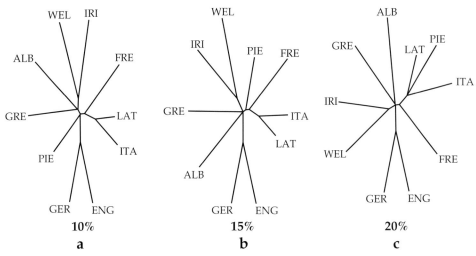

Figure 13.13. *'Borrowing' from LAT into PIE by percentage.*

Figure 13.13a, although it is not strictly within the Romance grouping. However, with 15 per cent 'borrowing', PIE has moved into the Romance subfamily (Fig. 13.13b), and at 20 per cent, its position is intermediate between LAT and ITA (Fig. 13.13c). The position of Proto-Indo-European on the similarity data appears to be between Figure 13.13b and Figure 13.13c.

To test the emerging hypothesis that additional influence of Latin on reconstructed Proto-Indo-European is responsible for the clustering of Proto-Indo-European with Romance in Figure 13.11, we replotted this tree with Latin removed. The result is shown in Figure 13.14. Proto-Indo-European does not quite join the tree at the root of the Indo-European cluster; rather, it is associated with the root of the Greek subgroup. It might be expected, however, that any immediate daughter of the proto-language might exert some effect of short edge attraction, being older and in all probability closer to the proto-system than would be the case for its own daughters. The location of Proto-Indo-European in this case is nonetheless much closer to that of PIE or ancestral language F in the simulations where 'borrowing' from Latin was not assumed, than to its position in the real similarity tree including Latin. We might be tempted to conclude that Proto-Indo-European has a favourite daughter.

Trees, simulations, and Nostratic

Before turning to other implications and possible applications of our methods, we must supply some content for the term 'borrowing' which we have used as a convenient but potentially misleading label for the apparently greater than expected contribution of Latin to Proto-Indo-European phonology which seems to emerge from the modified similarity data considered above. It is true that the magnitude of this effect seems beyond that which might be expected from any daughter of a certain age, as the comparison with Classical Greek should show. Nonetheless, we

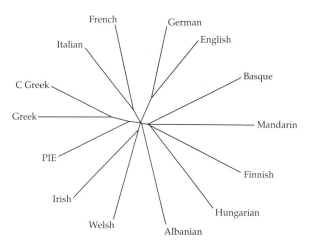

Figure 13.14. *Tree from modified similarity data, excluding Latin.*

should not allow the prediction of model results which will naturally follow from strictly averaged, simulated data, to lead us immediately to wholly negative conclusions when we find an apparent anomaly in real data. That is, the apparent bias towards Latin our similarity method suggests need not reflect badly on Proto-Indo-European reconstructions. On the contrary, Latin may indeed conserve features which can validly be reconstructed for Proto-Indo-European, but each of which is preserved in a different set of daughters, scattered across subfamily boundaries. That is, Latin may be more retentive and therefore truly closer to 'real' Proto-Indo-European than its sisters. In future work, more of those other sisters should also be included in the tree-drawing methodology, to assess whether similar results are achieved, or whether the effects are diluted as other daughters of equal or greater antiquity are included. One priority is then to include data from, for example, Sanskrit, Hittite and Old Irish; another is to retest using different Proto-Indo-European reconstructions, since clearly a method of this kind is only as good and as accurate as the data on which it operates.

Nonetheless, the possibility must be faced that there may be a general tendency in reconstruction for protolanguages to be based predominantly, and perhaps inordinately, on a single daughter or daughter branch, which may be the most archaic and conservative descendant, but might on the other hand be simply the best investigated or most liberally attested. If we regard realism in reconstruction as a valid goal (see Lass 1993), this kind of unwarranted bias would not advance us much towards it. Such potential bias, whether a general trend or a particular characteristic of Indo-European, would be relevant to Nostratic in that Proto-Indo-European (recent controversies over the consonant system notwithstanding) is typically regarded as one of the most securely reconstructed stocks within that larger putative family. Indeed, the reconstruction of Proto-Indo-European has already been through various cycles of proposals and emendations: take, for instance, the nineteenth-century hypothesis that the protolanguage strongly resembled Sanskrit, and the later realization that Sanskrit changes, notably the merger of *e, *a, *o as /a/, would have to be reversed to produce a more realistic picture of Proto-Indo-European. Of course, what we are considering here in terms of influence from Latin is not so far-reaching as this; and we are not suggesting that any wholesale revision of our reconstructions would be required. The effects are likely to be more minor, but also therefore more subtle, and less easy to detect: and they are likely to have more of an impact on higher-order groupings precisely because Proto-Indo-European has been subject to so much research and discussion. That is, it is not impossible that Proto-Indo-European itself should turn out to be the favourite daughter of Nostratic.

The implications for Nostratic are substantially greater, however, if such potential bias is a general trend for protolanguages. First, favourite daughters may themselves have borrowed from some source outside the family, making the establishment of unwarranted links more likely. Randomization across equally weighted daughter languages would minimize the effects of borrowing, but this might not be so if one daughter were favoured. This might not be a problem in data concentrating on basic vocabulary; but attempts to reconstruct Nostratic, for instance, naturally attempt to go beyond lists of one or two hundred words. Dolgopolsky (1998), for instance, is particularly concerned with linguistic palaeontology and the investigation of hypotheses on the homeland and culture of the speakers of Proto-Nostratic, and it follows that he is particularly concerned with cultural, rather than basic vocabulary.

It is also notable that, within work on Nostratic, the favourite daughter is not a new phenomenon. Perhaps the best-known case is that of Semitic relative to its larger family group, Afroasiatic. As Bomhard (1984, 133) notes,

> the comparative-historical study of the Afroasiatic Language Family is still in its infancy: Even though the Semitic and Egyptian branches have been scientifically investigated rather thoroughly, several of the other branches are only now being examined, and there remain many modern Afroasiatic languages that are scarcely even known.

Bomhard's (1984) reconstruction of Proto-Afroasiatic is therefore necessarily largely based on existing reconstructions of Proto-Semitic. Again, this has clear implications for the reconstruction of Proto-Nostratic, particularly given Bomhard & Kerns' (1994, 34) argument that Afroasiatic itself 'stands apart as an extremely ancient, independent branch' of Nostratic.

Problems of bias in longer-range reconstructions will be further compounded if they are combined with the problematic practice of 'reaching down'; that is, the identification of a form in a single language of a subgroup as a Nostratic cognate, even though this form could not be reconstructed for the subgroup as a whole. Ringe (1995, 60) notes that a considerable number of Illič-Svityč's etymologies exhibit reaching down, arguing that 'this is problematic in attempts to prove doubtful relationships, because it effectively multiplies the domains in which one is searching for comparanda, thereby multiplying the incidence of chance resemblances as well'. The whole problem of chance resemblances, and the issue of how best to guard against them, has been central to recent debate on long-range reconstructions. It might be thought that this debate has relatively little bearing on Nostratic, since 'Nostraticists maintain that they do use the comparative method' (Ringe 1995, 70), rather than more controversial methods like Greenberg's (1987) multilateral comparison. However, note that Bomhard at least describes his method as based partly on Greenberg's, and partly on traditional comparative and internal reconstruction (Bomhard & Kerns 1994, 3–4). Even if the comparative method is followed, some critics contend that 'It is neither sensible nor provident to look for a family tree of family trees' (Dixon 1997, 152), particularly if comparison is not stepwise, but rather involves several family groups at a time. In particular, there is widespread disquiet about the possibility that the comparative method might indeed be applied in long-range comparative work, but without the usual rigour in the determination of permissible phonological or semantic matches. As Lass (1997, 161) puts it, 'one man's etymology is another man's word-list.' And Ringe (1995) goes further, claiming that his mathematical comparison of 205 of Illič-Svityč's Nostratic roots to various probability curves shows the Nostratic results are indistinguishable from chance resemblances, under the simplest model he applies.

It would seem, then, that not all work on Nostratic is based on the comparative method. Furthermore, when the comparative method is used, it is not always applied rigorously. Our work on computational tree-drawing suggests yet another problem: one can use the comparative method, without relying on lax phonological or semantic criteria, and in a traditional step-by-step manner, and still find problems which accumulate all the way up the tree from language to family and family to superfamily, simply because there is bias towards a single daughter, perhaps only at the lowest level of the tree, and perhaps repeatedly right up into the highest reaches. Our findings therefore support Ringe's (1995, 71) assertion that 'use of the comparative method does not necessarily lead to clearly correct results'.

On the other hand, however, our computational methods also constitute a possible method of checking for and identifying bias towards particular languages or groups in comparison and reconstruction. If such bias can be detected, it can then be explored, to ascertain whether in a particular case it is justifiable; problematic but unavoidable, if for instance work on the family as a whole is not far advanced; or a candidate for correction. Furthermore, in cases where a family has been little investigated, our tree-drawing methods might themselves be a useful initial contribution, giving an outline indication of potential subgrouping, whether based on lexicostatistical or similarity techniques, which can then be explored further. As we saw for the links of Indo-European with Finno-Ugric which our statistical analysis supported earlier, such methods can also indicate those proposed links between higher-level groupings which might be worthy of further consideration. In addition, as historical linguists increasingly collaborate with scientists from other disciplines, like archaeology and genetics, where quantitative work is a way of life, it is incumbent on us to develop testable, transparent and verifiable models ourselves, to allow cross-disciplinary comparisons to be properly assessed. And, questions of bias apart, it would be extremely useful to have a diagnostic for assessing the relative retentiveness of languages in a family, to discern those which lie closest to the root for a particular set of data or area of the grammar, and which might therefore be of disproportionate utility in reconstruction. Just as quantitative methods deriving from concordances have identified hitherto unsuspected authorship of texts, or attempted but undetected imitation, so computational methods of the type outlined here might allow historical linguists to identify expected patterns and exceptions in our proposals of linguistic relatedness, whether remote and speculative or apparently well-characterized and understood.

References

Bomhard, A.R., 1984. *Towards Proto-Nostratic: a New Approach*. Amsterdam: Benjamins.

Bomhard, A.R. & J.C. Kerns, 1994. *The Nostratic Macrofamily: a Study in Distant Linguistic Relationship*. Berlin: Mouton de Gruyter.

Cavalli-Sforza, L.L., P. Menozzi & A. Piazza, 1994. *The History and Geography of Human Genes*. Princeton (NJ): Princeton University Press.

Dixon, R.M.W., 1997. *The Rise and Fall of Languages*. Cambridge: Cambridge University Press.

Dolgopolsky, A., 1998. *The Nostratic Macrofamily and Linguistic Palaeontology*. (Papers in the Prehistory of Languages.) Cambridge: The McDonald Institute for Archaeological Research.

Fitch, W. & E. Margoliash, 1967. Construction of phylogenetic trees. *Science* 155, 279–84.

Greenberg, J.H., 1987. *Language in the Americas*. Stanford (CA): Stanford University Press.

Lass, R., 1993. How real(ist) are reconstructions?, in *Historical Linguistics: Problems and Perspectives*, ed. C. Jones. London: Longman, 156–89.

Lass, R., 1997. *Historical Linguistics and Language Change*. Cambridge: Cambridge University Press.

Lohr, M., in prep. Genetic Classification and the Celtic Languages. Unpublished Ph.D. dissertation, University of Cambridge.

Lohr, M., R. McMahon & A. McMahon, 1998a. Modelling language evolution: trees and language history. Poster presented at the Second International Conference on the Evolution of Language, London.

Lohr, M., R. McMahon & A. McMahon, 1998b. Genetic classification and biological methodology. Paper presented at the Linguistics Association of Great Britain Spring Meeting, Lancaster.

Ringe, D.A., 1995. 'Nostratic' and the factor of chance. *Diachronica* 12(1), 55–74.

Ruvolo, M., 1987. Reconstructing genetic and linguistic trees: phenetic and cladistic approaches, in *Biological Metaphor and Cladistic Classification*, eds. H.M. Hoenigswald & L.F. Wiener. Philadelphia (PA): University of Pennsylvania Press, 193–216.

Sokal, R.R. & P.H.A. Sneath, 1963. *Principles of Numerical Taxonomy*. San Francisco (CA): W.H. Freeman.

Swadesh, M., 1950. Salish internal relationships. *International Journal of American Linguistics* 16, 157–67.

Part IV
Perspectives from the Daughter Families

Chapter 14

Afroasiatic and the Nostratic hypothesis

David Appleyard

Afroasiatic as a super-family or phylum, comprising six member families (Berber, Chadic, Cushitic, Egyptian, Omotic, Semitic) is classified first and foremost on the basis of grammatical morpheme correspondence. Lexical comparison should play a secondary, though none the less important role in classification. Following these principles, the morphological arguments for including Afroasiatic in a 'Nostratic' super-phylum seem weak. There are also serious methodological issues involved relating to questions such as the effects of 'language areal' features, as well as models of language development and relationship, most notably those implicit in the 'punctuated equilibrium' model of change and the theory of interacting trends of divergence and convergence. Following a more generally based discussion, the paper proceeds to examine some individual etymologies proposed in NM and finds that the lexical evidence in NM for Afroasiatic inclusion, at least, in 'Nostratic' is also too insubstantial to prove the case.

In his introduction to Aharon Dolgopolsky's book *The Nostratic Macrofamily and Linguistic Palaeontology* (hereafter *NM*), Colin Renfrew reminds us that individual comparative linguists tend to be either 'lumpers' or 'splitters'. That is, we are either what have been called 'long-rangers', quick to see and actively seek genetic connections between families of languages forming even larger linguistic units, or we set our sights much lower down the relationship scale and work more closely on identifying and quantifying smaller units such as language families or even branches of families. As a preparative to the present discussion, I must confess from the start that I am essentially a 'splitter' who is perhaps (if rather somewhat romantically) attracted by the ideas of the 'lumpers', but who is not convinced and doubts the methodological integrity of 'lumping'. I will say more of this later.

What is Afroasiatic?

The languages subsumed by Dolgopolsky under the term 'Nostratic' with which I am most familiar belong to two or three divisions of what is now more usually and widely called Afroasiatic. I cannot however claim to be an expert in all Afroasiatic member families. Incidentally, whilst I do not find terminological quibbles generally edifying, I should point out that the name Hamito-Semitic that Dolgopolsky uses throughout *NM* — though in his list of languages admittedly mentioning Afroasiatic in brackets — has now generally fallen out of fashion and Greenberg's term 'Afroasiatic' is preferred, at least in the English-speaking academic world, for the obvious reason that the term Hamito-Semitic (or even worse Semito-Hamitic) might give the erroneous impression that somehow the Semitic family stands apart from, or in a superior position to the remaining members. The word 'Hamitic' additionally has unhappy connotations from earlier schools of ethnology and romantic anthropology, and should now be avoided. I will therefore use Afroasiatic throughout the following discussion. The term Afroasiatic (also Afro-Asiatic, and its peculiarly Russian-coined variant Afrasian) covers a considerable number of languages — Dolgopolsky's list mentions about 125 by name, with quite a few etcs., and the complete list even of living languages is certainly considerably larger, probably at least double, even allowing for the familiar hesitation between languages and dialects. Consensus opinion further classifies these languages into six major groups (Berber, Chadic, Cushitic, Egyptian, Omotic, Semitic), as Dolgopolsky does in his data, though even here scholarly opinion is not unanimous. At least two leading scholars (Zaborski and Lamberti) in the Afroasiatic field have often argued for a closer unity between Cushitic and Omotic, which was the original view before Omotic was re-classified. Afroasiatic is not a single family in the sense that Indo-European, Kartvelian or Dravidian are. From my understanding of the other language groupings that are included in *NM*, Afroasiatic is in classificational terms probably more akin to (though less contentious than) Altaic: that is, a grouping of distinct language families into what has been called a super-family or phylum. For instance, whilst the degree of relationship between the languages of the Semitic family is probably qualitatively not too dissimilar from that of the Indo-European languages, and the two families could in classificational terms stand on a similar footing, the internal relationship between the members of the Chadic and Cushitic families, on the other hand, is certainly much more diffuse. At the opposite end of the scale the Berber languages are close enough to have been considered (incorrectly I would judge) as a dialect cluster, especially by most French scholars who dominate the field of Berber studies. The fifth member of the phylum, Egyptian, is to all intents and purposes a single language with some dialectal variation, apparently social as well as regional, but with of course an extraordinary, even unique time dimension. The remaining member, Omotic, is the most recent to enter the comparative field on a sound footing, having only been 'identified' as a separate member of the phylum at the close of the 1960s, a status which is, as I have said, disputed by some scholars who still prefer to see it as a part of Cushitic. Whether or not we accept the thesis that Omotic is a separate family (and I do, for reasons that will be apparent later on), the internal classifications of the group that have been proposed (see Hayward 1990) seem to follow a fairly orthodox middle-sized family model.

Another factor that begs particular consideration when dealing with Afroasiatic is that the nature and, I would say, even the quality of the data available from individual languages and different member families is extremely disparate and uneven. On the first hand, two of the families include some of the earliest recorded human languages: Egyptian (from the beginning of the third millennium BCE) and from Semitic, Old Akkadian (from the middle of the third millennium BCE). In addition, there are of course extensive ancient written records of many other Semitic languages, as well, from each of the branches of that family: Ugaritic, Canaanite languages such as Phoenician and Hebrew, various forms of Old Aramaic, Classical Arabic, Classical Ethiopic (Ge'ez), and various Epigraphic South Arabian languages (especially Sabaean), to name but the most obvious. From amongst the remaining Afroasiatic member families, however, only Berber has any pre-modern attestation and this, the Numidian or Libyan inscriptions dating from the second century BCE, is far too scant to provide much data for the historical linguist. The majority of Afroasiatic languages, including all the Chadic, Cushitic and Omotic languages, are only known from modern times. What is more, the extent and sometimes the quality of the data on these languages is much less than is desirable. This is a consideration that is particularly pertinent when reviewing the data in *NM*. As will be apparent later, some of the lexical citations supplied either come from unreliable sources or are not corroborated by other sources.

The existence of a considerable corpus of ancient Afroasiatic material spanning more than three millennia, something that is shared, I believe, only with Indo-European amongst the language families subsumed under 'Nostratic', whilst an enviable resource for the comparativist, does bring its own peculiar problems. There are two considerations when dealing with ancient data: comparison of data across a spectrum of time-depths, and the problem associated in using ancient language data recorded in a variety of writing systems. Firstly, in comparing, say, a feature or an item from the Egyptian of the Pyramid Texts with a feature or item from a modern Chadic language like Mubi, or a modern Semitic language like Chäha, one is obviously not comparing like with like. In practice this may not produce excessively distorted results but it could be argued, and indeed has been argued, that it is methodologically suspect. In an ideal situation, should not the linguist compare data of the same, or roughly the same time band? Modern data with modern data, so Chäha with Mubi (or better still Mubi with Hausa, and Chäha with Jibbali, for instance, keeping in the first instance within the broad family bounds), Old Egyptian with Old Akkadian, or Proto-Semitic with Proto-Cushitic, and so on. A more important consideration concerns the handling of ancient written sources, something that is especially relevant to some of the Afroasiatic field, namely the interpretation of the ancient data so that it can be used alongside material collected by trained linguists and recorded with all the rigour of modern descriptive method. I am, of course, thinking especially but not solely of Egyptian, whose writing system ignores vocalic phonemes, and even the interpretation of the consonantal symbols of which is, in recent decades, undergoing a considerable revision (Loprieno 1995; Satzinger 1997). The traditional transcription, which Dolgopolsky follows with some slight modifications of symbol (e.g. ꝫ for traditional grapheme <d̠>, where others use ɟ or ǧ), conceals quite a different phonetic reality if the most recent suggestions are correct. The fact, for instance, that <d̠> = /ɟ/, etc., was probably phonetically a voiceless glottalized affricate [tʃʼ] (i.e. č' in more the familiar Afroasiaticist transcription) from Old Egyptian through to the immediately pre-Coptic period (where not depalatalized to t) is interesting but not a major revision. A more substantial revision concerns the phonemes traditionally transcribed as <ḥ> (= glottalized [x'] and not as might be expected [ħ]), and especially <ꝫ>, now interpreted as originally a rhotic [ʀ] and only in later stages a glottal [ʔ], and <'> (Dolgopolsky's ˁ). Internal evidence suggests that the last was in part, in some dialects and at some stages of Egyptian, realized in some words originally as [d] and thence devoiced as [t], as well as [ˁ] elsewhere. This means that in making cognate sets for Egyptian items incorporating <'>, one has to be conscious of both possibilities. The Late Egyptian variant m-dj (and Coptic nta-) 'in the hand of' corresponding to Middle Egyptian m-ˁ illustrates this well.

The second consideration in assessing and evaluating language data for comparative work is, as I have suggested above, the reliability and even the size and range of the source material. Data on many Chadic, Cushitic and Omotic languages, most obviously, are restricted to at best brief grammatical sketches and more often just word-lists or antiquated glossaries, not infrequently without verification. We should also not forget that even in the erstwhile long studied Semitic family not all the modern languages have been described with equal thoroughness: there is much still to be done in the field of Modern South Arabian, for example (though Johnstone's dictionaries are a major resource). This means not only that the linguistic picture is woefully incomplete, but more importantly for the exercise in hand that it can also be unreliable. I do not, however, mean to imply that Dolgopolsky is unaware of these problems, nor that they are exclusive to Afroasiatic languages. They are rather considerations that are sometimes ignored in comparative lexical work and especially in work of the 'macro-comparativist' kind. Looking at the Afroasiatic material in *NM*, single language citations are not unusual as representatives of whole families. A great deal of inferential weight can therefore sit on little data that may in the end be suspect and cannot be corroborated from more recent or more reliable dictionaries, and so the argument for a particular comparison necessarily is weakened.

What makes a language Afroasiatic?

What then are the considerations, the pieces of linguistic evidence, that contribute to the viability of the idea of a phylum such as Afroasiatic, and that should therefore be equally essential in considering more remote level groupings that are proposed such as Nostratic? Conventional wisdom has usually concentrated on morphological comparison, that is to increase the probability that languages A...N, or language families A...N, are related there should be a shared body of grammatical morphemes, what Bender has called 'grammemes' (Bender 1990). Comparative lexical evidence is of course also part of the picture, and I will return to this aspect later, but I would maintain that grammatical morphemes must have priority in weighing up the evidence. These are the morphemes referring to the fundamental grammatical categories of the language, such as pronouns, demonstratives, markers of grammatical case, markers of tense-aspect-mood, markers of valency in verbs, and so on, as appropriate to the language type. This is not the same as questions of language typology, such as whether a language or language family marks 'gender' or 'class' in nouns, or whether the nominal system is of an 'ergative' or 'nominative' type, for instance. These typological features can and do change even radically in the history of a language. For example, Egyptian, which has the longest continuous recorded history of any language, of about 4500 years progressively from Old Egyptian to Coptic, has moved particularly in its verbal typology progressively from a complex fusional morphological type through degrees of periphrastic, isolating and/or agglutinating structures back to a complex fusional typology in Coptic (Hodge 1970). As an illustration, the principal narrative past-tense form in Old Egyptian, sɟm-f 'he heard', tentatively vocalized as sVɟ'mif (Loprieno 1995, 77), was replaced in Middle Egyptian in this function by sɟm-n-f (sa'ɟimnif) which already existed in Old Egyptian probably as some kind of resultative or present perfect and which is usually analyzed as consisting of a verbal noun bound with a prepositional phrase, 'a hearing to him'; this in turn was superseded in Late Egyptian by the periphrastic construction jr-f sʲm lit. 'he did a hearing', which is the origin of Coptic af'soːtəm. The latter is synchronically analyzable as *tense* {a} + *person* + {f} + *verb base (infinitive)* {soːtəm}, as much a fusional form as Old Egyptian sʲm-f (Loprieno 1995, 91ff.).

This 'linguistic cycle' is, as Hodge says, presumably a universal phenomenon; it is just that with Egyptian we are in a position to see it in action without recourse to reconstructing preceding or intermediate stages. However, it seems a general principle that a good number of grammatical morphemes persist throughout a language's history (Hodge 1975), in the example above the third masculine pronominal morpheme {f}, for instance. If this is the case with a 'real' language through time, then it should be equally a feature of reconstructed proto-languages.

The comparative linguist should be and is of course concerned with other levels of linguistic analysis. Running hand in hand with morphological comparison, and of necessity validating the results, is phonological comparison: the establishment of predictable patterns of sound change. This can only be done properly through lexical comparison for the obvious reason of a much greater size of corpus, and the results of structured lexical comparison would be expected to confirm the morphological. However, I would add a word of caution here: as much as we are all aware of the need rigorously to identify and adhere to patterns of regular sound change, anyone who has done extensive work on lexical comparison is conscious of instances that do not 'fit': to take an example from the area I know best, a Proto-Central Cushitic (Agaw) root *kamb-/*kʊmb- with the meaning 'cold' can be readily reconstructed from evidence in 'real' languages, and similarly a Proto-East Cushitic root *k'ab[b]- with exactly the same meaning. Yet the correspondence Proto-East Cushitic *k':PA. *k is not the regular one. Evidence from elsewhere in Afroasiatic, such as Egyptian <qb> 'cold' (n.), <qbb> 'cool' (vb.) [> Coptic kbob] and maybe Mocha (Omotic) 'k'ɐwo, supports a glottalized velar initial, which should have a reflex *q in Proto-Agaw. A correspondence between medial NC and CC [where N = homorganic nasal, and C = any (stop) consonant] is not unknown in Cushitic and Semitic, and though sporadic and not predictable would not be a cause for concern. Is the inclusion of the Agaw forms in this cognate set therefore to be rejected, contrary to appearances, because Agaw k- is not the regular correspondent of Proto-East Cushitic (and Proto-Cushitic) *k'-? Strict adherence to patterns of regular sound change would say yes. There are however quite a few apparent instances of Proto-Agaw *k = Proto-East Cushitic *k' (Appleyard 1996, 197).

To cite a contrary example, where a comparison has been proposed and is accepted by some, though the 'fit' is rather weak, the Proto-Agaw for 'bone' can be reconstructed as *ŋac. Attempts are usually made (most recently Orël & Stolbova 1995, 333) to connect this with the widespread Afroasiatic root *k'∇s (Egyptian qs, Coptic kas, Berber i-ɣəs, Proto-Omotic *k'as-/*k'us-, Proto-Chadic *ha-k'as[i]-) via something such as *N∇-k'∇c'. Such a linkage, however, would require irregular correspondences in both consonants: *ŋ ≠ *k' (or even *n+k'), *s ≠ *č'. An exact fit as far as the consonants are concerned, however, would be Proto-East Cushitic *moč'- 'bone' (Arvanites 1991, 240) with reflexes in Yaaku moč'o 'bone' and Somali madʒin 'limb'. The equation is, however, further complicated by such as Proto-Highland East Cushitic *mik'e and thence Sidamo mik'-iččo, which is probably the source of such as Dobase mik'ačče, etc., which seems to have led Orël & Stolbova to propose a Proto-Afroasiatic variant with final **č' alongside **s. Furthermore, there are near look-alikes elsewhere in Cushitic such as Beja míita 'bone', Oromo mita 'joint', Arbore mittá 'joint', Elmolo mótolač 'ankle' etc., though here the progressive mismatch č' ≠ k' ≠ t perhaps becomes too much.

With as long a time-depth as must be proposed for such constructs as Nostratic, how much more likely are such deviations from supposedly regular sound correspondences to occur? Heretical as it may seem, should we not be asking whether insistence on strict rules of sound correspondence are appropriate here? Of course, if this supposition is accepted, it would perversely make the reconstruction of proto-languages at such remote time depths all the more problematical.

In the field of comparative work across the Afroasiatic phylum the major name must be that of Diakonoff, whose pioneering study of 1965 (*Semito-Hamitic Languages*) has been to a great extent superseded by his major 1988 revision with the revised title *Afrasian Languages*. For Afroasiatic Diakonoff (1986, cited and reported by Blažek 1989, as well as Diakonoff 1988) has proposed the following list of morphemes reconstructable on the basis of evidence from all or most of the constituent families of the phylum. Some seem to me better substantiated than others as pertaining to the whole of Afroasiatic. In particular, I would emphasize the personal pronouns, gender markers, and the verb-stem derivational formants, and maybe some of the case markers, as the most diagnostic.

- a system of grammatical gender marking: masc. *-Vw/-Vy, fem. *-V̦i > *-ay/-aa; the latter is largely superseded as feminine marker by the marker of the old 'inactive' noun class -(a)t, the familiar feminine marker and one of the early diagnostics for inclusion in the Afroasiatic phylum. The vowel i is, however, associated with the feminine in several pronominal forms, often contrasting with a masculine u. At an even earlier level, Diakonoff sees remains of a noun-class system (with markers such as *-(a)b, *-(a)ħ, *-(a)l/r, *(a)n, *-(a)t).

- a grammatical case system with an original binary opposition: nominative or ergative *-i/-u: absolute *-a/-Ø. The principal evidence for this comes from Cushitic and Semitic, with possible traces in Egyptian and maybe Berber, though there is some dispute about the last.

- a system of spatial cases (e.g. locative-terminative/dative *-š; comitative/dative *-d; ablative *-k; locative-adverbialis *-m; directive *-l; ablative *-f/p). These appear variously as prepositions and postpositions, or case suffixes in a more conventional sense.

- a system of three categories of number: singular, dual and plural. As the oldest marker of the plural in nouns Diakonoff proposes an infix *-a(a)- before the gender marker (hence *-a(a)w, *-a(a)t) or the last consonant of the stem. A plural marker *-(aa)n that is often proposed elsewhere Diakonoff suggests may have a pronominal demonstrative origin (cf. plural pronouns). As the category of dual occurs only in Egyptian and the older Semitic languages along with, it is claimed, a few (?) remains in Berber, it would seem to me less reconstructable at the Proto-Afroasiatic level.

- a system of 'stirpes', or verb derivation expressing principally different argument structures from the base form, such as causative and passive-reflexive, with the following markers: *šV- essentially causative-factitive; *tV- originally denoting 'a change in the direction of action', and usually with reflexive, reciprocal and eventually passive function, to which we may also add an autobenefactive or 'middle' sense in Cushitic; *nV-/mV- with reflexive function, and thence sometimes passive. It is not clear whether this is one or two formatives: only Berber has both n- and m-, but mainly the latter; Semitic and Egyptian have the formative n- (but only as a rare and restricted formant in the latter), Cushitic has -m, Omotic has -n but also some traces of -m, and Chadic may have traces of n- (Lieberman 1986). In Berber, Cushitic, Semitic and apparently Omotic combinations of these formatives also occur. The formative elements themselves further appear to be of pronominal origin, and are identical in form to pronominal/demonstrative roots.

To these, most importantly, we can add much of the personal pronoun system, which has indeed been used more than any other part of the morphology as the Afroasiatic diagnostic *par excellence*. The reconstructed system (and the actual system in some languages) includes a fundamental division into two sets with different grammatical functions: Set A with subject function, and Set B with various oblique functions such as possessive and object, and includes both free and bound (clitic) forms. A recurrent confusion between the sets can be observed both between families and languages within families.

The most recent attempt to correlate all the Afroasiatic data is Blažek's (1995) whose reconstructions at the Proto-Afroasiatic level are as follow. I feel that there is a fair amount of imaginative and highly speculative reconstruction here, and would not necessarily endorse all the forms exactly, but the underlying patterns seem well reasoned and justifiable. Dolgopolsky's own reconstructions (1988) present a picture that differs from this in a few details.

	Set A		Set B	
	sg.	pl.	sg.	pl.
1	*ʔaku	*muni (inclusive)	*[ʔ]ya/i/u	(*muni) (inclusive)
		*hina/u (exclusive)		*na/i/u (exclusive)
2mas	*ta	*tunwa	*ku	*kunwa
2fem	*ti	*tinya	*ki	*kinya
3mas	*šu	*šunwa	*šu	*šunwa
3fem	*ši	*šinya	*ši	*šinya

As an illustration of a contentious reconstruction which is immediately relevant to the question of Afroasiatic and the Nostratic hypothesis, I would mention only the 1st person inclusive *muni that Blažek reconstructs. A 1st person pronoun *mV is proposed as a Nostratic grammatical morpheme, but the Afroasiatic evidence is problematic — and indeed Dolgopolsky excludes reference to Afroasiatic in this instance [NM, p. 17]. Whilst the distinction between categories of 1st plural inclusive and exclusive is found in a range of Cushitic, Omotic and Chadic languages, the inclusive *muni form is based exclusively on Chadic evidence. Indeed the reconstruction of a 1st person pronominal form in *m- for Proto-Afroasiatic is to my mind contentious anyway. Aside from Chadic where it occurs widely in the plural (inclusive where that category exists), m- is found as a first-person marker only in some languages belonging to one sub-branch of Cushitic (Northern Highland East Cushitic), and there as part of the person marking of the first singular and plural, presumably as a kind of pronominal adjunct, in some tenses (Sim 1988). I would maintain that this kind of lop-sided distribution does not permit the reconstruction of an *m- form for the whole of Afroasiatic. There may be other reasons for the Highland East Cushitic forms than retention of a supposed Afroasiatic morpheme lost everywhere else except Chadic. The m- element in the former has, for instance, been ingeniously explained

(Tosco 1996) as due to the re-interpretation of a morpheme borrowed from neighbouring Gurage (Semitic) languages, where it has nothing to do with person marking.

In addition to the *m- form, other Nostratic reconstructions for the 1st person pronoun are proposed: a first person singular 'replacement form' **ʔakE (a sort of deictic, for which see *inter alia* Greenberg 1991, 131ff.), 1st sing. 'oblique form' **Hoy∇, 1st plural 'exclusive' *n|ń∇. The two pronouns **ʔakE and **Hoy∇ are admittedly more substantial than the typical CV Nostratic grammatical morpheme. Even here, though, chance coincidence cannot be ruled out — after all for Proto-Austronesian Benedict (1975, 203) reconstructs a first-person pronoun **[w]aku/[w]aqu, and even a 'form of restricted occurrence' *[ʔ]ya, and Bender (1989, 13) suggests a Proto-Nilo-Saharan first-person singular **akʷai!

To return to Afroasiatic, as a development of this proposed proto-system, the following forms can be reconstructed for Proto-Semitic essentially through (a) the addition of a prefixed *ʔan- (topicalizer ?) to the first and second persons of set A, and (b) the development of set B into separate suffixed (possessive, verbal object) and independent (oblique case) forms. The resulting system is fairly similar to what can be reconstructed for Proto-Cushitic, too (Appleyard 1986), and as such may, in principle at least, more properly describe a shared stage earlier than Proto-Semitic. The prefixed *ʔan- also occurs in the first persons in Egyptian: sg. jnk (jaˈnak), pl. jnn (jaˈnan); in Berber: sg. *ənakkʷ (pl. *ənakkʷani is a pluralized form of the singular); and in Chadic: sg. *ʔani/a/u.

	Set A		Set B	
	sg.	pl.	sg.	pl.
1	*ʔanʔaku, *ʔanʔa (> *ʔanaaku, *ʔanaa)	*hinna, *[ʔa]nihna/u < *ʔan+hina/u	*-ya/-ii // *-ʔa // *-nii † *y[iw]aa	*-na/i/u
2mas	*ʔanta	*ʔantumu/ʔantunu	*-ka *kuwaa	*-kumu/-kunu
2fem	*ʔanti	*ʔantin[n]a	*-ki (*kuwaa) *	*-kin[n]a
3mas	*šuwa	*šumu/šunu	*-šuu *šuwaa	*-šumu/-šunu
3fem	*šiya	*šin[n]a	*-šaa/-šii *šiyaa	*-šin[n]a

† possessive *-ya/-ii; dative *-[ʔ]a; object *-nii

* a distinct independent second feminine singular form *kima[a] (or some such) can be proposed for other families: Proto-Berber *kamm, Proto-Chadic *ki[m]/ *kV̄m, Old Egyptian cm, cmt (= *čim, *čiˈmat).

It is also worth pointing out that the Omotic evidence presents some features which are difficult to reconcile with this picture of the personal pronouns, most obviously the first and second person forms of the independent pronouns, which for Proto-North Omotic have to be reconstructed as *ta and *ne, respectively. Various attempts have been made to explain these forms, which look distressingly the inverse of what might be expected, but none is to my mind really convincing. Nilo-Saharan influence has also been suggested. The first and second plural pronouns look more promising with forms reconstructable as *nV̄ and *ʔintV̄, respectively. The picture looks even more obscured when we turn to South Omotic where we find the following scheme: 1sg. *ʔi-/ʔa-; 2sg. *ya-; 1pl. *wo-; 2pl. *ye-, where at least some Nilotic influence is more readily detectable.

Another category of grammatical morphemes that is often held up as an Afroasiatic diagnostic, the almost 'classical' test in fact, is the ʔ-t-y-n patterning of personal marking in finite verbs, the so-called 'block pattern'. This can be best exemplified by the Proto-Semitic prefix-conjugation:

	sg.	pl.
1	*ʔa-	*ni-
2mas	*ti-	*ti-...-uu †
2fem	*ti-...-ii †	*ti-...-aa/-na †
3mas	*yi-	*yi-...-uu †
3fem	*ti-	*yi-/ti-...-aa/-na †

† the suffixed elements contributing gender and number marking are in these forms specific to Semitic.

However, this ʔ-t-y-n block pattern occurs only in Semitic, Berber and Cushitic. It does not occur in Egyptian, Chadic or Omotic. There are reasons for supposing that Semitic, Berber and Cushitic form a sub-group of families within the phylum, and if this is the case then the block pattern should be better seen as a subsequent development within that group rather than a common Afroasiatic feature lost in the other families.

I have expatiated at some length on the question of grammatical morphemes and to what extent some of these can be reconstructed for Proto-Afroasiatic to demonstrate the type of evidence that I believe is the most persuasive argument for the reality of proposing an Afroasiatic phylum. The same kind of evidence (the reconstruction of pronoun systems, nominal and verbal inflexion, and nominal and verbal derivational systems) has been produced for other language families and phyla, such as Indo-European, Kartvelian, Uralic, Dravidian, and so on (I do not know about Altaic). It is this kind of evidence that is more persuasive than lists of lexical comparisons. Even in the example of language families or phyla with less morphological 'baggage', such as Sino-Tibetan, there is, I believe, a body of evidence of this sort, pronouns and derivational affixes, to make a substantial case. As far as Nostratic is concerned, on the other hand, I find the 'evidence' too diffuse, less convincing. Although the purpose of *NM* is obviously to put the case for lexical data of the kind that is useful to the linguistic palaeontologist and the interface between historical linguistics and archaeology, Dolgopolsky does indeed provide us with a brief list of a few grammatical morpheme reconstructs [*NM*, p. 17] and more can be found elsewhere (Kaiser & Shevoroshkin 1988). The Afroasiatic 'evidence' for some of these is either easily contestable or highly suspect, however, and what is marginally more convincing is very little indeed (I have already discussed first person singular **$^{\circ}$akE and **HoyV, above): first person **n|ńV, second person **tV and **kV, interrogative **mi, causative **sV, negative-indefinite **ma. To these might be added a couple of more items from Illič-Svityč's list: locative particle **dV, 'directive' particle **kV, demonstrative pronoun **nV. These are, moreover, somewhat insubstantial in form, comprising simply a single consonant and a single vowel, and mostly what one might call consonants of low markedness, at that.

One final word on morphology: given what we can observe about typological change from languages with long recorded histories, such as Egyptian, I think it is legitimate to ask, how is it possible to make such precise statements as Dolgopolsky does about the typology of Proto-Nostratic as 'proto-Nostratic was a highly analytical language . . . with a rigid word order . . . and grammatical meanings expressed by word order, postpositions and grammatical pronouns' [*NM*, p. 17]? One is reminded of the famous attempt by Illič-Svityč to compose a poem in Proto-Nostratic, or the fables in Proto-Indo-European composed by some from an earlier generation of scholars.

Lexical comparison in Afroasiatic

I have suggested that morphological evidence is more persuasive than lexical for a very specific reason. I would imagine everyone agrees that language change receives impetus through two different mechanisms, which may act independently or more often than not interact in differing degrees at different times in a language's history: divergence through splitting up of original speech communities and convergence through diffusion across adjacent language communities (Dixon 1997, 15ff.); this is complementary to constant internal processes of change from generation to generation. Diffusion, or borrowing as it has been called more crudely, can affect all levels of linguistic structure, from phonology to morphology, from syntax to lexis. No aspect of linguistic structure is sacrosanct. Yet, I think it would also be generally agreed that some areas of a language are more open to the effects of diffusion than others: it would seem a general tendency that syntax and lexis and maybe phonology are more amenable to change through diffusion — vocabulary, syntactic patterns and phonetic and phonological features are more likely to be 'borrowed' than grammatical morphemes and maybe grammatical typologies. This can be readily illustrated from the area of Afroasiatic with which I am most familiar: the Semitic, Cushitic and Omotic languages of Ethiopia. The changing patterns of interaction over millennia between speakers of various languages from these three families within the region (or regions) of Ethiopia have meant that there is not only a large body of shared vocabulary but also a host of areal features at other levels of language structure: glottalized consonants (including implosives); avoidance of larger consonant clusters than CC; a special negative copula; a converb (sometimes less correctly called gerundive) form of the verb; a tendency towards multiple compound tenses especially in main clauses; a formal distinction between main and subordinate verbs; a polar contrastive particle, to mention but the most interesting and those that are not obviously shared with other Afroasiatic languages outside the area (Ferguson 1976). To these may be added a number of distinctive patterns of lexicalization (Hayward 1991), which of course is not the same as shared lexical items. There are, however, very few if any grammatical morphemes found across the languages of the area other than what can be attributed to a common Afroasiatic inheritance, of course. The picture I present here is something of a simplification. It is evident that we have to identify a number of subsidiary language areas within the overall Ethiopian 'macro-area' (Zaborski 1991), and within each sub-area more subtle patterns of influence can be observed.

All this does not mean, however, that lexical evidence is to be discounted. It has to be handled with greater circumspection. This is not simply because lexis, the words that are the most 'tangible' and 'discernible' element of a language that can be consciously perceived by speakers, is probably generally, if not at all times universally, the most open to diffusion. An additional and very important consideration is that different areas of the lexicon are liable to be susceptible to the effects of diffusion in differing degrees. Scholars in the field have been used to speaking of 'basic' vocabulary for many years and, as is well known, the notion that some vocabulary is less likely to be borrowed forms the underlying principle of lexicostatistics. Even here, though, considerable caution has to be exercised — it is evident that no area of the lexicon, no semantic field is totally immune from borrowing: one might suppose that items denoting universal features of the environment such as 'moon', 'cloud', 'stone', 'day(time)', 'salt' and 'water', or names of body parts such as 'tongue', 'brain', 'knee', 'ear', 'lung' and 'hair' would not be likely to be borrowed, but all of these items in Amharic, a Semitic language of Ethiopia, have indeed been borrowed from various of the neighbouring Cushitic languages, whilst other Ethiopian Semitic languages retain items of inherited Semitic origin for many of these.

The whole of the Ethiopian region, as I have said above, is demonstrably a complex of interlocking areas of diffusion, not only in typological and grammatical features, but obviously even more so in the field of lexicon. This makes it very difficult to undertake comparative lexical studies with a view to establishing just what vocabulary is to be seen as belonging to the various proto-languages, exactly the kind of information that is necessary if Proto-Cushitic is to be reconstructed from Proto-Agaw, Proto-Highland East Cushitic, Proto-Lowland East Cushitic, and so on, and thence to more remote levels such as Proto-Afroasiatic. For instance, to take a couple of the Amharic examples mentioned above: the Amharic item wɨha 'water' has cognates in other South Ethiopic languages, such as Chäha ixa, Argobba ɐhʷa, Endägäñ ɨhɨ, but other South Ethiopic languages and all of North Ethiopic retain what we know from comparative evidence to be the inherited Semitic root: e.g. Silt'i mɐy, Harari mii, Ge'ez may, etc. So there appears to be no problem; some South Ethiopic languages have borrowed the item for 'water'. However, the Amharic form wɨha (which also appears dialectally and in earlier Amharic as wɐha) with initial w-, lacking from the other South Ethiopic items, looks as if it has been influenced by Highland East Cushitic forms such as Hadiyya woʔo and Sidamo waho, whilst the other South Ethiopic items without initial w- look more like Central Cushitic (Agaw) forms such as Bilin ʕak'ʷ, Kemant axʷ, Awngi aɣu. It is debatable even whether the two Cushitic roots are related to one another. Even more complex, and illustrative of the cross-currents of lexical borrowing and diffusion within the Ethiopian region, are the various items for 'salt': Amharic has č'ɛw, with cognates mostly in North Ethiopic, e.g. Ge'ez s'ew, and which is of Central Cushitic (Agaw) origin, Proto-Agaw *čəw-a. Aside from Argobba, which has been regarded as a divergent dialect of Amharic, and the now extinct Gafat, the rest of South Ethiopic appears to have items of Lowland East Cushitic origin, e.g. Chäha aso, Silt'i asɛbo, Muher assɛwɐ, to which we may compare Somali ʕusbo, Oromo ašabóo, etc., and Omotic forms such as Mocha 'hič'iwo, and Kaffa ičebo, which may be either cognate or borrowed. A quite different root occurs in some other East Cushitic and Omotic languages alike: e.g. Gawwada sóqo, Hadiyya sook'ide, Zayse sóoge, Benchnon žegᵗ etc. The Semitic root occurring throughout Asian Semitic is found here only in Ge'ez, as mɛlh. Incidentally, further complicating the situation, the common Semitic root in its Arabic form, milh, has been borrowed into a small number of Lowland East Cushitic languages, such as Somali where it appears as milih, and Saho mulhu[u]; note also Beja miilak. The commodity salt has since ancient times been used as a currency across the Horn of Africa. It is therefore not surprising that the lexical items for 'salt' in the region show a distribution that betrays more the effects of diffusion than genetic affiliation.

All this means that in comparing lexical data from such a complex area as Ethiopia and the Horn the researcher has to be sensitive to probable zones of diffusion, in different places and equally at different times in the past. Ethiopian Semitic, various Cushitic branches, and Omotic have interacted with one another, and the latter in turn have interacted with various Nilo-Saharan languages. If this is true of Ethiopia, how equally true it must be across the Afroasiatic area. Indeed, it is evident from the lexicon that at various stages in (pre-)history Egyptian and Semitic have been subject to mutual borrowing: Central Semitic *yamm- 'sea' [NM, no. 13] appears in Late Egyptian as ym (Coptic yom) superseding the idiom wʔɟ wrr 'the great green'. Similarly, Central Semitic (Canaanite) ʔayyaal- 'deer' appears in Late Egyptian as jyr, ʔywr (? = a'yuːl) (Coptic [e]yuːl) [NM, no. 37]. Belonging to a much older stratum, it has been proposed that the hieroglyphic grapheme <d> (= phoneme /d/ probably realized in Old Egyptian as [t']), which has the form of a hand [▭], was devised at the time a cognate (cf. <ˤ> = dj mentioned above), or borrowed form of Semitic yad- 'hand' was in use. Later stages of Egyptian have a quite different root in this meaning: ɟr-t (Coptic 'toːre). In more recent times, Berber has been heavily influenced by Semitic (Arabic), but we just do not know what earlier influences and contacts the family may have had except that with the greater eastward spread of the family in ancient times than at present, Egyptian is likely to have been in direct contact. Even wider zones of diffusion are relevant to Chadic languages, including extensive interaction with languages subsumed under the (sometimes disputed) macro-family headings of both Nilo-Saharan and Niger-Congo (see for instance, Bonvini 1995). For the comparative Afroasiaticist, however, the interaction of various of the member families in varying degrees must be a pivotal consideration in assessing the validity of reconstructed lexical forms: to put it crudely, just what is borrowed and what is inherited? The more recent results of diffusion may be easily detectable, but deep-level influence is another matter.

Again, to repeat the argument made above, if it is true of Afroasiatic that there have been many layers of diffusion between adjacent languages and families of the phylum, and between them and adjacent languages of other families, then given the putatively much greater time-depth that would have to be allowed for a macro-family would the scope for the cross-currents of diffusion be not all the greater for 'Nostratic'? Indeed, some have seen the traces of an ancient contact between Proto-Indo-European and just Semitic — or as those who propose a West-Asian, Levantine 'home' for Afroasiatic would have it, between Proto-Indo-European and Proto-Afroasiatic. Others, such as Saul Levin and Carlton Hodge, would go further and propose a genetic link between Semitic and Indo-European, something of a one-sided view, I imagine, to the Nostraticist! The apparent obvious connection, for instance, between Proto-Semitic *θawr- (Dolgopolsky's *'θawar-) 'bull' and Proto-Indo-European *tawro- [NM, no. 41], or Proto-Semitic *wayn- 'wine' and Proto-Indo-European *woyno-, may be adduced in such cases, but as Dolgopolsky suggests this are surely to be explained as due to diffusion.

Afroasiatic linguistic palaeontology

Diakonoff's name is without doubt the most prominent, and the most eminent, in the question of linking Afroasiatic linguistic hypotheses with the supposed location, movements and cultures of peoples in prehistory. Originally (Diakonoff 1965) he suggested an Afroasiatic 'homeland' or 'Urheimat' in the southeastern Sahara which was a more amenable environment at the date he proposes for the Proto-Afroasiatic speech community than today. From there he took the speakers of the various proto-languages to their later locations, including the Proto-Semitic speakers who passed into Western Asia 'within the period from the 5th and the middle of the 4th millennium BC'. Later (Diakonoff 1988) he seems to have favoured the hypothesis proposed by his student Militariev that the home of Afroasiatic was in Western Asia, and that whilst Semitic 'stayed put', speakers of the other families migrated into Africa. The latter thesis of course fits nicely with the Nostratic hypothesis — witness the map in *NM* (p. xv) (Fig. 2 in the Introduction, this volume). Needless to say, I find this all highly speculative, and I would question the very premise upon which this kind of linguistic palae-ontology is constructed. Militariev's arguments (e.g. Militariev 1996) rest on lexical links he sees between Proto-Afroasiatic (Afrasian) and both North Cauca-sian and Sumerian, for which there is clearly no reason whatsoever to see an African origin. The reconstructions for Afroasiatic, where I am best able to judge, are speculative to say the least. For instance, a Proto-Agaw form *layl- 'bee', which I do not dispute (indeed, the reconstruction is my own, but properly is North-Agaw only) is linked with such Southern Cushitic forms as Dahalo nàla 'honey', Asax naɬa 'bee', and Chadic Bolewa lála 'spider', Banana lòlònà 'fly' to provide a proto-Afroasiatic reconstruction **laHl-, which is in turn linked with Sumerian làl 'honey' and which Militariev speculates is borrowed from Central Cushitic — presumably he means that part of Proto-Afroasiatic which later de-veloped into Cushitic! The vocabulary range seems to be dominated by animal names (ram, boar, ass, dog, snake, various kinds of bird, fox, etc.) with a few other terms referring to the environment and human relationships — a familiar inventory.

Undoubtedly the best reasoned study of this kind, relating linguistic ma-terial, and in particular vocabulary with prehistory is Diakonoff's study on Se-mitic and Afroasiatic vocabulary in the fields of animal husbandry and agriculture (Diakonoff 1981). In that study he applies a degree of sensitivity not only to the linguistic data and such questions as the effects of taboo and associated seman-tic shift, but also incorporates arguments from the fields of palaeobotany and palaeozoology. He is also sensitive to the different levels of relationship be-tween Afroasiatic languages, moving progressively through a 'Common Afrasian' level to an 'East–West Afrasian' grouping comprising Berber, Cushitic (but he includes Omotic here too) and Semitic, and finally to Semitic alone. His conclu-sions as far as early Semitic speakers in Western Asia are concerned seem to me well argued. The problem arises when one tries to apply this method to earlier putative stages, and is well illustrated by what Diakonoff himself says about Proto-Afroasiatic terminology in the field of domestic plant and animal names: only four terms are proposed as reconstructable by him (to use Diakonoff's transcriptions), *sām-/*samm- 'edible (non-cereal) plant', *lu̯ʔ-, *li̯ʔ- 'wild bull of the species *Bos primigenius*', *kal/r[∇]- 'dog', and *kʷ∇r- 'bull kept for breed-ing, *Bos taurus africanus*'. Other items, some of which also appear in *NM* [e.g.

no. 18], can only be reconstructed for later phases.

Vocabulary of this sort, plant and animal names (especially when domesticated), even simple artefacts and technology ('flint knife', 'bow', 'arrow', 'basket', 'rope', etc.), and cultural terminology, is especially likely to be diffused across adjacent languages and language families along with the products and ideas; so, for example, 'vessel' [*NM*, no. 23], where Egyptian kc (> Bohairic Coptic kaɟi) is usually explained as borrowed from Semitic (e.g. Aramaic kaːs[aː], Hebrew koːs). Unfortunately, this is the kind of vocabulary that concerns the linguistic palaeontologist, but the tendency for this kind of vocabulary to spread surely greatly reduces its reliability as a means of divining the type of material culture associated with the speakers of a putative proto-language.

Discussion of specific items

I would like to conclude this paper with a few comments on specific Afroasiatic entries in *NM*. First of all, however, a couple of general remarks are needed to set the following remarks in context. Dolgopolsky cites Afroasiatic material by family: Semitic, Berber, Cushitic, Omotic, Egyptian, Chadic, with family-level or lower level reconstructed proto-forms in some instances, and not in a reconstructed Proto-Afroasiatic form. This is for the obvious reason that reliable Proto-Afroasiatic reconstructions have not been made — and I would argue that they are not likely to be made, at least in the sense that Indo-Europeanist and Uralicist colleagues, for instance, are able to do. There are two recent (part-)dictionaries of Proto-Afroasiatic, Ehret's (1995) and Orël & Stolbova's (1995), but both have incurred a considerable degree of reservation and even censure from the Afroasiaticist academic community, not without reason I would add. There is not even a comprehensive comparative dictionary of Proto-Semitic that the researcher can use as a single source-book for reliable reconstructions. The Proto-Semitic reconstructions in *NM* are Dolgopolsky's own, and sometimes are at variance with the traditional forms (cf. *'θawar- and *θawr-, mentioned above) such as Fronzaroli's (1961; 1964–71). Besides Dolgopolsky's own early Cushitic reconstructions (1973), which have been subsequently modified and refined in a number of his articles, there are published reconstructions, not always whole dictionaries as such, of several branches of Cushitic (Black 1974; Sasse 1979; 1982; Hudson 1989; Arvanites 1991; Ehret 1980; 1987) and Chadic (Jungraithmayr & Shimizu 1981; Jungraithmayr & Ibriszimow 1994; Stolbova 1996), and for Berber I am only aware of one source (Prasse 1972–74). A comparative Omotic dictionary, let alone the reconstruction of Proto-Omotic lexicon, has not yet been seriously begun.

This form of citation by family allows to see at a glance, however, the unequal distribution of attestations of supposed Afroasiatic roots. Of the 102 entries of Dolgopolsky's 124 items in *NM* that include supposed Afroasiatic attestations, 36 consist of items occurring only in Semitic, and not an insubstantial number of these consist of attestations from a single language (nos. 16, 17, 24, 25, 30, 33, 46, 51, 60, 66, 70, 72, 85, 99, 107). Others comprise attestations from a single branch of Semitic only, especially Central Semitic (i.e. Aramaic-Canaanite-Arabic), some with possible cognates in other families of the phylum (nos. 13, 22, 47, 57, 63, 74, 86, 115, 122, 123). A major concern here is that there are reasons to believe that Semitic (especially in Western Asia) may have been a participant in a diffusion area that included Indo-European, as well as ancient languages of Eastern Anatolia and the Caucasus. It is clearly not good practice to reconstruct a lexeme at the Proto-Afroasiatic level when existing forms occur only in one family. Obviously, in order to reconstruct an item at the Proto-Afroasiatic level it would be ideal, but is hardly ever the case, that attestations are found in all member families. It should also be borne in mind that Afroasiatic is not a single layer with six equal constituents: Berber, Cushitic and Semitic would seem to form a sub-group (suggested by morphological comparison), and whilst at a deep level Cushitic and Omotic represent quite distinct members of the phylum, because of millennia of contact the two have to some degree grown together, especially in the area of the lexicon. Therefore, in order to propose a reconstructed lexeme at the Afroasiatic level, attested forms should occur at the very least in two, or better three families, and those attestations should be from a range of languages from within the family, and preferably from more than one branch or sub-branch. None of Dolgopolsky's Afroasiatic forms occurs in more than four of the six families (only nos. 22, 23, and 80 have supposed attestations in four families each), each with a serious question about the validity of some of the occurrences or their relevance to the discussion:

[22] The Semitic root *kadd- 'jar' occurs only in Central Semitic, whilst the supposedly extended form *k'adir- etc. (Dolgopolsky's *ḳVdVr-) also has a single Modern South Arabian attestation. There is really no evidence, however, that these are the same root — for one thing, what about the apparent deglottalization of the initial consonant (k: k' is not a permissible comparison according to the 'rules'!), and for another, what evidence is there for a nominal extension in *-r? The Omotic and Chadic forms cited show

considerable variation in the articulation not only of the initial, but also the medial consonant.

[23] Whilst the Semitic root *kaʔas- 'cup, vessel' is fairly incontroversial, the Egyptian item kc is, as said above, more probably a borrowing, and for Cushitic only one attestation is recorded, Khamtanga (Agaw) kʷəskʷəsa 'water-jug', and even then this has cognate forms in Ethiopian Semitic — an instance of diffusion, but which way?

[80] Again, whilst the Semitic root *θ'urar-/*θ'ir[a]r- (Fronzaroli *θ'urr-) 'flint' is incontroversial, the Egyptian cognate cited, Coptic čo:r 'cut' is usually regarded as a late borrowing from Arabic ẓarra (ḍarra).

Of the twelve or so entries with unqueried representations from three Afroasiatic families, the following require some comment:

[1]   Attestations are minimal from each family: 1 Semitic (Arabic ʔibratᵘⁿ 'syca-more'), 1 Cushitic (Oromo abruu, which incidentally has a variant arbuu), and 1 unqueried Chadic instance (Giziga ʔurof); Hausa ɓaure is queried.

[3]   Dolgopolsky sees two Semitic roots here *ʔar[y]ay- 'lion or similar' and *ʔarway- 'gazelle' [5], where traditional Semitic reconstruction sees as one *ʔarway- 'wild animal', closely reflecting the form and meaning of Geʻez ʔarwe.

[13]   The Semitic (actually Central Semitic only) root *yamm- 'sea' was men-tioned above in connection with the Egyptian borrowing ym. Dolgopolsky adds here Proto-Berber *ʔam- and Proto-Chadic *H∇-y∇m- 'water'. No men-tion is made, however, of the Proto-Semitic root *may- 'water', which oc-curs in all branches of the family and which has a genuine Egyptian cognate, as opposed to a borrowing, in mw (Coptic mow). There are probable Cushitic cognates in the word for 'tear', which looks like an ancient compound meaning 'water of the eye': Proto-East Cushitic *ʔilm-; Proto-Southern Cushitic *ʔilimá- (Ehret 1980, 291); Proto-Agaw *ʔərəŋʷ-. This root is one of the few that no one would dispute being Common Afroasiatic.

[19]   Here Semitic is represented solely by the single Arabic root mlɟ 'suck', which has cognates elsewhere in the family. Cushitic is represented by the

single Somali root maal-, which does not seem to have cognates elsewhere. One might ask, on what justification is the third consonant missing? Thirdly, the Egyptian noun mnɟ 'breast' (Bohairic Coptic em'not) may in fact be a derivative in the well-known prefix m- from a putative *nɟ cognate with a Cushitic root *nu[u]g 'suck' (Takács 1997, 232). Evidence for an Afroasiatic root **mlg would therefore seem to be virtually non-existent.

[20] Whilst a root *halab- 'milk' is totally uncontroversial for Semitic, the So-mali term that Dolgopolsky supplies, halable, does not seem to occur in any of the (large) modern dictionaries and is, I would suggest, simply the Arabic halab with the Somali suffix/enclitic -le meaning 'having, holding'.

[31] Aside from Chadic, the root *g∇∇g- 'road' occurs in three branches of the Cushitic family: Beja giig- 'go away'; Agaw (Bilin) gug 'road'; Highland East Cushitic Hadiyya (and closely related Kambatta) googo which may, how-ever, be an assimilation form of Proto-Highland East Cushitic *doogo with the same meaning, reconstructable from forms occurring in other High-land East Cushitic languages.

[36] It does not seem to me possible to reconstruct a Proto-Cushitic *gʷrħ 'ante-lope' on the basis of the data; what, for instance, is the explanation of the apparent -m suffix in Sidamo guruʔm-iččo, or indeed the -fiya 'suffix' of Chadic Ngizim gɜ̀ràfiyà? If Sidamo guruʔm-iččo is acceptable, what about Sidamo gaarran-čo, which is also glossed as 'antelope'?

[68] There are two Semitic (only Ethiopian) and Cushitic reflexes of the sup-posed single Nostratic root meaning 'marrow' or 'brain' that can be typi-fied as *ʔang[ʷ]aʕ- and *hangʷal-, respectively. The fact that the Semitic occurrences are confined to Ethiopia should immediately alert one to the likelihood that one is dealing with an Ethiopian term spread into Ethio-pian Semitic by diffusion. Indeed, the second version of the root occurs in a range of forms that suggest borrowing both ways, so that it is impossible to say whether one is dealing with an originally Semitic or Cushitic item. Incidentally, the Borana Oromo form ɛngu that Dolgopolsky cites is un-known to me, and does not occur in any recent dictionary or grammar of Borana; instead the usual surrii is recorded in the sense of 'brain'. This is a good example of how cautious one needs to be about using isolated forms recorded in out-of-the-way word lists.

[98]   The reflexes of a supposed Semitic root *k'rp 'peel (vb); bark (n.)' are restricted to Arabic and Ethiopian Semitic, although an apparent variant *k'lp does occur much more widely: Akkadian qilpu 'skin'; Hebrew qa:laɸ 'peel, strip'; Aramaic (Syriac) qəlaɸ, also qəlaɸta: 'foreskin'; Arabic qalafa 'peel', also qulfat^un 'foreskin' Soqotri k'alifoh 'bark'. The further apparent variant *k'rb, seen in Arabic qirbat^un 'water skin', is otherwise only found in Ethiopia, in both Semitic (Amharic and North Ethiopic only) and Cushitic (Beja and Agaw, but not Southern Agaw) languages. This very compact regional distribution is strongly suggestive of diffusion, but I would not be so confident as Dolgopolsky to suggest that the Cushitic items are borrowed from Semitic. Incidentally the Ge'ez item *k'ɐrb 'eyelid' that Dolgopolsky cites is doubtless more properly k'ɐrrɨb and a variant of the usual k'ɐrnɨb and as such does not belong here.

[113]   The Semitic plural forms Arabic nisuuna 'women', Hebrew naši:m, Aramaic nəšayya: (Syriac nɛšše:) corresponding to singulars from the Proto-Semitic root *ʔanθ-at-, which occurs in all branches, are confined to Central Semitic. There is obviously contamination here with the Proto-Semitic root usually reconstructed as *ʔaniš- 'man', *ʔinaaš- 'men, people' (as Dolgopolsky suggests). To the two Central Cushitic forms that Dolgopolsky cites (Bilin ʔusɐri, Khamtanga (actually) wɐsrɐy) can be added Kemant yusɐy; however, the reconstruction of a supposed Proto-Agaw *n̩s-at- cannot be defended; for one thing there would be no other reason to propose a syllabic nasal as part of the Proto-Agaw phonemic inventory than this item. Although not without its problems, the only really feasible reconstruction for Proto-(North) Agaw based on the attested forms would be *ʔus-ɐRi.

[116]   Semitic *ʔimm- (*ʔumm-) 'mother' is not controversial, but terms for 'mother' and 'father' are far from ideal for macro-comparisons. Indeed, Dolgopolsky says of the Highland East Cushitic *ama (the only Cushitic occurrence) that he reconstructs, 'this . . . may be an independent Lallwort without etymological connection with the Semitic and Berber words'. If that is true for one branch of one family, can it not also be true for other families?

[118]   Much the same issues as were raised over the item for 'mother' [116] can be repeated for this Afroasiatic root for 'father'. The presence of a bilabial

occlusive is common in terms for 'father', including appellatives, across the world.

It would be tiresome to go through every item in *NM* in this detailed fashion here, though inevitably there are comments on individual entries that could be made along the lines of the preceding. The picture that emerges, however, is fairly conclusive, I feel. The Afroasiatic entries in *NM* look rather scant and weak to me in comparison, say, with the Indo-European or the Uralic.

Conclusion: are macro-groupings viable constructs?

New theories (Dixon 1997) about the development of languages through time, inspired by the 'New Biology' model of species development, are calling into question the universality of the traditional genetic relationship model as typified by the family-tree diagram. Biologists are far from unanimous in accepting this model of development, and linguists are equally not likely to want to take it on board without reservation. Everyone would agree, however, that languages change constantly and that borrowing from adjacent, dominant or influential languages is part of that mechanism of language development alongside internal change in inherited material. Everyone would, I think, also agree that language change is not a steady process, but evidently occurs in fits and starts. What might be new is the understanding that all levels of language form and structure, from the phonetic to the lexical, from grammatical morphs to syntactic patterns, are open to borrowing, to the effects of diffusion. Also a relatively new concept and implicit in this is that languages can grow to be more alike, can in fact merge, just as much as they can diverge and grow apart. Dixon's argument is that sudden environmental and social events affecting speakers of a language or languages can rapidly accelerate the processes of change, whilst periods of stability or equilibrium can lead to the development of linguistic areas through the diffusion of features and ultimately to convergence. This 'punctuated equilibrium' model therefore forces us to consider whether such macro-groupings as Nostratic could have arisen through convergence as much as through the processes of genetic affiliation, by gluing together the family-trees of several language families. He also suggests (Dixon 1997, 28ff.) that the pre-eminence of family-tree model in the thinking of historical and comparative linguists arose because it was first worked out for, and fits well the facts of the Indo-European family which has essentially developed in regions and during periods of great change in human society, not least the spread of agriculture into Europe. The same model must have applied at least at varying points in time and various places in those language families subsumed under Afroasiatic. However, it is evident that at other points in time and in other places periods of comparative equilibrium have led to diffusion of features and convergence, if not the actual merging of languages. The Ethiopian area is a case in point, and I am sure is far from being the only one. The theory of punctuated equilibrium in language development to my mind may well explain why linguists have been, and still are, at variance over the classification of Omotic and Cushitic. If we are prepared to postulate that two different language families, Omotic and Cushitic, have operated upon and influenced one another over millennia then their similarities, at all levels and not just lexical, may be due to diffusion rather than a particularly close genetic relationship, such as those who speak of 'Cushomotic' or Omotic as 'West Cushitic' wish to propose. Nonetheless, there is still a fundamental level of grammatical morphemic ('grammemic') and indeed lexical commonalities that both share differently with other Afroasiatic languages, and not so much with one another to the exclusion of other families, so as to persuade me that Omotic is Afroasiatic as much as Cushitic is. I am not, however, convinced that the evidence, and in particular that put forward in *NM*, is of the same order such as to persuade that Afroasiatic is part of the macro-grouping called Nostratic. I do not mean to deny altogether the possibility of Nostratic — as I hinted at the beginning of this paper, it would be exciting if it were true — and maybe it does work for some of the proposed member families and phyla: a genetic link between Indo-European and Kartvelian, or between Indo-European and Uralic, has been proposed before — and, of course, between Semitic and/or Afroasiatic and Indo-European, though the validity of this I reject. Dixon indeed suggests a different scenario (1997, 100) that could explain apparent connections between Indo-European and Uralic, which I feel is a viable model elsewhere. He may also be unnecessarily harsh when he says (1997, 44), 'There is no reputable historical linguist, anywhere in the world, who accepts the claims of Greenberg and the Nostraticists', but he does raise serious questions as to whether such macro-families, if indeed a reality, could ever be scientifically identified. There has to be more than lists of vocabulary, for the reasons that I hope are apparent from the preceding discussion. I am conscious that archaeologists and prehistorians are excited by the prospects that these concepts of macro-families lay before them, but I would advise them that the majority of comparative and historical linguists are far more cautious than *NM*, even if they are not all outright dismissive of the idea.

References

Appleyard, D.L., 1986. Agaw, Cushitic and Afroasiatic: the personal pronoun revisited. *Journal of Semitic Studies* 31(2), 195–236.

Appleyard, D.L., 1996. Preparing a comparative Agaw dictionary, in Griefenow-Mewis & Voigt (eds.), 185–200.

Arvanites, L., 1991. *The Glottalic Phonemes of Proto Eastern Cushitic*. Ann Arbor (MI): University Microfilms International. Ph.D. Thesis. University of California, Los Angeles.

Bausi, A. & M. Tosco (eds.), 1997. *Afroasiatica Neapolitana: Contributi presentati all'8° Incontro di Linguistica Afroasiatica (Camito-Semitica)*. Naples: Istituto Universitario Orientale.

Bender, M.L., 1989. Nilo-Saharan Pronouns/demonstratives, in *Topics in Nilo-Saharan Linguistics*, ed. M.L. Bender. Hamburg: Helmut Buske Verlag, 1–34.

Bender, M.L., 1990. A survey of Omotic grammemes, in *Linguistic Change and Reconstruction Methodology*, ed. P. Baldi. (Trends in Linguistics, Studies and Monographs 45.) Berlin & New York (NY): Mouton de Gruyter, 661–95.

Benedict, P.K., 1975. *Austro-Thai Language and Culture, with a Glossary of Roots*. New Haven (CT): HRAF Press.

Black, P., 1974. *Lowland East Cushitic: Subgrouping and Reconstruction*. Ann Arbor (MI): University Microfilms International. Ph.D. Thesis, Yale University.

Blažek, V., 1989. A new contribution to comparative-historical Afrasian linguistics. *Asian and African Studies* 24, 203–22.

Blažek, V., 1995. The microsystems of personal pronouns in Chadic, compared with Afroasiatic, in Ibriszimow & Leger (eds.), 36–57.

Bonvini, E., 1995. À propos et en marge de 'Greater Chadic': le cas de voltaïque, in Ibriszimow & Leger (eds.), 85–117.

Diakonoff, I.M., 1965. *Semito-Hamitic Languages*. Moscow: Nauka.

Diakonoff, I.M., 1981. Earliest Semites in Asia. *Altorientalische Forschungen* 8, 23–74.

Diakonoff, I.M., 1988. *Afrasian Languages*. Moscow: Nauka.

Dixon, R.M.W., 1997. *The Rise and Fall of Languages*. Cambridge: Cambridge University Press.

Dolgopolsky, A., 1973. *Sravnitel'no-istoricheskaja fonetika kushitskix jazykov*. Moscow: Nauka.

Dolgopolsky, A., 1988. On etymology of pronouns and classification of the Chadic languages, in *Fucus: a Semitic/Afrasian Gathering in Remembrance of Albert Ehrman*. Amsterdam & Philadelphia (PA): John Benjamins, 201–20.

Dolgopolsky, A., 1998. *The Nostratic Macrofamily and Linguistic Palaeontology*. (Papers in the Prehistory of Languages.) Cambridge: The McDonald Institute for Archaeological Research.

Ehret, C., 1980. *The Historical Reconstruction of Southern Cushitic Phonology and Vocabulary*. Berlin: Dietrich Reimer Verlag.

Ehret, C., 1987. Proto-Cushitic reconstruction. *Sprache und Geschichte in Afrika* 8, 7–180.

Ehret, C., 1995. *Reconstructing Proto-Afroasiatic (Proto-Afrasian): Vowels, Tone, Consonants, and Vocabulary*. Berkeley (CA): University of California Press.

Ferguson, C.A., 1976. The Ethiopian language area, in *Language in Ethiopia*, eds. M.L. Bender, J.D. Bowen, R.L. Cooper & C.A. Ferguson. London: Oxford University Press, 63–76.

Fronzaroli, P., 1961. Prospettive di metodo statistico nella classificazione delle lingue semitiche. *Rendiconti dell'Accademia Nazionale dei Lincei. Classe di Scienze morali, storiche e filologiche* Serie VIII, 16, 348–80.

Fronzaroli, P., 1964–71. Studi sul lessico commune semitico. I. Oggetto e metodo della ricerca. *Rendiconti dell'Accademia Nazionale dei Lincei. Classe di Scienze morali, storiche e filologiche* Serie VIII, 19, 155–72. II. L'uomo e l'età. Serie VIII, 19, 243–80. III. I fenomeni naturali Serie VIII, 20, 135–50. IV. La religione; Serie VIII, 20, 246–69. V. La natura selvatica; Serie VIII, 23, 267–303. VI. La natura domestica; Serie

VIII, 24, 285–320. VII. L'alimentazione; Serie VIII, 26, 603–42.

Greenberg, J.H., 1991. Some problems of Indo-European, in *Sprung from Some Common Source. Investigations into the Prehistory of Languages*, eds. S.M. Lamb & E.D. Mitchell. Stanford (CA): Stanford University Press, 125–40.

Griefenow-Mewis, C. & R.M. Voigt (eds.), 1996. *Cushitic and Omotic Languages: Proceedings of the Third International Symposium. Berlin, March 17–19, 1994*. Köln: Rüdiger Köppe Verlag.

Hayward, R.J. (ed.), 1990. *Omotic Language Studies*. London: School of Oriental and African Studies.

Hayward, R.J., 1991. À propos patterns of lexicalization in the Ethiopian language area, in *Ägypten im afro-orientalischen Kontext. Aufsätze zur Archäologie, Geschichte und Sprache eines unbegrenzten Raumes. Gedenkschrift Peter Behrens*, eds. D. Mendel & U. Claudi. Köln: Universität zu Köln, 139–56.

Hodge, C.T., 1970. The linguistic cycle. *Language Sciences* 13, 1–7.

Hodge, C.T., 1975. Egyptian and survival, in *Hamito-Semitica: Proceedings of a Colloquium held by the Historical Section of the Linguistics Association (Great Britain) at the School of Oriental and African Studies, University of London*, eds. J. Bynon & T. Bynon. The Hague & Paris: Mouton, 171–91.

Hudson, G., 1989. *Highland East Cushitic Dictionary*. Hamburg: Buske Verlag.

Ibriszimow, D. & R. Leger with G. Schmitt (eds.), 1995. *Studia Chadica et Hamito-Semitica*. (Akten des Internationalen Symposions zur Tschadsprachenforschung Johann Wolfgang Goethe-Universitat Frankfurt am Main.) Köln: Rüdiger Köppe Verlag.

Jungraithmayr, H. & D. Ibriszimow, 1994. *Chadic Lexical Roots*, vol. 1: *Tentative Reconstruction, Grading, Distribution and Comments*, vol. 2: *Documentation*. Berlin: Dietrich Reimer Verlag.

Jungraithmayr, H. & K. Shimizu, in collaboration with N.P. Knowlton, 1981. *Chadic Lexical Roots: a First Evaluation of the Marburg Chadic Word Catalogue*. Berlin: Dietrich Reimer Verlag.

Kaiser, M. & V. Shevoroshkin, 1988. Nostratic. *Annual Review of Anthropology* 17, 309–29.

Lieberman, S.J., 1986. The Afro-Asiatic background of the Semitic N-Stem: towards the origins of the stem-afformatives of the Semitic and Afro-Asiatic verb. *Bibliotheca Orientalis* 43(5/6), 578–627.

Loprieno, A., 1995. *Ancient Egyptian: a Linguistic Introduction*. Cambridge: Cambridge University Press.

Militariev, A.Y., 1996. Home for Afrasian: African or Asian? Areal linguistic arguments, in Griefenow-Mewis & Voigt (eds.), 13–32.

NM = Dolgopolsky 1998.

Orël, V.E. & O.V. Stolbova, 1995. *Hamito-Semitic Etymological Dictionary: Materials for a Reconstruction*. Leiden: E.J. Brill.

Prasse, K.G., 1972–74. *Manuel de Grammaire Touaregue* (tăhăggărt), vols. I–III: *Phonétique, écriture et pronom*; vols. IV–V: *Nom*; vols. VI–VII: *Verbe*. Copenhagen: Akademisk Forlag.

Sasse, H.J., 1979. The consonant phonemes of Proto-East-Cushitic (PEC). A first approximation. *Afroasiatic Linguistics* 7(1), 1–67.

Sasse, H.J., 1982. *An Etymological Dictionary of Burji*. Hamburg: Buske Verlag.

Satzinger, H., 1997. Egyptian in the Afroasiatic frame: recent egyptological issues with an impact on comparative studies, in Bausi & Tosco (eds.), 27–48.

Sim, R., 1988. The diachronic derivation of the verb in Northern Highland East Cushitic, in *Cushitic-Omotic. Papers from the International Symposium on Cushitic and Omotic Languages*, eds. M. Bechhaus-Gerst & F. Serzisko. Hamburg: Helmut Buske Verlag, 433–52.

Stolbova, O.V., 1996. *Studies in Chadic Comparative Phonology*. Moscow: Diaphragma Publishers.

Takács, G., 1997. Selected new Egypto-Afrasian correspondences from the field of anatomical terminology, in Bausi & Tosco (eds.), 225–50.

Tosco, M., 1996. The Northern Highland East Cushitic verb in an areal perspective, in Griefenow-Mewis & Voigt (eds.), 71–99.

Zaborski, A., 1991. Ethiopian language subareas, in *Unwritten Testimonies of the African Past. Proceedings of the International Symposium*, eds. S. Pilaszewicz & E. Rzewuski. Warsaw: Wydnawnictwa Uniwersytetu Warszawskiego, 123–34.

Chapter 15

On Semitohamitic comparison[1]

Rainer Voigt

Asked to give an expertise on a new book by Professor Dolgopolsky, *The Nostratic Macrofamily and Linguistic Palaeontology* (hereafter *NM*), recently published by the McDonald Institute for Archaeological Research, I should like first to stress my scholarly scientific background as a Semitist and Semitohamitist.[2] From a methodological point of view, I regard Indo-European[3] studies as the pilot discipline in the field of linguistics. This standpoint has of course some bearing on my evaluation of Dolgopolsky's work and the Nostratic hypothesis in general.

1. Methodology

General methodological deliberations are not debated in Dolgopolsky's contribution but rather intensively in the Introduction by Professor Renfrew. Although his position is well known from his work, he undertakes a critical assessment of different opinions and positions established in the field of prehistory. This field has been described by the author as a field 'where historical linguistics, prehistoric archaeology and molecular biology overlap in an area of uncertain methodologies' (p. vii). The main problem is whether there will be any connexion of such different disciplines as linguistics, archaeology and biology, all of which work using methods that are quite different from each other. The domains of linguistics and archaeology seem to be more suitable for being joined than those of linguistics and biology. But one should not forget that strict overlapping and coincidence between both domains cannot be reached. There will always be a gap between them. This gap might be traversed under certain favourable circumstances when evidence from the side of linguistics and from that of archaeology does speak in favour of a specific overlapping and connexion between them. So, I think one can remain sceptical about the concrete cases of such a difficult procedure without ruling out the possibility of its realization.

As Semitist and Semitohamitist, I should not like to take up the case of Indo-European and its archaeological localization (see e.g. Renfrew 1987 & cf. Zimmer 1990) but rather that of Semitohamitic. This language family has been well established for a long time although its limits have varied to a certain degree in the history of that discipline. The common homeland of the Semitohamitic peoples as viewed from more internal evidence is generally seen in the northern part of Africa where living conditions were much more favourable ten thousand years ago. However, if Semitohamitic is linguistically connected with Indo-European — which is, in fact, an old and still attractive idea — then probably the localization of its homeland must be reconsidered.

The localization of the Semitohamitic homeland within the Fertile Crescent as advocated by some Nostraticists[4] has one important disadvantage which so far has not been properly stressed in the discussion, i.e. that it does not have regard to the linguistic 'enracinement' of Semitohamitic within Africa. This language family is deeply rooted in Africa insofar as one can find many Semitohamitic traces in other 'non-related' African languages. I should like to refer to the history of Semitohamitic classification, which provides some interesting cases. Carl Meinhof (1912), for example, has classed Ful, Masai and Nama among the Hamitic languages of Africa. Although this concept has been given up subsequently on account of more detailed linguistic research, his linguistic arguments are sometimes not fully disproved by hinting at the real cognate relationship of the languages under question. There remains something valuable or interesting that should be considered in future research. Other scholars have stressed the relationship with the Nilotic language group (Hohenberger 1958) or the similarity to some Saharan and West African languages (as in the work of Mukarovsky). Even Meroitic has been read and interpreted as a Semitohamitic language (Böhm 1988). Instead of favouring the idea of expanding the Semitohamitic family in Africa by adding some new members to it, which might be necessary in the future, I should like to argue that the observation of resemblances between Semitohamitic and other African languages must have an impact on our picture of the early historic development of this language family. That is why no (or rather few) special Semitohamitic connections have been postulated so far to non-related Near Eastern languages (except Indo-European). This, indeed, should be expected if the origin of this language group was in that area.

The rooting of Semitohamitic in Africa has been posited already by Leo Reinisch in 1873 in his *Der einheitliche Ursprung der Sprachen der alten Welt, nachgewiesen durch Vergleichung der afrikanischen, erythräischen und indogermanischen Sprachen mit Zugrundelegung des Teda*, i.e. 'the common origin of the languages of the Old World demonstrated through comparison of African, SH and IE languages on the basis of Teda'. Although his methodology does not correspond to the later achievements of this great scholar,[5] this work marks an important step in the history of the discipline.

Quite remarkably, the comparison of Semitohamitic with African languages is continuing to produce surprising results, as has been done in a manner that is partly quite convincing in the case of the Mande-Chadic comparisons as detected by Mukarovsky (1987). These observations are hardly compatible with the Nostratic theory according to which the original homeland of Semitohamitic was located in the Fertile Crescent. Then, the early 'Hamites' (resp. Hamites) would be those Semitohamites who did not stay in the Near East, like their brothers, the Semites, but migrated to Africa. Because of the comparatively late date of this presumed migration one would expect fewer similarities to other African languages. By the way, it was as early as in the nineteenth century that an Asiatic origin of the Hamites (and the speakers of other African language groups) was posited. R. Lepsius in his Nubian grammar (1880) speaks about the genetic unity of Semitic, Hamitic and Japhetic languages ('Japhetischen (Indogermanischen) Sprachen', p. xxiv) by calling it an 'einheitlicher aber dreigetheilter Völker-Quell'.[6] When — according to Lepsius — nobody would doubt ('niemand bezweifelt') that their homeland ('die Urheimath der drei Völkerstämme') was in Mesopotamia ('in oder in der Nähe der Mesopotamischen Ebenen') one can infer from this that this idea was not expressed by Lepsius for the first time. Eleven years later, A.W. Schleicher (1891) stresses the common home-land of the three language families ('die Urheimath der drei Sprachfamilien') in Asia. He assumed several waves of migration from the Near East to Africa which led eventually to the total peopling of that continent. The time when the fourth and latest great wave of immigration brought about the settling of the Hamites in North and East Africa is called 'Quartärzeit'. Evidently, this strange model has lost all its attraction since then. Nowadays, Africa in general is regarded as having always been populated during its history. With the Nostratic theory of a Near Eastern homeland of the huge language phylum that comprises Indo-European as well as Semitohamitic one has to assume again the immigration of all 'Hamites', i.e. the Semitohamites without the Semites, into North and North East Africa. This model appears hardly acceptable since it does not consider the continuing desertification of the Sahara in the last ten thousand years.

2. Methodology in Dolgopolsky's work

Contrary to Greenberg's methodology,[7] A. Dolgopolsky adheres to the method of comparative historical linguistics which has been practised by Indo-Europeanists for a long time by using the genealogical tree model and — what is more important — by relying on recurrent sound correspondences and by excluding mono- and biradical reconstructions (except for short morphemes, of course). Many reconstructions by other scholars not based on these principles are, in my view, not contributions on which one may build up further work successfully. Mention should be made here of the reconstruction by C. Ehret (1995) who works exclusively with verb extensions, as an *h 'amplificative', *w 'inchoative/denominative', *ɣ^w 'complementive', *ʕ 'partive (> andative)', *r 'diffusive', i.e. a total of 39 verb extensions (in his numeration). To many scholars, it is the very number of those verb extensions (not the idea of verb extensions which might have existed in an early stage of the language family) that will be the main obstacle to accepting this kind of reconstruction.

Another example is given in the Semitohamitic comparative contributions by C.T. Hodge (e.g. 1991) who works with short proto-roots and root extensions as well. What he calls consonant ablaut — probably on the basis of a different understanding of sound correspondences — does not conform with Indo-European linguistic practice.

3. The Semitohamitic material in Dolgopolsky's work

The Semitic material in NM is — without any doubt — reliable and correct. Different approaches can only point to the transcription, the interpretation of sound changes and the reconstruction of Proto-Semitic words.

One small detail refers to the transcription of Arabic ض which should be rendered according to the modern pronunciation of Arabic as ḍ (or ḍ) and not as z̧ which marks a 'uvularized ("emphatic")' 'voiced lateral fricative' (*NM*, p. 12). This realization possibly needs to be reconstructed for the early stage of Arabic but since other Arabic characters are transcribed to the modern usage ḍ should not make an exception. On the other hand, it is doubtful to reconstruct a fricative for this voiced lateral. The modern realization as a uvularized ('emphatic') ḍ (i.e. ḍ) could only be explained by positing a Proto-Arabic affricate realization ḍˡ (or $^{d}z^{e}$).

As to the reconstruction of Proto-Semitic, I should like to disagree primarily in one specific matter, i.e. the reconstruction of noun classes that have been traditionally considered as monosyllabic nouns (*1V23- without inflexion). See the following list of bisyllabic nouns mainly stressed on the first syllable:

          *'ʔibar 'sycamore' (p. 20)

          *'θalag 'snow' (p. 22)

          *'ḳarVχ 'ice' (p. 23)

          *'kaʔas 'vessel' (p. 31)

          *'naʕVl 'sinew, tie' (p. 36)

*'θawar 'bull, calf' (p. 43)

*'gadiy 'kid, lamb' (p. 48)

*buṭ(u)n/m 'pistachio tree/nut' (p. 52)

(*'dag or) *da'wag 'fish' (p. 62)

*'θu/irar 'sharp stone' (p. 65)

*gu/iḏ(V)ʕ 'tree trunk' (p. 68)

The author has already (Dolgopolsky 1986) propounded his ideas on the Proto-Semitic origin of these bisyllabic nouns without finding so far a genuine critical appraisal by other scholars. In general, Dolgopolsky has convincingly demonstrated that not all monosyllabic fVʕl nouns found in Arabic have at any rate to be attributed to the proto-language. His arguments in favour of splitting up the traditional fVʕl noun classes are (Dolgopolsky 1986, 72f.) as follows:

1. different treatment of Proto-Semitic nouns traditionally reconstructed as *faʕl in Classical Ethiopic, compare kalb (< *kalb-) 'dog' with ʔəlf (< *ʔalip, trad. *ʔalp-) 'thousand';

2. different treatment of Proto-Semitic nouns traditionally reconstructed as *fawl and *fayl in Classical Ethiopic, compare ʕawd (*ʕawd-) 'circle, around' with yom (< *yawam-, trad. *yawm-) 'day', resp. ʕayn (< *ʕayn-) 'eye' with bet (< *bayat-, trad. *bayt-) 'house';

3. different plurals of segolate forms in Hebrew, compare zayit (< *zayt-) pl. zêtîm 'olive' with tayiš (< *tayaš-, trad. *tayš-), pl. təyåšîm 'he-goat';

4. twofold representation of Proto-Semitic *aʔ in Akkadian (as â resp. ê), compare kâsu (< *kaʔs-) 'cup' (Hebr. kôs) with rêšu (< *raʔis¹-) 'head';

5. different vowels in the second syllable of Aramaic nouns in the *status absolutus*, compare ksap (st. emph. kaspå) 'silver' (Hebr. kᵉsep) with lhem (st. emph. laḥmå) 'bread' (Hebr. leḥem).

I do not consider the different plural formations with or without an intrusive a in the plural (§ 3) as an argument in favour of an original faʕal noun (as opposed to faʕl). The internal a that springs up between the second and third radical is due to a specific development connected with the formation of the plural as in *tayš > (sg.) tayiš, (pl.) *tayaš-îm > təyåšim 'he-goat'; zêtîm (*zayt-îm) is then a later formation analogical to st. constr. zêʸt and other forms that show a vowel contraction. This 'plural stem' (*faʕal-) as it might be called for the present is neither a characteristic of the lexeme nor a real internal plural. Its true nature will be disclosed in a forthcoming contribution.

The different representation of Proto-Semitic *fawl- and *fayl- in Classical Ethiopic as fol (e.g. sor 'bull') versus fawl (e.g. ʕawd) resp. fel (e.g. bet) versus fayl (e.g. ʕayn) is not easy to explain. The idea of Dolgopolsky to assume different

Proto-Semitic forms (monosyllabic *fawl- versus bisyllabic *fawal- resp. *fayl-versus *fayal-) is very attractive. Since so far no distinctive factor has been determined in order to explain the Classical Ethiopic forms the argumentation of Dolgopolsky seems to be conclusive. On the other hand, by resolving the Classical Ethiopic problem, a new problem arises in Arabic of how to account for the fact that according to the Arabic sound laws awa (or aṷa) resp. aya (or aįa) should yield aa as in ǧaar^{un} (< *ǧawar-) 'neighbour'. Including the nouns with strong radicals Dolgopolsky posits a great number of bisyllabic nouns that have become monosyllabic in Arabic. Since there are bisyllabic nouns in Arabic to be reconstructed for the proto-language it will be difficult to explain the development of only some proto-Semitic bisyllabic nouns to monosyllabic nouns as maintained by Dolgopolsky. The question is so important that it would need further elaboration.

Among the eleven nouns reconstructed with two vowels[8] I should like to accept only *'θalag 'snow' on behalf of Aram. st. abs. tlag (st. emph. talgå) and probably *'kaʔas 'vessel' on behalf of Samaritan Hebrew kuwwås. In my view the other nouns are characterized by a monosyllabic structure (without relevant stress, i.e. *1V23 instead of *'1V2V3 as well as *1V'2V3).

Generally it should be stressed that words with identical second and third radical must be monosyllabic (*1V22 or *1V2:) since the second part of the long consonant resp. the vowel length cannot be separated from its first part. Therefore, a reconstructed form *'θu/irar 'sharp stone' should be replaced by the form *'θu/irr. Only secondarily can the two identical consonants be separated.

On the other hand, an additional vowel in the Proto-Semitic form as reconstructed by Dolgopolsky and rejected by others does not change the picture of the proto-language dramatically. For the sake of a comparison within Nostratic or even within Semitohamitic the existence of a vowel lacking in the reconstruction of some words might be regarded as irrelevant. It has, indeed, a bearing on the derivation of extant Semitic forms from Proto-Semitic.

Whereas a reconstruction within the closely related Semitic family is a rather easy procedure, Semitohamitic comparative work is still in its initial stage. In this field a kind of scientific agreement has not yet been reached since the sound laws that connect the sound systems of the different language groups are still controversial.

From the two comparative dictionaries published in 1995, viz. Orël & Stolbova's *Hamito-Semitic Etymological Dictionary* and Ehret's *Reconstructing Proto-Afroasiatic*, that of Vladimir Orël and Olga Stolbova is more in line with traditional etymological research. A closer look at this work reveals several weak points that will not lead, however, to detraction from the merits of this first comprehensive survey of the Semitohamitic vocabulary.[9] The comparative Semitohamitic material presented by Dolgopolsky is to a high degree reliable and plausible. A comparison between the works mentioned could not be undertaken in this context. Only three examples will be given here.

1. The word for 'milk' is reconstructed by Orel & Stolbova as *ḥalib- and by Dolgopolsky as *ḥa'lab-. Both vocalizations of the triradical root do occur in Semitic. The difference in vocalization (e.g. Hebrew etc. ḥålåb, Arabic etc. ḥalib) is explained by Orël & Stolbova through 'assimilation of vowels' whereas Dolgopolsky has posited for ḥali:b a secondary type of adjective, which appears to be more plausible. Dolgopolsky gives an explanation of the Akkadian form ḥilpu (as a loanword from West Semitic) which has been noted only as 'irregular' by Orël & Stolbova.

2. Whereas Orël & Stolbova reconstruct for 'lion' (including 'hyena') one item *ʔa-ruw/*ʔa-ruy-, Dolgopolsky posits two Nostratic words: *ʔüřVwV 'large feline' and *ʔořu 'antelope (male), deer' which have led to different words in Semitic (e.g. Hebrew ʔărî 'lion' and Akkadian arwium 'gazelle'). Although these words might be related, their separation appears to be more realistic. In general, an advantage of Dolgopolsky's work is the consequent notation of tone in Chadic. Contrary to Orël & Stolbova the many Chadic words with the meaning 'lion, leopard' are given with tones (which are distinctive in these languages).

3. The SH word for 'goat, sheep' is given by Orël & Stolbova as *bag- without a third radical that is correctly reconstructed by Dolgopolsky (*NM*, p. 45f.) on the basis of the Cushitic forms with ʕ, cf. Iraqw bēʕi and the loans in Ethiosemitic as Tigrinya bäggiʕ, bäggǝʕ (not 'bägʕi', p. 46). See his rich documentation of this lexeme in Ethiosemitic (with the new theory to regard Classical Ethiopic bǝḥkʷ as cognate), Cushitic and Chadic (with a lot of languages).

As to the Semitohamitic comparisons with Egyptian which do not occur frequently, many of them must be revised according to the system of sound correspondences as posited by O. Rössler. Accordingly, a comparison of Eg. ꜥw.t 'Kleinvieh' with IE *xowi- 'sheep' and its derivation from Nostratic *ɣ/gawV (p. 44) does not appear to be in accordance with the insight that Eg. ꜥ, although later on matched with Semitic ʕ, is etymologically not a laryngeal but a dental-sibilant. A comparison of Egyptian s3.ty 'kind' (p. 88) with any other Semitohamitic (and Nostratic) words cannot be successful on behalf of the interpretation of 3 as [dz]. Indeed, this sound traditionally transcribed as ḏ is to be reconstructed as a voiceless emphatic affricate, i.e. č̣ [tš̟ʔ].

Some further remarks on specific points:

[13]   The Berber formative called 'article' by many scholars has the form *wa-
       (not *ʔa-) as we know from demonstratives as Kabyle m. wa, waği(ni), f.
       ta, taği(ni).

[58]   The reconstruction *'buṭ(u)n/m 'pistachio tree/nut' is based on differ-
       ent reflexes with n (as Hebrew *båṭnåh, pl. båṭnîm) and m (as Arabic
       buṭmᵘⁿ 'terebinth tree'). It is more natural to assume a proto-form with a
       labial nasal (m) which was later on assimilated to the preceding dental.
       The evidence for a Nostratic etymon *buṭV (without nasal) appears to
       be very weak since only Turkish bitrik is given as cognate.

[89]   The Semohamitic form most similar to 'Indo-Eur. *ser(w)- "vein, thread"'
       and 'Altaic *sirwV "sinew, tendon" is not a South Cushitic form contain-
       ing a root dʕr but Classical Ethiopic śərw 'sinew, tendon'.

[111] Some East Cushitic nouns for 'father/mother-in-law' show a remarkable
       similarity to the numeral 'three', e.g. Somali soddoh 'mother-in-law' —
       saddeh 'three', Boraana soddaa 'in law' — sadii 'three' so that one might
       think of a historical connection between them.

[118] The Proto-Semitic word for 'father' is not a biradical *ʔa'b- (with phone-
       mic stress) but a triradical *ʔabu- (showing the nominal form faʕl- of
       the root √ʔbu). The forms with declensional affixes (*ʔabu-u >) ʔabuu,
       (*ʔabu-i >) ʔabii, (*ʔabu-a >) ʔabaa are retained in many Semitic lan-
       guages before personal suffixes.

[119] As to the word for 'child, beget' in Agaw languages, Classical Ethiopic
       ʔəgʷal 'child, offspring', which has been traditionally connected with
       Arabic ʕigl, Hebrew ʕegel 'calf', has probably to be derived from Agaw
       (Bilin) ʔəq̇ʷra 'child'.

Even if one does not like to accept all etymologies proposed one will always find
stimulating remarks on specific Semitohamitic languages, among them especially those from the Cushitic language family (cf. Dolgopolsky 1973).

4. Nostratic comparisons in Dolgopolsky's work

I do not feel competent enough to judge the comparison of Semitohamitic with
other language families. But on the basis of more general considerations I must
confess to some doubt about the reliability of a reconstruction that goes back so
many millennia as necessary in order to reach the Proto-Altaic or Proto-Dravidian

knot. As expressed in the introduction, A. Dolgopolsky does not rely on the morphological structure of the languages to be compared. Instead, he opines that the grammatical structure of Proto-Nostratic was 'analytical with a rigid word order' (*NM*, p. 17). Evidently, the grammatical structure of the proto-language must have undergone drastic changes in the later development of the language phylum. By emphasizing on the morphological structure of a language — as I should like to do — one will come to the conclusion that only Indo-European is a suitable candidate for a genetic relationship with Semitohamitic. In fact, in my opinion the most convincing comparisons proposed in *NM* are those among SH and IE.

There are many quite convincing Nostratic comparisons that go far beyond SH and IE. A great deal of them must be attributed to loans. Especially the words for animals (as 'hyena', 'lion', 'leopard', 'monkey', 'bull, calf'), cereals, 'basket, vessel', weapons (as 'spear') and 'piece of leather (used esp. as footwear)' are to be considered as loanwords ('Kulturwörter') which sometimes show a great diffusion throughout the Afroeurasian continent.

Notes

1. In marginem of A. Dolgopolsky's *Nostratic Macrofamily and Linguistic Palaeontology*, Cambridge 1998.
2. Following my teacher Otto Rössler, I use the term Semitohamitic rather than Hamitosemitic. A hyphen in these terms (Semito-Hamitic resp. Hamito-Semitic) should be avoided. In his *The Languages of Africa* Greenberg did 'suggest the name Afroasiatic' (1963, 50) but he did not use this term, except for the headline, in the resp. chapter on Afroasiatic (pp. 42–65). According to him, the 'term Hamito-Semitic is so well-entrenched that it will no doubt continue to be used'.
3. By the way, the use of this term does not imply the classification of this language group into an Indian and a European branch.
4. This is based on the theory that there is a correlation between the distribution of the Nostratic languages and that of farming dispersal, see Renfrew 1996.
5. His glottogonic methodology becomes evident in the following passage cited by Petráček (1987, 11) that 'von einem ursprünglichen Laute nach und nach eine gewisse Summe von Lauten sich herausgebildet hat'.
6. These three language families constitute the 'Noachische Völkerfamilie' (p. xxv) since Noah is — according to Genesis 8 — the father of Sem, Ham and Japheth. In the nineteenth century, the common origin of these language families was a *communis opinio.* Several works dealing with this relationship are mentioned in Burrini 1978; 1979.
7. See the first chapter on 'The principles of genetic linguistic classificatiom' in his *Language in the Americas* (1987), where he speaks frankly about his 'deviation from what has become virtually a compulsory practice among American Indianists: the use of sound correspondence tables and asterisked reconstructed forms' (p. 1). With

reference to his classificational work on African languages (*The Languages of Africa*, Bloomington 1963), he avers that the 'particularly striking sound correspondences' referred to occasionally in this work 'figured in no essential way as part of my method'.

8. Some of them do not show a vowel between the second and third radical in the reconstructed Nostratic form, as in *ʔibrE 'fig tree', *ḳoʔć/cV 'basket', *ńo/aɣ/ʕlE 'sinew', *ḳožʕV 'tree trunk', *čürV 'flint-stone'.

9. Another important contribution is the 'Historical comparative vocabulary of Afrasian' by I.M. Diakonoff and other Russian scholars. This translation of an earlier Russian work not easily available in the West has been published in the *St Petersburg Journal of African Studies* in several instalments since 1993.

References

Böhm, G., 1988. *Die Sprache der Aithiopen im Lande Kusch*. Wien: Afro-Pub.

Burrini, G., 1978 & 1979. Profilo storico degli studi sul camito-semitico. *Annuali dell' Istituto Orientale di Napoli* 38, 113–53; 39, 351–84.

Diakonoff, I.M., A.G. Belova, A.Ju. Militarev & V.Ja. Porkhomovsky, 1993–95. Historical comparative vocabulary. *St Petersburg Journal of African Studies* 2, 5–28; 3, 5–26; 4, 7–38; 5, 4–32; etc.

Dolgopolsky, A.B., 1973. *Sravnitel'no-istoričeskaja slovar' fonetika kušitskix jazykov*. Moscow: Nauka.

Dolgopolsky, A.B., 1986. Semitic nomina segolata in Ethiopic, in *Ethiopian Studies: Proceedings of the 6th International Conference (Tel-Aviv 1980)*, ed. G. Goldenberg. Rotterdam: Balkema-Boston, 71–90.

Ehret, C., 1995. *Reconstructing Proto-Afroasiatic (Proto-Afrasian) Vowels, Tone, Consonants, and Vocabulary*. Berkeley (CA): University of California.

Greenberg, J.H., 1963. *Languages of Africa*. (Publications of the Indiana University Research Center in Anthropology, Folklore, and Linguistics, 25.) Bloomington (IN): Indiana University Press.

Greenberg, J.H., 1987. *Language in the Americas*. Stanford (CA): Stanford University Press.

Hodge, C.T., 1991. Indo-European and Afroasiatic, in *Sprung from Some Common Source: Investigations into the Prehistory of Languages*, eds. S.M. Lamb & E.D. Mitchell. Stanford (CA): Stanford University Press, 141–65.

Hohenberger, J., 1958. *Semitisches und hamitisches Sprachgut im Masai - Mit vergleichendem Wörterbuch*. Sachsenmühle: Selbstverlag des Verf.

Illič-Svityč, B.M., 1971–84. *Opyt sravnenija nostratičeskix jazykov*. 3 vols. Moscow: Nauka.

Lepsius, R., 1880. *Nubische Grammatik mit einer Einleitung über die Völker und Sprachen Afrikas*. Berlin: Hertz.

Meinhof, C., 1912. *Die Sprachen der Hamiten*. Hamburg: Friederichsen.

Mukarovsky, H.G., 1987. *Mande-Chadic Common Stock: a Study of Phonological and Lexical Evidence*. Vienna: Afro-Pub.

Orël, V.E. & O.V. Stolbova, 1995. *Hamito-Semitic Etymological Dictionary: Materials for a Reconstruction*. (Handbuch der Orientalistik, I. 18.) Leiden: Brill.

Petráček, K., 1987. Leo Reinisch: Der einheitliche Ursprung der Sprachen der alten Welt und die afrikanische Urheimat der semitohamitischen und semitischen Sprachen, in *Leo Reinisch: Werk und Erbe*, ed. H.G. Mukarovsky. Vienna: Österreichische Akademie der Wissenschaften, 309–32.

Reinisch, L., 1873. *Der einheitliche Ursprung der Sprachen der alten Welt, nachgewiesen durch Vergleichung der afrikanischen, erythräischen und indogermanischen Sprachen mit Zugrundelegung des Teda*. Vienna: Braunmüller. (Reprinted in 1973, Wiesbaden: Sändig.)

Renfrew, C., 1987. *Archaeology and Language: the Puzzle of Indo-European Origins*. London: Cape.

Renfrew, C., 1989. The origins of Indo-European languages. *Scientific American* 261(4) (October), 82–90.

Renfrew, C., 1996. Language families and the spread of farming, in *The Origins and Spread of Agriculture and Pastoralism in Eurasia*, ed. D.R. Harris. London: University College London, 70–92.

Rössler, O., 1971. Das Ägyptische als semitische Sprache, in *Christentum am Roten Meer*, vol. 1, eds. F. Altheim & R. Stiehl. Berlin: de Gruyter, 263–326.

Schleicher, A.W., 1891. *Afrikanische Petrefakten: Ein Versuch die grammatischen Bildungen und Formwurzeln der afrikanischen Sprachen durch Sprachvergleichung festzustellen*. Berlin: Fröhlich.

Sherratt, A. & S. Sherratt, 1988. The archaeology of Indo-European: an alternative view. *Antiquity* 62, 584–95.

Zimmer, S., 1990. The investigation of Proto-Indo-European history: methods, problems, limitations, in *When Worlds Collide: the Indo-Europeans and the Pre-Indo-Europeans*, eds. T.L. Markey & J.A.C. Greppin. Ann Arbor (MI): Karoma, 311–44.

Chapter 16

The current state of Nostratic linguistics

Alan S. Kaye

General remarks on the nature of comparative-historical linguistics are offered focusing on the process of reconstruction and reconstructed forms in prototype languages. Nostratic background material is presented with special attention given to the methodological problems involved in the establishment of hypertaxa. The current literature is discussed with mention of some of the older research in this area, with particular consideration of Aharon Dolgopolsky's The Nostratic Macrofamily and Linguistic Palaeontology *(hereafter* NM*). Remarks concentrate on the data from members of the Afroasiatic phylum presented by the author.*

The fact that scholars can disagree bespeaks a vibrant field in which enormous strides have been made in the past and which will surely continue to advance in the years ahead.[1] Dissent is one way science progresses; dissent and debate eventually lead to consensus. Thus, the following remarks, while critical of Aharon Dolgopolsky's new book (*NM*) are also intended to be constructive. My sole purpose is to allow the discipline of comparative-historical linguistics to make headway — NOT merely to express disagreement for its own sake. I do not intend my tone to be harsh or negative (yet I plan to call a spade a spade), nor do I invoke the derogatory and debunking spirits which have sometimes characterized the partisan debate concerning the proposed Amerind macrophylum proposed by Joseph H. Greenberg — a Nostratic-like hypertaxon stemming from Greenberg (1987). I doubt very much that Professor Dolgopolsky will be persuaded by this essay to abandon or even modify his position, although he might be swayed to alter a few points of detail. So the best I can hope for is for both of us to politely agree to disagree. All this boils down to the following perspective: Nostratic can be viewed, in many ways, as a religion: either you believe or you do not; O ye of little faith . . ., etc. My position will become clearer in what follows. Incidentally, linguistics has been viewed as a religion before. As Norval Smith has succinctly pointed out: 'There are certain obvious parallels between practising Christianity or Islam and practising linguistics or surgery' (1989, 198).

Nostratic

Dolgopolsky is, of course, by no means the first linguist to propose hypertaxa (see Lass 1997, 160), such as Nostratic — the genetic consortium among the following phyla: Afroasiatic-Indo-European-Dravidian (Colin Renfrew calls it 'Dravidian', p. xi, but also 'Elamo-Dravidian', p. xv, assuming a direct link with Elamite — a theory he hyperbolically claims has been proven by David McAlpin of the University of London (Renfrew 1991, 57); the latter term also occurs in Bomhard & Kerns (1994, 26–7) Altaic-Kartvelian-Uralic-Yukaghir (Renfrew, *NM* p. xi, refers to both 'Uralic' and 'Uralic-Yukaghir'; the latter term is also used by Bomhard & Kerns (1994, 25–6), and Dolgopolsky calls it 'Uralic' and also 'Uralic-Yukaghir', p. 7). Dolgopolsky continues the efforts of the Moscow School (led by his former colleague Vladislav M. Illič-Svityč (d. 1966 in a car accident) — see Illič-Svityč (1971–84) by producing yet another book-length venture on Nostratic, in which he postulates what he considers the evidence for it; and, in my opinion, he certainly will not be the last Nostraticist, distant genetic affiliations having become more fashionable research topics today than they were in previous years (see, e.g. Shevoroshkin 1989a,b). Greenberg (1997b) believes all the languages called Nostratic are related but do not constitute a family. He is of the opinion that Indo-European is more closely related to Uralic and languages in northern Asia than to Afroasiatic — a point of view Greenberg notes is identical to that of Bomhard (1996). Only time will tell which other languages and language families will become part of Nostratic. Greenberg (1997b, 187) embraces Nostratic as a grouping of related languages, but NOT a language family. He states further that Allan Bomhard 'has come to share a view almost identical to my own' (Greenberg 1997b). Campbell (1997b, 284) is of the opinion that Greenberg's Eurasiatic hypothesis is compatible with Nostratic; however, this is incorrect, if one interprets matters very literally.

Even global etymologies have been proposed, as linguists dare to talk about Proto-World (see Blažek 1989; Ruhlen 1994; Salmons 1992; 1997 for discussion). Interestingly enough, Proto-World (called this, but also referred to as Proto-Human, Proto-Language and other designations as well) was the cover story of the November 5, 1990 *US News and World Report* (pp. 60–70).[2] Haas (1969, 101) correctly puts her finger on why scholars indulge in this sort of activity: 'But classificatory schemes tend to be overrated, and suggestions of connections of great antiquity seem more glamorous than recent ones'. She is also correct, I believe, in the following observation: 'Consequently there will probably never be an end to new classificatory schemes'.

From the coining of the term 'Nostratic' (<Latin nostrās 'our countryman', related to noster 'our'; however, the introduction by Renfrew (*NM*, p. ix), incorrectly states it is from the non-existent Latin nostras 'our countryman' (following Trask (1996, 381), and the aforementioned *US News and World Report* erroneously states it means 'our language', p. 65) by the Danish linguist Holger Pedersen in 1903, according to Renfrew (Lass 1997, 160) states it originally stems from Pedersen (1924, ch. 8²), already extant in Sweet (1900) and Anderson (1879) before him, to Bomhard & Kerns (1994) and Joseph & Salmons (1998), the pursuit of distant genetic relationships has attracted many researchers (see Kaye (1985) for the history of a proposed Indo-European-Semitic hypertaxon going back to 1836, and Kaye (1992) on one of the most pioneering of these researchers, Edward Sapir, who was the first to think about the relationship between Sino-Tibetan and Nadene, although he never published anything on this theory (today's 'Dene-Caucasian' or 'Dene-Sino-Caucasian', on which see Campbell (1997b, 287), a topic later researched especially by two Russian linguists, S. Starostin and S. Nikolaev — see Shevoroshkin & Manaster Ramer (1991) and Starostin (1989)). One obvious result of this activity is that the Nostratic field now has a sizeable bibliography.[3] As a case in point, Bomhard & Kerns (1994) list 150 pages of references, including 17 items by Dolgopolsky, the last of which was published in 1989 (pp. 714–864).

There can be no doubt that the Nostratic hypothesis is today largely associated with Russian scholarship on the subject,[4] to the point where even American fellow Nostraticist Allan Bomhard has often felt like an outsider, and this is how he expressed it in his own words (pers. comm.). Indeed, one can easily note many parallels between the Nostratic and Japhetic hypotheses. Japhetidology was the invention of Nikolaj Jakovlevič Marr (1865-1934). Thomas (1957) has investigated the Marrist Georgian–Semitic relationship and his Japhetic, Semitic, and Hamitic branches of the Noëtic family. In 1922, without ever studying Dravidian languages, Marr added them to the Japhetic family, too (1957, 38). Burushaski, Elamite, Sumerian, and Basque were also considered Japhetic languages. It would be possible to explore Nostratic–Japhetic parallels further; however, this would be tangential to our major concerns in this essay. Even the pages of *Pravda* (e.g. May 23, 1950, 3–4) carried a discussion of Marr: 'On N. Ya. Marr's Research Methods' (translated in Murra *et al.* 1951, 32–5), and of course, Joseph Stalin's essay, 'Marxism and problems in linguistics' criticized Marr's work (*Pravda*, June 20, 1950, available in English translation by Foreign Languages Press, Peking 1972).

Language relatedness and comparative-historical linguistic methodology

At the outset, it should be stressed that no linguist can conclusively demonstrate from Dolgopolsky's comparisons the fallaciousness of Nostratic (despite some downright errors which will be pointed out in the course of our discussion of his etymologies), or that his phonological version of Nostratic (as opposed to that of other Nostraticists) is incorrect. There are, to be sure, differences of opinion among Nostraticists in this regard. One thing is sure, though: either Bomhard or Dolgopolsky is wrong in certain protophonemes and their sound correspondences. Obviously, both of them cannot be right and both of their proposed cognate sets are in conflict in many cases. Furthermore, some linguists accept Indo-European and Afroasiatic as belonging to the same family (Saul Levin, Carleton T. Hodge, e.g.); however, Levin (1995) does not accept Nostratic becasue the comparisons proposed do not convince him (more on this later), whereas Hodge (1998) does accept it, but with major differences from Bomhard & Kerns (1994), especially over the Indo-European glottalic theory (which is accepted by many of today's leading Indo-Europeanists and by Allan Bomhard as well). Furthermore, no linguist can prove (in any meaningful sense of the term, at least) that any two or more languages and/or language families are genetically unrelated. Dyen (1970, 440) finds 78 possible Proto-Indo-European-Proto-Austronesian cognates, yet does not waver in his steadfast belief in the likelihood that an Austronesian–Indo-European relationship cannot be demonstrated.

The mere fact that one finds no evidence of genetic relationship does not necessarily mean that one does not exist. There is, of course, always the possibility that Indo-European and Afroasiatic are, in fact, related (see Levin 1995 or Hodge 1998), and there is even the possibility that all the purported Nostratic languages belong to one family (including, according to Bomhard & Kerns (1994, 2), Elamite in Elamo-Dravidian, 'possibly' Sumerian, and Chukchi-Kamchatkan (going back, we are told, to Dolgopolsky's 'very earliest writings'), Eskimo-Aleut, and Gilyak (Nivkh) (1994, 3)), or even that all languages are related (specifically, if one accepts monogenesis,[5] as do Joseph H. Greenberg and many others as well). But there *always* has to be, in my opinion, a substantial amount of evidence in favour of the acceptance of a language family or hypertaxon. Indeed, it seems to me that one can unequivocally state that language unrelatedness is impossible to verify (according to Ruhlen (1989), Nostratic is related to Amerind, which is accepted by V. Shevoroshkin in the introduction to Shevoroshkin (1989b, 7), for which see Campbell (1997b, 328–9), yet this is not mentioned in *NM*; thus presumably, Dolgopolsky does not consider the evidence in favour of this hypertaxon to be 'substantial' enough, whereas the opposite holds true for the establishment of a family, phylum, or hypertaxon of languages, the ultimate and absolute proof of which rests, to be sure, as has always been and should always be the case, on the proven, established procedures of comparative-historical linguistic methodology (which are too well known to need elaboration here; however, see Shevoroshkin & Manaster Ramer (1991) for distant comparison, Lehmann (1994) for some enlightening remarks on distant comparison which needed to be stressed, and Newman (1995) for the position that the comparative method is unnecessary for the establishment of relatedness). It should be emphasized that the establishment of genetic ties is directly dependent, in my view, on the *rigour* of the enforcement of the comparative method, which establishes the relatedness of languages (see, e.g. Gamkrelidze & Ivanov 1990 on Indo-European). Thus, very few linguists can agree with V. Shevoroshkin, who is quoted as saying: 'It is *easy* (emphasis mine) to show all languages are related. These things are mainly done with correct methods in Russia' (Hagman 1990, 55). Most linguists would surely agree with Moscati *et al.* (1964, 17) when they proclaim:

> . . . the 'Aryo-Semitic' (Ascoli) or 'Nostratic' (Pedersen, Cuny) hypothesis which is claimed as a common ancestor of Hamito-Semitic and Indo-European. Such conjectures are, however, very highly speculative, especially on account of deep-seated morphological divergences between those groups, although the inflexional structure appears to be common to both. A more reliable explanation is to be sought in the common Mediterranean environment . . . Such limited links as may exist between Indo-European and Hamito-Semitic should not, therefore, be regarded as a heritage from a 'parent' language, but rather as a haphazard collection of isoglosses not unconnected with the geographical proximity of the two groups and certain historical contacts between them.

Most, if not all, historical linguists of any persuasion, as they read this volume, will want to examine the proposed comparisons, i.e. alleged cognates (see further below), and weigh the evidence presented before pronouncing judgement as to the merit of the author's hypothesis of cognates (e.g. Egyptian ḥwn 'boy, young man; [one's] child, son' (p. 89) and Estonian väi 'daughter's husband' and loanwords (e.g. Proto-Dravidian vanna '(elder) brother's wife' < Prakrit vahuṇṇī– 'husband's elder brother's wife (p. 89)) among the alleged Nostratic languages. The sole question is and should be whether the author proves a genetic relationship beyond a reasonable doubt. My assumption is that the basis for the validity of this hypothesis relies on the classical (Neogrammarian) comparative method, as I have stated above. This is a very important point to keep in mind because, given other sets of assumptions or presuppositions, several different perspectives may be entertained. However, we always wind up coming full circle, I think, looking for cognate sets based on the regularity postulate and the principle of systematic sound correspondences which recur in cognate after cognate (I should say alleged cognate after alleged cognate since the concept of 'false friends' is always present; e.g. Greek theós and Latin deus 'god'.[6] On this last point, Lass remarks (1997, 169, note 86): 'Ringe (1995) shows that the so-called Nostratic correspondences are not significantly different from the kinds of resemblances that could arise purely by chance, and that Nostratic is an unredeemable promissory note'. Although Nostratic resemblances look to me like a random curve, I must agree with Bernard Comrie (pers. comm., 18 July 1998), who has convinced me that Ringe (1995) has NOT proven that it is a random curve. Comrie is also of the opinion that there should be a mathematician somewhere who is capable of tackling the problem. If it can be proven that Nostratic resemblances are indeed random, then Nostratic should disintegrate at once (although it probably will not happen thus). Ringe (manuscript a) has cast further doubt on Nostratic, since chance similarities cannot be ruled out. Ringe claims that '. . . the results of this comparison show graphically that Nostraticists have NOT demonstrated greater-than-chance similarity between the language families which they claim are distantly related' (1995, 71). Sheila Embleton (pers. comm., 30 August 1998) writes: 'Ringe (1995) has not demonstrated that Nostratic resemblances are random. But he also COULD NOT demonstrate it. He has only demonstrated that the resemblances are indistinguishable from random.'

Furthermore, some of the claims in the literature, such as the following statement by Shevoroshkin, cannot be taken as factual: 'Nostratic reconstruction, as proposed by both Illič-Svityč and Dolgopolsky in 1964 independently, is a very precise and powerful instrument of comparative-historical linguistics' (1989b, 7). Also, when asked if he could 'converse with a 50,000-year-old man', Shevoroshkin replied: 'It would take a while . . . The problem is that what looks one way on paper might be differently pronounced. We don't know where the stress is' (Hagman 1990, 55). Unfortunately, there is a tendency among anthropologists, archaeologists, and culture historians, e.g. to consider as gospel the aforementioned kinds of statements, which are, sadly, perpetually quoted and requoted.[7] Imagine an introductory linguistics student reading in a linguistics textbook that Finnish is related to many American Indian languages — the thesis of Shevoroshkin (1989b, 7) *contra* remarks by Lyle Campbell. Then, too, we have Greenberg & Ruhlen (1992, 98–9), who postulate English milk and its cognates throughout Nostratic and Eurasiatic (the latter = Afroasiatic, Uralic, Dravidian, Eskimo-Aleut, and Amerind) with their remark that the 'probability for a random similarity among six families is about one in 10 billion' (1992, 98). Campbell (1997b, 410) is right to point to onomatopoeia and baby (child) language as factors here, and refers the reader to the further criticisms launched by Hock (1993). The statistics quoted here by Greenberg & Ruhlen (1992) demonstrate a misunderstanding of probability theory as applied to language.

My role as splitter among lumpers

It is my intention in this study to scrutinize some of the comparisons in *NM* and offer a conclusion as to the claim that the so-called Nostratic languages descend from a common ancestral source or protolanguage. I think that any reader of *NM* will, of necessity, need to execute what I have carried out. If this is done properly, I believe that one will be forced to conclude that the author's case has NOT been proven, since the burden of proof in these matters must rest with the proponent (see Newman (1995) for the opposing position to my notion of 'burden of proof'). The seeming resemblances discussed by the author are, in my view, the result of either language contact (= linguistic diffusion), i.e. linguistic borrowing, or pure chance, i.e. random resemblance — NOT the result of descent from a common ancestor, *Proto-Nostratic. In the case of the former, one should bear in mind that, since the majority of today's population are at least bilingual (McMahon 1994, 200), one can hypothesize that languages have been in contact from their beginning and have thus influenced one another. So many of these alleged cognates might actually be borrowings, such as no. 1, 'sycamore tree', where Arabic is the sole representative of the Semitic languages. And besides, this Nostratic word only shows up elsewhere in the phylum in Dravidian. Kamil V. Zvelebil, a Dravidianist, objects (this volume) to the Proto-Dravidian reconstruction. He proposes Proto-Dravidian *irt-, which does not look like Dolgopolsky's *ibr- at all. I asked the very question by Zvelebil (this volume, p. 363): 'So what has happened to the reflex of the Nostratic bilabial stop?' Professor Dolgopolsky had no answer to the aforementioned question at the symposium, nor could he explain how a Dravidian scholar, such as Zvelebil, could have posed this question to begin with.

It should be pointed out, moreover, that some of the lexemes should not have been used (nursery words), such as no. 117 'mother' and no. 118 'daddy', for very well-known reasons. I shall reserve judgement on the author's *Nostratic Dictionary* (in preparation) until I have had the opportunity to study all of the etymologies offered in that work. I am in full agreement with the late Robert Austerlitz, who so eloquently put it: 'I cannot say that I enjoy my role as splitter among lumpers, but since I believe in academic freedom much more fervently that I disbelieve in long-range groupings (LRGs), I will state my objections to lumping in a spirit of complete open-mindedness: I will believe the lumpers when they convince me' (1991, 353). I cannot accept Nostratic until the proposed cognates add up to a persuasive picture.[8] This point of view is quite different from that of Hodge (1998), who disagrees with Bomhard & Kerns (1994) on many details and seems, on occasion, to be quite lukewarm about Nostratic but does accept it, yet maintains that Indo-European and Afroasiatic, as closely related daughter languages, go back to a common origin, which he calls Lislakh (not a part of the Nostratic theory). Others, who also relate Indo-European with Egyptian and Semitic, have expressed grave doubts about lexical comaprisons. Abel (1886, 5) writes: 'But further I am quite convinced that it is only by an accurate examination of the grammar of languages that we can pronounce a decisive judgement on their affinities.' And: 'On the one hand, a great resemblance of sound in two words will sometimes prove nothing, or leave the judgment in great incertainty' (Abel 1886, 5). The latter pronouncement indeed explains many of the 1030 proto-roots of Common Indo-European–Semitic postulated by Brunner (1969), such as Latin en 'in' and Akkadian in(a) 'in' (1969, 21).

The bulk of Dolgopolsky's book discusses 125 alleged cognates among the Nostratic languages (pp. 20–98). I say 'alleged', as I have already maintained, as I cannot prove that these are not *ultimately* cognates (this may perhaps be provable one day when more evidence is offered, and/or when methods, procedures, or strategies improve beyond today's severe limitations of the classical comparative method). I can only say that for the moment, the alleged cognates do not appear to be genuine, since I see little or no evidence in the form of recurring systematic sound correspondences and plausible semantic matches to justify such a conclusion — certainly not on the scale established for the recognized linguistic families, such as Indo-European or Afroasiatic. The systematic sound correspondences listed on pp. 102–5 are far from convincing, either qualitatively or quantitatively, since the 124 or 125 comparisons (the index has 125, but no. 124 corresponds to no. 123 in the text, and no. 125 to no. 124) can be explained by means other than a genetic relationship. To complicate matters even more, what are we to make of the author's asterisked reflexes in many of the proto-daughter languages with single and double question marks (cf. a notation with a triple question mark in the body of the text itself, p.

71 — see below). I count, for example, 23 question-marked Proto-Berber phonemic reflexes alone. Proto-Egyptian is loaded with 27 question marks in addition to many blank spaces, i.e. no reflex at all offered from Proto-Nostratic, such as *č̣. Many of the 125 proposed etymologies have single and double question marks. Consider the triple question mark in the equation of Proto-Nostratic *ʒ́iryu/ű 'vein, sinew' > Iraqw dēʕarắmo 'root, sinew' (pp. 70–71). The alleged Korean cognate /sir/ 'thread', we note, has only one question mark attached to it (p. 71). What exactly are the linguistic differences denoted by single, double, and triple question marks? We are forced to agree with Colin Renfrew's remark calling Nostratic research 'these intriguing speculations' (p. xvi).

As an Afroasiaticist, I disappointingly note that, amazingly, there has not been one full-fledged reconstruction of Proto-Berber phonology and lexicon. There is not even one Berber etymological dictionary. In fact, Ehret (1995) states that he has decided not even to bother with Berber data in his reconstruction of Proto-Afroasiatic because Berber is the most aberrant daughter phylum phonologically (see Kaye 1996 for the details of this serious error). This is enigmatic indeed, especially in light of the fact that most Afroasiaticists place the Afroasiatic *Urheimat* in North Africa, although Renfrew believes that 'it has always seemed to me that the only coherent process underlying the Afroasiatic linguistic unity must be the dispersal of sheep and goats, and later cereals, from the Jordan–Palestine area across to North Africa . . .' (1998, 184).

There are several versions of Proto-Afroasiatic which have so far been published (see Kaye 1996; 1997) with many unresolved problems, and yet today's linguists are expected to accept the present version of Proto-Nostratic phonology without batting an eyelid (pp. 102–5). It strikes me as quite odd that linguistics could possess a comparative Nostratic dictionary without also having a comparative Semitic counterpart, and so on. As is well known, not even a single comparative Semitic dictionary has ever been published, although Stanislav Segert and David Cohen have attempted such projects (the latter scholar's is partially complete, however). We do not even possess an etymological dictionary of Arabic, and yet, strangely enough, two Afroasiatic comparative dictionaries were published in 1995 (by Ehret and Orël & Stolbova on which see above). How can we know so much about Proto-Nostratic when we have so little knowledge of Proto-Berber or Proto-Arabic? The latter offers numerous stumbling blocks in its reconstruction; e.g. the word for 'good' is modern Arabic dialects uses different roots (kuwayyis, mniih, ṭayyib, zeen, mizyan, samih, ḥasan, seme, etc.) which make it notoriously difficult to decide which one is Proto-Arabic. Indeed, more work is needed on Proto-Afroasiatic phonology, since scholars remain in the process of refining ideas about Proto-Cushitic, Proto-Chadic, and so on. This entire situation, obvious to the specialists, is very puzzling and difficult, if not impossible, to explain. How can the author so boldly reconstruct Proto-Nostratic without simultaneously, at least, offering reconstructions in some of the descendant protolanguages? This question is very germane to the issue of the relative chronology of Afroasiatic and Nostratic. Nichols (1998, 140), for example, maintains that Proto-Afroasiatic is at least 12,000 years old: 'This is by far the oldest securely demonstrated linguistic lineage on Earth' (Nichols 1998, 140). How can this fact be reconciled with another, viz., that Proto-Nostratic dates from 15,000 BC to 12,000 BC (according to Dolgopolsky 1994)?

Comments on Colin Renfrew's introduction to *NM*

Before examining the data presented by Dolgopolsky, we will first comment on the introduction by Colin Renfrew, Director of the McDonald Institute for Archaeological Research, Cambridge, England (pp. vii–xxii). Renfrew, seeking confirmation for the origin of agriculture in Anatolia, has long been on record as favouring the Nostratic hypothesis. Consider the following:

> This somewhat expanded version of the wave-of-advance model has the effect of situating the ancestral languages of the Indo-European, Afro-Asiatic and Dravidian groups quite close together in the Near East about 10,000 years ago. Although still hypothetical, this picture finds remarkable support from recent work in linguistics and genetics.
>   More than 20 years ago the Soviet linguists Vladislav M. Illich-Svitych and Aron Dolgopolsky proposed a number of European language families . . . they called Nostratic. The recognition of superfamilies, which may represent a breakthrough in linguistics, is still regarded as controversial (1991, 57).[9]

We read at the beginning of Renfrew's remarks in *NM* that much research on Nostratic 'is published in Russian and is little known in the west' (p. vii). This is not exactly the case, I believe, especially in view of Shevoroshkin & Markey (1986), Kaiser & Shevoroshkin (1988), Shevoroshkin (1989b), Bomhard & Kerns (1994), and Joseph & Salmons (1998), among other publications. Then on the next page we read that *NM* 'presents for the first time a full and rich illustration, with a large vocabulary, of the central tenet of the Nostratic hypothesis' (p. viii). However, this is not true because Bomhard & Kerns (1994, 195–714), e.g. present 601 Nostratic proto-roots. It is, moreover, difficult for me to comprehend how this book's mere 125 comparisons can compete with the 2000 'known' Nostratic roots as of the early 1990s (see p. 26 and also Dolgopolsky 1994, 2838). In addition to Bomhard & Kerns (1994), there are also Bomhard

(1984; 1990), and Shevoroshkin & Markey (1986) (see the critical remarks in Kaye 1985 and 1988).

Calling the term 'Nostratic' 'somewhat ethnocentric' (p. ix), Renfrew then mentions Dolgopolsky's term 'Boreic', which is, I believe, virtually unknown in the literature, and Joseph H. Greenberg's designation 'Eurasiatic' (p. ix); however, the latter term represents a hypertaxon quite different from Nostratic, since it is asserted that Indo-European and Afroasiatic are not so closely related (as they are in the development from Proto-Nostratic). Renfrew knows all of this, of course, since he observes that Greenberg includes Eskimo-Aleut, Chukchi-Kamchatkan, Ainu, and Gilyak, but not Afroasiatic, Kartvelian, and Dravidian in his Eurasiatic designation (p. xii).

We shall at this point turn specifically to Professor Renfrew's observations on Afroasiatic. He states that the term 'Hamito-Semitic' 'coincides *to a considerable extent* (emphasis mine) with the grouping recognized by Joseph Greenberg (1963)[10] and termed by him "Afroasiatic"' (p. xi). It must be pointed out that the terms 'Hamito-Semitic' (also 'Semito-Hamitic') and 'Afroasiatic' (plus other terms, such as Igor M. Diakonoff's 'Afrasian', 'Erythraic', etc.) are exactly equivalent today for almost everyone (see Kaye & Daniels (1992) on the earlier hyphenated designation, Afro-Asiatic, as well). The map of the Afroasiatic family includes the 'Omotic' branch, which is not accepted by all specialists (p. xii). Zaborski, a noted authority, rejects 'Omotic' and considers these languages to be West Cushitic (1992, 36). Renfrew's source (Ruhlen 1991) is less reliable (p. xii) than Bright (1992), which is much better for standard views on the intricacies of genetic classification.

Concerning the relationship between Japanese and Korean and their inclusion within Altaic, we learn from Renfrew (p. xii) that Dolgopolsky believes they are Altaic (and thus are mentioned in some of the tome's comparisons). Samuel E. Martin has long maintained the aforementioned theory (see Martin 1991). As I understand it, the Japanese–Korean–Altaic hypothesis is still controversial and not accepted by all linguists, while some would also place Ainu in the Altaic family. Comrie does make clear, however, that Japanese–Korean–Ainu 'is widely promoted at present' (1992, 49). Miller (1991) discusses the pros and cons of Japanese, e.g. as an Altaic language, remarking: 'The anti-Altaic position of Clauson and Doerfer is, to be sure, the "latest word" in many, perhaps in most, Altaic scholarly circles today' (1991, 324). The late Robert Austerlitz, who did extensive work on many so-called Altaic languages, never bought the Altaic family (1991, 360). It is puzzling to try to understand how the experts seem split, yet the non-specialist Nostraticists seem not to be divided at all in this regard. Recently, Greenberg (forthcoming b), not a specialist in Altaic particularly, has come out in favour of Altaic, calling its existence 'a certainty' (see further Austerlitz 1991, 92).

Let us turn to an examination of Renfrew's 'Problems with macrofamilies' (pp. xvi–xix). He begins with such phraseology as 'these intriguing speculations' (p. xvi). I certainly agree that the Nostratic hypothesis can best be referred to an 'intriguing speculation' (see again, note 1). As we read about 'lumpers' and 'splitters' we come away with the clear impression that Joseph H. Greenberg's multiple lexical comparisons (see Bengtson & Ruhlen 1997; Salmons 1997) and the four families of African linguistic classification '. . . (one of them Afroasiatic, as discussed above) was initially criticized upon methodological grounds' (p. xvii) were shouted down erroneously but 'it has been adopted almost universally' (p. xvii). It is important to realize that the Afroasiatic (= Hamito-Semitic) phylum was recognized as a distinct entity long before Greenberg's research into African linguistic classification was published (Greenberg 1963, and before that Greenberg 1950). All Greenberg basically did was to relabel (and somewhat refine) the term 'Hamito-Semitic', which has also been done, incidentally, by others subsequently (see, e.g. Hodge 1972 for the redesignation 'Lisramic').

One closing comment on Renfrew's final section, 'How to judge?' (pp. xix–xx), will now be offered. He remarks that the 125 examples offered in this book are waiting to be examined by specialists. He states: 'To a layman it seems improbable in the extreme that the equivalences which he shows would be the product of purely random variations among words which in fact have no genetic relationship. But that is an assessment by a non-specialist' (p. xx). The layman may well marvel that English cook and cookie are not related (see Trask 1996, 345–6), English much and Spanish mucho are not related, or that Persian bad 'bad' is *not* cognate with English bad. Imagine — identical meanings and identical phonemic structures! He may be further confused when told that Persian and English both belong to the Indo-European language family, and fail to comprehend, at the same time, that Armenian erku ([jɛrgú] according to my informant) 'two' is, phoneme for phoneme, cognate with English two, Gothic twai, German zwei, Sanskrit dvā, Greek dúō, Latin duo, Russian dva, etc., < Proto-Indo-European *dwō. It is well known that Proto-Indo-European *dw- > erk- in Armenian. Renfrew is correct when he ends with the pronouncement that 'it is for the historical linguists in the first instance to decide whether the evidence on offer is sufficient to lead to the general acceptance of the hypothesis' (*NM*, p. xx). Considering that the hypothesis was initially formulated approximately a century ago (see Renfrew, p. ix), along with so many others which have lumped one or more different linguistic phyla into various hypertaxa, the evidence so far presented has been insufficient to convince more than a handful of historical linguists that Nostratic (or Amerind, for that matter, and others) is anything other than fanciful linguistics based on the practice of unsound etymology. As with the Armenian example mentioned above, it should be obvious that the proper way to etymologize is to discover the systematic sound correspondences among languages — in addition to formulating the *Lautgesetze*.[11] If one does this properly, it is easy to understand how Amharic ləj 'child' is cognate with Arabic walad 'child' and Hebrew yɛlɛd 'boy'. It is unfortunate that many etymologists become involved in what has been referred to as 'word games' (see Jasanoff & Nussbaum 1996 for many concrete examples). So we can apparently still have all languages originating from Hebrew, the primordial language, and so on.[12] See the general discussion on very remote relations in Trask (1996, 376–404), which contains remarks on Nostratic (381–4) and Greenberg's multilateral comparisons (384–90). Trask, incidentally, concludes (this volume) that the evidence in favour of Nostratic is unconvincing insofar as he is concerned.

Classification of the Nostratic languages

Before turning our attention to the comparisons themselves, we shall address the classification of Nostratic languages proposed by the author (pp. 5–8). We shall comment on the first two language families only, Indo-European and Afroasiatic. First of all, we are completely baffled as to why a reader needs to be confronted with a list of these languages in this publication, when this information is readily available in many places. Linguists already are (or certainly should be) familiar with some of the listed members of the, for example, Germanic subfamily (p. 5): 'Swedish, Danish, Norwegian, Old High German, Middle High German, modern German dialects, Yiddish, Old English, Middle English, and English'. Secondly, some misinformation is presented in this section. Sogdian should be listed as a Middle Iranian language (after Middle Persian or Pahlavi), and not with the Neo-Iranian languages, Tajik and Kurdish (Payne 1992). Thirdly, under Semitic, Eblaitic (sic.) is called 'Eastern (sic.) Semitic' with a question mark following. One can safely remove this doubt, since Krebernik has conclusively demonstrated that Eblaite is to be classified as an early Akkadian (East Semitic) dialect (1996, 249). Fourthly, under Semitic, we read that Ethiosemitic is divided into Old Ethiopian and Ge'ez. There is no justification for this division (Wolf Leslau, pers. comm., 1 May 1998).

Let us now take up the approximately 150 Chadic languages. What would prompt Dolgopolsky to list half a page of them (p. 6)? Does the general historical linguist somehow gain anything from all these languages listed here? Has s/he ever heard of (or cared about) Ndam or Banana, two such languages?

Surely, the classification of Dravidian or Altaic is available in the standard handbooks, compendia, and encyclopedias of various sorts. I would hope that any reader would refer to the leading authorities on these matters of classification, and I see no reason for Dolgopolsky to devote his time to 'a more detailed and comprehensive classification of languages (and dialects)' in his *Nostratic Dictionary* (p. 8).

Transcription

Turning to a discussion of the transcription signs and other symbols used (pp. 11–16), many of which are awkward, some linguists, without question, will have difficulty in relating to them. It would make much more sense for the author to have used IPA symbolization throughout (correction from IPhA, p. 14). Notwithstanding the typographical errors (*allophons* for *allophones*, *german* for *German*, p. 11; *falligh* for *falling*, *un* for *an*, p. 15), we note that /g/ is defined as a 'voiced uvular stop' (p. 14). One should correct this to 'velar' since [G] is the correct symbol in common use for a uvular.

There is also the matter in inconsistency of the definitions themselves. /ɣ/, for instance, is called a 'voiced velar fricative', but /ð/ is a 'voiced fricative dental' (for voiced dental fricative), and /ɸ/ is defined as a 'fricative voiceless bilabial consonant' (for voiceless bilabial fricative — why mention 'consonant' at all here?). The awkward order of 'front low vowel' (p. 13) is matched by the symbol /ä/. In English, one normally refers to a low front vowel /æ/. Similarly, one talks of high front vowels and not front high ones (p. 13). I shall refrain from expatiating on the other infelicities of this sort (such as 'consonantic' for 'consonantal', p. 16, 'preconsonantic', and 'postconsonantic', p. 48), since they will be obvious to the reader (see also note 3).

There are 16 uncertainty signs (pp. 15–16). These are, unfortunately, user-unfriendly. Dolgopolsky uses a blank (or white) ∇ with borders (= a large ⱴ) or V for an unspecified vowel (p. 15). Why both when V is standard? Does the reader need to be told that * is a 'sign of reconstruction', or that ? represents 'a questionable Nostratic etymology, or a questionable cognate (p. 15)? In a similar vein, we are told that a protolanguage is 'the common ancestor of languages in a family' (p. 18). We might as well be told what a language is, too, not to mention dialect, word, verb, and so on.

The Nostratic 'miti' phenomenon

We will now focus our attention on the etymologies *per se* presented by the author. First, I would like to take up the 'miti' phenomenon. Dolgopolsky states: 'Among the most important resemblances is that of the personal pronouns and inflectional person-markers of the 1ˢᵗ and 2ⁿᵈ persons ('*mV [*mi in Dolgopolsky 1992] for 'I' . . . *tū̌ > ti for 'thou' . . .') (p. 17). This is, similarly, the perspective of Bomhard & Kerns who maintain: 'Proto-Nostratic *mi- or *me- 'I' and *tʰi or *tʰe 'thou' have particular importance, since, as forcefully demonstrated by John C. Kerns . . ., pronouns, being among the most stable elements in a language, are a particularly strong indicator of genetic relationship' (1994, 2). Ruhlen (1992, 5–6) states that these pronouns are Proto-Eurasiatic. The pronoun argument is given extensive treatment by Campbell (1997b, 240–52) going back to a 1787 observation by Jonathan Edwards that Mohegan and Hebrew had similar pronouns (Campbell 1997b, 241). Shevoroshkin (1989b, 7) states that, since grammatical elements are almost never borrowed, the obvious conclusion can be used as indicative of a genetic relationship. This point of view is, without question, erroneous. My own perspective on pronouns is the complete opposite of the above. Here, I believe, we should all agree with Meillet (1958), who represents the epitome of a sane and reasonable comparative-historical linguistics, quoted in Campbell (1997a, 349):

> It goes without saying that in order to establish genetic relatedness of languages one must disregard everything that can be explained by general conditions common to all languages. For instance, pronouns must be short words, clearly composed of easily pronounced sounds, generally without consonant clusters. The consequence is that PRONOUNS ARE SIMILAR IN ALMOST ALL LANGUAGES, though this does not imply a common origin . . . THEREFORE, PRONOUNS MUST BE USED WITH CAUTION IN ESTABLISHING RELATEDNESS OF LANGUAGES.

Contemporary linguists, of course, have continued to write on this topic, and the final word is still not in. Refuting Nichols & Peterson (1996), Campbell is, in my estimation, absolutely correct to maintain: 'These recurrent sounds in the world's pronoun systems are not wholly accidental, but neither are they, as I have attempted to show here, due to a single historical development' (1997b, 349). Now, the Nostraticists would have us believe that the similarities in the 'miti' pronouns could NOT be due to sheer coincidence, whereas I think that the opposite is true.

Christopher Ehret (this volume) notes *mi 'I, me' in Bantu (Niger-Congo). Is this compelling evidence to add two African subbranches to the Nostratic macrofamily? Trask (1996, 381) maintains that some Nostraticists have added additional families to Nostratic, viz. Chukchi-Kamchatkan, Eskimo-Aleut, Sumerian, Nilo-Saharan and Niger-Congo). I believe it is much more reasonable to conclude that nasals occur in first-person pronouns for perhaps the same reason they occur in 'mama'. Dento-alveolars occur in second-person pronouns for the same reason they occur in 'dada'. Again, to my way of thinking, Campbell's viewpoint is right on the mark (Campbell 1997b, 349):

> The reader may ask why pronouns[13] tend to have nasal consonants, a finding confirmed in N[ichols] and P[eterson]'s comparisons across the languages of their sample. Clearly, there is nothing particularly special about the n:m pronoun pattern. Languages tend to have nasals in pronominal forms for a variety of reasons: because they are unmarked sounds and hence recur with frequency, increasing the possibility of their occurrence *by chance* [emphasis mine: ASK];

because they are perceptually the most salient consonants and therefore are very useful in signalling important grammatical markers, and because some sounds (a small set) are used over and over commonly in short grammatical markers in languages and this makes the nasals (members of that set) pop up in grammatical markers, including in pronouns, with considerable frequency.

Sheer coincidence in language

At this point, let us shift to the matter of sheer coincidence in language ('by chance' — see above).[14] One of the best cases of this phenomenon in the vast scholarly literature of which I am aware concerns the bound pronominal suffixes of Proto-Eastern Miwok and Late Common Indo-European. Campbell (1997b) uses research by Callaghan (1980) to buttress his view that the occurrence of n and m and k in first- and second-person pronouns in New Guinea and America is coincidental. Saul Levin, well-known for two books relating Indo-European and Semitic languages, emphatically rejects Nostratic, and would consider the resemblances presented by Dolgopolsky to be purely coincidental. Levin's (1995) skepticism towards Nostratic, especially the Nostratic of Illič-Svityč, as well as the research of Möller (1906) and (1911), is expressed as follows:

> The results of Möller's research — and that of his direct successors — never struck me as sufficient to establish the Nostratic super-family and the proto-Nostratic language which they aimed at, embracing IE and Semitic together with its African relatives. So I am *a fortiori* skeptical of Illich-Svitych's research . . . He vastly enlarges the super-family to take in also Kartvelian, Uralic, Dravidian, and Altaic, and thus to cover a great expanse of Asia — east all the way to Korea and south to the tip of India. The etymological data, which he gathered with such admirable diligence, I draw upon gladly and gratefully, insofar as they are *cogent* [emphasis mine: ASK] . . .; but his

enterprise on the whole suffers from too much vagueness, on both the phonetic and semantic side . . .

In his attempt to demonstrate the original kinship of those enormously varied languages, Illich-Svitych could not help but push the age of their proto-Nostratic source far, far back into the dim past. [Dolgopolsky (1994) dates Proto-Nostratic at 15,000 to 12,000 BC — ASK.] So his method of comparative linguistics has yielded few solid results (1995, 5).

I believe most historical linguists will, incidentally, say exactly the same thing about Levin (1995). Strangely enough, I believe Levin may be aware of the possibility of some of the pitfalls in his book when he compares some 'possible remote cognates' to the Semitic root mlʔ 'full' (1995, 182). He compares forms in Tagalog, Malay, Turkish, Mandarin Chinese, etc., noting: 'A method has yet to be worked out for distinguishing between relevant and coincidental similarities, when the languages show only a few, not enough to disclose a recurrent pattern of phonetic correspondences' (Levin 1995, 182). My sentiments precisely!

This book is also about linguistic palaeontology, and a few remarks on this subject may now be apropos. What do we know about Proto-Indo-European culture as a direct reflection of reconstructed Proto-Indo-European? In this regard, we agree with Lehmann (1970), who remarks:

And when we discuss linguistic paleontology in our classes on Indo-European historical linguistics, our remarks are diffident, almost embarrassed. Clearly the linguistic palaeontologists had overextended themselves, to the point of elimination. We could cite a variety of ways in which they overplayed their hand. The one most directly pertinent for linguistics is the role they assigned to the language in their reconstruction of Indo-European culture.

Lehmann (1970, 2) makes a very solid case for his plea for the abandonment of 'fanciful constructions we find at the beginning of this century'. He goes on to affirm: 'The basic sources of the paleontologist must be texts and archeological data. Deductions from language must be related to these, examined as commentaries on them, but not used as primary sources' (Lehmann 1970, 2). Lehmann (1970) is filled with examples of linguists overplaying their palaeontological hands. There are a few linguistic palaeontologists, however, such as Lehmann's own University of Texas colleague, Edgar C. Polomé. Cf. his thoughts about 'Reconstructing Indo-European culture and religion' (1982, 296–315); 'The reconstruction of proto-Bantu (sic.) culture from the lexicon' (1982, 316–28); 'Indo-European culture, with special attention to religion' (1982, 329–52); and 'Lexical data and cultural contacts: a critique of the study of prehistoric isoglosses and borrowings' (1982, 353–68). Needless to say, there are some highly controversial issues in this field which will take us well beyond the limits of this paper.

343

Discussion of the etymologies (by number)

I shall restrict my comments to those items where I have some knowledge to share rather than make any remark that such and such an etymology is not convincing. Indeed, there are numerous problems with almost every etymology proposed. I take the liberty and cite the Proto-Nostratic form in the following for the benefit of those who do not have *NM* directly in front of them.

Trask (1996, 354–5) has a brief discussion of linguistic palaeontology, and Gamkrelidze & Ivanov (1990, 114–15) write on Indo-European linguistic palaeontology. My remarks which follow this immediately focus on linguistic matters (my interest) rather than linguistic palaeontological ones.

1. 'Fig tree': *ibrE. Doniach (1972, 1237) gives qayqab jummayzī as 'sycamore' in Arabic (correction from 'sycomore', p. 20). The cited Arabic data are not in Lane (1863.I, 5–6) nor in Wehr (1974). The root ʔbr basically means 'needle' in Arabic. Steingass (1884, 3) states that in addition to the primary meaning, it can also mean 'fruit of the sycamore tree', but not 'sycamore tree'; further, Steingass also states that it means 'malice'. In my view, since the fruit of the sycamore tree was envisaged as having thorns, there was a semantic extension of the basic sememe 'needle'. Would it be fair or right to compare the Arabic meaning 'malice' with something similar in Altaic or Indo-European? As has been said many times before, one can find almost any meaning possible for a root in some Arabic dictionary or other. To put it in other words, it is very easy indeed to misuse the infinity of the Arabic lexicon.

I wish to thank Allan Bomhard who referred me to Steingass (1884) in this instance. Bomhard, too, rejects the Nostratic etymology presented in *NM*. See his paper for the details (this volume).

Gragg (1982) does not list Oromo abru; however (Appleyard, this volume) has located abruu and a metathesized form, arbuu.

5. 'Antelope (male)': *ʔoř[u]. Leslau (1987, 40) considers Hebrew ʔaryē 'lion' the cognate (following Wagner). Dolgopolsky lists Geʕez ʔarwē 'wild beast' here as well as in no. 3, i.e. as going back to two distinct protoforms with a note stipulating: 'merger of two roots'. This is very unlikely.

6. 'Monkey': *maŋ[g]V̄. The Afroasiatic evidence is certainly meager (only Mubi, East Chadic).

The author's comment on the English word 'monkey' seems countered by my Webster's which states 'prob. < Middle Low German Moneke, name applied in the beast epic *Reynard the Fox* (*Webster's New World Dictionary* 1960, 950). *Webster's New Universal Dictionary* (1989, 925) adds more material to confirm the older position and changes 'probably' to 'apparently'.

It is interesting to note that Sergei A. Starostin rejects this etymology (public comment made at the Nostratic symposium, 17 July 1998, and also in his written paper: 'On the whole, a very dubious case').

7 & 8. 'Snow': *šűŋU and *čaĺ[U]g∇. It is unclear why these two words for 'snow' should rule out a tropical country as the Nostratic *Urheimat*. Is it not possible that, as is the case today, one can have a word for 'snow' without first-hand experience of living with it personally? In view of the aforementioned perspective, the Egyptian cognate (?) 'haily weather' seems difficult to explain. Many Egyptians today, as probably in yesteryear, have no first-hand knowledge of hail, yet certainly know what it is.

The phonetic correspondences in this match are particularly problematic. So, too, is the case of Japanese shimo 'frost'.

Also, how can one demonstrate that Arabic Θalj 'snow' = Yakut tohō- 'to break ice in a river'. (The Syriac word mentioned has, incidentally, two errors in its native orthographic rendition; see further note 16.)

9. 'Hoar-frost': *č¬[a]RʔV. There are two mistakes in the Arabic script rendition. This Arabic word is not to be found in Wehr (1974) nor in Lane (1863).

10. 'Ice, hoarfrost; to freeze': *k¬ir[u]qa. The cited Berber and Cushitic words, from the etymon qrr 'cold', are *not* cognate with the cited root k̞rq (PS *k̞rx), but rather with qrr. Cf. Arabic qarr 'cold' (Wehr 1974, 752) and Hebrew qar 'cold' with cognates throughout Semitic (Leslau 1987, 444). Dolgopolsky states: 'The Berber and Egyptian roots may alternatively go back to Nostr. *K̞arh∇ 'ice, hoar-frost'. However, no Egyptian root was mentioned, and the Proto-Nostratic root has */q/ and not */h/.

13. 'Water body' (sic.) (correct to 'body of water'): *yam∇. Gordon (1965, 411) notes that Akkadian yāmu and possibly Arabic yamm- are borrowed from northwest Semitic. Orël & Stolbova (1995, 258) reconstruct Proto-Afroasiatic *ham- 'water' = also *ham- in Proto-West and East Chadic. The Proto-Chadic form given is incorrect (p. 25). This is *yam- (Bomhard & Kerns 1994, 471), following Illič-Svityč (1971–84.I, 279–80). Paul Newman (pers. comm., 15 June 1998) reports that Proto-Chadic 'water' is *am(V), without an initial consonant (Newman 1977).

17. 'Cereals': *gaL∇. Relating Arabic ɣallat 'cereals' and Hittite halki- grain seems far-fetched. Why not also compare to English millet, which is closer to the Arabic form than the Hittite word? Is this possible further evidence for Proto-World?

18. 'Kernel, grain': *xänt ¬∇. The Arabic script has the plain <t> for the correct emphatic <ṭ>.

19. 'Breast': *mälge. The root mlg (Arabic mlj 'suck') is Greenberg & Ruhlen's (1992) Proto-World root. See further Hock (1993). It is surprising indeed that Dolgopolsky does not mention the alleged wider connections. Appleyard (this volume) denies the existence of Proto-Afroasiatic *mlg and sees the m- as a prefix to *ng (based on research by Gábor Takács).

20. 'White': *halb∇. There is no need to say: 'New Assyrian Akkadian'. 'New Assyrian' suffices. This is similar to saying 'Cairene Egyptian Arabic'. It is obvious that Cairene refers to Egyptian.

28. 'Sinew', 'to tie together': *ńoɣ/ʕIE. The cited Ge'ez form has a short /u/ and not a long one. Leslau (1987, 382) states that Dillmann considers the connection with Hebrew and Arabic naʕal 'shoe' 'with reservations'.

29. 'Spear': *p/p¬ešqE. Karekare pasku is listed as fasku by Orël & Stolbova (1995, 421). Is this a free variation, or is one of the forms erroneous?

32. 'To follow the tracks': *[d]EʕS∇. Wehr (1974, 282) glosses this root 'to trample, crush'. The root does not occur in Lane (1863). The last sentence here should read 'if' rather than 'of'.

33. 'Spike, spear, to pierce': *šuby∇. Arabic sbb 'pierce' is not listed in Wehr (1974, 292). Its basic meaning is 'cut': sabbahu 'He pierced him in the anus' and sabba 'anus' (Lane 1863.II, 1284).

34. 'To hit (the target)': *t¬ap¬∇. The semantic connections among the alleged cognates of Greek 'place', Anglo-Saxon 'tolerate', Afroasiatic 'know', and Dravidian 'appointed time' are obscure.

37. 'Deer': *ʔEl/li. Dolgopolsky states that 'the origin of h- is mysterious in the Ge'ez form'. It is reminiscent, however, of other Semitic ʔ and h alternations (e.g. Form IV of the perfect in Hebrew vs Arabic/Aramaic).

38. '(Young) deer': *boča. Arabic bðx means 'haughty, proud' (Wehr 1974, 48; Lane 1863.I, 173). Lane (1863.I) also cites biðx and baðix 'a camel that brays much' and baiðax 'corpulent woman'.

41. 'Bull; calf': *čuRV. I do not believe many historical linguists would agree with the cognates: Arabic Θawr 'bull' and English steer. The latter < Proto-Indo-European *stā- 'stand', whereas the Arabic has nothing at all to do with that root (*The American Heritage College Dictionary* (1993, 1330); the IE etymologies are penned by Harvard University's well-known Indo-Europeanist, Calvert Watkins).

46. 'Wild boar': *ʕ∇p¬∇r∇. Since this word only occurs in Arabic and Indo-European, is it not possible to view it as a borrowing? The same Semitic root means 'dust'.

49. 'Kid, young goat': *gadi. This root is a good example of a look-alike. The explanation that Proto-Indo-European has /ay/ before the /d/, whereas Afroasiatic has /iy/ after the /d/ by metathesis is *ad hoc*.

52. 'Small carnivore': *k¬un/ñ∇(ŕ∇). Why is the Arabic <qndr> 'beaver' cited as 'with unknown vowels'? This word does not occur in Wehr (1974) nor in Lane (1863). Doniach (1972, 106) gives the very close qundus as one of three possible translations for 'beaver'.

54. '(A kind of) fig tree': *ʒ/ǯugb∇. Arabic ʔazgab- means 'grape-vine' (Lane 1863.III, 1234), and not a 'big fig tree'. The Central Chadic acúwa 'fig tree' cited by Dolgopolsky is *not* the Proto-Central Chadic *tiyin- cited by Orël & Stolbova (1995, 502).

55. 'Edible cereals or fruit': *b[i]ŕ[uw]qa. The Arabic 'terebinth tree' is buṭm ~ buṭum (Lane 1863.I, 219), and *not* the forms cited (p. 53).

64. 'To bake': *ʔäPHi. The Arabic cognate is mīfan with a short /a/ — not a long one (Leslau 1987, 10). How is Pero ápò 'bake' reconciled with Proto-West Chadic *has- 'roast, bake' (Orël & Stolbova 1995, 275)?

65. 'Food made of ground cereals, flour': *qUbźⱯ. The Afroasiatic evidence is contradicted by Chadic data which point to *xu- as a prefix, according to Orël & Stolbova (1995, 298–9). They, however, reconstruct Proto-Afroasiatic *xubuʒ- 'cereal'.

Sergei A. Starostin (this volume) questions the Altaic data. Leslau (1987, 257) cites Arabic xubz as being a Ge'ez loanword, according to Theodor Nöldeke. Leslau (1987) even doubts the connection with the false Hebrew cognate, hăbittīm 'pans for baking'. Thus, it is difficult to reconstruct this as a Proto-Semitic word, let alone a Proto-Afroasiatic one.

66. 'Meat': *[ʔ]omśa. The cited Arabic forms are not to be found in Wehr (1974) nor in Lane (1863).

70. 'Soft parts of the animal's body': *ń[a]K¬U. Arabic niqy- 'marrow' is not to be found in Wehr (1974) nor in Lane (1863). It seems that very obscure Arabic words often figure in the equation.

The Proto-Turkic *yakri and Proto-Indo-European *yek^{w}ṛ(t-) seem a long way from Proto-Nostratic ńaḳU.

71. 'Egg': *muǹa(-t/dⱯ). There are six listings for 'testicle' and six different roots for 'egg' in Orël & Stolbova (1995). Not one of these coincides with the data presented here.

The reconstruction is not quite the same in Bomhard & Kerns (1994, 671), viz. *mun- or *mon-, which = Illič-Svityč (1971.II, 72–3) *muɲa.

72. 'Egg or white of egg' (sic.) for 'egg white': *ʔuħ/xi. I could not find any attestation of the cited ʔawħ or ʔāħ 'egg white' in Syro-Lebanese Arabic. Seven native speakers consulted had never heard it. They all used bayāḍ ilbēḏa or ilbayāḏ.

It is difficult to see how Old Japanese u enters the picture here. I leave my comment preceding as is for I had no way of knowing when I originally wrote that sentence that Starostin would note that the datum (attributed to him by Dolgopolsky) is erroneous. Starostin says this was an error in his paper, and also commented orally at the conference on the source of the error.

74. 'Fish': *doTgiHU. It is difficult to see the connection between Hebrew dāɣ and Standard Japanese ùo. Could the latter word be a Chinese borrowing from ü with a second tone (Pinyin yú)?

Cf. Bomhard & Kerns (1994, 269) = Illič-Svityč (1971.I, 219) no. 67, *diga.

79. 'Honey': *madu. Orël & Stolbova (1995) give three different roots for 'honey'. None of them is close to Proto-Nostratic *madu. Ehret (1995, 126) gives Proto-Afroasiatic *-dăb- ~ *-dĭb- > Arabic dibs. Cf. Bomhard & Kerns (1994, 665–6), who reconstruct *madw- ~ *mədw-.

83. 'Stone': *kiw[∇]hE. The Ge'ez and Arabic forms are taken from Leslau (1987, 280). Why does the author not mention in his comparisons Hebrew koaḥ 'strength', which according to two authorities belongs here (quoted by Leslau 1987)? This is odd, especially when one considers the fact that Dolgopolsky usually lists unnecessary cognates to establish the intended comparison, e.g. mentioning several modern South Arabian languages for one gloss where one would suffice.

84. 'Trunk (log)': *boruʕ/ɣ∇. Leslau (1987, 102) states that Akkadian burū is connected here by von Soden 'with reservations'. It is somewhat strange that von Soden, an expert Semitist, can express doubt about an Akkadian cognate in his realm of Semitic linguistics, whereas the author connects this word with English bridge.

The Syriac cognate listed is incorrect. It should be būryā.

90. 'Thorn, hook' (< 'tooth'): *ʔeẑeKU. The cited šikk-at 'weapon, edge' is perhaps related to Arabic šakk-at 'jab (with the point of a weapon)' listed in Wehr (1974, 481). Lane (1863.IV, 1583) glosses šikk-at as 'arms or weapons that are worn'. A much better proposal for a cognate to Biblical Hebrew šek 'thorn', pl. šikkīm (p. 71) is Arabic šawk 'thorns' (Wehr 1974, 494). This could be an irregular sibilant correspondence, since normally Arabic s = Hebrew š. How can all of the aforementioned relate with Proto-Turkic *il- 'hang on (smth.)'?

95. 'Hide, skin': *t¬o[w]qa. Bole ḍiší <Proto-Afroasiatic *dihus and Proto-Chadic *diHus- 'hide, skin', not *ḍk (Orël & Stolbova 1995, 160). Further, this is related to Arabic dahasa 'to cut; skin' (Orël & Stolbova 1995).

98. '(Kind of) bark, skin': *k¬oRup¬∇. Leslau (1987, 440) states that qarb 'eyelid' is a secondary formation from qərnəb. Thus it cannot be listed, since it was originally a quadriliteral.

99. 'To skin, to bark': *K¬ož∇. Arabic qašā is not listed in Wehr (1974) nor is it in Lane (1863). The equation of this with Classical Mongolian qoltusum ~ qoltasum seems far-fetched.

100. 'Piece of leather (used especially as footwear)': *K¬oR∇Hp¬/p∇. The proposed Proto-Chadic *krp is Proto-Afroasiatic *kabel/r 'shoe, sandal', according to Orël & Stolbova (1995, 308), which they further derive from *kab- 'shoe, sandal'. Paul Newman (pers. comm., 15 June 1998) has some severe reservations about the aforementioned Proto-Chadic reconstruction.

105. 'Sinciput': *t¬EqmE. Unfortunately, the phonetic gymnastics, including metathesis, strains credulity.

109. A woman of the other exogamous moiety: *kälu/ǘ. Is it not strange that this root survives only in Semitic and not in the rest of Afroasiatic?

114. 'Father, head of a family': *Hić/cx∇. Leslau (1987, 210) states that Dillmann connects this root with Arabic jzy reward. Dolgopolsky does not mention this connection, which must mean he does not accept it. However, he posits Hungarian ös 'ancestor' as a cognate, along with Classical Mongolian eʒen 'lord'!

115. 'Pater familias' (or 'owner'?): *ʔediN∇. The above-mentioned Classical Mongolian eʒen is cited as a cognate here, too! However, this time < Proto-Altaic *edin. The previous gloss did not cite a Proto-Altaic form. Why not?

One normally refers to Palmyrene (Aramaic) and not 'Palmyrian' (p. 91). Cf. Lipiński (1997, 667). Dolgopolsky does, however, use the correct term on p. 96.

116–18. 'Mother, mommy, daddy': *ʔemA; *ʔ[ä]y∇; *ʔaba. The author's discussion is marred by his own admission: 'The common origin of Hamito-Semitic, Altaic, and Dravidian stems is questionable, since each of these may be an independent nursery word creation' (p. 94). These types of words cannot be used for reconstruction purposes, as is well known.

Skinner (1996) also includes words of this type; e.g. 'mother' = Hausa māma (which also means 'breast' (1996, 195)). One must be careful using the comparisons offered in this book.

121. 'To make magic, cast spells': *ʔarba. The author states that the Biblical Hebrew ʔrb < *'be cunning'. The Arabic (uncited) ʔariba could belong here (= 'be skillful'), but not Arabic ʔaraba 'tighten' (Wehr 1974, 12). Old Arabic ʔaruba 'be cunning' is cited by Lane (1863.I, 44).

123. 'To exercise magic force': *ʕ/ɣal/l∇. Arabic šiwāṭ ~ šuwáṭ 'injure' is not to be found in Wehr nor in Lane (1863). Arabic šayyaṭa means 'to burn', and *not* 'expose (smbd.) to death, to ruin' (Wehr 1974, 497). Also, we read that Arabic šṭn means 'oppose (smbd.)'; rather, it means 'fasten' (Wehr 1974, 472). Arabic štm is another (unconnected) root and should not, in my view, be listed here.

124. 'To tell a story, pronounce magic\ritual texts': *tul∇. The cited Arabic tuwal-'magic art, witchcraft' is not listed in Wehr (1974) nor in Lane (1863). (It should be noted that no. 125 on p. 116 = no. 124; no. 124 on p. 116 = no. 123, etc.)

Conclusion

The science of etymology is first and foremost an exercise in being reasonable. A careful etymologist working within the domain of Afroasiatic is Wolf Leslau, who consistently hesitates to accept 'unlikely' connections which are improbable à la Dillmann; e.g. Ge'ez qās 'drawers covering the thigh' and Arabic kawt (1987, 445). Another cautious etymologist, the late Robert Austerlitz whom we have mentioned previously, examined the proposed Nostratic cognates to Indo-European polis 'city' (advanced by Illič-Svityč 1971–84.3), and concludes that it is 'more reasonable' (1991, 360) to assume borrowing rather than a genetic relationship. This is also, in part, my conclusion about Dolgopolsky's Nostratic comparisons offered in *NM*. It is far more reasonable to assume that either linguistic borrowing through language contact or pure chance accounts for the similarities among the languages discussed in *NM*.[15] Thus the Nostratic hypothesis must remain just that — a hypothesis, and an extremely unlikely one to boot!

Notes

1. I quite agree with Dixon, who proclaims that it is unlikely that we will ever be able to prove monogenesis or polygenesis, and it will 'never be possible for linguists to recover the structure of 'proto-World' . . . (1997, 143). M. Picard is highly critical of what he calls the 'general lack of concern for precision and rigor' exemplified by global etymologists Merritt Ruhlen and John D. Bengtson (in a co-authored chapter 'Global Etymologies' in Ruhlen (1994). It is tempting to compare Picard's finicky points against global etymologies with exactly the same points one can launch against Nostratic etymologies.

    Bender (1993) has also examined the case of global etymologies and has concluded that they are 'an illusion' (1993, 203). I think that an overwhelming percentage of today's linguists would totally agree with him. His current position further substantiates his (1969) investigation in which he demonstrated:

> For languages from unrelated families, the occurrence of 'cognates' based on establishing CVC correspondences is indeed random and follows the Poisson approximation to the normal distribution quite closely . . . Types and degrees of language contact phenomena, and ways of separating such phenomena from those of genetic relationship may not be susceptible to purely mathematical determination. The best that can be expected at this point is that mathematics can tell us whether it is worthwhile looking for genetic relationship in cases where it is not obvious (1969, 530–31).

2. Pedersen (1931, 338) mentions 'Nostratic languages' only twice in his final chapter, Chapter 8, 'Linguistic affinities of the Indo-Europeans, home, and civilization'. He defines the term as encompassing the world's most highly civilized nations together with degraded polar races and perhaps negroes' (Pedersen 1931). The concluding sentence of the book is still, in my opinion, valid 74 years after publication: 'Or will it all resolve itself into a suspicion that all the languages of the earth are related to one another — a doctrine which, in spite of Trombetti's eloquent plea, we still have no prospect of proving, or even of beginning to prove? (sic.)' (p. 339).

3. Dixon (1997, 44) is unafraid to call it as he sees it: 'There is no reputable historical linguist, anywhere in the world, who accepts the claims of Greenberg and the Nostraticists'. Further: 'These "trained comparativists" have been "trained" by aficionados of the Nostratic school . . . No more need be said' (1997, 135, note 11). And finally, Dixon (1997, 40) calls the alleged Nostratic cognates 'phono-semantic lookalikes (sic.)' (quoting James A. Matisoff) and 'spectacular — but vacuous — speculations' (1997, 44), and also refers to Nostratic linguistics as 'nonsensical' (1997, 39, note 8). Finally, he expresses critical sentiments towards non-linguists; e.g. Colin Renfrew's *Archaeology and Language* (London: Jonathan Cape, 1987): '[he] lacks an appropriate training in the methodology of historical linguistics for his work to constitute a linguistically significant contribution to the debate' (1997, 48, note 15).

It is important to note that the 'long rangers' do occasionally feel persecuted. Greenberg (forthcoming a, 2) writes: 'The genetic interpretation of widespread resemblance in both sound and meaning in large groups of languages, e.g. in the Americas, as somehow due to language contact over vast areas and in the most stable elements of language, however implausible on common sense grounds, is basically a reaction by specialists to any evidence of wider connections which would sometimes put in jeopardy their languages and/or falsify already published negative statements'. Greenberg (1997a) remarks that Edward Sapir's 'Algic' stock (= Algonquian, Wiyot, and Yurok) took 43 years to become accepted; however, years before Mary R. Haas proved Sapir right about his classification, it was Greenberg who pointed out to her that he thought Sapir was correct on the matter (1997a, 670).

4. This does not imply that all Russian linguists endorse the Nostratic hypothesis. See Anttila & Embleton (1988, 85), who ask why Boris A. Serebrennikov's article was used to represent the anti-Nostratic position in Shevoroshkin & Markey (1986), when presumably, there are better essays which do the job more effectively.

5. According to Ringe (1992, 1), 'the consensus of opinion among mainstream historical linguists is that while all human languages are likely to be genetically related, the remoter relationships cannot be demonstrated by reliable linguistic methods because the languages in question have diverged too much'. This statement seems hyperbolic, since there are quite a few mainstream historical linguists, including this writer, who do not fit into that categorization. In the last century, William Dwight Whitney, although an Indo-Europeanist, proclaimed that all American Indian languages 'prob-

ably are all descended from a single parent language' (quoted in Haas 1978, 141).

6. Hamp notes, quite correctly (1992, 97): 'Only later did Verner and Leskien improve the strictness of requirement for phonological correspondences to the point where unerring equations were (and are) demanded and thoroughly non-obvious equations became possible and convincing. After this it was possible for Pedersen to assert with confidence that Albanian gj [ǵ] or [ɟ] is the regular reflex of Indo-European *ś- before IE accented syllabic.'

7. One would do well to heed the warning of Johanna Nichols (1996, 65): 'Perhaps the greatest single need in this area is for nonlinguists to be made aware of just how much genetic diversity exists among the world's languages'. She is also of the opinion that 'paleodemography and linguistic geography support polygenesis' (1998, 165).

8. I agree with Johanna Nichol's perspective (1996, 52): 'Kaiser and Shevoroshkin (1988, 313–15) offer grammatical evidence for Nostratic which again consists of individual endings and lexical roots of fairly abstract semantics, with no requirement of paradigmaticity. Taken as individual root morphemes, such comparative evidence has a high probability of occurrence and is not even close to individual-identifying; that is, it is of no diagnostic value'.

9. There is surely an affinity between linguistics and archaeology as Renfrew (1987) and Mallory (1989) clearly demonstrate. However, other works, such as Mellars (1998) and his large bibliography (1998, 109–15), are less relevant for the Nostratic hypothesis in that they focus on the more distant past.

10. It was Greenberg (1950) which originally discussed Greenberg's ideas on Hamito-Semitic classification. Trask (1996, 385) also erroneously states that Greenberg 'scrapp[ed] the venerable but clearly creaky "Hamito-Semitic" family in favour of an Afro-Asiatic family', not realizing that both of these today are merely different names for the same family. Greenberg was, however, the originator of the South Cushitic subbranch of Cushitic and refined some earlier notions about Chadic, etc. *NM* uses the creaky term.

11. I do not wish to minimize the importance of semantic changes. As with the examples in the phonological realm, one must strive, at all times, to be reasonable. There are consistencies in semantic changes cross-linguistically, which allow for plausible semantic developments (see Wilkins 1996, 298–300 for details).

12. Mozeson (1989) is one such sad example which preaches monogenesis. One of the quotes on the back cover (blurb) of the volume summarizes what it contains: 'Fascinating . . . you have gone further than anyone in developing the concept of Hebrew as the mother of all languages'. (Rabbi Pinchas Stolper, Executive Vice-President, Union of Orthodox Jewish Congregation [sic.] of America). The tone of the alleged cognates presented is set by the author (1989, 3): 'Only after mastering Hebrew can a person fully understand words in English, Basque, or Swahili'.

Another even sadder specimen of 'scholarship' along these lines is Ismail (1989). It is most difficult to say anything at all about this book lest it be dignified. Other recent misuses of similarity (see Hamp 1992) include Josephson (1987), Key (1981), and Key (1984). Campbell (1997b, 261) rightly dismisses this latter publication as 'far-fetched'. I have already commented in print on a classic illustration from yesteryear (Kaye 1988, viz. Leesberg 1903). Need I say more? To be sure, there are numerous other authors who misuse similarity. Incidentally, Campbell (1997b, 206–59) has a fine discussion of the methodology used to determine distant genetic relationships in addition to the proposals concerning various American Indian languages (1997b,

260–329), including Nostratic-Amerind (1997b, 328–9).

And, of course, in the age of the internet, web sites, and the information superhighway, one is now confronted with Proto-Nostratic and Proto-Language (= Proto-World) essays (see Ryan & Ishinan 1998). Ehret (1995) is, incidentally, the source used for Afroasiatic therein. One example of Ryan & Ishinan's cognates may suffice (no. 4): IE eir- 'pole' = Arabic ʔayr 'penis'.

13. Paul Newman (pers. comm., June 1998) is correct to remark here that 'a specific shared ASYMMETRY in a pronominal SYSTEM can indeed be significant in demonstrating relatedness', the details of which can be found in Newman (1980, 15ff.).

14. See the solid discussion in Nichols (1996, 52–6, 64–7). Proto-Nostratic *wete 'water' is mentioned as possibly occurring in ten to fifteen of the world's languages totally by chance. Although the numbers 10–15 might not be correct, surely no one can argue with the approximation 'a few'. Ringe (manuscript b) demonstrates that if one compares 68 languages, the probability of finding a match of a CVC root is over 90 per cent. Multilateral comparison, according to this essay, gives results 'easily within the expected range of chance resemblances' (manuscript b, 3).

15. I must caution the reader that there are many typographical and stylistic infelicities in the book, some of which have been pointed out in the text (typical are examples, such as *aspect* for *aspects*, p. 98, or '. . . but are not any more today', which occurs twice in succession in the same paragraph, p. 18).

I would also like to mention that I do not comprehend why scripts were used in this book, although they are impressive, beautiful, and certainly take up considerable space; e.g. Hebrew, Syriac, Ethiopic, Greek, Cyrillic, Arabic — but not Armenian, Devanāgari, Japanese, Korean, Mongolian, etc. The comparative linguist does not need reference in any script; rather, all that is needed is an accurate (phonemic) IPA transcription.

Acknowledgements

I wish to thank Paul Newman for reading a preliminary version of this essay and making a number of very valuable suggestions, most of which I have been able to incorporate. I am also grateful to my student, Laurence Surfas, who offered many useful comments which led to an improved final version, and to Wolf Leslau, with whom I had the opportunity to review many of the issues I discuss in this endeavour. Joseph H. Greenberg also offered useful comments. Needless to say, the usual disclaimers apply.

References

Abel, C., 1886. *Einleitung in ein Aegyptisch-Semitisch-Indoeuropaeisches Wurzelwörterbuch.* Wiesbaden: Dr Martin Sändij.

Anderson, N., 1879. *Studien zur Vergleichung der indogermanischen und finnisch-ugrischen Sprachen.* Leipzig: K.F. Koehler.

Anttila, R. & S. Embleton, 1988. Review of Shevoroshkin & Markey (1986). *Canadian Journal of Linguistics* 33(1), 79–89.

Asher, R.E. (ed.), 1994. *The Encyclopedia of Language and Linguistics*. 10 vols. Oxford: Pergamon Press.

Austerlitz, R., 1991. Alternatives in long-range comparison, in Lamb & Mitchell (eds.), 353–64.

Baldi, P. (ed.), 1990. *Linguistic Change and Reconstruction Methodology*. Berlin: Mouton de Gruyter.

Bender, M.L., 1969. Chance CVC correspondences in unrelated languages. *Language* 45(3), 519–31.

Bender, M.L., 1993. Are global etymologies valid? *General Linguistics* 33(4), 191–210.

Bengtson, J. & M. Ruhlen, 1997. In defense of multilateral comparison. *California Linguistic Notes* 25(1), 3–4, 57.

Blažek, V., 1989. Materials for global etymologies, in Shevoroshkin 1989a, 37–40.

Bomhard, A., 1984. *Toward Proto-Nostratic*. Amsterdam: John Benjamins.

Bomhard, A., 1990. A survey of the comparative phonology of the so-called Nostratic languages, in Baldi (ed.), 331–58.

Bomhard, A., 1996. *Reconstructing Proto-Nostratic: Comparative Phonology, Morphology, and Vocabulary*. Charleston (SC): Signum.

Bomhard, A. & J.C. Kerns, 1994. *The Nostratic Macrofamily*. Berlin: Mouton de Gruyter.

Bright, W. (ed.), 1992. *International Encyclopedia of Linguistics*. 4 vols. Oxford: Oxford University Press.

Brunner, L., 1969. *Die gemeinsamen Wurzeln des semitischen und indogermanischen Wortschatzes*. Bern: Francke Verlag.

Callaghan, C.A., 1980. An Indo-European type paradigm in Proto Eastern Miwok, in Klar *et al.* (eds.), 331–8.

Campbell, L., 1997a. Amerindian personal pronouns: a second opinion. *Language* 73, 339–51.

Campbell, L., 1997b. *American Indian Languages: the Historical Linguistics of Native America*. Oxford: Oxford University Press.

Cardona, G., H.M. Hoenigswald & A. Senn (eds.), 1970. *Indo-European and Indo-Europeans*. Philadelphia (PA): University of Pennsylvania Press.

Comrie, B., 1992. Altaic languages, in Bright (ed.), vol. I, 47–51.

Cooper, J. & G.M. Schwartz (eds.), 1996. *The Study of the Ancient Near East in the 21st Century*. Winona Lake (IN): Eisenbrauns.

Davis, G.L. & G. Iverson (eds.), 1992. *Explanation in Historical Linguistics*. Amsterdam: John Benjamins.

Dixon, R.M.W., 1997. *The Rise and Fall of Languages*. Cambridge: Cambridge University Press.

Dolgopolsky, A., 1994. Nostratic, in Asher (ed.), vol. 5, 2838.

Dolgopolsky, A., 1998. *The Nostratic Macrofamily and Linguistic Palaeontology*. (Papers in the Prehistory of Languages.) Cambridge: The McDonald Institute for Archaeological Research.

Doniach, N.S., 1972. *The Oxford English–Arabic Dictionary of Current Usage*. Oxford: Oxford University Press.

Durie, N. & M. Ross (eds.), 1996. *The Comparative Method Reviewed*. Oxford: Oxford University Press.

Dyen, I., 1970. Background noise or evidence in comparative linguistics: the case of the Austronesian-Indo-European hypothesis, in Cardona *et al.* (eds.), 431–40.

Ehret, C., 1995. *Reconstructing Proto-Afrasiatic (Proto-Afrasian)*. Berkeley (CA): University of California Press.

Gamkrelidze, T.V. & V.V. Ivanov, 1990. The early history of Indo-European languages. *Scientific American* (March), 110–16.

Gordon, C.H., 1965. *Ugaritic Textbook*. Rome: Pontificium Institutum Biblicum.

Gragg, G.B., 1982. *Oromo Dictionary*. East Lansing: African Studies Center, Michigan State University.

Greenberg, J.H., 1950. Studies in African linguistic classification, part IV: Hamito-Semitic. *Southwestern Journal of Anthropology* 6, 47–63.

Greenberg, J.H., 1963. *The Languages of Africa*. Bloomington (IN): Supplement to *International Journal of American Linguistics*. (Correction from Stanford University Press, *NM*, p. xxi.)

Greenberg, J.H., 1987. *Language in the Americas*. Stanford (CA): Stanford University Press.

Greenberg, J.H., 1997a. Mary Haas, Algic, and the scientific consensus. *Anthropological Linguistics* 39(4), 668–72.

Greenberg, J.H., 1997b. The Indo-European first and second person pronouns in the perspective of Eurasiatic, especially Chukotkan. *Anthropological Linguistics* 39(2), 187–95.

Greenberg, J.H., forthcoming a. Are there mixed languages?, in *A Festschrift for V. Ivanov.*

Greenberg, J.H., forthcoming b. Does Altaic exist? Proofs version marked 'forthcoming', in *A Festschrift for V. Shevoroshkin.*

Greenberg, J.H. & M. Ruhlen, 1992. Linguistic origins of native Americans. *Scientific American* 267(5), 94–9.

Haas, M.R., 1969. *The Prehistory of Languages*. The Hague: Mouton.

Haas, M.R., 1978. *Language, Culture, and History*. Stanford (CA): Stanford University Press.

Hagman, H., 1990. Tracking mother (sic.) of 5000 tongues. *Insight* (February 5), 54–5.

Hamp, E.P., 1992. On misusing similarity, in Davis & Iverson (eds.), 95–103.

Hock, H., 1993. SWALLOTALES: Chance and the 'world etymology' MALIQ'A 'swallow, throat'. *Chicago Linguistics Society* 29, 215–38.

Hodge, C.T., 1972. Lisramic. *Language Sciences* 20, 13–16.

Hodge, C.T., 1998. Continuing toward Nostratic. *Eurasian Studies Yearbook* 70, 15–27.

Illič-Svityč, V.N., 1971–84. *Essays of Comparison of the Nostratic Languages* (= *Opyt Sravnenija Nostraticheskikh Jazykov*). 3 vols. Moscow: Nauka.

Ismail, T.A., 1989. *Classic Arabic as the Ancestor of Indo-Europian* (sic.) *Languages and Origin of Speech* (sic.). Cairo: AL Ahram Press (sic.).

Jablonski, N.G. & L.C. Aiello (eds.), 1998. *The Origin and Diversification of Language.* (Wattis Symposium Series in Anthropology; Memoirs of the California Academy of Science 24.) San Francisco (CA): California Academy of Sciences.

Jasanoff, J. & A. Nussbaum, 1996. Word games: the linguistic evidence in Black Athena, in Lefkowitz & Rogers (eds.), 177–205.

Joseph, B. & J. Salmons, 1998. *Nostratic: Sifting the Evidence*. Amsterdam: John Benjamins.

Josephson, N.S., 1987. *Greek Linguistic Elements in the Polynesian Languages*. Heidelberg: Carl Winter Universittsverlag.

Kaiser, M. & V. Shevoroshkin, 1988. Nostratic. *Annual Review of Anthropology* 17, 309–29.

Kaye, A.S., 1975. Review of Swadesh (1971). *Romance Philology* 29, 241–8.

Kaye, A.S., 1985. Review of Bomhard (1984). *Language* 61(4), 887–8.

Kaye, A.S., 1988. Review of Shevoroshkin and Markey (1986). *Journal of Afroasiatic Languages* 2(2), 222–6.

Kaye, A.S., 1992. Distant genetic relationship and Edward Sapir. *Semiotica* 91(3/4), 273–300.

Kaye, A.S., 1996. Review of Ehret (1995). *Canadian Journal of Linguistics* 41(3), 278–82.

Kaye, A.S., 1997. Review of Orël & Stolbova (1995). *Bulletin of the School of Oriental and African Studies* 69(2), 365–7.

Kaye, A.S. & P. Daniels, 1992. Comparative Afroasiatic and general genetic linguistics. *Word* 43(3), 429–58.

Key, M.R., 1981. *Intercontinental Linguistic Connections*. Irvine (CA): University of California, Irvine.

Key, M.R., 1984. *Polynesian and American Linguistic Connections*. Lake Bluff (IL): Jupiter Press.

Klar, K., M. Langdon & S. Silver (eds.), 1980. *American Indian and Indo-European Studies: Papers in Honor of Madison S. Beeler.* The Hague: Mouton.

Krebernik, M., 1996. The linguistic classification of Eblaite: methods, problems, and results, in Cooper & Schwartz (eds.), 233–49.

Lamb, S.M. & E.D. Mitchell (eds.), 1991. *Sprung from Some Common Source: Investigations into the Prehistory of Languages.* Stanford (CA): Stanford University Press.

Lane, E.W., 1863. *An Arabic–English Lexicon*. 8 vols. London: Williams & Norgate.

Lass, R., 1997. *Historical Linguistics and Language Change*. Cambridge: Cambridge University Press.

Leesberg, A.C.M., 1903. *Comparative Philology: a Comparison Between Semitic and American Languages*. Leiden: E.J. Brill.

Lefkowitz, M. & G. Rogers (eds.), 1996. *Black Athena Revisited*. Chapel Hill (NC): University of North Carolina Press.

Lehmann, W.P., 1970. Linguistic structure as diachronic evidence on proto-culture, in Cardona *et al.* (eds.), 1–10.

Lehmann, W.P., 1994. DCM [distant comparison] vs CM [comparative method]. *California Linguistic Notes* 24(2), 1, 3.

Leslau, W., 1987. *Comparative Dictionary of Ge'ez*. Wiesbaden: Otto Harrassowitz.

Levin, S., 1995. *Semitic and Indo-European: the Principal Etymologies*. Amsterdam: John Benjamins.

Lipiński, E., 1997. *Semitic Languages: Outline of a Comparative Grammar*. Leuven: Peeters.

McMahon, A.M.S., 1994. *Understanding Language Change*. Cambridge: Cambridge University Press.

Mallory, J.P., 1989. *In Search of the Indo-Europeans: Language, Archaeology and Myth*. London: Thames and Hudson.

Martin, S.E., 1991. Recent research on the relationships of Japanese and Korean, in Lamb & Mitchell (eds.), 269–92.

Meillet, A., 1958. *Linguistique historique et linguistique générale*. Paris: Champion.

Mellars, P., 1998. Neanderthals, Modern Humans and the archaeological evidence for language, in Jablonski & Aiello (eds.), 89–115.

Miller, R.A., 1991. Genetic connections among the Altaic languages, in Lamb & Mitchell (eds.), 293–327.

Möller, H., 1906. *Semitisch und Indogermanisch*, Teil 1: *Konsonanten*. Kopenhagen: H. Hagerup.

Möller, H., 1911. *Vergleichendes indogermanisch-semitisches Wörterbuch*. Göttingen: Vandenhoeck and Ruprecht.

Moscati, S., A. Spitaler, E. Ullendorff & W. von Soden, 1964. *An Introduction to the Comparative Grammar of the Semitic Languages*. Edited by S. Moscati. Wiesbaden: Otto Harrassowitz.

Mozeson, I.E., 1989. *The Word: the Dictionary that Reveals the Hebrew Source of English*. New York (NY): Shapolsky Publishers.

Murra, J., R.M. Hankin & F. Holling, 1951. *The Soviet Linguistic Controversy*. New York (NY): Kings Crown Press.

Newman, P., 1977. Chadic classification and reconstructions. *Afroasiatic Linguistics* 5, 1–42.

Newman, P., 1980. *The Classification of Chadic within Afroasiatic*. Leiden: Universitaire Pers.

Newman, P., 1995. *On Being Right: Greenberg's African Linguistic Classification and the Methodological Principles which Underlie It*. Bloomington (IN): Nigerian Languages Institute and African Studies Program, Indiana University.

Nichols, J., 1996. The comparative method as heuristic, in Durie & Ross (eds.), 39–71.

Nichols, J., 1998. The origin and dispersal of languages: linguistic evidence, in Jablonski & Aiello (eds.), 127–70.

Nichols, J. & D.A. Peterson, 1996. The Amerind personal pronouns. *Language* 72, 336–71.

Orël, V. & O. Stolbova, 1995. *Hamito-Semitic Etymological Dictionary*. Leiden: E.J. Brill.

Payne, J.R., 1992. Iranian languages, in Bright (ed.), 228–33.

Pedersen, H., 1931 (orig. 1924). *The Discovery of Language*. Trans. by J.W. Spargo. Bloomington (IN): Indiana University Press.

Picard, M., 1998. The case against global etymologies: evidence from Algonquian. *International Journal of American Linguistics* 64(2), 141–7.

Polomé, E., 1982. *Language, Society, and Paleoculture*. Stanford (CA): Stanford University Press.

Renfrew, C., 1987. *Archaeology and Language: the Puzzle of Indo-European Origins*. Cambridge: Cambridge University Press.

Renfrew, C., 1991. The origins of the Indo-European languages, in Wang (ed.) [originally 1989], 46–58.

Renfrew, C., 1998. The origins of world linguistic diversity: an archaeological perspective, in Jablonski & Aiello (eds.), 171–92.

Ringe, D.A., 1992. *On Calculating the Factor of Chance in Language Comparison*. Philadelphia (PA): The American Philosophical Society.

Ringe, D.A., manuscript a. The problem of binary comparison.

Ringe, D.A., manuscript b. How hard is it to match CVC-roots?

Ringe, D.A., 1995. Nostratic and the factor of chance. *Diachronica* 12(1), 55–74.

Ruhlen, M., 1989. Nostratic-Amerind cognates, in Shevoroshkin (ed.) 1989a, 75–83.

Ruhlen, M., 1991. *A Guide to the Worlds Languages*, vol. I. Stanford (CA): Stanford University Press [originally 1987].

Ruhlen, M., 1992. Multiregional evolution or Out of Africa: the linguistic evidence. Preliminary version. Symposium on Prehistoric Mongoloid Dispersals. Tokyo: The University of Tokyo. November 16, 1992.

Ruhlen, M., 1994. *On the Origin of Languages*. Stanford (CA): Stanford University Press.

Ryan, P.C. & Ishinan, 1998. Proto-language phonemes in IE and Afrasian (Egyptian and Arabic) (Nostratic hypothesis). World Wide Web: www.geocities.com/Athens/Forum/2803/comparison. AFRASIAN.3.html.

Salmons, J., 1992. A look at the data for a global etymology: *tik 'finger', in Davis & Iverson (eds.), 207–28.

Salmons, J., 1997. Global etymology as pre-Copernican linguistics. *California Linguistic Notes* 25(1), 5–7, 60.

Shevoroshkin, V. (ed.), 1989a. *Reconstructing Languages and Cultures*. Bochum: Brockmeyer.

Shevoroshkin, V. (ed.), 1989b. *Explorations in Language Macrofamilies*. Bochum: Brockmeyer.

Shevoroshkin, V., 1989c. A symposium on the deep reconstruction of languages and cultures, in Shevoroshkin (ed.) 1989a, 6–8.

Shevoroshkin, V. & A. Manaster Ramer, 1991. The remote relations of languages, in Lamb & Mitchell (eds.), 178–99.

Shevoroshkin, V. & T.L. Markey (eds.), 1986. *Typology, Relationship, and Time*. Ann Arbor (MI): Karoma.

Skinner, N., 1996. *Hausa Comparative Dictionary*. Cologne: Rüdiger Köppe Verlag.

Smith, N., 1989. *The Twitter Machine*. Oxford: Blackwell.

Starostin, S.A., 1989. Nostratic and Sino-Caucasian, in Shevoroshkin (ed.) 1989b, 42–66.

Steingass, F.J., 1884. *Arabic–English Dictionary*. New Delhi: Cosmo Publications. (Reprinted 1978.)

Swadesh, M., 1971. *The Origin and Diversification of Language*. Edited by J. Sherzer. Chicago (IL): Aldine-Atherton.

Sweet, H., 1900. *The History of Languages*. London: J.M. Dent.

Thomas, L.L., 1957. *The Linguistic Theories of N. Ja. Marr*. (University of California Publications in Linguistics 14.) Berkeley (CA): University of California Press.

Trask, R.L., 1996. *Historical Linguistics*. London: Arnold.

Wang, W.S-Y. (ed.), 1991. *The Emergence of Language: Development and Evolution*. New York (NY): W.H. Freeman.

Wehr, H., 1974. *A Dictionary of Modern Written Arabic*. Edited by J Milton Cowan. Wiesbaden: Otto Harrassowitz.

Wilkins, D.P., 1996. Semantic change and the search for cognates, in Durie & Ross (eds.), 264–304.

Zaborski, A., 1992. Afroasiatic languages, in Bright (ed.), vol. I, 36–7.

Chapter 17

The Dravidian perspective

Kamil V. Zvelebil

There is an evergrowing enthusiasm for linguistic superdivergence, resulting in drawing ever larger 'trees' and sooner or later combining Indo-European with South Caucasian, Uralic, Altaic, Elamite, Dravidian, Afro-Asiatic — and even Korean, Japanese and Eskimo-Aleut, if megalocomparison is pushed far enough. Holger Pedersen's '*nostratic*' macrofamily (although, if I am not mistaken, it was the famous British phonetician Henry Sweet, 1845–1912, who used the term round 1900 for the first time) is ardently enlarged. However, we should not forget that there may have been a converse process of convergence at work as the *historical norm*, whereby what are genetically unrelated and merely con-tiguous, neighbouring, or intertrading languages become fused into *Sprachbunde*; maybe, after all, Trubetzkoy *was* right (see Collinge 1995).

It has been suggested, as Colin Renfrew writes in his excellent and ex-tremely lucidly and elegantly written Introduction to Dolgopolsky's *The Nostratic Macrofamily and Linguistic Palaeontology* (hereafter *NM*), that individual lin-guists tend to be either 'lumpers' or 'splitters'. I don't think I belong to either group exclusively, and yet I agree with Renfrew that to say, as Dixon does, that no 'respectable historical linguist anywhere in the world' would accept the claims of the Nostraticists, is to close the eyes to ever growing and pretty serious evi-dence. A dismissive tone like this can hardly be maintained in face of the word-lists offered by Dolgopolsky, even from the Dravidianist's point of view which is, after all, why I offer my comments. When we look at the sound-shapes and the meanings of a number of items, including a few grammatical features, we have to admit that *something other than chance* is operating. The question is, of course, what is it, this 'something other'.

On the other hand, the grammatical structure of the languages in ques-tion has so far been scarcely considered. Phonology and grammar must be taken rigorously into account; so-called multilateral comparison of lexical similarities is not sufficient to convince us.

I have tried — very briefly and rather impressionistically, to point out some lexical, phonological and morphosyntactic similarities in my valedictory lecture at Utrecht University in 1990 (Zvelebil 1991a), and again in a paper published in India in 1991 (Zvelebil 1991b), drawing attention to items chosen from Elamite, Dravidian, Mongolian and Japanese. This approach was inspired by Colin Renfrew's papers and his book of 1987. I hypothesized about the possibility of considering the existence of a linguistic phylum which would include Elamite and Dravidian, Altaic and Japanese. Looking at Dolgopolsky's work we have to face our first basic problem: not yet have all those 'families' which are taken for granted been equally established as far as their proto-forms are concerned; thus there is a great difference in precision and completeness between, say, a (still hypothetical but generally fully accepted and firmly established) Proto-Indo-European on the one hand, and Proto-Dravidian on the other hand (not to speak of, for example, a Proto-Altaic!). Second: some of these proto-families themselves are still extremely hypothetic and not at all generally accepted — witness, e.g. Elamo-Dravidian (which I am in favour of but which is certainly far from being so well and validly established as Indo-European; and yet it is taken almost for granted, even with its date of 10,000–8000 BCE, and even by a scholar as cautious as Colin Renfrew). Dolgopolsky's inclusion of Korean and Japanese in Altaic (and, consequently, within the Nostratic macrofamily) will certainly be hardly universally accepted. Renfrew, on p. xii, of his 'Introduction' mentions the disagreement between the Nostraticists and Greenberg in these rather fundamental matters of inclusion or non-inclusion of certain language families in the macrofamily. One consequence of all this is that, methodologically, the results based on, say, Proto-Indo-European, will be much more complete, precise, convincing and acceptable than the results gained, e.g. from Proto-Altaic or Proto-Dravidian.

Let me now offer some more concrete observations from the Dravidian perspective.

On pp. 5–8, Dolgopolsky offers what he calls 'classification' of the Nostratic languages. Speaking from the Dravidian perspective, I would hardly call this 'classification' (for the problems of classification of Dravidian, cf. the recent papers by Emeneau, Krishnamurti and myself, see references; Emeneau even maintains that 'it must by now be obvious that to attempt to count the Dravidian "languages" is still premature. No "theory" is likely to help us, in the still prevailing state of inadequate fieldwork and the data to be thereby provided'). However, Dolgopolsky promises us 'more detailed and comprehensive classification' in his *Nostratic Dictionary* under preparation. It is perhaps necessary to stress once more that, when it comes to Korean and Japanese, most linguists consider these two languages as having no known external affiliation; to classify them as 'Altaic' is hardly acceptable.

A Dravidianist can find only a small number of Proto-Dravidian reconstructions which would be either unacceptable or rather doubtful. Dolgopolsky has clearly worked very carefully with the *Dravidian Etymological Dictionary* (Burrow & Emeneau 1984) which is on the whole a most reliable source (although, as e.g. J. Vacek has recently attempted to show us [see references], even the entries in this great work will have to be reconsidered and probably rearranged; in a paper yet to be published Vacek says,

> many of the DEDR etyma seem to need re-arrangements, occasionally some of the items contain words which may better be related with other etyma either as whole lexical units, or the respective words have several meanings so different that they should rather be split according to the respective meanings into two [exceptionally even more] homophones with different etymological background. (Vacek in press)

Another very positive feature of the Dolgopolsky approach (I am again speaking from the Dravidian perspective) seems to be his caution and a great deal of common sense. Nevertheless, in a paper by Kaiser & Shevoroshkin (1988) it is stated that Dolgopolsky 'composed a list of the fifteen most stable lexemes', among which he has included, as the Proto-Dravidian reconstruction, 1st person plural inclusive ('we and you') as *ma-/*mā-, while Dravidian *nā-m is regarded as 'we-exclusive'. Now this is one of the points I cannot accept. It is the concensus among Dravidianists (e.g. Emeneau, Krishnamurti, Subrahmanyam, Zvelebil) that the 1st person inclusive is Proto-Dravidian *nā-m, while 1st person exclusive is reconstructed as *yā-m. The suggested reconstructed *ma-/*mā- is almost certainly a mistake.

When it comes to the reconstructible Nostratic lexical stock, I have (from the point of a Dravidianist) classified these reconstructions as (a) convincing, (b) ingenious but problematic/in need of additional comments, (c) weak and unconvincing. I have to admit that the first two groups represent a majority of cases, at least after a preliminary, somewhat hasty assessment, in spite of a certain degree of semantic 'looseness' or even undue latitude.

Let me quote as a rather convincing reconstruction no. 100 which posits something like *ḲVRVHp/pV, where capital letters denote 'classes of phonemes' and the symbol V an 'unspecified vowel' [with the meaning 'piece of leather (used esp. as footwear)']: this Dolgopolsky finds in Indo-European, Hamito-Semitic and Dravidian: for Indo-European, cf. e.g. Latin *carpisculum* '(a kind of) shoe' or Czech (old and dialectal) krp- 'high boot' (I would add: we find in older Czech literature krpec 'sandal', whereas the Czech škrpál 'light shoe' is a loanword from Italian scarpa); for Hamito-Semitic e.g. Kola krap, and for Dravidian, the correct reconstruction *ker-V-pp- 'footwear (sandals, etc.)'. Indeed, the Tamil, Malayalam etc. forms with the initial c- are secondary, due to palatalization under the impact of the following -e. The semantics, in general, fits well. Let us apply basic principles of historical-comparative method to this item:

1. There is identity or close similarity in meaning ('footwear');
2. There is general agreement in sound-shape (k + vowel + r + vowel + pp [vowel]);
3. We can explain differences in the sound-shapes (if any) by valid phonological rules (as e.g. Proto-Dravidian *k- before front vowels > c- [in Tamil-Malayalam etc.]);
4. If there are semantic differences, they are not so striking as to annul or endanger the underlying semantic identity/similarity (cf. all those meanings quoted under [100]);
5. We may more or less rule out borrowing or diffusion (this is indeed a problem, but as far as the Dravidian perspective is concerned, I believe the item is not an 'undetected loan').

Hence the conclusion, always tentative and very hypothetic would be: the Indo-European *kerəp-/*krep- in the meaning of 'a kind of footwear', the Hamito-Semitic *krp, 'footwear' and the Dravidian *kerVppV- 'footwear' indeed seem to be related, and (hence?) derived from a common source (the only alternative being borrowing/diffusion). It would seem to me to be — to say the least — very odd, almost unbelievable, that this close similarity in phonetic shape and in meaning should be attributed to 'pure' chance. However, even this item, this reconstruction is not quite unproblematic (*why the initial glottalization?*).

I find other more or less convincing or clever reconstructions (always, mind you, viewed from the Dravidianist's perspective) in items 2 + 4 (*Dravidian Etymological Dictionary* 2579 Tamil civiṅki 'Indian lynx; hunting leopard': Kannada sivaṅgi 'the tiger-wolf, the hyaena; a leopard used in hunting', Telugu civāgi etc. 'hyaena' where Dolgopolsky suggests that the Proto-Dravidian *civ-V-ṅk-i manifests a coalescence of two Nostratic etyma, 'leopard' and 'hyaena' — a clever and perhaps even plausible suggestion); in item 22 (to which I would add the Czech plural kotce [still in use] 'merchants' sheds, small market', cf. also English cottage); in items 37 plus 47 (where, if he is right, the Malto ilaru 'mouse deer' has to be removed from *Dravidian Etymological Dictionary* 476; but perhaps he is wrong, and the Proto-Dravidian reconstruction should rather be *ir-al-ay, not *il(ar)V- as he suggests, and the Malto form rather a case of metathesis!); in item 64 (Dravidian *avi- v. 'be boiled, cooked'); in item 67 (Dravidian kuṭ- 'intestines'); in items 71 (Dravidian *muṇṭ-ay > *muṭṭ-ay 'egg') etc. I do have a few remarks on several other entries in Dolgopolsky's list: thus item [11]: I would rather reconstruct Proto-Dravidian *cav-a/*cuv-a instead of simply *cava- 'brackish/saline earth' (cf. entry 2674[b] uvar in the etymological dictionary). I find the semantics in no. 20 rather unconvincing: 'white' (e.g. Latin): 'milk' (e.g. Hamito-Semitic): 'swan' (e.g. Czech): 'be clear (of liquids)' (Dravidian): this and other items show the author's immense erudition, along with an imagination somewhat unbridled. In item no. 23 I would rather reconstruct Proto-Dravidian *kuy- than *ku/oc-a (cf. the Kota and Toda forms); and there is a mistake in the Tulu form which should be kusave, not *kisave. In entry 62 there are a few slight mistakes: it is not the 'old' but the modern, contemporary Czech form mrkev, whereas the form mrkva is precisely Old Czech (incidentally, qualified as 'pre-IE' even in the Czech etymological dictionary of 1966/1978); the Old Indian forms should be muraṅgī-, muruṅgī- with long final vowel. Items 95–6: this may indeed be *one* etymon in Dravidian, not two (cf. the etymological dictionary entry 3559), reconstructible as *tol- < **tok-al (> toval) < ***tuk-al/*tol-k — <**tul-k-a > tokka (however complicated this may appear). Some entries must be taken with great caution (which Dolgopolsky admits): he is rather careful when it comes to entries 112, 116, 118, 123 etc., admitting, e.g. in 118, a 'questionable' common origin of the forms in question; explaining, in 116, the Dravidian *amma 'mother' rather as Lallwort-creation; admitting, for Dravidian *vanna '(elder) brother's wife' (item 112) a possibility of borrowing from Prakrit (although this caution is based on the quoted etymological dictionary).

There are, from the Dravidian perspective, reconstructions which I would certainly hesitate to accept. Thus entry 84, for two reasons: the semantics (Nostratic 'trunk' ('log'): Dravidian 'hilt of a sword') is not convincing and, besides, the Malayalam and Telugu forms contain mistakes. I would not accept item 87 because the Proto-Dravidian form should rather be *kaṟ-, and not *kaṇṇ- 'sprout, shoot' (cf. the etymological dictionary entries 1165, 1185, 1353 & 1370); the Dravidian *kāmp- certainly does not belong here.

One of the most striking examples of a non-acceptable procedure is found right in no. 1: the word for 'fig tree' is reconstructed as Nostratic *ʔibrE. The cognates are found only (!) in Hamito-Semitic and Dravidian. I cannot speak for Hamito-Semitic, but the Proto-Dravidian forms reconstructed as *ir-~iṟ- do not show any reflex of the Nostratic *-b-. The Proto-Dravidian reconstruction, according to Dolgopolsky, should be rather something like *ibr- which is impossible for Proto-Dravidian since the regular reflex of Nostratic medial *-b- should be Proto-Dravidian *-v-; hence, we would expect a Proto-Dravidian reconstruction *ivr-/*ivṟ-. But a Dravidianist's analysis will yield at best a Proto-Dravidian *itt- < **iṟt- (even this is not yet certain). So what has happened to the reflex of the Nostratic bilabial stop?

Another interesting entry is no. 75: '(a kind of) fish'. The problem with Dravidian is the length: the only possible Dravidian reconstruction is *mīn- (cf. Sanskrit mīna-), with long vowel. How to account for the length? By a laryngeal in pre-Dravidian (as Bh. Krishnamurti would probably suggest)? Let me stress once more that these are very preliminary remarks. I would also like to ask: is it in fact worthwhile to submit the Nostraticists' results — as presented so far — to a detailed, painstaking, time-consuming scrutiny? Can the relationship of the languages in question indeed be documented using the well-tried comparative methods of historical linguistics?

I do certainly agree with Colin Renfrew when he says that the 'prospect is . . . a very exciting one' (*NM*, ix). And let me also add that the courage and wisdom exhibited by Colin Renfrew when he made possible the organization of the Symposium on the Nostratic hypothesis in order to encourage research 'at the uncertain frontiers of knowledge' is to be admired and congratulated. I do therefore *not* agree with some opinions expressed thus far that the Symposium on which this book is based was premature. On the contrary, I would say that it is most useful and valuable, if only to give special attention to the two matters which are, to my mind, of fundamental importance; the *methodological problems* connected with the possibility to establish linguistic 'macrofamilies' in general; and the problem of perspective: do we need to, indeed, can we, with the help of current methodology, establish such 'macrofamilies'? Stated somewhat differently: is not the notion of a Nostratic hyperfamily rather a matter of *belief*? V. Blažek (1989) even speaks of 'global etymologies' and of something called 'Proto-World'. Soon we may find ourselves facing something that we could call 'Proto-Human' language. This I do find not only premature, but, at this state of our knowledge, rather rash, an exercise which is not based on standard, legitimate, and accepted methods of historical and comparative linguistics. When I see the Nostratic consonant chart, the reconstructed phonemic inventory (*NM*, 101) and as I try to find my way through the 'transcription signs and other symbols' on pp. 11–16 of the work under review, I am reminded (do allow me to be somewhat frivolous at this point) of what Emperor Joseph II said to Mozart in Forman's movie *AMADEUS* at the performance of *Die Entführung aus dem Serail*: '*Too many notes!*'

In conclusion I would like to stress that, unless we are faced with regular sound correspondences, well established and explained; with well-explained exceptions to such correspondences; with solid comparison of grammatical structures, with well-explained divergencies of meanings, the Nostratic hypothesis (not to speak of a 'Proto-World' or a 'Proto-Human' linguistic hypothesis) will be no more than a thrilling and provocative speculation based on conjectures. Perhaps (to paraphrase what Emeneau wrote in *Language* 54 (1978), 201–10), more data, more precision, even a more sophisticated theory and, in particular, a new and well-functioning *methodology* are needed to combine typology and history, as well as phonemic, grammatical and semantic resemblances and similarities 'to everyone's satisfaction'. On the other hand, as Emeneau says, 'it seems a pity to neglect an opportunity when it is under one's nose.' That is, we should not *reject* the Nostratic hypothesis out of hand. On the contrary, we should subject its results to objective, rigorous scrutiny, to see not what we want to see, but what is (or is not) actually there. If I were asked — as a Dravidianist — to answer the question raised at the end of Colin Renfrew's Introduction (*NM*, p. xx), I would answer, 'no, the evidence on offer is not [yet] sufficient to lead to the *general acceptance* of the hypothesis'. However, I would like to add: it does seriously stimulate further research, and to a Dravidianist it offers some fresh and interesting insights even though he may not accept them as valid. Nevertheless, non-linguists should not, according to my opinion, readily embrace the Nostratic hypothesis without utmost caution and, I would even dare to say, without a great deal of distrust, as long as it either does not agree with the well-tried and well-established, standard and legitimate, methodological principles of historical and comparative linguistics; or, as an alternative, as long as it does not work out its 'own' solid, well-tried specific methodology valid for distant genetic relationships.

References

Blažek, V., 1989. Materials for global etymologies, in *Reconstructing Languages and Cultures*, ed. V. Shevoroshkin. Bochum: Brockmeyer, 37–40.

Burrow, T. & M.B. Emeneau, 1984. *A Dravidian Etymological Dictionary*. 2nd edition. Oxford: Clarendon Press.

Collinge, N.E., 1995. History of historical linguistics, in *Concise History of Language Sciences*, eds. E.F.K. Koerner & R.E. Asher. Oxford: Pergamon, 203–12.

Emeneau, M.B., 1978. Review of *Defining a Linguisitic Area: South Asia*, by Colin P. Masica. *Language* 54, 201–10.

Emeneau, M.B., n.d. How many Dravidian languages are there? Unpublished paper written after 1991.

Kaiser, M. & V. Shevoroshkin, 1988. Nostratic. *Annual Review of Anthropology* 17, 309–29.

Krishnamurti, B., 1998. Proto-Dravidian laryngeal *H revisited. *PILC Journal of Dravidic Studies* 7(2), 145–65.

Renfrew, C., 1987. *Archaeology and Language: the Puzzle of Indo-European Origins*. London: Jonathan Cape.

Sweet, H., 1900. *The History of Languages*. London: J.M. Dent.

Vacek, J., in press. 'To grow, to rise, to be great' in Dravidian and Altaic. *Archív Orientální* 64 (1996), 295–334; 'Tamil etymological notes 1' (to be published in *Archív Orientální*).

Zvelebil, K.V., 1991a. Long-Range Linguistic Comparisons: the Case of Dravidian. Valedictory Lecture, Utrecht, 1991.

Zvelebil, K.V., 1991b. Long-range language comparison in new models of language development: the case of Dravidian. *PILC Journal of Dravidic Studies* 1(1) (January), 21–31.

Zvelebil, K.V., 1997. Language list for Dravidian. *Archív Orientální* 65, 175–90.

Chapter 18

Altaic evidence for Nostratic

Alexander Vovin

It seems to me that Dolgopolsky's *The Nostratic Macrofamily and Linguistic Palaeontology* (hereafter *NM*) was not the best basis for the discussion of the validity of the Nostratic hypothesis. Dolgopolsky's goal in the book is to reconstruct Nostratic homeland and habitat and not to prove the hypothesis itself. In order to discuss the hypothesis itself, in my opinion, it would be better to wait for Dolgopolsky's forthcoming *Nostratic Dictionary*, as it will undoubtedly include some of the strongest Nostratic etymologies that, for obvious reasons, were not provided in this book, since it deals with linguistic palaeontology. Still, I believe it is necessary for a discussant to answer both questions that the present symposium asks: is the Nostratic hypothesis viable and did Dolgopolsky succeed in reconstructing Nostratic habitat on the basis of linguistic data?

The first question, I think, can be answered cautiously in the affirmative. It seems that the Nostratic hypothesis is still viable in spite of an overwhelming number of murky etymologies that I am going to discuss below. After a careful scrutiny that removes the majority of at least the Altaic etymologies presented in Dolgopolsky's book, there still remains a core that appears to support the Nostratic hypothesis. However, the second question should be answered in the negative: *NM* fails to provide a cogent reconstruction of Nostratic habitat from the viewpoint of an Altaicist again owing to the fact that the majority of etymologies in this book are untenable for one reason or another. The remaining number of reliable etymologies is too small to come to any impressive conclusions and, what is more important, the picture of Near Eastern Urheimat suggested by Dolgopolsky for all Nostratic families, including Altaic, is in sharp contradiction with everything that can be reconstructed on the basis of internal Altaic data using the same linguistic palaeontology method.

First of all, I will review all Altaic etymologies presented by Dolgopolsky in *NM*, dividing them into acceptable and unacceptable classes. The latter is further subdivided into several subclasses due to the nature of problems that compelled me to reject them: correspondence problems, reconstruction problems, limited attestation, poor or dubious attestation, obvious or possible loanwords, ghost words, semantics problems and morphological problems.

Some statistics

There are 80 Altaic etymologies among 124 entries in the book. I did not include in these 80 those that Dolgopolsky himself considered as dubious connections. Among these 80, I would characterize only 26 as good etymologies that can stand close scrutiny. The remaining 54 are, unfortunately, either totally unacceptable or problematic. Thus the ratio of acceptable to unacceptable is approximately 1:2, which is, in my opinion, not entirely encouraging, but promising.

Acceptable etymologies and some additions and corrections to them

In this part I shall discuss etymologies that can be accepted. In certain cases I tried to make corrections or additions from the viewpoint of an Altaicist, that could improve a given comparison.

Nostratic *ʔoŕ[u] 'antelope' (no. 5), 'deer' is well supported by both Tungusic *oron 'reindeer' and Written Mongolian oruŋgu, Khalkha orongo, etc. 'a kind of small dark antelope with long flat horns'.

Nostratic *šüŋV 'snow' (no. 7) is a very good etymology with reliable reflexes in both Tungusic and Mongolic. Turkic reflexes are more questionable, since they are found only in Qypchaq languages, that is at the very bottom of the Turkic tree. Japanese simo (OJ simwo[1] < proto-Japanese *sima-[C]u or *simu-[C]a) 'frost', however, does not belong here, since it is related to Tungusic *xima(n)[-] '[to] snow' > Evenki imanna, Oroch imasa, Nanai simana, Manchu nimanggi 'snow' (Tsintsius 1975, 312–13) rather than to Tungusic *süŋü 'snow' (Tsintsius 1977, 90–91).[2]

Under no. 14, Nostratic *moRE 'water body', we find only Mongolic *mören 'river' (Written Mongolian mören etc.). It is also necessary to add here Middle Korean múl 'water', Old Japanese myina, myidu 'water' (< *mi- < *mi[ri]), Tungusic *mu: <**mu[r]u. Also, possibly Turkic -mur in *yaɣ-mur 'rain' (the interpretation of this word as 'falling water' faces certain structural problems).

For no. 15, Nostratic *qaRp|pV 'to harvest cereal', besides the Turkic, Mongolic, and Tungusic forms cited by Dolgopolsky, one can also add Old Japanese apa 'millet' < proto-Japanese *àpá.

Nostratic *ṭapaV 'to hit (the target)' (no. 34) is well supported by Turkic *tap- 'to find, hit the target', and Mongolic *taɣa- (< *taba-) which both have reliable attestations in many languages. However, the root may be onomatopoetic.

Nostratic ʔElĭli 'deer' (no. 37) is well supported by both Turkic *elik 'female roebuck' and Mongolic *ili 'young deer'.

Nostratic *buKa 'bovine' (no. 39) is well supported by both Turkic *buqa 'bull' and Mongolic *buqa 'id.'. It is also possible to add Tungusic *buka 'id.' > Evenki buka, Solon buxa 'id.', Manchu buxa gurgu 'wild bull', buxa 'wild animal' (Tsintsius 1975, 103–4).

Nostratic *poḲu 'pack, wild cattle' (no. 48) is well supported by Altaic *p'ök'ür$_2$ 'bovine, bull, ox'. Dolgopolsky lists only Turkic *[h]ökür$_2$[3] and Mongolic *hüker 'bull, ox'. Tungusic *pukur 'ox, cattle' (> Evenki hukur, Solon uxur, Even høken) can be also added here.

Nostratic *ḲuSV 'nut' (no. 56) is well supported by Turkic *qusïq 'nut', Mongolic *qusïyan 'nut', and Tungusic *xusikta 'nut'. It seems possible to add also Old Japanese kusa 'seed' (Omodaka 1967, 255).

Under Nostratic *ḲolV '(large) fish' (no. 73) we find *both* Mongolic *qolisun 'fish-skin' and Mongolic *qalimu 'whale' as well as *both* Tungusic *xol-sa 'fish' and Tungusic *kalima 'whale', although the last one is considered by Dolgopolsky to be a possible loanword from Mongolic (that is unlikely due to the fact that Tungusic k- : Mongolic k- more often than not reflects genuine cognates (Vovin 1997, 277)). This is the same methodological impossibility that is also present in no. 58 (see below): it is impossible to have two different reflexes of the same Nostratic root in a given language, unless one of them is a loanword, since otherwise it violates the principle of correspondence regularity. This etymology is further plagued by other problems as well: the reason for reconstructing *xol-sa is unclear to me — the stem just appears to be *xol[o]-, and different Tungusic languages exhibit different suffixation, but the plural suffix *-sa is not attested in any of them, according to Tsintsius data (1977, 14–15). The first Dolgopolsky pair seems to be preferable to the words for 'whale' since the latter would have unexplained 'suffixes' -ma and -mu. If Dolgopolsky can provide typologically similar examples when 'fish' becomes a 'fish-skin' as in this case in Mongolic, this one may eventually turn into a very strong etymology. Also it is possible to add Middle Korean kwòlày 'whale' and with less certainty Old Japanese kudira 'id.' (< *kuntira ?<**kultira), which is much more problematic.

Nostratic *tüRV 'hard-roe' (no. 77) is well supported by both Mongolic *türisün and Tungusic *türe:kse 'fish eggs', 'roe'. Tungusic data cited by Dolgopolsky could be further supplemented by Manchu turi 'peas.' Is Korean twulwu/twuli 'round' related, too?

Nostratic *tile[ʔa]ĺo 'stone, heap of stones' (no. 82) is perfectly supported by Altaic *tiol$_2$a ~ *tia:l$_2$a 'stone' (I would rather reconstruct proto-Altaic *tiol$_2$o for the reasons outlined below) with reflexes in all five branches of Altaic (reconstructions below are mine): Japanese *(d)ísò -, Korean *twòló-k, Tungusic *ʒolo Mongolic *čila-ɣun, and Turkic *dịa:l₂ 'stone'. Dolgopolsky honestly notes that the initial *č- in Mongolic is irregular: it should have been a form with an initial *ʒ-.

There are also other corrections that are necessary. Thus, in Dolgopolsky's presentation it looks like proto-Japanese *dísì 'stone' is reflected in Old Japanese as isagwo 'sand'. This is not true, as isi 'stone' is well attested in Old Japanese (and also in Middle Japanese as ísì).[4] Moreover, Old Japanese isagwo (Middle Japanese íságó 3.1) 'sand' is unlikely to be a reflex of ísì 2.2b 'stone', for two reasons. First, these words belong to two different accent classes, the former to high atonic HHH (3.1), and the latter to high tonic HL (2.2b). Second, isagwo 'sand' being three syllables long is a compound by default, as there are no three- and more syllable long roots in Japanese, consisting of isa-n[o]-kwo, where -n < genetive marker -no, and kwo is a general term referring to small objects, e.g. Old Japanese kwo 'child', 'egg'. Its first component isa- is likely to be related to the Old Japanese word íswó 'beach' 2.1 < proto-Japanese *isa-[C]u or *isu-Ca. Note that both isagwo HHH (3.1) and iswo HH (2.1) belong to high atonic classes, that further supports this etymology. Old Japanese isagwo 'sand' < *isa-n[o]-kwo then probably has an etymology 'beach pebbles' < 'beach's eggs,' that has hardly anything to do with 'stone.'

In spite of the fact that the distinction between Old Japanese vowels /yi/ (phonetically [i]) and /iy/ (phonetically probably [i]) was not preserved after coronals, there is oblique evidence that Old Japanese isi 'stone' has to be reconstructed as proto-Japanese *(d)iso-: there are several placenames in Japan called Iso-no kami 'Top of a stone' (not located in the vicinity of the sea and therefore not to be confused with Iso-no kami 'Top of a beach') that indicate that the second syllable vowel was *iy, that has a diphthongal origin: iy < *o-[C]i or *u-[C]i.[5]

Middle Korean word :twolh does not have a vowel length as given by Dolgopolsky, but the rising pitch that, as was convincingly demonstrated by Ramsey on the basis of internal Korean data (Ramsey 1991), indicates that a stem was once disylabic *tòlʌ́, with accent pattern LH and the unrounded back mid-high vowel /ʌ/ in the second syllable, that is a neutralized [+back] vowel, that may reflect any pre-proto-Korean back vowel. However, in this case it was most likely a rounded mid-high *o, since there is also *o in the first syllable.

Tungusic *ʒola with vowel /a/ in the second is unwarranted by evidence: all Tungusic languages that preserve the vowel in the second syllable have /o/

and not /a/ (Tsintsius 1977, 263).

Nostratic *ǯirɣulü 'vein, sinew' (no. 89) is supported by Altaic *sirwü reconstructed by Dolgopolsky on the basis of Mongolic *sirbü-sün 'sinew, tendon', Tungusic *sire-kte 'sinew, thread', and (with a question mark) 'Old Korean (eleventh century) sirll "thread", Korean sil id.'. Several corrections are in order. First, a discovery of 'Old Korean'[6] materials of the eleventh century would be a huge scholarly sensation: none are known so far. The word is not attested in the early twelfth-century Chinese–Korean vocabulary 'Kyelim yusa', either, the word for 'thread' being represented there by a loan from Chinese (Kang 1991, 83). The first time the word sil 'thread' is attested is in the late Middle Korean of the fifteenth century (Yu 1964, 499). The crucial part, overlooked by Dolgopolsky, is that it has rising pitch :sil, that shows that the word in proto-Korean was disyllabic *sìlú (see the discussion pertaining to no. 82 above), where vowel /u/ stands for any [-back] vowel. Thus, we can see that the Korean form ultimately fits quite well with Tungusic *sire-kte. The Mongolic form is probably also related but it is more problematic due to *-b- in it, which does not correspond regularly to *-Ø- in Tungusic and Korean.[7]

Nostratic *ʔeʐekU 'thorn, hook' (no. 90) seems to be solidly supported by Mongolic *elgü- 'hang on (smth.), hang on a hook' and Tungusic *elgu 'hook'. Dolgopolsky is more careful about inclusion of Turkic *i:l- 'hang on (smth.)', but actually it might fit it well, provided Turkic vowel length can be explained as a compensatory length due to the loss of the second syllable.

Nostratic *toŕV 'bark' (no. 82), *Ḳa[pʔlʕ][E] 'bark' (no. 83), *ḲayerV 'bark, film' (no. 84), *Ḳaɬ[ü] 'skin, film, bark' (no. 97) all have excellent Altaic etymologies.

Korean pi- 'cut as with a sickle' used to support Nostratic *piχlɣɣA 'sharp bone, sharp tool' (no. 101) exists, but means in the standard language 'be empty', and not 'cut'. The form in question is actually Korean pey- 'to cut (with a sharp-edged instrument)', that is attested in some subdialects of Kyengsang and Cenla as pi:- or, more rarely, pi- (Choy 1978, 1371). The word is attested as pèhi- in Middle Korean (Yu 1964, 377), adding more credibility to Dolgopolsky's comparison, which together with Manchu fe- 'mow' may be taken as an acceptable Altaic etymology.

Nostratic *[ṭ]äχlḷa 'spleen' (no. 103) is supported very well by Mongolic *deli-gün and Turkic *da:l 'id.'.

Nostratic *tEqmE 'sinciput, crown of the head, top, tip' (no. 105) may be an acceptable etymology, but there is room for doubt and two corrections on the Altaic side are in order. First, Tungusic *tuŋu- and *t[ü]mV- 'crown of the head' are two different words, and not phonetic variants of one and the same word, since there is no interlanguage variation -ŋ-/-m- in Tungusic. Since Nostratic *-m- is supposed to be reflected as Altaic *-m-, and not Altaic *-ŋ-, I would leave aside *tuŋu- and use only reflexes of Tungusic *t[ü]mV-. Note, however, that some vowel correspondences for *t[ü]mV within Tungusic are irregular. Proto-Japanese *tumu-ri 'head' (> Middle Japanese tuburi, Early Modern Japanese tuburi, tumuri, Shuri çiburu 'head') can be added further to strengthen the etymology (contrary to Starostin, who compared it with Tungusic *tuŋu-, and reconstructed proto-Altaic *t'uŋu- (1991, 279)), unless Martin is right that it might be from the *tumu-[a]ra-Ci 'round thing' (Martin 1987, 556). Difference in meaning with Mongolic *teme-sün 'edges of a net, border of a hem or a mat' may be too great to include it in the same etymology. I would suggest that proto-Japanese *tuma 'rim, edge' (> Old Japanese tuma and Middle Japanese túmà, Japanese tuma etc.) is more likely to be compared with the Mongolic word in spite of the fact that a separate explanation is required to explain a correspondence of Old Japanese u: Mongolic e in the first syllable.

Nostratic *ñiḲa 'jugular vertebra, neck, nape of the neck' (no. 108) is well supported by Mongolic *niɣur-sun 'spinal marrow, spinal cord' and Tungusic *niki-(n) 'neck, vertebra'. Turkic *yaqa 'collar' is more problematic.

Nostratic *kälulü 'a woman of the other exogamous society' (no. 109), and *küda 'a man of the other moiety' (no. 110) are well supported by Altaic evidence.

Nostratic *ʔemA 'mother' (no. 118) is well supported by Altaic data, but a couple of additions and corrections are necessary. Middle Korean ámh (and not ám as Dolgopolsky cites it) 'wife, woman', 'female (in compounds)', is less likely to belong here than Middle Korean émà-:nim, émí 'mother'. Also, Old Japanese omo and Eastern Old Japanese amo can be further added to the Altaic list (Omodaka 1967, 49, 164).

Nostratic *ʔaba 'father' (no. 119) is also well supported by Altaic data. Middle Korean àpá-:nim 'father' should be cited along with Middle Korean àpí 'father' provided by Dolgopolsky, since the latter represents a dimunitive form ap-i < *apa-i.

Unacceptable etymologies

We must now consider the etymologies that must be rejected. I classify them below into several groups depending on reason.

Correspondences problems

This is one of the worst cases, as lack in regularity of correspondences degrades the Nostratic theory to the 'mass-comparison' exercises by 'Proto-worlders', that might be amusing but are hardly worth any serious consideration.

For no. 6 *maŋ[g]V 'monkey', Dolgopolsky provides Tungusic *moño 'monkey' reconstructed solely on the basis Manchu moño 'id.'. The word is not attested in other Tungusic languages but this is not a very serious problem, since Manchu represents the top branching-off node. It is much more disturbing that in spite of the Tungusic reflex *-ŋ- of Nostratic **-ŋ- listed on p. 105 we obviously have a palatal *-ñ- here.

Under no. 8, *čaĺ[U]gV 'snow', 'hoar-frost', Dolgopolsky gives Altaic *cal₂ka > Turkic *to:l₂ 'ice' (with sufficient attestations in daughter languages) and Tungusic *ʒalka 'fine snow' > Neghidal ʒalka- 'to snow (of fine snow)'. Here Dolgopolsky does a small disservice to Nostratic by reconstructing a *nominal* stem in proto-Tungusic on the basis of his citation of an actually attested *verbal* stem in only one language. Meanwhile, there is also Neghidal ʒalka 'fine snow', as well as Udehe ʒaka- 'to snow (of fine snow)', that perfectly corresponds to Neghidal form (Tungusic clusters *-lk- and *-lg- > Udehe -k-, -g-). Thus, actually there is a basis for a proto-Tungusic *ʒalka 'fine snow', since the word is attested in two languages belonging to two different subgroups within Tungusic, but this is not obvious from Dolgopolsky's presentation. However, this is a small problem compared to a real one with correspondences problem: Altaic does not have a *c, but only *č, moreover the latter is never reflected as *t in proto-Turkic (Starostin 1991 argued for the *d as a reflex of proto-Altaic *č, but most of his examples are not persuasive). Moreover, Turkic *t does not correspond to Tungusic *ʒ in any of existing Altaic reconstructions, nor is there such a correspondence in Dolgopolsky's own list. Indeed, according to the list of correspondences on p. 104, Nostratic *č- must be reflected as both Turkic *č- and Tungusic *č (Dolgopolsky uses the palatal ſ sign for both Turkic and Tungusic).

Under Nostratic *yaŋ[y]V 'sinew, tendon, bow(weapon)' (no. 26) Dolgopolsky provides Turkic *ʒa:ñ 'bow', 'arrow'. Although the evidence for reconstructing initial Turkic *ʒ rather than *y is more than meager, and most specialists would rather have just *ya:ñ, it is not crucial here, as Turkic *y- (or *ʒ- in Dolgopolsky's reconstruction) may be a reflex of the following proto-Altaic phonemes: *d, *ʒ, *l, *n, *ñ, and *y. In this case, however, we also have an Old Japanese cognate ya 'arrow' < proto-Japanese *ya, that suggests Proto-Altaic *da:ñ or *ʒa:ñ, neither of these being compatible with Nostratic reconstruction for two reasons: we would expect Turkic (and Altaic) *ŋ and not *ñ for Nostratic *ŋ according to Dolgopolsky's own correspondences on p. 105 (see also no. 6 where the same discrepancy in correspondences in observed), and Altaic *y-, not *d- or *ǯ- for Nostratic *y-.

Neither Classical Mongolian soyuga 'eyetooth, tusk' nor Manchu suyfun 'awl' can be reflexes of Nostratic *šubyV 'spike, spear, to pierce' (no. 33), because Nostratic *-b- corresponds to -b- in both these languages, according to Dolgopolsky's chart of correspondences on p. 102. Morphological composition of the Mongol word is not clear, but it is quite possible that it is ultimately a Tibetan loanword: so 'tooth'. Manchu suyfun clearly contains suffix -fun typical for nouns denoting instruments or tools of various kinds (cf. sektefun 'cushion', from sekte- 'to spread', 'to make (a bed)').

Under Nostratic *buṭV 'pistachio tree/nut' (no. 58) we find *both* Old Turkic buturɣa:q 'thorn tree which is shaped like a pistachio tree' and bitrik 'pistachio nut'. It is, however, methodologically impossible that both would be reflexes of the Nostratic form. In addition, the attestation in Altaic is limited to Turkic.

Nostratic *doTgiHU 'fish' (no. 74) at a first glance seems to be well supported by Middle Japanese iwo[8] < proto-Japanese *(d)iwo and Mongolic *ǯiɣa-sun 'id.'. However, proto-Japanese *-w- does not reflect Altaic velars, but only Altaic *-b-. Meanwhile, Mongolic *-ɣ- may reflect both Altaic *-g- and *-b-. Thus, the Altaic form is likely to be *dibV, and it is not compatible with Nostratic. I also have grave doubts about Tungusic *ǯoglyi 'lenok' (kind of fish), due to the fact that: a) reconstruction of Tungusic *-g- here is speculative; b) neither Tungusic *-g- nor *-y- corresponds to Old Japanese -w-; c) there is a considerable difference in vocalism and semantics. For the sake of clarity, it is necessary to add that there is no basis for reconstructing proto-Japanese *(d)iwua with [ua] in the last syllable, as Old Japanese does not preserve the contrast between vowels [wo] and [o̬] after [w]. Korean -chi, a suffix used in the names of fishes (e.g. sam-chi 'mackerel'), is likely to belong here too, as it goes back to proto-Korean *cVHi ?'fish',[9] where proto-Korean *-H- may reflect both velar *-g- and labial *-b- (Vovin 1995).

Nostratic *HićlcχV 'father, head of a family' (no. 114) and Nostratic *ʔediNV 'pater familias' (no. 115) are both reflected in Mongolic as *eǯen 'owner, master, lord'. This obviously is even more impossible than to have two different reflexes in a language of a single Nostratic etymon as above in no. 58. The first of these etymologies is more likely to be supported by Classical Mongolian ečige 'father', Khalkha eceg 'id.', etc., and not by Mongolic *eǯen. However, Sarï-Yughur ise 'owner, master', isolated in Turkic cannot possibly belong here, since Turkic *-č- is reflected in Sarï-Yughur as -ǯ'- and not as -s- (Tenishev *et al.* 1984, 247).

As for no. 115, if Mongolic *eǯen 'owner, master, lord' is indeed from pre-Mongolic *edin as Dolgopolsky suggests, then it is likely to be a Turkic loanword, since Turks were masters of the steppe prior to Mongols. Thus, at its best both no. 114 and no. 115 end up being etymologies with limited attestation, the first supported only by Mongolic *ečige 'father', and the second by Turkic *edi 'master'.

Reconstruction problems

This is also a very serious problem, as it demonstrates that histories of individual languages are ignored or sacrificed for the sake of a Nostratic etymology.

Under no. 3, *ʔ[ü]ŕVwV 'large feline', Dolgopolsky cites proto-Turkic *irbil₂[č] 'leopard'. Although the forms irbiz/irbič (and not irbiš as given by Dolgopolsky which is a ghost) are attested already in Old Turkic (Sevortian 1974, 346), a number of Turkic languages have a form ilbirs or ilvirs (Sevortian 1974, 374), that presents certain problems not only in reconstruction of Turkic archetype, but also in comparing the Turkic form to other Nostratic forms.

Under no. 23, *ḳoʔćlcV 'basket', Dolgopolsky provides Tungusic *xa[u-xan 'kettle, basket' on the basis of Oroch xačuan, Ulchi xačoan, Orok xačuɣan, Nanai xačoxã, Kili xačã and Manchu xačuxan mečen. For starters, the word does not mean 'kettle', but 'pot', 'cauldron', a metal object obviously unlikely to exist in the Mesolithic Nostratic community, and only in one language — Kili — do we find it meaning 'box made of birch bark' (Tsintsius 1975, 464–65). However, the very fact that Nanai, Orok and Ulchi initial x- corresponds to initial x- and not to Ø- in Manchu and Oroch, demonstrates that in all southern Tungusic languages this word is a loanword from Manchu. The only exception is the Kili word that is unlikely to be connected both phonetically and semantically to the Manchu word. Finally, Manchu xačuxan in xačuxan mečen is a form that underwent typical postvocalic nasal loss. The original Manchu form is xančuxan 'pot' that Tsintsius provides right in front of xačuxan mečen (1975, 465).

Altaic reflex *k[']ür₂änä 'marten, polecat' of Nostratic *kun|ĥV(ŕV) 'small carnivore' (no. 52), based on Turkic *k[']ür₂en 'polecat' (reconstruction of a tentative aspiration in Turkic is completely spurious) amd Mongolic *kürene 'polecat', involves metathesis, that of course could have happened theoretically, but can hardly be trusted as a reliable way to search for external etymologies.

Altaic reflexes of Nostratic *mar[y]V '(mul-, black-)berries' are represented by Korean melwu, 'Southwestern Korean' melE and Turkic *bürü 'strawberry'. First, there is no form melE in Cenla dialects (so-called 'Southwestern Korean'), but there is a form melɣwu in Cenla, as well as melɣuy in Ceycwuto, and similar archaic forms with -g- in other dialects (Choy 1978, 756–7). Furthermore, this -g- is supported by Middle Korean spelling with 'syllabification' mèlɢùy 'wild grapes'. Thus, the Korean form obviously does not reflect Nostratic *mar[y]V. Furthermore, Turkic *bürü is based exclusively on Quba Azeri müri, which is just one dialect of a single Turkic language. Thus, Altaic does not offer much for the reconstruction of Nostratic *mar[y]V.

Nostratic *q[u]ʒV 'intestines, pluck' (no. 67) is supported exclusively by Tungusic *[x]uʒa 'disembowel a bear', 'pluck a bear'. However, the reconstruction of an intial *x- in this word is not just uncertain as Dolgopolsky indicates, it is spurious, as there is absolutely no evidence that would support it, since none of the languages cited by Dolgopolsky preserves Tungusic initial *x-: Even uʒaq 'disembowel a bear', Neghidal uddo-nin 'bear's pluck' (Tsintsius 1977, 249).

There is absolutely no internal evidence supporting reconstruction of Tungusic *xü:k-kte 'tooth' with a final -k in the root, inspired solely by the Nostratic *ḳ[a]k[w]V 'tooth, claw, hook' (no. 91) which it is supposed to support. It should be just *xü:-kte which goes nicely together with Middle Japanese kiba 'fang' 2.2b < Proto-Japanese *ku[/o]-[C]i-n[o]-pa 'fang-tooth' (Martin 1987, 450). Besides, Manchu weihe 'tooth' simply does not belong here: there are no regular phonetic correspondences between Tungusic *xü:-kte and Manchu weihe.

Limited attestation

This is the largest group among rejected etymologies. It brings up a very important methodological question: what etymology can be considered to be Altaic? It is obvious that for Dolgopolsky a word is Altaic if it is attested in just one out of five Altaic branches and in any other Nostratic family or families. While the scenario under which a proto-Altaic word survives only in one branch is theoretically possible, the frequent abuse of this possibility (and this is exactly what happens in *NM*: 16 etymologies out of 80 Altaic etymologies used in the book belong to this cathegory (20 per cent)) leads to a low credibility of the proposal itself. Certainly, a word attested only in one branch may invite other explanations, such as loanword scenario or chance. For example, there might be a case of an early loanword when it would show the same correspondences as genuine cognates. It is much better to be on the safe side and not to consider such etymologies to be Altaic. I use a rule of thumb according to which a word must be well attested in two Altaic families to be accepted as Altaic.

Under no. 11, *Sah[i]bV 'desert', Turkic *sa:y has much wider attestations (Dolgopolsky cites only Old Turkic sa:y and Chagatay say): the word is also attested in Old Uighur, Koman, Old Qypchaq, and Turkmen (Clauson 1972, 858). It looks like a good etymology but, unfortunately, attestation in Altaic is limited to Turkic.

Turkic *bal 'honey', listed under no. 21 as a reflex of Nostratic **mayẑV 'tasty beverage', does not have parallels in other Altaic languages. Moreover, it is believed that the word itself may be an early Indo-European loanword in Turkic (Sevortian 1978, 47).

Nostratic *ḷoŋKa 'to bend' (no. 27) includes only Tungusic *luŋkE 'to bow' (rather 'to stoop', 'to bend forward', which is in its turn is based exclusively on Evenki luŋkin- and Even nⱺŋkʌ- (Tsintsius 1975, 510–11)). Although the author of these lines proposed that Even represents a special group within Tungusic, branching off at the second highest level (Vovin 1993), in the traditional classification both are believed to be closely related languages belonging to the same Northern Tungusic subgroup.

Nostratic *ɢoki 'track' (no. 31) is supported only by Turkic *Kog(V) 'follow, chase, hunt' (well attested within Turkic).

Nostratic *boča '(young) deer' (no. 38) is supported only by Tungusic *buča 'a kind of a deer' (with decent attestations within Tungusic).

Nostratic *k[ä]ȼV 'wild goat' (no. 44) is supported only by Turkic *käči 'id.' (attested only in Oghuz and Qypchaq languages).

Nostratic *bUyẑV 'fur-bearing animal' (no. 50) is supported only by Mongolic *bul[u]ɣan 'sable' > Middle Mongolian bulu'an, Classic Mongolian bulaɣan, etc. In addition, the semantics are too broad: it ranges from 'marten' in IE and 'sable' in Altaic to 'tiger' in Dravidian.

Nostratic *[ḳ]ür[w]V 'hard-roe', 'spawn' (no. 78) is well supported by Tungusic *xụrbe 'to spawn' (more exact reconstruction will be *xürbe, though: Dolgopolsky correctly reconstructs [ü] in other cases if Northern Tungusic, Oroch, and Udehe /i/ corresponding to Orok, Ulchi, and Nanai /u/, e.g. see nos. 7 and 77), but its Turkic attestation is limited to Azeri kürü 'hard-roe'.

Nostratic *č̣[ü]rV 'flintstone, knife' (no. 80) is supported only by Tungusic *ʕuru-[k]an 'knife'. Tungusic attestations are reliable, but the word is not attested in other Altaic languages. In addition, there is the same mistake in reconstruction as above in no. 78: *ʕuru-[k]an should be *ʕüru-[k]an.

Nostratic *buRV 'flint' (no. 81) is similarly supported only by Tungusic *bụrV 'flint' > Evenki buru, Solon boro, Even bur, Solon boro, Oroch bu, burakta, Udehe bu:, Ulcha, Orok buraqta, Nanai boraqta, Kili buraxta 'flint', Neghidal burokta 'amber'. For the sake of clarity, Neghidal form burokta probably does not belong here in spite of being included together with other Tungusic forms in Tsintsius

(1975, 114): Neghidal reflex of Tungusic *u̯ is /o/ like in Nanai, and not /u/ like in other Tungusic languages (Tsintsius 1949, 87). Besides, Neghidal burokta means 'amber', which is quite different from 'flint'. Solon boro 'flint' is suspicious, too, because Solon's reflex of Tungusic *u̯ is /u/, and not /o/.

Only Tungusic *talu 'birch bark' supports Nostratic *tal[U]ya 'skin, pelt' (no. 96).

Only Mongolic *qoruβu 'cataract, spot in the eye' (itself a teleological reconstruction, as there is no evidence that in this particular word Classical Mongolian -γ- < Mongolic *-β-) supports Nostratic *ḳoRup̣V '(kind of) bark, skin' (no. 98).

Only Mongolic *qoltu-sun 'bark (of a tree)' supports Nostratic *ḲôẑV 'to skin' (no. 99).

Only Tungusic *bene- 'wife's sibling' supports Nostratic *[ɦχV]wänlnV 'relative [of a younger/the same generation] of the other moiety' (no. 112).

Both Nostratic *ʔarba 'to make magic, cast spells' (no. 121) and Nostratic *ʕ[a]lV 'to burn sacrifices, use magic means' (no. 122) utilize only Turkic data. For the latter, Dolgopolsky also cites (with double question mark) Korean alcin alcin ha- 'to deceive', but it is an obvious onomatopoetic word.

Poor or dubious attestations

This is an even worse case than the previous one, since the word used for Nostratic comparisons is poorly attested even within one single Altaic branch. Unfortunately, this is the case: a number of words used in Nostratic reconstructions are attested only at the lowest levels, sometimes a single attestation in a subdialect of a single dialect of just one language is projected not only at the Proto-Turkic, Proto-Mongolic, Proto-Tungusic, Proto-Korean, or Proto-Japanese level, but to the Proto-Altaic itself. Although it is not theoretically impossible that a Nostratic word would survive in only one Turkic, Mongolic, etc. language, when a considerable number of examples turns out to be based on this extremely limited evidence, it, frankly speaking, does disservice to the Nostratic theory: why do examples with more reliable attestations appear less frequently than suspicious cases?

Under no. 2, *ĉ[i]bVγV 'hyena', we find Tungusic *cib/pka 'wolf' that is 'reconstructed' exclusively on the basis of cipkaku: 'wolf' found only in the Ayan subdialect of the eastern dialect of Evenki (in addition Dolgopolsky does not quite cite the word correctly: he has cipkaku with a short /u/ in the last syllable, while in fact the word has long /u:/ according to Tsintsius 1997, 399). Keeping in mind that many Altaic languages have a name for 'wolf' tabooed, it might be too brave to give Nostratic status to the Ayan Evenki form.

It seems dubious that Nostratic *m[u]rḳV(-ŋḲV) (no. 62), a murky reconstruction by itself, will be preserved only in Evenki muɲi 'tendon'.

Nostratic *çUḷV 'stalk, stick' (no. 85) is supported only by Solon co:ʃcoxu 'transverse perches of the roof' (Dolgopolsky does not indicate vowel length (Tsintsius 1977, 406)). However, this word is attested only in Ivanovskii's materials (Ivanovskii 1894), and is not supported by other sources in Solon. Vowel length is suspicious, as there seems to be no primary length in Solon. Although I was not able to locate the source of the word in Written Mongolian, Khalkha Mongolian and Buriat, I suspect that it may be a loan from one of surrounding Mongolian dialects, some of which are very poorly studied at the present. In addition, the morphological composition of the word is unclear.

Nostratic *ḳoǯʕV 'tree trunk' (no. 86) is supported only by Mongolic *qoǯuliɣula 'tree trunk, stump' > Classical Mongolian qoǯuɣula, qoǯiɣula and Khalha xozuul 'id.'. However, it is very likely that the Mongolic word has quite a transparent internal etymology: qozui- (phonetic variant of ɣozui- 'be be erect, rise, stick up') + -ɣula, a collective suffix.[10]

Obvious and possible loanwords

Poor attestations always involve the danger that a genuine Nostratic etymon presented may turn out to be a loanword from some other language.

Under no. 9, *č[a]ʀʔV 'hoarfrost', Dolgopolsky gives Mongolic *car > Written Mongolian car (actually čar), Khalkha, Kalmyk car 'layer of frost on the surface of snow', and Teleut čarim 'id.' as attestation in Turkic. However, both Altaic etymologies are suspicious. It is strange that the Nostratic word survived only in Teleut out of all Turkic languages. Mongolic attestations are more varied, but there are not many native monosyllabic Mongolic words, so a Mongolic *car is suspect. Indeed, I believe that Teleut čarim and possibly Mongolic *car are rather recent loans from Tibetan 'khyag.rum or 'khyag.rom 'ice', 'frost', that in Central Tibetan colloquial pronounciation adapted by Mongols would become [čarum] (Jäschke 1883, 7).

Altaic evidence for Nostratic *ḳir[u]qa 'ice', 'hoarfrost', 'to freeze' (no. 10) looks good superficially. But Turkic *kʰira-gu 'snow', 'hoarfrost' (the basis of the reconstruction of an aspirated *k'- in Turkic remains unclear) is suspicious: to the best of my knowledge there is no *-gu suffix in Turkic, and, therefore, the word is likely to be a loan from Mongolian kira-ɣu(n) 'hoarfrost' (listed below with a question mark by Dolgopolsky), since -ɣu(n) is a rather productive suffix in Mongolian. Thus, strictly speaking, the Mongolian word may be an inherited

Nostratic word, but not the Turkic. It is a different matter, of course, with Turkish and Gagauz kirç 'hoarfrost', which are also cited in *NM*; since these words exhibit different suffixation they may indeed be cognates, but the problem is that they are attested on the lowest level in Turkic, both Turkish and Gagauz belonging to the same Oghuz subgroup of Turkic.

I suspect that Classical Mongolian des and Khalkha des 'following, next, subsequent, second', which is cited by Dolgopolsky as the only Altaic reflex of Nostratic *[d]EʕSV 'to follow the tracks' (no. 32) is really a Tibetan loanword: de-s 'therefore', 'sledovatel'no' (Roerich 1985, 4.189), 'after that', that is an ablative case form of the Tibetan demonstrative pronoun de 'that'.

Ghost words and meanings
Although Dolgopolsky seems to be quite moderate in that respect, he also does not quite escape a tradition of the Moscow Nostratic school of providing ghost words and meanings that for some linguists of that school (but not all!) almost became a virtue.

Nostratic *gurHa 'antelope' (no. 36) would look very impressive, but both Middle Korean kwòlání and Korean kolani (Dolgopolsky gives kolanni as 'New Korean' form, but there is no such form in any Korean dialect (Choy 1978, 902–3)) do not mean 'deer' but 'elk'. Taking into consideration that some Korean dialects have forms with -ŋ- rather than with -n-: Kyengsang Namto koraŋi, Kyensang Namto and Cenla Namto korɛŋi, and Cenla Namto korɛŋ (Choy 1978, 902–3), it is possible to believe that this word represents a Palaeosiberian substratum word in Korean, cf. proto-Chukchi-Koryak *qoraŋi (Chukchi qoraŋi, Koryak qoyaŋi) 'reindeer'. It is also necessary to mention that there are no three-syllable long native roots in Korean. Removing Korean kolani from this etymology leaves only Mongolic *gu:ran (the basis for reconstruction of the long vowel in the first syllable is unclear to me) 'antelope'. Its other Nostratic counterparts are found only in Cushitic. Not an excitingly wide attestation.

Under no. 72, *ʔuhχi 'egg' (p. 60), we find Old Japanese u 'egg', that, I am afraid, simply does not exist. Dolgopolsky refers to personal communication with Starostin in 1976, but I suspect that the latter was mislead by two very similar Chinese characters: 卯 that has a reading u 'hare (only as the fourth of the zodiac signs, contraction of Middle Japanese usagi 'hare') and 卵 tamago 'egg'. Unfortunately, two dots inside the second character make all the difference.

To support Nostratic *golatḲE 'popliteal space (back of the knee), armpit' (no. 106), Dolgopolsky cites (again with reference to Starostin) Middle Korean òkóm (wòkwóm in Yale system of transliteration) and Phyengyang oɡim (phonetic transcription, the same as Standard Seoul okum in Yale system of transliteration) 'polpiteal space, armpit'. Dolgopolsky is misled here by Starostin, who should have known that a disyllabic word in Middle Korean ending in -wom is likely to be a nominalization of a verbal stem. Indeed it is: Korean ok- means 'bends [inside]' (intr.), and both Middle Korean wòk-wóm and Korean ok-um are nominalizations of this stem. In addition, neither Korean form means 'armpit', but just 'the inside curve of the knee or of the elbow' — this can be easily checked with any of the reliable dictionaries of Modern Korean, such as Martin *et al.* 1967.

Poor and incorrect semantics
This might be the most speculative and subjective area, where individual tastes differ. Yet, I cannot accept the following etymologies that, I believe, stretch the semantics beyond the limit.

Nostratic *SiwVŋgE 'leopard' (no. 4) is supported only by Tungusic *sibi[g]e 'large beast of prey' (> Evenki sibige: 'wolf' (miscited by Dolgopolsky as sibige without vowel length in the last syllable), Even heweye/hewye 'bear', Oroch si:wi 'nickname of a mythological dog'). In spite of the fact that most feline carnivores will definitely freeze to death in the regions of the Northern Tungus people or even Oroch habitat, it is still strange that the word for a feline changes to a word for a canine (?) or a bear, leaving aside the correspondences and reconstructional problems: thus, e.g. despite the fact that Evenki and Even forms are brought together in the same entry in Tsintsius (1977, 75), Evenki -i- does not correspond to Even -e- (Tsintsius 1949, 82–5).

I fail to see how Turkic *t'ul₂E- 'to hobble (a horse)' (no. 30), can be compared semantically to either Nostratic *tul[i][g]V 'catch with a net' or Tungusic *tule- 'to cast (a fishing net)'.

Altaic *a:bV 'wild game, hunt' (rather *a:ba, since the vowel of the second syllable is well supported by both Mongolic and Tungusic) is unlikely to mean 'wild game', as Dolgopolsky indicates, because this meaning is attested only in some Turkic languages (in Oghuz, Qarluq, and Qypchaq subgroups), but not in Mongolic or Tungusic that have only the meaning 'hunt' (Dolgopolsky does not provide Tungusic parallels), but there is Manchu aba, Solon awa 'hunt', and Nanai abala- 'to hunt' (Tsintsius 1975, 7). Therefore the comparison with Nostratic *ɣlɡawV 'wild sheep/goats' turns out to be spurious.

Morphological problems

There always will be cases when an attractive etymology can become less attractive due to the lack of clarity in morphological structure of some of its constituents.

Under no. 25, *ʕǀɣaŕK̲[u] 'sinew' we find Turkic *arka:-n 'lasso', 'thick rope' and Classical Mongolian arɣamǯi 'rope, tether', 'tie with a rope' along with related forms in several modern Mongolic languages. The Turkic connection seems to be viable, but the Mongolian one presents certain problems: Mongolic -ǯi- might be a denominal verbal suffix (Poppe 1964, 65), but there is no noun *arɣam in Mongolic to the best of my knowledge. Although there is no way to demonstrate with certainty that -m- in arɣamji is a suffix, if it is, it can be only a suffix of deverbal nouns (Poppe 1964, 47). Thus, Mongolic *arɣa- would be a verb, that further complicates the comparison with Turkic. Therefore, the safest way is to believe for the time being that Mongolic connection is dubious, and thus this etymology will end up in the class of etymologies with limited attestation.

Under no. 53, Nostratic *dik̲V 'edible cereals or fruit', we find Altaic *diK > *diK-ktä, which represents a teleological reconstruction. It is based on Tungusic *ǯikte 'berry' and Turkic *yigdä 'jujube tree or its fruit'. However, we ran into several problems here. First, -kte is a collective suffix in Tungusic, and the stem is just *ǯi-. There is no evidence that it can be reconstructed as *ǯik. On the other hand, to the best of my knowledge, there is no suffix -dä in Turkic that we can safely segment in this word. Thus, both Turkic and Tungusic parallels are better excluded for the moment.

Nostratic *molǀlV- 'to pound, gnaw/smash into pieces' (no. 63) is supported by proto-Altaic reconstruction *mölV based exclusively on Mongolic *mölǯi- < **möl-di- 'to gnaw into pieces'. Unfortunately, the Proto-Altaic form is completely teleological: there is the Mongolic denominal verbal suffix -ǯi- (cf. bayan 'rich', bayaǯi-qu 'to get rich'), but there is no nominal stem möl- attested in Mongolic that would support Dolgopolsky's segmentation. Nor is there any internal Mongolic evidence that would support a reconstruction of the Altaic vowel in the second syllable.

Nostratic *ñ[a]K̲U 'soft parts of the animal's body (liver, marrow, suet)' (no. 70) is supported exclusively by Old Turkic and Old Uighur yaqŕi 'suet, fat (of an animal)' on the basis of which Dolgopolsky surprisingly reconstructs Turkic *yakŕi with an initial *y- instead of an initial *ǯ- that he reconstructs in other cases (see, e.g. no. 26). It appears that a choice for *y- or *ǯ- for Proto-Turkic in Dolgopolsky reconstruction is dictated by Nostratic reconstruction, in spite of the fact that there is no *y-/*ǯ- contrast reconstructable on the basis of the Turkic internal evidence. This amounts to the reconstruction 'from above' that is not methodologically acceptable. The major problem with no. 70, however, is a simple fact that there is no suffix -ri in Old Turkic that we could safely segment in this word.

Combined problems

In one case, it is necessary to reject an etymology on the basis of several at first glance not very significant problems. However, when combined, these problems do not look very reassuring.

Nostratic *čuRV 'bull, calf' (no. 41) is supported by Tungusic *čur-/*čir-, Classical Mongolian ʒari 'wild deer', and in Turkic by Altay, Teleut, Quu-Kizhi, Küärik, and Baraba čar 'ox'. First, it is questionable whether Evenki forms čurup and čirak, and čirap as well as Neghidal čirap, are cognate at all: I do not know of any other examples with interdialectal correspondences u:i and p:k within Evenki itself. Probably we are faced with a complex picture of interdialect borrowing here that needs further clarification before using these data for long-range external comparisons. Besides, all attestations are limited, since they are confined to Northern Tungusic. The same can be said about Mongolic (the form ʒari is attested only in Classical Mongoplian), and Turkic attestations are confined to Khakass and Qyrghyz subgroups of Northeastern Turkic. In addition, the correspondence between Tungusic [u/i] and Turko-Mongolian [a] is problematic. All these pitfalls make a Nostratic origin of these forms more than dubious.

Nostratic and Altaic linguistic palaeontology

Finally, I would like to offer some thoughts regarding the viability of Dolgopolsky's proposal that the Nostratic macrofamily originated in West Asia. As I have mentioned above, the number of etymologies remaining after scrutiny is too small on which to base any far-reaching conclusions.

In addition, I think that internal Altaic evidence contradicts Dolgopolsky's proposal. While I do not know where the homeland of the Nostratic macrofamily was, I believe that the Altaic homeland was definitely in East Asia, and not West Asia, and even more specifically in Manchuria.

Several pieces of evidence can be offered for this point of view that was first put forward by Ramstedt (1957, 15). First, the homelands of all five branches of Altaic can be traced either to the East (Tungusic, Korean, Japanese) or to the West (Turkic, Mongolic) of the Great Khingan mountain range in Manchuria.

Movement of Altaic speakers to the West occurred only in comparatively recent times, and there is no other independent piece of evidence apart from Dolgopolsky's theory demonstrating that originally they came from the opposite direction to Manchuria. In any case, it would be too long a hike from West Asia to Manchuria to arrive in one piece. Furthermore, using the same linguistic palaeontology method for Altaic, we will arrive at a picture quite different from West Asia and typical for East Asia.

Although there are two Altaic words for 'snow', both of them have limited attestation. Much better is represented the word for 'ice': Altaic *bur$_2$[V] > Turkic buz, Tungusic bukse, Old Japanese pyi 'ice',[11] Middle Korean èl-úm 'ice' < *(b)elV- 'freeze'. This is a very typical picture for Manchuria that does not have a lot of snow, but where rivers freeze to their bottom.

There is some evidence that Altaic speakers, or at least the easternmost of them, knew the sea: Altaic *badaR 'sea' > Old Japanese wata, Middle Korean pàlól, pàtáh 'id.', ʔYakut badara:n 'swamp'; Altaic *tal[Vy] 'sea' > Old Turkic taluy, Written Mongolian dalay 'id.', Tungusic *dala-n 'flood'; Altaic *la:mu 'sea' > Tungusic *la:mu 'sea', Old Japanese namyi 'wave'; Altaic *sima 'island' > Old Japanese sima, Middle Korean :syem 'id.'; Altaic *kalim[V] 'whale' > Tungusic *kalim[V], Written Mongolian qalimu 'id.' (see above, no. 73); Altaic *kani 'crab' > Old Japanese kani, Middle Korean :key 'id.'; Altaic *sampa 'mackerel' > Old Japanese saba, Korean sam-chi 'id.'.

Altaic speakers lived in the area where mountains were covered by thick forests: Middle Japanese mori 'forest', Old Korean mwolwo, Middle Korean :mwoy 'mountain', Tungusic mo: 'tree', Mongolic *mo[r]-dun 'tree'. Mountains covered with forests are quite typical of northeast Asia, but not of southwest Asia. It is also possible that there was bamboo in Altaic motherland that historically did not grow in southwestern Asia: Old Japanese takey, Middle Korean táy 'bamboo'.

Finally, it is significant that none of the etymologies proposed by Dolgopolsky that more or less uncontroversially point to the southwest Asia, are found in Altaic: there are no 'lion', 'leopard', 'hyena', or 'fig tree'.

Therefore, I am able to come to the following conclusions:

1. Altaic data seem to support Nostratic theory in general, although Nostraticists frequently use them indiscriminately, and significant clean-up work must be done before jumping to any far-reaching conclusions.

2. Nostratic homeland in southwest Asia is not supported by Altaic data, and if it is indeed the case, a significant deal of explaining must be done with regard to how and when such a distant migration could have occurred.

Notes

1. The earliest attestation of Old Japanese simwo 'frost' is in 'Man'yôshû' V:804. It is traditionally believed that the contrast between Old Japanese syllables of /mwo/ and /mo̠/ was lost by this time, however recently John Bentley came up with a reliable statistical analysis showing that the book V of 'Man'yôshû' preserves this contrast pretty well, and that, therefore, the spellings found in book V are reliable (Bentley 1997).
2. See Vovin 1994, 247–8 on OJ /si/ as a reflex of PA *k'i or *k'i.
3. Since the word is not attested in Khaladzh, the initial h- is really spurious. It is obviously prophetic in Uighur and Uzbek, as no regular correspondences for initial h- in these languages can be established.
4. The necessity of citing Middle Japanese forms alongside with Old Japanese is due to the fact that we do not have reliable data on Old Japanese accentuation. Middle Japanese accentuation of the eleventh century appears to be almost identical to the reconstructed proto-Japanese, although there are some problems concerning textual evidence for the class 2.5 (for details see relevant chapter in Martin 1987).
5. There is a morphonological alternation for Old Japanese stems ending in -iy (including those after coronal where distinction seems to be neutralized): they appear with vowel -iy in isolation and before all case markers except genitive -no̠, before which and in compounds they end in vowel -o̠ or -u: cf. kiy 'tree', ko̠-no̠ 'tree-GEN', sati 'hunt', satu-yumyi 'hunting bow', tukiy 'moon', tuku-ywo 'moon[lit] night'.
6. Defining eleventh-century Korean as Old Korean is unwarranted: according to almost universally accepted periodization of the history of the Korean language by Yi Kimun (Lee Ki-moon), the period of tenth to fourteenth century is defined as 'Early Middle Korean' (Yi 1961, 84).
7. In the system correspondences proposed by Starostin there is an Altaic *-w- that is reflected as *-b- in Mongolic, *-Ø- in Korean, and *-w- or *-y- in Tungusic (Starostin 1991, 2). In my opinion all the etymologies with *-w- suggested in Starostin 1991 are dubious; and even if they were not in this particular case Tungusic would still have an irregular reflex *-Ø- instead of expected *-w- or *-y-.
8. The word iwo 'fish' is not attested phonetically on Old Japanese, but appears in the cited man'yôgana spelling in early Heain dictionaries 'Shinsen jikyô' and Wamyôshô (9th century).
9. Korean aspirates ph, th, ch, kh, go back to clusters *CH or *HC, where C is a voiceless stop and H is a voiceless velar (Ramsey 1991.)
10. -ɣula occurs most frequently with numerals in Written Mongolian, but is not limited to them (Poppe 1964, 55). Alternatively it may be that this -ɣula is related to deverbal nominal suffic -qalŋ that occurs in both Middle Mongolian (Street 1957, 58) and Written Mongolian (Poppe 1964, 47).
11. Attested phonetically only in usura-pyi 'thin ice' in MYS XX:4476.

References

Bentley, J., 1997. PO and MO in Old Japanese. Unpublished M.A. thesis, University of Hawai'i at Mânoa.

Choy, H., 1978. *Hankwuk pangen sacen* [*A Dictionary of Korean Dialects*]. Seoul: Hyenmunsa.

Clauson, G., 1972. *An Etymological Dictionary of the Pre-Thirteenth Century Turkish*. Oxford: Clarendon Press.

Ivanovskii, A.O., 1894. *Mandjurica. Obraztsy solonskogo i dakhurskogo iazykov* [*Samples of Solon and Daghur Language*]. Saint-Petersburg.

Jäschke, H., 1883. *Tibetan Grammar*. London: Trübner & Co.

Kang, S., 1991. *Kyelim yusa Kolye pangen yenkwu* [*A Study of Koryo Vocabulary in the 'Kyelim yusa'*]. Seoul: Sengkyukwan tayhakkyo chwulphanpu.

Martin, S.E., 1987. *The Japanese Language Through Time*. New Haven (CT) & London: Yale University Press.

Martin , S.E., Y.H. Lee, S.-U. Chang, 1967. *A Korean–English Dictionary*. New Haven (CT) & London: Yale University Press.

Omodaka, H. (ed.), 1967. *Jidai betsu kokugo daijiten. Jôdai hen* [*Big Dictionary of National Language by Periods*, vol. 1: *Old Japanese period*]. Tokyo: Sanseidô.

Poppe, N., 1964. *Grammar of Written Mongolian*. Wiesbaden: Otto Harrassowitz.

Ramsey, S.R., 1991. Proto-Korean and the origin of the Korean accent, in *Studies in the Historical Phonology of Asian Languages*, eds. W.G. Boltz & M.C. Shapiro. Amsterdam & Philadelphia (PA): John Benjamins Publishing Co., 213-38.

Ramstedt, G.J., 1957. *Einführung in die Altaische Sprachwissenschaft*, I: *Lautlehre*. Bearbeitet und heraus gegeben von Pentti Aalto. Helsinki: Suomalais-Ugrilaisen Seura.

Roerich, N., 1983–1990. *Tibetsko–Russko–Angliiskii Slovar's Sansritskimi Paralleliami* [*Tibetan–English–Russian Dictionary with Sanskrit Parallels*]. 11 vols. Moscow: Nauka.

Sevortian, E., 1974, 1978, 1980. *Etymologicheskii slovar' tiurkskikh iazykov*. Moscow: Nauka.

Starostin, S., 1991. *Altaiskaia problema i proiskhozdenie iaponskogo iazyka* [*The Altaic Problem and the Origins of the Japanese Language*]. Moscow: Nauka.

Street, J., 1957. *The Language of the Secret History of the Mongols*. New Haven (CT): American Oriental Society.

Tenishev, E., L.S. Levitskaia, L.A. Pokrovskaia, A.A. Iuldashev, N.Z. Gadzhieva, K.M. Musaev, N.A. Baskakov, V.D. Arakin & A.A. Kovshova, 1984. *Sravnitel'no-istoricheskaia grammatika tiurkskikh iazykov: Fonetika* [*Historical-Comparative Grammar of Turkic Languages: Phonetics*]. Moscow: Nauka.

Tsintsius, V., 1949. *Sravnitel'naia fonetika tunguso-man'chzhurskikh iazykov* [*A Comparative Phonetics of Manchu-Tungusic Languages*]. Leningrad: Gosudarstvennoe uchebno-pedagogicheskoe izdatel'stvo.

Tsintsius, V. (ed.), 1975. *Sravnitel'nyi slovar' tunguso-man'chzhurskikh iazykov* [*A Comparative Dictionary of Manchu-Tungusic Languages*], vol. 1. Leningrad: Nauka.

Tsintsius, V. (ed.), 1977. *Sravnitel'nyi slovar' tunguso-man'chzhurskikh iazykov* [*A Comparative Dictionary of Manchu-Tungusic Languages*], vol. 2. Leningrad: Nauka.

Vovin, A., 1993. Towards a new classification of Tungusic languages. *Eurasian Studies Yearbook* 65, 99–113.

Vovin, A., 1994. Genetic affiliation of Japanese and methodology of linguistic comparison. *Journal de la Société Finno-Ougrienne* 85, 241–56.

Vovin, A., 1995. Once again on the accusative marker in Old Korean. *Diachronica* XII, 2.

Vovin, A., 1997. Voiceless velars in Manchu. *Journal de la Société Finno-Ougrienne* 87, 263–80.

Yi, K., 1961. *Kwuke sa kaysel* [*A Sketch of the History of the Korean Language*]. Seoul: Thap chwulphansa.

Yu, C., 1964. *Yico e sacen* [*Dictionary of Korean Language of Yi Dynasty Period*]. Seoul: Yonsey tayhakkyo chwulphanpu.

Chapter 19

Some thoughts on the Nostratic theory and its historical implications

Denis Sinor

These provisional, preliminary remarks were prepared for a Symposium on the Nostratic Macrofamily held in the McDonald Institute for Archaeological Research, at the University of Cambridge, July 17–18th 1998. Put in simple terms, the task set for the participants was to comment on A. Dolgopolsky's book The Nostratic Macrofamily and Linguistic Palaeontology *(hereafter NM) specially prepared for the conference. My remarks are grouped in two parts. In the first of them, I will scrutinize some of the etymologies proposed in NM; in the second, I will present some of my views concerning the linguistic methods used and the historical conclusions that may be drawn on the basis of the linguistic evidence.*

1. Comments on individual etymologies

In conformity with the request made by the organizers of the Nostratic Symposium to the effect that 'Participants who have expertise in a particular language family are urged to focus on the quality of the evidence in that domain', I will concentrate on the evidence gathered in *NM* from the Uralic (Finno-Ugric and Samoyed) and Altaic (Turkic, Mongol, and Tunguz) material, a corpus in which I might claim some expertise. I disclaim any knowledge of most of the languages mentioned in sections II, III, and VI of the classification of the Nostratic languages as given in *NM*, nor am I familiar with the relevant linguistic literature. Because of my inability to judge the material culled from languages belonging to the above-mentioned sections (referred to as 'the other languages') I will presume that all these reconstructed forms are correct and represent generally acceptable material.

In the time limit given for the preparation of this paper I found it impossible to submit to detailed analysis all 124 etymologies proposed by Dolgopolsky in *NM*. Only some random samples chosen *sine ira et studio* will be the subject of this enquiry.

6. 'Monkey'. No Uralic forms are given and the Altaic group is represented by one single form taken from Manchu. Thus in this entry we have a motley assembly of one Hamito-Semitic, one Manchu, and one Dravidian word with hints to English monkey and some Romance words, though we are assured that 'nothing is known about their possible connection with Nostratic'.

7. 'Snow'. There can be no justification for positing a Uralic *Urform* for the clearly regional (Finnish and Lappish) words cited. The same remark is valid also for the reconstructed Turkic *seng 'ice flow, block of ice' which rests on the basis of only two words occurring in two, closely related Turkic dialects. Through borrowings these two words may, perhaps, be linked with the Tunguz or Mongol words cited.

13. 'Water body'. *NM* reconstructs a Nostratic *yamV which may or may not be accurate (I plead ignorance) but is certainly valid for Samoyed which has its correspondence in Tunguz forms such as Manchu, Oroch, Orok, Ude, namu 'great river; sea' (Sinor 1975, 250). So in this etymon we would have a Hamito-Semitic word with correspondences limited to Siberian languages. Some distance!

15. 'To harvest (cereal)'. Within Altaic, Common Turkic arpa 'barley' appears to be a word of civilization. Manchu arfa 'barley' is clearly a loan from Mongol since no parallels exist in the other Tunguz languages. One would hesitate to separate Mongol arbay 'barley' from the Turkic forms, though the final -y may be difficult to explain. But there are other problems. *NM* postulates a Nostratic initial *q-. Middle Mongolian does have an initial h- which, in most cases continues *p- but occasionally also *q-. (See the all-important but often forgotten article, Pelliot 1944.) But the Middle Mongol word, as *NM* rightly notes, has a vocalic initial: arbay (see Poppe 1938, 104). One might have expected a *harba(y) form. But this not very significant objection pales in comparison with the semantic problems posed by the equation. I just find it impossible to accept the equation of the verb 'to harvest' with 'barley'.

17. 'Cereals'. No Altaic or Uralic data are cited.

22. 'To wicker, wattle (wall, building)'. For Altaic, *NM* cites no Mongol or

Tunguz reflexes and Turkic is represented by only two words of identical form (qat-) taken from two adjacent Siberian dialects spoken by people who, most probably, were Turkicized just a few centuries ago. They constitute no acceptable evidence for the reconstruction of Proto-Turkic *qat, let alone for Proto-Altaic. Yet *NM* uses them, though admittedly with a cautionary question mark, for positing an Altaic *qat-.

24. 'Basket, box'. The 'Uralic' forms correctly cited are all taken from Finno-Ugric. Their relation with the Indo-European forms is very likely. Somewhat surprisingly, the word is not attested in Turkic, Mongol, or Tunguz. On the extraordinarily wide distribution of name of containers, see Sinor (1995; 1996).

26. 'Sinew, tendon', 'bow (weapon)'. There seems to be no compelling reason to derive Common Turkic ya 'bow' from *yań. The loss of the final remains unexplained. The Turkic forms are probably related to Tunguz nu and Mongol numun 'bow' (see Sinor 1978, 324). Turkic y- may continue *y-, *j-, *n-, *d-. The Tunguz and Mongol forms suggest here an initial Altaic *n-. *NM* gives neither Mongol nor Tunguz correspondences.

28. 'Sinew; to tie together'. For Uralic, Rédei (1988–91.I, 317) posits a *ńele (ńōle) form 'arrow' a meaning common to *all* the other forms cited. Tentatively, Rédei suggests links with Tunguz Evenki ńur 'arrow'. (For a complete listing of Tunguz forms see Cincius 1975, 648.) For anyone using the weapon, 'arrow' and 'bow' are very different objects.

36. 'Antelope, male antelope'. In Dolgopolsky's presentation the Hamito-Semitic words are linked with Classical Mongol (Lessing 1960, 368) gura(n) 'roebuck, wild goat, antelope'. The word occurs in more Tunguz dialects than indicated, Manchu has gûran. Some Turkic dialects have borrowed it from Mongol. More interestingly, the word is attested as far west as in Bashkir qoralai 'wild goat' complete with the archaic Mongol suffix -lai. (Novikova 1972, 128). Thus this word appears to have a fascinating history but there is no reason to posit a Proto-Altaic origin.

37. 'Deer'. The Turkic and Mongol forms cited do belong together, and may continue an *ilik. Yukagir is not a Uralic language. No Uralic forms are listed.

39. 'Bovine'. Turkic and Mongol words such as buqa 'bull' are cited. The very similarity of all these words suggests their relatively recent incorporation into Turkic, Mongol, and Tunguz. *NM* does not cite the Tunguz forms. The word appears also in the Ugrian languages and in Samoyed, probably as loan. The comparison appears to have merit, but why would the forms have remained unchanged over the millennia? No Uralic equivalents are given in *NM*. It may be relevant to note that in Sinor (1962), where I examined to some depth Altaic names for bovines, only four words out of eleven were present in Turkic and Mongolian and even these correspondences could be explained as early borrowings.

44. 'Wild goat'. The comparison with Common Turkic käči is defensible. No Mongol, Tunguz or Uralic parallels are given but they exist such as Classical Mongol quča 'ram'. The Mongol word was borrowed by Evenki, Manchu and other Tunguz dialects. There is no reason to believe that it can be posited for Proto-Altaic.

45. 'Billy goat, ram'. The comparison with Turkic/Mongol/Tunguz bugu 'deer' is tempting.

46. 'Wild boar'. The entry contains neither Uralic nor Altaic data.

48. 'Pack, wild cattle'. Although plausible at first sight, the comparison of Indo-European *peku-forms with an Altaic *pökür is untenable. In the words of Clauson (1956, 186), 'pökür is a mere figment of the imagination'. The initial h- which appears in Middle Mongolian and in some modern Mongol dialects is a secondary 'cockney h' and does not continue an Altaic *p-. For a more detailed treatment of the question, with further references, see Sinor (1962, 315–18).

50. 'Fur-bearing animal'. For Uralic, Dolgopolsky reconstructs possibly on his own authority a *buyžV-type form (if I can interpret *NM*'s impossibly complicated and unrealistic transcription system correctly) which compares unfavourably with Rédei's more credible *pojta 'ermine' (1988–91.I, 390). This is a purely Samoyed word with not even Finno-Ugric relatives. For phonetic reasons I can envisage no link between either of these forms and Mongol bulagan 'sable'.

54. '(A kind of) fig tree'. No Uralic or Altaic forms are given.

55. '(A kind of) edible fruit'. No Uralic or Altaic forms are given.

56. 'Nut'. The Altaic forms listed, e.g. Old Turkic qusıq do belong together and may be linked with Indo-European forms. Where is the Nostratic element in this equation?

61. 'Fruit of a leguminous plant'. The entry lists neither Uralic nor Altaic parallels.

64. 'To bake, prepare food on hot stones', postulates on the basis of an Old Turkic word äpmäk 'bread' a Proto-Turkic verb *äp 'to bake'. However, *NM* probably bases the equation on Clauson (1972, 12), misinterpreting the arcane system of abbreviations used in this excellent work. Old Turkic has no such word.

71. 'Egg, testicle'. No Altaic words are listed.

75. 'A kind of fish'. No Altaic words are given.

76. 'A kind of fish'. No Altaic words are given. The Indo-European forms stand for the generic 'fish'.

79. 'Honey'. An old stand-by for the macro-comparatist, once used by myself (Sinor 1944, 237). Inexplicably, *NM* does not adduce the Uralic forms listed in Rédei (1988–91.I, 273), certainly linked with Indo-European material. Nor does he mention the oft-quoted Chinese *miet, certainly a member of this family of words of civilization.

84. 'Trunk, log'. The Finno-Ugric words derived from *pora 'raft' (for a listing see Rédei 1988–91.I, 395) may have a link with the Nostratic form posited though I fail to see how this can be reconstructed from the Indo-European words listed. No Altaic connection is suggested.

88. 'Pole, long piece of wood'. *NM*'s tentative suggestion that Mongol joruga 'arrow with a horn head' belongs to this group may be dismissed on se-

mantic grounds. Were the etymology acceptable — *NM* marks it with two question marks — it would link only Mongol to 'the other languages'.

91. 'Tooth'. *NM* cites only Tunguz forms, clearly based on Cincius (1975–77.I, 300). It should be remarked that Cincius' splendid work is a *comparative* and not an *etymological* dictionary, a simple listing of similar forms with cognate meanings. Manchu weihe cannot be linked with the other Tunguz words of a *kVk type. It is unjustifiable to posit a Proto-Altaic form on the evidence of only Tunguz data.

92. 'Bark'. *NM* cites e.g. Old Turkic toz, Mongol durusun. While one might disagree in the detail with the presentation of the Altaic data, the etymology is acceptable and well known. No Uralic forms are given.

93. 'Bark'. The word listed for 'the other languages' may have connections with the Uralic words. Rédei (1988–91.I, 180) justifiably suggests a Proto-Uralic *kora. There are at least two reasons to reject categorically the possibility of any connection between this form and the Turkic words adduced by *NM*. In opposition to Uralic -r-, these have all an intervocalic -b-/-w- (such as Old Turkic qavuq). I know of no -r- > -v- development that could justify this etymology. Also, I balk at the semantic somersault needed to group under the semantic heading 'bark' words meaning 'bran'. This is an etymology gone terribly awry.

102. 'Bile'. Uralic piša (Rédei 1988–91.I, 384) has no parallel in Altaic.

108. 'Jugular vertebra, neck, nape'. The assemblage seems tempting, were it not that the reconstruction (according to Illič-Svityč) of the Altaic *ńika is probably unjustified. *NM* posits a Mongol *nigursun where the asterisk is actually superfluous since this is in fact the Classical Mongol form. Most likely, niɣur-sun is a metathetical form of Classical Mongol niru-ɣu 'back, spine, backbone' well represented in Tunguz languages, e.g. Evenki ńiri 'vertebra'. The Mongol and Tunguz forms can be found assembled in Kolesnikova (1972, 58–9) who posits an Altaic *ńirū form.

119. 'Child'. No Mongol, Tunguz or Uralic correspondences to Common Turkic ogul are given, nor are Indo-European forms cited. So what is the basis of the Nostratic etymology?

121. 'To make magic, to cast spells'. *NM* offers this as a questionable Nostratic etymology. While no Mongol or Tunguz parallels are adduced, the Turkic words cited appear to be relevant.

2. General comments on the theoretic background

In order to help in the evaluation of their usefulness for the clarification of early Eurasian history, and also for the sake of simplicity, let us assume for a moment that all the etymologies presented in *NM* are correct. While such a happy state of affairs would allow for several historical conclusions to be drawn, there is at least one that lies outside the circle of their scholarly effectiveness. Used on their own, without having recourse to morphological correspondences, they do not prove the genetic relationship of the proto-languages which they represent. Morphological correspondences provide the key to the reconstruction of any proto-language. In the words of Sammalahti (1988, 479) 'It is quite clear that the sorting of the morpheme stock is the most critical part of the research'. The weakest point of the Altaic hypothesis is precisely the fundamental morphological divergences that separate the Northern Tunguz from the Mongol languages.

I would not suggest that lexical correspondences can shed no light on the history of language families. However, it should be borne in mind that the validity of any reconstructed form depends on the amount of information on which it is based. Regrettably, most of the posited forms listed in *NM* rest on a handful of haphazardly collected words, fished out from the virtually limitless vocabulary of perhaps a hundred or more languages. Among the above-cited 35 etymons, eleven (nos. 17, 24, 46, 54, 55, 61, 71, 75, 76, 84 & 102) have no Altaic data at all, while a further four (nos. 22, 44, 119 & 121) contain only Turkic but no Mongol or Tunguz words. One looks in vain for Uralic data in nine sets (nos. 6, 17, 39, 44, 46, 54, 55, 92 & 119).

In scrutinizing the etymologies presented in *NM*, it is important to bear in mind that while there seems to be a consensus that the known Uralic languages have a common ancestry, the genetic relationship of Turkic, Mongol, and Tunguz languages is subject to grave doubts and has been seriously challenged. Proto-Altaic would probably be the closest relation to Proto-Uralic but the genetic relationship of the two cannot be demonstrated convincingly (see Sinor 1988a). The main difficulty lies in the shakiness of attempts to reconstruct Proto-Altaic (Sinor 1963). If there were no Proto-Altaic, how could it be part of Nostratic? How can a Nostratic proto-language be reconstructed on the basis of proto-languages that may have never existed?

In *NM* there are some serious methodological lapses in the reconstruction of Proto-Altaic forms. Many, if not most, of the posited Proto-Altaic forms suffer from the fatal flaw that they are attested in only one of the three Altaic groups and, even worse, there is often one single word that stands for the whole family. One cannot compare identical words. What can be the scholarly value of an Altaic *guran 'antelope' (no. 36) reconstructed on the basis of *one* Mongol word guran; how can we posit (no. 44) a Proto-Altaic word on the strength of *one* Turkic word käči 'goat'? It is inadmissible to posit an *Urform* on the evidence of one or two closely related languages. No scholar of repute would posit an Indo-European ancestor for two words represented only in Italian and Spanish. And yet a similar procedure is used, even twice, in no. 7 and in no. 22. In the second instance, on the basis of *one* Turkic word qat- 'to weave, plait, twist' (Tofa and Tuvin are virtually identical Turkic languages) Dolgopolsky posits an Altaic *qat, even though there are neither Mongol nor Tunguz reflexes to be found. No student of Indo-European vocabulary expects to find one and the same word in the vocabulary of each and every Indo-European language, but few, if any would posit for Proto-Indo-European a word reconstructed on the basis of, say, a Bavarian dialect and Sogdian. Entry no. 6 represents this type of reasoning. As pointed out above, one single Tunguz word, Manchu monio (= moño) is called upon to represent the whole Altaic family.

Janhunen's statement (1982, 23) that 'Proto-Uralic . . . is probably the most ancient unambiguously established parent language in Eurasia' must be taken with some reservations, partly because, as he points out (1982, 40), it rests on a mere 140 etymologies. The strength of the material lies in the choice of this vocabulary; thus about 30 items refer to the body and functions of the body. From an infinitely greater corpus, *NM* lists but seven words (nos. 102–8) pertaining to anatomy. None of them has an unequivocal meaning, none of them refers to easily identifiable parts of the body such as head, foot, hand. In *NM* two conclusions are drawn from this meager material. The first, that 'the speakers of Nostratic had a fairly good knowledge of anatomy' is rather self-evident. Is there a people that does not have it? The second conclusion, however, is most unlikely. It implies that the Nostratic people had more interest in the parts of a body of an animal than in those of themselves. I very much doubt that this was the case. It would be a very 'inhuman' attitude.

Many of the historical conclusions drawn in *NM* go beyond the limits of credibility. It is said (p. 19) that the lexical stock 'suggests subtropical climatic conditions in the original home of Nostratic'. Here I must say that, as I see it, *NM* has a peculiar concept of what constitutes the subtropical regions. According to geographic conventions known to me, these do not include southern Europe. Dolgopolsky seems to use the term for what others call the 'temperate zone'. In *NM* (p. 19), a Middle European or Siberian homeland for Nostratic is ruled out by the presence in the Nostratic vocabulary of words like 'fig tree' (no. 1), or 'lion/hyena' (no. 2), 'large feline' (no. 3), 'leopard' (no. 4). Let us take these examples one by one. For no. 1 *NM* lists neither Uralic, nor Altaic, nor Indo-European forms. So, by what right might this word be posited for 'Nostratic'? The same remark applies also to no. 2 where one single word taken from an Evenki subdialect serves to reconstruct a form compatible with the Nostratic construct. Moreover, the meaning of the word is 'wolf'. Entry no. 3 lists Turkic and Mongol words of the irbis 'leopard'-type. They appear only in a few north-ern Turkic languages and in Mongol, that is not exactly in a subtropical region. Of course, 'large felines' live outside the subtropical zone and, yes, also in Sibe-ria. And what about the tiger of Manchuria? The same remarks apply also to no. 4 'leopard', an entry with only Tunguz data. If we suppose (I do not) that the words here listed warrant the positing of a Nostratic proto-form, then the Tunguz reflexes contradict the theory of a subtropical homeland. If, however, we view these as loans, or words of civilization, then they are useless for the reconstruc-tion of a Nostratic form. And what about the Tunguz word oron '*domesticated reindeer*' cited in no. 5 with the qualifier 'domesticated' omitted? Would it also point toward a subtropical homeland? I hardly think so. Oro is probably a re-gional, sub-arctic technical term which might even be linked with Finnish poro 'domesticated reindeer' for which no accepted etymology exists (Sinor 1975, 255). Dolgopolsky lists four reconstructed words (nos. 7, 8, 9 & 10) for 'snow, frost' and expresses the view (p. 19) that their presence rules out the possibility of a tropical Nostratic homeland. One should remember that any language may and does have words for concepts of which its speakers have no direct experi-ence, but the bulk of the material presented in *NM* would point to a homeland located in a temperate zone. Of course all such speculation should take into account the climatic changes that occurred during the Mesolithic, and notably the warming trends present in most regions of Eurasia.

Conclusions? At the end of these desultory remarks I would hesitate to put forward any. Yet a few general thoughts generated by the perusal of *NM* may be worth recording. I see no *a priori* reason for not believing in linguistic macro-families but we should bear in mind that the peoples who today, or at any time in history, speak or spoke languages related to one another are not necessarily ethnically or racially related. Lapp is just as certainly a Finno-Ugric language as it is beyond doubt that anthropologically the Lapps differ not only from the Finno-Ugrians but also from all other European peoples. One cannot but speculate on the number of ethnic units that, in the course of millennia changed their language, while taking over into their new mother tongue elements of that which they had gradually abandoned. If we believe in the monogenesis of the human race, belief in the existence of one Proto-Proto-Proto~ language becomes unavoidable. If we do not, it becomes necessary to assume the existence of several Proto-Proto-Proto~ languages, one for each newly formed human group. Through such a process we reach the realm of pure fantasy.

Having a closer look at the continental mass of Eurasia I can see no reason why we should doubt the possibility of several languages descending from the language(s) used by the first human group or groups. All this seems most likely. I also believe in the possibility of reconstructing with more or less accuracy the ancestry of *some* of the languages present or past.

What I do not believe is the possibility to attribute any objective chronology to the development of languages. Since linguistic changes do not occur at a steady pace, prior to the existence of written records there are no criteria for figuring out the point in time when they happened. Drastic changes may occur within a very short time-span as exemplified by the change in English vocabulary following the Norman Conquest. As a corollary of my disbelief in the possibility of dating any linguistic change not vouchsafed by written records, I find it impossible to attribute with any degree of certainty any given language to any given prehistoric civilization. Of course it is *more likely* that the Mesolithic people living somewhere in the Ural region spoke Proto-Uralic than, say, Proto-Cushitic but with many hundreds of languages disappearing in historical times, it is just as likely that they used a language of which no trace whatsoever remains.

The disappearance of languages which we can still witness in our own times is a fact not to be ignored in comparative linguistics. Namely, languages do not disappear without leaving traces in other languages and many word correspondences may trace their origin to a common linguistic substratum now no longer identifiable. Many years ago Marcel Cohen (1926, 83) coined the term '*mot bouchon*' for words which, as it were, float aimlessly on the ocean of the vocabularies, remnants of languages submerged by the surge of Hamito-Semitic, Indo-European or other major linguistic groups.

To satisfy my own curiosity rather than with the intent of making a scholarly statement, I glanced at what Chinese sources may have to say about the languages of the Northern Barbarians in the period corresponding roughly speaking to the first millennium AD. For this purpose I used for guide Eberhard (1942). Of the 59 descriptions given of peoples living in Central Eurasia only 18 contain any indication of their languages. Of these only three are identifiable today. Four are said to be identical with or similar to these known languages. In three cases the sources state that the language of the given people is not like a known language; in eight cases it is said that the language used is similar to a language now unknown. Because of practical considerations the Chinese have always paid attention to the languages of the peoples with whom they had diplomatic or military contacts, so the linguistic waste these figures represent is really quite frightening: of the 59 peoples mentioned the language of only three can be identified and for another three we may make educated guesses.

I must here confess my feeling of unease when I notice some of the conclusions reached by the methods of linguistic palaeontology. In the preceding pages and elsewhere (e.g. Sinor 1969) I have hinted at some of the pitfalls that endanger the unwary, willing to draw far-reaching conclusions from the existence or non-existence of a word in a given linguistic corpus. Stronger emphasis may be required *Caveant consules ne quid detrimenti respublica capiat.* Let me just give some random examples. The English knew mountains and lakes before they borrowed these words from the French, the Karakalpaks were aware of the fact that trees have bark even before they borrowed Russian beresta to name it. From a variety of languages similar examples could be cited by the thousands. However, my favorite remains the case of the Hungarians word for 'coitus', which happens to be a Turkic loanword. Should we assume that the Hungarians had no sexual relationships prior to their acquiring from the Turks the only relevant word of their vocabulary? One may wonder why they have not become extinct. Since, with small variations, the word banana occurs in a very great number of Indo-European, Uralic, and Altaic languages, are we to conclude that the homeland of the peoples speaking these languages lay somewhere in the West Indies? Since Dolgopolsky assumes (p. 61) a Proto-Mongol word *qalimu 'whale' (in fact this is simply the Classical Mongol form elevated at the rank of an *Urform*), should we conclude that the Proto-Mongols were whale-hunters? Perhaps in the Gobi when the land was still under water?

In his introduction to *NM* (p. xiii) Renfrew argues for caution on negative linguistic evidence to be used in the description of the homeland or the civilization of prehistoric peoples, but Dolgopolsky does not heed the warning. When it comes to speculating about the civilization of the Nostratic people, *NM* does not shy away from an *argumentum ex silentio*. The *absence* of a common Nostratic word for a large body of water is for Dolgopolsky a valid argument (p. 26) for the localization in Southwestern Asia of the ancestral Nostratic homeland. Surprisingly, *NM* no. 13 (see above) does give a Nostratic word for a large body of water.

For the purpose of placing the Nostratic homeland, the name of trees would be more revealing than those of the monkey or the hyena, yet *NM* cites only the fig tree (no. 1) the name of which he traces only in Hamito-Semitic and Dravidian. It should cause no wonder that it is unknown in Evenki or Ostiak. On page 33, following the Nostratic etymology no. 24 for 'basket, box', we are told that 'according to the lexical data, the speakers of the Nostratic languages had no agriculture, no husbandry, *no pottery* [my emphasis]. Hence, they did not belong to the Neolithic epoch'. Yet in this very same entry no. 24 *NM* justifiably compares Uralic and Indo-European *pVd-type words meaning 'kettle'. Since the production of pottery vessels certainly antedated those made of metal, the historical conclusion drawn is unwarranted.

Perhaps the most astonishing statement in *NM* is made on page 28 where the reader is told that 'milk as food exists only in societies with husbandry'. This is linguistic palaeontology gone berserk. Two questions arise: 1) Is there milk that is not food?; 2) Instead of breast-feeding did Nostratic mothers nourish their babies with Nestlé products? Surely, if there is one food that is universally known everywhere where mammals live or have lived, it must be milk. Were I a believer in *argumenta ex silentio*, the absence of a common word for 'milk' might alone suffice for me to doubt the genetic relationship of any two languages. Were we to follow Dolgopolsky's penchant for the use of negative evidence, we would have to conclude that the Nostratic people had no heads since no common word exists for that part of the body.

A perusal of *NM* appears to justify the biblical encouragement 'seek and ye shall find'. With semantic criteria applied very liberally, it is not very surprising that in the immense lexicon represented by the complete vocabulary of so many Proto-Languages which may or may not have existed, similar roots may be found. I am not particularly surprised that for 15 of *NM*'s 124 etyma, Trask (this volume) was able to suggest 15 equivalents in Basque, a language which neither Dolgopolsky nor he himself would include in the Nostratic group. I completely agree with Trask's statement that 'chance resemblances between arbitrary languages are by no means so difficult to find as is sometimes suggested'. Coincidences of the same order of magnitude between Nostratic and Nilo-Saharan are given by Ehret (this volume). The whole Nostratic undertaking could become much more convincing if comparisons were focused on well-defined semantic categories, as, for instance, exemplified by Friedrich (1970) on *Proto-*

Indo-European Trees. Much can be said for the method used by Dmitrieva (1972), little known even among Altaists. Her enquiry proceeds from the plant, with its Latin name indicated, or its parts (such as 'bark' or 'bud') and lists its appellations in the various Altaic languages, irrespective of whether these are related or not. Unfortunately she leaves it to her readers to categorize and analyze the lessons to be drawn from her 139 sets. A similar approach used for Nostratic data, whatever its results may be, would carry more conviction than what appears to be a haphazard hunt for correspondences.

There can be no doubt that the gathering of a corpus of words taken from many languages spoken in adjacent areas can be of great service in the endeavour to shed light on some aspects of prehistory. Because of this Professor Dolgopolsky deserves the gratitude of all who labour in the field of Eurasian prehistory. At the time depth at which the Nostratic hypothesis is situated, the distinction between loan words and words genetically linked may not be made. Of course, for the student of prehistory, loanwords can be as enlightening as are words genetically related and it is my hope that the material to be gathered between the covers of a vast Nostratic comparative dictionary — similar to that compiled by Cincius (1975–77) for Tunguz — would give an impetus to their study.

References

Cincius, V.I. (ed.), 1972. *Ocherki sravnitelnoy leksikologii altajskikh jayzkov.* Leningrad: Nauka.

Cincius, V.I., 1975–77. *Sravnitel'nyj slovar' tunguso-man'chzhurskikh jazykov,* vols. I–II. Leningrad: Nauka.

Clauson, G., 1956. The case against the Altaic theory. *Central Asiatic Journal* 2, 181–7.

Clauson, G., 1972. *An Etymological Dictionary of Pre-Thirteenth-Century Turkish.* Oxford: Clarendon Press.

Cohen, M., 1926. Sur le nom d'un contenant en entrelacs dans le monde méditerranéen. *Bulletin de la Société de Linguistique de Paris* 27, 81–120.

Dmitrieva, L.V., 1972. Nazvaniya rasteniy v tjurkskikh I drugikh altayskikh yazykakh, in Cincius (ed.), 151–223.

Dolgopolsky, A., 1998. *The Nostratic Macrofamily and Linguistic Palaeontology.* (Papers in the Prehistory of Languages.) Cambridge: The McDonald Institute for Archaeological Research. Abbreviated *NM*.

Eberhard, W., 1942. *Kultur und Siedlung der Randvölker Chinas.* Leiden: Brill.

Friedrich, O., 1970. *Proto-Indo-European Trees: the Arboreal System of a Prehistoric People.* Chicago (IL): University of Chicago Press.

Hajdú, P., 1979. Language contacts in north-west Siberia. *Fenno-Ugrica Suecana* 2, 19–31.

Janhunen, J., 1982. On the structure of Proto-Uralic. *Finnisch-ugrische Forschungen* 44, 23–42.

Kolesnikova, V.D., 1972. Nazvaniya chastey tela cheloveka v altayskikh yazykakh, in Cincius (ed.), 71–103.

Lessing, F.D. (ed.), 1960. *Mongolian–English Dictionary.* Berkeley & Los Angeles (CA): University of California Press.

NM = Dolgopolsky 1998.

Novikova, K.A., 1972. Inoyazichnie êlementi v tunguso-man'chzhurskoj leksike otnosjashchejsja k zhivotnomu miru, in Cincius (ed.), 104–50.

Pelliot, P., 1944. Les formes avec et sans q- (k-) initial en turc et en mongol. *T'oung Pao* 37, 73–101.

Poppe, N., 1938. *Mongol'skij slovar' Mukaddimat al-Adab*. Moscow: Trudy Instituta Vostokovedenika xiv.

Rédei, K., 1988–91. *Uralisches Etymologisches Wörterbuch*, vols. I–III. Budapest: Akadémiai Kiadó.

Renfrew, C., 1998. Introduction: the Nostratic hypothesis, linguistic macrofamilies and prehistoric studies, in Dolgopolsky, vii–xxii.

Sammalahti, P., 1988. Historical phonology of the Uralic languages, in Sinor (ed.) 1988a, 478–554.

Sinor, D., 1944. Ouralo-altaïque - Indo-Européen. *T'oung Pao* 37, 226–47. (Reprinted in Sinor 1990.)

Sinor, D., 1962. Some Altaic names for bovines. *Acta Orientalia Academiae Scientiarum Hungaricae* 15, 309–24. (Reprinted in Sinor 1990.)

Sinor, D., 1963. Observations on a new comparative Altaic phonology. *Bulletin of the School of Oriental and African Studies* 26, 133–44. (Reprinted in Sinor 1990.)

Sinor, D., 1969. Geschichtliche Hypothese und Sprachwissenschaft in der ungarischen, finnisch-ugrischen and uralischen Sprachgeschichtsforschung. *Ural-Altaische Jahrbücher* 41, 173–81.

Sinor, D., 1975. Uralo-Tunguz lexical correspondences, in *Researches in Altaic Languages*, ed. L. Ligeti. Budapest: Akadémiai Kiadó, 245–65 (Reprinted in Sinor 1990.)

Sinor, D., 1978. Altaica and Uralica, *in Studies in Finno-Ugric Linguistics in Honor of Alo Raun*, ed. D. Sinor. (Uralic and Altaic Series 131.) Bloomington (IN): Indiana University Press, 319–32. (Reprinted in Sinor 1990.)

Sinor, D. (ed.), 1988a. *The Uralic Languages: Description, History, Foreign Influences*. Leiden: Brill.

Sinor, D., 1988b. The problem of the Ural–Altaic relationship, in Sinor (ed.) 1988a, 706–41.

Sinor, D., 1990. *Essays in Comparative Altaic Linguistics*. (Uralic and Altaic Series 143.) Bloomington (IN): Indiana University Press.

Sinor, D., 1995. On vessels, bags, coffins and melons: musing over Turkic qap. *Acta Orientalia Academiae Scientiarum Hungaricae* 42, 457–64.

Sinor, D., 1996. Some Altaic terms for containers, in *Proceedings of the 38th Permanent International Altaistic Conference (PIAC), Kawasaki, Japan: August 7–12, 1995*, ed. G. Stary. Wiesbaden: Harrassowitz, 345–57.

Part V
Conclusions

Chapter 20

Towards a future history of macrofamily research

Daniel Nettle

The Nostratic hypothesis has been with us now for around seventy-five years (Renfrew 1998, ix), and the observation from which it departs — a possible relationship between members of the main language families of Western Eurasia and North Africa — is evidently sufficiently strong to continue to generate linguistic interest and scholarship, not just, as is sometimes alleged, in Russia and its diaspora (see, as well as the papers in this volume, Collinder 1965; Bomhard 1984; Bomhard & Kerns 1994; Campbell 1990; Hegedűs 1992; Joseph & Salmons 1998; Greenberg in prep.). However, it is clear that the validity of Nostratic is not accepted by the majority of the profession of historical linguistics. Dixon's (1997, 44) recent assessment that 'there is no reputable historical linguist, anywhere in the world, who accepts the claims of . . . the Nostraticists' is certainly an overstatement, but the insight that most linguists do not feel compelled by what they have read to accept Nostratic is a true one (see Appleyard, Comrie, Campbell, Sinor, Trask, Zvelebil, all in this volume).

On the other hand, the proponents of Nostratic see nothing in the scepticism of their colleagues which would lead them to abandon their position, for if the Nostratic hypothesis is not proven, it is not, for them, discredited either. Indeed, Nostraticists frequently express the frustration that they feel the evidence that they have put forward to be ample, and would like to know just what more they would need to do to have their position accepted. As this volume and the conference which preceded it so clearly show, the issue appears to be at an impasse, with the goal of a consensus on the Nostratic question way off in the distance, and no real consensus even on the more immediate question of how to get from here to there. The Nostraticists feel that they have provided the means, but the unconvinced demur. Interested non-specialists, like the editors of this volume, are at a loss to find the concord in this discord.

A glance elsewhere in historical linguistics reveals that the Nostratic case is not an isolated one. As well as Nostratic (or the overlapping but no less controversial Eurasiatic), there is an impressive list of other hypothesized macrofamilies in the world: Austric, Australian, Indo-Pacific, Amerind (and several sub-proposals for grouping the languages of the Americas), and Sino-Caucasian, to name but a few. What is remarkable about this list is not the existence of so many controversial hypotheses, which would betoken a science in vibrant health, but rather the observation that almost all of them are stuck at the same log-jam as Nostratic. That is, proponents consider them demonstrated, and have in some cases moved on to other work, whilst the unconvinced feel no compulsion to change their minds. In fact, a similar situation also obtains in the case of some groupings which have been more widely accepted, such as Altaic, Nilo-Saharan, Khoisan, and even Niger-Congo. Whilst advocates (who are more numerous than in the cases listed previously) feel these to be firmly inside the perimeter of the known, it is quite common to find figures of high authority in the field listing them as unfounded speculations (see, for a selection of views, Unger 1990; Austerlitz 1991; Nichols 1992; Sands 1995; Nurse 1997; Dixon 1997; Campbell 1998a; this volume). In a mature science, it might be comforting to think that this situation is not possible. For a given hypothesis, there should be consensus that it has been confirmed or that the evidence is insufficient, with a few cases where the jury is still out. But for so many of the basic explanatory entities of a small field to have indeterminate status, with some considering them uncontroversially true whilst others of equal eminence dismiss them almost without further comment, would seem to be a matter for consternation.

This point should not be overstated; there are hundreds of language families which are well established. The sets of families used by typologists as a sampling frame, such as the 250 or so of Nichols (1992), as well as many of their sub-units, are generally uncontroversial. Moreover, the existence of some indeterminate theories may be an irreducible feature of the historical sciences, in which hypotheses cannot be tested by experiment, but instead singular historical events must be reconstructed through fragmentary and decaying evidence. Nonetheless, the Nostratic problem is of wider import, for in considering it we consider the problems of historical linguistics more generally.

When faced with frank and persistent disagreement, it is often fruitful to stand back from the details of the case and think clearly at a conceptual level about the methods being used to advance knowledge. The purpose of this concluding paper, then, is not to discuss specific points of evidence, which is anyway far beyond my expertise, nor to summarize, or adjudicate between, the differing views on Nostratic found in the pages of this volume. Rather, I wish to think about how the problems of assessing hypothesized macrofamilies might be solved. This paper aims, then, at a future history of this controversy. If the paper seems to concentrate too much on the failings of the Nostratic case as presented so far, this is not through a desire to detract from the achievements of its supporters, rather, it is through an interest in what more, positively, can be done to advance the issue. Many of the points I will make have been made elsewhere in the growing literature on distant linguistic relationships (see e.g. Ringe 1992; McMahon & McMahon 1995; Nichols 1996; Campbell 1998b), but there is no harm in setting them out again with special attention to Nostratic, the subject of this volume.

We can easily conceive of a situation in, say, thirty years, where, despite brilliant scholarly endeavour and the accumulation of more alleged evidence, in the form of etymologies, for Khoisan, Nostratic, Austric and Sino-Caucasian, those hypotheses still retain the status which Matthews (1997, 247) pithily ascribes to them now: the sort of hypotheses you believe to the extent you believe that sort of hypothesis. Equally, we can conceive of a situation in which the impasse is broken. That is, some of the macrofamilies are definitely confirmed and some definitely abandoned, and enquiry has been able to progress. The question this paper seeks to address, then, is that of what linguistics needs to do for the latter future history — the one which is surely desirable — to happen. This is a question which is above all about methodology.

The question of methodology

Dunbar (1995) suggests that the key attribute determining the progress of a scientific paradigm is the rate at which incorrect hypotheses can be eliminated. By this criterion, comparative linguistics would appear to progress only haltingly. If Nostratic is wrong, it shows no sign of being eliminated after seventy-five years; whilst if it is right, its converse, that the languages in question do not descend from a common ancestor, is an incorrect hypothesis which shows no sign of being dislodged. Belief in a proposition and belief in its opposite should not be able to persist in a small scholarly community who agree on basic phenomena, models and rational principles (though it often does; we all hope this is due to transitional phenomena). In this section and the next, then, we consider the kinds of methodological developments which would be required for a faster turnover of hypotheses to be achieved.

Moving beyond the Great Scholar

Linguistic comparison has often been the work of the brilliant individual scholar. The hypothesized macrofamilies we have before us are the fruits of gargantuan labours by highly dedicated individuals (Illič-Svityč and Dolgopolsky for Nostratic; Starostin for Sino-Caucasian; Greenberg for Amerind, and so on). The results of their labours, which rightly inspire our respect, often go beyond the knowledge of any of their commentators and thus become difficult to assess. Methodologies are also applied in somewhat idiosyncratic ways. Dolgopolsky (unlike Greenberg) certainly adheres to the standard comparative method of historical linguistics. However, the comparative method is a method only in a weak sense. A method in a strong sense is a well-defined formal algorithm, such as the methods of numerical taxonomy (McMahon, Lohr and McMahon, this volume). With such a method, any two investigators starting from the same data will achieve precisely the same result as long as the method has in fact been applied. This is true whether or not they are trained biologists and indeed whether or not they are human; for methods in this strong sense can always be implemented by computers.

The comparative method in linguistics is not really a method in the same way. It is a loose collection of general principles for demonstrating related-ness between a group of languages and for reconstructing the ancestral forms (though these two parts are sometimes separated; see Durie & Ross 1996a; Nichols 1996). Different people with different degrees of knowledge or different assess-ments of evidence may come up with substantially different results, without either having departed from the 'method'. Add to this the dispute about whether the method has been applied too loosely in particular cases (Campbell, this volume), and we see that the possibilities for indeterminacy are great.

It is perhaps as a result of this methodological indeterminacy that debates on the results of comparison can often assume a rather *ad hominem* character. Enthusiasts for some grouping point to the great learning and long apprentice-ship in comparison with the scholar who produced a particular work. Opponents of Nostratic address cultural factors within Russia which might have favoured the emergence of a Nostratic school (Décsy, this volume; Dixon 1997, 39).

As Chomsky has pointed out in a different context (Chomsky 1979, 6–7), the extent to which an individual's background is thought relevant in a discipline is in inverse proportion to the quality of the methods that discipline has for judging the arguments themselves. In mathematics, for example, such characteristics are completely irrelevant, and no-one ever asks about them; but then, mathematics has strong, person-free formal methods for eliminating in-correct arguments. In the humanities, where the picture is less clear, the status of the investigator has always had some relevance. I would venture to suggest that for macrofamily studies to have a successful future, the *ad hominem* factor needs to be minimized, and should ideally become completely irrelevant. Knowl-edge only progresses on a firm footing to the extent that ideas are considered on their merits and their evidentiary basis, and become completely divorced from the individuals who produce them.

This has implications for the way research is produced. Good comparativists already cite the supporting etymologies for all their hypothesized forms. However, in other historical sciences, researchers are required to make public, in a unified format, all the data on which their conclusions are based, not just those which support the hypothesis. Human genetics has deve-loped the GenBank system for this very purpose. Ideally, the entire sample universe should be available to anyone who wishes to investigate the evidence underlying the claim. Where this has been done for the vocabulary of specific semantic fields across several language families, it has proved useful for the reconstruction of both genetic and areal relationships (Sinor, this volume).

In a successful future for macrofamily research, then, the relevant forms from as many of the world's languages as possible, and all reconstructed nodes, would be made available, in a unified transcription, on a large public database, against which claims could be checked. Furthermore, the methods used in arriving at a cognate set or claim would be specified by authors in painstaking detail as a condition of publication anywhere. This is a serious constraint; unless any reasonably literate person, regardless of training or prior belief about the hypothesis, can replicate the reconstruction, then the claim is not science but falls into the realm of the imagination. Ideally, it would be desirable to see methods implementable by computers which are blind to the hypothesis under investigation and whose algorithms can be justified and published. McMahon, Lohr and McMahon (this volume) suggest promising routes down this road.

Such measures as these would constitute a cultural revolution for a discipline which began in the humanities tradition. However, if the limits of the knowable are to be pushed back further than their present position, which is what the Nostratic claim entails doing, they may be necessary.

The right kind of evidence

The sheer quantity of evidence for Nostratic produced by Illič-Svityč and Dolgopolsky is by now considerable (and will further increase with the publication of Dolgopolsky's *Nostratic Dictionary*, by the McDonald Institute). One might well wonder how much more they would have to produce for the hypothesis to gain general acceptance.

However, the acceptance of a hypothesis of genetic relationship is dependent not so much upon quantity of evidence as on evidence of a certain type. A successful resolution of macrofamily controversies would require scholars to concentrate on producing evidence with this in mind.

A fundamental distinction needs to be made between the evidence which is used to test the hypothesis that the Nostratic languages are related, and the evidence which can be interpreted once the relatedness is proven. For example, there may be forms of Nostratic origin which are only preserved in two or three families (say, Indo-European and Semitic). Once the Nostratic hypothesis is confirmed, then, if the sound correspondences are right, such forms can be identified as Nostratic retentions. However, they cannot legitimately be used in the initial demonstration of Nostratic, because before Nostratic is proved there are more parsimonious non-genetic explanations, such as IE-Semitic borrowing. To give another hypothetical example, there may be forms in some contemporary Semitic languages which cannot be reconstructed to Proto-Afroasiatic, but which are nonetheless of Nostratic origin. The fact that they cannot be reconstructed to Proto-Afroasiatic is just an accident of preservation, which, once the Nostratic hypothesis is proven, can be seen as such and the underlying Nostratic identity recognized. However, before Nostratic is proven, it is quite illegitimate to 'reach down' and compare a contemporary form from one family with a reconstructed one from a different family, principally because in doing so one greatly increases the probability of finding chance resemblances (to which we return below). Similar observations apply to forms in which the sound correspondences are not completely regular; once the hypothesis is proven, one can accommodate them by invoking conditioning factors and so on; but to admit them in the stage of the proof of the hypothesis vastly increases the window through which chance resemblances and borrowing may be mistaken for genetic relatedness.

Furthermore, the great bulk of the evidence adduced so far for Nostratic is lexical, whereas accepted proofs of genetic relatedness generally depend upon whole grammatical paradigms, ideally including morphological idiosyncracies, being identified as cognate (Nichols 1996). I would suggest, then, that a successful resolution of macrofamily controversies would depend upon their advocates producing a small, high-quality body of evidence to make the inital demonstration. This body of evidence would include only core vocabulary and grammatical morphemes; it would include only forms which are attested in all or most daughter families, are reconstructible to the proto-language of those families, and in which the sound correspondences are regular and the semantic shifts not too great. This evidence might not be extensive, but it would do more to achieve consensus than a much larger body of more variable data. Once this evidence had been accepted, researchers could go on to interpret the more problematic cases.

It is clear that the evidence published to date falls some way short of these desiderata for demonstrating the Nostratic hypothesis. Of the 245 cognate sets in Illič-Svityč (1971), 154 are supported by evidence from only 2 or 3 of the constituent families, with only 5 being found in all 6 families (Ringe 1995, 57). Similar limitations of attestation apply to Illič-Svityč (1989) and *NM* (see Campbell 1998b; this volume). Over half of the sets in *NM* are found in only two or three of the six constituent families, with only 15 of the 124 being found in five or six.

Over one third of the sets in *NM* involve 'reaching down'. Such methods vastly increase the probability of finding chance lookalikes, since there are, for example, around 250 Afroasiatic languages in which to search for matches (see below for more discussion of the problem of chance resemblances). Finally, in *NM*, although a chart of sound correspondences is produced, around 35 of the 124 sets violate these correspondences in some way (Campbell, this volume), and over 90 per cent of sets contain some kind of uncertainty signs. No tabulation is given of the frequency of occurrence of each correspondence, or the ratio of the correspondence's occurrence to its violation.

These observations are not intended as a criticism of *NM* or of Illič-Svityč's works. None of these was prepared as an initial proof of the Nostratic hypothesis; *NM*, for example, is a work of linguistic palaeontology, which sets out to discover, assuming the Nostratic hypothesis is true, what we can infer about the Nostratic lifeway. My intention is rather to consider what kind of work would be needed to achieve greater consensus about Nostratic or any other macrofamily, in the hope that the challenge will be taken up.

The question of the hypothesis to be tested

The key to scientific enquiry is hypothesis testing, and a definitive test of the Nostratic hypothesis is what seems to have eluded us so far. There is thus a need to clarify conceptually what the hypothesis is and just how a test might be carried out.

The work of comparativists tends to rest on positive evidence. That is, sets of cognates are put forward which are consistent with, and best explained by, the common descent of the languages in question. This procedure has been relatively successful with such families as Bantu, Polynesian and Indo-European, since the evidence is reasonably clear in these cases. Where the cognate sets are more obscure or problematic, due to the accretion of historical change, the accumulation of positive evidence becomes less compelling. It is primarily this problem that leads us to the difficulty recovering the truth in cases of distant comparison, and leads to the commonplace amongst cautious linguists that there is time depth beyond which scientific statements about relatedness are impossible (see, e.g. Nichols 1992; 1994). I would suggest, then, that to push the time horizon back further, the problem of hypothesis testing needs to be reconsidered.

Null hypotheses and positive evidence

As I have said, the usual method of argumentation in comparative linguistics is to put forward a hypothesis, and then list evidence consistent with it and thus supportive of it. Where the evidence is so clear that other explanations (chance and borrowing) can be eliminated, this procedure is effective enough. However, as a scientific methodology, it is rather unsophisticated.

We owe to Popper (1968) the insight that empirical knowledge advances not by the proof of true propositions, which is problematic owing to the well-known philosophical problems associated with induction from particular to general statements, but by the falsification of untrue propositions. Thus scientists, in best practice, do not list the evidence in support of a theory. Rather they contrive experiments or observations which could potentially falsify it. A theory's acceptance (which is always tentative) should rest on the range of falsificatory trials it has withstood, compared to its rivals. The reason that falsificatory rather than confirming evidence is sought is that any theory is compatible with an indefinitely large number of real world observations, many of which are also compatible with its rivals. Merely listing these observations thus gives no logical grounds for accepting the whole theory. However, a single case where the theory makes a clear prediction which is not empirically met gives strong logical justification for rejecting the theory (Chalmers 1978).

Now this view of good scientific methodology is an idealization, and not straightforwardly applicable to the current case. In practice, positive evidence is often used to justify belief in a hypothesis, and hypotheses are not abandoned even in the face of counter-examples if the hypothesis has numerous explanatory achievements and if no better alternative is available. Moreover, in the historical sciences, the absence of a relationship or the non-occurrence of an event can never be demonstrated, so falsification is more provisional. At best we can say that there is no convincing evidence.

The general principle of falsificationism can nonetheless be adopted and applied in the case of hypotheses of distant linguistic relationship. Simply producing supportive cognate sets, which are, by the nature of the relationship under investigation, equivocal, can never resolve the issue by itself, since any individual cognate set will be compatible with the alternative hypotheses of chance and borrowing. Rather we have to force the different hypotheses we could hold about the relationship of the set of languages under investigation to make contradictory predictions, and see which is falsified by the evidence.

Scientific investigations always depart from a Null Hypothesis, and if this is falsified, adopt a prespecified alternative, which, in the simplest case is just the negation of the Null. The Null Hypothesis, the one we aim to test, should not be the hypothesis that the Nostratic languages are all related in a genetic sense. It should instead be the hypothesis that they are unrelated in a genetic sense. This can be justified in general and specific terms. In general, the Null Hypothesis should always be the most conservative possible (that is, the hypothesis which assumes least about the world). This is an important methodological principle which, like the related Occam's razor, saves us from unwarranted inferences about the world. More specifically, the hypothesis that the Nostratic languages are related in a genetic sense is not a viable Null, since, as stated, it is not directly falsifiable. It can never be shown that two languages are unrelated, since the hypothesis of their relatedness is entirely compatible with the observation that historical change has destroyed or mutated the evidence in any particular domain we care to investigate.

We should start, then, from the Null Hypothesis of no genetic relationship. This is falsifiable in the standard way, and if we can falsify it, then we have rational grounds for accepting the Nostratic hypothesis. We merely have to specify the predictions that this Null Hypothesis makes about the Nostratic daughter languages.

Unfortunately, this is where the matter becomes more complex. Most naïvely, one might assume that the Null Hypothesis of unrelatedness entails prediction (P1):

(P1) There will be no items which correspond in form and meaning across the daughter languages of the Nostratic group.

If this really were the prediction entailed by the hypothesis, then Nostratic would already be confirmed, but so would the relatedness of almost any languages one might care to name. This is because a certain number of items will correspond in form and meaning by chance alone. The prediction (P1) should thus be replaced by (P2):

(P2) The resemblances in form and meaning across the daughter languages of the Nostratic group will not exceed the level expected by chance.

The problem, of course, is determining the level expected by chance. Given that the number of phonemes is finite (and their arrangements into words constrained by universal phonotactic principles), the number of matches we should expect by chance is probably quite high. Bender (1969) estimates that a match rate of more than 7 per cent would be required to refute the hypothesis of chance in short roots, allowing for a limited degree of semantic shift. If the amount of semantic shift or sound change admitted is increased, this figure increases exponentially. Ringe (1992) extends similar reasoning to multilateral comparison and concludes that if the number of languages is large then the probability of finding a match for any given root by chance becomes extremely large. This is a criticism primarily aimed at Greenberg's (1963; 1987) methods, and not the Nostraticists, who use more traditional comparison of proto-languages. This radically restricts the possibilities of chance resemblance. However, as we have seen, *NM* makes extensive use of 'reaching down', or using forms not from proto-languages but from their daughters. Every time this is done, the probability of a chance match is vastly increased, and in the limit, 'reaching down' reduces the comparative method to a form of multilateral comparison.

Ringe's probabilistic reasoning makes a clear prediction; if resemblances are due to chance, then the number of matches attested in two families will exceed those found in three, which will be more than those in four and so on. There is nothing in Illič-Svityč's (1971) data which is inconsistent with such a distribution (Ringe 1995). This does not, of course, mean that the cognate sets are the results of chance; merely that we may not be able to reject the Null Hypothesis that they are.

Nothing has been said so far of the requirement of regular sound correspondences, which is the major point which differentiates the Nostraticists from Greenberg. Regular sound correspondences, properly applied, vastly reduce the likelihood that the resemblances involved are just chance. However, they do not reduce this probability to zero. The more times a sound correspondence is observed, the more unlikely it is to have arisen by chance, but correspondences can easily be set up if each correspondence is found in only a few examples. For the workings of chance to be dismissed, then, it would be necessary to tabulate how many instances of each sound correspondence were found in the data set, and to show this was greater than chance expectation. A perfectly regular but trivial set of correspondences can be set up for any two unrelated languages if each correspondence is required to occur only a very few times (see Trask, this volume, for a discussion).

Any work aiming to demonstrate a hypothesis of distant linguistic relationship, then, would be required to lay out not just its correspondences but also their frequency of occurrence and, moreover, could claim no data as cognate which violated them. This is not because there are no forms in language which violate regular sound changes; there are, and they stem from analogy and various forms of special conditioning (Campbell 1996). It is rather the methodological principle that, once the requirement of regular sound change has been introduced as a way of limiting the chance resemblance problem, it would be self-defeating to relax it on an *ad hoc* basis. To do so generally would reduce the comparative method to multi-lateral comparison.

Evidence forcing the rejection of the Null Hypothesis, then, would have to show not just that there were resemblances between the daughter languages, but that these resemblances exceeded the expectation of chance. The expectation of chance could be arrived at in two ways. The first would be to use a theoretical model based on the probabilities of phoneme occurrence (Ringe 1992). This, however, becomes mathematically intractable, owing to the complex and changeable nature of word forms (the second phoneme of a form in one language can correspond to the first in another, and so on). Furthermore, languages do not assemble their lexicons with random number tables; universal human principles of nursery forms, ease of articulation, onomatopoeia, and so on, are at work, and these increase the level of non-genetic similarity we should expect to find. The second way would be to use an outgroup of languages thought to be unrelated to Nostratic, and show that the level of resemblances to be found between these and the Nostratic languages is significantly lower than that observed within Nostratic.

Various attempts to use such an outgroup have been made across the literature on distant comparison. Campbell (1988) and Matisoff (1990), aiming at *reductio ad absurdum* of Greenberg (1987), find ample matches between Finnish and 'Amerind', and between Proto-Sino-Tibetan and 'Amerind' respectively. Dyen (1970) finds 73 lexical and 3 grammatical resemblances between Proto-Indo-European and Proto-Austronesian, which he takes to be indicative of the high level of 'background noise' we can expect in comparison at this depth (see also Trask's Basque–Nostratic 'matches' in this volume). In this context the apparent resemblances raised in this volume between Nostratic and Sino-Caucasian (Starostin), between Nostratic and Salishan (Shevoroshkin), and between Nostratic and Nilo-Saharan and Niger-Congo (Ehret), though proposed with a friendly intent to macrofamily studies, appear potentially damaging to the Nostratic hypothesis. This is because, for that hypothesis to be true, it would have to be the case that the resemblances within the Nostratic languages were significantly greater than those found using languages which lie outside it. Finding a similar degree of resemblance in other phyla might lead to either the revision of the hypothesis, or the conclusion that we are merely observing the level of background similarity of human languages.

Even if the problem of chance were solved, the equally serious problem of borrowing remains, and this is where the greatest challenge to the Nostratic idea lies. The lexical items common to different Western Eurasian language families may reflect an ancient linguistic area. These societies have had a history of intimate contact, exchange and shift for millennia. All of these are powerful mechanisms for the transfer of items from language to language. The Nostratic hypothesis explicitly claims that the existence of similar forms in the daughter families is due to common origin and not to borrowing. We must therefore replace (P2) with (P3) as the prediction to be tested in order to falsify the Null Hypothesis:

(P3) The resemblances in form and meaning across the daughter languages of the Nostratic group will not exceed the level expected by the combination of chance and borrowing.

The problem with testing (P3) is that no clear discussion has been had about what the expected level of borrowing between contiguous languages is. Distant comparison has generally rested on two assumptions. The first is, as Welmers (1970, 4) puts it, that external influences (borrowing) 'are insignificant when compared with internal change', and the second is that borrowings can be identified and eliminated on an *ad hoc* basis. It is not clear that these two assumptions are valid.

The first issue, the relative level of borrowing, depends heavily on the wider social context. It may be true that the level of borrowing in core vocabulary is low in recent European languages (Dixon 1997, 10), but then the social context is highly atypical of human history; large, complex societies, often monolingual, and with a marked tendency for endogamy within the language group (Barbujani & Sokal 1990). In small societies, such as must have been typical of the Mesolithic and early Neolithic, multilingualism is the norm and the level of borrowing in all parts of the language, including core vocabulary and morphology, can be extremely high (see, for instance, Thurston 1987 on New Britain, Grace 1996 on New Caledonia, Dixon 1997 on Australia, Appleyard, this volume, on Ethiopia, Nettle 1998 on the Central Nigerian Highlands). There are theoretical models which predict that this should be so, because the probability of spread of a new variant, be it of internal or external origin, can be argued to be related to population size (Nettle forthcoming).

This effect is exacerbated by two further factors. Firstly, small societies tend not to be self-sustaining in biological terms, as incest-avoidance principles conspire with limited cohorts of eligible women to force men to seek wives beyond the local group. Linguistic exogamy provides an extremely powerful vector for the transmission of items between languages, even in the absence of prestige differences between languages. In Nettle (1998), I showed that a hundred years or so of regular intermarriage between speakers of a Benue-Congo language and its Chadic neighbours had led to the transfer of a significant proportion of core vocabulary and several productive morphological patterns. In the small societies of ten thousand years ago, how common must this pattern have been? Second, the ethnographic record shows that small societies are historically unstable, frequently being broken up and dispersed or absorbed by neighbours (Soltis *et al.* 1995). Every time this happens, language shift occurs, with all the potential for substratal change which that affords.

The second assumption of most comparisons is that borrowings can easily be identified and eliminated. Once again, this may be true for Europe in historical times, where we have the written record, and a good historical understanding of the social context. However, it is not obvious that ancient borrowings can generally be detected on the basis of synchronic evidence alone. Borrowings become naturalized to the phonological system of the recipient language, and in the process often take on regular sound correspondences to the donor language. This can be observed in, for example, the regular p:f correspondence between English and Hausa.

English	Hausa	
pencil	fensìr	
passenger	fasànjàà	
pound	fâm	
primary	firamàre	etc.

It is unclear how, after several millennia of further evolution and in the absence of historical data, the loan status of such forms could be detected. The languages of Eurasia have had many opportunities to borrow from one another;

there may have been borrowing between daughter languages, which we are in danger of taking for origin of common ancestry if we admit 'reaching down' or, far worse, borrowing between proto-languages, which will be difficult to eliminate even in forms reconstructible to the proto-languages of the constituent families (for a discussion of some 'Nostratic' forms which can also be explained by prehistoric language contact, see Gamkrelidze *et al.* 1995).

A successful demonstration of the genetic status of Nostratic, then, would have to provide a reasoned analysis of what the expected (or maximum plausible) level of ancient borrowing is, and show that the cognates found exceed this level. Distributional arguments would have to be employed to do this. The requirement that cognates only be accepted in the initial testing of the hypothesis if they are found in all or most of the daughter families will help to eliminate undetected borrowings. The pattern of distribution should also differ between borrowings and ancestral forms. Borrowings will generally be found in language families that are geographically adjacent, and the greater the geographic distance between two families, the fewer should be the shared forms owing to borrowing (though prehistoric adjacency might be hard to judge). One could even model the expected fall off of borrowings against distance, using the theory of migration-drift equilibrium from genetics (Rogers & Harpending 1986). Inherited cognates, on the other hand, will show no such effect; they are just as likely to be retained in two distant families as in two adjacent ones. If the hypothesis of genetic origin is correct, then, the number of cognates linking the different families should be a uniform distribution. This hypothesis could easily be tested and would seem to provide a way of discriminating between inheritance and areal effects.

The problem of borrowing can also be addressed by attending to the kind of evidence found. Cultural words should be treated with suspicion and, above all, cognate morphological paradigms should be sought, for whilst individual words can wander around freely, the probability of whole paradigms being transmitted by diffusion is minimal. It is this kind of reasoning that rules out contact as an explanation for even the most divergent branches of Indo-European.

However it is done, the problems of ancient borrowings and linguistic areas must be addressed; this is perhaps the most serious obstacle for any proposed macrofamily to overcome. Whatever tests are in the end devised to scrutinize macrofamilies, they must first be calibrated on language families which are generally accepted, since the criteria for demonstration of a macrofamily should not be raised higher than that for entities which are already established.

Conclusions

In this paper, I have tried to suggest some of the ways in which questions of distant linguistic relationship would have to be clarified in order for the controversies of today to subside in the future. If, as Ehret (this volume) suggests, the time for deep comparison has come, then the time has come for convincing and reliable methods to facilitate it. This means that advocates of any proposed genetic grouping of languages must accept the challenge of showing that what I have labelled prediction (P3) is false. That is, they must show systematically that the resemblances observed in form and meaning exceed the level expected by the combination of chance and borrowing. If the comments in this paper are correct, this means less effort should be addressed to accumulating further etymologies, and more to the quality of those etymologies; less effort for trawling for new data, and more to hypothesis testing; less effort to the accumulation of positive evidence for macrofamilies, and more to the question of what the expected levels of resemblance owing to chance and borrowing might be, so that the simpler possibilities can be rejected with conviction. These remarks are not intended to be critical of the vast labours of those who have pioneered macrofamily studies. The papers in this volume amply testify to their extraordinary achievements in uncovering resemblances between the languages of Eurasia and North Africa. However, to ascertain the significance of those resemblances, and thus turn their labours into solid inferences about human history, is a separate endeavour, and this represents the challenge for the future.

Acknowledgements

The author is grateful to all the particpants in the Nostratic symposium for their discussion of these matters, and in many cases for comments on the manuscript. Special thanks go to Professor Aharon Dolgopolsky and my co-editor Colin Renfrew.

References

Austerlitz, R., 1991. Alternatives to long-range comparison, in *Sprung from Some Common Source: Investigations into the Prehistory of Languages*, eds. S.M. Lamb & E.D. Mitchell. Stanford (CA): Stanford University Press, 353–64.

Barbujani, G. & R.R. Sokal, 1990. Zones of sharp genetic change in Europe are also linguistic boundaries. *Proceedings of the National Academy of Sciences of the U.S.A.* 87, 1816–19.

Bender, M.L., 1969. Chance CVC correspondences in unrelated languages. *Language* 45, 519–51.

Bomhard, A.R., 1984. *Toward Proto-Nostratic: a New Approach to the Comparison of Proto-Indo-European and Proto-Afroasiatic*. Amsterdam: John Benjamins.

Bomhard, A.R. & J.C. Kerns, 1994. *The Nostratic Macrofamily: a Study in Distant Linguistic Relationship*. Berlin: Mouton.

Campbell, L., 1988. Review of Greenberg 1987. *Language* 64, 591–615.

Campbell, L., 1990. Indo-European and Uralic trees. *Diachronica* 7, 149–80.

Campbell, L., 1996. On sound change and challenges to regularity, in Durie & Ross (eds.), 72–89.

Campbell, L., 1998a. *Historical Linguistics: an Introduction*. Edinburgh: Edinburgh University Press.

Campbell, L., 1998b. How to show languages are related: methods for distant linguistic comparison, in *Handbook of Historical Linguistics*, eds. R.D. Janda & B.D. Joseph. Oxford: Blackwell.

Campbell, L., 1998c. Nostratic: a personal assessment, in Joseph & Salmons (eds.), 107–52.

Chalmers, A.F., 1978. *What is this Thing Called Science?* Milton Keynes: Open University Press.

Chomsky, N.A., 1979. *Language and Responsibility*. New York (NY): Pantheon.

Collinder, B., 1965. *An Introduction to the Uralic Languages*. Berkeley (CA): University of California Press.

Dixon, R.M.W., 1997. *The Rise and Fall of Languages*. Cambridge: Cambridge University Press.

Dolgpolosky, A., 1998. *The Nostratic Macrofamily and Linguistic Palaeontology*. (Papers in the Prehistory of Languages.) Cambridge: The McDonald Institute for Archaeological Research.

Dunbar, R.I.M., 1995. *The Trouble with Science*. London: Faber & Faber.

Durie, M. & M.D. Ross, 1996a. Introduction, in Durie & Ross (eds.), 1–38.

Durie, M. & M.D. Ross (eds.), 1996b. *The Comparative Method Reviewed: Regularity and Irregularity in Language Change*, eds. M. Durie & M.D. Ross. Oxford: Oxford University Press.

Dyen, I., 1970. Background 'noise' or 'evidence' in comparative linguistics: the case of the Austronesian-Indo-European hypothesis, in *Indo-European and Indo-Europeans*, eds. G. Cardona, H. Hoenigswald & A. Senn. Philadelphia (PA): University of Pennsylvania Press.

Gamkrelidze, T.V., V.V. Ivanov, R. Jakobson & J. Nichols, 1995. *Indo-European and the Indo-Europeans*. Berlin: Mouton.

Grace, G.W., 1996. Regularity of change in what?, in Durie & Ross (eds.), 157–79.

Greenberg, J.H., 1963. *The Languages of Africa*. Bloomington (IN): Indiana University Press.

Greenberg, J.H., 1987. *Language in the Americas*. Stanford (CA): Stanford University Press.

Greenberg, J.H., in prep. *Indo-European and its Closest Relatives: the Eurasiatic Language Family*. Stanford (CA): Stanford University Press.

Hegedűs, I., 1992. *Bibliographica Nostratica 1960–1990: a List of Publications on, or Relevant for, the Nostratic Hypothesis*. Szombathely: Seminar für Uralische Phililogie der Berzsenyi-Hochschule.

Illič-Svityč, V.M., 1971. *Opyt sravnenija nostraticeskix jazykov (semitoxamitshij, kartvel'skij, indoevropejski, ural'skij, dravidijskij, altajjskij)*, part 1. Moscow: Nauka.

Illič-Svityč, V.M., 1989. The relationship of the Nostratic family language: a probabilistic evaluation of the similarities in question, in *Explorations in Language Macrofamilies*, ed. V. Sheroroshkin. Bochum: Brockmeyer, 111–21.

Joseph, B.D. & J. Salmons (eds.), 1998. *Nostratic: Sifting the Evidence*. Amsterdam: John Benjamins.

Matisoff, J., 1990. On megalocomparison. *Language* 66, 106–20.

Matthews, P., 1997. *The Concise Oxford Dictionary of Linguistics*. Oford: Oxford University Press.

McMahon, A. & R. McMahon, 1995. Linguistics, genetics and archaeology: internal and external evidence in the Amerind controversy. *Transactions of the Philological Society* 93, 125–226.

Nettle, D., 1998. *The Fyem Language of Northern Nigeria*. Munich: Lincom Europa.

Nettle, D., forthcoming. Is the rate of linguistic change constant? *Lingua*.

Nichols, J., 1992. *Linguistic Diversity in Space and Time*. Chicago (IL): University of Chicago Press.

Nichols, J., 1994. The spread of language around the Pacific rim. *Evolutionary Anthropology* 3, 206–15.

Nichols, J., 1996. The comparative method as heuristic, in Durie & Ross (eds.), 39–71.

NM = Dolgopolsky 1998.

Nurse, D., 1997. The contribution of linguistics to the study of history in Africa. *Journal of African History* 38, 359–91.

Popper, K., 1968. *The Logic of Scientific Discovery*. London: Hutchinson.

Renfrew, C., 1998. Introduction: the Nostratic hypothesis, linguistic macrofamilies and prehistoric studies, in Dolgpolosky, vii–xxii.

Ringe, D.A., 1992. On calculating the factor of chance in language comparison. *Transactions of the American Philosophical Society* 82, 1–110.

Ringe, D.A., 1995. 'Nostratic' and the factor of chance. *Diachronica* 12, 55–74.

Rogers, A. & H. Harpending, 1986. Migration and genetic drift in human populations. *Evolution* 40, 1312–27.

Sands, B.E., 1995. Evaluating Claims of Distant Linguistic Relationship: the Case of Khoisan. Unpublished Ph.D. thesis, UCLA.

Soltis, J., R. Boyd & P.J. Richerson, 1995. Can group-functional behaviors evolve by cultural group selection? An empirical test. *Current Anthropology* 36, 473–94.

Thurston, W., 1987. *Processes of Change in the Languages of North-Western New Britain*. (Pacific Linguistics B-99.) Canberra: Australian National University.

Unger, J.M., 1990. Summary report of the Altaic panel, in *Linguistic Change and Reconstruction Methodology*, ed. P. Baldi. Berlin: Mouton, 479–82.

Welmers, W.E., 1970. Language change and language relationships in Africa. *Language Sciences* 12, 1–8.